1953

Essays

IN MODERN
LITERARY
CRITICISM

Essays in

MODERN LITERARY
CRITICISM

Edited by RAY B. WEST, Jr.

Rinehart & Company, Inc.   NEW YORK · TORONTO

Preface

Ideally, the student of modern criticism would read the criticism of his age against a background of traditional writings which would include the works of Aristotle and Plato, perhaps Horace and Boileau, certainly Dryden, Pope, and Johnson. He would possess at least a general idea of the critical attitudes of secondary figures such as Longinus, Goethe, Sidney, and Wordsworth. He would be aware of the principal concepts of philosophy, particularly as they dealt with aesthetics, from the age of Greece to the present, understanding the shifts in attitude between Greek and Christian philosophies, between Medieval and Renaissance ideas, between orthodox Christianity and the Reformation. He would have formulated in his own mind certain distinctions between Classicism and Romanticism, Idealism and Realism, Naturalism and Surrealism. He would, in addition to being well-read in the literature of all time, possess a certain knowledge of history and the arts of sculpture, painting, and music.

But it is idle to talk of the ideal student. No teacher ever meets him, and it is the student before him in the classroom with whom he must concern himself. At best he can usually assume that the student has had a few of the traditional courses in literature, that he knows something about the development of philosophic and critical ideas from Plato to Dryden— sometimes to Coleridge, and that, since courses in Modern Criticism are seldom required for degrees, that he has a somewhat unusual curiosity about the theories and techniques of modern writing. The point I am trying to make is that such an assumption is necessary. No teacher has the time in a single term, or even in the occasional two-term courses, to cover all of the necessary background. His problem becomes one of deciding just how much he can afford to supply; that is, where he can begin in order to do the most complete and satisfying job of teaching.

This also is the question of the anthologist—the first, at least, and undoubtedly the most difficult one: Where shall I begin? The questions which follow from this present their own difficulties, but they are not unrelated. The second, the most obvious, question is, What shall I include? The problem for the teacher is one of time. For the anthologist it is space. The book should not be too large to handle easily in the classroom. It should not cost too much. But even aside from these restrictions, only a certain number of pages can be crowded into any volume. In planning our book then, shall we apportion a certain number of pages to a review of traditional, older material? In the present volume this question has been answered in the negative, for the reason that there are already available many anthologies containing such material. To have reprinted Aristotle's *Poetics,* for instance, would have robbed our book of at least two examples of modern criticism which are less easily available in the library or in other anthologies.

Shall we then leave out all preliminary material and provide the student only with writings which can, strictly speaking, be called "modern"? The danger would be that the student might see contemporary criticism as an isolated and unique activity, unrelated to the criticism of the past. Also, there is usually a very specific, though highly complex, relationship between the writing of any age and the age which immediately precedes it. The opportunity to see such material without the obscuring impedimenta which surround it in its own times is seldom given. This volume begins, therefore, with a brief survey of those writings from the nineteenth and early twentieth centuries which seem to have exerted the most *direct* influence upon the body of critical writing which we mean when we speak of "Modern Criticism."

The question of "influence" is an elusive and difficult one, and in the selection of essays in Section I, titled "The Background of Modern Criticism," we cannot hope to have satisfied everyone. In the first place, it seemed necessary to keep this section as brief as possible. Certain important nineteenth-century writings were omitted—writings which did not exert a direct influence, but against which modern criticism was primarily in rebellion. The writings of Wordsworth, Wilde, and Tolstoy, for instance, interesting in themselves, seemed less valuable to the student of modern criticism than examples from Coleridge, Arnold, and James. Remy de Gourmont was selected as an example of the French concern with style, which is not unrelated to Coleridge's interests, and which has played so important a role in contemporary criticism from Ezra Pound to Kenneth Burke. The relationship to modern criticism of the last three authors included is more complex and will be discussed at greater length in the introduction to Section I. Croce, Santayana, and Babbitt each expressed ideas concerning the nature of literature which represented a shift in attitude from certain dominant ideas of the nineteenth century, and they also contributed ideas and attitudes which the body of recent criticism has been forced to consider with extreme seriousness.

Section II, entitled "Modern Critical Theory," presents those writings by present-day critics which attempt to define the function of criticism in terms of our age, in terms of specific technical problems, and in terms of certain clearly defined areas of thought. In short, the primary concern of the articles in this section is definition. The categories into which they have been placed are not arbitrary, but neither are they exclusive. If such division propagates the weakness of all categorizing (the attempt to reduce complex matters to the flatness of simple topic headings), it is hoped that something, at least, is to be gained over the opposite method, which would be simply to lump all of the material together under a single heading, such as "definition" or "special problems." Essays have been included in this section when their central emphasis is upon the theory of criticism as opposed to its practice.

The final section deals with what must eventually become the central preoccupation of any body of criticism, and it is titled "The Practice of Criticism." Here the division into subsections, according to the particular genre with which the critic is concerned, is justified on the grounds that this is not only how the student has been taught to view critical problems, it is how the critic himself has thought. Certainly many problems overlap, particularly such theoretical problems as were discussed in Section II. Yet the techniques differ in significant ways, and it is easier, as a rule, to see Henry James's problems in terms of Dostoievsky or André Gide, than in terms of Pope or Wordsworth. Likewise, the essays within each subsection have been ordered according to the chronological sequence of their subjects because this is the order in which the student is accustomed to consider them. The historical perspective is not here of major importance; it is hoped, merely, that the student will be aided by discovering a familiar organization. Such arrangement also makes visible the relatively wide time-range covered by modern critics, who sometimes are thought to be primarily concerned with their own contemporaries.

Seven years have passed since I first considered the possibility of collecting a volume of critical writings which would contain those essays which I, as a student and as a teacher, had found exciting and profitable. Since then the perspective of modern criticism has been constantly shifting. For me this is an indication of its living quality, and I hope that at least a small portion of that quality survives in this book. Criticism should be no more static than the literature which it examines, yet one of the most interesting facts about the writing done over the past forty years is that it continues to impress its value upon the reader coming upon it for the first time. What is that value? In a certain sense, it is the value of ideas.

The excitement may lie occasionally in the novelty of those ideas, though most often it exists in the freshness of old ideas seen in a new context. Over and above the value of ideas themselves, however, is the value of the ideas in relation to works of literature. This is merely to say what has been said many times before—that criticism cannot stand alone, that it exists only in relation to the works of art which it examines and for the purpose of making that literature more readily available to all who would enjoy and understand it.

Finally, I should seem ungrateful if I did not acknowledge the advice of critics and scholars who have at various times seen and commented upon the proposed contents of this book. Allen Tate, F. Cudworth Flint, Robert Penn Warren, R. P. Blackmur, Austin Warren, Lionel Trilling, Donald Stauffer, W. K. Wimsatt, Jr., Moody E. Prior, Paul Engle, and Warren Carrier have made valuable suggestions, but none of them has seen the table of contents in its final form and may not be held responsible for its shortcomings. I am also indebted to Harry Goldgar and L. R. Lind for assistance in translating the foreign passages which occur in the various articles and to E. F. McGuire for assistance with the bibliography.

RAY B. WEST, JR.

Iowa City
September, 1952

Contents

I

The Background of
Modern Criticism

Introduction

THE importance of Samuel Taylor Coleridge to modern criticism has become increasingly obvious in recent years. F. R. Leavis, a Cambridge scholar and a significant "modern" critic, has called Coleridge criticism's "modern instaurator." Herbert Read has written: ". . . it is my contention that criticism derives its penetrative power from the use of the systematic method he [Coleridge] had established by his philosophical speculations." Allen Tate speaks of Coleridge's direct influence, which he believes to have been "very great," but Mr. Tate is impressed also by the indirect influence as it comes to us through Edgar Allan Poe, Charles Baudelaire, and the French symbolists. Equally important is the nearness of Coleridge's concern with problems of language and poetic diction to our own interests in the twentieth century—interests which we see reflected, for instance, in the writings of such critics as I. A. Richards, William Empson, Kenneth Burke, and Cleanth Brooks.

Yet to speak of Coleridge's "influence" does not mean that the modern critic has, necessarily, accepted wholly either the philosophical viewpoint or the methods of Coleridge. Mr. Tate holds strong reservations concerning the value of much of Coleridge's writings, feeling that they lead us eventually away from the poem into what has become known as the psychology of poetry. He feels, apparently, much as T. S. Eliot does concerning our interest in Matthew Arnold. Eliot wrote: ". . . the revival of interest in Arnold in our time—and I believe he is admired and read not only more than Carlyle and Ruskin, but than Pater—is a very different thing from the influence he exerted in his own time. We go to him for refreshment and for the companionship of a kindred point of view to our own, but not as a discipline." In both Coleridge and Arnold, that is, we recognize insights which have become the critical touchstones of our own day; for instance, the insistence upon the organic wholeness of a work of art, with emphasis upon the unity of effect in Coleridge (the psychological consideration) and upon the unity of construction (the formal structure) in Arnold. Yet in both we see mirrored the confusions and contradictions of our age as well: the difficulty in distinguishing between content and technique (truth and beauty), in apprehending and defining their qualities and the manner in which they affect the sensibility and the intellect of the reader. Is the recognizable effect of a work of art the result of the objective structure and form, or is it primarily the result of a subjective receptability of the reader? Such problems were central in much of the criticism of the nineteenth century, and they have become primary concerns of our own day.

Eric R. Bentley has written: "The New Criticism stems from such books as T. S. Eliot's *The Sacred Wood* (1920) and J. Middleton Murry's *The Problem of Style* (1925)." But here we are concerned with tracing it even further back—to its roots in the nineteenth century. Mr. Bentley makes this clear: "Eliot and Murry," he says, "are linked with the previous age, especially through the writer whom Eliot has called 'the critical conscience of a generation,' Remy de Gourmont." Gourmont, a French critic of the turn of the century, provides a link between the end of the last century and the beginning of our own. His concept of style as the result of intuition and sensibility owes something to the transcendental Danish philosopher Sören Kierkegaard as well as to the French philosopher Henri Bergson.

However, such influences are seldom as direct as they seem. Gourmont's influence upon such early writers as Murry, Eliot, and Ezra Pound cannot be doubted. In America, at least, it is doubtful that many writers had even heard of Kierkegaard and Bergson until the second quarter of the century, and the influence of Gourmont himself came to them primarily at second hand through Murry and Eliot. The somewhat similar writings of the Italian philosopher Benedetto Croce were, however, made known in America early in the century by an American scholar and writer, Joel Spingarn. Mr. Spingarn served the cause of criticism in America by beginning the rescue of it from academic scholars, whose preoccupations were primarily with biographical data and the social conditions surrounding the inception of a work. His aim was laudable in that it attempted to focus attention upon the work itself. His critical attitude, which he called anti-Aristotelian, was, however, too subjective and soft-minded to attract the hardier spirits of his time. He went beyond Gourmont to Anatole France for his definition of the critic's function, describing the act as ". . . a sensitive soul detailing his 'adventure among masterpieces.' "

Croce's aim, while similar to Gourmont's in its emphasis upon the psychological effect and the subjective quality of a work of art, had a sounder philosophical basis than the romantic attitudes of Anatole France and Joel Spingarn. Art was, for him, a special province of human knowledge, but its effect was not achieved through the logic of truth so much as through the intuitive perception (that is, the emotional and imaginative perception) of its particular kind of beauty. The creative act was, for him, the "intuitive expression" of ". . . the whole man: the man who thinks and wills, and loves, and hates; who is strong and weak, sublime and pathetic, good and wicked; man in the exultation and agony of living; and together with the man, integral with him, it is all nature in its perpetual labour of evolution." It is not too difficult to see here the relationship between Croce's intuitive and sensitive artist and Gourmont's artist whose whole being is expressed through the medium of his technical accomplishments—"Style is the man." It makes little difference, therefore, whether we see our modern critics as influenced by Gourmont or by Croce. In either case, they were directed toward a consideration of the relationship of the artist to his work, the relationship of the work to its audience.

Contemporary with Spingarn was another academic, Irving Babbitt, who was a teacher of T. S. Eliot at Harvard (a writer, incidentally, whose importance to Eliot's thinking has never been sufficiently acknowledged), but who was as unlike Gourmont and Croce as it is possible to imagine. While Spingarn called himself an anti-Aristotelian, Babbitt thought of himself as a traditionalist and a classicist. He attacked French romanticism as subjective, personal, and relativistic. He did not deny the existence of a certain measure of the intuitive (he called it "taste"), but he insisted upon a controlling standard, "a code of outer rules by which this sensibility was disciplined and held in check." He emphasized the importance of formal structure as opposed to what he considered unbridled experimentalism, traditional standards as opposed to what he called the irresponsible relativism of science in our times. In all of this we can see his influence upon Eliot, and perhaps less directly upon such modern critics as John Crowe Ransom, Allen Tate, Robert Penn Warren, and Yvor Winters. The point at which all of these critics (with the possible exception of Winters) found it impossible to follow Babbitt was in the implications of his writing that literature was primarily a form of ethical instruction, similar in effect to philosophy and religion.

Nevertheless, in the extremes of Spingarn and Babbitt exist those contradictions which Mr. Tate found to have existed in Coleridge's view of poetry and which have carried over as a central preoccupation of our times: Platonism vs. Aristotelianism, subjectivism vs. objectivism, intuition vs. formal judgment. Such problems are not, of course, generally stated in such broad terms. However, they do underlie almost every consideration of the value of a work of art. When Remy de Gourmont says, ". . . style is as personal as the colour of the eyes or the sound of the voice," he is emphasizing the subjective nature of a work of art. Yet the very concept of something which may be called "style" suggests a thing existing apart from its user—a technique. When T. S. Eliot uses a term such as "objective correlative" to explain the function of an action in a drama, he is stressing the separate and independent existence of that action, but he does not deny that the successful "imagining" of the objective sequence of events had its origin in the genius (the sensibility) of its author. Such distinctions in the broad sense, though the critic is dependent upon them, belong rightfully to the realm of philosophy, or within that branch of philosophy known as aesthetics.

Benedetto Croce is, of course, primarily a philosopher. Another modern philosopher whose concern with aesthetics parallels the interests of the modern critic is George Santayana. Perhaps one reason we hear so little about Santayana's views on art is that there is so little disagreement between him and the assumptions of contemporary criticism. His aesthetic views represent an attempt to bridge the contradictions mentioned above. What is beauty? How is it achieved? How is it perceived and recognized? A general statement of his answers would differ little from the conclusions of criticism: "Beauty is pleasure regarded as the quality of a thing . . . beauty is constituted by the objectification of pleasure. It is pleasure objectified." Yet a thing of beauty is not wholly unrelated to its maker, the time in which it is created, or the materials from which it is fashioned. Its principal aim is not utility, or even knowledge; yet to call it mere "entertainment" is hedonistic and does not suggest its real value. It must not be without moral value, yet its concern with morals differs from that of the philosophical treatise or the religious tract. Santayana's distinctions are, finally, similar to Coleridge's divisions of science and art. Science is concerned with utility, art with ornament; but the real distinction is that utility suggests an extrinsic value, a value outside itself, and is thus servile—the value of art (beauty) is intrinsic, thus free.

Some such assumption as this was behind the critical writings of Henry James, although confined wholly to problems of fiction. He saw art as probably the highest form of human expression and fiction as one of the highest forms of art. Its structure was organic (as was the structure of poetry for Coleridge); the truths which it revealed were implicit rather than explicit, as they are in music or in painting. But the criticism of fiction has not until very recently become an important preoccupation of modern criticism. The history of the present interest in Henry James probably began with the enthusiasm of Ezra Pound soon after James's death, but did not become general until sometime following the publication of the James issue of *Hound & Horn* in 1934. Since 1940 it is probably no exaggeration to say that the major portion of our critics have turned from a concern with problems of poetry to an interest in the criticism of fiction, and in almost every case the critical concepts of James have been at the center of their work.

The essays in this opening section, then, deal primarily with general problems, but are selected to indicate those problems which modern critics have considered most pertinent to our times. A reasonably clear understanding of such problems is necessary to any real appreciation or understanding of much of the writing done during the second quarter of our century.

FROM BIOGRAPHIA LITERARIA, XIV

SAMUEL TAYLOR COLERIDGE

OCCASION OF THE LYRICAL BALLADS, AND THE OBJECTS ORIGINALLY PROPOSED—PREFACE TO THE SECOND EDITION—THE ENSUING CONTROVERSY, ITS CAUSES AND ACRIMONY—PHILOSOPHIC DEFINITIONS OF A POEM AND POETRY WITH SCHOLIA

DURING the first year that Mr. Wordsworth and I were neighbours, our conversations turned frequently on the two cardinal points of poetry, the power of exciting the sympathy of the reader by a faithful adherence to the truth of nature, and the power of giving the interest of novelty by the modifying colours of imagination. The sudden charm, which accidents of light and shade, which moonlight or sunset diffused over a known and familiar landscape, appeared to represent the practicability of combining both. These are the poetry of nature. The thought suggested itself—(to which of us I do not recollect)—that a series of poems might be composed of two sorts. In the one, the incidents and agents were to be, in part at least, supernatural; and the excellence aimed at was to consist in the interesting of the affections by the dramatic truth of such emotions, as would naturally accompany such situations, supposing them real. And real in this sense they have been to every human being who, from whatever source of delusion, has at any time believed himself under supernatural agency. For the second class, subjects were to be chosen from ordinary life; the characters and incidents were to be such as will be found in every village and its vicinity, where there is a meditative and feeling mind to seek after them, or to notice them, when they present themselves.

In this idea originated the plan of the LYRICAL BALLADS; in which it was agreed, that my endeavours should be directed to persons and characters supernatural, or at least romantic; yet so as to transfer from our inward nature a human interest and a semblance of truth sufficient to procure for these shadows of imagination that willing suspension of disbelief for the moment, which constitutes poetic faith. Mr. Wordsworth, on the other hand, was to propose to himself as his object, to give the charm of novelty to things of every day, and to excite a feeling analogous to the supernatural, by awakening the mind's attention to the lethargy of custom, and directing it to the loveliness and the wonders of the world before us; an inexhaustible treasure, but for which, in consequence of the film of familiarity and selfish solicitude, we have eyes, yet see not, ears that hear not, and hearts that neither feel nor understand.

With this view I wrote THE ANCIENT MARINER, and was preparing among other poems, THE DARK LADIE, and the CHRISTABEL, in which I should have more nearly realized my ideal, than I had done in my first attempt. But Mr. Wordsworth's industry had proved so much more successful, and the number of his poems so much greater, that my compositions, instead of forming a balance, appeared rather an interpolation of heterogeneous matter. Mr. Wordsworth added two or three poems written in his own character, in the impassioned, lofty, and sustained diction, which is characteristic of his genius. In this form the LYRICAL BALLADS were published; and were presented by him, as an experiment, whether subjects, which from their nature rejected the usual ornaments and extra-colloquial style of poems in general, might not be so managed in the language of ordinary life as to produce the pleasurable interest, which it is the peculiar business of poetry to impart. To the second edition he added a preface of considerable length; in which, notwithstanding some passages of apparently a contrary import, he was understood to contend for the extension of this style to poetry of all kinds, and to reject as vicious and indefensible all phrases and forms of speech that were not included in what he (unfortunately, I think, adopting an equivocal expression) called the language of real life. From this preface, prefixed to poems in which it was impossible to deny the presence of original genius, however mistaken its direction might be deemed, arose the whole long-continued controversy. For from the conjunction of perceived power with supposed heresy I explain the inveteracy and in some instances, I grieve to say, the acrimonious passions, with which the controversy has been conducted by the assailants.

Had Mr. Wordsworth's poems been the silly, the childish things, which they were for a long time described as being; had they been really distinguished from the compositions of other poets merely by meanness of language and inanity of thought; had they indeed contained nothing more than what is found in the parodies and pretended imitations of them; they must have sunk at once, a dead weight, into the slough of oblivion, and have dragged the preface along with them. But year after year increased the number of Mr. Wordsworth's admirers. They were found too not in the lower classes of the reading public, but chiefly among young men of strong sensibility and meditative minds; and their admiration (inflamed perhaps in some degree by opposition) was distinguished by its intensity, I might almost say, by its religious fervour. These facts, and the intellectual energy of the author, which was more or less consciously felt, where it was outwardly and even boisterously denied, meeting with sentiments of aversion to his opinions, and of alarm at their consequences, produced an eddy of criticism, which would of itself have borne up the poems by the violence with which it whirled them round and round. With many parts of this preface in the sense attributed to them and which the words undoubtedly seem to authorize, I never concurred; but on the contrary objected to them as erroneous in principle, and as contradictory (in appearance at least) both to other parts of the same preface, and to the author's own practice in the greater part of the poems themselves. Mr. Wordsworth in his recent collection has, I find, degraded this prefatory disquisition to the end of his second volume, to be read or not at the reader's choice. But he has not, as far as I can discover, announced any change in his poetic creed. At all events, considering it as the source of a controversy, in which I have been honoured more than I deserve by the frequent conjunction of my name with his, I think it expedient to declare once for all, in what points I coincide with the opinions supported in that preface, and in what points I altogether differ. But in order to render myself intelligible I must previously, in as few words as possible, explain my views, first, of a Poem; and secondly, of Poetry itself, in kind, and in essence.

The office of philosophical disquisition consists in just distinction; while it is the privilege of the philosopher to preserve himself constantly aware, that distinction is not division. In order to obtain adequate notions of any truth, we must intellectually separate its distinguishable parts; and this is the technical process of philosophy. But having so done, we must then restore them in our conceptions to the unity, in which they actually coexist; and this is the result of philosophy. A poem contains the same elements as a prose composition; the difference therefore must consist in a different combination of them, in consequence of a different object being proposed. According to the difference of the object will be the difference of the combination. It is possible, that the object may be merely to facilitate the recollection of any given facts or observations by artificial arrangement; and the composition will be a poem, merely because it is distinguished from prose by metre, or by rhyme, or by both conjointly. In this, the lowest sense, a man might attribute the name of a poem to the well-known enumeration of the days in the several months;

> "Thirty days hath September,
> April, June, and November," &c.

and others of the same class and purpose. And as a particular pleasure is found in anticipating the recurrence of sounds and quantities, all compositions that have this charm superadded, whatever be their contents, *may* be entitled poems.

So much for the superficial form. A difference of object and contents supplies an additional ground of distinction. The immediate purpose may be the communication of truths; either of truth absolute and demonstrable, as in works of science; or of facts experienced and recorded, as in history. Pleasure, and that of the highest and most permanent kind, may result from the attainment of the end; but it is not itself the immediate end. In other works the communication of pleasure may be the immediate purpose; and though truth, either moral or intellectual, ought to be the ultimate end, yet this will distinguish the character of the author, not the class to which the work belongs. Blest indeed is that state of society, in which the immediate purpose would be baffled by the perversion of the proper ultimate end; in which no charm of diction or imagery could exempt the BATHYLLUS even of an Anacreon, or the ALEXIS of Virgil, from disgust and aversion!

But the communication of pleasure may be the immediate object of a work not metrically composed; and that object may have been in a high degree attained, as in novels and romances. Would then the mere superaddition of metre, with or without rhyme, entitle these to the name of poems? The answer is, that nothing can permanently please, which does not contain in itself the reason why it is so, and not otherwise. If metre be superadded, all other parts must be made consonant with it. They must be such, as to justify the perpetual and distinct attention to each part, which an exact correspondent recurrence of accent and sound are calculated to excite. The final definition then, so deduced, may be thus worded. A poem is that species of composition, which is opposed to works of science, by proposing for its *immediate* object pleasure, not truth; and from all other species—(having *this* object in common with it)—it is discriminated by proposing to itself such delight from the *whole,* as is compatible with a distinct gratification from each component *part*.

Controversy is not seldom excited in consequence of the disputants attaching each a different meaning to the same word; and in few instances has this been more striking, than in disputes concerning the present subject. If a man chooses to call every composition a poem, which is rhyme, or measure, or both, I must leave his opinion uncontroverted. The distinction is at least competent to characterize the writer's intention. If it were subjoined, that the whole is likewise entertaining or affecting, as a tale, or as a series of interesting reflections, I of course admit this as another fit ingredient of a poem, and an additional merit. But if the definition sought for be that of a *legitimate* poem, I answer, it must be one, the parts of which mutually support and explain each other; all in their proportion harmonizing with, and supporting the purpose and known influences of metrical arrangement. The philosophic critics of all ages coincide with the ultimate judgment of all countries, in equally denying the praises of a just poem, on the one hand, to a series of striking lines or distiches, each of which, absorbing the whole attention of the reader to itself, becomes disjoined from its context, and forms a separate whole, instead of a harmonizing part; and on the other hand, to an unsustained composition, from which the reader collects rapidly the general result unattracted by the component parts. The reader should be carried forward, not merely or chiefly by the mechanical impulse of curiosity, or by a restless desire to arrive at the final solution; but by the pleasureable activity of mind excited by the attractions of the journey itself. Like the motion of a serpent, which the Egyptians made the emblem of intellectual power; or like the path of sound through the air;—at every step he pauses and half recedes, and from the retrogressive movement collects the force which again carries him onward. *Praecipitandus est liber spiritus,*[1] says Petronius most happily. The epithet, *liber,* here balances the preceding verb; and it is not easy to conceive more meaning condensed in fewer words.

But if this should be admitted as a satisfactory character of a poem, we have still to seek for a definition of poetry. The writings of Plato, and Jeremy Taylor, and Burnet's Theory of the Earth, furnish undeniable proofs that poetry of the highest kind may exist without metre, and even without the contradistinguishing objects of a poem. The first chapter of Isaiah—(indeed a very large portion of the whole book)—is poetry in the most emphatic sense; yet it would be not less irrational than strange to assert, that pleasure, and not truth was the immediate object of the prophet. In short, whatever specific import we attach to the word, Poetry, there will be found involved in it, as a necessary consequence, that a poem of any length neither can be, nor ought to be, all poetry. Yet if an har-

---

[1] [The free spirit must be brought down.]

monious whole is to be produced, the remaining parts must be preserved in keeping with the poetry; and this can be no otherwise effected than by such a studied selection and artificial arrangement, as will partake of one, though not a peculiar property of poetry. And this again can be no other than the property of exciting a more continuous and equal attention than the language of prose aims at, whether colloquial or written.

My own conclusions on the nature of poetry, in the strictest use of the word, have been in part anticipated in some of the remarks on the Fancy and Imagination in the early part of this work. What is poetry?—is so nearly the same question with, what is a poet?—that the answer to the one is involved in the solution of the other. For it is a distinction resulting from the poetic genius itself, which sustains and modifies the images, thoughts, and emotions of the poet's own mind.

The poet, described in ideal perfection, brings the whole soul of man into activity, with the subordination of its faculties to each other according to their relative worth and dignity. He diffuses a tone and spirit of unity, that blends, and (as it were) *fuses,* each into each, by that synthetic and magical power, to which I would exclusively appropriate the name of Imagination. This power, first put in action by the will and understanding, and retained under their irremissive, though gentle and unnoticed, control, *laxis effertur habenis,*[1] reveals itself in the balance or reconcilement of opposite or discordant qualities; of sameness, with difference; of the general with the concrete; the idea with the image; the individual with the representative; the sense of novelty and freshness with old and familiar objects; a more than usual state of emotion with more than usual order; judgment ever awake and steady self-possession with enthusiasm and feeling profound or vehement; and while it blends and harmonizes the natural and the artificial, still subordinates art to nature; the manner to the matter; and our admiration of the poet to our sympathy with the poetry. Doubtless, as Sir John Davies observes of the soul—(and his words may with slight alteration be applied, and even more appropriately, to the poetic Imagination)—

> Doubtless this could not be, but that she turns
>   Bodies to *spirit* by sublimation strange,
> As fire converts to fire the things it burns,
>   As we our food into our nature change.

> From their gross matter she abstracts *their* forms,
>   And draws a kind of quintessence from things;
> Which to her proper nature she transforms
>   To bear them light on her celestial wings.

---

[1] [Is swept along with reins loose.]

Thus does she, when from *individual states*
She doth abstract the universal kinds;
Which then re-clothed in divers names and fates
Steal access through the senses to our minds.

Finally, Good Sense is the Body of poetic genius, Fancy its Drapery, Motion its Life, and Imagination the Soul that is everywhere, and in each; and forms all into one graceful and intelligent whole.

THE FUNCTION OF CRITICISM AT THE PRESENT TIME

MATTHEW ARNOLD

Many objections have been made to a proposition which, in some remarks of mine on translating Homer, I ventured to put forth; a proposition about criticism, and its importance at the present day. I said that "of the literature of France and Germany, as of the intellect of Europe in general, the main effort, for now many years, has been a critical effort; the endeavour, in all branches of knowledge, theology, philosophy, history, art, science, to see the object as in itself it really is." I added, that owing to the operation in English literature of certain causes, "almost the last thing for which one would come to English literature is just that very thing which now Europe most desires,—criticism"; and that the power and value of English literature was thereby impaired. More than one rejoinder declared that the importance I here assigned to criticism was excessive, and asserted the inherent superiority of the creative effort of the human spirit over its critical effort. And the other day, having been led by an excellent notice of Wordsworth, published in the *North British Review,* to turn again to his biography, I found, in the words of this great man, whom I, for one, must always listen to with the profoundest respect, a sentence passed on the critic's business, which seems to justify every possible disparagement of it. Wordsworth says in one of his letters:—

"The writers in these publications" (the *Reviews*), "while they prosecute their inglorious employment, cannot be supposed to be in a state of mind very favourable for being affected by the finer influences of a thing so pure as genuine poetry."

And a trustworthy reporter of his conversation quotes a more elaborate judgment to the same effect:—

"Wordsworth holds the critical power very low, infinitely lower than the inventive; and he said to-day that if the quantity of time consumed in writing critiques on the works of others were given to original composition, of whatever kind it might be, it would be much better employed; it would make a man find out sooner his own level, and it would do infinitely less mischief. A false or malicious criticism may do much injury to the minds of others; a stupid invention, either in prose or verse, is quite harmless."

It is almost too much to expect of poor human nature, that a man capable of producing some effect in one line of literature, should, for the greater good of society, voluntarily doom himself to impotence and obscurity in another. Still less is this to be expected from men addicted to the composition of the "false or malicious criticism" of which Wordsworth speaks. However, everybody would admit that a false or malicious criticism had better never have been written. Everybody, too, would be willing to admit, as a general proposition, that the critical faculty is lower than the inventive. But is it true that criticism is really, in itself, a baneful and injurious employment? is it true that all time given to writing critiques on the works of others would be much better employed if it were given to original composition, of whatever kind this may be? Is it true that Johnson had better have gone on producing more *Irenes* instead of writing his *Lives of the Poets?* nay, is it certain that Wordsworth himself was better employed in making his Ecclesiastical Sonnets than when he made his celebrated Preface, so full of criticism, and criticism of the works of others? Wordsworth was himself a great critic, and it is to be sincerely regretted that he has not left us more criticism; Goethe was one of the greatest of critics, and we may sincerely congratulate ourselves that he has left us so much criticism. Without wasting time over the exaggeration which Wordsworth's judgment on criticism clearly contains, or over an attempt to trace the causes,—not difficult, I think, to be traced,—which may have led Wordsworth to this exaggeration, a critic may with advantage seize an occasion for trying his own conscience, and for asking himself of what real service, at any given moment, the practice of criticism either is, or may be made, to his own mind and spirit, and to the minds and spirits of others.

The critical power is of lower rank than the creative. True; but in assenting to this proposition, one or two things are to be kept in mind. It is undeniable that the exercise of a creative power, that a free creative activity, is the true function of man; it is proved to be so by man's finding in it his true happiness. But it is undeniable, also, that men may have the sense of exercising this free creative activity in other ways than in producing great works of literature or art; if it were not so, all but a very few men would be shut out from the true happiness of all men; they may have it in well-doing, they may have it in learning, they may have it even in criticising. This is one thing to be kept in mind. Another is, that the exercise of the creative power in the production of great works of literature or art, however high this exercise of it may rank, is not at all epochs and under all conditions possible; and that therefore labour may be vainly spent in attempting it, and may with more fruit be used in preparing for it, in rendering it possible. This creative power works with elements, with materials; what if it has not those materials, those elements, ready for its use? In that case it must surely wait till they are ready. Now, in literature, —I will limit myself to literature, for it is about literature that the question arises,—the elements with which the creative power works are ideas; the best ideas on every matter which literature touches, current at the time; at any rate we may lay it down as certain that in modern literature no manifestation of the creative power not working with these can be very important or fruitful. And I say *current* at the time, not merely accessible at the time; for creative literary genius does not principally show itself in discovering new ideas, that is rather the business of the philosopher; the grand work of literary genius is a work of synthesis and exposition, not of analysis and discovery; its gift lies in the faculty of being happily inspired by a certain intellectual and spiritual atmosphere, by a certain order of ideas, when it finds itself in them; of dealing divinely with these ideas, presenting them in the most effective and attractive combinations, making beautiful works with them, in short. But it must have the atmosphere, it must find itself amidst the order of ideas, in order to work freely; and these it is not so easy to command. This is why great creative epochs in literature are so rare; this is why there is so much that is unsatisfactory in the productions of many men of real genius; because, for the creation of a master-work of literature two powers must concur, the power of the man and the power of the moment, and the man is not enough without the moment; the creative power has, for its happy exercise, appointed elements, and those elements are not in its own control.

Nay, they are more within the control of the critical power. It is the business of the critical power, as I said in the words already quoted, "in all branches of knowledge, theology, philosophy, history, art, science, to see the object as in itself it really is." Thus it tends, at last, to make an intellectual situation of which the creative power can profitably avail itself. It tends to establish an order of ideas, if not absolutely true, yet true by comparison with that which it displaces; to make the best ideas prevail.

Presently these new ideas reach society, the touch of truth is the touch of life, and there is a stir and growth everywhere; out of this stir and growth come the creative epochs of literature.

Or, to narrow our range, and quit these considerations of the general march of genius and of society,—considerations which are apt to become too abstract and impalpable,—every one can see that a poet, for instance, ought to know life and the world before dealing with them in poetry; and life and the world being in modern times, very complex things, the creation of a modern poet, to be worth much, implies a great critical effort behind it; else it would be a comparatively poor, barren, and short-lived affair. This is why Byron's poetry had so little endurance in it, and Goethe's so much; both had a great productive power, but Goethe's was nourished by a great critical effort providing the true materials for it, and Byron's was not; Goethe knew life and the world, the poet's necessary subjects, much more comprehensively and more thoroughly than Byron. He knew a great deal more of them, and he knew them much more as they really are.

It has long seemed to me that the burst of creative activity in our literature, through the first quarter of this century, had about it in fact something premature; and that from this cause its productions are doomed, most of them, in spite of the sanguine hopes which accompanied and do still accompany them, to prove hardly more lasting than the productions of far less splendid epochs. And this prematureness comes from its having proceeded without having its proper data, without sufficient materials to work with. In other words, the English poetry of the first quarter of this century, with plenty of energy, plenty of creative force, did not know enough. This makes Byron so empty of matter, Shelley so incoherent, Wordsworth even, profound as he is, yet so wanting in completeness and variety. Wordsworth cared little for books, and disparaged Goethe. I admire Wordsworth, as he is, so much that I cannot wish him different; and it is vain, no doubt, to imagine such a man different from what he is, to suppose that he could have been different; but surely the one thing wanting to make Wordsworth an even greater poet than he is,—his thought richer, and his influence of wider application,—was that he should have read more books, among them, no doubt, those of that Goethe whom he disparaged without reading him. But to speak of books and reading may easily lead to a misunderstanding here. It was not really books and reading that lacked to our poetry at this epoch; Shelley had plenty of reading. Coleridge had immense reading. Pindar and Sophocles—as we all say so glibly, and often with so little discernment of the real import of what we are saying—had not many books; Shakespeare was no deep reader. True; but in the Greece of Pindar and Sophocles, in the England of Shakespeare, the poet lived in a current of ideas in the highest degree animating and nourishing to the creative power; society was, in the fullest measure, permeated by fresh thought, intelligent and alive; and this state of things is the true basis for the creative power's exercise, in this it finds its data, its materials, truly ready for its hand; all the books and reading in the world are only valuable as they are helps to this. Even when this does not actually exist, books and reading may enable a man to construct a kind of semblance of it in his own mind, a world of knowledge and intelligence in which he may live and work; this is by no means an equivalent to the artist for the nationally diffused life and thought of the epochs of Sophocles or Shakespeare; but, besides that it may be a means of preparation for such epochs, it does really constitute, if many share in it, a quickening and sustaining atmosphere of great value. Such an atmosphere the many-sided learning and the long and widely-combined critical effort of Germany formed for Goethe, when he lived and worked. There was no national glow of life and thought there as in the Athens of Pericles or the England of Elizabeth. That was the poet's weakness. But there was a sort of equivalent for it in the complete culture and unfettered thinking of a large body of Germans. That was his strength. In the England of the first quarter of this century there was neither a national glow of life and thought, such as we had in the age of Elizabeth, nor yet a culture and a force of learning and criticism such as were to be found in Germany. Therefore the creative power of poetry wanted, for success in the highest sense, materials and a basis; a thorough interpretation of the world was necessarily denied to it.

At first sight it seems strange that out of the immense stir of the French Revolution and its age should not have come a crop of works of genius equal to that which came out of the stir of the great productive time of Greece, or out of that of the Renaissance, with its powerful episode the Reformation. But the truth is that the stir of the French Revolution took a character which essentially distinguished it from such movements as these. These were, in the main, disinterestedly intellectual and spiritual movements; movements in which the human spirit looked for its satisfaction in itself and in the increased play of its own activity: the French Revolution took a political, practical character. This Revolution—the object of so much blind love and so much blind hatred,—found indeed its motive-power in the intelligence of men, and not in their practical sense;—this is what distinguishes it from the English Revolution of Charles the First's time; this is what makes it a more spiritual event than our Revolution, an event of much more powerful and world-wide interest, though practically less successful—it appeals to an order of ideas which are universal, certain, permanent. 1789 asked of a thing, Is it rational? 1642 asked of a thing, Is it legal? or, when it went furthest, Is it according to conscience? This is the English fashion, a fashion to be treated, within its own sphere, with the highest respect; for its success, within its own sphere, has been prodigious. But what is law in one place is not law in another; what is law here to-day is not law even here to-morrow; and as for conscience, what is binding on one man's conscience is not binding on another's. The old woman who threw her stool at the head of the surpliced minister in the Tron Church at Edinburgh obeyed an impulse to which millions of the human race may be permitted to remain strangers. But the prescriptions of reason are absolute, unchanging, of universal validity; *to count by tens is the easiest way of counting*—that is a proposition of which every one, from here to the Antipodes, feels the force; at least I should say so if we did not live in a country where it is not impossible that any morning we may find a letter in the *Times* declaring that a decimal coinage is an absurdity. That a whole nation should have been penetrated with an enthusiasm for pure reason, and with an ardent zeal for making its prescriptions triumph, is a very remarkable thing, when we consider how little of mind, or anything so worthy and quickening as mind, comes into the motives which alone, in general, impel great masses of men. In spite of the extravagant direction given to this enthusiasm, in spite of the crimes and follies in which it lost itself, the French Revolution derives from the force, truth, and universality of the ideas which it took for its law, and from the passion with which it could inspire a multitude for these ideas, a unique and still living power; it is—it will probably long remain—the greatest, the most animating event in history. And as no sincere passion for the things of the mind, even though it turn out in many respects an unfortunate passion, is ever quite thrown away and quite barren of good, France has reaped from hers one fruit, the natural and legitimate fruit, though not precisely the grand fruit she expected: she is the country in Europe where *the people* is most alive.

But the mania for giving an immediate political and practical application to all these fine ideas of the reason was fatal. Here an Englishman is in his element: on this theme we can all go for hours. And all we are in the habit of saying on it has undoubtedly a great deal of truth. Ideas cannot be too much prized in and for themselves, cannot be too much lived with; but to transport them abruptly into the world of politics and practice, violently to revolutionise this world to their bidding,—that is quite another thing. There is the world of ideas and there is the world of practice; the French are often for suppressing the one and the English the other; but neither is to be suppressed. A member of the House of Com-

litical and practical so much that ideas easily become objects of dislike in his eyes, and thinkers "miscreants," because ideas and thinkers have rashly meddled with politics and practice. This would be all very well if the dislike and neglect confined themselves to ideas transported out of their own sphere, and meddling rashly with practice; but they are inevitably extended to ideas as such, and to the whole life of intelligence; practice is everything, a free play of the mind is nothing. The notion of the free play of the mind upon all subjects being a pleasure in itself, being an object of desire, being an essential provider of elements without which a nation's spirit, whatever compensations it may have for them, must, in the long run, die of inanition, hardly enters into an Englishman's thoughts. It is noticeable that the word *curiosity,* which in other languages is used in a good sense, to mean, as a high and fine quality of man's nature, just this disinterested love of a free play of the mind on all subjects, for its own sake,—it is noticeable, I say, that this word has in our language no sense of the kind, no sense but a rather bad and disparaging one. But criticism, real criticism, is essentially the exercise of this very quality; it obeys an instinct prompting it to try to know the best that is known and thought in the world, irrespectively of practice, politics, and everything of the kind; and to value knowledge and thought as they approach this best, without the intrusion of any other considerations whatever. This is an instinct for which there is, I think little original sympathy in the practical English nature, and what there was of it has undergone a long benumbing period of check and suppression in the epoch of concentration which followed the French Revolution.

But epochs of concentration cannot well endure for ever; epochs of expansion, in the due course of things, follow them. Such an epoch of expansion seems to be opening in this country. In the first place all danger of a hostile forcible pressure of foreign ideas upon our practice has long disappeared; like the traveller in the fable, therefore, we begin to wear our cloak a little more loosely. Then, with a long peace the ideas of Europe steal gradually and amicably in, and mingle, though in infinitesimally small quantities at a time, with our own notions. Then, too, in spite of all that is said about the absorbing and brutalising influence of our passionate material progress, it seems to me indisputable that this progress is likely, though not certain, to lead in the end to an apparition of intellectual life; and that man, after he has made himself perfectly comfortable and has now to determine what to do with himself next, may begin to remember that he has a mind, and that the mind may be made the source of great pleasure. I grant it is mainly the privilege of faith, at present, to discern this end to our railways, our business, and our fortune-making; but we shall see if, here as elsewhere, faith is not in the end the true prophet. Our ease, our travelling, and our unbounded liberty to hold just as hard and securely as we please to the practice to which our notions have given birth, all tend to beget an inclination to deal a little more freely with these notions themselves, to canvass them a little, to penetrate a little into their real nature. Flutterings of curiosity, in the foreign sense of the word, appear amongst us, and it is in these that criticism must look to find its account. Criticism first; a time of true creative activity, perhaps,—which, as I have said, must inevitably be preceded amongst us by a time of criticism,—hereafter, when criticism has done its work.

It is of the last importance that English criticism should clearly discern what rules for its course, in order to avail itself of the field now opening to it, and to produce fruit for the future, it ought to take. The rules may be given in one word; by being *disinterested*. And how is it to be disinterested? By keeping aloof from practice; by resolutely following the law of its own nature, which is to be a free play of the mind on all subjects which it touches; by steadily refusing to lend itself to any of those ulterior, political, practical considerations about ideas, which plenty of people will be sure to attach to them, which perhaps ought often to be attached to them, which in this country at any rate are certain to be attached to them quite sufficiently, but which criticism has really nothing to do with. Its business is, as I have said, simply to know the best that is known and thought in the world, and by in its turn making this known, to create a current of true and fresh ideas. Its business is to do this with inflexible honesty, with due ability; but its business is to do no more, and to leave alone all questions of practical consequences and applications, questions which will never fail to have due prominence given to them. Else criticism, besides being really false to its own nature, merely continues in the old rut which it has hitherto followed in this country, and will certainly miss the chance now given to it. For what is at present the bane of criticism in this country? It is that practical considerations cling to it and stifle it; it subserves interests not its own; our organs of criticism are organs of men and parties having practical ends to serve, and with them those practical ends are the first thing and the play of mind the second; so much play of mind as is compatible with the prosecution of those practical ends is all that is wanted. An organ like the *Revue des Deux Mondes,* having for its main function to understand and utter the best that is known and thought in the world, existing, it may be said, as just an organ for a free play of the mind, we have not; but we have the *Edinburgh Review,* existing as an organ of the old Whigs, and for as much play of the mind as may suit its being that; we have the *Quarterly Review,* existing as an organ of the Tories, and for as much play of mind as may suit its being that; we have the *British Quarterly Review,* existing as an organ of the political Dissenters, and for as much play of mind as may suit its being that; we have the *Times,* existing as an organ of the common, satisfied, well-to-do Englishman, and for as much play of mind as may suit its being that. And so on through all the various factions, political and religious, of our society; every faction has, as such, its organ of criticism, but the notion of combining all factions in the common pleasure of a free disinterested play of mind meets with no favour. Directly this play of mind wants to have more scope, and to forget the pressure of practical considerations a little, it is checked, it is made to feel the chain. We saw this the other day in the extinction, so much to be regretted, of the *Home and Foreign Review;* perhaps in no organ of criticism in this country was there so much knowledge, so much play of mind; but these could not save it. *The Dublin Review* subordinates play of mind to the practical business of Roman Catholicism, and lives. It must needs be that men should act in sects and parties, that each of these sects and parties should have its organ, and should make this organ subserve the interests of its action; but it would be well, too, that there should be a criticism, not the minister of these interests, not their enemy, but absolutely and entirely independent of them. No other criticism will ever attain any real authority or make any real way towards its end,—the creating a current of true and fresh ideas.

It is because criticism has so little kept in the pure intellectual sphere, has so little detached itself from practice, has been so directly polemical and controversial, that it has so ill accomplished, in this country, its best spiritual work; which is to keep man from a self-satisfaction which is retarding and vulgarising, to lead him towards perfection, by making his mind dwell upon what is excellent in itself, and the absolute beauty and fitness of things. A polemical practical criticism makes men blind even to the ideal imperfection of their practice, makes them willingly assert its ideal perfection, in order the better to secure it against attack; and clearly this is narrowing and baneful for them. If they were reassured on the practical side, speculative considerations of ideal perfection they might be brought to entertain, and their spiritual horizon would thus gradually widen. Mr Adderley says to the Warwickshire farmers:—

"Talk of the improvement of breed! Why, the race we ourselves represent, the men and women, the old Anglo-Saxon race, are the best breed in the whole world. . . . The absence of a too enervating climate, too unclouded skies, and a too luxurious nature, has produced so vigorous a race of people, and has rendered us so superior to all the world."

Mr Roebuck says to the Sheffield cutlers:—

"I look around me and ask what is the state of England? Is not property safe? Is not every man able to say what he likes? Can you not walk from one end of England to the other in perfect security? I ask you whether, the world over or in past history, there is anything like it? Nothing. I pray that our unrivalled happiness may last."

Now obviously there is a peril for poor human nature in words and thoughts of such exuberant self-satisfaction, until we find ourselves safe in the streets of the Celestial City.

> Das wenige verschwindet leicht dem Blicke
> Der vorwärts sieht, wie viel noch übrig bleibt—

says Goethe; "the little that is done seems nothing when we look forward and see how much we have yet to do." Clearly this is a better line of reflection for weak humanity, so long as it remains on this earthly field of labour and trial. But neither Mr Adderley nor Mr Roebuck is by nature inaccessible to considerations of this sort. They only lose sight of them owing to the controversial life we all lead, and the practical form which all speculation takes with us. They have in view opponents whose aim is not ideal, but practical; and in their zeal to uphold their own practice against these innovators, they go so far as even to attribute to this practice an ideal perfection. Somebody has been wanting to introduce a six-pound franchise, or to abolish church-rates, or to collect agricultural statistics by force, or to diminish local self-government. How natural, in reply to such proposals, very likely improper or ill-timed, to go a little beyond the mark and to say stoutly, "Such a race of people as we stand, so superior to all the world! The old Anglo-Saxon race, the best breed in the whole world! I pray that our unrivalled happiness may last! I ask you whether, the world over or in past history, there is anything like it?" And so long as criticism answers this dithyramb by insisting that the old Anglo-Saxon race would be still more superior to all others if it had no church-rates, or that our unrivalled happiness would last yet longer with a six-pound franchise, so long will the strain, "The best breed in the whole world!" swell louder and louder, everything ideal and refining will be lost out of sight, and both the assailed and their critics will remain in a sphere, to say the truth, perfectly unintelligent, a sphere in which spiritual progression is impossible. But let criticism leave church-rates and the franchise alone, and in the most candid spirit, without a single lurking thought of practical innovation, confront with our dithyramb this paragraph on which I stumbled in a newspaper immediately after reading Mr Roebuck:—

"A shocking child murder has just been committed at Nottingham. A girl named Wragg left the workhouse there on Saturday morning with her young illegitimate child. The child was soon afterwards found dead on Mapperly Hills, having been strangled. Wragg is in custody."

Nothing but that; but, in juxtaposition with the absolute eulogies of Mr Adderley and Mr Roebuck, how eloquent, how suggestive are those few lines! "Our Old Anglo-Saxon breed, the best in the whole world!"—how much that is harsh and ill-favoured there is in this best! *Wragg!* If we are to talk of ideal perfection, of "the best in the whole world," has any one reflected what a touch of grossness in our race, what an original shortcoming in the more delicate spiritual perceptions, is shown by the natural growth amongst us of such hideous names,—Higginbottom, Stiggins, Bugg! In Ionia and Attica they were luckier in this respect than "the best race in the world"; by the Ilissus there was no Wragg, poor thing! And "our unrivalled happiness";—what an element of grimness, bareness, and hideousness mixes with it and blurs it; the workhouse, the dismal Mapperly Hills,—how dismal those who have seen them will remember;—the gloom, the smoke, the cold, the strangled illegitimate child! "I ask you whether, the world over or in past history, there is anything like it?" It may be so, one is inclined to answer; but at any rate, in that case, the world is very much to be pitied. And the final touch,—short, bleak and inhuman: *Wragg is in custody.* The sex lost in the confusion of our unrivalled happiness; or shall I say, the superfluous Christian name lopped off by the straightforward vigour of our old Anglo-Saxon breed? There is profit for the spirit in such contrasts as this; criticism serves the cause of perfection by establishing them. By eluding sterile conflict, by refusing to remain in the sphere where alone narrow and relative conceptions have any worth and validity, criticism may diminish its momentary importance, but only in this way has it a chance of gaining admittance for those wider and more perfect conceptions to which all its duty is really owed. Mr Roebuck will have a poor opinion of an adversary who replies to his defiant songs of triumph only by murmuring under his breath, *Wragg is in custody;* but in no other way will these songs of triumph be induced gradually to moderate themselves, to get rid of what in them is excessive and offensive, and to fall into a softer and truer key.

It will be said that it is a very subtle and indirect action which I am thus prescribing for criticism, and that, by embracing in this manner the Indian virtue of detachment and abandoning the sphere of practical life, it condemns itself to a slow and obscure work. Slow and obscure it may be, but it is the only proper work of criticism. The mass of mankind will never have any ardent zeal for seeing things as they are; very inadequate ideas will always satisfy them. On these inadequate ideas reposes, and must repose, the general practice of the world. That is as much as saying that whoever sets himself to see things as they are will find himself one of a very small circle; but it is only by this small circle resolutely doing its own work that adequate ideas will ever get current at all. The rush and roar of practical life will always have a dizzying and attracting effect upon the most collected spectator, and tend to draw him into its vortex; most of all will this be the case where that life is so powerful as it is in England. But it is only by remaining collected, and refusing to lend himself to the point of view of the practical man, that the critic can do the practical man any service, and it is only by the greatest sincerity in pursuing his own course, and by at last convincing even the practical man of his sincerity, that he can escape misunderstandings which perpetually threaten him.

For the practical man is not apt for fine distinctions, and yet in these distinctions truth and the highest culture greatly find their account. But it is not easy to lead a practical man,—unless you reassure him as to your practical intentions, you have no chance of leading him,—to see that a thing which he has always been used to look at from one side only, which he greatly values, and which, looked at from that side, quite deserves, perhaps, all the prizing and admiring which he bestows upon it,—that this thing, looked at from another side, may appear much less beneficent and beautiful, and yet retain all its claims to our practical allegiance. Where shall we find language innocent enough, how shall we make the spotless purity of our intentions evident enough, to enable us to say to the political Englishman that the British constitution itself, which, seen from the practical side, looks such a magnificent organ of progress and virtue, seen from the speculative side,—with its compromises, its love of facts, its horror of theory, its studied avoidance of clear thoughts,—that, seen from this side, our august constitution sometimes looks,—forgive me, shade of Lord Somers!—a colossal machine for the manufacture of Philistines? How is Cobbett to say this and not be misunderstood, blackened as he is with the smoke of a lifelong conflict in the field of political practice? how is Mr Carlyle to say it and not be misunderstood, after his furious raid into this field with his *Latter-day Pamphlets?* how is Mr Ruskin, after his pugnacious political economy? I say, the critic must keep out of the region of immediate practice in the political, social, humanitarian sphere, if he wants to make a beginning for that more free speculative treatment of things, which may perhaps one day make its benefits felt even in this sphere, but in a natural and thence irresistible manner.

Do what he will, however, the critic will still remain exposed to frequent misunderstandings, and nowhere so much as in this country. For here people are particularly indisposed even to comprehend that without this free disinterested treatment of things, truth and the highest culture are out of the question. So immersed are they in practical life, so accustomed to take all their notions from this life and its processes, that they are apt to think that truth and culture themselves can be reached by the processes of this life, and that it is an impertinent singularity to think of reaching them in any other. "We are all *terrae filii,*" [1] cries their eloquent advocate; "all Philistines together. Away with the notion of proceeding by any other way than the way dear to the Philistines; let us have a social movement, let us organise and combine a party to pursue truth and new thought, let us call it *the liberal party,* and let us all stick to each other, and back each other up. Let us have no nonsense about independent criticism, and intellectual delicacy, and the few and the many. Don't let us trouble ourselves about foreign thought; we shall invent the whole thing for ourselves as we go along. If one of us speaks well, applaud him; if one of us speaks ill, applaud him too; we are all in the same movement, we are all liberals, we are all in pursuit of truth." In this way the pursuit of truth becomes really a social, practical, pleasurable affair, almost requiring a chairman, a secretary, and advertisements; with the excitement of a little resistance, an occasional scandal, to give the happy sense of difficulty overcome; but, in general, plenty of bustle and very little thought. To act is so easy, as Goethe says; to think is so hard! It is true that the critic has many temptations to go with the stream, to make one of the party movement, one of these *terrae filii;* it seems ungracious to refuse to be a *terrae filius,* [2] when so many excellent people are; but the critic's duty is to refuse, or, if resistance is vain, at least to cry with Obermann: *Périssons en résistant.* [3]

How serious a matter it is to try and resist, I had ample opportunity of experiencing when I ventured some time ago to criticise the celebrated first volume of Bishop Colenso. The echoes of the storm which was then raised I still, from time to time, hear grumbling round me. That storm arose out of a misunderstanding almost inevitable. It is a result of no little culture to attain to a clear perception that science and religion are two wholly different things; the multitude will for ever confuse them; but happily that is of no great real importance, for while it imagines itself to live by its false science, it does really live by its true religion. Dr Colenso, however, in his first volume did all he could to strengthen the confusion, and to make it dangerous. He did this with the best intentions, I freely admit, and with the most candid ignorance that this was the natural effect of what he was doing; but, says Joubert, "Ignorance, which in matters of

---

[1] [Sons of the earth.]
[2] [Son of the earth.]
[3] [Let us die fighting.]

morals extenuates the crime, is itself, in intellectual matters, a crime of the first order." I criticised Bishop Colenso's speculative confusion. Immediately there was a cry raised: "What is this? here is a liberal attacking a liberal. Do not you belong to the movement? are not you a friend of truth? Is not Bishop Colenso in pursuit of truth? then speak with proper respect of his book. Dr Stanley is another friend of truth, and you speak with proper respect of his book; why make these invidious differences? both books are excellent, admirable, liberal; Bishop Colenso's perhaps the most, because it is the boldest, and will have the best practical consequences for the liberal cause. Do you want to encourage to the attack of a brother liberal his, and your, and our implacable enemies, the *Church and State Review* or the *Record,*—the High Church rhinoceros and the Evangelical hyaena? Be silent, therefore; or rather speak, speak as loud as ever you can! and go into ecstasies over the eight hundred and odd pigeons." But criticism cannot follow this coarse and indiscriminate method. It is unfortunately possible for a man in pursuit of truth to write a book which reposes upon a false conception. Even the practical consequences of a book are to genuine criticism no recommendation of it, if the book is, in the highest sense, blundering. I see that a lady who herself, too, is in pursuit of truth, and who writes with great ability, but a little too much, perhaps, under the influence of the practical spirit of the English liberal movement, classes Bishop Colenso's book and M. Renan's together, in her survey of the religious state of Europe, as facts of the same order, works, both of them, of "great importance"; "great ability, power, and skill"; Bishop Colenso's, perhaps, the most powerful; at least, Miss Cobbe gives special expression to her gratitude that to Bishop Colenso "has been given the strength to grasp, and the courage to teach, truths of such deep import." In the same way, more than one popular writer has compared him to Luther. Now it is just this kind of false estimate which the critical spirit is, it seems to me, bound to resist. It is really the strongest possible proof of the low ebb at which, in England, the critical spirit is, that while the critical hit in the religious literature of Germany is Dr Strauss's book, in that of France M. Renan's book, the book of Bishop Colenso is the critical hit in the religious literature of England. Bishop Colenso's book reposes on a total misconception of the essential elements of the religious problem, as that problem is now presented for solution. To criticism therefore, which seeks to have the best that is known and thought on this problem, it is, however well meant, of no importance whatever. M. Renan's book attempts a new synthesis of the elements furnished to us by the Four Gospels. It attempts, in my opinion, a synthesis, perhaps premature, perhaps impossible, certainly not successful. Perhaps we shall always have to acquiesce in Fleury's sentence on such recastings of the Gospel-story: *Quiconque s'imagine la pouvoir mieux écrire, ne l'entend pas.*[1] M. Renan had himself passed by anticipation a like sentence on his own work, when he said: "If a new presentation of the character of Jesus were offered to me, I would not have it; its very clearness would be, in my opinion, the best proof of its insufficiency." His friends may with perfect truth rejoin that at the sight of the Holy Land, and of the actual scene of the Gospel-story, all the current of M. Renan's thoughts may have naturally changed, and a new casting of that story irresistibly suggested itself to him; and that this is just a case for applying Cicero's maxim; Change of mind is not inconsistency—*nemo doctus unquam mutationem consilii inconstantiam dixit esse.* Nevertheless, for criticism, M. Renan's first thought must still be the truer one, as long as his new casting so fails more fully to commend itself, more fully (to use Coleridge's happy phrase about the Bible) to *find* us. Still M. Renan's attempt is, for criticism, of the most real interest and importance, since, with all its difficulty, a fresh synthesis of the new Testament *data,* is the very essence of the religious problem, as now presented; and only by efforts in this direction can it receive a solution.

Again, in the same spirit in which she judges Bishop Colenso, Miss Cobbe, like so many earnest liberals of our practical race, both here and in America, herself sets vigorously about a positive reconstruction of religion, about making a religion of the future out of hand, or at least setting about making it. We must not rest, she and they are always thinking and saying, in negative criticism, we must be creative and constructive; hence we have such works as her recent *Religious Duty,* and works still more considerable, perhaps, by others, which will be in every one's mind. These works often have much ability; they often spring out of sincere convictions, and a sincere wish to do good; and they sometimes, perhaps, do good. Their fault is (if I may be permitted to say so) one which they have in common with the British College of Health, in the New Road. Every one knows the British College of Health; it is that building with the lion and the statue of the Goddess Hygeia before it; at least I am sure about the lion, though I am not absolutely certain about the Goddess Hygeia. This building does credit, perhaps, to the resources of Dr Morrison and his disciples; but it falls a good deal short of one's idea of what a British College of Health ought to be. In England, where we hate public interference and love individual enterprise, we have a whole crop of places like the British College of Health; the grand name

---

[1] [Whoever supposes that he can write it better, don't listen to him.]

without the grand thing. Unluckily, creditable to individual enterprise as they are, they tend to impair our taste by making us forget what more grandiose, noble, or beautiful character properly belongs to a public institution. The same may be said of the religions of the future of Miss Cobbe and others. Creditable, like the British College of Health, to the resources of their authors, they yet tend to make us forget what more grandiose, noble, or beautiful character properly belongs to religious constructions. The historic religions, with all their faults, have had this; it certainly belongs to the religious sentiment, when it truly flowers, to have this; and we impoverish our spirit if we allow a religion of the future without it. What then is the duty of criticism here? To take the practical point of view, to applaud the liberal movement and all its works,—its New Road religions of the future into the bargain,—for their general utility's sake? By no means; but to be perpetually dissatisfied with these works, while they perpetually fall short of a high and perfect ideal.

In criticism, these are elementary laws; but they never can be popular, and in this country they have been very little followed, and one meets with immense obstacles in following them. That is a reason for asserting them again and again. Criticism must maintain its independence of the practical spirit and its aims. Even with well-meant efforts of the practical spirit it must express dissatisfaction, if in the sphere of the ideal they seem impoverishing and limiting. It must not hurry on to the goal because of its practical importance. It must be patient, and know how to wait; and flexible, and know how to attach itself to things and how to withdraw from them. It must be apt to study and praise elements that for the fulness of spiritual perfection are wanted, even though they belong to a power which in the practical sphere may be maleficent. It must be apt to discern the spiritual shortcomings or illusions of powers that in the practical sphere may be beneficent. And this without any notion of favouring or injuring, in the practical sphere, one power or the other; without any notion of playing off, in this sphere, one power against the other. When one looks, for instance, at the English Divorce Court,—an institution which perhaps has its practical conveniences, but which in the ideal sphere is so hideous; an institution which neither makes divorce impossible nor makes it decent, which allows a man to get rid of his wife, or a wife of her husband, but makes them drag one another first, for the public edification, through a mire of unutterable infamy,—when one looks at this charming institution, I say, with its crowded trials, its newspaper reports, and its money compensations, this institution in which the gross unregenerate British Philistine has indeed stamped an image of himself, —one may be permitted to find the marriage theory of Catholicism refreshing and elevating. Or when Protestantism, in virtue of its supposed rational and intellectual origin, gives the law to criticism too magisterially, criticism may and must remind it that its pretensions, in this respect, are illusive and do it harm; that the Reformation was a moral rather than an intellectual event; that Luther's theory of grace no more exactly reflects the mind of the spirit than Bossuet's philosophy of history reflects it; and that there is no more antecedent probability of the Bishop of Durham's stock of ideas being agreeable to perfect reason than of Pope Pius the Ninth's. But criticism will not on that account forget the achievements of Protestantism in the practical and moral sphere; nor that, even in the intellectual sphere, Protestantism, though in a blind and stumbling manner, carried forward the Renaissance, while Catholicism threw itself violently across its path.

I lately heard a man of thought and energy contrasting the want of ardour and movement which he now found amongst young men in this country with what he remembered in his own youth, twenty years ago. "What reformers we were then!" he exclaimed; "what a zeal we had! how we canvassed every institution in Church and State, and were prepared to remodel them all on first principles!" He was inclined to regret, as a spiritual flagging, the lull which he saw. I am disposed rather to regard it as a pause in which the turn to a new mode of spiritual progress is being accomplished. Everything was long seen, by the young and ardent amongst us, in inseparable connection with politics and practical life. We have pretty well exhausted the benefits of seeing things in this connection, we have got all that can be got by so seeing them. Let us try a more disinterested mode of seeing them; let us betake ourselves more to the serener life of the mind and spirit. This life, too, may have its excesses and dangers; but they are not for us at present. Let us think of quietly enlarging our stock of true and fresh ideas, and not, as soon as we get an idea or half an idea, be running out with it into the street, and trying to make it rule there. Our ideas will, in the end, shape the world all the better for maturing a little. Perhaps in fifty years' time it will in the English House of Commons be an objection to an institution that it is an anomaly, and my friend the Member of Parliament will shudder in his grave. But let us in the meanwhile rather endeavour that in twenty years' time it may, in English literature, be an objection to a proposition that it is absurd. That will be a change so vast, that the imagination almost fails to grasp it. *Ab integro soeclorum nascitur ordo.*[1]

If I have insisted so much on the course which criticism must take

---

[1] [The march of the centuries begins anew.—VIRGIL.]

where politics and religion are concerned, it is because, where these burning matters are in question, it is most likely to go astray. In general, its course is determined for it by the idea which is the law of its being; the idea of a disinterested endeavour to learn and propagate the best that is known and thought in the world, and thus to establish a current of fresh and true ideas. By the very nature of things, as England is not all the world, much of the best that is known and thought in the world cannot be of English growth, must be foreign; by the nature of things, again, it is just this that we are least likely to know, while English thought is streaming in upon us from all sides, and takes excellent care that we shall not be ignorant of its existence; the English critic, therefore, must dwell much on foreign thought, and with particular heed on any part of it, which, while significant and fruitful in itself, is for any reason specially likely to escape him. Judging is often spoken of as the critic's one business, and so in some sense it is; but the judgment which almost insensibly forms itself in a fair and clear mind, along with fresh knowledge, is the valuable one; and thus knowledge, and ever fresh knowledge, must be the critic's great concern for himself; and it is by communicating fresh knowledge, and letting his own judgment pass along with it,—but insensibly, and in the second place, not the first, as a sort of companion and clue, not as an abstract lawgiver,—that he will generally do most good to his readers. Sometimes, no doubt, for the sake of establishing an author's place in literature, and his relation to a central standard (and if this is not done, how are we to get at our *best in the world?*) criticism may have to deal with a subject-matter so familiar that fresh knowledge is out of the question, and then it must be all judgment; an enunciation and detailed application of principles. Here the great safeguard is never to let oneself become abstract, always to retain an intimate and lively consciousness of the truth of what one is saying, and, the moment this fails us, to be sure that something is wrong. Still, under all circumstances, this mere judgment and application of principles is, in itself, not the most satisfactory work to the critic; like mathematics, it is tautological, and cannot well give us, like fresh learning, the sense of creative activity. To have this sense is, as I said at the beginning, the great happiness and the great proof of being alive, and it is not denied to criticism to have it; but then criticism must be sincere, simple, flexible, ardent, ever widening its knowledge. Then it may have, in no contemptible measure, a joyful sense of creative activity; a sense which a man of insight and conscience will prefer to what he might derive from a poor, starved, fragmentary, inadequate creation. And at some epochs no other creation is possible.

Still, in full measure, the sense of creative activity belongs only to genuine creation; in literature we must never forget that. But what true man of letters ever can forget it? It is no such common matter for a gifted nature to come into possession of a current of true and living ideas, and to produce amidst the inspiration of them, that we are likely to underrate it. The epochs of Æschylus and Shakespeare make us feel their preeminence. In an epoch like those is, no doubt, the true life of literature; there is the promised land, towards which criticism can only beckon. That promised land it will not be ours to enter, and we shall die in the wilderness; but to have desired to enter it, to have saluted it from afar, is already, perhaps, the best distinction among contemporaries; it will certainly be the best title to esteem with posterity.

THE ART OF FICTION

HENRY JAMES

I SHOULD not have fixed so comprehensive a title to these few remarks, necessarily wanting in any completeness upon a subject the full consideration of which would carry us far, did I not seem to discover a pretext for my temerity in the interesting pamphlet lately published under this name by Mr. Walter Besant. Mr. Besant's lecture at the Royal Institution—the original form of his pamphlet—appears to indicate that many persons are interested in the art of fiction, and are not indifferent to such remarks as those who practise it may attempt to make about it. I am therefore anxious not to lose the benefit of this favourable association, and to edge in a few words under cover of the attention which Mr. Besant is sure to have excited. There is something very encouraging in his having put into form certain of his ideas on the mystery of story-telling.

It is a proof of life and curiosity—curiosity on the part of the brotherhood of novelists as well as on the part of their readers. Only a short time ago it might have been supposed that the English novel was not what the French call *discutable*. It had no air of having a theory, a conviction, a consciousness of itself behind it—of being the expression of an artistic faith, the result of choice and comparison. I do not say it was necessarily the worse for that: it would take much more courage than I possess to intimate that the form of the novel as Dickens and Thackeray (for instance) saw it had any taint of incompleteness. It was, however, *naïf* (if I may help myself out with another French word); and evidently if it be destined to suffer in any way for having lost its *naïveté* it has now an idea of making sure of the corresponding advantages. During the period I have alluded to there was a comfortable, good-humoured feeling abroad that a novel is a novel, as a pudding is a pudding, and that our only business with it could be to swallow it. But within a year or two, for some reason or other, there have been signs of returning animation—the era of discussion would appear to have been to a certain extent opened. Art lives upon discussion, upon experiment, upon curiosity, upon variety of attempt, upon the exchange of views and the comparison of standpoints; and there is a presumption that those times when no one has anything particular to say about it, and has no reason to give for practice or preference, though they may be times of honour, are not times of development—are times, possibly, even a little of dulness. The successful application of any art is a delightful spectacle, but the theory too is interesting; and though there is a great deal of the latter without the former I suspect there has never been a genuine success that has not had a latent core of conviction. Discussion, suggestion, formulation, these things are fertilising when they are frank and sincere. Mr. Besant has set an excellent example in saying what he thinks, for his part, about the way in which fiction should be written, as well as about the way in which it should be published; for his view of the "art," carried on into an appendix, covers that too. Other labourers in the same field will doubtless take up the argument, they will give it the light of their experience, and the effect will surely be to make our interest in the novel a little more what it had for some time threatened to fail to be—a serious, active, inquiring interest, under protection of which this delightful study may, in moments of confidence, venture to say a little more what it thinks of itself.

It must take itself seriously for the public to take it so. The old superstition about fiction being "wicked" has doubtless died out in England; but the spirit of it lingers in a certain oblique regard directed toward any story which does not more or less admit that it is only a joke. Even the most jocular novel feels in some degree the weight of the proscription that was formerly directed against literary levity: the jocularity does not always succeed in passing for orthodoxy. It is still expected, though perhaps people are ashamed to say it, that a production which is after all only a "make-believe" (for what else is a "story"?) shall be in some degree apologetic—shall renounce the pretension of attempting really to represent life. This, of course, any sensible, wide-awake story declines to do, for it quickly perceives that the tolerance granted to it on such a condition is only an attempt to stifle it disguised in the form of generosity. The old evangelical hostility to the novel, which was as explicit as it was narrow, and which regarded it as little less favourable to our immortal part than a stage-play, was in reality far less insulting. The only reason for the existence of a novel is that it does attempt to represent life. When it relinquishes this attempt, the same attempt that we see on the canvas of the painter, it will have arrived at a very strange pass. It is not expected of the picture that it will make itself humble in order to be forgiven; and the analogy between the art of the painter and the art of the novelist is, so far as I am able to see, complete. Their inspiration is the same, their process (allowing for the different quality of the vehicle) is the same, their success is the same. They may learn from each other, they may explain and sustain each other. Their cause is the same, and the honour of one is the honour of another. The Mahometans think a picture an unholy thing, but it is a long time since any Christian did, and it is therefore the more odd that in the Christian mind the traces (dissimulated though they may be) of a suspicion of the sister art should linger to this day. The only effectual way to lay it to rest is to emphasise the analogy to which I just alluded—to insist on the fact that as the picture is reality, so the novel is history. That is the only general description (which does it justice) that we may give of the novel. But history also is allowed to represent life; it is not, any more than painting, expected to apologise. The subject-matter of fiction is stored up likewise in documents and records, and if it will not give itself away, as they say in California, it must speak with assurance, with the tone of the historian. Certain accomplished novelists have a habit of giving themselves away which must often bring tears to the eyes of people who take their fiction seriously. I was lately struck, in reading over many pages of Anthony Trollope, with his want of discretion in this particular. In a digression, a parenthesis or an aside, he concedes to the reader that he and this trusting friend are only "making believe." He admits that the events he narrates have not really happened, and that he can give his narrative any turn the reader may like best. Such a betrayal of a sacred office seems to me, I confess, a terrible crime; it is what I mean by the attitude of apology, and it shocks me every whit as much in Trollope as it would have shocked me in Gibbon or Macaulay. It implies that the novelist is less occupied in looking for the truth (the truth, of course I mean, that he assumes, the premises that we must grant him, whatever they may be) than the historian, and in doing so it deprives him at a stroke of all his standing-room. To represent and illustrate the past, the actions of men, is the task of either writer, and the only difference that I can see is, in proportion as he succeeds, to the honour of the novelist, consisting as it does in his having more difficulty in collecting his evidence, which is so far from being purely literary. It seems to me to give him a great character, the fact that he has at once so much in common with the philosopher and the painter; this double analogy is a magnificent heritage.

It is of all this evidently that Mr. Besant is full when he insists upon the fact that fiction is one of the *fine* arts, deserving in its turn of all the honours and emoluments that have hitherto been reserved for the success-ful profession of music, poetry, painting, architecture. It is impossible to insist too much on so important a truth, and the place that Mr. Besant demands for the work of the novelist may be represented, a trifle less ab-stractly, by saying that he demands not only that it shall be reputed artistic, but that it shall be reputed very artistic indeed. It is excellent that he should have struck this note, for his doing so indicates that there was need of it, that his proposition may be to many people a novelty. One rubs one's eyes at the thought; but the rest of Mr. Besant's essay confirms the revelation. I suspect in truth that it would be possible to confirm it still further, and that one would not be far wrong in saying that in addition to the people to whom it has never occurred that a novel ought to be ar-tistic, there are a great many others who, if this principle were urged upon them, would be filled with an indefinable mistrust. They would find it difficult to explain their repugnance, but it would operate strongly to put them on their guard. "Art," in our Protestant communities, where so many things have got so strangely twisted about, is supposed in certain circles to have some vague injurious effect upon those who make it an important consideration, who let it weigh in the balance. It is assumed to be op-posed in some mysterious manner to morality, to amusement, to instruc-tion. When it is embodied in the work of the painter (the sculptor is another affair!) you know what it is: it stands there before you, in the honesty of pink and green and a gilt frame; you can see the worst of it at a glance, and you can be on your guard. But when it is introduced into literature it becomes more insidious—there is danger of its hurting you before you know it. Literature should be either instructive or amusing, and there is in many minds an impression that these artistic preoccupa-tions, the search for form, contribute to neither end, interfere indeed with both. They are too frivolous to be edifying, and too serious to be diverting; and they are moreover priggish and paradoxical and superfluous. That, I think, represents the manner in which the latent thought of many people who read novels as an exercise in skipping would explain itself if it were to become articulate. They would argue, of course, that a novel ought to be "good," but they would interpret this term in a fashion of their own, which indeed would vary considerably from one critic to an-other. One would say that being good means representing virtuous and aspiring characters placed in prominent positions; another would say that it depends on a "happy ending," on a distribution at the last of prizes, pensions, husbands, wives, babies, millions, appended paragraphs, and cheerful remarks. Another still would say that it means being full of incident and movement, so that we shall wish to jump ahead, to see who was the mysterious stranger, and if the stolen will was ever found, and shall not be distracted from this pleasure by a tiresome analysis or "description." But they would all agree that the "artistic" idea would spoil some of their fun. One would hold it accountable for all the description, another would see it revealed in the absence of sympathy. Its hostility to a happy ending would be evident, and it might even in some cases render any ending at all impossible. The "ending" of a novel is, for many persons, like that of a good dinner, a course of dessert and ices, and the artist in fiction is regarded as a sort of meddlesome doctor who forbids agreeable aftertastes. It is therefore true that this conception of Mr. Besant's of the novel as a superior form encounters not only a negative but a positive indifference. It matters little that as a work of art it should really be as little or as much of its essence to supply happy endings, sympathetic characters, and an objective tone, as if it were a work of mechanics: the association of ideas, however incongruous, might easily be too much for it if an eloquent voice were not sometimes raised to call attention to the fact that it is at once as free and as serious a branch of literature as any other.

Certainly this might sometimes be doubted in presence of the enormous number of works of fiction that appeal to the credulity of our generation, for it might easily seem that there could be no great character in a commodity so quickly and easily produced. It must be admitted that good novels are much compromised by bad ones, and that the field at large suffers discredit from overcrowding. I think, however, that this injury is only superficial, and that the superabundance of written fiction proves nothing against the principle itself. It has been vulgarised, like all other kinds of literature, like everything else to-day, and it has proved more than some kinds accessible to vulgarisation. But there is as much difference as there ever was between a good novel and a bad one: the bad is swept with all the daubed canvases and spoiled marble into some unvisited limbo, or infinite rubbish-yard beneath the back-windows of the world, and the good subsists and emits its light and stimulates our desire for perfection. As I shall take the liberty of making but a single criticism of Mr. Besant, whose tone is so full of love of his art, I may as well have done with it at once. He seems to me to mistake in attempting to say so definitely beforehand what sort of an affair the good novel will be. To indicate the danger of such an error as that has been the purpose of these few

pages; to suggest that certain traditions on the subject, applied *a priori,*
have already had much to answer for, and that the good health of an art
which undertakes so immediately to reproduce life must demand that it
be perfectly free. It lives upon exercise, and the very meaning of exercise
is freedom. The only obligation to which in advance we may hold a novel,
without incurring the accusation of being arbitrary, is that it be interesting.
That general responsibility rests upon it, but it is the only one I can think of.
The ways in which it is at liberty to accomplish this result (of interesting us)
strike me as innumerable, and such as can only suffer from being marked
out or fenced in by prescription. They are as various as the temperament of
man, and they are successful in proportion as they reveal a particular mind,
different from others. A novel is in its broadest definition a personal, a direct impression of life: that, to begin with, constitutes its value, which is
greater or less according to the intensity of the impression. But there will be
no intensity at all, and therefore no value, unless there is freedom to feel
and say. The tracing of a line to be followed, of a tone to be taken, of a
form to be filled out, is a limitation of that freedom and a suppression of
the very thing that we are most curious about. The form, it seems to me,
is to be appreciated after the fact; then the author's choice has been made,
his standard has been indicated; then we can follow lines and directions
and compare tones and resemblances. Then in a word we can enjoy one
of the most charming of pleasures, we can estimate quality, we can apply
the test of execution. The execution belongs to the author alone; it is what
is most personal to him, and we measure him by that. The advantage, the
luxury, as well as the torment and responsibility of the novelist, is that
there is no limit to what he may attempt as an executant—no limit to his
possible experiments, efforts, discoveries, successes. Here it is especially
that he works, step by step, like his brother of the brush, of whom we
may always say that he has painted his picture in a manner best known
to himself. His manner is his secret, not necessarily a jealous one. He
cannot disclose it as a general thing if he would; he would be at a loss
to teach it to others. I say this with a due recollection of having insisted
on the community of method of the artist who paints a picture and the
artist who writes a novel. The painter *is* able to teach the rudiments of
his practice, and it is possible, from the study of good work (granted the
aptitude), both to learn how to paint and to learn how to write. Yet it remains true, without injury to the *rapprochement,*[1] that the literary artist
would be obliged to say to his pupil much more than the other, "Ah, well,
you must do it as you can!" It is a question of degree, a matter of delicacy.

---

[1] [Reconciliation.]

If there are exact sciences, there are also exact arts, and the grammar of painting is so much more definite that it makes the difference.

I ought to add, however, that if Mr. Besant says at the beginning of his essay that the "laws of fiction may be laid down and taught with as much precision and exactness as the laws of harmony, perspective, and proportion" he mitigates what might appear to be an extravagance by applying his remark to "general" laws, and by expressing most of these rules in a manner with which it would certainly be unaccommodating to disagree. That the novelist must write from his experience, that his "characters must be real and such as might be met with in actual life"; that "a young lady brought up in a quiet country village should avoid descriptions of garrison life," and "a writer whose friends and personal experiences belong to the lower middle-class should carefully avoid introducing his characters into society"; that one should enter one's notes in a commonplace book; that one's figures should be clear in outline; that making them clear by some trick of speech or of carriage is a bad method, and "describing them at length" is a worse one; that English Fiction should have a "conscious moral purpose"; that "it is almost impossible to estimate too highly the value of careful workmanship—that is, of style"; that "the most important point of all is the story," that "the story is everything": these are principles with most of which it is surely impossible not to sympathise. That remark about the lower middle-class writer and his knowing his place is perhaps rather chilling; but for the rest I should find it difficult to dissent from any one of these recommendations. At the same time, I should find it difficult positively to assent to them, with the exception, perhaps, of the injunction as to entering one's notes in a commonplace book. They scarcely seem to me to have the quality that Mr. Besant attributes to the rules of the novelist—the "precision and exactness" of "the laws of harmony, perspective, and proportion." They are suggestive, they are even inspiring, but they are not exact, though they are doubtless as much so as the case admits of: which is a proof of that liberty of interpretation for which I just contended. For the value of these different injunctions—so beautiful and so vague—is wholly in the meaning one attaches to them. The characters, the situation, which strike one as real will be those that touch and interest one most, but the measure of reality is very difficult to fix. The reality of Don Quixote or of Mr. Micawber is a very delicate shade; it is a reality so coloured by the author's vision that, vivid as it may be, one would hesitate to propose it as a model: one would expose one's self to some very embarrassing questions on the part of a pupil. It goes without saying that you will not write a good novel unless you possess the sense of reality; but it will be difficult to give you a recipe for calling that sense into being. Humanity is immense, and reality has a myriad forms, the most one can affirm is that some of the flowers of fiction have the odour of it, and others have not; as for telling you in advance how your nosegay should be composed, that is another affair. It is equally excellent and inconclusive to say that one must write from experience; to our supposititious aspirant such a declaration might savour of mockery. What kind of experience is intended, and where does it begin and end? Experience is never limited, and it is never complete; it is an immense sensibility, a kind of huge spider-web of the finest silken threads suspended in the chamber of consciousness, and catching every air-borne particle in its tissue. It is the very atmosphere of the mind; and when the mind is imaginative—much more when it happens to be that of a man of genius—it takes to itself the faintest hints of life, it converts the very pulses of the air into revelations. The young lady living in a village has only to be a damsel upon whom nothing is lost to make it quite unfair (as it seems to me) to declare to her that she shall have nothing to say about the military. Greater miracles have been seen than that, imagination assisting, she should speak the truth about some of these gentlemen. I remember an English novelist, a woman of genius, telling me that she was much commended for the impression she had managed to give in one of her tales of the nature and way of life of the French Protestant youth. She had been asked where she learned so much about this recondite being, she had been congratulated on her peculiar opportunities. These opportunities consisted in her having once, in Paris, as she ascended a staircase, passed an open door where, in the household of a *pasteur,* some of the young Protestants were seated at table round a finished meal. The glimpse made a picture; it lasted only a moment, but that moment was experience. She had got her direct personal impression, and she turned out her type. She knew what youth was, and what Protestantism; she also had the advantage of having seen what it was to be French, so that she converted these ideas into a concrete image and produced a reality. Above all, however, she was blessed with the faculty which when you give it an inch takes an ell, and which for the artist is a much greater source of strength than any accident of residence or of place in the social scale. The power to guess the unseen from the seen, to trace the implication of things, to judge the whole piece by the pattern, the condition of feeling life in general so completely that you are well on your way to knowing any particular corner of it—this cluster of gifts may almost be said to constitute experience, and they occur in country and in town, and in the most differing stages of education. If experience consists of impressions, it may be said that impressions *are* experience, just as (have we not seen it?) they are the very air we breathe. Therefore, if I should certainly say to a novice, "Write from experience and from experience only," I should feel that this was rather a tantalising monition if I were not careful immediately to add, "Try to be one of the people on whom nothing is lost!"

I am far from intending by this to minimise the importance of exactness—of truth of detail. One can speak best from one's own taste, and I may therefore venture to say that the air of reality (solidity of specification) seems to me to be the supreme virtue of a novel—the merit on which all its other merits (including that conscious moral purpose of which Mr. Besant speaks) helplessly and submissively depend. If it be not there they are all as nothing, and if these be there, they owe their effect to the success with which the author has produced the illusion of life. The cultivation of this success, the study of this exquisite process, form, to my taste, the beginning and the end of the art of the novelist. They are his inspiration, his despair, his reward, his torment, his delight. It is here in very truth that he competes with life; it is here that he competes with his brother the painter in *his* attempt to render the look of things, the look that conveys their meaning, to catch the colour, the relief, the expression, the surface, the substance of the human spectacle. It is in regard to this that Mr. Besant is well inspired when he bids him take notes. He cannot possibly take too many, he cannot possibly take enough. All life solicits him, and to "render" the simplest surface, to produce the most momentary illusion, is a very complicated business. His case would be easier, and the rule would be more exact, if Mr. Besant had been able to tell him what notes to take. But this, I fear, he can never learn in any manual; it is the business of his life. He has to take a great many in order to select a few, he has to work them up as he can, and even the guides and philosophers who might have most to say to him must leave him alone when it comes to the application of precepts, as we leave the painter in communion with his palette. That his characters "must be clear in outline" as Mr. Besant says—he feels that down to his boots; but how he shall make them so is a secret between his good angel and himself. It would be absurdly simple if he could be taught that a great deal of "description" would make them so, or that on the contrary the absence of description and the cultivation of dialogue, or the absence of dialogue and the multiplication of "incident," would rescue him from his difficulties. Nothing, for instance, is more possible than that he be of a turn of mind for which this odd, literal opposition of description and dialogue, incident and description, has little meaning and light. People often talk of these things as if they had a kind of internecine distinctness, instead of melting into each other at every breath, and being intimately associated parts of one general effort of expression. I cannot imagine composition existing in a series of blocks, nor conceive, in any novel worth discussing at all, of a passage of description that is not in its intention narrative, a passage of dialogue that is not in its intention descriptive, a touch of truth of any sort that does not partake of the nature of incident, or an incident that derives its interest from any other source than the general and only source of the success of a work of art—that of being illustrative. A novel is a living thing, all one and continuous, like any other organism, and in proportion as it lives will it be found, I think, that in each of the parts there is something of each of the other parts. The critic who over the close texture of a finished work shall pretend to trace a geography of items will mark some frontiers as artificial, I fear, as any that have been known to history. There is an old-fashioned distinction between the novel of character and the novel of incident which must have cost many a smile to the intending fabulist who was keen about his work. It appears to me as little to the point as the equally celebrated distinction between the novel and the romance—to answer as little to any reality. There are bad novels and good novels, as there are bad pictures and good pictures; but that is the only distinction in which I see any meaning, and I can as little imagine speaking of a novel of character as I can imagine speaking of a picture of character. When one says picture one says of character, when one says novel one says of incident, and the terms may be transposed at will. What is character but the determination of incident? What is incident but the illustration of character? What is either a picture or a novel that is *not* of character? What else do we seek in it and find in it? It is an incident for a woman to stand up with her hand resting on a table and look at you in a certain way; or if it be not an incident I think it will be hard to say what it is. At the same time it is an expression of character. If you say you don't see it (character in *that* —*allons donc!*), this is exactly what the artist who has reasons of his own for thinking he *does* see it undertakes to show you. When a young man makes up his mind that he has not faith enough after all to enter the Church as he intended, that is an incident, though you may not hurry to the end of the chapter to see whether perhaps he doesn't change once more. I do not say that these are extraordinary or startling incidents. I do not pretend to estimate the degree of interest proceeding from them, for this will depend upon the skill of the painter. It sounds almost puerile to say that some incidents are intrinsically much more important than others, and I need not take this precaution after having professed my sympathy for the major ones in remarking that the only classification of the novel that I can understand is into that which has life and that which has it not.

The novel and the romance, the novel of incident and that of character—these clumsy separations appear to me to have been made by critics and readers for their own convenience, and to help them out of some of their occasional predicaments, but to have little reality or interest for the producer, from whose point of view it is of course that we are attempting to consider the art of fiction. The case is the same with another shadowy category which Mr. Besant apparently is disposed to set up— that of the "modern English novel"; unless indeed it be that in this matter he has fallen into an accidental confusion of standpoints. It is not quite clear whether he intends the remarks in which he alludes to it to be didactic or historical. It is as difficult to suppose a person intending to write a modern English as to suppose him writing an ancient English novel: that is a label which begs the question. One writes the novel, one paints the picture, of one's language and of one's time, and calling it modern English will not, alas! make the difficult task any easier. No more, unfortunately, will calling this or that work of one's fellow-artist a romance—unless it be, of course, simply for the pleasantness of the thing, as for instance when Hawthorne gave this heading to his story of *Blithedale*. The French, who have brought the theory of fiction to remarkable completeness, have but one name for the novel, and have not attempted smaller things in it, that I can see, for that. I can think of no obligation to which the "romancer" would not be held equally with the novelist; the standard of execution is equally high for each. Of course it is of execution that we are talking—that being the only point of a novel that is open to contention. This is perhaps too often lost sight of, only to produce interminable confusions and cross-purposes. We must grant the artist his subject, his idea, his *donnée:* [1] our criticism is applied only to what he makes of it. Naturally I do not mean that we are bound to like it or find it interesting: in case we do not our course is perfectly simple—to let it alone. We may believe that of a certain idea even the most sincere novelist can make nothing at all, and the event may perfectly justify our belief; but the failure will have been a failure to execute, and it is in the execution that the fatal weakness is recorded. If we pretend to respect the artist at all, we must allow him his freedom of choice, in the face, in particular cases, of innumerable presumptions that the choice will not fructify. Art derives a considerable part of its beneficial exercise from flying in the face of presumptions, and some of the most interesting experiments of which it is capable are hidden in the bosom of common things. Gustave Flaubert has written a story about the devotion of a servant-girl to a parrot, and the production, highly finished as it is, cannot on the whole be called a success. We are perfectly

---

[1] [His given point of departure.]

free to find it flat, but I think it might have been interesting; and I, for my part, am extremely glad he should have written it; it is a contribution to our knowledge of what can be done—or what cannot. Ivan Turgénieff has written a tale about a deaf and dumb serf and a lap-dog, and the thing is touching, loving, a little masterpiece. He struck the note of life where Gustave Flaubert missed it—he flew in the face of a presumption and achieved a victory.

Nothing, of course, will ever take the place of the good old fashion of "liking" a work of art or not liking it: the most improved criticism will not abolish that primitive, that ultimate test. I mention this to guard myself from the accusation of intimating that the idea, the subject, of a novel or a picture, does not matter. It matters, to my sense, in the highest degree, and if I might put up a prayer it would be that artists should select none but the richest. Some, as I have already hastened to admit, are much more remunerative than others, and it would be a world happily arranged in which persons intending to treat them should be exempt from confusions and mistakes. This fortunate condition will arrive only, I fear, on the same day that critics become purged from error. Meanwhile, I repeat, we do not judge the artist with fairness unless we say to him, "Oh, I grant you your starting-point, because if I did not I should seem to prescribe to you, and heaven forbid I should take that responsibility. If I pretend to tell you what you must not take, you will call upon me to tell you then what you must take; in which case I shall be prettily caught. Moreover, it isn't till I have accepted your data that I can begin to measure you. I have the standard, the pitch; I have no right to tamper with your flute and then criticise your music. Of course I may not care for your idea at all; I may think it silly, or stale, or unclean; in which case I wash my hands of you altogether. I may content myself with believing that you will not have succeeded in being interesting, but I shall, of course, not attempt to demonstrate it, and you will be as indifferent to me as I am to you. I needn't remind you that there are all sorts of tastes: who can know it better? Some people, for excellent reasons, don't like to read about carpenters; others, for reasons even better, don't like to read about courtesans. Many object to Americans. Others (I believe they are mainly editors and publishers) won't look at Italians. Some readers don't like quiet subjects; others don't like bustling ones. Some enjoy a complete illusion, others the consciousness of large concessions. They choose their novels accordingly, and if they don't care about your idea they won't, *a fortiori,* care about your treatment."

So that it comes back very quickly, as I have said, to the liking: in spite of M. Zola, who reasons less powerfully than he represents, and who will not reconcile himself to this absoluteness of taste, thinking that there are certain things that people ought to like, and that they can be made to like. I am quite at a loss to imagine anything (at any rate in this matter of fiction) that people *ought* to like or to dislike. Selection will be sure to take care of itself, for it has a constant motive behind it. That motive is simply experience. As people feel life, so they will feel the art that is most closely related to it. This closeness of relation is what we should never forget in talking of the effort of the novel. Many people speak of it as a factitious, artificial form, a product of ingenuity, the business of which it is to alter and arrange the things that surround us, to translate them into conventional, traditional moulds. This, however, is a view of the matter which carries us but a very short way, condemns the art to an external repetition of a few familiar *clichés,* cuts short its development, and leads us straight up to a dead wall. Catching the very note and trick, the strange irregular rhythm of life, that is the attempt whose strenuous force keeps Fiction upon her feet. In proportion as in what she offers us we see life *without* rearrangement do we feel that we are touching the truth; in proportion as we see it *with* rearrangement do we feel that we are being put off with a substitute, a compromise and convention. It is not uncommon to hear an extraordinary assurance of remark in regard to this matter of rearranging, which is often spoken of as if it were the last word of art. Mr. Besant seems to me in danger of falling into the great error with his rather unguarded talk about "selection." Art is essentially selection, but it is a selection whose main care is to be typical, to be inclusive. For many people art means rose-colored windowpanes, and selection means picking a bouquet for Mrs. Grundy. They will tell you glibly that artistic considerations have nothing to do with the disagreeable, with the ugly; they will rattle off shallow commonplaces about the province of art and the limits of art till you are moved to some wonder in return as to the province and the limits of ignorance. It appears to me that no one can ever have made a seriously artistic attempt without becoming conscious of an immense increase—a kind of revelation—of freedom. One perceives in that case—by the light of a heavenly ray—that the province of art is all life, all feeling, all observation, all vision. As Mr. Besant so justly intimates, it is all experience. That is a sufficient answer to those who maintain that it must not touch the sad things of life, who stick into its divine unconscious bosom little prohibitory inscriptions on the end of sticks, such as we see in public gardens—"It is forbidden to walk on the grass; it is forbidden to touch the flowers; it is not allowed to introduce dogs or to remain after dark; it is requested to keep to the right." The young aspirant in the line of fiction whom we continue to imagine will do nothing without taste, for in that case his freedom would be of little use to him; but the first advantage of his taste will be to reveal to him the absurdity of the little sticks and tickets. If he have taste, I must add, of course he will have ingenuity, and my disrespectful reference to that quality just now was not meant to imply that it is useless in fiction. But it is only a secondary aid; the first is a capacity for receiving straight impressions.

Mr. Besant has some remarks on the question of "the story" which I shall not attempt to criticise, though they seem to me to contain a singular ambiguity, because I do not think I understand them. I cannot see what is meant by talking as if there were a part of a novel which is the story and part of it which for mystical reasons is not—unless indeed the distinction be made in a sense in which it is difficult to suppose that any one should attempt to convey anything. "The story," if it represents anything, represents the subject, the idea, the *donnée* of the novel; and there is surely no "school"—Mr. Besant speaks of a school—which urges that a novel should be all treatment and no subject. There must assuredly be something to treat; every school is intimately conscious of that. This sense of the story being the idea, the starting-point, of the novel, is the only one that I see in which it can be spoken of as something different from its organic whole; and since in proportion as the work is successful the idea permeates and penetrates it, informs and animates it, so that every word and every punctuation-point contribute directly to the expression, in that proportion do we lose our sense of the story being a blade which may be drawn more or less out of its sheath. The story and the novel, the idea and the form, are the needle and thread, and I never heard of a guild of tailors who recommended the use of the thread without the needle, or the needle without the thread. Mr. Besant is not the only critic who may be observed to have spoken as if there were certain things in life which constitute stories, and certain others which do not. I find the same odd implication in an entertaining article in the *Pall Mall Gazette,* devoted, as it happens, to Mr. Besant's lecture. "The story is the thing!" says this graceful writer, as if with a tone of opposition to some other idea. I should think it was, as every painter who, as the time for "sending in" his picture looms in the distance, finds himself still in quest of a subject—as every belated artist not fixed about his theme will heartily agree. There are some subjects which speak to us and others which do not, but he would be a clever man who should undertake to give a rule—an *index expurgatorius* [1]—by which the story and the no-story should be known apart. It is impossible (to me at least) to imagine any such rule which shall not be altogether arbitrary.

---

[1] [A list (of books) requiring expurgation.]

The writer in the *Pall Mall* opposes the delightful (as I suppose) novel of *Margot la Balafrée* to certain tales in which "Bostonian nymphs" appear to have "rejected English dukes for psychological reasons." I am not acquainted with the romance just designated, and can scarcely forgive the *Pall Mall* critic for not mentioning the name of the author, but the title appears to refer to a lady who may have received a scar in some heroic adventure. I am inconsolable at not being acquainted with this episode, but am utterly at a loss to see why it is a story when the rejection (or acceptance) of a duke is not, and why a reason, psychological or other, is not a subject when a cicatrix is. They are all particles of the multitudinous life with which the novel deals, and surely no dogma which pretends to make it lawful to touch the one and unlawful to touch the other will stand for a moment on its feet. It is the special picture that must stand or fall, according as it seem to possess truth or to lack it. Mr. Besant does not, to my sense, light up the subject by intimating that a story must, under penalty of not being a story, consist of "adventures." Why of adventures more than of green spectacles? He mentions a category of impossible things, and among them he places "fiction without adventure." Why without adventure, more than without matrimony, or celibacy, or parturition, or cholera, or hydropathy, or Jansenism? This seems to me to bring the novel back to the hapless little *rôle* of being an artificial, ingenious thing—bring it down from its large, free character of an immense and exquisite correspondence with life. And what *is* adventure when it comes to that, and by what sign is the listening pupil to recognise it? It is an adventure—an immense one—for me to write this little article; and for a Bostonian nymph to reject an English duke is an adventure only less stirring, I should say, than for an English duke to be rejected by a Bostonian nymph. I see dramas within dramas in that, and innumerable points of view. A psychological reason is, to my imagination, an object adorably pictorial; to catch the tint of its complexion—I feel as if that idea might inspire one to Titianesque efforts. There are few things more exciting to me, in short, than a psychological reason, and yet, I protest, the novel seems to me the most magnificent form of art. I have just been reading, at the same time, the delightful story of *Treasure Island,* by Mr. Robert Louis Stevenson, and, in a manner less consecutive, the last tale from M. Edmond de Goncourt, which is entitled *Chérie.* One of these works treats of murders, mysteries, islands of dreadful renown, hairbreadth escapes, miraculous coincidences and buried doubloons. The other treats of a little French girl who lived in a fine house in Paris, and died of wounded sensibility because no one would marry her. I call *Treasure Island* delightful, because it appears to me to have succeeded wonderfully in what it attempts; and I venture to bestow no epithet upon *Chérie,* which strikes me as having failed deplorably in what it attempts—that is in tracing the development of the moral consciousness of a child. But one of these productions strikes me as exactly as much of a novel as the other, and as having a "story" quite as much. The moral consciousness of a child is as much a part of life as the islands of the Spanish Main, and the one sort of geography seems to me to have those "surprises" of which Mr. Besant speaks quite as much as the other. For myself (since it comes back in the last resort as I say, to the preference of the individual), the picture of the child's experience has the advantage that I can at successive steps (an immense luxury, near to the "sensual pleasure" of which Mr. Besant's critic in the *Pall Mall* speaks) say Yes or No, as it may be, to what the artist puts before me. I have been a child in fact, but I have been on a quest for a buried treasure only in supposition, and it is a simple accident that with M. de Goncourt I should have for the most part to say No. With George Eliot, when she painted that country with a far other intelligence, I always said Yes.

The most interesting part of Mr. Besant's lecture is unfortunately the briefest passage—his very cursory allusion to the "conscious moral purpose" of the novel. Here again it is not very clear whether he be recording a fact or laying down a principle; it is a great pity that in the latter case he should not have developed his idea. This branch of the subject is of immense importance, and Mr. Besant's few words point to considerations of the widest reach, not to be lightly disposed of. He will have treated the art of fiction but superficially who is not prepared to go every inch of the way that these considerations will carry him. It is for this reason that at the beginning of these remarks I was careful to notify the reader that my reflection on so large a theme have no pretension to be exhaustive. Like Mr. Besant, I have left the question of the morality of the novel till the last, and at the last I find I have used up my space. It is a question surrounded with difficulties, as witness the very first that meets us, in the form of a definite question, on the threshold. Vagueness, in such a discussion, is fatal, and what is the meaning of your morality and your conscious moral purpose? Will you not define your terms and explain how (a novel being a picture) a picture can be either moral or immoral? You wish to paint a moral picture or carve a moral statue: will you not tell us how you would set about it? We are discussing the Art of Fiction; questions of art are questions (in the widest sense) of execution; questions of morality are quite another affair, and will you not let us see how it is that you find it so easy to mix them up? These things are so clear to Mr. Besant that he has deduced from them a law which he sees embodied in English Fiction, and which is "a truly admirable thing and a great cause for congratulation." It is a great cause for congratulation indeed when such thorny problems become as smooth as silk. I may add that in so far as Mr. Besant perceives that in point of fact English Fiction has addressed itself preponderantly to these delicate questions he will appear to many people to have made a vain discovery. They will have been positively struck, on the contrary, with the moral timidity of the usual English novelist; with his (or with her) aversion to face the difficulties with which on every side the treatment of reality bristles. He is apt to be extremely shy (whereas the picture that Mr. Besant draws is a picture of boldness), and the sign of his work, for the most part, is a cautious silence on certain subjects. In the English novel (by which of course I mean the American as well), more than in any other, there is a traditional difference between that which people know and that which they agree to admit that they know, that which they see and that which they speak of, that which they feel to be a part of life, and that which they allow to enter into literature. There is the great difference, in short, between what they talk of in conversation and what they talk of in print. The essence of moral energy is to survey the whole field, and I should directly reverse Mr. Besant's remark and say not that the English novel has a purpose, but that it has a diffidence. To what degree a purpose in a work of art is a source of corruption I shall not attempt to inquire; the one that seems to me least dangerous is the purpose of making a perfect work. As for our novel, I may say lastly on this score that as we find it in England today it strikes me as addressed in a large degree to "young people," and that this in itself constitutes a presumption that it will be rather shy. There are certain things which it is generally agreed not to discuss, not even to mention, before young people.[1] That is very well, but the absence of discussion is not a symptom of the moral passion. The purpose of the English novel—"a truly admirable thing, and a great cause for congratulation"—strikes me therefore as rather negative.

There is one point at which the moral sense and the artistic sense lie very near together; that is in the light of the very obvious truth that the deepest quality of a work of art will always be the quality of the mind of the producer. In proportion as that intelligence is fine will the novel, the picture, the statue partake of the substance of beauty and truth. To be constituted of such elements is, to my vision, to have purpose enough. No good novel will ever proceed from a superficial mind; that seems to me an axiom which, for the artist in fiction, will cover all needful moral

---

[1] Cf. *Our Mutual Friend,* Bk. I, Ch. XI: "The question about everything was, would it bring a blush into the cheek of the young person?"

ground: if the youthful aspirant take it to heart it will illuminate for him many of the mysteries of "purpose." There are many other useful things that might be said to him, but I have come to the end of my article, and can only touch them as I pass. The critic in the *Pall Mall Gazette,* whom I have already quoted, draws attention to the danger, in speaking of the art of fiction, of generalising. The danger that he has in mind is rather, I imagine, that of particularising, for there are some comprehensive remarks which, in addition to those embodied in Mr. Besant's suggestive lecture, might without fear of misleading him be addressed to the ingenuous student. I should remind him first of the magnificence of the form that is open to him, which offers to sight so few restrictions and such innumerable opportunities. The other arts, in comparison, appear confined and hampered; the various conditions under which they are exercised are so rigid and definite. But the only condition that I can think of attaching to the composition of the novel is, as I have already said, that it be sincere. This freedom is a splendid privilege, and the first lesson of the young novelist is to learn to be worthy of it. "Enjoy it as it deserves," I should say to him; "take possession of it, explore it to its utmost extent, publish it, rejoice in it. All life belongs to you, and do not listen either to those who would shut you up into corners of it and tell you that it is only here and there that art inhabits, or to those who would persuade you that this heavenly messenger wings her way outside of life altogether, breathing a superfine air, and turning away her head from the truth of things. There is no impression of life, no manner of seeing it and feeling it, to which the plan of the novelist may not offer a place; you have only to remember that talents so dissimilar as those of Alexandre Dumas and Jane Austen, Charles Dickens and Gustave Flaubert have worked in this field with equal glory. Do not think too much about optimism and pessimism; try and catch the colour of life itself. In France to-day we see a prodigious effort (that of Émile Zola, to whose solid and serious work no explorer of the capacity of the novel can allude without respect), we see an extraordinary effort, vitiated by a spirit of pessimism on a narrow basis. M. Zola is magnificent, but he strikes an English reader as ignorant; he has an air of working in the dark; if he had as much light as energy, his results would be of the highest value. As for the aberrations of a shallow optimism, the ground (of English fiction especially) is strewn with their brittle particles as with broken glass. If you must indulge in conclusions, let them have the taste of a wide knowledge. Remember that your first duty is to be as complete as possible—to make as perfect a work. Be generous and delicate and pursue the prize."

OF STYLE OR WRITING

REMY DE GOURMONT

> Et ideo confiteatur eorum stultitia, qui arte scientiaque im-
> munes, de solo ingenio confidentes, ad summa summe canenda
> prorumpunt; a tanta praesuntuositate desistant, et si anseres
> naturali desidia sunt, nolint astripetam aquilam imitari.[1]
>
> Dante: *Dé vulgari eloquio.*

DEPRECIATION of "writing"—that is, writing as an art—is a precaution taken from time to time by worthless writers. They believe it sound, but it is the sign of their mediocrity and the avowal of a secret regret. It is not without chagrin that the impotent man gives up the pretty woman whose limpid eyes invite him, and there must be bitterness in the disdain publicly proclaimed by one who confesses utter ignorance of his trade, or absence of the gift without which exercise of that trade is an imposture. Yet some of these poor creatures actually pride themselves upon their poverty. They declare that their ideas are rare enough not to need fine clothing; that the newest, richest imagery is merely the veil thrown by vanity over the emptiness of the thought; that what matters, after all, is the substance and not the form, the spirit and not the letter, the thing and not the word; and they can continue like this a long time, for they have at their command a whole flock of facile commonplaces which, however, fool nobody. We should pity the first group and despise the second, replying to neither, unless it be to say this: that there are two literatures, and that they belong to each other.

Two literatures. This is a prudent and provisional form of ex-

---

[1] [And therefore let those who, innocent of art and science, and trusting to genius alone, rush forward to sing of the highest subjects in the highest style, confess their folly and cease from such presumption; and if in their natural sluggishness they are but geese, let them abstain from imitating the eagle soaring to the stars. (Translated by A. G. Ferrers Howell and Philip H. Wicksteed in *The Portable Dante;* The Viking Press, 1947, p. 638).]

pression intended to divert the mob by according it a share in the landscape, a view of the garden which it may not enter. If there were not two
literatures and two provinces, it would be necessary to cut at once the
throats of nearly all French writers—a dirty job and one in which, for
my part, I should blush to have a hand. Enough, then. The boundary is
established. There are two sorts of writers: the writers who write and
the writers who do not write—just as there are voiceless singers and singers with voices.

The disdain for style would seem to be one of the conquests of 1789.
At least, prior to the democratic era, it had been taken for granted that
the one way to treat writers who did not write was to ridicule them. From
Pisistratus to Louis XVI, the civilized world was unanimous on this point
—a writer must know how to write. This was the Greek view, and the
Romans loved fine style to such a degree that they came to write very
badly through wishing to write too well. Saint Ambrose esteemed eloquence so highly that he regarded it as one of the gifts of the Holy Spirit
—*vox donum Spiritus*—and Saint Hilary of Poitiers, in chapter thirteen
of his *Treatise on the Psalms,* does not hesitate to call bad style a sin. It
cannot, then, be from Roman Christianity that we have derived our present
indulgence for uncouth literature. Still, inasmuch as Christianity is necessarily responsible for all modern aggressions against external beauty, it
might be supposed that the taste for bad style was one of those Protestant
importations that befouled France in the eighteenth century—contempt
for style and moral hypocrisy being Anglican vices.[1]

However, if the eighteenth century wrote badly, it did so unconsciously. It thought that Voltaire wrote well, especially in verse, and reproached Ducis only with the barbarousness of his models. It had an ideal.
It did not admit that philosophy might be an excuse for bad literature. It
rhymed everything, from the treatises of Isaac Newton to garden manuals
and cook-books. This lust for putting art and fine language where they
did not belong, led to the adoption of a medium style calculated to ele-
vate all vulgar subjects and to degrade all the others. With the best of
intentions, the eighteenth century ended by writing as if it were the most
refractory to art in the world's history. England and France signed, at that
time, a literary pact destined to endure till the arrival of Chateaubriand,
whose *Génie du Christianisme* [2] sounded its solemn dissolution. From the

---

[1] On the importance and influence of Protestantism at this time, see the work
of E. Hugues, pilfered by Protestant writers for the last twenty-five years: *Histoire de
la Restauration du Protestantisme en France au XVIIIᵉ siècle* (1872).

[2] A book so little known and disfigured in its pious editions. Nothing could be
less pious, however, or less edifying, after the first volume, than this curious and con-

appearance of this book, which opens the century, there has been but one way for a writer to have talent, namely, to know how to write—no longer in the manner of La Harpe, but in accordance with the examples of an unconquered tradition as old as the first awakening of beauty in human intelligence.[1]

But the eighteenth century manner corresponded only too well to the natural tendencies of a democratic civilization. Neither Chateaubriand nor Victor Hugo was able to abrogate the organic law which sends the herd plunging down to the green plain where there is grass, and where there will be nothing but dust, once it has passed. It was soon deemed useless to cultivate a landscape destined to popular devastations, so there sprang up a literature without style, just as there are highroads without grass, without shade, and without wayside springs.

II

Writing is a trade, and I should rather see it catalogued between cobbling and carpentry, than separated from the other manifestations of human activity. Thus set apart, it can be virtually denied existence under colour of according it special honour, and so far removed from every vital interest that it will die of its isolation. Given, however, its place in one of the symbolic niches along the great gallery, it suggests apprenticeship and the handling of tools. It repels impromptu vocations. It is severe and uninviting.

Writing is a trade, but style is not a science. "Style is the man," and that other formula, "Style is inviolable," offered by Hello, mean exactly the same thing, namely, that style is as personal as the colour of the eyes or the sound of the voice. One can learn to write; one cannot learn to have a style. A writer can dye his style, as he does his hair, but he must begin over again every morning, and have no distractions. It is so little possible to acquire a style, that one is often lost in the course of a lifetime. When the vital force diminishes, writing suffers. Practice, which improves other gifts, often spoils this one.

Writing is very different from painting or modelling. To write or to speak is to make use of a faculty necessarily common to all men—a primordial and unconscious faculty which cannot be analyzed without the com-

---

fused encyclopedia, where we find *René* and statistical tables, *Atala* and a catalogue of Greek painters. It is a universal history of civilization and a plan of social reconstruction.

[1] In speaking of the eighteenth century, exception must always be made of the grandiose and solitary Buffon, in his tower at Montbard, who was, in the modern sense of these words, a scientist, a philosopher, and a poet.

plete anatomy of the intelligence. That is why all treatises on the art of writing, whether they number ten pages or ten thousand, are but vain sketches. The question is so complex that it is hard to know where to attack it. It has so many sharp points, and is such a thicket of thorns and thistles that, instead of plunging straight into it, one goes around, and that is wiser.

To write, as Flaubert and Goncourt understood it, is to exist, to be one's self. To have a style is to speak, in the midst of the common language, a peculiar dialect, unique and inimitable, yet so constituted as to be at once the language of all and the language of an individual. Style is self-evident. To study its mechanism is useless to the point where uselessness becomes a positive menace. That which can be recomposed from the products of stylistic distillation bears the same resemblance to the style distilled, that a perfumed paper rose bears to a real rose.

Whatever be the fundamental importance of a "written" work, possession of style enhances its value. It was Buffon's opinion that all the beauties found in a well-written book, "all the relations which constitute style, are so many truths quite as useful for the mind as those forming the substance of the subject, and perhaps even more precious." And, despite the common disdain, this is also the common opinion, since the books of the past which still live, live only by virtue of their style. Were the contrary possible, such a contemporary of Buffon as Boulanger, author of *L'Antiquité dévoilée,* would not be unknown to-day, for there was nothing mediocre about the man but his way of writing. And is it not because he almost always lacked style, that another contemporary, Diderot, has never enjoyed more than a few hours of reputation at a time, and that as soon as people stop talking about him, he is forgotten?

It is because of this incontestable preponderance of style that the invention of plots is of no great importance in literature. To write a good novel or a lasting drama, one must either select a subject so banal that it is absolutely nil, or invent one so new that genius alone can get anything out of it—*Romeo and Juliet,* or *Don Quixote.* Most of Shakespeare's tragedies are merely a succession of metaphors embroidered on the canvas of the first story that came to his hand. Shakespeare invented nothing but his lines and his phrases. His images being new, their novelty necessarily communicated life to the characters. If *Hamlet,* idea for idea, had been written by Christopher Marlowe, it would be merely an obscure, clumsy tragedy, cited as an interesting sketch. M. de Maupassant, who invented the majority of his themes, is a lesser storyteller than Boccaccio, who invented none of his. Besides, the invention of subjects is limited, though infinitely flexible. But, change the age, and you change the story. If M. Aicard had genius, he would not have translated *Othello;* he would have remade it, just as the youthful Racine remade the tragedies of Euripides. If man did not have style as a means of achieving variety, everything would be said in the first hundred years of a literature. I am quite willing to admit that there are thirty-six situations for novels and dramas, but a more general theory can, as a matter of fact, recognize four only. Man, taken as the centre, may have relations with himself, with other men, with the other sex, with the infinite—God or Nature. A piece of literature falls necessarily into one of these four categories; but were there in the world one theme only, and that *Daphnis and Chloe,* it would suffice.

One of the excuses made by writers who do not know how to write, is the diversity of genres. They believe that one genre calls for style, and that another does not. A novel, they say, should not be written in the same tone as a poem. True; but absence of style means absence of tone also, and when a book lacks "writing," it lacks everything. It is invisible or, as we say, it passes unnoticed. And that is as it should be. After all, there is but one genre, poetry, and but one medium, verse; for beautiful prose must have a rhythm which will make us doubt whether it be merely prose. Buffon wrote nothing but poems, as did Bossuet and Chateaubriand and Flaubert. If the *Époques de la Nature* stirs the admiration of scientists and philosophers, it is none the less a sumptuous epic. M. Brunetière spoke with ingenious boldness of the evolution of the genres. He showed that Bossuet's prose is but one of the cuts in the great lyric forest where Victor Hugo later was a woodsman. But I prefer the idea that there are no genres, or that there is but one only. This, moreover, is in closer accord with the latest theories of science and philosophy. The idea of evolution is about to disappear before that of permanence, perpetuity.

Can one learn to write? Regarded as a question of style, this amounts to asking if, with application, M. Zola could have become Chateaubriand, or if M. Quesnay de Beaurepaire, had he taken pains, could have become Rabelais: if the man who imitates precious marbles by spraying pine panels with a sharp shake of his brush, could, properly guided, have painted the *Pauvre Pêcheur,* or if the stone-cutter, who chisels the depressing fronts of Parisian houses in the Corinthian manner, might not, perhaps, after twenty lessons, execute the *Porte d'Enfer* or the tomb of Philippe Pot?

Can one learn to write? If, on the other hand, the question be one of the elements of a trade, of what painters are taught in the academies, all that can indeed be learned. One can learn to write correctly, in the neutral manner, just as engravers used to work in the "black manner." One can learn to write badly—that is to say, properly, and so as to merit a prize for literary excellence. One may learn to write very well, which is another way of writing very ill. How melancholy they are, those books which are well-written—and nothing more!

III

M. Albalat has, then, published a manual entitled *The Art of Writing Taught in Twenty Lessons*. Had this work appeared at an earlier date, it would certainly have found a place in the library of M. Dumouchel, professor of literature, and he would have recommended it to his friends Bouvard and Pécuchet: "Then," as Flaubert tells us, "they sought to determine the precise constitution of style, and, thanks to the authors recommended by Dumouchel, they learned the secret of all the genres." However, the two boys would have found M. Albalat's remarks somewhat subtle. They would have been shocked to learn that *Télémaque* is badly written and that Mérimée would gain by condensation. They would have rejected M. Albalat and set to work on their biography of the Duc d'Angoulême without him.

Such resistance does not surprise me. It springs, perhaps, from an obscure feeling that the unconscious writer laughs at principles, at the art of epithets, and at the artifice of the three graduated impulses. Had M. Albalat known that intellectual effort, and especially literary effort, is, in very large measure, independent of consciousness, he would have been less imprudent and hesitated to divide a writer's qualities into two classes: natural qualities and qualities that can be acquired. As if a quality—that is to say a manner of being and of feeling—were something external to be added like a colour or an odour. One becomes what he is—without wishing to even, and despite every effort to oppose it. The most enduring patience cannot turn a blind imagination into a visual imagination, and the work of a writer who sees the landscape, whose aspect he transposes into terms of literary art, is better, however awkward, than after it has been retouched by someone whose vision is void, or profoundly different. "But the master alone can give the salient stroke." I can see Pécuchet's discouragement at this. The master's stroke in artistic literature—even the salient stroke—is necessarily the very one on which stress should not have been laid. Otherwise the stroke emphasizes the detail to which it is customary to give prominence, and not that which had struck the unskilled but sincere inner eye of the apprentice. M. Albalat makes an abstraction of this almost always unconscious vision, and defines style as "the art of grasping the value of words and their interrelations." Talent, in his opinion, consists "not in making a dull, lifeless use of words, but in discovering the *nuances,* the images, the sensations, which result from their combinations."

Here we are, then, in the realm of pure verbalism—in the ideal region of signs. It is a question of manipulating these signs and arranging them in patterns that will give the illusion of representing the world of sensations. Thus reversed, the problem is insoluble. It may well happen, since all things are possible, that such combinations of words will evoke life—even a determinate life—but more often they will remain inert. The forest becomes petrified. A critique of style should begin with a critique of the inner vision, by an essay on the formation of images. There are, to be sure, two chapters on images in Albalat's book, but they come quite at the end. Thus the mechanism of language is there demonstrated in inverse order, since the first step is the image, the last the abstraction. A proper analysis of the natural stylistic process would begin with the sensation and end with the pure idea—so pure that it corresponded not only to nothing real, but to nothing imaginative either.

If there were an art of writing, it would be nothing more or less than the art of feeling, the art of seeing, the art of hearing, the art of using all the senses, whether directly or through the imagination; and the new, serious method of a theory of style would be an attempt to show how these two separate worlds—the world of sensations and the world of words—penetrate each other. There is a great mystery in this, since they lie infinitely far apart—that is to say, they are parallel. Perhaps we should see here the operation of a sort of wireless telegraphy. We note that the needles on the two dials act in unison, and that is all. But this mutual dependence is, in reality, far from being as complete and as clear as in a mechanical device. When all is said, the accords between words and sensations are very few and very imperfect. We have no sure means of expressing our thoughts, unless perhaps it be silence. How many circumstances there are in life, when the eyes, the hands, the mute mouth, are more eloquent than any words.[1]

IV

M. Albalat's analysis is, then, bad, because unscientific. Yet from it he has derived a practical method of which it may be said that, while incapable of forming an original writer—he is well aware of this himself—it might possibly attenuate, not the mediocrity, but the incoherence, of

---

[1] An attempt will be made some day in a study in the *World of Words,* to determine whether words have really a meaning—that is to say, a constant value.

speeches and publications to which custom obliges us to lend some attention. Besides, even were this manual still more useless than I believe it to be, certain of its chapters would nevertheless retain their expository and documentary interest. The detail is excellent, as, for example, the pages where it is shown that the idea is bound up in the form, and that to change the form is to modify the idea. "It means nothing to say of a piece of writing that the substance is good, but the form is bad." These are sound principles, though the idea may subsist as a residue of sensation, independently of the words, and, above all, of a choice of words. But ideas stripped bare, in the state of wandering larvae, have no interest whatever. It may even be true that such ideas belong to everybody. Perhaps all ideas are common property. But how differently one of them, wandering through the world, awaiting its evocator, will be revealed according to the word that summons it from the Shades. What would Bossuet's ideas be worth, despoiled of their purple? They are the ideas of any ordinary student of theology, and, uttered by him, such a farrago of stupid nonsense would shock and shame those who had listened to it intoxicated in the Sermons and Oraisons. And the impression will be similar if, having lent a charmed ear to Michelet's lyric paradoxes, we come across them again in the miserable mouthings of some senator, or in the depressing commentaries of the partisan press. This is the reason why the Latin poets, including the greatest of them all, Virgil, cease to exist when translated, all looking exactly alike in the painful and pompous uniformity of a normal student's rhetoric. If Virgil had written in the style of M. Pessonneaux, or of M. Benoist, he would be Benoist, he would be Pessonneaux, and the monks would have scrapped his parchments to substitute for his verses some good lease of a sure and lasting interest.

Apropos of these evident truths, M. Albalat refutes Zola's opinion that "it is the form which changes and passes the most quickly," and that "immortality is gained by presenting living creatures." So far as this second sentence can be interpreted at all, it would seem to mean that what is called life, in art, is independent of form. But perhaps this is even less clear? Perhaps it will seem to have no sense whatever. Hippolytus, too, at the gates of Troezen, was "without form and without colour"; only he was dead. All that can be conceded to this theory is that, if a beautiful and original work of art survives its century and, what is more, the language in which it was written, it is no longer admired except as a matter of imitation, in obedience to the traditional injunction of the educators. Were the Iliad to be discovered to-day, beneath the ruins of Herculaneum, it would give us merely archaeological sensations. It would interest us in precisely the same degree as the *Chanson de Roland;* but a comparison of the two poems would then reveal more clearly than at present their correspondence to extremely different moments of civilization, since one is written entirely in images (somewhat stiff, it is true) while the other contains so few that they have been counted.

There is, moreover, no necessary relation between the merit of a work and its duration. Yet, when a book has survived, the authors of "analyses and extracts conforming to the requirements of the academic programme" know very well how to prove its "inimitable" perfection, and to resuscitate (for the brief time of a lecture) the mummy which will return once more to its linen bands. The idea of glory must not be confused with that of beauty. The former is entirely dependent upon the revolutions of fashion and of taste. The second is absolute to the extent of human sensations. The one is a matter of manners and customs; the other is firmly rooted in the law.

The form passes, it is true, but it is hard to see just how it could survive the matter which is its substance. If the beauty of a style becomes effaced or falls to dust, it is because the language has modified the aggregate of its molecules—words—as well as these molecules themselves, and because this internal activity has not taken place without swellings and disturbances. If Angelico's frescos have "passed," it is not that time has rendered them less beautiful, but that the humidity has swollen the cement where the painting has become caked and coated. Languages swell and flake like cement; or rather, they are like plane-trees, which can live only by constantly changing their bark, and which, early each spring, shed on the moss at their feet the names of lovers graven in their very flesh.

But what matters the future? What matters the approval of men who will not be what we should make them, were we demiurges? What is this glory enjoyed by man the moment he quits the realm of consciousness? It is time we learned to live in the present moment, to make the best of the passing hour, bad though it may be, and to leave to children this concern for the future, which is an intellectual weakness—though the naïveté of a man of genius. It is highly illogical to desire the immortality of works, when affirming and desiring the mortality of the soul. Dante's Virgil lived beyond life, his glory grown eternal. Of this dazzling conception there is left us but a little vain illusion, which we shall do well to extinguish entirely.

This does not mean, however, that we should not write for men as if we were writing for angels, and thus realize, according to our calling and our nature, the utmost of beauty, even though passing and perishable.

V

M. Albalat shows excellent judgment in suppressing the very amusing distinctions made by the old manuals between the florid style and the simple style, the sublime and the moderate. He deems justly that there are but two sorts of style: the commonplace and the original. Were it permitted to count the degrees from the mediocre to the bad, as well as from the passable to the perfect, the scale of shades and of colours would be long. It is so far from the *Légende de Saint-Julien l'Hospitalier* to a parliamentary discourse, that we really wonder if it is the same language in both cases—if there are not two French languages, and below them an infinite number of dialects almost entirely independent of one another. Speaking of the political style, M. Marty-Laveaux [1] thinks that the people, having remained faithful in its speech to the traditional diction, grasps this very imperfectly and in a general way only, as if it were a foreign language. He wrote this twenty-seven years ago, but the newspapers, more widely circulated at present, have scarcely modified popular habits. It is always safe to estimate in France that, out of every three persons, there is one who reads a bit of a paper now and then by chance, and another who never reads at all. At Paris the people have certain notions concerning style. They have a special predilection for violence and wit. This explains the popularity, rather literary than political, of a journalist like Rochefort, in whom the Parisians have for a long time found once more their ancient ideal of a witty and wordy cleaver of mountains.

Rochefort is, moreover, an original writer—one of those who should be cited among the first to show that the substance is nothing without the form. To be convinced of this, one has only to read a little further than his own article in the paper which he edits. Yet we are perhaps fooled by him. We have been, it appears, for fully half a century, by Mérimée, from whom M. Albalat quotes a page as a specimen of the hackneyed style. Going farther, he indulges in his favourite pastime; he corrects Mérimée and juxtaposes the two texts for our inspection. Here is a sample:

Bien qu'elle ne fût pas insensible au plaisir *ou à la vanité d'inspirer un sentiment sérieux à* un homme aussi léger *que l'était Max dans son opinion,* elle n'avait jamais pensé que cette affection pût devenir *un jour* dangeureuse *pour son repos.* [2]

Sensible au plaisir d'attirer sérieusement un homme aussi léger, elle n'avait jamais pensé que cette affection pût devenir dangeureuse. [3]

---

[1] *De l'Enseignement de notre langue.*

[2] [(M. Albalat has italicized everything he deems banal or useless.) While she was not insensitive to the pleasure or the vanity of inspiring a serious sentiment in a

It cannot, at least, be denied that the severe professor's style is economical, since it reduces the number of lines by nearly one-half. Subjected to this treatment, poor Mérimée, already far from fertile, would find himself the father of a few thin opuscules, symbolic thenceforth of his legendary dryness. Having become the Justin of all the Pompeius Troguses, Albalat places Lamartine himself upon the easel to tone down, for example, *la finesse de sa peau rougissante comme à quinze ans sous les regards,* to *sa fine peau de jeune fille rougissante.*[1] What butchery! The words stricken out by M. Albalat are so far from being hackneyed that they would, on the contrary, correct and counteract the commonplaceness of the improved sentence. This surplusage conveys the exceedingly subtle observation of a man who has made a close study of women's faces—a man more tender than sensual, and touched by modesty rather than by carnal prestige. Good or bad, style cannot be corrected. Style is inviolable.

M. Albalat gives some very amusing lists of *clichés,* or hackneyed phrases; but this criticism, at times, lacks measure. I cannot accept as *clichés* "kindly warmth," "precocious perversity," "restrained emotion," "retreating forehead," "abundant hair," or even "bitter tears," for tears can be "bitter" and can be "sweet." It should be understood, also, that the expression which exists as a *cliché* in one style, can occur as a renewed image in another. "Restrained emotion" is no more ridiculous than "simulated emotion," while, as for "retreating forehead," this is a scientific and quite accurate expression, which one has only to be careful about employing in the proper place. It is the same with the others. If such locutions were banished, literature would become a kind of algebra and could no longer be understood without the aid of long analytical operations. If the objection to them is that they have been overworked, it would be necessary to forego all words in common use as well as those devoid of mystery. But that would be a delusion. The commonest words and most current expressions can surprise us. Finally, the true *cliché,* as I have previously explained, may be recognized by this, that, whereas the image which it conveys, already faded, is halfway on the road to abstraction, it is not yet sufficiently insignificant to pass unperceived and to take its place among the signs which owe whatever life they may possess to the will of the intelligence.[2]

---

man as gay as was Max in her opinion, she had never thought that this affection could one day become dangerous to her peace of mind.]

[3] [Sensitive to the pleasure of attracting seriously a man so gay, she had never thought that this affection could become dangerous.]

[1] [The delicacy of her skin blushing under these stares as if she were fifteen *becomes* her delicate girl's skin blushing.]

[2] See the chapter on the cliché, in my book, *L'Esthétique de la Langue française* (author's note).

Very often, in the *cliché,* one of the words has kept a concrete sense, and what makes us smile is less its triteness than the coupling of a living word with one from which the life has vanished. This can be seen clearly in such formulas as: "in the bosom of the Academy," "devouring activity," "open his heart," "sadness was painted on his face," "break the monotony," "embrace principles." However, there are *clichés* in which all the words seem alive—*une rougeur colora ses joues;* [1] others in which all seem dead —*il était au comble des ses voeux.* [2] But this last was formed at a time when the word *comble* was thoroughly alive and quite concrete. It is because it still contains the residue of a sensible image that its union with *voeux* displeases us. In the preceding example the word *colorer* has become abstract, since the concrete verb expressing this idea is *colorier,* and goes badly with *rougeur* and *joues.* I do not know just where a minute work on this part of the language, in which the fermentation is still unfinished, would lead us; but no doubt in the end it would be quite easy to demonstrate that, in the true notion of the *cliché,* incoherence has its place by the side of triteness. There would be matter in such a study for reasoned opinions that M. Albalat might render fruitful for the practice of style.

VI

It is to be regretted that he has dismissed the subject of periphrasis in a few lines. We expected an analysis of this curious tendency to replace by a description the word which is the sign of the thing in question. This malady, which is very ancient, since enigmas have been found on Babylonian cylinders (that of the wind very nearly in the terms employed by our children), is perhaps the very origin of all poetry. If the secret of being a bore consists of saying everything, the secret of pleasing lies in saying just enough to be, not understood even, but divined. Periphrasis, as handled by the didactic poets, is perhaps ridiculous only because of the lack of poetic power which it indicates; for there are many agreeable ways of not naming what it is desired to suggest. The true poet, master of his speech, employs only periphrases at once so new and so clear in their shadowy half-light, that any slightly sensual intelligence prefers them to the too absolute word. He wishes neither to describe, to pique the curiosity, nor to show off his learning; but, whatever he does, he employs periphrases, and it is by no means certain that all those he creates will remain fresh long. The periphrasis is a metaphor, and thus has the same

---

[1] [A blush colored her cheeks.]
[2] [He had reached the fulfillment of his desires.]

life-span as a metaphor. It is far indeed from the vague and purely musical periphrases of Verlaine:

> *Parfois aussi le dard d'un insecte jaloux*
> *Inquiétait le col des belles sous les branches,*[1]

to the mythological enigmas of a Lebrun, who calls the silkworm

> *"L'amant des feuilles de Thisbé."* [2]

Here M. Albalat appropriately quotes Buffon to the effect that nothing does more to degrade a writer than the pains he takes to "express common or ordinary things in an eccentric or pompous manner. We pity him for having spent so much time making new combinations of syllables only to say what is said by everybody." Delille won fame by his fondness for the didactic periphrasis, but I think he has been misjudged. It is not fear of the right word that makes him describe what he should have named, but rather his rigid system of poetics, and his mediocre talent. He lacks precision because he lacks power, and he is very bad only when he is not precise. But whether as a result of method or emasculation, we are indebted to him for some amusing enigmas:

> *Ces monstres qui de loin semblent un vaste écueil.*

> *L'animal recouvert de son épaisse croûte,*
> *Celui dont la coquille est arrondie en voûte.*

> *L'équivoque habitant de la terre et des ondes.*

> *Et cet oiseau parleur que sa triste beauté*
> *Ne dédommage pas de sa stérilité.*[3]

It should not, however, be thought that the *Homme des Champs,* from which these charades are taken, is a poem entirely to be despised.

---

[1] [Sometimes too, the sting of a jealous insect
Would disturb the neck of the beauties under the branches.]

[2] [The lover of the leaves of Thisbe.]

[3] [These monsters who from afar seemed a vast reef.

The animal covered with his thick armour,
He whose shell is rounded like a vault.

The ambiguous inhabitant of the earth and the waves.

And this talking bird whose sad beauty
Does not make up for his sterility.]

The Abbé Delille had his merits and, once our ears, deprived of the pleasures of rhythm and of number, have become exhausted by the new versification, we may recover a certain charm in full and sonorous verses which are by no means tiresome, and in landscapes which, while somewhat severe, are broad and full of air.

> . . . *Soit qu'une fraîche aurore*
> *Donne la vie aux fleurs qui s'empressent d'éclore,*
> *Soit que l'astre du monde, en achevant son tour,*
> *Jette languissamment les restes d'un beau jour.*[1]

VII

Yet M. Albalat asks how it is possible to be personal and original. His answer is not very clear. He counsels hard work and concludes that originality implies an incessant effort. This is a very regrettable illusion. Secondary qualities would, doubtless, be easier to acquire, but is concision, for example, an absolute quality? Are Rabelais and Victor Hugo, who were great accumulators of words, to be blamed because M. de Pontmartin was also in the habit of stringing together all the words that came into his head, and of heaping up as many as a dozen or fifteen epithets in a single sentence? The examples given by Albalat are very amusing; but if Gargantua had not played as many as two hundred and sixteen different and agreeable games under the eye of Ponocrates, we should feel very sorry, though "the great rules of the game are eternal."

Concision is sometimes the merit of dull imaginations. Harmony is a rarer and more decisive quality. There is no comment to be made on what Albalat says in this connection, unless it be that he believes a trifle too much in the necessary relations between the lightness or heaviness of a word, for example, and the idea which it expresses. This is an illusion which springs from our habits of thought, and an analysis of the sounds destroys it completely. It is not merely, says Villemain, imitation of the Greek or the Latin *fremere* that has given us the word *frémir;* it is also the relation of its sound to the emotion expressed. *Horreur, terreur, doux, suave, rugir, soupirer, pesant, léger,* come to us not only from Latin, but from an intimate sense which has recognized and adopted them as analogous to the impression produced by the object.[2] If Villemain, whose opinion

---

[1]   [. . . Either that a fresh dawn
Gives life to the flowers that are anxious to bloom,
Or that the star of the world, completing its course
Casts forth languidly the fragments of a beautiful day.]
[2] *L'Art d'ecrire,* p. 138.

M. Albalat accepted, had been better versed in linguistics, he would doubt-less have invoked the theory of roots, which at one time gave to his non-sense an appearance of scientific force. As it stands, the celebrated orator's brief paragraph would afford very agreeable matter for discussion. It is quite evident that if *suave* and *suaire* invoke impressions generally re-mote from each other, this is not because of the quality of their sound. In English, *sweet* and *sweat* are words which resemble each other. *Doux* is not more *doux* than *toux* and the other monosyllables of the same tone. Is *rugir* more violent than *rougir* or *vagir*? *Léger* is the contraction of a Latin word of five syllables, *leviarium*. If *légère* carries with it its own meaning, does *mégère* likewise? *Pesant* is neither more nor less heavy than *pensant*, the two forms being, moreover, doublets of a single Latin original, *pensare*. As for *lourd*, this is *luridus*, which meant many things; yellow, wild, sav-age, strange, peasant, heavy—such, doubtless, is its genealogy. *Lourd* is no more heavy than *fauve* is cruel. Think also of *mauve* and *velours*. If the English *thin* means the same as the French *mince*, how does it happen that the idea of its opposite, *épais*, is expressed by *thick?* Words are nega-tive sounds which the mind charges with whatever sense it pleases. There are coincidences, chance agreements, between certain sounds and certain ideas. There are *frémir, frayeur, froid, frileux, frisson*.[1] Yes; but there are also: *frein, frère, frêle, frêne, fret, frime*,[2] and twenty other analogous sonorities, each of which is provided with a very different meaning.

M. Albalat is more successful in the balance of the two chapters where he treats successively word harmony and sentence harmony. He is right in calling the Goncourts' style *un style désécrit*.[3] This is still more strikingly true applied to Loti, in whose work there are no longer any sentences. His pages are thickets of phrases. The tree has been felled, its branches have been lopped; there is nothing left but to make faggots of them.

Beginning with the ninth lesson, *L'Art d'écrire* becomes still more didactic, and we encounter Invention, Disposition and Elocution. I should find it hard to explain just how M. Albalat succeeds in separating these three phases of composition, which are really one. The *art of developing a subject* has been refused me by Providence. I leave all that to the un-conscious, nor do I know anything more of the *art of invention*. I believe that an author invents by reversing the method of Newton—that is, without ever thinking about it, while, as for elocution, I should hesitate to trust myself to the method of recasting. One does not recast, one re-

---

1 [Tremble, terror, co'd, chil'y, a shiver.]
2 [Brake, brother, frail, ash (tree), freight (cargo), sham.]
3 [An unwritten (formless) style.]

makes, and it is so tedious to do the same thing twice, that I approve of those who throw the stone at the first turn of the sling. But here is what proves the inanity of literary counsels: Théophile Gautier wrote the complicated pages of *Capitaine Fracasse* at odd moments on a printer's table, among half-opened bundles of papers, in the stench of oil and ink, and it is said that Buffon recopied eighteen times the *Époques de la Nature.*[1] This divergence is of no importance, since, as M. Albalat should have said, there are writers who make their corrections mentally, putting on paper only the swift or sluggish product of the unconscious, while there are others who need to see exteriorized what they have written, and to see it more than once, in order to correct it—that is, to understand it. Yet, even in the case of mental corrections, exterior revision is often profitable, provided, as Condillac puts it, the writer knows how to stop, to bring to a conclusion.[2] But too often the demon of Betterment has tormented and sterilized intelligence. It is also true that it is a great misfortune to lack self-criticism. Who will dare to choose between the writer who does not know what he is doing, and the one who, endowed with a double nature, can watch himself as he works? There is Verlaine and there is Mallarmé. One must follow the bent of one's own genius.

M. Albalat excels in definitions. "Description is the animated depiction of objects." He means that, in order to describe, a writer must, like a painter, place himself before the landscape, whether this be real or imaginary. Judging by the analysis that he makes of a page of *Télémaque,* it seems clear that Fénelon was only moderately endowed with visual imagination, and more moderately still with the gift of words. In the first twenty lines of the description of Calypso's grotto, the word *doux* occurs three times, and the verb *former* four. This has, indeed, become for us the very type of the inexpressive style, but I persist in believing that it once had its freshness and grace, and that the appeal which it made when it appeared was not unjustified. We smile at this opulence of gilt paper and painted flowers—the ideal of an archbishop who had remained a theological student—and forget that no one had described nature since *Astrée.* Those sweet oranges, those syrups diluted with spring-water, were refreshments fit for Paradise. It would be cruel to compare Fénelon, not with Homer, but even with the Homer of Leconte de Lisle. Translations too well done—those that may be said to possess literary literalness—have

---

[1] [Ages of Nature.] Or rather, had them copied by his secretaries. He afterwards reworked the clean copy. There is a whole volume on this subject: *Les Manuscrits de Buffon,* by P. Flourens, Paris, Garnier, 1860.

[2] There is, on this point, a pretty passage from Quintilian, quoted by M. Albalat, p. 213.

in fact the inevitable result of transforming into concrete, living images everything which had become abstract in the original. Did λευκοβραχίων [1] mean one who had white arms, or was it merely a wornout epithet? Did λευκάκανθα [2] suggest an image such as *blanche épine,*[3] or a neutral idea like *aubépine,*[4] which has lost its representative value? We cannot tell; but, judging dead languages by the living, we must suppose that most of the Homeric epithets had already reached the stage of abstraction in Homer's own time.[5] It is possible that foreigners may find in a work as outworn for us as *Télémaque,* the same pleasure which we derive from the *Iliad* done in bas-relief by Leconte de Lisle. *Mille fleurs naissantes émaillaient les tapis verts* [6] is a *cliché* only when read for the hundredth time. New, the image would be ingenious and pictorial. Poe's poems, translated by Mallarmé, acquired a life at once mysterious and precise which they do not possess to the same degree in the original, and, from Tennyson's *Mariana,* agreeable verse full of commonplaces and padding, grey in tone, the same poet, by substituting the concrete for the abstract, made a fresco of lovely autumnal colouring. I offer these remarks merely as a preface to a theory of translation. They will suffice here to indicate that, where it is a question of style, comparison should be made only between texts in the same language and belonging to the same period.

It is very difficult, after fifty years, to appreciate the real originality of a style. To do so, one should have read all the notable books in the order of their publication. It is at least possible to judge of the present, and also to accord some weight to the contemporary opinions of a work. Barbey d'Aurevilly found in Georges Sand a profusion of *anges de la destinée,*[7] of *lampes de la foi,*[8] and of *coupes de miel,*[9] which certainly were not invented by her any more than the rest of her washed-out style; but "these decrepit tropes" would have been none the better if she had invented them. I feel sure that the cup, whose brim has been rubbed with honey, goes back to the obscure ages of pre-Hippocratic medicine. Hackneyed expressions enjoy a long life. M. Albalat notes justly "that there are images which can be renewed and rejuvenated." There are many

---

1 [With white arms, or shoulders.]

2 [White thorn.]

3 [White thorn.]

4 [Hawthorne.]

5 I take it for granted that the reader no longer believes that the Homeric poems were composed at haphazard by a multitude of rhapsodists of genius, and that it was enough to string these improvisations together to get the *Iliad* and the *Odyssey.*

6 [A thousand flowers in birth enamelled the green carpets.]

7 [Angels of destiny.]

8 [Lamps of faith.]

9 [Goblets of honey.]

such, and among them some of the commonest; but I cannot see that, in calling the moon the *morne lampe,*[1] Leconte de Lisle has been very successful in freshening up Lamartine's *lampe d'or.*[2] M. Albalat, who gives evidence of wide reading, should attempt a catalogue of metaphors by subject: the moon, the stars, the rose, the dawn, and all the "poetic" words. We should thus obtain a collection of a certain utility for the study of words and psychology of elementary emotions. Perhaps we should learn at last why the moon is so dear to poets. Meanwhile he announces his next book, *La Formation du style par l'assimilation des auteurs;*[3] and I suppose that, once the series is complete, everyone will write well— that there will henceforth be a good medium style in literature, as there is in painting and in the other fine arts, which the State protects so successfully. Why not an Académie Albalat, as well as an Académie Julian?

Here, then, is a book which lacks almost nothing except not having a purpose, except being a work of pure and disinterested analysis; but, were it to have an influence, were it to multiply the number of honourable writers, it would deserve our maledictions. Instead of putting the manual of literature and all the arts within the reach of all, it would be wiser to transport their secrets to the top of some Himalaya. Yet there are no secrets. To be a writer, it is enough to have natural talent for the calling, to practise with perseverance, to learn a little more every morning, and to experience all human sensations. As for the art of "creating images," we are obliged to believe that this is absolutely independent of all literary culture, since the loveliest, truest and boldest images are enclosed in the words we use every day—age-old products of instinct, spontaneous flowering of the intellectual garden.

---

[1] [Gloomy lamp.]
[2] [Lamp of gold.]
[3] [The Formation of Style by the Assimilation of Authors.]

THE DEFENCE OF POETRY

BENEDETTO CROCE

In English literature the classical *Defence of Poetry* is that of Shelley, though to speak exactly there are two; for that of Philip Sidney, belonging to the Renaissance, sets out from a point of view very distant from our own. Shelley's work was written in 1821 to refute the assertion that poetry can no longer find a place in mature civilization; or, as Vico would have said, "in fully developed mind." The theory of the death of poetry, or of its superannuation in the modern world, was not peculiar to Hegel, who gave it its most extreme and most systematic form, but sprang up in many places in the early decades of the nineteenth century. There were various reasons for this, but the chief, and perhaps a fundamental one, was the habit of confusing, or too closely connecting, images of art with religious myths. Shelley pointed to poetry as the eternal source of all intellectual, moral, and civil vitality, and claimed that it was a specially necessary corrective for times when the selfish and mechanical principle, represented by Mammon, threatens to prevail, and when the body has become too unwieldy for that which animates it. In fact, it was for his own times that he sought the aid of poetry, times when, in spite of their splendid culture, he thought that the intellect was excessively honoured. He foresaw a dangerous disproportion between the accumulated growth of moral, historical, political, and economic science on the one hand and, on the other, the failing forces of imagination, with all those kindred generous impulses which alone can quicken abstract knowledge to a fruitful and beneficent activity.

Thirty years before Shelley, Friedrich Schiller had been moved in like manner to invoke the aid of art and poetry for the salvation of a humanity tossed unceasingly from the extreme of servitude to the extreme of anarchy, and unable to foresee any other end to its troubles than in some blind force, which might settle with a strong hand the dispute between these rival principles. While Schiller was writing, the crisis of the French Revolution was developing with terrible rapidity. The theo-

The 1933 Deneke Lecture "The Defence of Poetry," by Benedetto Croce, is reprinted by permission of The Clarendon Press, Oxford.

retical programme of that revolution was the triumph of reason and liberty underfoot. The consequences, in countries not yet affected by the movement, were a growing hostility of governments to a liberty which seemed their obvious enemy, and a design to uphold and fortify tyranny and oppression; while, at the same time, among their subject peoples, the promised reign of liberty and reason raised an ever stronger enthusiasm and more irresistible agitation. How was it possible to avoid or to mitigate this ominous clash between the state of nature, where might is right, and the state of reason and liberty? The former was incapable of really rising to the latter, and, after spasmodic efforts, only relapsed into brutality. The latter was unable to stoop to the former or to assimilate it, and striving, consistently with its theory, to realize itself by uncompromising and impatient methods, became so violent, tyrannical, and bloody as to provoke reaction. Or, to ask the same question in terms of psychology, how could the sensuous, passionate man be raised to the level of the rational man, without a deterioration in which each party would rival the other, and finally both sink to the same depth of monstrosity and degradation? Schiller could see no solution except to set up, as a mediator between the sensuous and the rational man, a third, the artist.[1] Between the state of nature and the state of reason he set the state of art or poetry, which has gone beyond the first and not attained the second; which is no longer purely passive [2] or passionate, but is not yet ethically active; [3] which has gained aesthetic but not moral freedom. Such a state has escaped from nature but has not yet developed itself in any definite sphere; it covers rather the totality of human faculties, training and exercising them all as in some noble kind of play.

Do we too live in an age that might justify once more an appeal to poetry for the succour which Schiller and Shelley implored of it? I think all who heard such a question would, with one voice, eagerly answer: Yes.

In fact, no day passes without our all hearing the universal complaint that lofty motives have now vanished from our world; that the only aim of life is victory in the fight for riches, the only pleasure that of the body; that the one spectacle which can stir us to excitement or admiration is the strange and reckless exhibition of physical force; that our only emulation is in the fierce struggle for pre-eminence between nations or classes. The sublime and sacred watchwords, which stirred the hearts of former ages, are either a mere laughingstock, or quite meaningless for a generation who knows not what to make of them, and which cannot compre-

---

[1] *L'uomo estetico.*

[2] *passività.*

[3] *pratica attività.*

hend the power and fascination that they exercised, or seem to have exercised, upon its fathers and grandfathers, who still mumble the tale. The dreams, the enthusiasms, the despondencies *de grands amants ou de grands citoyens,*[1] as the poet calls them, have become a byword. Science interests us only when it can afford new methods of production; philosophy only when it lends itself to adorn the aims of particular classes, governments, and nations with sophistic formulas or shameless lies; art only when it panders to the mental and spiritual vacuity of its audience by elaborate staging, discordant imagery, or the vain promise of new and strange sensations. The old religion loses every day more of what respectability it still possessed as a practical institution, by making terms with the powers of this world and, in return for its services, pocketing a bribe or snatching a material advantage. As a spiritual institution it offers an asylum to those who through laziness or disillusion are weary of thinking and acting on their own responsibility. Our civilization is technically perfect and spiritually barbarous; ravenous of wealth and indifferent to good; utterly insensible to all that ought to move the human conscience. All its powers seem employed in selfish aggression or defence. This is the dense atmosphere in which we are stifled, which painfully chokes and crushes every freedom of heart, every delicate sensibility, every quickness of mind. But if some fresh rain of poetry should permeate it, what recreation would it bring, what ampler breath, what heightened spirits! Then we should renew our sense of the eternal human drama, of the tragedies and glories of our kind; we should see things once more in their true proportions and relations, in their harmonious hierarchy; we should fall in love again with love and with loving-kindness; we should renew our scorn for all that is base and abject, and vulgar; our hearts would reopen to hope and joy, to manly grief, to the relief of tears, to frank and cleansing laughter—the laughter so seldom heard in a world where it is outfaced by sarcasm, by sly leers, or by shameless ribaldry.

In point of objective truth it is easy to see how much exaggeration and illusion there is in such a picture of the modern world. That it is no historical portrait we have already hinted by borrowing the tones of the stricken and complaining hearts who bewail its character. Rather it is the vision which contemporaries have of a development in which they are actors, and which they endure in their own persons. Consequently, when they balance the necessary contrasts of new and old, the necessary losses and innovations, they are apt to see in the course of the struggle nothing but what offends them and arouses their protest, their opposition,

---

[1] [great lovers or great citizens.]

and rebellion. It is from such hostile criticism that they compose their picture, which accordingly, is the prejudiced portrayal of a dreaded enemy, coloured by the injuries received or feared from him. To paint a true picture of the whole process they would obviously have to include themselves, and many like themselves, who resist it or work in an opposite and complementary sense, not to mention that mute, inglorious host of good and honest men who are the underlying fabric which holds human society together. Instead of this, in the strife and fury of passion they forget both themselves and these others; their imagination sees the whole field occupied by the triumphant and ravaging hordes of the enemy. That is why in every age almost identical complaints are heard, and the same gloomy pictures painted; just objects of irony, sometimes, to the cultivated and the reflective. But granting all this, every age, besides what all have in common, has its proper difficulties and problems. If it would be ingenuous to take for historic truth the pessimistic picture projected by the fears of a combatant, it would be stupid to overlook the peculiar physiognomy and character of every age. On the most calm and careful consideration, we have to admit two important points. The first is that the vast improvement in means of production and in economy of labour during the nineteenth and early twentieth centuries has left its mark on the general character, and has overshadowed other elements of human experience, which struggled painfully against its undue preponderance. The second is that the world war has further weakened the resistance of our higher spiritual powers by mowing down millions of young lives, by cutting short or hampering the education of millions more, by breaking the tradition of culture, and by elevating to power new classes ignorant or contemptuous of that tradition. All this suffices to prove that the crudity and barbarism complained of, if not the only characteristics of modern society, are yet, after all deductions, real enough; it suffices to justify our renewed appeal to poetry as a saviour of the world.

But, in such an appeal, what are we really asking? What do we in fact expect of poetry, and what can it give? Both Shelley and Schiller had pretty clear ideas on the nature of poetry and its function in individual and social life. They firmly grasped the disinterested nature of the aesthetic activity, which Schiller defined as free from any definite aim,[1] and spiritually effective precisely by this unpracticalness.[2] Shelley forbade art to pursue moral ends, but recognized its power to purge the human mind of base desires, to rouse our enthusiasm for love and for all that is good or

---

[1] *particolare determinazione.*

[2] *indeterminazione.* Cf. Schiller, *Letters on the Aesthetic Education of Mankind,* xxii.

noble, to enlarge the mind by rendering it the receptacle of a thousand un-
apprehended combinations of thought. He understood, moreover, the regeneration of truths which poetry effects in face of the intellectual algebra
which tends to conventionalize them; poetry, he says, "purges from our
inward sight the film of familiarity which obscures from us the wonder of
our being." But both Schiller and Shelley, in developing the arguments of
their discussions, either attributed to poetry a good deal more than it can
really do, and thus lost sight of its true and simple nature, or assigned to it
a particular task which is not appropriate to it. In neither of them is the
scientific elaboration of the thesis worthy of its primary and fundamental
idea.

Shelley, in fact, was carried away by his sense of the infinite value
of this spiritual activity, and gave it absolute supremacy over all others,
making it the first author of every human achievement and the source of
all civilization. Poets are for him the unacknowledged legislators of the
world, its "true princes," as Tommaso Campanella would have called them,
in contrast to "the pretenders," who oppose them with physical force. Poets
are not only the authors of language and of music, of the dance, and architecture, and statuary, and painting: they are the institutors of laws, and
the founders of civil society, and the inventors of the arts of life, and the
teachers who draw into a certain propinquity with the beautiful and the
true, that partial apprehension of the agencies of the invisible world which
is called religion. Poetry is indeed something divine. It is at once the
centre and circumference of knowledge; it is that which comprehends all
science, and that to which all science must be referred. Without the exertions of the philosophers, of Locke, Hume, Gibbon, Voltaire, and Rousseau, who put to flight the shades of slavish credulity and ignorance, and
shook off the chains of tyrants, a little more nonsense would have been
talked for a century or two, and a few more heretics might have been
burnt. But if neither Dante, Petrarch, Boccaccio, Shakespeare nor Milton,
had ever existed; if Raphael and Michelangelo had never been born; if a
revival of the study of Greek literature had never taken place; the human
mind could never have been awakened to the invention of the grosser sciences or that application of analytical reasoning to the aberrations of
society, which it is now attempted to exalt over the direct expression of
the inventive and creative faculty itself. The dark ages were therefore
the dark ages because in them the poetical principle decayed, and
despotism and superstition proportionately flourished. Poetry is not only
what is so called in the restricted sense, what it expressed in words and
verses. The true poetry of Rome was fashioned in its institutions and in
the deeds of its heroic history, in Camillus and Regulus, in the senators

seated before the invading Gauls, in the stolid resistance of the republic
after Cannae. Poetry is philosophy and philosophy is poetry. Plato and
Bacon were great poets; Shakespeare, Dante, and Milton are great philosophers.

Such statements have, no doubt, an element of truth—without which
they could not have issued from the mind of Shelley—namely that poetry,
being an eternal category of the human spirit, can be discovered in every
individual, in every achievement, and in every action of our life. Their
element of error consists in overlooking or forgetting that the other categories also—logical thought, will, morality—must, like poetry, have their
place in every person and in every act. Consequently a captious criticism
might give the supremacy in turn to logical thought, will, and morality,
thus making the whole world, which for Shelley revolved on the axis of
poetry, revolve on the axis of any of these categories. Poetry, far from
gaining by being expanded over the whole world, loses its proper and
distinctive character, and therewith its proper strength and efficacy. Nor,
in truth, can we say that this proper and distinctive character is comprised
in Shelley's definition of poetry, so often re-echoed, as "the record of the
best and happiest moments of the happiest and best minds." This is in fact
rather a poetical or imaginative expression than a technical definition, and
indeed the whole *Defence* has a movement which is a good deal more
poetical than reasoned or critical.

Schiller, for his part, demanded from poetry, and in general from
aesthetic education, the solution of the problem of development from a
state of violence to a state of freedom, from sense and passion to reason.
This was the problem which the eighteenth century had solved in its own
way by its faith in the irresistible power of enlightenment through reason.
Before reason all errors were to melt away; spiritual and temporal arms
were to fall from the hands of priests and despots, and the natural goodness
of men was to celebrate its final triumph. It was the same problem as that
offered by Kant's conception of an absolute, unyielding moral law which
subdues and expels the passions with no aid save its own fearless and
heroic strength. Schiller could no longer believe in the miracles of mere
reason; he could not accept the hard and fast Kantian opposition between
feeling and morality, between impulse and duty, nor the eradication and
suppression of the former by the latter. To him the old problem appeared
in a new guise, as the political problem of his own day, as the quest for
a mediator between old and new, between the actual and the ideal. He
was equally unable to satisfy himself with the solution of the Jacobins or
with that of the reactionaries, both alike ruinous; he longed for a genuine
and substantial progress towards reason and liberty. But, in inserting a

third state between the two which he assumed, he was treating Kant's problem, which was really dialectical or metaphysical, psychologically. For in actual fact there is not first the state of nature or feeling and then the state of freedom or reason, nor is there an intermediate aesthetic state; but only the unceasing alternation from the one moment or factor to the other, from feeling to reason, from random impulse [1] to moral freedom. In such an alternation poetry can have no place, except in the sense, already explained, that poetry pervades all things as the unity of all-pervasive spirit does. Accordingly, the logical problem which Schiller had in mind reduced itself to the problem of the nature of development or evolution, and his political problem to that of finding in the actual some point of contact with the ideal, in the old some seed of the new. He had, therefore, both to criticize and to respect, both to abolish and to retain, the old and actual, if he would really achieve the new and ideal. A similar solution was in fact reached by the historically-minded liberal policy of the nineteenth century, among whose prophets Schiller, with his theory of Aesthetic Education, must be included. But poetry and art have a sphere both wider and narrower than this political principle, or, more truly, the aesthetic problem belongs to a different branch of inquiry. The education dreamed of by Schiller, which, by cultivating all man's various faculties harmoniously, should train him for life without engaging him in any one path of life leading to this or the other particular object, was evidently not pure poetry or aesthetic education. Rather it was liberal education and general culture, not narrowly intellectual or rationalistic, nor yet narrowly artistic and imaginative, but directed alike on the reason and the imagination, on the will and the conscience, and harmonizing all together.

Having noted the varieties in the conception of poetry in two great minds, both exceptionally rich in poetic genius, if we now set ourselves to define that conception, it is certainly not, as might be suspected, with the idea of discovering and revealing it for the first time, *nondum auditum indictumque prius.*[2] The conception of poetry, like other fundamental conceptions, needs no discovery, because it has always been present in man's mind since his spirit first created poetry, which is as much as to say *ab eterno.*[3] But from time to time it is useful in particular discussions to reaffirm it against new confusions and errors which tend to obscure it, though, at the same time, by stimulating it to clearer consciousness and stronger emphasis, they keep it sound and vigorous. The subject of our discussion is the way in which poetry can help to preserve or refresh man's

---

[1] *l'arbitrio.*
[2] [Not yet heard and said before.]
[3] [from the eternal.]

superior nature in its contest with his inferior, morality in its contest with expediency. And since the way suggested by Schiller and Shelley has been shown impossible, or their descriptions of it vague and loose, we must, for this purpose, reaffirm the true conception of poetry; not only in order to correct, in some degree, their aesthetic theories, but still more to contend against other current theories which confuse or replace it by conceptions of different nature and application.

It is certainly unnecessary to-day to attack "oratorical" poetry. For more than a century and a half it has been condemned in theory by aesthetics or the philosophy of art, and attacked in practice by critics, both in its form of solemn poems or decorous odes designed to inculcate political, moral, and religious virtue, or to expound the great truths of philosophy and science, and also in its lighter, more palatable form of satire, epigram, and playful or "occasional" verse. Such things have their uses, but, in spite of Aristotle's warning, they have been falsely called poetry because they were written in verse. Yet criticism distinguishes them from true poetry, and even in single poems distinguishes the poetical portions from the oratorical, which it dismisses from its consideration. The same aesthetic tendency has made itself felt in various ways in the plastic and pictorial arts, where sharp distinctions have been drawn between "literature," which is a subject edifying or in general "oratorical," and "painting" which is the poetic element; between "illustrative" and "decorative" values, and many more. In Italy, at least, the same tendency begins to show itself also in musical criticism. The only proper object of aesthetic consideration to-day is the poetry which is nothing but poetry or, as it is also called, "pure poetry."

Unfortunately into this very conception of "pure" poetry, as opposed to oratory, has been insinuated another, which is its opposite and its corruption, which might indeed be called a conception of a poetry that is "impure" because contaminated with a questionable sensationalism. To avoid misunderstanding, it might be better to call the poetry thus set before us as our ideal, "mystical-voluptuous," since its mark is the union of sensual gratification with turgid emotion, as if in this sensuality we fathomed the mystery of the universe and attained a kind of beatific ecstasy. This ideal of poetry and of the arts is connected, in devious ways, with what is called "decadence," whose chief symptoms consist precisely in the confusion of matter with form, of the sensuous with the ideal, of pleasure with morality; so that the former are disguised and honoured as the latter, and a witches' banquet celebrated where the devil sits enthroned and worshipped.

Such an impure conception of pure poetry excludes, or pretends to exclude, from poetry all the meaning of words, concentrating on the mere sound. But people who have banished all meaning naturally cannot dwell in this night of not-being. They have to elaborate a kind of significance of their own out of the mere nervous titillation, or "suggestion," as they call it, which arouses no clear image, but only the possibility of innumerable images and thoughts, varying from reader to reader and from moment to moment, linked solely by threads of contiguity, contrast, and other forms of the so-called association of ideas.

We need not trouble to attack poets who boast of such doctrines, since there is no causal connexion between theories of poetry and poetic creation. Men of poetic genius, holding these or even worse doctrines, have done very beautiful work; and, on the other hand, men with the best theories and no genius write cold insipidities which naturally remain unread. The fact that our modern Maevius and Bavius, and Suffenus may generally be found under the banner of "pure poetry" only means that this happens to be the fashion and that mediocrity always follows the fashion. But the theory concerns us for its own sake and as a theory, since, if we took it for true, it would destroy the very conception of poetry and annihilate the problem before us. As a principle of practical criticism it has, hitherto at least, had little or no importance, for it has occurred to nobody to apply it in a history of poetry. Past poetry, indeed, answers badly to the demands of this theory, and worst in the supreme poets, in Homer, Sophocles, Dante, and Shakespeare, who give it the lie direct. Accordingly, the so-called critics of this school usually either neglect all past art, as if it had been condemned by some peculiar law of its nature literally to pass away, or else they pronounce that all former poets were unfortunate, since, in the course of composition, they lost sight of that spark of inspiration which glimmers here and there in their verses. In practical criticism the theory has been little applied except for the consolation and honour of some beloved brother-artist, who is ready with mutual praise and admiration, instead of the laughter that would be more in place. Generally it is elaborated to serve as the criticism of the future for an art of the future, which, like so many futurisms, does not escape some suspicion of quackery.

Coming to the theory as such, if what it says were true, poetry would be nothing but a voluptuous thrill leading only to satiety, and comparable, as the name here suggested for it would imply, to barren sensuality, bearing no fruit in the life of the soul. It could receive nothing from thought or will and could give them nothing, nor could it compose with them the harmonious unity of the spirit. At best it would belong to that class of pleasures which satisfy physiological or pathological needs, like those of alcohol and tobacco, narcotics, stimulants, and aphrodisiacs. We need not exclude the possibility that the manufacturers and amateurs of these verbal or phonetic drugs labelled pure poems, granting that their physical raptures are no affectation but as real as they are capable of feeling, may be some kind of erotic maniacs.

Pure poetry, in the pure sense of the term, is certainly "sounds," and certainly it is not sounds which have a logical meaning like the sounds of prose. That is to say, it does not communicate a conception, a judgement, or an inference, nor the story of particular facts. But to say it has no logical meaning is not to say it is a mere physical sound without a soul, an embodied soul which is one with its body as that is with it. In order to distinguish the soul of truth in poetry from the soul of truth in prose, aesthetic science has borrowed and employs the word "intuition," and asserts that poetic intuition and poetic expression are brought forth at a single birth. It maintains also that poetic intuition cannot be translated into logical terms; it is something infinite that has no other equivalent than the melody in which it is expressed, and that may be sung but never rendered into prose. It is impossible to see what people mean when, in their desire to confine poetry to pure sound which is nothing but sound, they so often say that it is or ought to be pure "music": as if music could be mere sound and nothing more, and had not already a soul of its own, which would equally justify us in demanding that music should be poetry. It is a delusion to suppose that a verse delights us by any sounds with which it stimulates our ears to ecstasy. What it stimulates to ecstasy is our imagination, and thereby our emotion. There is a verse of Racine which Théophile Gautier used to scan and declaim with gusto, and which other disciples of preciosity are in the habit of citing as absolutely unmeaning and yet, or rather for that reason, the only beautiful verse which the poet ever succeeded in writing:

La fille de Minos et de Pasiphaé [1]

That is certainly beautiful, but not in virtue of the physical combination of its sounds. One might make infinite other combinations of such sounds without producing any effect of beauty. It is beautiful because these sounds, these syllables and accents, bring before us, in an instantaneous imaginative fusion, all that was mysterious and sinister, all that was divine and fiendish, all that was majestic and perverted, both in the person and in the parentage of Phaedra. And this is expressed by two epic names, that

---

[1] [The daughter of Minos and of Pasiphaë.]

of the royal Cretan legislator and that of his incestuous wife, at whose side rises, in our imagination, the brutal figure of the bull.

And while we are dealing with mistakes of this kind, I may perhaps be allowed to say that we should not lend too docile ears to similar errors of artists when they talk of their artistic aims and methods, or describe their inspired experience and the usual physical symptoms which precede, accompany, and follow it. Such accounts are not very weighty and do not deserve to be taken as philosophically or scientifically sound. Many years ago a man with one of the most purely poetic talents that I have ever intimately known—a poet of the Neapolitan dialect named Salvatore di Giacomo—told me that poetry always came to him in the shape of an overmastering stomach-ache; and, while he made the confession, his face exhibited every mark of agony and nausea. And lately, in a lecture given by an English poet this year at Cambridge,[1] I met with a mention of the same part of his anatomy. For there I read that poetry is a "secretion," like the resin which exudes from a pine-tree, or the pearl formed in a diseased oyster, and that its birth-place is in "the pit of the stomach." And this reminded me that Goethe too, in a like context, talked about the stomach: but his experience, on the contrary, was that if he were to conceive and bring forth good poetry this digestive organ must be in sound condition, and he concluded that, to judge from his extraordinary powers of creation, nobody ever had so fine a stomach as William Shakespeare. But whatever action poetic travail may have upon the stomach, or whatever the stomachic condition favourable for its completion, we are, none the less, entitled to reject the conclusion drawn in the Cambridge lecture quoted above, that poetry "is rather physical than intellectual," or only to accept it, in the sense perhaps intended, as a curiosity of whimsical paradox.

If, then, poetry is intuition and expression, the fusion of sound and imagery, what is the material which takes on the form of sound and imagery? It is the whole man: the man who thinks and wills, and loves, and hates; who is strong and weak, sublime and pathetic, good and wicked; man in the exultation and agony of living; and together with the man, integral with him, it is all nature in its perpetual labour of evolution. But the thoughts and actions and emotions of life, when sublimated to the subject-matter of poetry, are no longer the thought that judges, the action effectually carried out, the good and evil, or the joy and pain actually done

---

[1] *The Name and Nature of Poetry,* by A. E. Housman (Cambridge University Press, 1933).

or suffered. They are all now simply passions and feelings immediately assuaged and calmed, and transfigured in imagery. That is the magic of poetry: the union of calm and tumult, of passionate impulse with the controlling mind which controls by contemplating. It is the triumph of contemplation, but a triumph still shaken by past battle, with its foot upon a living though vanquished foe. Poetic genius chooses a straight path in which passion is calmed and calm is passionate; a path that has on one side merely natural feeling, and on the other the reflection and criticism which is twice removed from nature; a path from which minor talents find it but too easy to slip into an art either convulsed and distorted by passion, or void of passion and guided by principles of the understanding. Then they are called "romantic" or "classical." The man of poetic taste also treads this narrow path, in which he is permitted to share the delights of poetry. He knows how that delight is compounded· it is shot with pain; permeated by a strange sweetness and tenderness; torn between alternate impulses and repulsions, desire and renunciations, between the zest of life and the desire of death; yet always delight: the delight of perfect form and of beauty.

Is this enjoyment of poetry, this delight in beauty, rare or common? It is both: as a settled habit it is rare, reserved for select spirits who are born to it and trained by education; it is common, as the native tendency of all ingenuous minds. The place where it is hardest to find is precisely among the professional students of poetry and of its historical achievements. They seem gifted with a strange immunity, which lets them all their life handle the books of the poets, edit and annotate them, discuss their various interpretations, investigate their sources, furnish them with biographical introductions, and all without suffering so much contagion as to experience in their own persons the poetic fever. After all, it is much the same in religion, which is felt by lofty minds and by the humble plebs, but not by those who handle the sacred vessels, by the priests and sacristans, who go through their ritual unconcerned, and sometimes with little reverence.

If we call to mind the conception of poetry in its strict character, circumscribed within its proper limits, it must not only decline all those particular functions to which it has been invoked or bent against its nature, but also it must lose the supreme place of honour assigned to it by Shelley, when he called it the fountain of all the forms of civil life. We may indeed invoke it for the regeneration and refreshment and spiritual renewal of human society, but only in accordance with its own essence, not as if it could replace or spontaneously generate the other powers, capacities, and relations of man. In short, we must only look upon it as one among other paths leading to a single goal. Other paths lead there too: the paths of thought, of philosophy, of religion, of conscience, of political action. Not least, there is that path of activity which aims at the production of economic goods; an activity which, seriously carried on, is compelled to realize itself as part of the universal human activity on which all its own strength and permanence depend. Whichever of these paths we enter and pursue we must at least enter the others also, and we find in the end that they are not divergent nor even parallel, but join in a circle which is the rounded unity of the human spirit. And on every path there is the chance —though it is no chance when looked at in the contexture of the whole and as an incident of the world-drama—that an individual may stop half-way, as if exhausted, and never reach the goal that is set before him, but remain one-sided, incomplete, discordant. There is the philosopher who does not carry out the practical requirements of his philosophy but sees the better and follows the worse, or at least stands idle when he should be fulfilling his duties as a citizen and a soldier. There is the artistic genius who never effects the passage from the dreams of poetry to philosophic thought and consistent action. Both are half-men, *dimidiati viri*.[1] But this stunting of life, this breach which the individual makes at some point in the integrity of the spiritual circle, revenges itself, and often in the very region which is dearest to him. The philosopher of easy virtue or of loose morals feels his philosophic enthusiasm gradually dry up, and loses faith in his own thinking; the creator and lover of poetry who has exhausted his early stock of human experience gradually degenerates into the mere stylist or purveyor of belles-lettres. For our part, in the meantime, let us try, as our aptitudes and attainments may permit, to introduce others to the path of poetry, by which they may reach one of the unfailing fountains of perennial youth. Will they be disposed to follow us or will they refuse? Will they exchange expressions of ready sympathy, or will they accompany us with reluctance and even disgust, and turn out bad companions? Certainly I will not conceal a feeling, perhaps not peculiar to myself, which I have had during the last twenty years: a feeling that if I recite aloud a line or stanza of Dante or Petrarch or Foscolo, their voices find no echo: a sense of a surrounding atmosphere strange, hostile, and contemptuous; a sense of sacrilege in bringing into it those gentle and exalted words, born in a different world and addressed to a different world. But does such an experience imply that we must withdraw into ourselves; that we must keep silence; that we must hold such communion only with our own hearts, shyly, as becomes us when we dream over lost

---

[1] [of a half man.]

happiness? Or is it rather simply the signal that here is a barrier to be broken down? Let me picture to you a mythical scene of very different character. We are in a gathering of men and youths on edge with mutually hostile passions. They are opponents who mistrust one another, alienated by conflicting aims; each of them aloof and angry, on the defensive of his own narrow circumference. Suddenly somebody opens a book of poetry and begins to read: as the music flows on, as the images float before their eyes, something mysterious moves in their hearts, their souls incline to it, their imagination awakes. They follow the expressive rhythm in its theme, in its modulations, in its final harmony; and in these modulations and that harmony they begin, with wonder and emotion, to remember something in themselves that was sleeping, cold or buried—their common humanity. After that discovery, can they still look at one another as before? Can they any longer see themselves as utterly divided, as mortal enemies, when a bond has been forged between them, when all have had a momentary glimpse into the world of beauty, and learned that in that world they are brothers? Can such a moment of divine augury vainly vanish and leave not a trace upon their minds? Must it not bring the need for other such moments, and for much else of the same kind; not only for verses and poems, and music, and pictures, but for thoughts which illuminate and for deeds that uplift the heart?

It may be said, in discouragement of vain hopes and over-confidence, that the world is hard and heavy, and needs more than individual good-will and poetic fancies. But we know that, all the same, this hard and heavy world moves, or rather that it only exists in movement, and that it is moved by nothing but our united efforts; that each of us, great or small or tiny as he may be, in his relation to all the others is answerable for the world. If we too, as lovers of poetry, exert what strength we have, we shall have done the duty of our station.

THE NATURE OF BEAUTY

GEORGE SANTAYANA

It would be easy to find a definition of beauty that should give in a few words a telling paraphrase of the word. We know on excellent authority that beauty is truth, that it is the expression of the ideal, the symbol of divine perfection, and the sensible manifestation of the good. A litany of these titles of honour might easily be compiled, and repeated in praise of our divinity. Such phrases stimulate thought and give us a momentary pleasure, but they hardly bring any permanent enlightenment. A definition that should really define must be nothing less than the exposition of the origin, place, and elements of beauty as an object of human experience. We must learn from it, as far as possible, why, when, and how beauty appears, what conditions an object must fulfil to be beautiful, what elements of our nature make us sensible of beauty, and what the relation is between the constitution of the object and the excitement of our susceptibility. Nothing less will really define beauty or make us understand what aesthetic appreciation is. The definition of beauty in this sense will be the task of this whole book, a task that can be only very imperfectly accomplished within its limits.

The historical titles of our subject may give us a hint towards the beginning of such a definition. Many writers of the last century called the philosophy of beauty *Criticism,* and the word is still retained as the title for the reasoned appreciation of works of art. We could hardly speak, however, of delight in nature as criticism. A sunset is not criticised; it is felt and enjoyed. The word "criticism," used on such an occasion, would emphasize too much the element of deliberate judgment and of comparison with standards. Beauty, although often so described, is seldom so perceived, and all the greatest excellences of nature and art are so far from being approved of by a rule that they themselves furnish the standard and ideal by which critics measure inferior effects.

This age of science and of nomenclature has accordingly adopted a more learned word, *Æsthetics,* that is, the theory of perception or of susceptibility. If criticism is too narrow a word, pointing exclusively to our more artificial judgments, aesthetics seems to be too broad and to include within its sphere all pleasures and pains, if not all perceptions whatsoever. Kant used it, as we know, for his theory of time and space as forms of all perception; and it has at times been narrowed into an equivalent for the philosophy of art.

If we combine, however, the etymological meaning of criticism with that of aesthetics, we shall unite two essential qualities of the theory of beauty. Criticism implies judgment, and aesthetics perception. To get the common ground, that of perceptions which are critical, or judgments which are perceptions, we must widen our notion of deliberate criticism so as to include those judgments of value which are instinctive and immediate, that is, to include pleasures and pains; and at the same time we must narrow our notion of aesthetics so as to exclude all perceptions which are not appreciations, which do not find a value in their objects. We thus reach the sphere of critical or appreciative perception, which is, roughly speaking, what we mean to deal with. And retaining the word "aesthetics," which is now current, we may therefore say that aesthetics is concerned with the perception of values. The meaning and conditions of value is, then, what we must first consider.

Since the days of Descartes it has been a conception familiar to philosophers that every visible event in nature might be explained by previous visible events, and that all the motions, for instance, of the tongue in speech, or of the hand in painting, might have merely physical causes. If consciousness is thus accessory to life and not essential to it, the race of man might have existed upon the earth and acquired all the arts necessary for its subsistence without possessing a single sensation, idea, or emotion. Natural selection might have secured the survival of those automata which made useful reactions upon their environment. An instinct of self-preservation would have been developed, dangers would have been shunned without being feared, and injuries revenged without being felt.

In such a world there might have come to be the most perfect organization. There would have been what we should call the expression of the deepest interests and the apparent pursuit of conceived goods. For there would have been spontaneous and ingrained tendencies to avoid certain contingencies and to produce others; all the dumb show and evidence of thinking would have been patent to the observer. Yet there would surely have been no thinking, no expectation, and no conscious achievement in the whole process.

The onlooker might have feigned ends and objects of forethought, as we do in the case of the water that seeks its own level, or in that of the vacuum which nature abhors. But the particles of matter would have remained unconscious of their collocation, and all nature would have been insensible of their changing arrangement. We only, the possible spectators of that process, by virtue of our own interests and habits, could see any progress or culmination in it. We should see culmination where the result attained satisfied our practical or aesthetic demands, and progress wherever such a satisfaction was approached. But apart from ourselves, and our human bias, we can see in such a mechanical world no element of value whatever. In removing consciousness, we have removed the possibility of worth.

But it is not only in the absence of all consciousness that value would be removed from the world; by a less violent abstraction from the totality of human experience, we might conceive beings of a purely intellectual cast, minds in which the transformations of nature were mirrored without any emotion. Every event would then be noted, its relations would be observed, its recurrence might even be expected; but all this would happen without a shadow of desire, of pleasure, or of regret. No event would be repulsive, no situation terrible. We might, in a word, have a world of idea without a world of will. In this case, as completely as if consciousness were absent altogether, all value and excellence would be gone. So that for the existence of good in any form it is not merely consciousness but emotional consciousness that is needed. Observation will not do, appreciation is required.

We may therefore at once assert this axiom, important for all moral philosophy and fatal to certain stubborn incoherences of thought, that there is no value apart from some appreciation of it, and no good apart from some preference of it before its absence or its opposite. In appreciation, in preference, lies the root and essence of all excellence. Or, as Spinoza clearly expresses it, we desire nothing because it is good, but it is good only because we desire it.

It is true that in the absence of an instinctive reaction we can still apply these epithets by an appeal to usage. We may agree that an action is bad, or a building good, because we recognize in them a character which we have learned to designate by that adjective; but unless there is in us some trace of passionate reprobation or of sensible delight, there is no moral or aesthetic judgment. It is all a question of propriety of speech, and of the empty titles of things. The verbal and mechanical proposition, that passes for judgment of worth, is the great cloak of ineptitude in these matters. Insensibility is very quick in the conventional use of words. If we appealed more often to actual feeling, our judgments would be more diverse, but they would be more legitimate and instructive. Verbal judg-

ments are often useful instruments of thought, but it is not by them that
worth can ultimately be determined.

Values spring from the immediate and inexplicable reaction of vital
impulse, and from the irrational part of our nature. The rational part is
by its essence relative; it leads us from data to conclusions, or from parts
to wholes; it never furnishes the data with which it works. If any preference
or precept were declared to be ultimate and primitive, it would thereby be
declared to be irrational, since mediation, inference, and synthesis are the
essence of rationality. The ideal of rationality is itself as arbitrary, as much
dependent on the needs of a finite organization, as any other ideal. Only
as ultimately securing tranquillity of mind, which the philosopher in-
stinctively pursues, has it for him any necessity. In spite of the verbal propriety of saying that reason demands rationality, what really demands
rationality, what makes it a good and indispensable thing and gives it all
its authority, is not its own nature, but our need of it both in safe and economical action and in the pleasures of comprehension.

It is evident that beauty is a species of value, and what we have said
of value in general applies to this particular kind. A first approach to a
definition of beauty has therefore been made by the exclusion of all intellectual judgments, all judgments of matter of fact or of relation. To substitute judgments of fact for judgments of value, is a sign of a pedantic
and borrowed criticism. If we approach a work of art or nature scientifically,
for the sake of its historical connexions or proper classification, we do not
approach it aesthetically. The discovery of its date or of its author may
be otherwise interesting; it only remotely affects our aesthetic appreciation
by adding to the direct effect certain associations. If the direct effect were
absent, and the object in itself uninteresting, the circumstances would be
immaterial. Molière's *Misanthrope* says to the court poet who commends
his sonnet as written in a quarter of an hour,

> Voyons, monsieur, le temps ne fait rien à l'affaire,[1]

and so we might say to the critic that sinks into the archaeologist, show
us the work, and let the date alone.

In an opposite direction the same substitution of facts for values makes
its appearance, whenever the reproduction of fact is made the sole standard of artistic excellence. Many half-trained observers condemn the work
of some naïve or fanciful masters with a sneer, because, as they truly say,
it is out of drawing. The implication is that to be correctly copied from
a model is the prerequisite of all beauty. Correctness is, indeed, an element

---

[1] [See here, sir, time has nothing to do with it.]

of effect and one which, in respect to familiar objects, is almost indispensable, because its absence would cause a disappointment and dissatisfaction incompatible with enjoyment. We learn to value truth more and more as our love and knowledge of nature increase. But fidelity is a merit only because it is in this way a factor in our pleasure. It stands on a level with all other ingredients of effect. When a man raises it to a solitary pre-eminence and becomes incapable of appreciating anything else, he betrays the decay of aesthetic capacity. The scientific habit in him inhibits the artistic.

That facts have a value of their own, at once complicates and explains this question. We are naturally pleased by every perception, and recognition and surprise are particularly acute sensations. When we see a striking truth in any imitation, we are therefore delighted, and this kind of pleasure is very legitimate, and enters into the best effects of all the representative arts. Truth and realism are therefore aesthetically good, but they are not all-sufficient, since the representation of everything is not equally pleasing and effective. The fact that resemblance is a source of satisfaction justifies the critic in demanding it, while the aesthetic insufficiency of such veracity shows the different value of truth in science and in art. Science is the response to the demand for information, and in it we ask for the whole truth and nothing but the truth. Art is the response to the demand for entertainment, for the stimulation of our senses and imagination, and truth enters into it only as it subserves these ends.

Even the scientific value of truth is not, however, ultimate or absolute. It rests partly on practical, partly on aesthetic interests. As our ideas are gradually brought into conformity with the facts by the painful process of selection,—for intuition runs equally into truth and into error, and can settle nothing if not controlled by experience,—we gain vastly in our command over our environment. This is the fundamental value of natural science, and the fruit it is yielding in our day. We have no better vision of nature and life than some of our predecessors, but we have greater material resources. To know the truth about the composition and history of things is good for this reason. It is also good because of the enlarged horizon it gives us, because the spectacle of nature is a marvellous and fascinating one, full of a serious sadness and large peace, which gives us back our birthright as children of the planet and naturalizes us upon the earth. This is the poetic value of the scientific *Weltanschauung*.[1] From these two benefits, the practical and the imaginative, all the value of truth is derived.

---

[1] [World view.]

Aesthetic and moral judgments are accordingly to be classed together in contrast to judgments intellectual; they are both judgments of value, while intellectual judgments are judgments of fact. If the latter have any value, it is only derivative, and our whole intellectual life has its only justification in its connexion with our pleasures and pains.

The relation between aesthetic and moral judgments, between the spheres of the beautiful and the good, is close, but the distinction between them is important. One factor of this distinction is that while aesthetic judgments are mainly positive, that is, perceptions of good, moral judgments are mainly and fundamentally negative, or perceptions of evil. Another factor of the distinction is that whereas, in the perception of beauty, our judgment is necessarily intrinsic and based on the character of the immediate experience, and never consciously on the idea of an eventual utility in the object, judgments about moral worth, on the contrary, are always based, when they are positive, upon the consciousness of benefits probably involved. Both these distinctions need some elucidation.

Hedonistic ethics have always had to struggle against the moral sense of mankind. Earnest minds, that feel the weight and dignity of life, rebel against the assertion that the aim of right conduct is enjoyment. Pleasure usually appears to them as a temptation, and they sometimes go so far as to make avoidance of it a virtue. The truth is that morality is not mainly concerned with the attainment of pleasure; it is rather concerned, in all its deeper and more authoritative maxims, with the prevention of suffering. There is something artificial in the deliberate pursuit of pleasure; there is something absurd in the obligation to enjoy oneself. We feel no duty in that direction; we take to enjoyment naturally enough after the work of life is done, and the freedom and spontaneity of our pleasures is what is most essential to them.

The sad business of life is rather to escape certain dreadful evils to which our nature exposes us,—death, hunger, disease, weariness, isolation, and contempt. By the awful authority of these things, which stand like spectres behind every moral injunction, conscience in reality speaks, and a mind which they have duly impressed cannot but feel, by contrast, the hopeless triviality of the search for pleasure. It cannot but feel that a life abandoned to amusement and to changing impulses must run unawares into fatal dangers. The moment, however, that society emerges from the early pressure of the environment and is tolerably secure against primary evils, morality grows lax. The forms that life will farther assume are not to be imposed by moral authority, but are determined by the genius of the race, the opportunities of the moment, and the tastes and resources of individual minds. The reign of duty gives place to the reign of freedom, and the law and the covenant to the dispensation of grace.

The appreciation of beauty and its embodiment in the arts are activities which belong to our holiday life, when we are redeemed for the moment from the shadow of evil and the slavery to fear, and are following the bent of our nature where it chooses to lead us. The values, then, with which we here deal are positive; they were negative in the sphere of morality. The ugly is hardly an exception, because it is not the cause of any real pain. In itself it is rather a source of amusement. If its suggestions are vitally repulsive, its presence becomes a real evil towards which we assume a practical and moral attitude. And, correspondingly, the pleasant is never, as we have seen, the object of a truly moral injunction.

We have here, then, an important element of the distinction between aesthetic and moral values. It is the same that has been pointed to in the famous contrast between work and play. These terms may be used in different senses and their importance in moral classification differs with the meaning attached to them. We may call everything play which is useless activity, exercise that springs from the physiological impulse to discharge the energy which the exigencies of life have not called out. Work will then be all action that is necessary or useful for life. Evidently if work and play are thus objectively distinguished as useful and useless action, work is a eulogistic term and play a disparaging one. It would be better for us that all our energy should be turned to account, that none of it should be wasted in aimless motion. Play, in this sense, is a sign of imperfect adaptation. It is proper to childhood, when the body and mind are not yet fit to cope with the environment, but it is unseemly in manhood and pitiable in old age, because it marks an atrophy of human nature, and a failure to take hold of the opportunities of life.

Play is thus essentially frivolous. Some persons, understanding the term in this sense, have felt an aversion, which every liberal mind will share, to classing social pleasures, art, and religion under the head of play, and by that epithet condemning them, as a certain school seems to do, to gradual extinction as the race approaches maturity. But if all the useless ornaments of our life are to be cut off in the process of adaptation, evolution would impoverish instead of enriching our nature. Perhaps that is the tendency of evolution, and our barbarous ancestors amid their toils and wars, with their flaming passions and mythologists, lived better lives than are reserved to our well-adapted descendants.

We may be allowed to hope, however, that some imagination may survive parasitically even in the most serviceable brain. Whatever course history may take,—and we are not here concerned with prophecy,—the question of what is desirable is not affected. To condemn spontaneous and delightful occupations because they are useless for self-preservation shows an uncritical prizing of life irrespective of its content. For such a system the worthiest function of the universe should be to establish perpetual motion. Uselessness is a fatal accusation to bring against any act which is done for its presumed utility, but those which are done for their own sake are their own justification.

At the same time there is an undeniable propriety in calling all the liberal and imaginative activities of man play, because they are spontaneous, and not carried on under pressure of external necessity or danger. Their utility for self-preservation may be very indirect and accidental, but they are not worthless for that reason. On the contrary, we may measure the degree of happiness and civilization which any race has attained by the proportion of its energy which is devoted to free and generous pursuits, to the adornment of life and the culture of the imagination. For it is in the spontaneous play of his faculties that man finds himself and his happiness. Slavery is the most degrading condition of which he is capable, and he is as often a slave to the niggardness of the earth and the inclemency of heaven, as to a master or an institution. He is a slave when all his energy is spent in avoiding suffering and death, when all his action is imposed from without, and no breath or strength is left him for free enjoyment.

Work and play here take on a different meaning, and become equivalent to servitude and freedom. The change consists in the subjective point of view from which the distinction is now made. We no longer mean by work all that is done usefully, but only what is done unwillingly and by the spur of necessity. By play we are designating, no longer what is done fruitlessly, but whatever is done spontaneously and for its own sake, whether it have or not an ulterior utility. Play, in this sense, may be our most useful occupation. So far would a gradual adaptation to the environment be from making this play obsolete, that it would tend to abolish work, and to make play universal. For with the elimination of all the conflicts and errors of instinct, the race would do spontaneously whatever conduced to its welfare and we should live safely and prosperously without external stimulus or restraint.

In this second and subjective sense, then, work is the disparaging term and play the eulogistic one. All who feel the dignity and importance of the things of the imagination, need not hesitate to adopt the classification which designates them as play. We point out thereby, not that they have no value, but that their value is intrinsic, that in them is one of the sources of all worth. Evidently all values must be ultimately intrinsic. The useful is good because of the excellence of its consequences; but these must somewhere cease to be merely useful in their turn, or only excellent as means; somewhere we must reach the good that is good in itself and for its own sake, else the whole process is futile, and the utility of our first object illusory. We here reach the second factor in our distinction, between aesthetic and moral values, which regards their immediacy.

If we attempt to remove from life all its evils, as the popular imagination has done at times, we shall find little but aesthetic pleasures remaining to constitute unalloyed happiness. The satisfaction of the passions and the appetites, in which we chiefly place earthly happiness, themselves take on an aesthetic tinge when we remove ideally the possibility of loss or variation. What could the Olympians honour in one another or the seraphim worship in God except the embodiment of eternal attributes, of essences which, like beauty, make us happy only in contemplation? The glory of heaven could not be otherwise symbolized than by light and music. Even the knowledge of truth, which the most sober theologians made the essence of the beatific vision, is an aesthetic delight; for when the truth has no further practical utility, it becomes a landscape. The delight of it is imaginative and the value of it aesthetic.

This reduction of all values to immediate appreciations, to sensuous or vital activities, is so inevitable that it has struck even the minds most courageously rationalistic. Only for them, instead of leading to the liberation of aesthetic goods from practical entanglements and their establishment as the only pure and positive values in life, this analysis has led rather to the denial of all pure and positive goods altogether. Such thinkers naturally assume that moral values are intrinsic and supreme; and since these moral values would not arise but for the existence or imminence of physical evils, they embrace the paradox that without evil no good whatever is conceivable.

The harsh requirements of apologetics have no doubt helped them to this position, from which one breath of spring or the sight of one well-begotten creature should be enough to dislodge them. Their ethical temper and the fetters of their imagination forbid them to reconsider their original assumption and to conceive that morality is a means and not an end; that it is the price of human non-adaptation, and the consequence of the original sin of unfitness. It is the compression of human conduct within the narrow limits of the safe and possible. Remove danger, remove pain, remove the occasion of pity, and the need of morality is gone. To say "thou shalt not" would then be an impertinence.

But this elimination of precept would not be a cessation of life. The senses would still be open, the instincts would still operate, and lead all creatures to the haunts and occupations that befitted them. The variety of nature and the infinity of art, with the companionship of our fellows, would fill the leisure of that ideal existence. These are the elements of our positive happiness, the things which, amid a thousand vexations and vanities, make the clear profit of living.

Not only are the various satisfactions which morals are meant to secure aesthetic in the last analysis, but when the conscience is formed, and right principles acquire an immediate authority, our attitude to these principles becomes aesthetic also. Honour, truthfulness, and cleanliness are obvious examples. When the absence of these virtues causes an instinctive disgust, as it does in well-bred people, the reaction is essentially aesthetic, because it is not based on reflection and benevolence, but on constitutional sensitiveness. This aesthetic sensitiveness is, however, properly enough called moral, because it is the effect of conscientious training and is more powerful for good in society than laborious virtue, because it is much more constant and catching. It is κολοκἀγαθία [1] the aesthetic demand for the morally good, and perhaps the finest flower of human nature.

But this tendency of representative principles to become independent powers and acquire intrinsic value is sometimes mischievous. It is the foundation of the conflicts between sentiment and justice, between intuitive and utilitarian morals. Every human reform is the reassertion of the primary interests of man against the authority of general principles which have ceased to represent those interests fairly, but which still obtain the idolatrous veneration of mankind. Nor are chivalry and religion alone liable to fall into this moral superstition. It arises wherever an abstract good is substituted for its concrete equivalent. The miser's fallacy is the typical case, and something very like it is the ethical principle of half our respectable population. To the exercise of certain useful habits men come to sacrifice the advantage which was the original basis and justification of those habits. Minute knowledge is pursued at the expense of largeness of mind, and riches at the expense of comfort and freedom.

This error is all the more specious when the derived aim has in itself some aesthetic charm, such as belongs to the Stoic idea of playing one's part in a vast drama of things, irrespective of any advantage thereby accruing to any one; somewhat as the miser's passion is rendered a little normal when his eye is fascinated not merely by the figures of a bank account, but by the glitter of the yellow gold. And the vanity of playing a tragic part and the glory of conscious self-sacrifice have the same immediate fascination. Many irrational maxims thus acquire a kind of nobility. An object

---

[1] [Nobleness, goodness (of character and conduct).]

is chosen as the highest good which has not only a certain representative value, but also an intrinsic one,—which is not merely a method for the realization of other values, but a value in its own realization.

Obedience to God is for the Christian, as conformity to the laws of nature or reason is for the Stoic, an attitude which has a certain emotional and passionate worth, apart from its original justification by maxims of utility. This emotional and passionate force is the essence of fanaticism, it makes imperatives categorical, and gives them absolute sway over the conscience in spite of their one-sidedness and their injustice to the manifold demands of human nature.

Obedience to God or reason can originally recommend itself to a man only as the surest and ultimately least painful way of balancing his aims and synthesizing his desires. So necessary is this sanction even to the most impetuous natures, that no martyr would go to the stake if he did not believe that the powers of nature, in the day of judgment, would be on his side. But the human mind is a turbulent commonwealth, and the laws that make for the greatest good cannot be established in it without some partial sacrifice, without the suppression of many particular impulses. Hence the voice of reason or the command of God, which makes for the maximum ultimate satisfaction, finds itself opposed by sundry scattered and refractory forces, which are henceforth denominated bad. The unreflective conscience, forgetting the vicarious source of its own excellence, then assumes a solemn and incomprehensible immediacy, as if its decrees were absolute and intrinsically authoritative, not of to-day or yesterday, and no one could tell whence they had arisen. Instinct can all the more easily produce this mystification when it calls forth an imaginative activity full of interest and eager passion. This effect is conspicuous in the absolutist conscience, both devotional and rationalistic, as also in the passion of love. For in all these a certain individuality, definiteness, and exclusiveness is given to the pursued object which is very favourable to zeal, and the heat of passion melts together the various processes of volition into the consciousness of one adorable influence.

However deceptive these complications may prove to men of action and eloquence, they ought not to impose on the critic of human nature. Evidently what value general goods do not derive from the particular satisfactions they stand for, they possess in themselves as ideas pleasing and powerful over the imagination. This intrinsic advantage of certain principles and methods is none the less real for being in a sense aesthetic. Only a sordid utilitarianism that subtracts the imagination from human nature, or at least slurs over its immense contribution to our happiness, could fail to give these principles the preference over others practically as good.

If it could be shown, for instance, that monarchy was as apt, in a given case, to secure the public well-being as some other form of government, monarchy should be preferred, and would undoubtedly be established, on account of its imaginative and dramatic superiority. But if, blinded by this somewhat ethereal advantage, a party sacrificed to it important public interests, the injustice would be manifest. In a doubtful case, a nation decides, not without painful conflicts, how much it will sacrifice to its sentimental needs. The important point is to remember that the representative or practical value of a principle is one thing, and its intrinsic or aesthetic value is another, and that the latter can be justly counted only as an item in its favour to be weighed against possible external disadvantages. Whenever this comparison and balancing of ultimate benefits of every kind is angrily dismissed in favour of some absolute principle, laid down in contempt of human misery and happiness, we have a personal and fantastic system of ethics, without practical sanctions. It is an evidence that the superstitious imagination has invaded the sober and practical domain of morals.

We have now separated with some care intellectual and moral judgments from the sphere of our subject, and found that we are to deal only with perceptions of value, and with these only when they are positive and immediate. But even with these distinctions the most remarkable characteristic of the sense of beauty remains undefined. All pleasures are intrinsic and positive values, but all pleasures are not perceptions of beauty. Pleasure is indeed the essence of that perception, but there is evidently in this particular pleasure a complication which is not present in others and which is the basis of the distinction made by consciousness and language between it and the rest. It will be instructive to notice the degrees of this difference.

The bodily pleasures are those least resembling perceptions of beauty. By bodily pleasures we mean, of course, more than pleasures with a bodily seat; for that class would include them all, as well as all forms and elements of consciousness. Aesthetic pleasures have physical conditions, they depend on the activity of the eye and the ear, of the memory and the other ideational functions of the brain. But we do not connect those pleasures with their seats except in physiological studies; the ideas with which aesthetic pleasures are associated are not the ideas of their bodily causes. The pleasures we call physical, and regard as low, on the contrary, are those which call our attention to some part of our own body, and which make no object so conspicuous to us as the organ in which they arise.

There is here, then, a very marked distinction between physical and aesthetic pleasure; the organs of the latter must be transparent, they must not intercept our attention, but carry it directly to some external object. The greater dignity and range of aesthetic pleasure is thus made very intelligible. The soul is glad, as it were, to forget its connexion with the body and to fancy that it can travel over the world with the liberty with which it changes the objects of its thought. The mind passes from China to Peru without any conscious change in the local tensions of the body. This illusion of disembodiment is very exhilarating, while immersion in the flesh and confinement to some organ gives a tone of grossness and selfishness to our consciousness. The generally meaner associations of physical pleasures also help to explain their comparative crudity.

The distinction between pleasure and the sense of beauty has sometimes been said to consist in the unselfishness of aesthetic satisfaction. In other pleasures, it is said, we gratify our senses and passions; in the contemplation of beauty we are raised above ourselves, the passions are silenced and we are happy in the recognition of a good that we do not seek to possess. The painter does not look at a spring of water with the eyes of a thirsty man, nor at a beautiful woman with those of a satyr. The difference lies, it is urged, in the impersonality of the enjoyment. But this distinction is one of intensity and delicacy, not of nature, and it seems satisfactory only to the least aesthetic minds.[1]

In the second place, the supposed disinterestedness of aesthetic delights is not truly fundamental. Appreciation of a picture is not identical with the desire to buy it, but it is, or ought to be, closely related and preliminary to that desire. The beauties of nature and the plastic arts are not consumed by being enjoyed; they retain all the efficacy to impress a second beholder. But this circumstance is accidental, and those aesthetic objects which depend upon change and are exhausted in time, as are all performances, are things the enjoyment of which is an object of rivalry and is coveted as much as any other pleasure. And even plastic beauties can often not be enjoyed except by a few, on account of the necessity of travel

---

[1] Schopenhauer, indeed, who makes much of it, was a good critic, but his psychology suffered much from the pessimistic generalities of his system. It concerned him to show that the will was bad, and, as he felt beauty to be a good if not a holy thing, he hastened to convince himself that it came from the suppression of the will. But even in his system this suppression is only relative. The desire of individual objects, indeed, is absent in the perception of beauty, but there is still present that initial love of the general type and principles of things which is the first illusion of the absolute, and drives it on to the fatal experiment of creation. So that, apart from Schopenhauer's mythology, we have even in him the recognition that beauty gives satisfaction to some dim and underlying demand of our nature, just as particular objects give more special and momentary pleasures to our individualized wills. His psychology was, however, far too vague and general to undertake an analysis of those mysterious feelings.

or other difficulties of access, and then this aesthetic enjoyment is as selfishly pursued as the rest.

The truth which the theory is trying to state seems rather to be that when we seek aesthetic pleasures we have no further pleasure in mind; that we do not mix up the satisfactions of vanity and proprietorship with the delight of contemplation. This is true, but it is true at bottom of all pursuits and enjoyments. Every real pleasure is in one sense disinterested. It is not sought with ulterior motives, and what fills the mind is no calculation, but the image of an object or event, suffused with emotion. A sophisticated consciousness may often take the idea of self as the touchstone of its inclinations; but this self, for the gratification and aggrandizement of which a man may live, is itself only a complex of aims and memories, which once had their direct objects, in which he had taken a spontaneous and unselfish interest. The gratifications which, merged together, make the selfishness are each of them ingenuous, and no more selfish than the most altruistic, impersonal emotion. The content of selfishness is a mass of unselfishness. There is no reference to the nominal essence called oneself either in one's appetites or in one's natural affections; yet a man absorbed in his meat and drink, in his houses and lands, in his children and dogs, is called selfish because these interests, although natural and instinctive in him, are not shared by others. The unselfish man is he whose nature has a more universal direction, whose interests are more widely diffused.

But as impersonal thoughts are such only in their object, not in their subject or agent, since all thoughts are the thoughts of somebody: so also unselfish interests have to be somebody's interests. If we were not interested in beauty, if it were of no concern to our happiness whether things were beautiful or ugly, we should manifest not the maximum, but the total absence of aesthetic faculty. The disinterestedness of this pleasure is, therefore, that of all primitive and intuitive satisfactions, which are in no way conditioned by a reference to an artificial general concept, like that of the self, all the potency of which must itself be derived from the independent energy of its component elements. I care about myself because "myself" is a name for the things I have at heart. To set up the verbal figment of personality and make it an object of concern apart from the interests which were its content and substance, turns the moralist into a pedant, and ethics into a superstition. The self which is the object of *amour propre* is an idol of the tribe, and needs to be disintegrated into the primitive objective interests that underlie it before the cultus of it can be justified by reason.

The supposed disinterestedness of our love of beauty passes into another characteristic of it often regarded as essential,—its universality. The pleasures of the senses have, it is said, no dogmatism in them; that anything gives me pleasure involves no assertion about its capacity to give pleasure to another. But when I judge a thing to be beautiful, my judgment means that the thing is beautiful in itself, or (what is the same thing more critically expressed) that it should seem so to everybody. The claim to universality is, according to this doctrine, the essence of the aesthetic; what makes the perception of beauty a judgment rather than a sensation. All aesthetic precepts would be impossible, and all criticism arbitrary and subjective, unless we admit a paradoxical universality in our judgment, the philosophical implications of which we may then go on to develop. But we are fortunately not required to enter the labyrinth into which this method leads; there is a much simpler and clearer way of studying such questions, which is to challenge and analyze the assertion before us and seek its basis in human nature. Before this is done, we should run the risk of expanding a natural misconception or inaccuracy of thought into an inveterate and pernicious prejudice by making it the centre of an elaborate construction.

That the claim of universality is such a natural inaccuracy will not be hard to show. There is notoriously no great agreement upon aesthetic matters; and such agreement as there is, is based upon similarity of origin, nature, and circumstance among men, a similarity which, where it exists, tends to bring about identity in all judgments and feelings. It is unmeaning to say that what is beautiful to one man *ought* to be beautiful to another. If their senses are the same, their associations and dispositions similar, then the same thing will certainly be beautiful to both. If their natures are different, the form which to one will be entrancing will be to another even invisible, because his classifications and discriminations in perception will be different, and he may see a hideous detached fragment or a shapeless aggregate of things, in what to another is a perfect whole—so entirely are the unities of objects unities of function and use. It is absurd to say that what is invisible to a given being *ought* to seem beautiful to him. Evidently this obligation of recognizing the same qualities is conditioned by the possession of the same faculties. But no two men have exactly the same faculties, nor can things have for any two exactly the same values.

What is loosely expressed by saying that any one ought to see this or that beauty is that he would see it if his disposition, training, or attention were what our ideal demands for him; and our ideal of what any one should be has complex but discoverable sources. We take, for instance, a certain pleasure in having our own judgments supported by those of others; we are intolerant, if not of the existence of a nature different from

our own, at least of its expression in words and judgments. We are confirmed or made happy in our doubtful opinions by seeing them accepted
universally. We are unable to find the basis of our taste in our own experience and therefore refuse to look for it there. If we were sure of our
ground, we should be willing to acquiesce in the naturally different feelings and ways of others, as a man who is conscious of speaking his language
with the accent of the capital confesses its arbitrariness with gayety, and
is pleased and interested in the variations of it he observes in provincials;
but the provincial is always zealous to show that he has reason and ancient
authority to justify his oddities. So people who have no sensations, and do
not know why they judge, are always trying to show that they judge by universal reasons.

Thus the frailty and superficiality of our own judgments cannot brook
contradiction. We abhor another man's doubt when we cannot tell him
why we ourselves believe. Our ideal of other men tends therefore to include the agreement of their judgments with our own; and although we
might acknowledge the fatuity of this demand in regard to natures very
different from the human, we may be unreasonable enough to require that
all races should admire the same style of architecture, and all ages the
same poets.

The great actual unity of human taste within the range of conventional history helps the pretension. But in principle it is untenable.
Nothing has less to do with the real merit of a work of imagination than
the capacity of all men to appreciate it; the true test is the degree and
kind of satisfaction it can give to him who appreciates it most. The symphony would lose nothing if half mankind had always been deaf, as nine-
tenths of them actually are to the intricacies of its harmonies; but it would
have lost much if no Beethoven had existed. And more: incapacity to
appreciate certain types of beauty may be the condition *sine qua non* [1]
for the appreciation of another kind; the greatest capacity both for enjoyment and creation is highly specialized and exclusive, and hence the
greatest ages of art have often been strangely intolerant.

The invectives of one school against another, perverse as they are
philosophically, are artistically often signs of health, because they indicate a vital appreciation of certain kinds of beauty, a love of them that has
grown into a jealous passion. The architects that have pieced out the imperfections of ancient buildings with their own thoughts, like Charles V
when he raised his massive palace beside the Alhambra, may be condemned from a certain point of view. They marred much by their inter-

---

[1] [Indispensable.]

ference; but they showed a splendid confidence in their own intuitions, a proud assertion of their own taste, which is the greatest evidence of aesthetic sincerity. On the contrary, our own gropings, eclecticism, and archaeology are the symptoms of impotence. If we were less learned and less just, we might be more efficient. If our appreciation were less general, it might be more real, and if we trained our imagination into exclusiveness, it might attain to character.

There is, however, something more in the claim to universality in aesthetic judgments than the desire to generalize our own opinions. There is the expression of a curious but well-known psychological phenomenon, viz., the transformation of an element of sensation into the quality of a thing. If we say that other men should see the beauties we see, it is because we think those beauties *are in the object,* like its colour, proportion, or size. Our judgment appears to us merely the perception and discovery of an external existence, of the real excellence that is without. But this notion is radically absurd and contradictory. Beauty, as we have seen, is a value; it cannot be conceived as an independent existence which affects our senses and which we consequently perceive. It exists in perception, and cannot exist otherwise. A beauty not perceived is a pleasure not felt, and a contradiction. But modern philosophy has taught us to say the same thing of every element of the perceived world; all are sensations; and their grouping into objects imagined to be permanent and external is the work of certain habits of our intelligence. We should be incapable of surveying or retaining the diffused experiences of life, unless we organized and classified them, and out of the chaos of impressions framed the world of conventional and recognizable objects.

How this is done is explained by the current theories of perception. External objects usually affect various senses at once, the impressions of which are thereby associated. Repeated experiences of one object are also associated on account of their similarity; hence a double tendency to merge and unify into a single percept, to which a name is attached, the group of those memories and reactions which in fact had one external thing for their cause. But this percept, once formed, is clearly different from those particular experiences out of which it grew. It is permanent, they are variable. They are but partial views and glimpses of it. The constituted notion therefore comes to be the reality, and the materials of it merely the appearance. The distinction between substance and quality, reality and appearance, matter and mind, has no other origin.

The objects thus conceived and distinguished from our ideas of them, are at first compacted of all the impressions, feelings, and memories, which offer themselves for association and fall within the vortex of the amal-

gamating imagination. Every sensation we get from a thing is originally
treated as one of its qualities. Experiment, however, and the practical need
of a simpler conception of the structure of objects lead us gradually to
reduce the qualities of the object to a minimum, and to regard most perceptions as an effect of those few qualities upon us. These few primary
qualities, like extension which we persist in treating as independently real
and as the quality of a substance, are those which suffice to explain the order of our experiences. All the rest, like colour, are relegated to the subjective sphere, as merely effects upon our minds, and apparent or secondary
qualities of the object.

But this distinction has only a practical justification. Convenience and
economy of thought alone determine what combination of our sensations
we shall continue to objectify and treat as the cause of the rest. The right
and tendency to be objective is equal in all, since they are all prior to the
artifice of thought by which we separate the concept from its materials, the
thing from our experiences.

The qualities which we now conceive to belong to real objects are
for the most part images of sight and touch. One of the first classes of
effects to be treated as secondary were naturally pleasures and pains, since
it could commonly conduce very little to intelligent and successful action
to conceive our pleasures and pains as resident in objects. But emotions
are essentially capable of objectification, as well as impressions of sense;
and one may well believe that a primitive and inexperienced consciousness would rather people the world with ghosts of its own terrors and passions than with projections of those luminous and mathematical concepts
which as yet it could hardly have formed.

This animistic and mythological habit of thought still holds its own
at the confines of knowledge, where mechanical explanations are not found.
In ourselves, where nearness makes observation difficult, in the intricate
chaos of animal and human life, we still appeal to the efficacy of will and
ideas, as also in the remote night of cosmic and religious problems. But
in all the intermediate realm of vulgar day, where mechanical science has
made progress, the inclusion of emotional or passionate elements in the
concept of the reality would be now an extravagance. Here our idea of
things is composed exclusively of perceptual elements, of the ideas of form
and of motion.

The beauty of objects, however, forms an exception to this rule.
Beauty is an emotional element, a pleasure of ours, which nevertheless we
regard as a quality of things. But we are now prepared to understand
the nature of this exception. It is the survival of a tendency originally universal to make every effect of a thing upon us a constituent of its conceived

nature. The scientific idea of a thing is a great abstraction from the mass of perceptions and reactions which that thing produces; the aesthetic idea is less abstract, since it retains the emotional reaction, the pleasure of the perception, as an integral part of the conceived thing.

Nor is it hard to find the ground of this survival in the sense of beauty of an objectification of feeling elsewhere extinct. Most of the pleasures which objects cause are easily distinguished and separated from the perception of the object: the object has to be applied to a particular organ, like the palate, or swallowed like wine, or used and operated upon in some way before the pleasure arises. The cohesion is therefore slight between the pleasure and the other associated elements of sense; the pleasure is separated in time from the perception, or it is localized in a different organ, and consequently is at once recognized as an effect and not as a quality of the object. But when the process of perception itself is pleasant, as it may easily be, when the intellectual operation, by which the elements of sense are associated and projected, and the concept of the form and substance of the thing produced, is naturally delightful, then we have a pleasure intimately bound up in the thing, inseparable from its character and constitution, the seat of which in us is the same as the seat of the perception. We naturally fail, under these circumstances, to separate the pleasure from the other objectified feelings. It becomes, like them, a quality of the object, which we distinguish from pleasures not so incorporated in the perception of things, by giving it the name of beauty.

We have now reached our definition of beauty, which, in the terms of our successive analysis and narrowing of the conception, is value positive, intrinsic, and objectified. Or, in less technical language, Beauty is pleasure regarded as the quality of a thing.

This definition is intended to sum up a variety of distinctions and identifications which should perhaps be here more explicitly set down. Beauty is a value, that is, it is not a perception of a matter of fact or of a relation: it is an emotion, an affection of our volitional and appreciative nature. An object cannot be beautiful if it can give pleasure to nobody: a beauty to which all men were forever indifferent is a contradiction in terms.

In the second place, this value is positive, it is the sense of the presence of something good, or (in the case of ugliness) of its absence. It is never the perception of a positive evil, it is never a negative value. That we are endowed with the sense of beauty is a pure gain which brings no evil with it. When the ugly ceases to be amusing or merely uninteresting and becomes disgusting, it becomes indeed a positive evil: but a moral and practical, not an aesthetic one. In aesthetics that saying is true—often

so disingenuous in ethics—that evil is nothing but the absence of good: for
even the tedium and vulgarity of an existence without beauty is not itself
ugly so much as lamentable and degrading. The absence of aesthetic goods
is a moral evil: the aesthetic evil is merely relative, and means less of
aesthetic good than was expected at the place and time. No form in itself
gives pain, although some forms give pain by causing a shock of surprise
even when they are really beautiful; as if a mother found a fine bull pup
in her child's cradle, when her pain would not be aesthetic in its nature.

Further, this pleasure must not be in the consequence of the utility
of the object or event, but in its immediate perception; in other words,
beauty is an ultimate good, something that gives satisfaction to a natural
function, to some fundamental need or capacity of our minds. Beauty is
therefore a positive value that is intrinsic; it is a pleasure. These two circumstances sufficiently separate the sphere of aesthetics from that of ethics.
Moral values are generally negative, and always remote. Morality has to
do with the avoidance of evil and the pursuit of good: aesthetics only with
enjoyment.

Finally, the pleasures of sense are distinguished from the perception of
beauty, as sensation in general is distinguished from perception; by the
objectification of the elements and their appearance as qualities rather of
things than of consciousness. The passage from sensation to perception is
gradual, and the path may be sometimes retraced: so it is with beauty and
the pleasures of sensation. There is no sharp line between them, but it
depends upon the degree of objectivity my feeling has attained at the moment whether I say "It pleases me," or "It is beautiful." If I am self-
conscious and critical, I shall probably use one phrase; if I am impulsive
and susceptible, the other. The more remote, interwoven, and inextricable
the pleasure is, the more objective it will appear; and the union of two
pleasures often makes one beauty. In Shakespeare's LIVth sonnet are
these words:

> O how much more doth beauty beauteous seem
> By that sweet ornament which truth doth give!
> The rose looks fair, but fairer we it deem
> For that sweet odour which doth in it live.
> The canker-blooms have full as deep a dye
> As the perfumèd tincture of the roses,
> Hang on such thorns, and play as wantonly
> When summer's breath their maskèd buds discloses.
> But, for their beauty only is their show,
> They live unwooed and unrespected fade;
> Die to themselves. Sweet roses do not so:
> Of their sweet deaths are sweetest odours made.

One added ornament, we see, turns the deep dye, which was but show and mere sensation before, into an element of beauty and reality; and as truth is here the co-operation of perceptions, so beauty is the co-operation of pleasures. If colour, form, and motion are hardly beautiful without the sweetness of the odour, how much more necessary would they be for the sweetness itself to become a beauty! If we had the perfume in a flask, no one would think of calling it beautiful: it would give us too detached and controllable a sensation. There would be no object in which it could be easily incorporated. But let it float from the garden, and it will add another sensuous charm to objects simultaneously recognized, and help to make them beautiful. Thus beauty is constituted by the objectification of pleasure. It is pleasure objectified.

STANDARDS IN CRITICISM

IRVING BABBITT

We are told that Louis XIV once submitted a sonnet he had written to the judgment of Boileau, who said, after reading it: "Sire, nothing is impossible for your Majesty. You set out to write some bad verses, and you have succeeded." The point of this story, for the modern reader, lies not so much in the courage of the critic as in the meekness of the king. With the progress of democracy one man's opinion in literature has come to be as good as another's—a deal better, too, the Irishman would add—and such words as deference and humility are in a fair way to become obsolete. We can scarcely conceive to what an extent men once allowed their personal impressions to be overawed and held in check by a body of outer prescriptions. Only a century ago an Edinburgh reviewer could write: "Poetry has thus much at least in common with religion, that its standards were fixed long ago by certain inspired writers whose authority it is no longer lawful to question." Racine tells us that the audience was afraid, at the first performance of his comedy *Les Plaideurs,* that "it had not laughed according to the rules."

The revolt came at last from this tyranny of the "rules," and the

---

The selection "Standards in Criticism" from *Masters of Modern French Criticism,* by Irving Babbitt, is reprinted by permission of and arrangement with Houghton Mifflin Company, the authorized publishers.

romantic critics opposed to the neoclassic narrowness their plea for wider knowledge and wider sympathy; they would see before they began to oversee, and be historical rather than dogmatic; they would neither exclude nor conclude, but explain; above all, they would be appreciative, and substitute the fruitful criticism of beauties for the barren criticism of faults. The weakness of the whole school has been its proneness to forget that knowledge and sympathy are after all only the feminine virtues of the critic. Hence the absence of the masculine note in so much modern criticism; hence the tendency of judgment to be swallowed up completely in sympathy and comprehension—*tout comprendre, c'est tout pardonner.*[1] Renan, one of the most perfect embodiments of the ideal of wider knowledge and wider sympathy, says that when anyone was presented to him he tried to enter into this person's point of view and serve up to him his own ideas in advance. One thinks almost involuntarily of Dr. Johnson and how, when people disagreed with him, he "roared them down"; how men like Reynolds and Gibbon and Burke ventured to present their protest to him only in the form of a round robin, so that the awful Aristarch might not know on whom first to visit his wrath. It is of course well, and indeed indispensable, that the critic should cultivate the feminine virtues, but on condition, as Tennyson has put it, that he be man-woman and not woman-man. Through neglect of this truth criticism has tended in its development during the past century to become first a form of history, and then a form of biography, and finally a form of gossip. History and biography remind us in their gradual encroachments upon critical judgment of those mayors of the palace in Merovingian times who insinuated themselves under cover of the services they rendered and at last thrust themselves into their masters' place. It is true that judgment would not have been thus dispossessed if it had not first shown itself a *roi fainé-ant.*[2]

Sainte-Beuve himself, as we saw, labored during the latter part of his life to correct, or one might more fairly say to complete, his earlier method and to assert once more the supremacy of judgment. It is curious to trace the transformation of the militant romanticist of 1830 into the conservative who finally extols as the true type of the critic Malherbe and Boileau and Dr. Johnson. He follows these men in founding his own judgments for the most part on the traditional standards of the classicist; yet no one knew

---

[1] [To understand everything is to pardon everything.]

[2] [Idle king.] The *roi fainéants* were the tail end of the Merovingian dynasty, first kings of France, so named because they delegated all responsibility to regional subordinates.

better than Sainte-Beuve that these standards were doomed. "Let us be the last of our kind," he exclaims, "before the great confusion."

The "great confusion" that Sainte-Beuve foresaw is now upon us. I pointed out that he himself has been correctly defined in his influence on his successors, not as a defender of standards and judgment, but as a great doctor of relativity. Now nearly all recent criticism, so far as it is anything more than a form of gossip and small talk, may be roughly classified as either impressionistic or scientific; and it is in this doctrine of relativity that both impressionistic and scientific critics unite. The impressionist is interested in a book only as it relates itself to his sensibility, and his manner of praising anything that makes this appeal to him is to say that it is "suggestive." The scientific critic for his part is interested solely in the way a book is related as a phenomenon to other phenomena, and when it is the culminating point or the point of departure of a large number of these relationships, he says that it is "significant" (the favorite word of Goethe). If the impressionist is asked to rise above his sensibility and judge by a more impersonal standard, he answers that there is no such impersonal element in art, but only "suggestiveness," and is almost ready to define art with a recent French writer as an "attenuated hypnosis." If the scientific critic in turn is urged to get behind the phenomena and rate a book with reference to a scale of absolute values, he absconds into his theory of the "unknowable."

We may illustrate by a familiar passage from Taine, who is easily the most eminent of those who have attempted to make criticism scientific. "What do we see," he says in his *English Literature,* "under the fair glazed pages of a modern poem? A modern poet who has studied and traveled, a man like Alfred de Musset, Victor Hugo, Lamartine, or Heine, in a black coat and gloves, welcomed by the ladies, and making every evening his fifty bows and his score of *bons mots* in society; reading the papers in the morning, lodging as a rule on a second floor; not overgay, because he has nerves, and especially because, in this dense democracy where we stifle one another, the discredit of official dignities has exaggerated his pretensions, while increasing his importance, and because the keenness of his feelings in general rather disposes him to think himself a god."

Now in the first place the results of this attempt to infer from a poem the life and personality of the poet are strangely uncertain. We read in the recently published letters of John Richard Green that when Taine was in England getting information for the last volume of his *English Literature,* he began talking about Tennyson with Palgrave, a great friend of the laureate.

"Wasn't he in early youth rich, luxurious, fond of pleasure, self-indulgent?" Taine asked. "I see it all in his early poems—his riot, his adoration of physical beauty, his delight in jewels, in the abandonment of all to pleasure, in wine, and . . ."

"Stop! stop!" said Palgrave, out of all patience. "As a young man Tennyson was poor—he had little more than one hundred pounds a year, his habits were, as they still are, simple and reserved, he cared then as he cares now for little more than a chat and a pipe; he has never known luxury in your sense."

Taine thanked Palgrave for his information—and when the book came out Tennyson was found still painted as the young voluptuary of the critic's fancy.

Even assuming that Taine's inferences could be drawn correctly, he would have us fix our attention on precisely those features of a poem that are least poetical. The very prosaic facts he is looking for would be at least as visible in the writing of some mediocrity as in a work of the first order. It is, indeed, when Taine starts out to deal in this fashion with a poet of genius like Milton, to reduce *Paradise Lost* to a mere "sign," that the whole method is seen to be grotesquely inadequate. "Adam," says Taine in his critique of Milton, "is your true paterfamilias with a vote, an M.P., an old Oxford man," etc. He listens to the conversation of Adam and Eve, the first pair, only to hear "an English household, two reasoners of the period—Colonel Hutchinson and his wife. Good heavens! dress them at once"; and he continues in this vein for pages.

But, says M. Bourget, speaking for the impressionists, there is another way of approaching the volume of verse that Taine would treat solely from the point of view of its "significance"; and in rendering the "suggestiveness" of the volume to the impressionist sensibility, M. Bourget proceeds to employ a luxuriance of epithet that lack of space forbids our quoting. He asks us to imagine a young woman alone in her boudoir on an overcast winter afternoon. A vague melancholy steals upon her as she reclines at ease in her long chair; all aquiver with ineffable longing, she turns to her favorite poet. She does not surmise behind the delicately tinted pages of the beloved book the prosaic facts of environment, the obscure animal origins of talent that are so visible to Taine. What she does perceive is the dream of the poet—"the inexpressible and mysterious beyond that he has succeeded in throwing like a halo round his verses." For Taine the stanzas are a result; for the young woman "who intoxicates her heart with them so deliciously," they are a cause. "She does not care for the alembic in which the magic philter has been distilled, provided only this magic is operative, provided her reading culminates in an exquisite and trembling exaltation" and "suggests to her dreams either sweet or sad, but always productive of ecstasy." Who does not see, concludes M. Bourget, that entirely different theories of art are applied in the two ways of approaching the volume of verse?

The two theories are different, indeed; yet they are alike in this, that neither the "significance" of the volume to Taine nor its "suggestiveness" to M. Bourget affords any real means of escape from the quicksands of relativity to some firm ground of judgment. We may be sure that a third-rate bit of contemporary sentimentality will "suggest" more ineffable dreams to the young woman in the long chair than a play of Sophocles. To state the case more generally, how many books there are that were once infinitely suggestive and are still of the highest significance in literary history which yet intrinsically are now seen to be of very inferior value! This is eminently true of certain writings of Rousseau, to whom much of the peculiar exaggeration of the *sense propre* or individual sense that one finds in the impressionists can ultimately be traced. If the special modes of sensibility that impressionism exhibits go back to Rousseau, its philosophical theory may best be considered as a reappearance in modern thought of the ancient maxim that man is the measure of all things. This celebrated dictum became current at a decisive moment in Greek life and would indeed seem to sum up almost necessarily the point of view of any age that has cast off traditional standards. The all-important question is whether one interprets the maxim in the spirit of the sophists or in that of Socrates. The resemblance between the impressionistic and the sophistical understanding of the maxim is unmistakable; not only the individual man, but his present sensations and impressions are to be made the measure of all things. "All of us," says M. Anatole France, "judge everything by our own measure. How could we do otherwise, since to judge is to compare, and we have only one measure, which is ourselves; and this measure is constantly changing? We are all of us the sport and playthings of mobile appearances." Perhaps no recent writer has shown more of the Socratic spirit in his use of the maxim than Emerson. "A true man," he says, "belongs to no other time and place, but is the center of things. Where he is, there is nature. He measures you and all men and all events." Though Emerson thus asserts the maxim, he has not therefore succumbed, like M. France, to the doctrine of relativity and the feeling of universal illusion that accompanies it; on the contrary, he has attained to a new sense of the unity of human nature—a unity founded not on tradition but on insight. He says somewhere that he finds such an identity both of thought and sentiment in the best books of the world, that they seem to him to be the work of "one all-seeing, all-hearing gentleman." Now it is evidently this one all-seeing, all-hearing gentleman who is for Emerson the measure of all things. The individual man is the measure of all things only in so far as he has realized in himself this essential human nature. To be sure, the line is often hard to draw in practice between the two types of individualist. There were persons in ancient Athens—for example, Aristophanes in *The Clouds*—who treated Socrates as an ordinary sophist. In the same way, there are persons today who fail to see the difference between Emerson and an ordinary impressionist. "The source of Emerson's power," says Professor Santayana, "lay not in his doctrine but in his temperament."

Emerson's language is often indistinguishable from that of the impressionist. "I would write on the lintels of my doorpost, *whim*." "Dream delivers us to dream, and there is no end to illusion." "Life is a flux of moods." But he is careful to add that "there is that in us which changes not and which ranks all sensations and states of mind." The impressionist denies this element of absolute judgment and so feels free to indulge his temperament with epicurean indolence; at the same time he has the contemptuous indulgence for others that befits beings who are the "sport and playthings of mobile appearances." M. France says that he "despises men tenderly." We would reply in the words of Burke that the "species of benevolence which arises from contempt is no true charity." Impressionism has led to a strange increase in the number of dilettantes and *jouisseurs littéraires*,[1] who to the precept *de gustibus non*[2] have given developments that would certainly have surprised its author. The Horatian plea for an honest liberty of taste has its necessary corrective in the truth that is very bluntly stated in a Spanish proverb: "There are tastes that deserve the cudgel." We are told that Sainte-Beuve was once so offended by an outrageous offense to good taste in a remark of Nicolardot's that, yielding to an irresistible impulse, he kicked him out of the room. Dante, in replying to a certain opponent, says with the instinct of a true Italian, that he would like to answer such "bestiality not with words but with a knife." We must remember that "good taste" as formerly understood was made up of two distinct elements: first, one's individual sensibility, and secondly, a code of outer rules by which this sensibility was disciplined and held in check. The observance of these rules became for the community of well-bred people a sort of *noblesse oblige*,[3] and taste in this sense has been rightly defined by Rivarol as a man's literary honor. Now that the outer code has been abrogated, taste is not therefore delivered over to the caprices of a vagrant sensibility; taste is attained only when this sensibility is rectified

---

[1] [Literary voluptuaries.]

[2] [Concerning taste (there is) no (*disputandum est*) disputing.]

[3] [Rank imposes obligations.]

with reference to standards inwardly apprehended, and in this sense may be defined as a man's literary conscience; it is, in short, only one aspect of the struggle between our lower and higher selves. Some, indeed, would maintain that taste is not a thing thus to be won by an effort of the will, but is rather an inborn and incommunicable tact, a sort of mysterious election, a free gift of the muses to a predestined few; that in literature many are called and few are chosen. In the article "Goût" [1] of the *Philosophical Dictionary,* Voltaire discourses on the small number of the elect in matters of taste, and in almost the next article ("Grâce") [2] turns all his powers of mockery on those who assert the same doctrine in religion. Not only individuals but whole nations were once held to be under the reprobation of the muses. As Voltaire says sadly, *presque tout l'univers est barbare.*[3] Perhaps even today persons might be found who would regard as legitimate the famous query of Father Bouhours whether a German can have wit. There are only too many examples in Germany and elsewhere of how far infinite industry and good intentions are from sufficing for the attainment of taste. However it may be in theology, it remains true in literature, as Gautier remarks, that works without grace are of no avail.

But one may recognize an element of predestination in the problem of taste and not therefore acquiesce in the impressionist's preaching of the fatality and finality of temperament. Everyone, to be sure, has an initial or temperamental taste, but it is hard to say how far this taste may be transformed by subordinating it to the higher claims of our nature. Dr. Johnson says that if he had no duties and no reference to futurity he should spend his life in driving briskly in a post chaise with a pretty woman. Here then is the temperamental taste of Dr. Johnson, and if he had been a disciple of M. France, he might have accepted it as final. Boswell reports an outburst of Johnson on this very subject: "Do not, sir, accustom yourself to trust to *impressions.* By trusting to impressions, a man may gradually come to yield to them, and at length be subject to them, so as not to be a free agent, or what is the same thing in effect, to *suppose* that he is not a free agent. A man who is in that state should not be suffered to live; . . . there can be no confidence in him, no more than in a tiger."

Johnson would evidently have agreed with the Buddhists in looking on the indolent settling down of a man in his own temperament as the chief of all the deadly sins. A fulmination like the foregoing is good to clear the air after the debilitating sophistries of M. France. Yet we feel that Johnson's point of view implies an undue denial of the individual's right to

---

[1] [Taste.]
[2] [Virtue, goodness, beauty.]
[3] [Almost the entire universe is savage.]

his own impressions and that therefore it has become in some measure obsolete. It is well for us, after all, to have fresh and vivid and personal impressions; it is well for us, in short, to awaken our senses; but we should "awaken our senses that we may the better judge"—and not simply that we may the better enjoy. For instance, Walter Pater continually dwells on the need of awakening our senses, but when he speaks of "living in the full stream of refined sensation," when he urges us to gather ourselves together "into one desperate effort to see and touch," there is a hedonistic flavor in these utterances that can escape no one. On the other hand, there should be no ascetic denial of the value of the impression in itself. Brunetière is reported to have said to another critic, whom he suspected of intellectual epicureanism: *"You* always praise what pleases you; *I* never do." This is an asceticism of taste worthy of the spectator of Racine's comedy who wished to laugh according to the rules. And so Brunetière was led naturally into his reactionary attitude; seeing only the evil possibilities of individualism, he would have the modern man forego his claim to be the measure of all things and submit once more to outer authority. A certain type of seventeenth-century critic attempted to establish a standard that was entirely outside the individual. The impressionist has gone to the opposite extreme and set up a standard that is entirely within the individual. The problem is to find some middle ground between Procrustes and Proteus; and this right mean would seem to lie in a standard that is in the individual and yet is felt by him to transcend his personal self and lay hold of that part of his nature that he possesses in common with other men.

The impressionist not only refuses the individual man any such principle of judgment to which he may appeal from his fleeting impressions; he goes further and refuses men collectively any avenue of escape from universal illusion and relativity; he denies, in short, the doctrine embodied in the old church maxim, *"Securus judicat orbis terrarum,"* [1] a doctrine so fundamental, we may note in passing, that in the form attributed to Lincoln it has become the cornerstone of democracy: "You cannot fool all the people all the time." M. Anatole France is fond of insisting, like Sainte-Beuve before him, that there inheres in mankind as a whole no such power of righting itself and triumphing over its own errors and illusions. A whole chapter might be made up of passages from Sainte-Beuve on the vanity of fame. "Posterity has allowed three fourths of the works of antiquity to perish," says M. France in turn; "it has allowed the rest to be frightfully corrupted . . . In the little that it has kept there

---

[1] [Untroubled, he judges the world.]

are detestable books which are none the less immortal. Varius, we are told, was the equal of Virgil. He has perished. Aelian was an ass, and he survives. There is posterity for you," etc. Here again the contrast between the two types of individualist is absolute. "There is no luck in literary reputation," says Emerson. "They who make up the final verdict for every book are not the partial and noisy public of the hour, but a court as of angels; a public not to be bribed, not to be entreated, and not to be overawed decides upon every man's title to fame. Only those books come down which deserve to last. Blackmore, Kotzebue, or Pollock may endure for a night, but Moses and Homer stand forever. The permanence of all books is fixed by no effort friendly or hostile, but by their own specific gravity or the intrinsic importance of their contents to the constant mind of man."

We should add, then, in order to define our critical standard completely, that the judgment of the keen-sighted few in the present needs to be ratified by the verdict of posterity.

II

Modern

Critical Theory

Introduction

MANY approximate dates have been suggested as the beginning of "modern" literary criticism. Some say it began when J. Middleton Murry introduced the ideas and attitudes of Remy de Gourmont to the English in his *The Problem of Style* (1922). Others consider it to have originated with I. A. Richards' *The Principles of Literary Criticism* (1924). In America, the publication of Cleanth Brooks's *Modern Poetry and the Tradition* (1939) appears to have marked the moment when the critical ideas implicit in the earlier writings of T. S. Eliot, Ezra Pound, John Crowe Ransom, Yvor Winters, and Allen Tate were applied more or less systematically to the whole body of modern American and British poetry. Moreover, Mr. Brooks's volume seemed related in attitude and method to a book published in England nine years earlier by a former student of I. A. Richards—William Empson's *Seven Types of Ambiguity* (1930).

But the publication of books serves merely to sum up tendencies and to supply convenient dates. The fermentation which produced such volumes began during and after the first World War. The earliest writings of Ezra Pound and T. E. Hulme were a rebellion against certain prevailing ideas, identified generally as post-Victorianism in England and the Genteel Tradition in America, and they were based, in part at least, upon the more cautious and respectable-seeming reaction against nineteenth century romanticism of such writers as Matthew Arnold in England and Irving Babbitt in America. However, modern criticism did not become a recognizable influence until as late as the mid-thirties, until the time when it seemed, in America at least, to have inherited the appeal Babbitt and his followers had had for young scholars on university campuses, when it led the reaction against the excesses of Marxist critics of the late twenties and thirties, and when it pressed its objections against the dull, busy-work of so much traditional academic scholarship.

Before Irving Babbitt's death in 1933, his interests had broadened until they had become almost as extra-literary as the interests of the conventional scholars whom he attacked. He had attracted such talented students and scholars as Paul Elmer More, Stuart P. Sherman, G. R. Elliott,

Norman Foerster, T. S. Eliot, and Austin Warren. But, theoretically at least, Babbitt's reaction against the temper of his own age was unyielding. The younger critics (most of whom were themselves poets) found it necessary to work within the framework of their own times and in terms of certain very practical problems related to their own work. It is not difficult to see at this date how amazingly influential such writers as Ford Madox Ford, Ezra Pound, and T. S. Eliot were upon their contemporaries, Pound in particular, who, as Ernest Hemingway has said recently, "spawned a whole generation of poets."

Yet for many years their writings were known only by a small group of readers of such periodicals as *The Dial, The Seven Arts,* and *Hound & Horn.* With the founding of *The Southern Review* at Louisiana State University (1935), and with the publication of *Modern Poetry and the Tradition,* these critics began to make their influence felt upon university campuses. Through the pages of *The Southern Review,* and even in the more traditional scholarly journals, they attacked the conventional attitudes of literary scholarship. With the publication of a volume titled *Understanding Poetry* (1938), the two editors of *The Southern Review,* Cleanth Brooks and Robert Penn Warren, effected what has been called, perhaps with mild overstatement, "a revolution in the teaching of poetry in American universities."

During this period, a similar influence was being exerted in England by the Cambridge scholar, F. R. Leavis. As teacher, author, and editor of a critical review, *Scrutiny* (established 1932), he occupied a strategic position, and in one book alone (*Revaluation,* 1936), he has been said to present what ". . . amounts to a new view of English poetic tradition." Yet the germ of this view existed in the early criticism and poetry of Ezra Pound and T. S. Eliot or in the early attempts of I. A. Richards to construct critical principles for the evaluation of literature. Such a reservation does not detract from the achievement of Mr. Leavis. He has carried the characteristic methods of modern criticism (close analysis and revaluation) further, perhaps, than any modern critic. As a practicing critic and as an editor he has had much the same influence in England as Brooks and Warren have had in America.

Yet both the application of a name and the seeming coherence of ideas and influence as suggested above are somewhat misleading. Those critics most commonly identified as the "new critics," such authors as T. S. Eliot, Herbert Read, Allen Tate, Cleanth Brooks, John Crowe Ransom, William Empson, and Robert Penn Warren, insist that they are not presenting a *new* view of literature, but are regaining an *old* view, lost or obscured by the temper of our age and the demands of an outworn, pseudo-scientific scholarship. Those with the most right to be called "new" stem from the early attempts of I. A. Richards to establish a basis for the appreciation of literature in the admittedly *new* science of psychology. Yet even here there is no clear-cut basis for deciding who belongs. Certainly Maud Bodkin does, as do William Empson and Kenneth Burke; perhaps Edmund Wilson, less certainly Lionel Trilling and Mark Schorer. Yet most of us would not call these the "new critics." What basis then do we have for assuming a coherence or unity in modern criticism? How can we best express the agreement within disagreement which exists in contemporary criticism? Perhaps we should resort to a figure of speech and say merely that it is best to view modern criticism as a house with many rooms, its occupants living in an uneasy but on the whole respectful relationship to each other, that it is impossible and misleading to see it as a fixed belief or an organized crusade.

The manner in which the essays in this section are arranged is designed to illustrate both the amount of agreement concerning the nature of the problems with which modern criticism is engaged and the amount of disagreement concerning the means by which those problems may best be solved. These articles should also illustrate the search for standards (or criteria) by which special aspects of the general problems may be dealt with. The controversial nature of much of this writing should not be stressed except in the interests of scholarly inquiry into the various methods of modern criticism. How does one best get at values represented in a literary work? Allen Tate has said, wisely, that he admires any critic whose method allows the reader "to engage" the work—which leads him into literature, not away from it. Emphasis in this section, however, is not upon those writings which do illustrate "engagement" so much as it is upon those which attempt to set up attitudes and standards by which engagement may be accomplished, by which a work of art, finally, may be best understood and appreciated.

1. Function

ROMANTICISM AND CLASSICISM

T. E. HULME

I want to maintain that after a hundred years of romanticism, we are in for a classical revival, and that
the particular weapon of this new classical spirit, when
it works in verse, will be fancy. And in this I imply the superiority of fancy
—not superior generally or absolutely, for that would be obvious nonsense, but superior in the sense that we use the word good in empirical
ethics—good for something, superior for something. I shall have to prove
then two things, first that a classical revival is coming, and secondly, for
its particular purposes, fancy will be superior to imagination.

So banal have the terms Imagination and Fancy become that we
imagine they must have always been in the language. Their history as two
different terms in the vocabulary of criticism is comparatively short. Originally, of course, they both meant the same thing; they first began to be
differentiated by the German writers on aesthetics in the eighteenth century.

I know that in using the words "classic and romantic" I am doing a
dangerous thing. They represent five or six different kinds of antitheses,
and while I may be using them in one sense you may be interpreting them
in another. In this present connection I am using them in a perfectly precise
and limited sense. I ought really to have coined a couple of new words, but
I prefer to use the ones I have used, as I then conform to the practice of the
group of polemical writers who make most use of them at the present day,
and have almost succeeded in making them political catchwords. I mean
Maurras, Lasserre and all the group connected with *L'Action Française*.

At the present time this is the particular group with which the distinction is most vital. Because it has become a party symbol. If you asked a
man of a certain set whether he preferred the classics or the romantics, you
could deduce from that what his politics were.

"Romanticism and Classicism" by T. E. Hulme, from *Speculations,* ed. by H.
Read. Reprinted by permission of Routledge & Kegan Paul, Ltd.

The best way of gliding into a proper definition of my terms would be to start with a set of people who are prepared to fight about it—for in them you will have no vagueness. (Other people take the infamous attitude of the person with catholic tastes who says he likes both.)

About a year ago, a man whose name I think was Fauchois gave a lecture at the Odéon on Racine, in the course of which he made some disparaging remarks about his dullness, lack of invention and the rest of it. This caused an immediate riot: fights took place all over the house; several people were arrested and imprisoned, and the rest of the series of lectures took place with hundreds of gendarmes and detectives scattered all over the place. These people interrupted because the classical ideal is a living thing to them and Racine is the great classic. That is what I call a real vital interest in literature. They regard romanticism as an awful disease from which France had just recovered.

The thing is complicated in their case by the fact that it was romanticism that made the revolution. They hate the revolution, so they hate romanticism.

I make no apology for dragging in politics here; romanticism both in England and France is associated with certain political views, and it is in taking a concrete example of the working out of a principle in action that you can get its best definition.

What was the positive principle behind all the other principles of '89? I am talking here of the revolution in as far as it was an idea; I leave out material causes—they only produce the forces. The barriers which could easily have resisted or guided these forces had been previously rotted away by ideas. This always seems to be the case in successful changes; the privileged class is beaten only when it has lost faith in itself, when it has itself been penetrated with the ideas which are working against it.

It was not the rights of man—that was a good solid practical war-cry. The thing which created enthusiasm, which made the revolution practically a new religion, was something more positive than that. People of all classes, people who stood to lose by it, were in a positive ferment about the idea of liberty. There must have been some idea which enabled them to think that something positive could come out of so essentially negative a thing. There was, and here I get my definition of romanticism. They had been taught by Rousseau that man was by nature good, that it was only bad laws and customs that had suppressed him. Remove all these and the infinite possibilities of man would have a chance. This is what made them think that something positive could come out of disorder, this is what created the religious enthusiasm. Here is the root of all romanticism: that man, the individual, is an infinite reservoir of possibilities; and if you can so rearrange society by the destruction of oppressive order then these possibilities will have a chance and you will get Progress.

One can define the classical quite clearly as the exact opposite to this. Man is an extraordinarily fixed and limited animal whose nature is absolutely constant. It is only by tradition and organisation that anything decent can be got out of him.

This view was a little shaken at the time of Darwin. You remember his particular hypothesis, that new species came into existence by the cumulative effect of small variations—this seems to admit the possibility of future progress. But at the present day the contrary hypothesis makes headway in the shape of De Vries's mutation theory, that each new species comes into existence, not gradually by the accumulation of small steps, but suddenly in a jump, a kind of sport, and that once in existence it remains absolutely fixed. This enables me to keep the classical view with an appearance of scientific backing.

Put shortly, these are the two views, then. One, that man is intrinsically good, spoilt by circumstance; and the other that he is intrinsically limited, but disciplined by order and tradition to something fairly decent. To the one party man's nature is like a well, to the other like a bucket. The view which regards man as a well, a reservoir full of possibilities, I call romantic; the one which regards him as a very finite and fixed creature, I call the classical.

One may note here that the Church has always taken the classical view since the defeat of the Pelagian heresy and the adoption of the sane classical dogma of original sin.

It would be a mistake to identify the classical view with that of materialism. On the contrary it is absolutely identical with the normal religious attitude. I should put it in this way: That part of the fixed nature of man is the belief in the Deity. This should be as fixed and true for every man as belief in the existence of matter and in the objective world. It is parallel to appetite, the instinct of sex, and all the other fixed qualities. Now at certain times, by the use of either force or rhetoric, these instincts have been suppressed—in Florence under Savonarola, in Geneva under Calvin, and here under the Roundheads. The inevitable result of such a process is that the repressed instinct bursts out in some abnormal direction. So with religion. By the perverted rhetoric of Rationalism, your natural instincts are suppressed and you are converted into an agnostic. Just as in the case of the other instincts, Nature has her revenge. The instincts that find right and proper outlet in religion must come out in some other way. You don't believe in a God, so you begin to believe that man is a god. You don't believe in Heaven, so you begin to believe in a heaven on earth.

In other words, you get romanticism. The concepts that are right and proper in their own sphere are spread over, and so mess up, falsify and blur the clear outlines of human experience. It is like pouring a pot of treacle over the dinner table. Romanticism then, and this is the best definition I can give of it, is spilt religion.

I must now shirk the difficulty of saying exactly what I mean by romantic and classical in verse. I can only say that it means the result of these two attitudes towards the cosmos, towards man, in so far as it gets reflected in verse. The romantic, because he thinks man infinite, must always be talking about the infinite; and as there is always the bitter contrast between what you think you ought to be able to do and what man actually can, it always tends, in its later stages at any rate, to be gloomy. I really can't go any further than to say it is the reflection of these two temperaments, and point out examples of the different spirits. On the one hand I would take such diverse people as Horace, most of the Elizabethans and the writers of the Augustan age, and on the other side Lamartine, Hugo, parts of Keats, Coleridge, Byron, Shelley and Swinburne.

I know quite well that when people think of classical and romantic in verse, the contrast at once comes into their mind between, say, Racine and Shakespeare. I don't mean this; the dividing line that I intend is here misplaced a little from the true middle. That Racine is on the extreme classical side I agree, but if you call Shakespeare romantic, you are using a different definition to the one I give. You are thinking of the difference between classic and romantic as being merely one between restraint and exuberance. I should say with Nietzsche that there are two kinds of classicism, the static and the dynamic. Shakespeare is the classic of motion.

What I mean by classical in verse, then is this. That even in most imaginative flights there is always a holding back, a reservation. The classical poet never forgets this finiteness, this limit of man. He remembers always that he is mixed up with earth. He may jump, but he always returns back; he never flies away into the circumambient gas.

You might say if you wished that the whole of the romantic attitude seems to crystallise in verse round metaphors of flight. Hugo is always flying, flying over abysses, flying up into the eternal gases. The word infinite in every other line.

In the classical attitude you never seem to swing right along to the infinite nothing. If you say an extravagant thing which does exceed the limits inside which you know man to be fastened, yet there is always conveyed in some way at the end an impression of yourself standing outside it, and not quite believing it, or consciously putting it forward as a flourish. You never go blindly into an atmosphere more than the truth, an at-

mosphere too rarefied for man to breathe for long. You are always faithful
to the conception of a limit. It is a question of pitch; in romantic verse
you move at a certain pitch of rhetoric which you know, man being what
he is, to be a little high-falutin. The kind of thing you get in Hugo or
Swinburne. In the coming classical reaction that will feel just wrong. For
an example of the opposite thing, a verse written in the proper classical
spirit, I can take the song from Cymbeline beginning with "Fear no more
the heat of the sun." I am just using this as a parable. I don't quite mean
what I say here. Take the last two lines:

> Golden lads and girls all must,
> As chimney sweepers, come to dust.

Now, no romantic would have ever written that. Indeed, so ingrained is
romanticism, so objectionable is this to it, that people have asserted that
these were not part of the original song.

Apart from the pun, the thing that I think quite classical is the word
lad. Your modern romantic could never write that. He would have to write
golden youth, and take up the thing at least a couple of notes in pitch.

I want now to give the reasons which make me think that we are near-
ing the end of the romantic movement.

The first lies in the nature of any convention or tradition in art. A
particular convention or attitude in art has a strict analogy to the phenomena of organic life. It grows old and decays. It has a definite period of
life and must die. All the possible tunes get played on it and then it is exhausted; moreover its best period is its youngest. Take the case of the
extraordinary efflorescence of verse in the Elizabethan period. All kinds
of reasons have been given for this—the discovery of the new world and all
the rest of it. There is a much simpler one. A new medium had been given
them to play with—namely, blank verse. It was new and so it was easy to
play new tunes on it.

The same law holds in other arts. All the masters of painting are born
into the world at a time when the particular tradition from which they start
is imperfect. The Florentine tradition was just short of full ripeness when
Raphael came to Florence, the Bellinesque was still young when Titian was
born in Venice. Landscape was still a toy or an appanage of figure-painting
when Turner and Constable arose to reveal its independent power. When
Turner and Constable had done with landscape they left little or nothing
for their successors to do on the same lines. Each field of artistic activity is
exhausted by the first great artist who gathers a full harvest from it.

This period of exhaustion seems to me to have been reached in romanticism. We shall not get any new efflorescence of verse until we get a new technique, a new convention, to turn ourselves loose in.

Objection might be taken to this. It might be said that a century as an organic unity doesn't exist, that I am being deluded by a wrong metaphor, that I am treating a collection of literary people as if they were an organism or state department. Whatever we may be in other things, an objector might urge, in literature in as far as we are anything at all—in as far as we are worth considering—we are individuals, we are persons, and as distinct persons we cannot be subordinated to any general treatment. At any period at any time, an individual poet may be a classic or a romantic just as he feels like it. You at any particular moment may think that you can stand outside a movement. You may think that as an individual you observe both the classic and the romantic spirit and decide from a purely detached point of view that one is superior to the other.

The answer to this is that no one, in a matter of judgment of beauty, can take a detached standpoint in this way. Just as physically you are born that abstract entity, man, but the child of particular parents, so you are in matters of literary judgment. Your opinion is almost entirely of the literary history that came just before you, and you are governed by that, whatever you may think. Take Spinoza's example of a stone falling to the ground. If it had a conscious mind it would, he said, think it was going to the ground because it wanted to. So you with your pretended free judgment about what is and what is not beautiful. The amount of freedom in man is much exaggerated. That we are free on certain rare occasions, both my religion and the views I get from metaphysics convince me. But many acts which we habitually label free are in reality automatic. It is quite possible for a man to write a book almost automatically. I have read several such products. Some observations were recorded more than twenty years ago by Robertson on reflex speech, and he found that in certain cases of dementia, where the people were quite unconscious so far as the exercise of reasoning went, that very intelligent answers were given to a succession of questions on politics and such matters. The meaning of these questions could not possibly have been understood. Language here acted after the manner of a reflex. So that certain extremely complex mechanisms, subtle enough to imitate beauty, can work by themselves—I certainly think that this is the case with judgments about beauty.

I can put the same thing in slightly different form. Here is a question of a conflict of two attitudes, as it might be of two techniques. The critic, while he has to admit that changes from one to the other occur, persists in regarding them as mere variations to a certain fixed normal, just as a pendulum swings. I admit the analogy of the pendulum as far as movement, but I deny the further consequence of the analogy, the existence of the point of rest, the normal point.

When I say that I dislike the romantics, I dissociate two things: the part of them in which they resemble all the great poets, and the part in which they differ and which gives them their character as romantics. It is this minor element which constitutes the particular note of the century, and which, while it excites contemporaries, annoys the next generation. It was precisely that quality in Pope which pleased his friends, which we detest. Now, anyone just before the romantics who felt that, could have predicted that a change was coming. It seems to me that we stand just in the same position now. I think that there is an increasing proportion of people who simply can't stand Swinburne.

When I say that there will be another classical revival I don't necessarily anticipate a return to Pope. I say merely that now is the time for such a revival. Given people of the necessary capacity, it may be a vital thing; without them we may get a formalism something like Pope. When it does come we may not even recognize it as classical. Although it will be classical it will be different because it has passed through a romantic period. To take a parallel example: I remember being very surprised, after seeing the Post Impressionists, to find in Maurice Denis's account of the matter that they consider themselves classical in the sense that they were trying to impose all the same order on the mere flux of new material provided by the impressionist movement, that existed in the more limited materials of the painting before.

There is something now to be cleared away before I get on with my argument, which is that while romanticism is dead in reality, yet the critical attitude appropriate to it still continues to exist. To make this a little clearer: For every kind of verse, there is a corresponding receptive attitude. In a romantic period we demand from verse certain qualities. In a classical period we demand others. At the present time I should say that this receptive attitude has outlasted the thing from which it was formed. But while the romantic tradition has run dry, yet the critical attitude of mind, which demands romantic qualities from verse, still survives. So that if good classical verse were to be written to-morrow very few people would be able to stand it.

I object even to the best of the romantics. I object still more to the receptive attitude. I object to the sloppiness which doesn't consider that a poem is a poem unless it is moaning or whining about something or other. I always think in this connection of the last line of a poem of John Webster's which ends with a request I cordially endorse:

End your moan and come away.

The thing has got so bad now that a poem which is all dry and hard, a properly classical poem, would not be considered poetry at all. How many people now can lay their hands on their hearts and say they like either Horace or Pope? They feel a kind of chill when they read them.

The dry hardness which you get in the classics is absolutely repugnant to them. Poetry that isn't damp isn't poetry at all. They cannot see that accurate description is a legitimate object of verse. Verse to them always means a bringing in of some of the emotions that are grouped round the word infinite.

The essence of poetry to most people is that it must lead them to a beyond of some kind. Verse strictly confined to the earthly and the definite (Keats is full of it) might seem to them to be excellent writing, excellent craftsmanship, but not poetry. So much has romanticism debauched us, that, without some form of vagueness, we deny the highest.

In the classic it is always the light of ordinary day, never the light that never was on land or sea. It is always perfectly human and never exaggerated: man is always man and never a god.

But the awful result of romanticism is that, accustomed to this strange light, you can never live without it. Its effect on you is that of a drug.

There is a general tendency to think that verse means little else than the expression of unsatisfied emotion. People say: "But how can you have verse without sentiment?" You see what it is: the prospect alarms them. A classical revival to them would mean the prospect of an arid desert and the death of poetry as they understand it, and could only come to fill the gap caused by that death. Exactly why this dry classical spirit should have a positive and legitimate necessity to express itself in poetry is utterly inconceivable to them. What this positive need is, I shall show later. It follows from the fact that there is another quality, not the emotion produced, which is at the root of excellence in verse. Before I get to this I am concerned with a negative thing, a theoretical point, a prejudice that stands in the way and is really at the bottom of this reluctance to understand classical verse.

It is an objection which ultimately I believe comes from a bad metaphysic of art. You are unable to admit the existence of beauty without the infinite being in some way or another dragged in.

I may quote for purposes of argument, as a typical example of this kind of attitude made vocal, the famous chapters in Ruskin's *Modern Painters,* Vol. II, on the imagination. I must say here, parenthetically, that I use this word without prejudice to the other discussion with which I shall end the paper, I only use the word here because it is Ruskin's word. All

that I am concerned with just now is the attitude behind it, which I take to
be romantic.

Imagination cannot but be serious; she sees too far, too darkly, too sol-
emnly, too earnestly, ever to smile. There is something in the heart of everything, if we can reach it, that we shall not be inclined to laugh at. . . . Those
who have so pierced and seen the melancholy deeps of things, are filled with
intense passion and gentleness of sympathy. (Part III, Chap. III, § 9.)
There is in every word set down by the imaginative mind an awful undercurrent of meaning, and evidence and shadow upon it of the deep places out of
which it has come. It is often obscure, often half-told; for he who wrote it, in
his clear seeing of the things beneath, may have been impatient of detailed interpretation; for if we choose to dwell upon it and trace it, it will lead us always
securely back to that metropolis of the soul's dominion from which we may follow out all the ways and tracks to its farthest coasts. (Part III, Chap. III, § 5.)

Really in all these matters the act of judgment is an instinct, an absolutely unstateable thing akin to the art of the tea taster. But you must
talk, and the only language you can use in this matter is that of analogy.
I have no material clay to mould to the given shape; the only thing which
one has for the purpose, and which acts as a substitute for it, a kind of
mental clay, are certain metaphors modified into theories of aesthetic
and rhetoric. A combination of these, while it cannot state the essentially
unstateable intuition, can yet give you a sufficient analogy to enable you to
see what it was and to recognise it on condition that you yourself have
been in a similar state. Now these phrases of Ruskin's convey quite clearly
to me his taste in the matter.

I see quite clearly that he thinks the best verse must be serious. That
is a natural attitude for a man in the romantic period. But he is not content
with saying that he prefers this kind of verse. He wants to deduce his opinion like his master, Coleridge, from some fixed principle which can be
found by metaphysic.

Here is the last refuge of this romantic attitude. It proves itself to be
not an attitude but a deduction from a fixed principle of the cosmos.

One of the main reasons for the existence of philosophy is not that it
enables you to find truth (it can never do that) but that it does provide
you a refuge for definitions. The usual idea of the thing is that it provides
you with a fixed basis from which you can deduce the things you want in
aesthetics. The process is the exact contrary. You start in the confusion
of the fighting line, you retire from that just a little to the rear to recover,
to get your weapons right. Quite plainly, without metaphor this—it provides you with an elaborate and precise language in which you really can
explain definitely what you mean, but what you want to say is decided by

other things. The ultimate reality is the hurly-burly, the struggle; the metaphysic is an adjunct to clear-headedness in it.

To get back to Ruskin and his objection to all that is not serious. It seems to me that involved in this is a bad metaphysical aesthetic. You have the metaphysic which in defining beauty or the nature of art always drags in the infinite. Particularly in Germany, the land where theories of aesthetics were first created, the romantic aesthetes collated all beauty to an impression of the infinite involved in the identification of our being in absolute spirit. In the least element of beauty we have a total intuition of the whole world. Every artist is a kind of pantheist.

Now it is quite obvious to anyone who holds this kind of theory that any poetry which confines itself to the finite can never be of the highest kind. It seems a contradiction in terms to them. And as in metaphysics you get the last refuge of a prejudice, so it is now necessary for me to refute this.

Here follows a tedious piece of dialectic, but it is necessary for my purpose. I must avoid two pitfalls in discussing the idea of beauty. On the one hand there is the old classical view which is supposed to define it as lying in conformity to certain standard fixed forms; and on the other hand there is the romantic view which drags in the infinite. I have got to find a metaphysic between these two which will enable me to hold consistently that a neo-classic verse of the type I have indicated involves no contradiction in terms. It is essential to prove that beauty may be in small, dry things.

The great aim is accurate, precise and definite description. The first thing is to recognise how extraordinarily difficult this is. It is no mere matter of carefulness; you have to use language, and language is by its very nature a communal thing; that is, it expresses never the exact thing but a compromise—that which is common to you, me and everybody. But each man sees a little differently, and to get out clearly and exactly what he does see, he must have a terrific struggle with language, whether it be with words or the technique of other arts. Language has its own special nature, its own conventions and communal ideas. It is only by a concentrated effort of the mind that you can hold it fixed to your own purpose. I always think that the fundamental process at the back of all the arts might be represented by the following metaphor. You know what I call architect's curves—flat pieces of wood with all different kinds of curvature. By a suitable selection from these you can draw approximately any curve you like. The artist I take to be the man who simply can't bear the idea of that "approximately." He will get the exact curve of what he sees *apt !*

whether it be an object or an idea in the mind. I shall here have to change my metaphor a little to get the process in his mind. Suppose that instead of your curved pieces of wood you have a springy piece of steel of the same types of curvature as the wood. Now the state of tension or concentration of mind, if he is doing anything really good in this struggle against the in-grained habit of the technique, may be represented by a man employing all his fingers to bend the steel out of its own curve and into the exact curve which you want. Something different to what it would assume naturally.

There are then two things to distinguish, first the particular faculty of mind to see things as they really are, and apart from the conventional ways in which you have been trained to see them. This is itself rare enough in all consciousness. Second, the concentrated state of mind, the grip over oneself which is necessary in the actual expression of what one sees. To prevent one falling into the conventional curves of ingrained technique, to hold on through infinite detail and trouble to the exact curve you want. Wherever you get this sincerity you get the fundamental quality of good art without dragging in infinite or serious.

I can now get at that positive fundamental quality of verse which constitutes excellence, which has nothing to do with infinity, with mystery or with emotions.

This is the point I aim at, then, in my argument. I prophesy that a period of dry, hard, classical verse is coming. I have met the preliminary objection founded on the bad romantic aesthetic that in such verse, from which the infinite is excluded, you cannot have the essence of poetry at all.

After attempting to sketch out what this positive quality is, I can get on to the end of my paper in this way. That where you get this quality ex-hibited in the realm of the emotions you get imagination, and that where you get this quality exhibited in the contemplation of finite things you get fancy.

In prose as in algebra concrete things are embodied in signs or count-ers which are moved about according to rules, without being visualised at all in the process. There are in prose certain type situations and arrange-ments of words, which move as automatically into certain other arrange-ments as do functions in algebra. One only changes the X's and the Y's back into physical things at the end of the process. Poetry, in one aspect at any rate, may be considered as an effort to avoid this characteristic of prose. It is not a counter language, but a visual concrete one. It is a compromise for a language of intuition which would hand over sensations bodily. It always endeavours to arrest you, and to make you continuously see a physical thing, to prevent you gliding through an abstract process. It chooses fresh epithets and fresh metaphors, not so much because they are new, and we are tired of the old, but because the old cease to convey a physical thing and become abstract counters. A poet says a ship "coursed the seas" to get a physical image, instead of the counter word "sailed." Visual meanings can only be transferred by the new bowl of metaphor; prose is an old pot that lets them leak out. Images in verse are not mere decoration, but the very essence of an intuitive language. Verse is a pedestrian taking you over the ground, prose—a train which delivers you at a destination.

I can now get on to a discussion of two words often used in this connection, "fresh" and "unexpected." You praise a thing for being "fresh." I understand what you mean, but the word besides conveying the truth conveys a secondary something which is certainly false. When you say a poem or drawing is fresh, and so good, the impression is somehow conveyed that the essential element of goodness is freshness, that it is good because it is fresh. Now this is certainly wrong, there is nothing particularly desirable about freshness *per se*. Works of art aren't eggs. Rather the contrary. It is simply an unfortunate necessity due to the nature of language and technique that the only way the element which does constitute goodness, the only way in which its presence can be detected externally, is by freshness. Freshness convinces you, you feel at once that the artist was in an actual physical state. You feel that for a minute. Real communication is so very rare, for plain speech is unconvincing. It is in this rare fact of communication that you get the root of aesthetic pleasure.

I shall maintain that wherever you get an extraordinary interest in a thing, a great zest in its contemplation which carries on the contemplator to accurate description in the sense of the word accurate I have just analysed, there you have sufficient justification for poetry. It must be an intense zest which heightens a thing out of the level of prose. I am using contemplation here just in the same way that Plato used it, only applied to a different subject; it is a detached interest. "The object of aesthetic contemplation is something framed apart by itself and regarded without memory or expectation, simply as being itself, as end not means, as individual not universal."

To take a concrete example. I am taking an extreme case. If you are walking behind a woman in the street, you notice the curious way in which the skirt rebounds from her heels. If that peculiar kind of motion becomes of such interest to you that you will search about until you can get the exact epithet which hits it off, there you have a properly aesthetic emotion. But it is the zest with which you look at the thing which decides you to make the effort. In this sense the feeling that was in Herrick's mind when he wrote "the tempestuous petticoat" was exactly the same as that which in bigger and vaguer matters makes the best romantic verse. It doesn't matter an atom that one emotion produced is not of dignified vagueness, but on the contrary amusing; the point is that exactly the same activity is at work as in the highest verse. That is the avoidance of conventional language in order to get the exact curve of the thing.

I have still to show that in the verse which is to come, fancy will be the necessary weapon of the classical school. The positive quality I have talked about can be manifested in ballad verse by extreme directness and simplicity, such as you get in "On Fair Kirkconnel Lea." But the particular verse we are going to get will be cheerful, dry and sophisticated, and here the necessary weapon of the positive quality must be fancy.

Subject doesn't matter; the quality in it is the same as you get in the more romantic people.

It isn't the scale or kind of emotion produced that decides, but this one fact: Is there any real zest in it? Did the poet have an actually realised visual object before him in which he delighted? It doesn't matter if it were a lady's shoe or the starry heavens.

Fancy is not mere decoration added on to plain speech. Plain speech is essentially inaccurate. It is only by new metaphors, that is, by fancy, that it can be made precise.

When the analogy has not enough connection with the thing described to be quite parallel with it, where it overlays the thing it described and there is a certain excess, there you have the play of fancy—that I grant is inferior to imagination.

But where the analogy is every bit of it necessary for accurate description in the sense of the word accurate I have previously described, and your only objection to this kind of fancy is that it is not serious in the effect it produces, then I think the objection to be entirely invalid. If it is sincere in the accurate sense, when the whole of the analogy is necessary to get out the exact curve of the feeling or things you want to express—there you seem to me to have the highest verse, even though the subject be trivial and the emotions of the infinite far away.

It is very difficult to use any terminology at all for this kind of thing. For whatever word you use is at once sentimentalised. Take Coleridge's word "vital." It is used loosely by all kinds of people who talk about art, to mean something vaguely and mysteriously significant. In fact, vital and mechanical is to them exactly the same antithesis as between good and bad.

Nothing of the kind; Coleridge uses it in a perfectly definite and what

I call dry sense. It is just this: A mechanical complexity is the sum of its parts. Put them side by side and you get the whole. Now vital or organic is merely a convenient metaphor for a complexity of a different kind, that in which the parts cannot be said to be elements as each one is modified by the other's presence, and each one to a certain extent is the whole. The leg of a chair by itself is still a leg. My leg by itself wouldn't be.

Now the characteristic of the intellect is that it can only represent complexities of the mechanical kind. It can only make diagrams, and diagrams are essentially things whose parts are separate one from another. The intellect always analyses—when there is a synthesis it is baffled. That is why the artist's work seems mysterious. The intellect can't represent it. This is a necessary consequence of the particular nature of the intellect and the purposes for which it is formed. It doesn't mean that your synthesis is ineffable, simply that it can't be definitely stated.

Now this is all worked out in Bergson, the central feature of his whole philosophy. It is all based on the clear conception of these vital complexities which he calls "intensive" as opposed to the other kind which he calls "extensive," and the recognition of the fact that the intellect can only deal with the extensive multiplicity. To deal with the intensive you must use intuition.

Now, as I said before, Ruskin was perfectly aware of all this, but he has no such metaphysical background which would enable him to state definitely what he meant. The result is that he has to flounder about in a series of metaphors. A powerfully imaginative mind seizes and combines at the same instant all the important ideas of its poem or picture, and while it works with one of them, it is at the same instant working with and modifying all in their relation to it and never losing sight of their bearings on each other—as the motion of a snake's body goes through all parts at once and its volition acts at the same instant in coils which go contrary ways.

A romantic movement must have an end of the very nature of the thing. It may be deplored, but it can't be helped—wonder must cease to be wonder.

I guard myself here from all the consequences of the analogy, but it expresses at any rate the inevitableness of the process. A literature of wonder must have an end as inevitably as a strange land loses its strangeness when one lives in it. Think of the lost ecstasy of the Elizabethans. "Oh my America, my new found land," think of what it meant to them and of what it means to us. Wonder can only be the attitude of a man passing from one stage to another, it can never be a permanently fixed thing.

THE TEACHER'S MISSION

EZRA POUND

I

"Artists are the antennae of the race." If this statement is incomprehensible and if its corollaries need any explanation, let me put it that a nation's writers are the voltometers and steam-gauges of that nation's intellectual life. They are the registering instruments, and if they falsify their reports there is no measure to the harm that they do. If you saw a man selling defective thermometers to a hospital, you would consider him a particularly vile kind of cheat. But for 50 years an analogous treatment of thought has gone on in America without throwing any discredit whatever on its practitioners.

For this reason I personally would not feel myself guilty of manslaughter if by any miracle I ever had the pleasure of killing Canby or the editor of the *Atlantic Monthly* and their replicas, or of ordering a wholesale death and/or deportation of a great number of affable, suave, moderate men, all of them perfectly and smugly convinced of their respectability, and all incapable of any twinge of conscience on account of any form of mental cowardice or any falsification of reports whatsoever.

Criminals have no intellectual interests. Is it clear to the teacher of literature that writers who falsify their registration, sin against the well-being of the nation's mind? Is there any possible "voice from the audience" that can be raised to sustain the contrary? Is there any reader so humble of mind as to profess incomprehension of this statement?

In so far as education and the press have NOT blazoned this view during our time, the first step of educational reform is to proclaim the necessity of HONEST REGISTRATION, and to exercise an antiseptic intolerance of all inaccurate reports about letters—intolerance of the same sort that one would exercise about a false hospital chart or a false analysis in a hospital laboratory.

This means abolition of personal vanity in the reporting; it means abolition of this vanity whether the writer is reporting on society at large;

"The Teacher's Mission," from Ezra Pound's *Polite Essays,* published by New Directions, 1937, and reprinted with their permission and that of Ezra Pound.

on the social and economic order, or on literature itself. It means the abolition of local vanity. You would not tolerate a doctor who tried to tell you the fever temperature of patients in Chicago was always lower than that of sufferers from the same kind of fever in Singapore (unless accurate instruments registered such a difference).

As the press, daily, weekly, and monthly, is utterly corrupted, either from economic or personal causes, it is manifestly UP to the teaching profession to act for themselves without waiting for the journalists and magazine blokes to assist them.

The mental life of a nation is no one man's private property. The function of the teaching profession is to maintain the HEALTH OF THE NATIONAL MIND. As there are great specialists and medical discoverers, so there are "leading writers"; but once a discovery is made, the local practitioner is just as inexcusable as the discoverer himself if he fails to make use of known remedies and known prophylactics.

A vicious economic system has corrupted every ramification of thought. There is no possibility of ultimately avoiding perception of this. The first act is to recognize the disease, the second to cure it.

II

The shortcomings of education and of the professor are best tackled by each man for himself; his first act must be an examination of his consciousness, and his second, the direction of his will toward the light.

The first symptom he finds will, in all probability, be mental LAZINESS, lack of curiosity, desire to be undisturbed. This is not in the least incompatible with the habit of being very BUSY along habitual lines.

Until the teacher wants to know all the facts, and to sort out the roots from the branches, the branches from the twigs, and to grasp the MAIN STRUCTURE of his subject, and the relative weights and importances of its parts, he is just a lump of the dead clay in the system.

The disease of the last century and a half has been "abstraction." This has spread like tuberculosis.

Take the glaring example of "Liberty." Liberty became a goddess in the eighteenth century, and had a FORM. That is to say, Liberty was "defined" in the *Rights of Man* as "the right to do anything that doesn't hurt someone else." The restricting and highly ethical limiting clause was, within a few decades, REMOVED. The idea of liberty degenerated into meaning mere irresponsibility and the right to be just as pifflingly idiotic as the laziest sub-human pleased, and to exercise almost "any and every" activity utterly regardless of its effect on the commonweal.

I take a non-literary example, on purpose. Observing the same mental defection in literary criticism or in proclaimed programmes, we stigmatize writing which consists of "general terms." These general terms finally have NO meaning, in the sense that each teacher uses them with a meaning so vague as to *convey* nothing to his students.

All of which is inexcusable AFTER the era of "Agassiz and the fish" —by which I mean now that general education is in position to profit by the parallels of biological study based on EXAMINATION and COMPARISON of particular specimens.

All teaching of literature should be performed by the presentation and juxtaposition of specimens of writing and NOT by discussion of some other discusser's opinion *about* the general standing of a poet or author. Any teacher of biology would tell you that knowledge can NOT be transmitted by general statement without knowledge of particulars. By this method of presentation and juxtaposition even a moderately ignorant teacher can transmit most of what he knows WITHOUT filling the student's mind with a great mass of prejudice and error. The teaching may be incomplete but it will not be idiotic or vicious. Ridiculous prejudice in favour of known authors, or in favour of modern as against ancient, or ancient against modern work, would of necessity disappear.

The whole system of intercommunication via the printed page in America is now, and has been, a mere matter of successive *dilutions* of knowledge. When some European got tired of an idea he wrote it down, it was printed after an interval, and it was reviewed in, say, London, by a hurried and harassed reviewer, usually lazy, almost always indifferent. The London periodicals were rediluted by still more hurried and usually incompetent New York reviewers, and their "opinion" was dispersed and watered down via American trade distribution. Hence the 15 to 20 years' delay with which all and every idea, and every new kind of literature, reaches the "American reader" or "teacher."

The average reader under such a system has no means whatsoever of controlling the facts. He has been brought up on vague general statements, which have naturally blunted his curiosity. The simple ignorance displayed, even in the *English Journal,* is appalling, and the individuals cannot always be blamed.

A calm examination of the files of the *Little Review* for 1917–19 will show the time-lag between publication and reception of perfectly simple facts. The Douglas economics now being broadcast by Senator Cutting, and receiving "thoughtful attention from the Administration," were available in 1919, and mentionable in little magazines in America in 1920. Many people think they would have saved us from the crisis, and would have already abolished poverty, had they received adequate attention and open discussion, and started toward being put into effect at that time. I mention this to show that the time-lag in American publishing and teaching is NOT CONFINED to what are called "merely cultural subjects" but that it affects even matters of life and death, eating or starvation, the comfort and suffering of great masses of the people.

III

Our editor asks: What ought to be done?

1. Examination of conscience and consciousness, by each teacher for himself or herself.

2. Direction of the will toward the light, with concurrent sloughing off of laziness and prejudice.

3. An inexorable demand for the facts.

4. Dispassionate examination of the ideogramic method (the examination and juxtaposition of particular specimens—e.g., particular works, passages of literature) as an implement for acquisition and transmission of knowledge.

5. A definite campaign against human deadwood still clogging the system. A demand either that the sabotage cease, or that the saboteurs be removed.

As concomitant and result, there would naturally be a guarantee that the dismissal of professors and teachers *for having* EXAMINED facts and having discussed ideas, should cease. Such suppression of the searchers for Truth is NOT suited to the era of the New Deal, and should be posted on the pillar of infamy as a symptom of the Wilson-Harding-Coolidge-Hoover epoch. To remove any teacher or professor for his IDEAS, it should be necessary to prove that these ideas had been preached from malice and against the mental health of the nation. As in our LAW a man is assumed innocent until the contrary is proved, so a man must be assumed to be of good-will until the contrary is proved.

A man of good-will abandons a false idea as soon as he is made aware of its falsity, he abandons a mis-statement of fact as soon as corrected. In the case of a teacher misinforming his students, it is the business of his higher officers to INSTRUCT him, not merely to suppress him. In the case of professors, etc., the matter should be carried in open debate.

When the University of Paris was alive (let us say in the time of Abelard) even highly technical special debates were a public exhilaration. Education that does not bear on LIFE and on the most vital and immediate problems of the day is not education but merely suffocation and sabotage.

Retrospect is inexcusable, especially in education, save when used distinctly AS a leverage toward the future. An education that is not focused on the life of to-day and to-morrow is treason to the pupil. There are no words permitted in a polite educational bulletin that can describe the dastardliness of the American university system as we have known it. By which I don't mean that the surface hasn't been, often, charming. I mean that the *fundamental* perversion has been damnable. It has tended to unfit the student for his part in his era. Some college presidents have been chosen rather for their sycophantic talents than for their intellectual acumen or their desire to enliven and build intellectual life. Others with good intentions have seen their aims thwarted and their best intended plans sidetracked, and have been compelled to teeter between high aim and constriction. The evil, like all evil, is in the direction of the will. For that phrase to have life, there must be both will *and* direction.

There may have been an excuse, or may have been extentuating circumstances for my generation, but there can be no *further* excuse. When I was in prep school Ibsen was a joke in the comics, and the great authors of the weekly "literary" press and the "better magazines" were . . . a set of names that are now known only to "students of that period," and to researchers. Then came the Huneker-Brentano sabotage. New York's advanced set abandoned the Civil War, and stopped at the London nineties or the mid-European sixties and eighties. That is, the London nineties were maintained in New York up to 1915. Anything else was considered as bumptious silliness. The *Atlantic Monthly*'s view of French literature in 1914 was as comic as Huey Long's opinion of Aquinas. And the pretenders, the men who then set themselves up as critics and editors, still prosper, and still prevent contemporary ideas from penetrating the Carnegie library system or from reaching the teaching profession, until they have gathered a decade's mildew—or two decades' mildew.

The humblest teacher in grammar school CAN CONTRIBUTE to the national education if he or she refuses to let printed inaccuracy pass unreproved:

(A) By acquiring even a little accurate knowledge based on examination and comparison of PARTICULAR books.

(B) By correcting his or her own errors gladly and as a matter of course, at the earliest possible moment.

For example, a well-known anthology by a widely accepted anthologist contains a mass of simple inaccuracies, statements contrary to simple, ascertainable chronology. I have not seen any complaints. In the *English Journal* inaccuracies of fact occur that ought to be corrected NOT by established authors but by junior members of the teaching profession. This would lead inevitably to a higher intellectual morale. Some teachers would LIKE it, others would have to accept it because they would not be able to continue without it. False witness in teaching of letters OUGHT to be just as dishonourable as falsification in medicine.

THE FUNCTION OF CRITICISM

T. S. ELIOT

W_RITING_ several years ago on the subject of the relation of the new to the old in art, I formulated a view to which I still adhere, in sentences which I take the liberty of quoting, because the present paper is an application of the principles they express:

"The existing monuments form an ideal order among themselves, which is modified by the introduction of the new (the really new) work of art among them. The existing order is complete before the new work arrives; for order to persist after the supervention of novelty, the *whole* existing order must be, if ever so slightly, altered; and so the relations, proportions, values of each work of art toward the whole are readjusted; and this is conformity between the old and the new. Whoever has approved this idea of order, of the form of European, of English literature, will not find it preposterous that the past should be altered by the present as much as the present is directed by the past."

I was dealing then with the artist, and the sense of tradition which, it seemed to me, the artist should have; but it was generally a problem of order; and the function of criticism seems to be essentially a problem of order too. I thought of literature then, as I think of it now, of the literature of the world, of the literature of Europe, of the literature of a single country, not as a collection of the writings of individuals, but as "organic wholes," as systems in relation to which, and only in relation to which, individual works of literary art, and the works of individual artists, have their significance. There is accordingly something outside of the artist to which he owes allegiance, a devotion to which he must surrender and sacrifice himself in order to earn and to obtain his unique position. A com-

mon inheritance and a common cause unite artists consciously or unconsciously: it must be admitted that the union is mostly unconscious. Between the true artists of any time there is, I believe, an unconscious community. And, as our instincts of tidiness imperatively command us not to
leave to the haphazard of unconsciousness what we can attempt to do consciously, we are forced to conclude that what happens unconsciously we
could bring about, and form into a purpose, if we made a conscious attempt. The second-rate artist, of course, cannot afford to surrender himself to any common action; for his chief task is the assertion of all the
trifling differences which are his distinction: only the man who has so
much to give that he can forget himself in his work can afford to col-
laborate, to exchange, to contribute.

   If such views are held about art, it follows that *a fortiori* whoever
holds them must hold similar views about criticism. When I say criticism, I mean of course in this place the commentation and exposition of
works of art by means of written words; for of the general use of the word
"criticism" to mean such writings, as Matthew Arnold uses it in his essay,
I shall presently make several qualifications. No exponent of criticism (in
this limited sense) has, I presume, ever made the preposterous assumption
that criticism is autotelic activity. I do not deny that art may be affirmed
to serve ends beyond itself; but art is not required to be aware of these
ends, and indeed performs its function, whatever that may be, according
to various theories of value, much better by indifference to them. Criticism, on the other hand, must always profess an end in view, which, roughly
speaking, appears to be the elucidation of works of art and the correction
of taste. The critic's task, therefore, appears to be quite clearly cut out for
him; and it ought to be comparatively easy to decide whether he performs
it satisfactorily, and in general, what kinds of criticism are useful and what
are otiose. But on giving the matter a little attention, we perceive that
criticism, far from being a simple and orderly field of beneficent activity,
from which impostors can be readily ejected, is no better than a Sunday
park of contending and contentious orators, who have not even arrived
at the articulation of their differences. Here, one would suppose, was a
place for quiet co-operative labour. The critic, one would suppose, if he is
to justify his existence, should endeavour to discipline his personal prejudices and cranks—tares to which we are all subject—and compose his
differences with as many of his fellows as possible, in the common pursuit
of true judgment. When we find that quite the contrary prevails, we begin
to suspect that the critic owes his livelihood to the violence and extremity
of his opposition to other critics, or else to some trifling oddities of his own
with which he contrives to season the opinions which men already hold,

and which out of vanity or sloth they prefer to maintain. We are tempted to expel the lot.

Immediately after such an eviction, or as soon as relief has abated our rage, we are compelled to admit that there remain certain books, certain essays, certain sentences, certain men, who have been "useful" to us. And our next step is to attempt to classify these, and find out whether we establish any principles for deciding what kinds of book should be preserved, and what aims and methods of criticism should be followed.

II

The view of the relation of the work of art to art, of the work of literature to literature, of "criticism" to criticism, which I have outlined above, seemed to me natural and self-evident. I owe to Mr. Middleton Murry my perception of the contentious character of the problem; or rather, my perception that there is a definite and final choice involved. To Mr. Murry I feel an increasing debt of gratitude. Most of our critics are occupied in labour of obnubilation; in reconciling, in hushing up, in putting down, in squeezing in, in glozing over, in concocting pleasant sedatives, in pretending that the only difference between themselves and others is that they are nice men and the others of very doubtful repute. Mr. Murry is not one of these. He is aware that there are definite positions to be taken, and that now and then one must actually reject something and select something else. He is not the anonymous writer who in a literary paper several years ago asserted that Romanticism and Classicism are much the same thing, and that the true Classical Age in France was the Age which produced the Gothic cathedrals and—Jeanne d'Arc. With Mr. Murry's formulation of Classicism and Romanticism I cannot agree; the difference seems to me rather the difference between the complete and the fragmentary, the adult and the immature, the orderly and the chaotic. But what Mr. Murry does show is that there are at least two attitudes toward literature and toward everything, and that you cannot hold both. And the attitude which he professes appears to imply that the other has no standing in England whatever. For it is made a national, a racial issue.

Mr. Murry makes his issue perfectly clear. "Catholicism," he says, "stands for the principle of unquestioned spiritual authority outside the individual; that is also the principle of Classicism in literature." Within the orbit within which Mr. Murry's discussion moves, this seems to me an unimpeachable definition, though it is of course not all that there is to be said about either Catholicism or Classicism. Those of us who find ourselves supporting what Mr. Murry calls Classicism believe that men cannot get on without giving allegiance to something outside themselves. I am aware that "outside" and "inside" are terms which provide unlimited opportunity for quibbling, and that no psychologist would tolerate a discussion which shuffled such base coinage; but I will presume that Mr. Murry and myself can agree that for our purpose these counters are adequate, and concur in disregarding the admonitions of our psychological friends. If you find that you have to imagine it as outside, then it is outside. If, then, a man's interest is political, he must, I presume, profess an allegiance to principles, or to a form of government, or to a monarch; and if he is interested in religion, and has one, to a Church; and if he happens to be interested in literature, he must acknowledge, it seems to me, just that sort of allegiance which I endeavoured to put forth in the preceding section.. There is, nevertheless, an alternative, which Mr. Murry has expressed. "The English writer, the English divine, the English statesman, inherit no rules from their forbears; they inherit only this: a sense that in the last resort they must depend upon the inner voice." This statement does, I admit, appear to cover certain cases; it throws a flood of light upon Mr. Lloyd George. But why *"in the last resort"?* Do they, then, avoid the dictates of the inner voice up to the last extremity? My belief is that those who possess this inner voice are ready enough to hearken to it, and will hear no other. The inner voice, in fact, sounds remarkably like an old principle which has been formulated by an elder critic in the now familiar phrase of "doing as one likes." The possessors of the inner voice ride ten in a compartment to a football match at Swansea, listening to the inner voice, which breathes the eternal message of vanity, fear, and lust.

Mr. Murry will say, with some show of justice, that this is a wilful misrepresentation. He says: "If they (the English writer, divine, statesman) dig *deep enough* in their pursuit of self-knowledge—a piece of mining done not with the intellect alone, but with the whole man—they will come upon a self that is universal"—an exercise far beyond the strength of our football enthusiasts. It is an exercise, however, which I believe was of enough interest to Catholicism for several handbooks to be written on its practice. But the Catholic practitioners were, I believe, with the possible exception of certain heretics, not palpitating Narcissi; the Catholic did not believe that God and himself were identical. "The man who truly interrogates himself will ultimately hear the voice of God," Mr. Murry says. In theory, this leads to a form of pantheism which I maintain is not European—just as Mr. Murry maintains that "Classicism" is not English. For its practical results, one may refer to the verses of *Hudibras.*

I did not realise that Mr. Murry was the spokesman for a considerable sect, until I read in the editorial columns of a dignified daily that "magnificent as the representatives of the classical genius have been in England, they are not the sole expressions of the English character, which remains at bottom obstinately 'humorous' and nonconformist." This writer is moderate in using the qualification *sole,* and brutally frank in attributing this "humorousness" to "the unreclaimed Teutonic element in us." But it strikes me that Mr. Murry, and this other voice, are either too obstinate or too tolerant. The question is, the first question, *not* what comes natural or what comes *easy* to us, but what is right? Either one attitude is better than the other, or else it is indifferent. But how can such a choice be indifferent? Surely the reference to racial origins, or the mere statement that the French are thus, and the English otherwise, is not expected to settle the question: which, of two antithetical views, is *right?* And I cannot understand why the opposition between Classicism and Romanticism should be profound enough in Latin countries (Mr. Murry says it is) and yet of no significance among ourselves. For if the French are *naturally* classical, why should there be any "opposition" in France, any more than there is here? And if Classicism is not natural to them, but something acquired, why not acquire it here? Were the French in the year 1600 classical, and the English in the same year romantic? A more important difference, to my mind, is that the French in the year 1600 *had already a more mature prose.*

III

This discussion may seem to have led us a long way from the subject of this paper. But it was worth my while to follow Mr. Murry's comparison of Outside Authority with the Inner Voice. For to those who obey the inner voice (perhaps "obey" is not the word) nothing that I can say about criticism will have the slightest value. For they will not be interested in the attempt to find any common principles for the pursuit of criticism. Why have principles, when one has the inner voice? If I like a thing, that is all I want; and if enough of us, shouting all together, like it, that should be all that *you* (who don't like it) ought to want. The law of art, said Mr. Clutton Brock, is all case law. And we can not only like whatever we like to like but we can like it for any reason we choose. We are not, in fact, concerned with literary *perfection* at all—the search for perfection is a sign of pettiness, for it shows that the writer has admitted the existence of an unquestioned spiritual authority outside himself, to which he has attempted to *conform.* We are not in fact interested in art. We will not worship Baal. "The principle of classical leadership is that obeisance is made to the office or to the tradition, never to the man." And we want, not principles, but men.

Thus speaks the Inner Voice. It is a voice to which, for convenience, we may give a name: and the name I suggest is Whiggery.

IV

Leaving, then, those whose calling and election are sure and return-ing to those who shamefully depend upon tradition and the accumulated wisdom of time, and restricting the discussion to those who sympathise with each other in this frailty, we may comment for a moment upon the use of the terms "critical" and "creative" by one whose place, on the whole, is with the weaker brethren. Matthew Arnold distinguishes far too bluntly, it seems to me, between the two activities; he overlooks the capital im-portance of criticism in the work of creation itself. Probably, indeed, the larger part of the labour of an author in composing his work is critical labour; the labour of sifting, combining, constructing, expunging, correct-ing, testing: this frightful toil is as much critical as creative. I maintain even that the criticism employed by a trained and skilled writer on his own work is the most vital, the highest kind of criticism; and (as I think I have said before) that some creative writers are superior to others solely be-cause their critical faculty is superior. There is a tendency, and I think it is a whiggery tendency, to decry this critical toil of the artist; to propound the thesis that the great artist is an unconscious artist, unconsciously in-scribing on his banner the words Muddle Through. Those of us who are Inner Deaf Mutes are, however, sometimes compensated by a humble con-science, which, though without oracular expertness, counsels us to do the best we can, reminds us that our compositions ought to be as free from defects as possible (to atone for their lack of inspiration), and, in short, makes us waste a good deal of time. We are aware, too, that the critical dis-crimination which comes so hardly to us has in more fortunate men flashed in the very heat of creation; and we do not assume that because works have been composed without apparent critical labour, no critical labour has been done. We do not know what previous labours have prepared, or what goes on, in the way of criticism, all the time in the minds of the creators.

But this affirmation recoils upon us. If so large a part of creation is really criticism, is not a large part of what is called "critical writing" really creative? If so, is there not creative criticism in the ordinary sense? The answer seems to be, that there is no equation. I have assumed as axiomatic that a creation, a work of art, is autotelic; and that criticism, by definition, is *about* something other than itself. Hence you cannot fuse creation with criticism as you can fuse criticism with creation. The critical activity finds its highest, its true fulfilment in a kind of union with creation in the labour of the artist.

But no writer is completely self-sufficient, and many creative writers have a critical activity which is not all discharged into their work. Some seem to require to keep their critical powers in condition for the real work by exercising them miscellaneously; others, on completing a work, need to continue the critical activity by commenting on it. There is no general rule. And as men can learn from each other, so some of these treatises have been useful to other writers. And some of them have been useful to those who were not writers.

At one time I was inclined to take the extreme position that the *only* critics worth reading were the critics who practised, and practised well, the art of which they wrote. But I had to stretch this frame to make some important inclusions; and I have since been in search of a formula which should cover everything I wished to include, even if it included more than I wanted. And the most important qualification which I have been able to find, which accounts for the peculiar importance of the criticism of practitioners, is that a critic must have a very highly developed sense of fact. This is by no means a trifling or frequent gift. And it is not one which easily wins popular commendations. The sense of fact is something very slow to develop, and its complete development means perhaps the very pinnacle of civilisation. For there are so many spheres of fact to be mastered, and our outermost sphere of fact, of knowledge, of control, will be ringed with narcotic fancies in the sphere beyond. To the member of the Browning Study Circle, the discussion of poets about poetry may seem arid, technical, and limited. It is merely that the practitioners have clarified and reduced to a state of fact all the feelings that the member can only enjoy in the most nebulous form; the dry technique implies, for those who have mastered it, all that the member thrills to; only that has been made into something precise, tractable, under control. That, at all events, is one reason for the value of the practitioner's criticism—he is dealing with his facts, and he can help us to do the same.

And at every level of criticism I find the same necessity regnant. There is a large part of critical writing which consists in "interpreting" an author, a work. This is not on the level of the Study Circle either; it occasionally happens that one person obtains an understanding of another, or a creative writer, which he can partially communicate, and which we feel to be true and illuminating. It is difficult to confirm the "interpretation" by external evidence. To any one who is skilled in fact on this level there will be evidence enough. But who is to prove his own skill? And for every success in this type of writing there are thousands of impostures. Instead of insight, you get a fiction. Your test is to apply it again and again to the original, with your view of the original to guide you. But there is no one to guarantee your competence, and once again we find ourselves in a dilemma.

We must ourselves decide what is useful to us and what is not; and it is quite likely that we are not competent to decide. But it is fairly certain that "interpretation" (I am not touching upon the acrostic element in literature) is only legitimate when it is not interpretation at all, but merely putting the reader in possession of facts which he would otherwise have missed. I have had some experience of Extension lecturing, and I have found only two ways of leading any pupils to like anything with the right liking: to present them with a selection of the simpler kind of facts about a work—its conditions, its setting, its genesis—or else to spring the work on them in such a way that they were not prepared to be prejudiced against it. There were many facts to help them with Elizabethan drama: the poems of T. E. Hulme only needed to be read aloud to have immediate effect.

Comparison and analysis, I have said before, and Remy de Gourmont has said before me (a real master of fact—sometimes, I am afraid, when he moved outside of literature, a master illusionist of fact), are the chief tools of the critic. It is obvious indeed that they *are* tools, to be handled with care, and not employed in an inquiry into the number of times giraffes are mentioned in the English novel. They are not used with conspicuous success by many contemporary writers. You must know what to compare and what to analyse. The late Professor Ker had skill in the use of these tools. Comparison and analysis need only the cadavers on the table; but interpretation is always producing parts of the body from its pockets, and fixing them in place. And any book, any essay, any note in *Notes and Queries,* which produces a fact even of the lowest order about a work of art is a better piece of work than nine-tenths of the most pretentious critical journalism, in journals or in books. We assume, of course, that we are masters and not servants of facts, and that we know that the discovery of Shakespeare's laundry bills would not be of much use to us; but we must always reserve final judgment as to the futility of the research which has discovered them, in the possibility that some genius will appear who will know of a use to which to put them. Scholarship, even in its humblest forms, has its rights; we assume that we know how to use it, and how to neglect it. Of course the multiplication of critical books and essays may create, and I have seen it create, a vicious taste for reading about works of art instead of reading the works themselves, it may supply opinion instead of educating taste. But *fact* cannot corrupt taste; it can at worst gratify one taste—a taste for history, let us say, or antiquities, or biography

—under the illusion that it is assisting another. The real corrupters are those who supply opinion or fancy; and Goethe and Coleridge are not guiltless—for what is Coleridge's *Hamlet:* is it an honest inquiry as far as the data permit, or is it an attempt to present Coleridge in an attractive costume?

We have not succeeded in finding such a test as any one can apply; we have been forced to allow ingress to innumerable dull and tedious books; but we have, I think, found a test which, for those who are able to apply it, will dispose of the really vicious ones. And with this test we may return to the preliminary statement of the polity of literature and of criticism. For the kinds of critical work which we have admitted, there is the possibility of co-operative activity, with the further possibility of arriving at something outside of ourselves, which may provisionally be called truth. But if any one complains that I have not defined truth, or fact, or reality, I can only say apologetically that it was no part of my purpose to do so, but only to find a scheme into which, whatever they are, they will fit, if they exist.

THE PRESENT FUNCTION OF CRITICISM

ALLEN TATE

> Nous avons une impuissance de prouver, invincible à tout le dogmatisme. Nous avons une idée de la vérité, invincible à tout le pyrrhonisme.[1]
>
> Pascal

I

WE are not very much concerned when we confess that communication among certain points of view is all but impossible. Let us put three persons together who soon discover that they do not agree. No matter; they quickly find a procedure, a program, an objective. So they do agree that there is some-

[1] [We have a powerlessness to verify, impervious to all dogmatism. We have an idea of truth, impervious to all skepticism.]

thing to be *done,* although they may not be certain why they are doing it, and they may not be interested in the results, the meaning of which is not very important: before they can consider the meaning they have started a new program. This state of mind is positivism. It assumes that the communication of ideas towards the formulation of truths is irrelevant to action; the program is an end in itself. But if we are interested in truth I believe that our intellectual confusion is such that we can merely write that interest upon the record of our time.

This essay represents a "point of view" which seems to have little in common with other points of view that are tolerated, and even applauded, today. It cannot be communicated at the level of the procedure and the program; it cannot, in short, be communicated to persons whose assumptions about life come out of positivism. (For positivism is not only a scientific movement; it is a moral attitude.) It has moved to contempt and rage persons whose intelligence I respect and admire.

The point of view here, then, is that historicism, scientism, psychologism, biologism, in general the confident use of the scientific vocabularies in the spiritual realm, has created or at any rate is the expression of a spiritual disorder. That disorder may be briefly described as a dilemma.

On the one hand, we assume that all experience can be ordered scientifically, an assumption that we are almost ready to confess has intensified if it has not actually created our distress; but on the other hand, this assumption has logically reduced the spiritual realm to irresponsible emotion, to what the positivists of our time see as irrelevant feeling; it is irrelevant because it cannot be reduced to the terms of positivist procedure. It is my contention here that the high forms of literature offer us the only complete, and thus the most responsible, versions of our experience. The point of view of this essay, then, is influenced by the late, neglected T. E. Hulme (and not this essay alone). It is the belief, philosophically tenable, in a radical discontinuity between the physical and the spiritual realms.

In our time the historical approach to criticism, in so far as it has attempted to be a scientific method, has undermined the significance of the material which it proposes to investigate. On principle the sociological and historical scholar must not permit himself to see in the arts meanings that his method does not assume. To illustrate some of the wide implications of this method I will try to see it as more than a method: it is the temper of our age. It has profoundly influenced our politics and our education.

What will happen to literature under the totalitarian society that is coming in the next few years—it may be, so far as critical opinion is concerned, in the next few months? The question has got to be faced by literary critics, who as men of explicit ideas must to a great extent define for imaginative literature the *milieu* in which it will flourish or decay. The first ominous signs of this change are before us. The tradition of free ideas is as dead in the United States as it is in Germany. For at least a generation it has suffered a slow extinction, and it may receive the *coup de grâce* from the present war. The suppression of the critical spirit in this country will have sinister features that the official Nazi censorship, with all its ruthlessness, has not yet achieved, for the Nazis are, towards opinion, crude, objective, and responsible. Although it has only a harsh military responsibility, this censorship is definite, and it leaves the profession of letters in no doubt of its standing. Under this regime it has no standing at all. Increasingly since 1933 the critical intelligence under National Socialism has enjoyed the choice of extinction or frustration in exile.

Could the outlook be worse for the future of criticism? In the United States we face the censorship of the pressure group. We have a tradition of irresponsible interpretation of patriotic necessity. We are entering a period in which we shall pay dearly for having turned our public education over to the professional "educationists" and the sociologists. These men have taught the present generation that the least thing about man is his intelligence, if he have it at all; the greatest thing his adjustment to Society (not to a good society): a mechanical society in which we were to be conditioned for the realization of a *bourgeois* paradise of gadgets and of the consumption, not of the fruits of the earth, but of commodities. Happily this degraded version of the myth of reason has been discredited by the course of what the liberal mind calls "world events"; and man will at any rate be spared the indignity of achieving it. What else can he now achieve? If history had dramatic form we might be able to see ourselves going down to destruction, with a small standard flying in the all but mindless hollow of our heads; and we should have our dignity to the end.

But this vision is too bright, too optimistic; for the "democracy" of appetites, drives, and stimulus-and-response has already affected us. What we thought was to be a conditioning process in favor of a state planned by Teachers College of Columbia University will be a conditioning equally useful for Plato's tyrant state. The actuality of tyranny we shall enthusiastically greet as the development of democracy, for the ringing of the democratic bell will make our political glands flow as freely for dictatorship as, hitherto, for monopoly capitalism.

This hypocrisy is going to have a great deal to do with literary criticism because it is going to have a very definite effect upon American thought and feeling, at every level. There is no space here to track down the intellectual pedigree of the attitude of the social scientist. As early as 1911 Hilaire Belloc published a neglected book called *The Tyrant State,* ir which he contended that the world revolution would not come out of the Second International. Nobody paid any attention to this prophecy; the Marxists ignored it for the obvious reason, and the liberals took it to mean that the world revolution would not happen at all. Belloc meant that the revolution was inherent in our pseudo-democratic intellectual tradition, buttressed by monopoly capitalism, and that the revolution would not proceed towards social justice, but would achieve the slave state. The point of view that I am sketching here looks upon the rise of the social sciences and their influence in education, from Comtism to Deweyism, as a powerful aid to the coming of the slave society. Under the myth of reason all the vast accumulation of *data* on social behavior, social control, social dynamics, was to have been used in building a pseudo-mystical and pseudo-democratic utopia on the Wellsian plan. In this vision of mindless perfection an elementary bit of historical insight was permitted to lapse: Plato had this insight, with less knowledge of history than we have. It is simply that, if you get a society made up of persons who have surrendered their humanity to the predatory impulses, the quickest way to improve matters is to call in a dictator; for when you lose the moral and religious authority, the military authority stands ready to supervene. Professor Dewey's social integration does not supervene. Under the actuality of history our sociological knowledge is a ready-made weapon that is now being used in Europe for the control of the people, and it will doubtless soon be used here for the same purpose.

To put this point of view into another perspective it is only necessary to remember that the intellectual movement variously known as positivism, pragmatism, instrumentalism, is the expression of a middle-class culture— a culture that we have achieved in America with so little consciousness of any other culture that we often say that a class description of it is beside the point. Matthew Arnold—in spite of his vacillating hopes for the middle class—said that one of its leading traits was lack of intelligence, and that industrialism, the creation of the middle class, had "materialized the upper class, vulgarized the middle class, and brutalized the lower class."

This lack of intelligence in our middle class, this vulgarity of the utilitarian attitude, is translatable into other levels of our intellectual activity. It is, for example, but a step from the crude sociologism of the normal school to the cloistered historical scholarship of the graduate school. We are all aware, of course, of the contempt in which the scholars hold the "educationists": yet the historical scholars, once the carriers of the humane tradition, have now merely the genteel tradition; the independence of judgment, the belief in intelligence, the confidence in literature, that informed the humane tradition, have disappeared; under the genteel tradition the scholars exhibit timidity of judgment, disbelief in intelligence, and suspicion of the value of literature. These attitudes of scholarship are the attitudes of the *haute bourgeoisie* [1] that support it in the great universities; it is now commonplace to observe that the uncreative money-culture of modern times tolerates the historical routine of the scholars. The routine is "safe," and it shares with the predatory social process at large a naturalistic basis. And this naturalism easily bridges the thin gap between the teachers' college and the graduate school, between the sociologist and the literary source-hunter, between the comptometrist of literary "reactions" and the enumerator of influences.

The naturalism of the literary scholar is too obvious to need demonstration here; his substitution of "method" for intelligence takes its definite place in the positivistic movement which, from my point of view, has been clearing the way for the slave state; and the scholar must bear his part of the responsibility for the hypocrisy that will blind us to the reality of its existence, when it arrives.

The function of criticism should have been, in our time, as in all times, to maintain and to demonstrate the special, unique, and complete knowledge which the great forms of literature afford us. And I mean quite simply, *knowledge,* not historical documentation and information. But our literary critics have been obsessed by politics, and when they have been convinced of the social determinism of literature, they have been in principle indistinguishable from the academic scholars, who have demonstrated that literature does not exist, that it is merely history, which must be studied as history is studied, through certain scientific analogies. The scholars have not maintained the tradition of literature as a form of knowledge; by looking at it as merely one among many forms of social and political expression, they will have no defense against the censors of the power state, or against the hidden censors of the pressure group. Have the scholars not been saying all along that literature is only politics? Well, then, let's suppress it, since the politics of poets and novelists is notoriously unsound. And the scholars will say, yes, let's suppress it—our attempt to convert literature into science has done better than that: it has already extinguished it.

II

What the scholars are saying, of course, is that the meaning of a work of literature is identical with their method of studying it—a method that dissolves the literature into its history. Are the scholars studying literature,

---

[1] [Upper middle-class.]

or are they not? That is the question. If they are not, why then do they continue to pretend that they are? This is the scholars' contribution to the intellectual hypocrisy of the positivistic movement. But when we come to the individual critics, the word hypocrisy will not do. When we think of the powerful semi-scientific method of studying poetry associated with the name of I. A. Richards, we may say that there is a certain ambiguity of critical focus.

Mr. Richards has been many different kinds of critic, one kind being an extremely valuable kind; but the rôle I have in mind here is that of *The Principles of Literary Criticism,* a curious and ingenious *tour de force* of a variety very common today. The species is: literature is not really nonsense, it is in a special way a kind of science; this particular variety is: poetry is a kind of applied psychology. I am not disposing of Mr. Richards, in a sentence; like everybody else of my generation I have learned a great deal from him, even from what I consider his errors and evasions; and if it is these that interest me now, it is because they get more attention than his occasional and profound insights into the art of reading poetry.

In *The Principles of Literary Criticism* there is the significant hocus-pocus of impulses, stimuli, and responses; there are even the elaborate charts of nerves and nerve-systems that purport to show how the "stimuli" of poems elicit "responses" in such a way as to "organize our impulses" towards action; there is, throughout, the pretense that poetry is at last a laboratory science. How many innocent young men—myself among them —thought, in 1924, that laboratory jargon meant laboratory demonstration! But for a certain uneasiness evinced by Mr. Richards in the later chapters, one could fairly see this book as a typical instance of the elaborate cheat that the positivistic movement has perpetrated upon the human spirit. For the uneasy conscience of one Richards, a thousand critics and scholars have not hesitated to write literary history, literary biography, literary criticism, with facile confidence in whatever scientific analogies came to hand.

With the candor of a generous spirit Mr. Richards has repudiated his early scientism: the critical conscience that struggled in the early work against the limitations of a positivist education won out in the end. What did Mr. Richards give up? It is not necessary to be technical about it. He had found that the picture of the world passed on to us by the poetry of all the pre-scientific ages was scientifically false. The *things* and *processes* pointed to by the poets, even the modern poets, since they too were backward in the sciences, could not be verified by any of the known scientific procedures. As a good positivist he saw the words of a poem as *referents,* and referents have got to refer to something—which the words of even the best poem failed to do. If Mr. Richards could have read Carnap and

Morris in the early twenties, he would have said that poems may *designate* but they do not *denote,* because you can designate something that does not exist, like a purple cow. Poems designate things that do not exist, and are compacted of *pseudo-statements,* Mr. Richards's most famous invention in scientese; that is, false statements, or just plain lies.

Perhaps the best way to describe Mr. Richards's uneasiness is to say that, a year or two later, in his pamphlet-size book, *Science and Poetry,* he came up short against Matthew Arnold's belief that the future of poetry was immense, that, religion being gone, poetry would have to take its place. The curious interest of Arnold's argument cannot detain us. It is enough to remember that even in *The Principles of Literary Criticism* Mr. Richards was coming round to that view. Not that poetry would bring back religion, or become a new religion! It would perform the therapeutic offices of religion, the only part of it worth keeping. In short, poetry would "order" our minds; for although science was true, it had failed to bring intellectual order—it had even broken up the older order of pseudo-statement; and although poetry was false, it would order our minds, whatever this ordering might mean.

To order our minds with lies became, for a few years, Mr. Richards' program, until at last, in *Coleridge on the Imagination* (1935), the Sisyphean effort to translate Coleridge into naturalistic terms broke down; and now, I believe, Mr. Richards takes the view that poetry, far from being a desperate remedy, is an independent form of knowledge, a kind of cognition, equal to the knowledge of the sciences at least, perhaps superior. The terms in which Mr. Richards frames this insight need not concern us here: I have sketched his progress towards it in order to remind you that the repudiation of a literal positivism by its leading representative in modern criticism has not been imitated by his followers, or by other critics who, on a different road, have reached Mr. Richards's position of ten years ago. They are still there. Whether they are sociologists in criticism or practitioners of the routine of historical "correlation," they alike subscribe to a single critical doctrine. It is the Doctrine of Relevance.

III

The Doctrine of Relevance is very simple. It means that the subject-matter of a literary work must not be isolated in terms of form; it must be tested (on an analogy to scientific techniques) by observation of the world that it "represents." Are the scene, the action, the relations of the characters in a novel, in some verifiable sense true? It is an old question. It has given rise in our time to various related sorts of criticism that frequently produce great insights. (I think here of Mr. Edmund Wilson's naturalistic interpretation of James's *The Turn of the Screw*. Mr. Wilson's view is not the whole view, but we can readily see that we had been missing the whole view until he added his partial view.)

The criterion of relevance, as we saw with Mr. Richards, has a hard time of it with an art like poetry. Of all the arts, poetry has a medium the most complex and the least reducible to any one set of correlations, be they historical, or economic, or theological, or moral. From the point of view of direct denotation of objects about all that we can say about one of Keats's odes is what I heard a child say—"It is something about a bird."

But with the novel the case is different, because the novel is very close to history—indeed, in all but the great novelists, it is not clearly set off from history. I do not intend here to get into Aristotle and to argue the difference between history and fiction. It is plain that action and character, to say nothing of place and time, point with less equivocation to observed or perhaps easily observable phenomena than even the simplest poetry ever does. The novel points with some directness towards history —or I might say with Mr. David Daiches, to the historical process.

I mention Mr. Daiches because his *The Novel and the Modern World* seems to me to be one of the few good books on contemporary fiction. Yet at bottom it is an example of what I call the Doctrine of Relevance, and I believe that he gains every advantage implicit in that doctrine, and suffers, in the range and acuteness of his perceptions, probably none of its limitations. I cannot do justice to Mr. Daiches's treatment of some of the best novelists of our time; my quotations from his final essay—which is a summary view of his critical position—will do him less than justice. His statement of his method seems to me to be narrower than his critical practice:

The critic who endeavors to see literature as a process rather than as a series of phenomena, and as a process which is bound up with an infinite series of ever wider processes, ought to realize that however wide his context, it is but a fraction of what it might be.

Admirable advice; but what concerns me in this passage is the assumption that Mr. Daiches shares with the historical scholar, that literature is to be understood chiefly as part of the historical process. He goes on to say:

The main object is to indicate relevance and to show how understanding depends on an awareness of relevance. That appreciation depends on understanding and that a theory of value can come only after appreciation, hardly need noting.

I must confess that after a brilliant performance of two hundred ten pages I feel that Mr. Daiches has let us down a little here. I am aware that he enters a shrewd list of warnings and exceptions, but I am a little disappointed to learn that he sees himself as applying to the novel a criterion of historical relevance not very different from the criterion of the graduate school. It is likely that I misunderstand Mr. Daiches. He continues:

The patterning of those events [in a novel], their relation to each other within the story, the attitude to them which emerges, the mood which surrounds them, the tone in which they are related, and the style of the writing are all equally relevant.

Yes: but relevant to what? And are they *equally* relevant? The equality of relevance points to historical documentation; or may we assume here that since the "main object is to indicate relevance," the critic must try to discover the relevance of history to the work? Or the work to history? What Mr. Daiches seems to me to be saying is that the function of criticism is to bring the work back to history, and to test its relevance to an ascertainable historical process. Does relevance then mean some kind of identity with an historical process? And since "understanding depends on awareness of relevance," is it understanding of history or of the novel; or is it of both at once? That I am not wholly wrong in my grasp of the terms relevance and process is borne out by this passage:

He [the critic] can neither start with a complete view of civilization and work down to the individual work of art, nor can he start with the particular work of art and work up to civilization as a whole; he must try both methods and give neither his complete trust.

Admirable advice again; but are there actually two methods here? Are they not both the historical method? When Mr. Daiches says that it is possible to start from the individual work of art and work *up* (interesting adverb, as interesting as the *down* to which you go in order to reach the work of art), he doubtless alludes to what he and many other critics today call the "formalist" method. Mr. Daiches nicely balances the claims of formalist and historian. The formalist is the critic who doesn't work up, but remains where he started, with the work of art—the "work in itself," as Mr. Daiches calls it, "an end which, though attainable, is yet unreal." Its unreality presumably consists in the critic's failure to be aware of the work's relevance to history. There may have been critics like Mr. Daiches's formalist monster, but I have never seen one, and I doubt that Mr. Daiches himself, on second thought, would believe he exists. (Or perhaps he was Aristotle, who said that the nature of tragedy is in its structure, not its reception by the audience.) I am not sure. As a critic of the novel Mr. Daiches is acutely aware of unhistorical meanings in literature, but as a critical theorist he seems to me to be beating his wings in the unilluminated tradition of positivism. That tradition has put the stigma of "formalism" upon the unhistorical meaning. Critics of our age nervously throw the balance in favor of the historical lump. Mr. Daiches's plea for it rests upon its superior inclusiveness; the historical scholar can make formal analyses against the background of history; he has it both ways, while the formalist has it only one, and that one "unreal." But here, again, Mr. Daiches's insight into the vast complexity of the critic's task prompts at least a rueful misgiving about the "wider context"; he admits the superiority of the historian, "though it may be replied that inclusiveness is no necessary proof of such superiority." At this point Mr. Daiches becomes a little confused.

I have the strong suspicion in reading Mr. Daiches (I have it in reading the late Marxists and the sociological and historical scholars) that critics of the positivist school would not study literature at all if it were not so handy in libraries; they don't really like it; or they are at any rate ashamed of it—because it is "unreal." The men of our time who have the boldness and the logical rigor to stand by the implications of their position are the new logical positivists at Chicago—Carnap and Morris, whom I have already mentioned; they are quite firm in their belief—with a little backsliding on the part of Morris [1]—that poetry, and perhaps all imaginative literature, is, in Mr. Arthur Mizener's phrase, only "amiable insanity": it designates but it does not denote anything real. I respect this attitude because it is barbarism unabashed and unashamed. But of the positivists who still hanker after literature with yearnings that come out of the humane tradition, what can be said? The ambiguity—or since we are in our mental climate and no longer with persons—the hypocrisy of our liberal intellectual tradition appears again; or let us say the confusion. Is Mr. Daiches wrestling with a critical theory, or is he only oscillating between the extremes of a dilemma? From the strict, logical point of view he is entitled merely to the positivist horn, as the general critical outlook of our age is so entitled.

This ought to be the end of literature, if literature were logical; it is not logical but tough; and after the dark ages of our present enlightenment it will flourish again. This essay has been written from a point of view which does not admit the validity of the rival claims of formalism and history, of art-for-art's-sake and society. Literature is the complete knowledge of man's experience, and by knowledge I mean that unique and formed intelligence of the world of which man alone is capable.

---

[1] Charles W. Morris, "Science, Art, and Technology," in *The Kenyon Review*, Autumn 1939. Mr. Morris argues that, although poetry is nonsense semantically, it is in the realm of "value."

A BURDEN FOR CRITICS

R. P. BLACKMUR

WHEN George Santayana made his apology for writing a system of philosophy—one more after so many, one more after a lifetime of self-denial—he put his plea for forgiveness on the ground that he was an ignorant man, almost a poet. No doubt there was some reservation in Santayana's mind when he made that plea; no doubt there is some in mine when I adapt it to myself. This essay does not introduce a system of criticism; it is only a plea that criticism take up some of its possibilities that have been in abeyance, or in corruption, for some time; and it may be that like Santayana's philosophy it will look like an approach to a system. If so, it is the system of an ignorant man, and there is nothing in it that does not remind itself at every turn that it is the kind of ignorance which goes with being almost a poet. Poetry is one of the things we do to our ignorance; criticism makes us conscious of what we have done, and sometimes makes us conscious of what can be done next, or done again.

That consciousness is the way we feel the critic's burden. By a burden, I mean both a weight and a refrain, something we carry and something that carries us along, something we have in possession and something that reminds us what we are. It is the burden of our momentum. In relation to it we get work done. Out of relation to it we get nothing done, except so far as we are swept along; and of course we are mainly swept along. The critic's job is to put us into maximum relation to the burden of our momentum, which means he has to run the risk of a greater degree of consciousness than his mind is fit for. He risks substituting the formulas of relation for the things related. I take it the critic is a relativist; but his relativism does not need to be either deterministic or positivistic, as in our time it usually is; he may rather be the relativist of insight, aspiration, vision. He is concerned with choice, not prescription, with equity not law; never with the dead hand, always with the vital purpose. He knows that the institution of literature, so far as it is alive, is made again at every instant. It is made afresh as part of the process of being known afresh;

what is permanent is what is always fresh, and it can be fresh only in performance—that is, in reading and seeing and hearing what is actually in
it at this place and this time. It is in performance that we find out relation
to momentum. Or put another way, the critic brings to consciousness the
means of performance.

Perform is a word of which we forget the singular beauty. Its meaning is: to furnish forth, to complete, to finish, in a sense which is influenced
by the ideas clustered in the word *form;* so that *performance* is an enlightening name for one of our richest activities, rich with extra life. If it is
the characteristic intent of the critic to see about the conditions of performance, it is his characteristic temptation to interfere with those conditions. He will find substitutes; he will make one condition do for every
condition; he will make precedent do for balance, or rote for authority;
and, worst of all, he will impose the excellence of something he understands upon something he does not understand. Then all the richness of
actual performance is gone. It is worth taking precautions to prevent that
loss, or at any rate to keep us aware of the risk.

The precautions of the past come down to us as mottoes; and for the
critic of literature in our time I would suggest three mottoes—all Latin—
as exemplary. *Omnis intellectus omniformis est:* [1] every mind is omniform,
every mind has latent in it all possible forms of the mind, even one's own
mind. The temptation is to make some single form of the mind seem omni-
competent; omnicompetence becomes omniscience and asserts for itself
closed authority based upon a final revelation. *Omnis intellectus omniformis
est.* This is a motto of the Renaissance, and leads us directly to a motto
of the high Middle Ages, which preceded, or initiated, rather than followed, an era of absolute authority; *fides quaerens intellectus.* [2] If the
temptation of the Renaissance was to put one's own version of the mind
in first place, the temptation of the Middle Ages was to identify God with
either one's own knowledge of him or with one's particular form of faith.
Fides quaerens intellectus is a motto meant to redeem that temptation;
for it is faith alone that may question the intellect, as it is only the intellect
that can curb faith. The very principle of balance, together with the radical
precariousness of its nature, lies in the reversibility of this motto. Just so,
the value of both these mottoes is heightened by putting them into relation
with a third, which is classical in its time, and which has to do primarily
neither with intellect nor faith but with the temptation of the moral sensibility. *Corruptio optimae pessima;* [3] in corruption the best is the worst.

---

[1] [Each mind is many-shaped (of all shapes).]
[2] [Faith seeking understanding.]
[3] [The corruption of the best is the worst (corruption).]

Here, in this motto, is that hard core of common sense—Cochrane's phrase —of which the Christian world has never got enough in its heritage from classical culture. It reminds the moral ego of its fatal temptation to forget that the ground it stands on is not its own, but other, various, and equal. Surely we have made the best in us the worst when we have either pushed an insight beyond its field or refused, when using one insight, to acknowledge the pressure of all those insights—those visions of value— with which it is in conflict. If we do not see this, we have lost the feeling of richness, the sense of relation, and the power of judgment; and without these we cannot, as conscious critics, bring our experience of literature to actual performance. We should know neither what to bring, nor what to look for.

All this is generality; it applies to literature chiefly in the sense that literature is one aspect among many of the general human enterprise. The horror for critics, of most aspects of that enterprise is that they are exigent in action and will by no means stand still for criticism until they are done for. The beauty of literature is that it is exigent in the mind and will not only stand still but indeed never comes fully into its life of symbolic action until criticism has taken up the burden of bringing it into performance and finding its relation to the momentum of the whole enterprise. Both what constitutes performance and the very nature of relation—that is to say, what must be done and what may be taken for granted—change from time to time. It seems likely that one reason there has been so little great literature is that at most times so little has been required of it: how often has a Virgil felt obligated to create the myth of imperial culture? It is even more likely that the ability to cope with the task was wanting when required: how often has a Dante turned up to put into actual order all that had been running into the disorder of the rigid intellect and the arbitrary will? Ordinarily, past times have required little of literature in the way either of creating or ordering a culture. The artist's task was principally to express the continuity of his culture and the turbulence that underlay it. That is perhaps why we find the history of criticism so much concerned with matters of decorum: that is to say, with conformity, elegance, rhetoric, or metrics: matters not now commonly found or considered in the reviews. In our own time—if I may be permitted the exaggerations of ignorance and of poetry—almost everything is required of the art and particularly of literature. Almost the whole job of culture, as it has formerly been understood, has been dumped into the hands of the writer. Possibly a new form of culture, appropriate to a massive urban society, is emerging: at any rate there are writers who write with a new ignorance and a new collective illiteracy: I mean the Luce magazines and Hollywood. But the old drives persist. Those who seem to be the chief writers of our time have found their subjects in attempting to dramatize at once both the culture and the turbulence it was meant to control, and in doing so they have had practically to create—as it happens, to re-create—the terms, the very symbolic substance, of the culture as they went along.

I do not mean that this has happened by arrogation on the part of the writers; I mean they have been left alone with this subject as part of the actual experience of life in our time: which is always the subject which importunes every serious writer if he is honest and can keep himself free of the grosser hallucinations. The actual is always the medium through which the visitation of the Muse is felt. Perhaps a distinction will clarify what is meant. It is getting on towards a century since Matthew Arnold suggested that poetry could perhaps take over the expressive functions of religion. Possibly Arnold only meant the functions of the Church of England and the lesser dissenting sects. Whatever he meant, it did not happen, it could not and it cannot happen. All poetry can do is to dramatize, to express, what has actually happened to religion. This it has done. It has not replaced or in any way taken over the functions of religion; but it has been compelled to replace the operative force of religion as a resource with the discovery, or creation, of religion as an aesthetic experience. The poet has to put his religion itself into his poetry along with his experience of it. Think, together, of the religious poetry of George Herbert and of T. S. Eliot: of how little Herbert had to do before he got to his poetry, of how much Eliot is compelled to put into his poetry before he is free to write it. Consider too—and perhaps this is more emphatic of what has happened— the enormous mass of exegetical criticism it has seemed necessary and desirable to apply to Eliot's poetry and indeed to the whole school of Donne. This criticism neither compares, nor judges; it elucidates scripture.

Let us put the matter as a question. Why do we treat poetry, and gain by doing so, after much the same fashion as Augustine treated the scriptures in the fifth century? Why do we make of our criticism an essay in the understanding of words and bend upon that essay exclusively every tool of insight and analysis we possess? Why do we have to recreate so much of the poem in the simple reading which is only the preface to total performance? Do we, like Augustine, live in an interregnum, after a certainty, anticipating a synthesis? If so, unlike Augustine, we lack a special revelation; we take what we can find, and what we find is that art is, as Augustine sometimes thought, a human increment to creation. If this is so, how, then, has it come about?

We know very well how it has come about, and we come late enough in the sequence of our time so that we can summarize it in what looks like an orderly form—or at any rate a poetic form. It composes into something we can understand. We come late in a time when the burden of descriptive and historical knowledge is greater than any man or group of men can encompass; when the labor by which our society gets along from day to day is not only divided but disparate and to the individual laborer fragmentary; and when, in an effort to cope with the burden of knowledge and the division of labor, we have resorted to the adulterative process called universal education.

As a natural effect of such a situation we have the disappearance or at least the submergence of tradition in the sense that it is no longer available at either an instinctive or a critical level but must be looked for, dug out, and largely re-created as if it were a new thing and not tradition at all. We have also a decay of the power of conviction of mastery; we permit ourselves everywhere to be overwhelmed by the accidents of our massive ignorance and by the apparent subjectivity of our individual purposes. Thus we have lost the field of common reference, we have dwindled in our ability to think symbolically, and as we look about us we see all our old unconscious skills at life disappearing without any apparent means of developing new unconscious skills.

We have seen rise instead a whole series of highly conscious, but deeply dubious and precarious skills which have been lodged in the sciences of psychology, anthropology, and sociology, together with the whole confusion of practices which go with urbanization. Consider how all these techniques have been developed along lines that discover trouble, undermine purpose, blight consciousness, and prevent decision; how they promote uncertainty, insecurity, anxiety, and incoherence; how above all they provide barriers between us and access to our common enterprise. Perhaps the unwieldy and unmanipulable fact of urbanization does more of the damage than the conscious techniques.

But this is not a diagnosis; it is a statement of sequence, a composition of things in relation. At the point where we arrest this sequence, and think in terms of what we can remember of our old culture, does it not seem plain to us what we have? Do we not have a society in which we see the attrition of law and rational wisdom and general craft? Do we not have an age anti-intellectual and violent, in which there is felt a kind of total responsibility to total disorder? Who looks ahead except to a panacea or a millennium which is interchangeable with an invoked anarchy, whether in the world or in the individual personality? Do we not above all each day wonderfully improve our chances of misunderstanding each other? These are the questions we ask of a living, not a dead, society.

They become more emphatic when we ask them about the schools of art and criticism which accompanied this shift in the structure of society. If we begin with Arnold's effort at the secularization of the old culture, it is easy to remind ourselves of the sequence that it began. Here it is, in very rough order. The hedonism in Pater, the naturalism of Zola, the impressionism of Anatole France, art for art as of the nineties, the naturalistic relativism of de Gourmont, the aestheticism of the psychologists, the rebirth of symbolism (as in Mallarmé and Yeats) the private mind, imagism and free verse, futurism, expressionism and expressive form, Dada and surrealism, dream literature, spontaneous or automatic form, anti-intellectual form, the school of Donne in English and American poetry, the stream of consciousness (that libel on Joyce), the revolution of the word, the new cult of the word. Some of these phrases will carry different meanings to different people; let us say that the general sequence runs towards some kind of autonomous and absolute creation and therefore towards total literalism.

That is on the positive side. On the negative side, every school on the list except Arnold's secularism, which was less a school than a plea for one, is an attack on disinterestedness of mind and imagination, though none of them meant to be so. And Arnold, who meant just the opposite, helped them at their business by seeing too much necessity in the offing. All of them either accepted or revolted violently against a predetermined necessity; none of them was able to choose necessity or to identify it with his will. None of them was apparently acquainted with the sense of our Latin mottoes. Their only causes were Lost Causes; their only individuals were atoms; they reflected their time, as schools must.

The world has about now caught up with these trains of ideas, these images, trends, habits, patterns, these tendencies towards either mass action or isolated action—equally violent whether in attraction or repulsion. It is a world of engineers and anarchs; rather like the Roman world when the impulse of Virgil and the Emperor Augustus had died out and the impulse of Benedict and Augustine had not yet altered the direction and aspect of the general momentum. It is a world alive and moving but which does not understand itself.

Of this world individual artists have given a much better account than the doctrines of their schools would suggest, and they have done so for two reasons. The arts cannot help reacting directly and conventionally to what is actual in their own time; nor can the arts help, whether consciously or not, working into their masterpieces what has survived of the full tradition—however they may contort or corrupt it. They deal with life or experience itself, both what is new and what is accumulated, inherited, still living. They cannot come *de novo*. They cannot help, therefore, creating at a disinterested level, despite themselves. That is why they constitute a resource of what is not new—the greater part of ourselves—and a means of focusing what is new, all that necessarily aggravates us and tears at our nerve ends in our friction with it. That is why Chartres Cathedral survives better than the schools of the Bishop of Chartres; though both were equally vital in their time.

Consider in this light what seem to be the masterpieces of our time. Consider the poetry of Eliot, Yeats, Valéry, Rilke; the novels of Joyce, Gide, Hemingway, Proust, Mann, Kafka; the plays of Shaw, Pirandello, O'Neill; the music of Stravinsky, Block, Bartók, Ravel, Satie, Schönberg; the painting of Matisse, Picasso, Rouault, Marin, Hartley; the sculpture of Maillol, Brancusi, Faggi, Lachaise, Zorach, Archipenko, Moore. Think also, but at another level, not easy to keep in strict parallel, of the architecture of Leviathan: the railway station at Philadelphia, the Pentagon, the skyscrapers, the gasoline stations, the highway systems, the East and West Side Highways, apartment houses each a small city, and the interminable multiple dwellings. Think too of the beautiful bridges which connect or traverse eyesores: the George Washington Bridge, the Pulaski Skyway. Lastly, for architecture, think of the National Parks, with their boulevards running at mountain peak.

What an expression of an intolerable, disintegrating, irrational world: a doomed world, nevertheless surviving, throwing up value after value with inexhaustible energy but without a principle in sight. And how difficult to understand the arts which throw up the values. Only Hemingway and Maillol in the roster above perhaps made works which seem readily accessible when seriously approached. Shaw is as difficult as Joyce, Mann as Kafka, if you really look into them. The difficulties arise, it seems to me, partly because of the conditions of society outlined above as they affect the audience and partly because of these same conditions as they affect the artist at his work. The two are not the same, though they are related. The audience is able to bring less to the work of art than under the conditions of the old culture, and the artist is required to bring more. What has changed its aspect is the way the institutions, the conceptions, the experience of culture gets into the arts. What has happened is what was said above: almost the whole job of culture has been dumped on the artist's hands.

It is at this point that we begin to get at the burden of criticism in our time. It is, to put it one way, to make bridges between the society and the arts: to prepare the audience for its art and to prepare the arts for their artists. The two kinds of preparation may sometimes be made in one structure; but there is more often a difference of emphasis required. Performance, the condition we are after, cannot mean the same thing to the audience and the artist. The audience needs instruction in the lost skill of symbolic thinking. The arts need rather to be shown how their old roles can be played in new conditions. To do either, both need to be allied to the intellectual habits of the time. Besides analysis, elucidation, and comparison, which Eliot once listed as the functions of criticism, criticism in our time must also come to judgment.

If we look at the dominant development in criticism in English during the last thirty years—all that Mr. Ransom means by the New Criticism—with its fineness of analysis, its expertness of elucidation, and its ramifying specialization of detail—we must see how natural, and at bottom how facile, a thing it has been. It has been the critics' way of being swept along, buoyed more by the rush than by the body of things. It is a criticism, that is, which has dealt almost exclusively either with the executive technique of poetry (and only with a part of that) or with the general verbal techniques of language. Most of its practitioners have been men gifted in penetrating the private symbolisms and elucidating the language of all that part of modern poetry we have come to call the school of Donne. With a different criticism possibly another part of modern poetry might have become dominant, say the apocalyptic school—though of course I cannot myself think so. In any case, it was a criticism created to cope with and develop the kind of poetry illustrated by Eliot's *Waste Land* and Yeats' *Tower,* two poems which made desperate attempts to reassert the tradition under modern conditions: Eliot by Christianity, Yeats by a private philosophy. Eminently suited for the *initial* stages of criticism of this poetry, it has never been suited to the later stages of criticism; neither Eliot nor Yeats has been compared or judged because there has been no criticism able to take those burdens. For the rest, the "new criticism" has been suited for *some* older poetry, but less because of the nature of the poetry than because of the limitation of the modern reader. For most older poetry it is not suited for anything but sidelights, and has therefore made misjudgments when applied. It is useless for Dante, Chaucer, Goethe, or Racine. Applied to drama, it is disfiguring, as it is to the late seventeenth- and all the eighteenth-century poetry. Yet it has had to be used and abused because there has seemed no other way of recreating—in the absence of a positive culture outside poetry—a verbal sensibility capable of coping with the poetry at all. In a stable society with a shared culture capable of convictions, masteries, and vital dogmas, such a criticism might have needed only its parallel developments for the novel and the play and the older forms of all literature; such a society does not need much criticism. But in an unstable society like ours, precisely because the burden put upon the arts is so unfamiliar and so extensive (it is always the maximum burden in intensity), a multiple burden is put upon criticism to bring the art to full performance. We have to compare and judge as well as analyze and elucidate. We have to make plain not only what people are reading, but also—as Augustine and the other fathers had to do with the scriptures— what they are reading about.

Here I do not wish to be misunderstood. Critics are not fathers of a new church. I speak from a secular point of view confronting what I believe to be a secular world which is not well understood; and I suppose what I want criticism to do can as well as not be described as the development of aesthetic judgment—the judgment of the rational imagination— to conform with the vast increase of material which seems in our time capable only of aesthetic experience. This is not to define a revelation or create a society. It is to define and explore the representations in art of what is actually going on in existing society. I see no reason why all forms of the word *aesthetic* cannot be restored to good society among literary critics by remembering its origin in a Greek word meaning to perceive, and remembering also its gradual historical limitation to what is perceived or felt—that is, what is actually there—in the arts. I have here the company of Bergson, who thought that the serious arts gave the aesthetic experience of the true nature of what the institutions of society are meant to control. And in another way, I have more support than I want in the philosophy of Whitehead, who found that the sciences in new growth, far from giving us knowledge with relation among its parts, give us instead abstractions good for practical manipulation but conformable only to a mystery. As a consequence, his philosophy of organism, with its attribution of feeling relations everywhere, is an aesthetic philosophy: in which knowledge comes to us as an aesthetic experience.

We do not need to go so far as Whitehead. The sort of thing that is wanted here to go on with seems to show clearly in James Joyce, whose *Ulysses* is the direct aesthetic experience of the breakdown of the whole Graeco-Christian world, not only in emotion but also in concept. Or again, Mann's *Magic Mountain* is the projected aesthetic experience of both that whole world and the sickness which is breaking it down. And again, Gide's *Counterfeiters* is a kind of gratuitous aesthetic—a free possibility—of what is happening along with the breakdown. Lastly, Eliot's religious poetry is a partly utopian and partly direct aesthetic experience of the actual Christian life today. That is what these works are about, and they cannot be judged aesthetically until full stock has been taken of what they are about. For us, they create their subjects; and indeed it is the most conspicuous thing about them that they do so. On each of these authors—even Eliot in his kind of reference—the whole substance of his subject is a necessary part of the aesthetic experience of it. It is for that reason that we have to judge the subject as well as what is done with it. To exaggerate only a little, in the world as it is, there is no way to get a mastery of the subject except in the aesthetic experience. How do we go about doing so?

That is, how does criticism enlarge its aesthetics to go with the enlargement of aesthetic experience. Here we must take again the risk of generalization, and we must begin with a generalization to get what the sciences have done with aesthetics out of the way. If we do not get rid of them by generalization we cannot get rid of them at all, for in detail their techniques are very tempting. Let us say then that psychology turns aesthetics into the mechanics of perception, that scientific logic turns it into semasiology, just as technical philosophers had already turned it into a branch of epistemology. All these studies are troublemakers and lead, like our social studies, to the proliferation of a sequence of insoluble and irrelevant problems so far as the critic of literature is concerned. Let us put it provisionally, that for the literary critic aesthetics comprises the study of superficial and mechanical executive techniques, partly in themselves, but also and mainly in relation to the ulterior techniques of conceptual form and of symbolic form. I do not say that one of these is deeper or more important than another, certainly not in isolation. But let us take them in the order given, and generalize a program of work.

By superficial and mechanical executive techniques I mean the whole rationale of management and manipulation through more or less arbitrary devices which can be learned, which can be made elegant, and which are to some extent the creatures of taste or fashion so far as particular choice is concerned. In some lucky cases they may be the sole preoccupation of the working artist, as in some unlucky cases they may be the one aspect of his work to which he seemingly pays least attention. In our own day they are troublesome to the extent that they are ignored in an abeyance from which they ought to be redeemed. It would seem to me, for example, that a considerable amount of potentially excellent verse fails to make its way because the uses of meter—in the sense that all verse has meter—are not well understood, though they are now beginning again to be played with: Mr. Eliot has just resorted to the metrics of Johnson and Milton. The critic who is capable of doing so ought to examine into the meters of his victims. Similarly, the full narrative mode is in little use by serious novelists, and the full dramatic mode is not in much more use; yet these are the basic modes of a man telling a story. If only because they are difficult, the critic ought to argue for them when he sees a weakness which might have been turned into a strength by their use. Again, and related to the two previous examples, there is a great deal of obscurity in modern writing which could be cleared up if writers could be forced (only by criticism) to develop a skill in making positive statement, whether generalized or particular, whether in verse or in prose. Statement may make art great and ought not to be subject to fashion.

And so on. The critic can have little authority as a pedagogue. The main study of executive techniques will always be, to repeat, in relation to the ulterior techniques of conceptual and symbolic form. By conceptual techniques I mean the rationale of what the artist does with his dominant convictions, or obsessions, or insights, or visions, and how they are translated into major stresses of human relations as they are actually experienced. Here we are concerned with the aesthetics of the idea in relation to the actual, of the rational to what is rationalized. In Dostoevsky, for example, we are interested in his conception of the Double only as we see what happens to it in the character of Versilov, or Raskolnikov, or Dmitri Karamazov. In Joyce's *Ulysses* it is not the Homeric pattern of father and son that counts, but what happens to the conception of intransigence in Stephen in concert and conflict with that transigent man Bloom. So in the later poems of Yeats, the concepts of the phases of the moon are interesting as they work or fail to work in the chaos and anarchy and order of actual lyric emotions. On a more generalized level, it is through concern with conceptual techniques that one notes that the European novels of greatest stature seem to follow, not the conceptual pattern of Greek tragedy but the pattern of Christian rebirth, conversion, or change of heart; which is why novels do not have tragic heroes. But examples are endless.

And all of them, as those just cited, would tend if pursued to lead us into the territory of symbolic techniques which underlies and transcends them. I am not satisfied with the term. By symbolic techniques I mean what happens in the arts—*what gets into the arts*—that makes them relatively inexhaustible so long as they are understood. I mean what happens in the arts by means of fresh annunciations of residual or traditional forces, whether in the language, culture, or institutions of the artist's society. I mean those forces which operate in the arts that are greater than ourselves and come from beyond or under ourselves. But I am not satisfied with the definitions any more than I am with the term. It may be I mean invokable forces, or raw forces, the force of reality, whatever reality may be, pressing into and transforming our actual experience. It is what bears us and what we cannot bear except through the intervention of one of the great modes of the mind, religion, philosophy, or art, which, giving us the illusion of distance and control, makes *them,* too, seem forces greater than ourselves. It is in the figure of Dante himself in *The Divine Comedy,* Faustus in

Doctor Faustus, Hamlet and Lear in *Hamlet* and *King Lear,* Emma Bovary in *Madame Bovary,* all the brothers in *The Brothers Karamazov.* It is in the conjunction of the gods of the rivers and of the sea with the Christian gods in Eliot's *Dry Salvages.* It is the force of reality pressing into the actuality of symbolic form. Its technique is the technique of so concentrating or combining the known techniques as to discover or release that force. It is for this purpose and in this way that the executive, conceptual, and symbolic techniques go rationally together: the logic, the rhetoric, and the poetic; they make together the rationale of that enterprise in the discovery of life which is art. But the arts are not life, though in the sense of this argument they may make a rationale for discovering life. Whether they do or not, and how far, is the act of judgment that is also the last act in bringing particular works of art to full performance. Because the arts are imperfect, they can be judged only imperfectly by aesthetic means. They must be judged, therefore, by the declaration and elucidation of identity in terms of the whole enterprise that they feed, and of which they are the play, the aesthetic experience. There is a confusion here that cannot be clarified, for it is a confusion of real things, as words are confused in a line of verse, the better the line the more completely, so that we cannot tell which ones govern the others. The confusion is, that it is through the aesthetic experience of it that we discover, and discover again, what life is, and that at present, if our account of it is correct, we also discover what our culture is. It is therefore worth while considering the usefulness of a sequence of rational critical judgments upon the art of our time as an aid in determining the identity, the meaning in itself, of present society. Such a sequence of judgments might transform us who judge more than the art judged.

Here, perhaps, is a good point to sweep some bad rubbish into the bins. Critical judgment need not be arrogant in its ambitions, only in its failures. Nor is it concerned with ranks and hierarchies, except incidentally. What I mean by judgment is what Aristotle would have meant by the fullest possible declaratory proposition of identity. Again, the ideal of judgment—no more to be reached by critics than by other men—is theological: as a soul is judged finally, quite apart from its history, for what it really is at the moment of judgment. Our human approximation of such judgment will be reached if we keep the ideal of it in mind and with that aid make our fullest act of recognition. Judgment is the critic's best recognition.

Thus it is now clear that my purpose in proposing a heavy burden for criticism is, to say the least of it, evangelical. What I want to evangelize in the arts is rational intent, rational statement, and rational technique; and I want to do it through technical judgment, clarifying judgment, and the judgment of discovery, which together I call rational judgment. I do not know if I should have enough eloquence to persuade even myself to consider such a burden for criticism, did I not have, this time not as precautions but as mentors, my three Latin mottoes. *Omnis intellectus omniformis est. Fides quaerens intellectus. Corruptio optima pessima.* They point the risk, and make it worth taking.

2. Beliefs

POETRY AND BELIEFS

I. A. RICHARDS

THE business of the poet, as we have seen, is to give order and coherence, and so freedom, to a body of experience. To do so through words which act as its skeleton, as a structure by which the impulses which make up the experience are adjusted to one another and act together. The means by which words do this are many and varied. To work them out is a problem for linguistic psychology, that embarrassed young heir to philosophy. What little can be done shows already that most critical dogmas of the past are either false or nonsense. A little knowledge is not here a danger, but clears the air in a remarkable way.

Roughly and inadequately, even in the light of present knowledge, we can say that words work in the poem in two main fashions. As sensory stimuli and as (in the *widest* sense) symbols. We must refrain from considering the sensory side of the poem, remarking only that it is *not* in the least independent of the other side, and that it has for definite reasons prior importance in most poetry. We must confine ourselves to the other function of words in the poem, or rather, omitting much that is of secondary relevance, to one form of that function, let me call it *pseudo-statement*.

It will be admitted—by those who distinguish between scientific statement, where truth is ultimately a matter of verification as this is understood in the laboratory, and emotive utterance, where "truth" is primarily acceptability *by* some attitude, and more remotely is the acceptability *of* this attitude itself—that it is *not* the poet's business to make scientific statements. Yet poetry has constantly the air of making statements, and important ones; which is one reason why some mathematicians cannot read it. They find the alleged statements to be *false*. It will be agreed that their approach to poetry and their expectations from it are mistaken. But what exactly is the other, the right, the poetic, approach and how does it differ from the mathematical?

The poetic approach evidently limits the framework of possible consequences into which the pseudo-statement is taken. For the scientific approach this framework is unlimited. Any and every consequence is relevant. If any of the consequences of a statement conflicts with acknowledged fact then so much the worse for the statement. Not so with the pseudo-statement when poetically approached. The problem is—just how does the limitation work? One tempting account is in terms of a supposed universe of discourse, a world of make-believe, of imagination, of recognised fictions common to the poet and his readers. A pseudo-statement which fits into this system of assumptions would be regarded as "poetically true"; one which does not, as "poetically false." This attempt to treat "poetic truth" on the model of general "coherence theories" is very natural for certain schools of logicians but is inadequate, on the wrong lines from the outset. To mention two objections, out of many; there is no means of discovering what the "universe of discourse" is on any occasion, and the kind of coherence which must hold within it, supposing it to be discoverable, is not an affair of logical relations. Attempt to define the system of propositions into which

O Rose, thou art sick!

must fit, and the logical relations which must hold between them if it is to be "poetically true"; the absurdity of the theory becomes evident.

We must look further. In the poetic approach the relevant consequences are not logical or to be arrived at by a partial relaxation of logic. Except occasionally and by accident logic does not enter at all. They are the consequences which arise through our emotional organisation. The acceptance which a pseudo-statement receives is entirely governed by its effects upon our feelings and attitudes. Logic only comes in, if at all, in

subordination, as a servant to our emotional response. It is an unruly servant, however, as poets and readers are constantly discovering. A pseudo-
statement is "true" if it suits and serves some attitude or links together
attitudes which on other grounds are desirable. This kind of "truth" is so
opposed to scientific "truth" that it is a pity to use so similar a word, but at
the present it is difficult to avoid the malpractice.[1]

This brief analysis may be sufficient to indicate the fundamental
disparity and opposition between pseudo-statements as they occur in poetry
and statements as they occur in science. A pseudo-statement is a form of
words which is justified entirely by its effect in releasing or organising our
impulses and attitudes (due regard being had for the better or worse or-
ganisations of these *inter se*); a statement, on the other hand, is justified by
its truth, *i.e.*, its correspondence, in a highly technical sense, with the fact
to which it points.

Statements true and false alike do, of course, constantly touch off attitudes and action. Our daily practical existence is largely guided by them.
On the whole true statements are of more service to us than false ones.
None the less we do not and, at present, cannot order our emotions and
attitudes by true statements alone. Nor is there any probability that we
ever shall contrive to do so. This is one of the great new dangers to which
civilisation is exposed. Countless pseudo-statements—about God, about
the universe, about human nature, the relations of mind to mind, about the
soul, its rank and destiny—pseudo-statements which are pivotal points in
the organisation of the mind, vital to its well-being, have suddenly become,
for sincere, honest and informal minds, impossible to believe as for centuries they have been believed.[2] The accustomed incidences of the modes
of believing are changed irrecoverably; and the knowledge which has dis-
placed them is not of a kind upon which an equally fine organisation of the
mind can be based.

---

[1] A pseudo-statement, as I use the term, is not necessarily false in any sense.
It is merely a form of words whose scientific truth or falsity is irrelevant to the
purpose at hand.

"Logic" in this paragraph is, of course, being used in a limited and conventional,
or popular sense.

[2] See Appendix. For the mind I am considering here, the question "Do I believe *x?*" is no longer the same. Not only the "What" that is to be believed but the
"How" of the believing has changed—through the segregation of science and its
clarification of the techniques of proof. This is the danger; and the remedy suggested
is a further differentiation of the "Hows." To these differences correspond differences
in the sense of "is so" and "being" where, as is commonly the case, "is so" and
"being" assert believings. As we admit this, the world that "is" divides into worlds
commensurable in respect of so-called "degrees of reality." Yet, and this is all-
important, these worlds have an order, with regard to one another, which is the
order of the mind; and interference between them imperils sanity.

This is the contemporary situation. The remedy, since there is no prospect of our gaining adequate knowledge, and since indeed it is fairly clear that genuine knowledge cannot meet this need, is to cut our pseudo-statements free from that kind of belief which is appropriate to verified statements. So released they will be changed, of course, but they can still be the main instruments by which we order our attitudes to one another and to the world. This is not a desperate remedy, for, as poetry conclusively shows, even the most important among our attitudes can be aroused and maintained without any believing of a factual or verifiable order entering in at all. We need no such beliefs, and indeed we must have none, if we are to read *King Lear*. Pseudo-statements to which we attach no belief and statements proper, such as science provides, cannot conflict. It is only when we introduce inappropriate kinds of believing into poetry that danger arises. To do so is from this point of view a profanation of poetry.

Yet an important branch of criticism which has attracted the best talents from prehistoric times until to-day consists of the endeavour to persuade men that the functions of science and poetry are identical, or that the one is a "higher form" of the other, or that they conflict and we must choose between them.

The root of this persistent endeavour has still to be mentioned; it is the same as that from which the Magical View of the world arose. If we give to a pseudo-statement the kind of unqualified acceptance which belongs by right only to certified scientific statements—and those judgments of the routine of perception and action from which science derives—, if we can contrive to do this, the impulses and attitudes with which we respond to it gain a notable stability and vigour. Briefly, if we can contrive to believe poetry, then the world *seems,* while we do so, to be transfigured. It used to be comparatively easy to do this, and the habit has become well established. With the extension of science and the neutralisation of nature it has become difficult as well as dangerous. Yet it is still alluring; it has many analogies with drug-taking. Hence the endeavours of the critics referred to. Various subterfuges have been devised along the lines of regarding Poetic Truth as figurative, symbolic; or as more immediate, as a truth of Intuition transcending human knowledge; or as a higher form of the same truth as reason yields. Such attempts to use poetry as a denial or as a corrective of science are very common. One point can be made against them all: they are never worked out in detail. There is no equivalent of Mill's *Logic* expounding any of them. The language in which they are framed is usually a blend of obsolete psychology and emotive exclamations.

The long-established and much-encouraged habit of giving to emotive utterances—whether pseudo-statements simple, or looser and larger wholes taken as saying something figuratively—the kind of assent which we give to unescapable facts, has for most people debilitated a wide range of their responses. A few scientists, caught young and brought up in the laboratory, are free from it; but then, as a rule, they pay no *serious* attention to poetry. For most men the recognition of the neutrality of nature brings about—through this habit—a divorce from poetry. They are so used to having their responses propped up by beliefs, however vague, that when these shadowy supports are removed they are no longer able to respond. Their attitudes to so many things have been forced in the past, over-encouraged. And when the world-picture ceases to assist there is a collapse. Over whole tracts of natural emotional response we are to-day like a bed of dahlias whose sticks have been removed. And this effect of the neutralisation of nature is only in its beginnings. However, human nature has a prodigious resilience. Love poetry seems able to out-play psychoanalysis.

A sense of desolation, of uncertainty, of futility, of the groundlessness of aspirations, of the vanity of endeavour, and a thirst for a life-giving water which seems suddenly to have failed, are the signs in consciousness of this necessary reorganisation of our lives.[1] Our attitudes and impulses are being compelled to become self-supporting; they are being driven back upon their biological justification, made once again sufficient to themselves. And the only impulses which seem strong enough to continue unflagging are commonly so crude that, to more finely developed individuals, they hardly seem worth having. Such people cannot live by warmth, food, fighting, drink, and sex alone. Those who are least affected by the change are those who are emotionally least removed from the animals. As we shall see at the close of this essay, even a considerable poet may attempt to find relief by a reversion to primitive mentality.

It is important to diagnose the disease correctly and to put the blame

---

[1] My debt to *The Waste Land* here will be evident. The original footnote seems to have puzzled Mr. Eliot and some other readers. Well it might! In saying, though, that he "had effected a complete severance between his poetry and all beliefs" I was referring not to the poet's own history, but to the technical detachment of the poetry. And the way in which he then seemed to me to have "realized what might otherwise have remained a speculative possibility" was by finding a new order through the contemplation and exhibition of disorder.

"Yes! Very funny this terrible thing is. A man that is born falls into a dream like a man falls into the sea. If he tries to climb out into the air as inexperienced people endeavour to do, he drowns—*nicht wahr?* . . . No! I tell you! The way is to the destructive element submit yourself, and with the exertions of your hands and feet in the water make the deep, deep, sea keep you up. So if you ask me how to be? In the destructive element immerse . . . that was the way." *Lord Jim,* p. 216. Mr. Eliot's later verse has sometimes shown still less "dread of the unknown depths." That, at least, seems in part to explain to me why *Ash Wednesday* is better poetry than even the best sections of *The Waste Land.*

in the right quarter. Usually it is some alleged "materialism" of science which is denounced. This mistake is due partly to clumsy thinking, but chiefly to relics of the Magical View. For even if the Universe were "spiritual" all through (whatever that assertion might mean; all such assertions are probably nonsense), that would not make it any more accordant to human attitudes. It is not what the universe is made of but how it works, the law it follows, which makes knowledge of it incapable of spurring on our emotional responses, and further, the nature of knowledge itself makes it inadequate. The contact with things which we therein establish is too sketchy and indirect to help us. We are beginning to know too much about the bond which unites the mind to its object in knowledge [1] for that old dream of a perfect knowledge which would guarantee perfect life to retain its sanction. What was thought to be pure knowledge, we see now to have been shot through with hope and desire, with fear and wonder; and these intrusive elements indeed gave it all its power to support our lives. In knowledge, in the "How?" of events, we can find hints by which to take advantage of circumstances in our favour and avoid mischances. But we cannot get from it a *raison d'être* or a justification of more than a relatively lowly kind of life.

The justification, or the reverse, of any attitude lies, not in the object, but in itself, in its serviceableness to the whole personality. Upon its place in the whole system of attitudes, which is the personality, all its worth depends. This is true equally for the subtle, finely compounded attitudes of the civilised individual as for the simpler attitudes of the child.

In brief, the imaginative life is its own justification; and this fact must be faced, although sometimes—by a lover, for example—it may be very difficult to accept. When it is faced, it is apparent that all the attitudes to other human beings and to the world in all its aspects, which have been serviceable to humanity, remain as they were, as valuable as ever. Hesitation felt in admitting this is a measure of the strength of the evil habit I have been describing. But many of these attitudes, valuable as ever, are, now that they are being set free, more difficult to maintain, because we still hunger after a basis in belief.

APPENDIX

Two chief words seem likely occasions of misunderstanding in the above: and they have in fact misled some readers. One is *Nature,* the other is *Belief.*

---

[1] Verifiable scientific knowledge, of course. Shift the sense of "knowledge" to include hope and desire and fear as well as reference, and what I am saying would no longer be true. But the relevant sense of "true" would have changed too. Its sanction would no longer be verifiability.

Nature is evidently as variable a word as can be used. Its senses range from the mere inconclusive THAT, in which we live and of which we are a part, to whatever would correspond to the most detailed and interconnected account we could attain of this. Or we omit ourselves (and other minds) and make Nature *either* what influences us (in which case we should not forget our metabolism), *or* an object we apprehend (in which case there are as many Natures as there are types of apprehension we care to distinguish). And what is "natural" to one culture is strange and artificial to another. (See *Mencius on the Mind,* chap III.) More deceptively, the view here being inseparable from the eye, and this being a matter of habitual speculation, we may talk, as we think, the same language, and yet put very different things into Nature; and what we then find will not be unconnected with what we have put in.

I have attempted some further discussion of these questions in Chapters VI and VII of *Coleridge on Imagination.*

Belief. Two "beliefs" may differ from one another: (1) In their objects (2) In their statements or expressions (3) In their modes (4) In their grounds (5) In their occasions (6) In their connections with other "beliefs" (7) In their links with possible action (8) And in other ways. Our chief evidence usually for the beliefs of other people (and often for our own) must be some statement or other expression. But very different beliefs may fittingly receive the same expression. Most words used in stating any speculative opinion are as ambiguous as "Belief"; and yet by such words belief-objects must be distinguished.

But in the case of "belief" there is an additional difficulty. Neither it nor its partial synonyms suggest the great variety of attitudes (3) that are commonly covered (and confused) by the term. They are often treated as though they were mere variations in degree. Of what? Of belief, it would be said. But this is no better than the parallel trick of treating varieties of love as a mere more or less only further differentiated by their objects. Such crude over-simplifications distort the structure of the mind, and, although favorite suasive devices with some well-intentioned teachers, are disastrous.

There is an ample field here awaiting a type of dispassionate inquiry which it has seldom received. A world threatened with ever more and more leisure should not be too impatient of important and explorable subtleties.

Meanwhile, as with "Nature," misunderstandings should neither provoke nor surprise. I should not be much less at my reader's mercy if I were to add notes doubling the length of this little book. On so vast a matter, even the largest book could contain no more than a sketch of how things have seemed to be sometimes to the writer.

3. *Intentions*

THE INTENTIONAL FALLACY

W. K. WIMSATT, JR., AND M. C. BEARDSLEY

> He owns with toil he wrote the following scenes;
> But, if they're naught, ne'er spare him for his pains:
> Damn him the more; have no commiseration
> For dullness on mature deliberation.
> > William Congreve, Prologue to *The Way of the World*

THE claim of the author's "intention" upon the critic's judgment has been challenged in a number of recent discussions, notably in the debate entitled *The Personal Heresy*, between Professors Lewis and Tillyard, and at least implicitly in periodical essays like those in the "Symposiums" of 1940 in the *Southern* and *Kenyon Reviews*.[1] But it seems doubtful if this claim and most of its romantic corollaries are as yet subject to any widespread questioning. The present writers, in a short article entitled "Intention" for a *Dictionary*[2] of literary criticism, raised the issue but were unable to pursue its implications at any length. We argued that the design or intention of the author is neither available nor desirable as a standard for judging

"The Intentional Fallacy" reprinted by permission of W. K. Wimsatt, Jr., and Monroe C. Beardsley.

[1] Cf. Louis Teeter, "Scholarship, and the Art of Criticism," *ELH*, V (Sept. 1938), 173–94; René Wellek, review of Geoffrey Tillotson's *Essays in Criticism and Research, Modern Philology*, XLI (May 1944), 262; G. Wilson Knight, *Shakespeare and Tolstoy*, English Association Pamphlet No. 88 (April 1934), p. 10; Bernard C. Heyl, *New Bearings in Esthetics and Art Criticism* (New Haven, 1943), pp. 66, 113, 149.

[2] *Dictionary of World Literature*, ed. Joseph T. Shipley (New York, 1942), pp. 326–339.

the success of a work of literary art, and it seems to us that this is a principle which goes deep into some differences in the history of critical attitudes. It is a principle which accepted or rejected points to the polar opposites of classical "imitation" and romantic expression. It entails many specific truths about inspiration, authenticity, biography, literary history and scholarship, and about some trends of contemporary poetry, especially its allusiveness. There is hardly a problem of literary criticism in which the critic's approach will not be qualified by his view of "intention."

"Intention," as we shall use the term, corresponds to *what he intended* in a formula which more or less explicitly has had wide acceptance. "In order to judge the poet's performance, we must know *what he intended*." Intention is design or plan in the author's mind. Intention has obvious affinities for the author's attitude toward his work, the way he felt, what made him write.

We begin our discussion with a series of propositions summarized and abstracted to a degree where they seem to us axiomatic, if not truistic.

1. A poem does not come into existence by accident. The words of a poem, as Professor Stoll has remarked, come out of a head, not out of a hat. Yet to insist on the designing intellect as a *cause* of a poem is not to grant the design or intention as a *standard*.

2. One must ask how a critic expects to get an answer to the question about intention. How is he to find out what the poet tried to do? If the poet succeeded in doing it, then the poem itself shows what he was trying to do. And if the poet did not succeed, then the poem is not adequate evidence, and the critic must go outside the poem—for evidence of an intention that did not become effective in the poem. "Only one *caveat* must be borne in mind," says an eminent intentionalist [1] in a moment when his theory repudiates itself; "the poet's aim must be judged at the moment of the creative act, that is to say, by the art of the poem itself."

3. Judging a poem is like judging a pudding or a machine. One demands that it work. It is only because an artifact works that we infer the intention of an artificer. "A poem should not mean but be." A poem can *be* only through its *meaning*—since its medium is words—yet it *is*, simply *is*, in the sense that we have no excuse for inquiring what part is intended or meant. [2] Poetry is a feat of style by which a complex of meaning is handled

---

[1] J. E. Spingarn, "The New Criticism," in *Criticism and America* (New York, 1924), pp. 24–25.

[2] As critics and teachers constantly do. "We have here a deliberate blurring. . . ." "Should this be regarded as ironic or as unplanned?" ". . . is the literal meaning intended . . . ?" ". . . a paradox of religious faith which is intended to exult. . . ." "It seems to me that Herbert intends. . . ." These examples are chosen from three pages of an issue of *The Explicator* (Fredericksburg, Va.) vol. II, no. 1

all at once. Poetry succeeds because all or most of what is said or implied is relevant; what is irrelevant has been excluded, like lumps from pudding and "bugs" from machinery. In this respect poetry differs from practical messages, which are successful if and only if we correctly infer the intention. They are more abstract than poetry.

4. The meaning of a poem may certainly be a personal one, in the sense that a poem expresses a personality or state of soul rather than a physical object like an apple. But even a short lyric poem is dramatic, the response of a speaker (no matter how abstractly conceived) to a situation (no matter how universalized). We ought to impute the thoughts and attitudes of the poem immediately to the dramatic *speaker,* and if to the author at all, only by a biographical act of inference.

5. If there is any sense in which an author, by revision, has better achieved his original intention, it is only the very abstract, tautological, sense that he intended to write a better work and now has done it. (In this sense every author's intention is the same.) His former specific intention was not his intention. "He's the man we were in search of, that's true"; says Hardy's rustic constable, "and yet he's not the man we were in search of. For the man we were in search of was not the man we wanted." [1]

. . . . .

"Is not a critic," asks Professor Stoll, ". . . a judge, who does not explore his own consciousness, but determines the author's meaning or intention, as if the poem were a will, a contract, or the constitution? The poem is not the critic's own." [2] He has diagnosed very accurately two forms of irresponsibility, one of which he prefers. Our view is yet different. The poem is not the critic's own and not the author's (it is detached from the author at birth and goes about the world beyond his power to intend about it or control it). The poem belongs to the public. It is embodied in language, the peculiar possession of the public, and it is about the human being, an object of public knowledge. What is said about the poem is subject to the same scrutiny as any statement in linguistics or in the general science of psychology or morals. Mr. Richards has aptly called the poem a *class*—"a class of experiences which do not differ in any character more than a certain amount . . . from a standard experience."

(Oct. 1943). Authors often judge their own works in the same way. See *This is My Best,* ed. Whit Burnett (New York, 1942), e.g., pp. 539–540.

[1] A close relative of the intentional fallacy is that of talking about "means" and "end" in poetry instead of "part" and "whole." We have treated this relation concisely in our dictionary article.

[2] E. E. Stoll, "The Tempest," *PMLA,* XLIV (Sept. 1932), 703.

And he adds, "We may take as this standard experience the relevant experience of the poet when contemplating the completed composition." Professor Wellek in a fine essay on the problem has preferred to call the poem "a system of norms," "extracted from every individual experience," and he objects to Mr. Richards' deference to the poet as reader. We side with Professor Wellek in not wishing to make the poet (outside the poem) an authority.

A critic of our *Dictionary* article, Mr. Ananda K. Coomaraswamy, has argued [1] that there are two kinds of enquiry about a work of art: (1) whether the artist achieved his intentions; (2) whether the work of art "ought ever to have been undertaken at all" and so "whether it is worth preserving." Number (2), Mr. Coomaraswamy maintains, is not "criticism of any work of art *qua* work of art," but is rather moral criticism; number (1) is artistic criticism. But we maintain that (2) need not be moral criticism: that there is another way of deciding whether works of art are worth preserving and whether, in a sense, they "ought" to have been undertaken, and this is the way of objective criticism of works of art as such, the way which enables us to distinguish between a skilful murder and a skilful poem. A skilful murder is an example which Mr. Coomaraswamy uses, and in his system the difference between the murder and the poem is simply a "moral" one, not an "artistic" one, since each if carried out according to plan is "artistically" successful. We maintain that (2) is an enquiry of more worth than (1), and since (2), and not (1) is capable of distinguishing poetry from murder, the name "artistic criticism" is properly given to (2).

II

It is not so much an empirical as an analytic judgment, not a historical statement, but a definition, to say that the intentional fallacy is a romantic one. When a rhetorician, presumably of the first century A.D., writes: "Sublimity is the echo of a great soul," or tells us that "Homer enters into the sublime actions of his heroes" and "shares the full inspiration of the combat," we shall not be surprised to find this rhetorician considered as a distant harbinger of romanticism and greeted in the warmest terms by so romantic a critic as Saintsbury. One may wish to argue whether Longinus should be called romantic,[2] but there can hardly be a doubt that in one important way he is.

---

[1] Ananda K. Coomaraswamy, "Intention," *The American Bookman,* I (Winter, 1944), 41–48.

[2] For the relation of Longinus to modern romanticism, see R. S. Crane, review of Samuel Monk's *The Sublime, Philological Quarterly,* XV (April, 1936), 165–66.

Goethe's three questions for "constructive criticism" are "What did the author set out to do? Was his plan reasonable and sensible, and how far did he succeed in carrying it out?" If one leaves out the middle question, one has in effect the system of Croce—the culmination and crowning philosophic expression of romanticism. The beautiful is the successful intuition—expression, and the ugly is the unsuccessful; the intuition or private part of art is *the* aesthetic fact, and the medium or public part is not the subject of aesthetic at all. Yet aesthetic reproduction takes place only "if all the other conditions remain equal."

Oil-paintings grow dark, frescoes fade, statues lose noses . . . the text of a poem is corrupted by bad copyists or bad printing.

The Madonna of Cimabue is still in the Church of Santa Maria Novella; but does she speak to the visitor of today as to the Florentines of the thirteenth century?

Historical interpretation labours . . . to reintegrate in us the psychological conditions which have changed in the course of history. It . . . enables us to see a work of art (a physical object) as its *author saw it* in the moment of production.[1]

The first italics are Croce's, the second ours. The upshot of Croce's system is an ambiguous emphasis on history. With such passages as a point of departure a critic may write a close analysis of the meaning or "spirit" of a play of Shakespeare or Corneille—a process that involves close historical study but remains aesthetic criticism—or he may write sociology, biography, or other kinds of non-aesthetic history. The Crocean system seems to have given more of a boost to the latter way of writing.

"What has the poet tried to do," asks Spingarn in his 1910 Columbia Lecture from which we have already quoted, "and how has he fulfilled his intention?" The place to look for "insuperable" ugliness, says Bosanquet, in his third *Lecture* of 1914, is the "region of insincere and affected art." The seepage of the theory into a non-philosophic place may be seen in such a book as Marguerite Wilkinson's inspirational *New Voices,* about the poetry of 1919 to 1931—where symbols "as old as the ages . . . retain their strength and freshness" through "Realization." We close this section with two examples from quarters where one might least expect a

---

[1] It is true that Croce himself in his *Ariosto, Shakespeare and Corneille,* trans. Douglas Ainslie (London, 1920) Chapter VII, "The Practical Personality and the Poetical Personality," and in his *Defence of Poetry,* trans. E. F. Carritt (Oxford, 1933), p. 24, has delivered a telling attack on intentionalism, but the prevailing drift of such passages in the *Aesthetic* as we quote is in the opposite direction.

taint of the Crocean. Mr. I. A. Richards' fourfold distinction of meaning into "sense," "feeling," "tone," "intention" has been probably the most influential statement of intentionalism in the past fifteen years, though it contains a hint of self-repudiation: "This function [intention]," says Mr. Richards, "is not on all fours with the others." In an essay on "Three Types of Poetry" Mr. Allen Tate writes as follows:

We must understand that the lines

> Life like a dome of many-colored glass
> Stains the white radiance of eternity

are not poetry; they express the *frustrated will* trying to compete with science. The *will* asserts a rhetorical proposition about the whole of life, but the *imagination* has not seized upon the materials of the poem and made them into a whole. Shelley's simile is imposed upon the material from above; it does not grow out of the material.

The last sentence contains a promise of objective analysis which is not fulfilled. The reason why the essay relies so heavily throughout on the terms "will" and "imagination" is that Mr. Tate is accusing the romantic poets of a kind of insincerity (romanticism in reverse) and at the same time is trying to describe something mysterious and perhaps indescribable, an "imaginative whole of life," a "wholeness of vision at a particular moment of experience," something which "yields us the quality of the experience." If a poet had a toothache at the moment of conceiving a poem, that would be part of the experience, but Mr. Tate of course does not mean anything like that. He is thinking about some kind of "whole" which in this essay at least he does not describe, but which doubtless it is the prime need of criticism to describe—in terms that may be publicly tested.

III

I went to the poets; tragic, dithyrambic, and all sorts. . . . I took them some of the most elaborate passages in their own writings, and asked what was the meaning of them. . . . Will you believe me? . . . there is hardly a person present who would not have talked better about their poetry than they did themselves. Then I knew that not by wisdom do poets write poetry, but by a sort of genius and inspiration.

That reiterated mistrust of the poets which we hear from Socrates may have been part of a rigorously ascetic view in which we hardly wish to participate, yet Plato's Socrates saw a truth about the poetic mind which the world no longer commonly sees—so much criticism, and that the most inspirational and most affectionately remembered, has proceeded from the poets themselves.

Certainly the poets have had something to say that the analyst and professor could not say; their message has been more exciting: that poetry should come as naturally as leaves to a tree, that poetry is the lava of the imagination, or that it is emotion recollected in tranquillity. But it is necessary that we realize the character and authority of such testimony. There is only a fine shade between those romantic expressions and a kind of earnest advice that authors often give. Thus Edward Young, Carlyle, Walter Pater:

I know two golden rules from *ethics,* which are no less golden in *Composition,* than in life. 1. *Know thyself;* 2dly, *Reverence thyself.*

This is the grand secret for finding readers and retaining them: let him who would move and convince others, be first moved and convinced himself. Horace's rule, *Si vis me flere,*[1] is applicable in a wider sense than the literal one. To every poet, to every writer, we might say: Be true, if you would be believed. Truth! there can be no merit, no craft at all, without that. And further, all beauty is in the long run only *fineness* of truth, or what we call expression, the finer accommodation of speech to that vision within.

And Housman's little handbook to the poetic mind yields the following illustration:

Having drunk a pint of beer at luncheon—beer is a sedative to the brain, and my afternoons are the least intellectual portion of my life—I would go out for a walk of two or three hours. As I went along, thinking of nothing in particular, only looking at things around me and following the progress of the seasons, there would flow into my mind, with sudden and unaccountable emotion, sometimes a line or two of verse, sometimes a whole stanza at once. . . .

This is the logical terminus of the series already quoted. Here is a confession of how poems were written which would do as a definition of poetry just as well as "emotion recollected in tranquillity"—and which the young poet might equally well take to heart as a practical rule. Drink a pint of beer, relax, go walking, think on nothing in particular, look at things, surrender yourself to yourself, search for the truth in your own soul, listen to the sound of your own inside voice, discover and express the *vraie vérité.*[2]

It is probably true that all this is excellent advice for poets. The young imagination fired by Wordsworth and Carlyle is probably closer to the verge of producing a poem than the mind of the student who has been

---

[1] [If you wish me to weep.—HORACE *De Arte Poetica.*]
[2] [Absolute truth.]

sobered by Aristotle or Richards. The art of inspiring poets, or at least of inciting something like poetry in young persons, has probably gone further in our day than ever before. Books of creative writing such as those issued from the Lincoln School are interesting evidence of what a child can do if taught how to manage himself honestly.[1] All this, however, would appear to belong to an art separate from criticism, or to a discipline which one might call the psychology of composition, valid and useful, an individual and private culture, yoga, or system of self-development which the young poet would do well to notice, but different from the public science of evaluating poems.

Coleridge and Arnold were better critics than most poets have been, and if the critical tendency dried up the poetry in Arnold and perhaps in Coleridge, it is not inconsistent with our argument, which is that judgment of poems is different from the art of producing them. Coleridge has given us the classic "anodyne" story, and tells what he can about the genesis of a poem, which he calls a "psychological curiosity," but his definitions of poetry and of the poetic quality "imagination" are to be found elsewhere and in quite other terms.

The day may arrive when the psychology of composition is unified with the science of objective evaluation, but so far they are separate. It would be convenient if the passwords of the intentional school, "sincerity," "fidelity," "spontaneity," "authenticity," "genuineness," "originality," could be equated with terms of analysis such as "integrity," "relevance," "unity," "function"; with "maturity," "subtlety," and "adequacy," and other more precise axiological terms—in short, if "expression" always meant aesthetic communication. But this is not so.

"Aesthetic" art, says Professor Curt Ducasse, an ingenious theorist of expression, is the conscious objectification of feelings, in which an intrinsic part is the critical moment. The artist corrects the objectification when it is not adequate, but this may mean that the earlier attempt was not successful in objectifying the self, or "it may also mean that it was a successful objectification of a self which, when it confronted us clearly, we disowned and repudiated in favor of another." [2] What is the standard by which we disown or accept the self? Professor Ducasse does not say. Whatever it may be, however, this standard is an element in the definition

---

[1] See Hughes Mearns, *Creative Youth* (Garden City, 1925) esp. pp. 10, 27–29. The technique of inspiring poems keeps pace today with a parallel analysis of the process of inspiration in successful artists. See Rosamond E. M. Harding, *An Anatomy of Inspiration,* Cambridge, 1940; Julius Portnoy, *A Psychology of Art Creation,* Philadelphia, 1942.

[2] Curt Ducasse, *The Philosophy of Art* (New York, 1929), p. 116.

of art which will not reduce to terms of objectification. The evaluation of the work of art remains public; the work is measured against something outside the author.

IV

There is criticism of poetry and there is, as we have seen, author psychology, which when applied to the present or future takes the form of inspirational promotion; but author psychology can be historical too, and then we have literary biography, a legitimate and attractive study in itself, one approach, as Mr. Tillyard would argue, to personality, the poem being only a parallel approach. Certainly it need not be with a derogatory purpose that one points out personal studies, as distinct from poetic studies, in the realm of literary scholarship. Yet there is danger of confusing personal and poetic studies; and there is the fault of writing the personal as if it were poetic.

There is a difference between internal and external evidence for the meaning of a poem. And the paradox is only verbal and superficial that what is (1) internal is also public: it is discovered through the semantics and syntax of a poem, through our habitual knowledge of the language, through grammars, dictionaries, and all the literature which is the source of dictionaries, in general through all that makes a language and culture; while what is (2) external is private or idiosyncratic; not a part of the work as a linguistic fact: it consists of revelations (in journals, for example, or letters or reported conversations) about how or why the poet wrote the poem—to what lady, while sitting on what lawn, or at the death of what friend or brother. There is (3) an intermediate kind of evidence about the character of the author or about private or semi-private meanings attached to words or topics by an author or by a coterie of which he is a member. The meaning of words is the history of words, and the biography of an author, his use of a word, and the associations which the word had for *him,* are part of the word's history and meaning.[1] But the three types of evidence, especially (2) and (3), shade into one another so subtly that it is not always easy to draw a line between examples, and hence arises the difficulty for criticism. The use of biographical evidence need not involve intentionalism, because while it may be evidence of what the author intended, it may also be evidence of the meaning of his words and the

---

[1] And the history of words *after* a poem is written may contribute meanings which if relevant to the original pattern should not be ruled out by a scruple about intention. Cf. C. S. Lewis and E. M. W. Tillyard, *The Personal Heresy* (Oxford, 1939), p. 16; Teeter, *loc. cit.,* pp. 183, 192; review of Tillotson's *Essays, TLS, XLI* (April, 1942), 174.

dramatic character of his utterance. On the other hand, it may not be all this. And a critic who is concerned with evidence of type (1) and moderately with that of type (3) will in the long run produce a different sort of comment from that of the critic who is concerned with type (2) and with (3) where it shades into (2).

The whole glittering parade of Professor Lowes' *Road to Xanadu,* for instance, runs along the border between types (2) and (3) or boldly traverses the romantic region of (2). " 'Kubla Khan,' " says Professor Lowes, "is the fabric of a vision, but every image that rose up in its weaving had passed that way before. And it would seem that there is nothing haphazard or fortuitous in their return." This is not quite clear—not even when Professor Lowes explains that there were clusters of associations, like hooked atoms, which were drawn into complex relation with other clusters in the deep well of Coleridge's memory, and which then coalesced and issued forth as poems. If there was nothing "haphazard or fortuitous" in the way the images returned to the surface, that may mean (1) that Coleridge could not produce what he did not have, that he was limited in his creation by what he had read or otherwise experienced, or (2) that having received certain clusters of associations, he was bound to return them in just the way he did, and that the value of the poem may be described in terms of the experiences on which he had to draw. The latter pair of propositions (a sort of Hartleyan associationism which Coleridge himself repudiated in the *Biographia*) may not be assented to. There were certainly other combinations, other poems, worse or better, that might have been written by men who had read Bartram and Purchas and Bruce and Milton. And this will be true no matter how many times we are able to add to the brilliant complex of Coleridge's reading. In certain flourishes (such as the sentence we have quoted) and in chapter headings like "The Shaping Spirit," "The Magical Synthesis," "Imagination Creatrix," it may be that Professor Lowes pretends to say more about the actual poems than he does. There is a certain deceptive variation in these fancy chapter titles; one expects to pass on to a new stage in the argument, and one finds—more and more sources, more about "the streamy nature of association." [1]

"Wohin der Weg?" [2] quotes Professor Lowes for the motto of his

---

[1] Chapters VIII, "The Pattern," and XVI, "The Known and Familiar Landscape," will be found of most help to the student of the poem.

For an extreme example of intentionalistic criticism, see Kenneth Burke's analysis of *The Ancient Mariner* in *The Philosophy of Literary Form* (Louisiana State University Press, 1941), pp. 22–23, 93–102. Mr. Burke must be credited with realizing very clearly what he is up to.

[2] [Where does the path go?]

book. "Kein Weg! Ins Unbetretene." [1] Precisely because the way is *un-betreten,* we should say, it leads away from the poem. Bartram's *Travels* contains a good deal of the history of certain words and romantic Floridan conceptions that appear in "Kubla Khan." And a good deal of that history has passed and was then passing into the very stuff of our language. Per-haps a person who has read Bartram appreciates the poem more than one who has not. Or, by looking up the vocabulary of "Kubla Khan" in the *Oxford English Dictionary,* or by reading some of the other books there quoted, a person may know the poem better. But it would seem to per-tain little to the poem to know that *Coleridge* has read Bartram. There is a gross body of life, of sensory and mental experience, which lies behind and in some sense causes every poem, but can never be and need not be known in the verbal and hence intellectual composition which is the poem. For all the objects of our manifold experience, especially for the intel-lectual objects, for every unity, there is an action of the mind which cuts off roots, melts away context—or indeed we should never have objects or ideas or anything to talk about.

It is probable that there is nothing in Professor Lowes' vast book which could detract from anyone's appreciation of either *The Ancient Mariner* or *Kubla Khan.* We next present a case where preoccupation with evidence of type (3) has gone so far as to distort a critic's view of a poem (yet a case not so obvious as those that abound in our critical journals).

In a well-known poem by John Donne appears the following quatrain:

> Moving of th' earth brings harmes and feares,
>   Men reckon what it did and meant,
> But trepidation of the spheares,
>   Though greater farre, is innocent.

A recent critic in an elaborate treatment of Donne's learning has written of this quatrain as follows:

. . . he touches the emotional pulse of the situation by a skillful allusion to the new and the old astronomy. . . . Of the new astronomy, the "moving of the earth" is the most radical principle; of the old, the "trepidation of the spheres" is the motion of the greatest complexity. . . . As the poem is a valediction for-bidding mourning, the poet must exhort his love to quietness and calm upon his departure; and for this purpose the figure based upon the latter motion (trepidation), long absorbed into the traditional astronomy, fittingly suggests the tension of the moment without arousing the "harmes and feares" implicit in the figure of the moving earth.[2]

---

[1] [No path into the unknown (untrod).]

[2] Charles M. Coffin, *John Donne and the New Philosophy* (New York, 1927), pp. 97–98.

The argument is plausible and rests on a well-substantiated thesis that Donne was deeply interested in the new astronomy and its repercussions in the theological realm. In various works Donne shows his familiarity with Kepler's *De Stella Nova,* with Galileo's *Siderius Nuncius,* with William Gilbert's *De Magnete,* and with Clavius's commentary on the *De Sphaera* of Sacrobosco. He refers to the new science in his Sermon at Paul's Cross and in a letter to Sir Henry Goodyer. In *The First Anniversary* he says the "new philosophy calls all in doubt." In the *Elegy on Prince Henry* he says that the "least moving of the center" makes "the world to shake."

It is difficult to answer argument like this, and impossible to answer it with evidence of like nature. There is no reason why Donne might not have written a stanza in which the two kinds of celestial motion stood for two sorts of emotion at parting. And if we become full of astronomical ideas and see Donne only against the background of the new science, we may believe that he did. But the text itself remains to be dealt with, the analyzable vehicle of a complicated metaphor. And one may observe: (1) that the movement of the earth according to the Copernican theory is a celestial motion, smooth and regular, and while it might cause religious or philosophic fears, it could not be associated with the crudity and earthiness of the kind of commotion which the speaker in the poem wishes to discourage; (2) that there is another moving of the earth, an earthquake, which has just these qualities and is to be associated with the tear-floods and sigh-tempests of the second stanza of the poem; (3) that "trepidation" is an appropriate opposite of earthquake, because each is a shaking or vibratory motion; and "trepidation of the spheres" is "greater far" than an earthquake, but not much greater (if two such motions can be compared as to greatness) than the annual motion of the earth; (4) that reckoning what it "did and meant" shows that the event has passed, like an earthquake, not like the incessant celestial movement of the earth. Perhaps a knowledge of Donne's interest in the new science may add another shade of meaning, an overtone to the stanza in question, though to say even this runs against the words. To make the geo-centric and helio-centric antithesis the core of the metaphor is to disregard the English language, to prefer private evidence to public, external to internal.

V

If the distinction between kinds of evidence has implications for the historical critic, it has them no less for the contemporary poet and his critic. Or, since every rule for a poet is but another side of a judgment by a

critic, and since the past is the realm of the scholar and critic, and the
future and present that of the poet and the critical leaders of taste, we
may say that the problems arising in literary scholarship from the intentional fallacy are matched by others which arise in the world of progressive
experiment.

The question of "allusiveness," for example, as acutely posed by the
poetry of Eliot, is certainly one where a false judgment is likely to involve the intentional fallacy. The frequency and depth of literary allusion
in the poetry of Eliot and others has driven so many in pursuit of full
meanings to the *Golden Bough* and the Elizabethan drama that it has become a kind of commonplace to suppose that we do not know what a
poet means unless we have traced him in his reading—a supposition redo-
lent with intentional implications. The stand taken by Mr. F. O. Matthiessen
is a sound one and partially forestalls the difficulty.

If one reads these lines with an attentive ear and is sensitive to their sudden
shifts in movement, the contrast between the actual Thames and the idealized
vision of it during an age before it flowed through a megalopolis is sharply conveyed by that movement itself, whether or not one recognizes the refrain to be
from Spenser.

Eliot's allusions work when we know them—and to a great extent even
when we do not know them, through their suggestive power.

But sometimes we find allusions supported by notes, and it is a very
nice question whether the notes function more as guides to send us where
we may be educated, or more as indications in themselves about the character of the allusions. "Nearly everything of importance . . . that is apposite to an appreciation of 'The Waste Land,' " writes Mr. Matthiessen
of Miss Weston's book, "has been incorporated into the structure of the
poem itself, or into Eliot's Notes." And with such an admission it may
begin to appear that it would not much matter if Eliot invented his sources
(as Sir Walter Scott invented chapter epigraphs from "old plays" and
"anonymous" authors, or as Coleridge wrote marginal glosses for *The
Ancient Mariner*). Allusions to Dante, Webster, Marvell, or Baudelaire,
doubtless gain something because these writers existed, but it is doubtful
whether the same can be said for an allusion to an obscure Elizabethan:

> The sound of horns and motors, which shall bring
> Sweeney to Mrs. Porter in the spring.

"Cf. Day, *Parliament of Bees*": says Eliot,

> When of a sudden, listening, you shall hear,
> A noise of horns and hunting, which shall bring
> Actaeon to Diana in the spring,
> Where all shall see her naked skin. . . .

The irony is completed by the quotation itself; had Eliot, as is quite conceivable, composed these lines to furnish his own background, there would be no loss of validity. The conviction may grow as one reads Eliot's next note: "I do not know the origin of the ballad from which these lines are taken: it was reported to me from Sydney, Australia." The important word in this note—on Mrs. Porter and her daughter who washed their feet in soda water—is "ballad." And if one should feel from the lines themselves their "ballad" quality, there would be little need for the note. Ultimately, the inquiry must focus on the integrity of such notes as parts of the poem, for where they constitute special information about the meaning of phrases in the poem, they ought to be subject to the same scrutiny as any of the other words in which it is written. Mr. Matthiessen believes the notes were the price Eliot "had to pay in order to avoid what he would have considered muffling the energy of his poem by extended connecting links in the text itself." But it may be questioned whether the notes and the need for them are not equally muffling. The omission from poems of the explanatory stratum on which is built the dramatic or poetic stuff is a dangerous responsibility. Mr. F. W. Bateson has plausibly argued that Tennyson's "The Sailor Boy" would be better if half the stanzas were omitted, and the best versions of ballads like "Sir Patrick Spens" owe their power to the very audacity with which the minstrel has taken for granted the story upon which he comments. What then if a poet finds he cannot take so much for granted in a more recondite context and rather than write informatively, supplies notes? It can be said in favor of this plan that at least the notes do not pretend to be dramatic, as they would if written in verse. On the other hand, the notes may look like unassimilated material lying loose beside the poem, necessary for the meaning of the verbal symbol, but not integrated, so that the symbol stands incomplete.

We mean to suggest by the above analysis that whereas notes tend to seem to justify themselves as external indexes to the author's *intention,* yet they ought to be judged like any other parts of a composition (verbal arrangement special to a particular context), and when so judged their reality as parts of the poem, or their imaginative integration with the rest of the poem, may come into question. Mr. Matthiessen, for instance, sees that Eliot's titles for poems and his epigraphs are informative apparatus, like the notes. But while he is worried by some of the notes and thinks that Eliot "appears to be mocking himself for writing the note at the same time that he wants to convey something by it," Mr. Matthiessen believes that the "device" of epigraphs "is not at all open to the objection of not being sufficiently structural." "The *intention,*" he says, "is to enable the poet to secure a condensed expression in the poem itself." "In each case

the epigraph is *designed* to form an integral part of the effect of the poem."
And Eliot himself, in his notes, has justified his poetic practice in terms of
intention.

The Hanged Man, a member of the traditional pack, fits my purpose in two
ways: because he is associated in my mind with the Hanged God of Frazer, and
because I associate him with the hooded figure in the passage of the disciples
to Emmaus in Part V. . . . The man with Three Staves (an authentic member
of the Tarot pack) I associate, quite arbitrarily, with the Fisher King himself.

And perhaps he is to be taken more seriously here, when off guard in a
note, than when in his Norton Lectures he comments on the difficulty of
saying what a poem means and adds playfully that he thinks of prefixing
to a second edition of *Ash Wednesday* some lines from *Don Juan:*

> I don't pretend that I quite understand
> My own meaning when I would be *very* fine;
> But the fact is that I have nothing planned
> Unless it were to be a moment merry.

If Eliot and other contemporary poets have any characteristic fault, it may
be in *planning* too much.[1]

Allusiveness in poetry is one of several critical issues by which we
have illustrated the more abstract issue of intentionalism, but it may be for
today the most important illustration. As a poetic practice allusiveness
would appear to be in some recent poems an extreme corollary of the romantic intentionalist assumption, and as a critical issue it challenges and
brings to light in a special way the basic premise of intentionalism. The
following instance from the poetry of Eliot may serve to epitomize the
practical implications of what we have been saying. In Eliot's "Love Song
of J. Alfred Prufrock," towards the end, occurs the line: "I have heard the
mermaids singing, each to each," and this bears a certain resemblance to a
line in a Song by John Donne, "Teach me to heare Mermaides singing,"
so that for the reader acquainted to a certain degree with Donne's poetry,
the critical question arises: Is Eliot's line an allusion to Donne's? Is Prufrock
thinking about Donne? Is Eliot thinking about Donne? We suggest that
there are two radically different ways of looking for an answer to this question. There is (1) the way of poetic analysis and exegesis, which inquires
whether it makes any sense if Eliot-Prufrock *is* thinking about Donne. In
an earlier part of the poem, when Prufrock asks, "Would it have been
worth while, . . . To have squeezed the universe into a ball," his words

---

[1] In his critical writings Eliot has expressed the right view of author psychology
(See *The Use of Poetry and the Use of Criticism*, Cambridge, 1933, p. 139 and "Tradition and the Individual Talent" in *Selected Essays*, New York, 1932), though his
record is not entirely consistent (See *A Choice of Kipling's Verse*, London, 1941,
pp. 10–11, 20–21).

take half their sadness and irony from certain energetic and passionate lines of Marvell "To His Coy Mistress." But the exegetical inquirer may wonder whether mermaids considered as "strange sights" (To hear them is in Donne's poem analogous to getting with child a mandrake root) have much to do with Prufrock's mermaids, which seem to be symbols of romance and dynamism, and which incidentally have literary authentication, if they need it, in a line of a sonnet by Gérard de Nerval. This method of inquiry may lead to the conclusion that the given resemblance between Eliot and Donne is without significance and is better not thought of, or the method may have the disadvantage of providing no certain conclusion. Nevertheless, we submit that this is the true and objective way of criticism, as contrasted to what the very uncertainty of exegesis might tempt a second kind of critic to undertake: (2) the way of biographical or genetic inquiry, in which, taking advantage of the fact that Eliot is still alive, and in the spirit of a man who would settle a bet, the critic writes to Eliot and asks what he meant, or if he had Donne in mind. We shall not here weigh the probabilities—whether Eliot would answer that he meant nothing at all, had nothing at all in mind—a sufficiently good answer to such a question—or in an unguarded moment might furnish a clear and, within its limit, irrefutable answer. Our point is that such an answer to such an inquiry would have nothing to do with the poem "Prufrock"; it would not be a critical inquiry. Critical inquiries, unlike bets, are not settled in this way. Critical inquiries are not settled by consulting the oracle.

4. Technique

TECHNIQUE AS DISCOVERY

MARK SCHORER

MODERN criticism, through its exacting scrutiny of literary texts, has demonstrated with finality that in art beauty and truth are indivisible and one. The Keatsian overtones of these terms are mitigated and an old dilemma solved if for beauty we substitute form, and for truth, content. We may, without risk of loss, narrow them even more, and speak of technique and subject matter. Modern criticism has shown us that to speak of content as such is not to speak of art at all, but of experience; and that it is only when we speak of the *achieved* content, the form, the work of art as a work of art, that we speak as critics. The difference between content, or experience, and achieved content, or art, is technique.

When we speak of technique, then, we speak of nearly everything. For technique is the means by which the writer's experience, which is his subject matter, compels him to attend to it; technique is the only means he has of discovering, exploring, developing his subject, of conveying its meaning, and, finally, of evaluating it. And surely it follows that certain techniques are sharper tools than others, and will discover more; that the writer capable of the most exacting technical scrutiny of his subject matter will produce works with the most satisfying content, works with thickness and resonance, works which reverberate, works with maximum meaning.

We are no longer able to regard as seriously intended criticism of poetry which does not assume these generalizations; but the case for fiction has not yet been established. The novel is still read as though its content has some value in itself, as though the subject matter of fiction has greater or lesser value in itself, and as though technique were not a primary but a supplementary element, capable perhaps of not unattractive embellishments upon the surface of the subject, but hardly of its essence. Or technique is thought of in blunter terms than those which one associates with poetry, as such relatively obvious matters as the arrangement of events to create plot; or, within plot, of suspense and climax; or as the means of revealing character motivation, relationship, and development; or as the use of point of view, but point of view as some nearly arbitrary device for the heightening of dramatic interest through the narrowing or broadening of perspective upon the material, rather than as a means toward the positive definition of theme. As for the resources of language, these, somehow, we almost never think of as a part of the technique of fiction—language as used to create a certain texture and tone which in themselves state and define themes and meanings; or language, the counters of our ordinary speech, as forced, through conscious manipulation, into all those larger meanings which our ordinary speech almost never intends. Technique in fiction, all this is a way of saying, we somehow continue to regard as merely a means to organizing material which is "given" rather than as the means of exploring and defining the values in an area of experience which, for the first time *then,* are being given.

Is fiction still regarded in this odd, divided way because it is really less tractable before the critical suppositions which now seem inevitable to poetry? Let us look at some examples: two well-known novels of the past, both by writers who may be described as "primitive," although their relative innocence of technique is of a different sort—Defoe's *Moll Flanders* and Emily Brontë's *Wuthering Heights;* and three well-known novels of this century—*Tono Bungay,* by a writer who claimed to eschew technique; *Sons and Lovers,* by a novelist who, because his ideal of subject matter ("the poetry of the immediate present") led him at last into the fallacy of spontaneous and unchangeable composition, in effect eschewed technique; and *A Portrait of the Artist as a Young Man,* by a novelist whose practice made claims for the supremacy of technique beyond those made by anyone in the past or by anyone else in this century.

Technique in fiction is, of course, all those obvious forms of it which are usually taken to be the whole of it, and many others; but for present purposes, let it be thought of in two respects particularly: the uses to which language, as language, is put to express the quality of the experience in question; and the uses of point of view not only as a mode of dramatic delimitation, but more particularly, of thematic definition. Technique is really what T. S. Eliot means by "convention": any selection, structure, or distortion, any form or rhythm imposed upon the world of action; by means of which, it should be added, our apprehension of the world of action is enriched or renewed. In this sense, everything is technique which is not the lump of experience itself, and one cannot properly say that a writer has no technique, or that he eschews technique, for, being a writer, he cannot do so. We can speak of good and bad technique, of adequate and inadequate, of technique which serves the novel's purpose, or disserves.

II

In the prefatory remarks to *Moll Flanders,* Defoe tells us that he is not writing fiction at all, but editing the journals of a woman of notorious character, and rather to instruct us in the necessities and the joys of virtue than to please us. We do not, of course, take these professions seriously, since nothing in the conduct of the narrative indicates that virtue is either more necessary or more enjoyable than vice. On the contrary, we discover that Moll turns virtuous only after a life of vice has enabled her to do so with security; yet it is precisely for this reason that Defoe's profession of didactic purpose has interest. For the actual morality which the novel enforces is the morality of any commercial culture, the belief that virtue pays—in worldly goods. It is a morality somewhat less than skin deep, having no relation to motives arising from a sense of good and evil, least of all, of evil-*in*-good, but exclusively from the presence or absence of food, drink, linen, damask, silver, and timepieces. It is the morality of measurement, and without in the least intending it, *Moll Flanders* is our classic revelation of the mercantile mind: the morality of measurement, which Defoe has completely neglected to measure. He fails not only to evaluate this material in his announced way, but to evaluate it at all. His announced purpose is, we admit, a pious humbug, and he meant us to read the book as a series of scandalous events; and thanks to his inexhaustible pleasure in excess and exaggeration, this element in the book continues to amuse us. Long before the book has been finished, however, this element has also become an absurdity; but not half the absurdity as that which Defoe did not intend at all—the notion that Moll could live a rich and full life of crime, and yet, repenting, emerge spotless in the end. The point is, of course, that she has no moral being, nor has the book any moral life. Everything is external. Everything can be weighed, measured, handled, paid for in gold, or expiated by a prison term. To this, the whole texture of the novel testifies— the bolts of goods, the inventories, the itemized accounts, the landlady's bills, the lists, the ledgers—all this which taken together comprises what we call Defoe's method of circumstantial realism.

He did not come upon that method by any deliberation; it represents precisely his own world of value, the importance of external circumstance to Defoe. The point of view of Moll is indistinguishable from the point of view of her creator. We discover the meaning of the novel (at unnecessary length, without economy, without emphasis, with almost none of the distortions or the advantages of art) in spite of Defoe, not because of him. Thus the book is not the true chronicle of a disreputable female, but the true allegory of an impoverished soul, the author's; not an anatomy of the criminal class, but of the middle class. And we read it as an unintended comic revelation of self and of social mode. Because he had no adequate resources of technique to separate himself from his material, thereby to discover and to define the meanings of his material, his contribution is not to fiction but to the history of fiction, and to social history.

The situation in *Wuthering Heights* is at once somewhat the same and yet very different. Here, too, the whole novel turns upon itself, but this time to its estimable advantage; here, too, is a revelation of what is perhaps the author's secret world of value, but this time, through what may be an accident of technique, the revelation is meaningfully accomplished. Emily Brontë may merely have stumbled upon the perspectives which define the form and the theme of her book. Whether she knew from the outset, or even at the end, what she was doing, we may doubt; but what she did and did superbly we can see.

We can assume, without at all becoming involved in the author's life but merely from the tone of somnambulistic excess which is generated by the writing itself, that this world of monstrous passion, of dark and gigantic emotional and nervous energy, is for the author, or was in the first place, a world of ideal value; and that the book sets out to persuade us of the moral magnificence of such unmoral passion. We are, I think, expected, in the first place, to take at their own valuation these demonic beings, Heathcliff and Cathy: as special creatures, set apart from the cloddish world about them by their heightened capacity for feeling, set apart, even, from the ordinary objects of human passion as, in their transcendent, sexless relationship, they identify themselves with an uncompromising landscape and cosmic force. Yet this is absurd, as much of the detail that surrounds it ("Other dogs lurked in other recesses") is absurd. The novelist Emily Brontë had to discover these absurdities to the girl Emily; her technique had to evaluate them for what they were, so that we are persuaded that it is not Emily who is mistaken in her estimate of her characters, but they who are mistaken in their estimate of themselves. The theme of the moral magnificence of unmoral passion is an impossible theme to sustain, and what interests us is that it was device—and this time, mere, mechanical device—which taught Emily Brontë—the needs of her temperament to the contrary, all personal longing and reverie to the contrary, perhaps—that this was indeed not at all what her material must mean as art. Technique objectifies.

To lay before us the full character of this passion, to show us how it first comes into being and then comes to dominate the world about it and the life that follows upon it, Emily Brontë gives her material a broad scope in time, lets it, in fact, cut across three generations. And to manage material which is so extensive, she must find a means of narration, points of view, which can encompass that material, and, in her somewhat crude concept of motive, justify its telling. So she chooses a foppish traveler who stumbles into this world of passionate violence, a traveler representing the thin and conventional emotional life of the far world of fashion, who wishes to hear the tale; and for her teller she chooses, almost inevitably, the old family retainer who knows everything, a character as conventional as the other, but this one representing not the conventions of fashion, but the conventions of the humblest moralism.

What has happened is, first, that she has chosen as her narrative perspective those very elements, conventional emotion and conventional morality, which her hero and heroine are meant to transcend with such spectacular magnificence; and second, that she has permitted this perspective to operate throughout a long period of time. And these two elements compel the novelist to see what her unmoral passions come to. Moral magnificence? Not at all; rather, a devastating spectacle of human waste; ashes. For the time of the novel is carried on long enough to show Heathcliff at last an emptied man, burned out by his fever ragings, exhausted and will-less, his passion meaningless at last. And it goes even a little further, to Lockwood, the fop, in the graveyard, sententiously contemplating headstones. Thus in the end the triumph is all on the side of the cloddish world, which survives.

Perhaps not all on that side. For, like Densher at the end of *The Wings of the Dove,* we say, and surely Hareton and the second Cathy say, "We shall never be again as we were!" But there is more point in observing that a certain body of materials, a girl's romantic daydreams, have, through the most conventional devices of fiction, been pushed beyond their inception in fancy to their meanings, their conception as a written book—that they, that is, are not at all as they were.

III

Technique alone objectifies the materials of art; hence technique alone evaluates those materials. This is the axiom which demonstrates itself so devastatingly whenever a writer declares, under the urgent sense of the importance of his materials—whether these are autobiography, or social ideas, or personal passions—whenever such a writer declares that he cannot linger with technical refinements. That art will not tolerate such a writer H. G. Wells handsomely proves. His enormous literary energy included no respect for the techniques of his medium, and his medium takes its revenge upon his bumptiousness. "I have never taken any very great pains about writing. I am outside the hierarchy of conscious and deliberate writers altogether. I am the absolute antithesis of Mr. James Joyce. . . . Long ago, living in close conversational proximity to Henry James, Joseph Conrad, and Mr. Ford Madox Hueffer, I escaped from under their immense artistic preoccupations by calling myself a journalist." Precisely. And he escaped—he disappeared—from literature into the annals of an era.

Yet what confidence! "Literature," Wells said, "is not jewelry, it has quite other aims than perfection, and the more one thinks of 'how it is done' the less one gets it done. These critical indulgences lead along a fatal path, away from every natural interest towards a preposterous emptiness of technical effort, a monstrous egotism of artistry, of which the later work of Henry James is the monumental warning. 'It,' the subject, the thing or the thought, has long since disappeared in these amazing works; nothing remains but the way it has been manipulated." Seldom has a literary theorist been so totally wrong; for what we learn as James grows for us and Wells disappears is that without what he calls "manipulation," there *is* no "it," no "subject" in art. There is again only social history.

The virtue of the modern novelist—from James and Conrad down—is not only that he pays so much attention to his medium, but that, when he pays most, he discovers through it a new subject matter, and a greater one. Under the "immense artistic preoccupations" of James and Conrad and Joyce, the form of the novel changed, and with the technical change, analogous changes took place in substance, in point of view, in the whole conception of fiction. And the final lesson of the modern novel is that technique is not the secondary thing that it seemed to Wells, some external machination, a mechanical affair, but a deep and primary operation; not only that technique *contains* intellectual and moral implications, but that it *discovers* them. For a writer like Wells, who wished to give us the intellectual and the moral history of our times, the lesson is a hard one; it tells us that the order of intellect and the order of morality do not exist at all, in art, except as they are organized in the order of art.

Wells' ambitions were very large. "Before we have done, we will have all life within the scope of the novel." But that is where life already is, within the scope of the novel; where it needs to be brought is into novels. In Wells we have all the important topics in life, but no good novels. He was not asking too much of art, or asking that it include more than it happily can; he was not asking anything of it—as art, which is all that it can give, and that is everything.

A novel like *Tono Bungay,* generally thought to be Wells' best, is therefore instructive. "I want to tell—*myself,"* says George, the hero, "and my impressions of the thing as a whole"—the thing as a whole being the collapse of traditional British institutions in the twentieth century. George "tells himself" in terms of three stages in his life which have rough equivalents in modern British social history, and this is, to be sure, a plan, a framework; but it is the framework of Wells' abstract thinking, not of his craftsmanship, and the primary demand which one makes of such a book as this—that means be discovered whereby the dimensions of the hero contain the experiences he recounts—is never met. The novelist flounders through a series of literary imitations—from an early Dickensian episode, through a kind of Shavian interlude, through a Conradian episode, to a Jules Verne vision at the end. The significant failure is in that end, and in the way that it defeats not only the entire social analysis of the bulk of the novel, but Wells' own ends as a thinker. For at last George finds a purpose in science. "I decided that in power and knowledge lay the salvation of my life; the secret that would fill my need; that to these things I would give myself."

But science, power, and knowledge are summed up at last in a destroyer. As far as one can tell Wells intends no irony, although he may here have come upon the essence of the major irony in modern history. The novel ends in a kind of meditative rhapsody which denies every value that the book had been aiming toward. For all the kinds of social waste which Wells has been describing, this is the most inclusive, the final waste. Thus he gives us in the end not a novel, but a hypothesis; not any individual destiny, but a theory of the future; and not his theory of the future, but a nihilistic vision quite opposite from everything that he meant to represent. With a minimum of attention to the virtues of technique, Wells might still not have written a good novel; but he would at any rate have established a point of view and a tone which would have told us what he meant.

To say what one means in art is never easy, and the more intimately one is implicated in one's material, the more difficult it is. If, besides, one commits fiction to a therapeutic function which is to be operative not on the audience but on the author, declaring, as D. H. Lawrence did, that "One sheds one's sicknesses in books, repeats and presents again one's emotions to be master of them," the difficulty is vast. It is an acceptable theory only with the qualification that technique, which objectifies, is under no other circumstances so imperative. For merely to repeat one's emotions, merely to look into one's heart and write, is also merely to repeat the round of emotional bondage. If our books are to be exercises in self-analysis, then technique must—and alone can—take the place of the absent analyst.

Lawrence, in the relatively late Introduction to his *Collected Poems,* made that distinction of the amateur between his "real" poems and his "composed" poems, between the poems which expressed his demon directly and created their own form "willy-nilly," and the poems which, through the hocus-pocus of technique, he spuriously put together and could, if necessary, revise. His belief in a "poetry of the immediate present," poetry in which nothing is fixed, static, or final, where all is shimmeriness and impermanence and vitalistic essence, arose from this mistaken notion of technique. And from this notion, an unsympathetic critic like D. S. Savage can construct a case which shows Lawrence driven "concurrently to the dissolution of personality and the dissolution of art." The argument suggests that Lawrence's early crucial novel, *Sons and Lovers,* is another example of meanings confused by an impatience with technical resources.

The novel has two themes: the crippling effects of a mother's love on the emotional development of her son; and the "split" between kinds of love, physical and spiritual, which the son develops, the kinds represented by two young women, Clara and Miriam. The two themes should, of course, work together, the second being, actually, the result of the first: this "split" is the "crippling." So one would expect to see the novel developed, and so Lawrence, in his famous letter to Edward Garnett, where he says that Paul is left at the end with the "drift towards death," apparently thought he had developed it. Yet in the last few sentences of the novel, Paul rejects his desire for extinction and turns toward "the faintly humming, glowing town," to life—as nothing in his previous history persuades us that he could unfalteringly do.

The discrepancy suggests that the book may reveal certain confusions between intention and performance.

One of these is the contradiction between Lawrence's explicit characterizations of the mother and father and his tonal evaluations of them. It is a problem not only of style (of the contradiction between expressed moral epithets and the more general texture of the prose which applies to them) but of point of view. Morel and Lawrence are never separated, which is a way of saying that Lawrence maintains for himself in this book the confused attitude of his character. The mother is a "proud, *honorable* soul," but the father has a "small, *mean* head." This is the sustained contrast; the epithets are characteristic of the whole, and they represent half of Lawrence's feelings. But what is the other half? Which of these characters is given his real sympathy—the hard, self-righteous, aggressive, demanding mother who comes through to us, or the simple, direct, gentle, downright, fumbling, ruined father? There are two attitudes here. Lawrence (and Morel) loves his mother, but he also hates her for compelling his love; and he hates his father with the true Freudian jealousy, but he also loves him for what he is in himself, and he sympathizes more deeply with him because his wholeness has been destroyed by the mother's domination, just as his, Lawrence-Morel's, has been.

This is a psychological tension which disrupts the form of the novel and obscures its meaning, because neither the contradiction in style nor the confusion in point of view is made to right itself. Lawrence is merely repeating his emotions, and he avoids an austerer technical scrutiny of his material because it would compel him to master them. He would not let the artist be stronger than the man.

The result is that, at the same time that the book condemns the mother, it justifies her; at the same time that it shows Paul's failure, it offers rationalizations which place the failure elsewhere. The handling of the girl, Miriam, if viewed closely, is pathetic in what it signifies for Lawrence, both as man and artist. For Miriam is made the mother's scapegoat, and in a different way from the way that she was in life. The central section of the novel is shot through with alternate statements as to the source of the difficulty: Paul is unable to love Miriam wholly, and Miriam can love only his spirit. These contradictions appear sometimes within single paragraphs, and the point of view is never adequately objectified and sustained to tell us which is true. The material is never seen as material; the writer is caught in it exactly as firmly as he was caught in his experience of it. "That's how women are with me," said Paul. "They want me like mad, but they don't want to belong to me." So he might have said, and believed it; but at the end of the novel, Lawrence is still saying that, and himself believing it.

For the full history of this technical failure, one must read *Sons and Lovers* carefully and then learn the history of the manuscript from the book called *D. H. Lawrence: A Personal Record,* by one E. T., who was Miriam in life. The basic situation is clear enough. The first theme—the crippling effects of the mother's love—is developed right through to the end; and then suddenly, in the last few sentences, turns on itself, and Paul gives himself to life, not death. But all the way through, the insidious rationalizations of the second theme have crept in to destroy the artistic coherence of the work. A "split" would occur in Paul; but as the split is treated, it is superimposed upon rather than developed in support of the first theme. It is a rationalization made from it. If Miriam is made to insist on spiritual love, the meaning and the power of theme one are reduced; yet Paul's weakness is disguised. Lawrence could not separate the investigating analyst, who must be objective, from Lawrence, the subject of the book; and the sickness was not healed, the emotion not mastered, the novel not perfected. All this, and the character of a whole career, would have been altered if Lawrence had allowed his technique to discover the full meaning of his subject.

A Portrait of the Artist as a Young Man, like *Tono Bungay* and *Sons and Lovers,* is autobiographical, but unlike these it analyzes its material rigorously, and it defines the value and the quality of its experience not by appended comment or moral epithet, but by the texture of the style. The theme of *A Portrait,* a young artist's alienation from his environment, is explored and evaluated through three different styles and methods as Stephen Dedalus moves from childhood through boyhood into maturity. The opening pages are written in something like the Ulyssesean stream of consciousness, as the environment impinges directly on the consciousness of the infant and the child, a strange, opening world which the mind does not yet subject to questioning, selection, or judgment. But this style changes very soon, as the boy begins to explore his surroundings; and as his sensuous experience of the world is enlarged, it takes on heavier and heavier rhythms and a fuller and fuller body of sensuous detail, until it reaches a crescendo of romantic opulence in the emotional climaxes which mark Stephen's rejection of domestic and religious values. Then gradually the style subsides into the austere intellectuality of the final sections, as he defines to himself the outlines of the artistic task which is to usurp his maturity.

A highly self-conscious use of style and method defines the quality of experience in each of these sections, and, it is worth pointing out in connection with the third and concluding section, the style and method evaluate the experience. What has happened to Stephen is, of course, a progressive alienation from the life around him as he progressed in his initiation into it, and by the end of the novel, the alienation is complete. The final portion of the novel, fascinating as it may be for the developing esthetic creed of Stephen-Joyce, is peculiarly bare. The life experience was not bare, as we know from *Stephen Hero;* but Joyce is forcing technique to comment. In essence, Stephen's alienation is a denial of the human environment; it is a loss; and the austere discourse of the final section, abstract and almost wholly without sensuous detail or strong rhythm, tells us of that loss. It is a loss so great that the texture of the notation-like prose here suggests that the end is really all an illusion, that when Stephen tells us and himself that he is going forth to forge in the smithy of his soul the uncreated conscience of his race, we are to infer from the very quality of the icy, abstract void he now inhabits, the implausibility of his aim. For *Ulysses* does not create the conscience of the race; it creates our consciousness.

In the very last two or three paragraphs of the novel, the style changes once more, reverts from the bare, notative kind to the romantic prose of Stephen's adolescence. "Away! Away! The spell of arms and voices; the white arms of roads, their promise of close embraces and the black arms of tall ships that stand against the moon, their tale of distant nations. They are held out to say: We are alone—come." Might one not say that the austere ambition is founded on adolescent longing? That the excessive intellectual severity of one style is the counterpart of the excessive lyric relaxation of the other? And that the final passage of *A Portrait* punctuates the illusory nature of the whole ambition?

For *Ulysses* does not create a conscience. Stephen, in *Ulysses,* is a little older, and gripped now by guilt, but he is still the cold young man divorced from the human no less than the institutional environment. The environment of urban life finds a separate embodiment in the character of Bloom, and Bloom is as lost as Stephen, though touchingly groping for moorings. Each of the two is weakened by his inability to reach out, or to do more than reach out to the other. Here, then, is the theme again, more fully stated, as it were in counterpoint.

But if Stephen is not much older, Joyce is. He is older as an artist not only because he can create and lavish his godlike pity on a Leopold

Bloom, but also because he knows now what both Stephen and Bloom mean, and *how much,* through the most brilliant technical operation ever made in fiction, they can be made to mean. Thus *Ulysses,* through the imaginative force which its techniques direct, is like a pattern of concentric circles, with the immediate human situation at its center, this passing on and out to the whole dilemma of modern life, this passing on and out beyond that to a vision of the cosmos, and this to the mythical limits of our experience. If we read *Ulysses* with more satisfaction than any other novel of this century, it is because its author held an attitude toward technique and the technical scrutiny of subject matter which enabled him to order, within a single work and with superb coherence, the greatest amount of our experience.

IV

In the United States during the last twenty-five years, we have had many big novels but few good ones. A writer like James T. Farrell apparently assumes that by endless redundancy in the description of the surface of American life, he will somehow write a book with the scope of *Ulysses.* Thomas Wolfe apparently assumed that by the mere disgorging of the raw material of his experience he would give us at last our epic. But except in a physical sense, these men have hardly written novels at all.

The books of Thomas Wolfe were, of course, journals, and the primary role of his publisher in transforming these journals into the semblance of novels is notorious. For the crucial act of the artist, the unique act which is composition, a sympathetic editorial blue pencil and scissors were substituted. The result has excited many people, especially the young, and the ostensibly critical have observed the prodigal talent with the wish that it might have been controlled. Talent there was, if one means by talent inexhaustible verbal energy, excessive response to personal experience, and a great capacity for auditory imitativeness, yet all of this has nothing to do with the novelistic quality of the written result; for until the talent is controlled, the material organized, the content achieved, there is simply the man and his life. It remains to be demonstrated that Wolfe's conversations were any less interesting as novels than his books, which is to say that his books are without interest as novels. As with Lawrence our response to the books is determined, not by their qualities as novels, but by our response to him and his qualities as a temperament.

This is another way of saying that Thomas Wolfe never really knew what he was writing *about. Of Time and the River* is merely a euphemism for "Of a Man and his Ego." It is possible that had his conception of himself and of art included an adequate respect for technique and the capacity to pursue it, Wolfe would have written a great novel on his true subject—the dilemma of romantic genius; it was his true subject, but it remains his undiscovered subject, it is the subject which *we* must dig out for him, because he himself had neither the lamp nor the pick to find it in and mine it out of the labyrinths of his experience. Like Emily Brontë, Wolfe needed a point of view beyond his own which would separate his material and its effect.

With Farrell, the situation is opposite. He knows quite well what his subject is and what he wishes to tell us about it, but he hardly needs the novel to do so. It is significant that in sheer clumsiness of style no living writer exceeds him, for his prose is asked to perform no service beyond communication of the most rudimentary kind of fact. For his ambitions the style of the newspaper and the lens of the documentary camera would be quite adequate, yet consider the diminution which Leopold Bloom, for example, would suffer, if he were to be viewed from these, the technical perspectives of James Farrell. Under the eye of this technique, the material does not yield up enough; indeed, it shrinks.

More and more writers in this century have felt that naturalism as a method imposes on them strictures which prevent them from exploring through all the resources of technique the full amplifications of their subjects, and that thus it seriously limits the possible breadth of esthetic meaning and response. James Farrell is almost unique in the complacency with which he submits to the blunt techniques of naturalism; and his fiction is correspondingly repetitive and flat.

That naturalism had a sociological and disciplinary value in the nineteenth century is obvious; it enabled the novel to grasp materials and make analyses which had eluded it in the past, and to grasp them boldly; but even then it did not tell us enough of what, in Virginia Woolf's phrase, is "really real," nor did it provide the means to the maximum of reality coherently contained. Even the Flaubertian ideal of objectivity seems, today, an unnecessarily limited view of objectivity, for as almost every good writer of this century shows us, it is quite as possible to be objective about subjective states as it is to be objective about the circumstantial surfaces of life. Dublin, in *Ulysses,* is a moral setting: not only a city portrayed in the naturalistic fashion of Dickens' London, but also a map of the modern psyche with its oblique and baffled purposes. The second level of reality in no way invalidates the first, and a writer like Joyce shows us that, if the artist truly respects his medium, he can be objective about both at once. What we need in fiction is a devoted fidelity to every technique which will help us to discover and to evaluate our subject matter, and more than that, to discover the amplifications of meaning of which our subject matter is capable.

Most modern novelists have felt this demand upon them. André Gide allowed one of his artist-heroes to make an observation which considerably resembles an observation we have quoted from Wells. "My novel hasn't got a subject . . . Let's say, if you prefer it, it hasn't got *one* subject . . . 'A slice of life,' the naturalist school said. The great defect of that school is that it always cuts its slice in the same direction; in time, lengthwise. Why not in breadth? Or in depth? As for me I should like not to cut at all. Please understand; I should like to put everything into my novel." Wells, with his equally large blob of potential material, did not know how to cut it to the novel's taste; Gide cut, of course—in every possible direction. Gide and others. And those "cuts" are all the new techniques which modern fiction has given us. None, perhaps, is more important than that inheritance from French symbolism which Huxley, in the glittering wake of Gide, called "the musicalization of fiction." Conrad anticipated both when he wrote that the novel "must strenuously aspire to the plasticity of sculpture, to the colour of painting, and to the magic suggestiveness of music—which is the art of arts," and when he said of that early but wonderful piece of symbolist fiction, *The Heart of Darkness,* "It was like another art altogether. That sombre theme had to be given a sinister resonance, a tonality of its own, a continued vibration that, I hoped, would hang in the air and dwell on the ear after the last note had been struck."

The analogy with music, except as a metaphor, is inexact, and except as it points to techniques which fiction can employ as fiction, not very useful to our sense of craftsmanship. It has had an approximate exactness in only one work, Joyce's final effort, an effort unique in literary history, *Finnegans Wake,* and here, of course, those readers willing to make the effort Joyce demands, discovering an inexhaustible wealth and scope, are most forcibly reminded of the primary importance of technique to subject, and of their indivisibility.

The techniques of naturalism inevitably curtail subject and often leave it in its original area, that of undefined social experience. Those of our writers who, stemming from this tradition, yet, at their best, achieve a novelistic definition of social experience—writers like the occasional Sherwood Anderson, William Carlos Williams, the occasional Erskine Caldwell, Nathaniel West, and Ira Wolfert in *Tucker's People*—have done so by pressing naturalism far beyond itself, into positively Gothic distortions. The structural machinations of Dos Passos and the lyrical interruptions of Steinbeck are the desperate maneuvers of men committed to a method of whose limitations they despair. They are our symbolists *manqué,* who end as allegorists.

Our most accomplished novels leave no such impressions of desperate and intentional struggle, yet their precise technique and their determination to make their prose work in the service of their subjects have been the measure of their accomplishment. Hemingway's *The Sun Also Rises* and Wescott's *The Pilgrim Hawk* are consummate works of art not because they may be measured by some external, neoclassical notion of form, but because their forms are so exactly equivalent with their subjects, and because the evaluation of their subjects exists in their styles.

Hemingway has recently said that his contribution to younger writers lay in a certain necessary purification of the language; but the claim has doubtful value. The contribution of his prose was to his subject, and the terseness of style for which his early work is justly celebrated is no more valuable, as an end in itself, than the baroque involutedness of Faulkner's prose, or the cold elegance of Wescott's. Hemingway's early subject, the exhaustion of value, was perfectly investigated and invested by his bare style, and in story after story, no meaning at all is to be inferred from the fiction except as the style itself suggests that there is no meaning in life. This style, more than that, was the perfect technical substitute for the conventional commentator; it expresses and it measures that peculiar morality of the stiff lip which Hemingway borrowed from athletes. It is an instructive lesson, furthermore, to observe how the style breaks down when Hemingway moves into the less congenial subject matter of social affirmation: how the style breaks down, the effect of verbal economy as mute suffering is lost, the personality of the writer, no longer protected by the objectification of an adequate technique, begins its offensive intrusion, and the entire structural integrity slackens. Inversely, in the stories and the early novels, the technique was the perfect embodiment of the subject and it gave that subject its astonishing largeness of effect and of meaning.

One should correct Buffon and say that style is the subject. In Wescott's *Pilgrim Hawk*—a novel which bewildered its many friendly critics by the apparent absence of subject—the subject, the story, is again in the style itself. This novel, which is a triumph of the sustained point of view, is only bewildering if we try to make a story out of the narrator's observations upon others; but if we read his observations as oblique and unrecognized observations upon himself the story emerges with perfect coherence, and it reverberates with meaning, is as suited to continuing reflection as the greatest lyrics.

The rewards of such respect for the medium as the early Hemingway and the occasional Wescott have shown may be observed in every good

writer we have. The involutions of Faulkner's style are the perfect
equivalent of his involved structures, and the two together are the perfect
representation of the moral labyrinths he explores, and of the ruined world
which his novels repeatedly invoke and in which these labyrinths exist.
The cultivated sensuosity of Katherine Anne Porter's style—as of Eudora
Welty's and Jean Stafford's—has charm in itself, of course, but no more
than with these others does it have esthetic value in itself; its values lie in
the subtle means by which sensuous details become symbols, and in the
way the symbols provide a network which is the story, and which at the
same time provides the writer and us with a refined moral insight by means
of which to test it. When we put such writers against a writer like William
Saroyan, whose respect is reserved for his own temperament, we are ap-
palled by the stylistic irresponsibility we find in him, and by the almost total
absence of theme, or defined subject matter, and the abundance of unwar-
ranted feeling. Such a writer inevitably becomes a sentimentalist because
he has no means by which to measure his emotion. Technique, at last, is
measure.

These writers, from Defoe to Porter, are of unequal and very different
talent, and technique and talent are, of course, after a point, two different
things. What Joyce gives us in one direction, Lawrence, for all his imperfections as a technician, gives us in another, even though it is not usually the
direction of art. Only in some of his stories and in a few of his poems, where
the demands of technique are less sustained and the subject matter is not
autobiographical, Lawrence, in a different way from Joyce, comes to the
same esthetic fulfillment. Emily Brontë, with what was perhaps her intuitive
grasp of the need to establish a tension between her subject matter and
her perspective upon it, achieves a similar fulfillment; and, curiously, in
the same way and certainly by intuition alone, Hemingway's early work
makes a moving splendor from nothingness.

And yet, whatever one must allow to talent and forgive in technique,
one risks no generalization in saying that modern fiction at its best has been
peculiarly conscious of itself and of its tools. The technique of modern
fiction, at once greedy and fastidious, achieves as its subject matter not
some singleness, some topic or thesis, but the whole of the modern consciousness. It discovers the complexity of the modern spirit, the difficulty
of personal morality, and the fact of evil—all the untractable elements
under the surface which a technique of the surface alone cannot approach.
It shows us—in Conrad's words, from *Victory*—that we all live in an "age
in which we are camped like bewildered travelers in a garish, unrestful
hotel," and while it puts its hard light on our environment, it penetrates,
with its sharp weapons, the depths of our bewilderment. These are not two

things, but only an adequate technique can show them as one. In a realist like Farrell, we have the environment only, which we know from the newspapers; in a subjectivist like Wolfe, we have the bewilderment only, which we record in our own diaries and letters. But the true novelist gives them to us together, and thereby increases the effect of each, and reveals each in its full significance.

Elizabeth Bowen, writing of Lawrence, said of modern fiction, "We want the naturalistic surface, but with a kind of internal burning. In Lawrence every bush burns." But the bush burns brighter in some places than in others, and it burns brightest when a passionate private vision finds its objectification in exacting technical search. If the vision finds no such objectification, as in Wolfe and Saroyan, there is a burning without a bush. In our committed realists, who deny the resources of art for the sake of life, whose technique forgives both innocence and slovenliness—in Defoe and Wells and Farrell—there is a bush but it does not burn. There, at first glance, the bush is only a bush; and then, when we look again, we see that, really, the thing is dead.

5. *Ideas and Morals*

THE ESTHETIC JUDGMENT AND THE ETHICAL JUDGMENT

NORMAN FOERSTER

I

"W E, it seems, are critical; we are embarrassed with second thoughts; we cannot enjoy anything for hankering to know whereof the pleasure consists; we are lined with eyes; we see with our feet; the time is infected with Hamlet's unhappiness—'Sicklied o'er with the pale cast of thought.'" These are the words

"The Esthetic Judgment and the Ethical Judgment," by Norman Foerster, from *The Intent of the Critic*, D. A. Stauffer, ed., reprinted by permission of Princeton University Press.

in which Emerson, a hundred years ago, characterized our modern age, an age of criticism.

It is sometimes remarked that there is something wrong with an age which goes in predominantly for criticism. Unhappily there are many other reasons for thinking that there is something wrong with our age. That is precisely why we need criticism. Our modern age, bent upon a return to Nature, has more and more prostituted the humanities—the civilizing forces of religion, philosophy, literature and the arts; and now the totalitarian states, employing with sinister effect the one great creative force of the modern world, science, are intent upon completing the return to Nature, the return to the primitive. These are the times that try men's souls, to see whether we still have souls. These are the times that try men's minds, to see whether we can clarify the phrases we glibly repeat to summon up courage, phrases such as "preserving the values of civilization," "preserving the democratic way of life," "preserving the dignity of man." Without a keener and more earnestly affirmative criticism than we have had, we shall not even know what we wish to preserve, or why it is worth preserving.

Because there is nearly everything wrong with our age, the kind of criticism which can render the greatest service is a general criticism, taking into account the whole of our civilization. Granted that our civilization is highly complex, still we shall have to deal with it in the light of a few simple ideas firmly established. The greater the degree of specialization— the more men are sundered from each other by their preoccupations—to the same extent the need grows for some kind of intellectual and spiritual clearing-house. I refer to the kind of criticism, ranging into diverse fields and vitally connecting them, exemplified in the nineteenth century by Carlyle, Ruskin, Arnold, and Emerson, in the early twentieth century by Chesterton, Babbitt, and More, and in the present day by Jacques Maritain and Lewis Mumford. Such men are not merely critics of literature, they are critics of the foundations of our whole culture.

II

I am to deal in this paper, however, not with general but with literary criticism. What is the task of literary criticism? Let me begin with some negations.

Literary criticism is not concerned with literary works in respect to their *causes*. In our scientific age, it has been customary to think of the intention of a literary work as the sum of many and diverse causes. These causes lie in the author's experience, external and internal, the relation between the world in which he lives, which spreads round him and also back into the past, and his own inner constitution, his developing capacities as man and artist. For each of his works, it is conceived, there is an intricate complex of causes, but we can never be sure that we have found all of them. The study of these causes is a form of history, a blend of literary history, intellectual history, and social history. As scholars know, it is a fascinating study in itself, and it may offer valuable hints to the literary critic, who must use all means to understand the work with which he is dealing. Possibly it is capable of offering more help to the critic than has sometimes been allowed for it by those, including myself, who have reacted against the exaggerated estimate of its services by the sons of Taine; no one, admittedly, has thought through with any finality the relations of the two fields of activity. Clearly, however, the historical study of literature is not literary criticism but at best a preparation for it.

Nor is literary criticism concerned with literary works in respect to their ulterior *effects*. When a work is published—given to the public—it produces (or so the author hopes) some effect upon the public. It may influence the direction of thought or feeling, as in the case of Emerson's *Essays*. It may even lead to more or less change in the realm of practical affairs, ethical, social, political. Thus, *Uncle Tom's Cabin* became one of the causes of the War Between the States, and latterly *The Grapes of Wrath* has begotten a vigorous social response. The high potency of the effects of literary works was a vital concern with Plato, who expelled from his republic all poets except those singing hymns to the gods and praises of famous men, and it is today a vital concern with the dictators of Europe. It has also been a vital concern with American Humanists and Neo-Scholastics, who, since Babbitt's book on *Literature and the American College,* have given fresh life to Matthew Arnold's contention that not science but great literature is the central instrument in the educational process of making men human. And it has been a vital concern with Marxist and other Leftist critics, who realize that literature may become one instrument in the process of making men socialists. Yet it must be admitted that all practical effects, whether good, bad, or indifferent, are extrinsic to the literary work, carrying us away from the work. As causes take us back, effects take us forward. The literary critic must not go either way: he must stay with the work itself: he must deal with its values intrinsically.

Now if there is any sense at all in the history of criticism from Greek antiquity to the present century, two kinds of value are inherent in literature, esthetic and ethical. Let it be granted at once that esthetic value and ethical value are interdependent and, in all strictness, blended inseparably; still, it has not been found possible to discuss them both adequately at one and the same time. Let it be granted also that, logically if not practically, esthetic value must come first, since this determines whether a piece of writing is literature or a piece of non-literary writing.

III

An essential task of the literary critic is to contemplate, analyze, and judge a literary work as a work of art, as a thing of beauty, in its esthetic character. Literature is an art, a form of skill in making, the thing made being a thing of beauty and therefore "a joy forever." The critic is interested, like the artist, in technique, the process of making, but especially he is interested in structure, the esthetic properties of the thing made, its architectonic features such as unity, balance, emphasis, rhythm, and the like, the shapely pattern resulting when all the materials, that is, the emotions, sense perceptions, images, allusions, ideas, ethical insights, have been brought into more or less complete interplay and fullness of tension. When the whole work finally springs to life in his mind, the critic experiences a delight, a joy in the thing of beauty, akin to that of the artist when his vision at length fell into shape. He has a revel similar to that of Mozart, who tells us that musical ideas came streaming to him, began to join one another and kindle his imagination, and formed in his mind into a larger and larger piece till the composition, though unwritten, was complete, and could be seen at a glance. "Then," he said, "I don't hear the notes one after another, as they are hereafter to be played, but it is as if in my fancy they were all at once. And that *is* a revel (*das ist nun ein Schmaus*)." Inferior works of art do not afford this esthetic experience, and in the greatest art the excitement is imperfect. The critic thus has esthetic exaltations, satisfactions, annoyances, boredoms, which it is his business, as a rational judge, to justify in terms of the esthetic qualities of the works themselves.

I need not say more concerning esthetic judgment; no responsible person questions that it is the business of the literary critic, as of all art critics. A suggestive fact must now be noted: that whereas criticism in the other arts is usually esthetic, criticism in the art of literature is usually not. Why this is I shall inquire presently. Here let me pay tribute to a group of distinguished critics who have so earnestly concentrated upon the esthetic aspect that they have developed a new expertness in the analysis of poetic patterns. Never before, at least in English and American letters, have we had so much close reading, sensitive discrimination, free-ranging alertness expressed in a subtle style suited to the task. I refer, of course, to men like T. S. Eliot, William Empson, John Crowe Ransom, Allen Tate, Cleanth Brooks, and R. P. Blackmur, who, though they have had other interests as well, have excelled in practical criticism of the esthetic aspect of poems.

That I am not disposed to underrate their achievement, or the importance of the esthetic point of view, I have perhaps indicated by sponsoring, at the University of Iowa, the recognition of imaginative writing as an art in the graduate school, taking the stand that a play, a novel, a book of verse is as pertinent and honorable in the training of a literary doctor as an academic study in language or literary history or literary criticism.

Having said this, I feel the freer to attack the heresy to which our esthetic critics are inclined, the heresy of the esthetic to which Poe, for example, subscribed. The heresy of the esthetic seems to me as bad as the heresy of the didactic. Both endeavor to make partial truth serve as the whole truth.[1] Both tend to take us away from literature, the one into problems of morals, the other into problems of esthetics. Indeed, esthetic critics, judging from their line of argument, appear to have scant interest in literature. They begin by speaking of literature; then they turn to the art of literature; then to the art of poetry; then to one kind of poetry, the lyric; and then to one kind of lyric, the metaphysical, in which the poem, as they put it, must not *mean* but *be,* in which substance and form are one, as in the art of music. Now, the view that music, the great modern art, is also the purest art came into vogue with romanticism, along with the corollary view that the essence of literature is lyricism. If music is the purest art, literature is obviously the impurest, so impure that we actually speak of "literature and the arts," as if literature were not an art at all.

But there is another way of ranking the arts, according to their degree of articulateness. From this point of view music is the least and literature the most articulate art. While literature often strives in vain to equal music in wedding form and substance, its special perfection is an articulateness for which the other arts often strive in vain. Whereas music, in the line of Sidney Lanier, is "Love in search of a word," literature begins with the word, and builds its structures in terms of sentences, that is to say, propositions. In literature, reason and the ethical imagination, contemplating man and the grounds of his happiness and unhappiness, speak to us with an incomparable fullness and clarity; and they do this with maximum facility in the drama, because the essence of drama, as of human life, is action, external action in relation to the inner springs of action. Conceived as the most articulate art, literature has its center, not in the lyric, but rather in the drama, which lies about midway between works like *The Education*

---

[1] Heresies of many sorts have thrived in modern culture because it is so divisive and specialist. The concept of the "economic man," whose activity is independent of moral and political considerations, is but one instance of our tendency to seek purity of thought and achieve unreality. The esthetic man is as artificial as the economic man, as George F. Thomas pointed out in his inaugural lecture at Princeton, "Religion in an Age of Secularism," 1940.

of Henry Adams or *The Flowering of New England,* where literature begins
to be differentiated from non-literary prose, and the poems of Vachel
Lindsay or Gertrude Stein, where literature is on the verge of passing over
into music. Or we might reasonably say that literature has its center in the
narrative poem or in the novel, since such works as the *Iliad* and *Wilhelm
Meister,* like *Hamlet* and *Ghosts,* are, whatever their personal content and
accent, primarily imaginative representations of life.[1]

IV

We have now come upon the explanation of the fact which I remarked
a while ago, that whereas criticism in the other arts is generally esthetic,
criticism in the field of literature tends to neglect the esthetic aspect. I deplore the neglect, but the reason for it seems plain enough: that the ethical
or philosophical aspect of literature is not only a legitimate but an indispensable concern of the literary critic. I believe that Aristotle was right in
thinking of imaginative literature as not only an art giving pleasure or
delight, but as a reasonable imitation of life, of human action and human
nature; in thinking of imaginative literature as philosophical in a way in
which history and science are not. I do not find it necessary to follow Max
Eastman and some of his successors in conceiving that all we *know* about
life is what science tells us and that the area in which poetry may disport is
fast shrinking to nothing. There is, and will always be, not only scientific
but human knowledge, that sort of knowledge that we derive from the
humanities, notably from literature, knowledge such as we may secure,
as Dr. Johnson recognized, by reading Shakespeare, "by reading human
sentiments in human language, by scenes from which a hermit may estimate
the transactions of the world, and a confessor predict the progress of the
passions." Not a little of Johnson's wisdom, which exceeded that of most
of our psychologists and sociologists of today, came from great literature.

That poetry contains wisdom was well understood not only by Johnson, but also by Sidney, Dryden, Coleridge, Shelley, Arnold, Emerson,
indeed pretty much everybody till we arrive at a few esthetic specialists
of the present day. Traditionally they thought of wisdom as instruction, and
conceived of the poet as a teacher, an unfortunate terminology because it

---

[1] Works like these, in their rich articulation, would be more competent than
lyrics to enlighten the proverbial Martian as to the nature of literature and the nature
of mundane life. The lyric, as a fine distillate, a terse comment or gloss upon the text
of life, is capable of an articulateness which is incisive rather than abundant. Its
special character is, however, unlimited implication, an inexhaustible indeterminate-
ness approaching that of music.

seems to emphasize the effects of literature, which are the province of the sociological and moral critic. The literary critic is concerned rather with the wisdom *inherent* in literature, with the judgment of its ethical soundness, the firmness and range of its imitation of life. He repeats the Horatian formula not because it is traditional but because its soundness has made it traditional, saying with Robert Frost, the wisest of our contemporary poets, that a poem "begins in delight and ends in wisdom," or with Paul Engle that a poem affords a "wise excitement" or "intense wisdom." He is content to say, if you insist, that delight is all, but in that case he will add at once that the delight comes from the wisdom expressed as well as from the expression of the wisdom.

If, then, literary criticism is an esthetic judgment, it is equally an ethical judgment, and both judgments are needed to determine the "greatness" of literary works. A poem like "A Psalm of Life" falls short on both counts: it is bungling in its art, stereotyped in its wisdom. A poem like "Tintern Abbey" is great esthetically; as we have come increasingly to see, it is ethically vital but unsound; in sum, this poem is a superb expression of unwisdom. On the other hand, the poem which Wordsworth addressed to Milton (along with some of his other sonnets deeply inspired by the nobility of the English tradition) has greatness on the two counts, is both finely formed and wisely conceived.

To estimate the greatness of literary works, which is the main business of literary criticism, what is needed is a rounded estimate, esthetic and ethical. In a truly rounded estimate, the two tasks will be inseparable, will interpenetrate as intimately as in the organic unity of the literary work itself. But in fact such an organic criticism is impossible, and indeed all interpretation and evaluation is, strictly speaking, inept. Change the words and you change the thought. Paraphrase and you rob the text of much of its meaning. Translate and you impoverish or else create a new thing. Say anything whatever about a piece of literature in either its esthetic or its ethical aspect and you dilute or denature what is there. The only completely scrupulous critic is, therefore, the completely silent critic. Since this asceticism is more than critic flesh can endure, critics may be permitted to go on criticizing as well as they can, turning, again and again, consciously or not, from one kind of judgment to the other, violating the simultaneity of literature by resorting to alternation. Or they may be permitted to let one kind of judgment preponderate, because it is the kind in which they are interested or gifted, provided that they leave room, in their total theory, for others to practise more fully the other kind of judgment. Unfortunately some critics will be tempted to go farther, to become exclusive and intolerant, to employ one of the two judgments and decry the other. Preoccupied with a half-truth, such critics will fall into the heresy of estheticism or the heresy of didacticism.[1]

V

The theory of literary criticism I have sketched is that of the so-called Neo-Humanists. Why have they so inadequately practised it? Why has their interest in the esthetic properties of literature always been so definitely secondary, their interest in its ethical properties so definitely primary? Why did Babbitt and More, the leaders of the group, display an increasing aloofness even from literature? Why did the author of so many accomplished literary studies in the Shelburne series select as his crowning achievement a profound study of the Christian religion? And why did Babbitt, one of whose first books was on the modern confusion of the arts, attain his most substantial achievement in a book on democracy and close his career with a book on Hindu religion?

I have already answered these questions by saying that More and Babbitt were general critics. They were convinced that there is nearly everything wrong with modern civilization. Living in a time of complacent naturalism, when the idea of progress promised a Utopia and science a method for attaining it, they made themselves unpopular by asserting that such a deluded program could only lead to the destruction of our civilization. To others, such as the socialists, who saw something fundamentally wrong in our civilization but who sought a remedy in a new economic system, they replied that the higher issues must be faced before the lower, since "the economic problem will be found to run into the political problem, and the political problem in turn into the philosophical problem, and the philosophical problem itself to be almost indissolubly bound up at last with the religious problem." Believing that our civilization had gone wrong on first principles, they were not content to be literary critics; they were general critics, and finally religious critics.

That it is possible to serve the same high ends without leaving the field of literary criticism has been shown most clearly, perhaps, by a scholar deeply influenced by them, G. R. Elliott of Amherst College. His *Cycle*

---

[1] From the Greeks till the late nineteenth century, the greater peril was didacticism; since the *Décadents* it has been estheticism.

Treating the ethical quality of the artifact as but one element in a system of relationships on a par with such other elements as rhythm, imagery, and diction, an accomplished group of critics today has tended to a confined and unwholesome estheticism which contrasts with the wide and free humanity of literature itself. As I. A. Richards suggests, many naturally superior critical minds, reacting against the "wild asses" who crudely applied the criterion of moral effect, "have virtually shut themselves up in a paddock."

of Modern Poetry, published in that year of economic hubris and nemesis, 1929, is not a work of philosophy, nor a work in which literature is merely used as material for philosophic purposes; it is a genuine piece of literary criticism, in which a sensitive esthetic discrimination interplays with keen ethical insight. With this double awareness Mr. Elliott considers the whole cycle of English poetry since the eighteenth century, beginning with Shelley and Byron, ending with Hardy, Frost, and their immediate successors. This great poetic impulse, as he conceives, is "now pretty well exhausted": "Poetry today, in England and America, is groping for a fresh direction." Mr. Elliott's prevailing theme is the subjection of modern poetry; his purpose, to show how it may attain freedom. "Perhaps never before," he says, "has poetry been so widely eager and experimental and, at the same time, so shortly tethered." He finds it tethered on one side to art because of a mistaken notion of the relation of poetry to art, and on the other side to something which is lacking large human meanings. His conclusion is that our poetry can rewin its freedom only by traversing anew "the great zones of the religious and moral imagination" with the aid of Milton "as a living classic and as our chief guide." A serious effort at poetic freedom will compel us to transcend modern ideas of human freedom. To illustrate, Mr. Elliott contrasts Whitman's declaration at the close of the Civil War: "Be not disheartened, affection shall solve the problems of freedom yet," with what Milton wrote at the close of the English Civil War: "Instead of fretting with vexation, or thinking that you can lay the blame on anyone but yourselves, know that to be free is the same thing as to be pious, to be wise, to be temperate and just, to be frugal and abstinent, and lastly, to be magnanimous and brave." Whitman's sentence, Mr. Elliott comments, "is the theme of nineteenth century poetry: its social unreality is now glaring; it is a worn-out imagining." But the passage from Milton "speaks to us, in our post-war era, like the voice of destiny close to our ear."

There may be many reasons, as the general critic could point out, why we need to deepen our notion of freedom, but Mr. Elliott, as literary critic, is concerned with one reason only: to restore the health of modern poetry. He wishes to free poetry from its deforming aberrations by returning it to the great tradition. Once reconnected with a truly usable past, it will have some chance to move forward to a central creativeness, instead of deploying barrenly in technical experiment. To become great once more, poetry needs a humane philosophy.[1]

---

[1] In the decade since *The Cycle of Modern Poetry* appeared, efforts have been extended to find a usable past in the poetry of Milton's century, especially in that of Donne, but with emphasis on a shift in technique rather than on a return to a humane

VI

Now, the prominence given by humanist critics—even by Mr. Elliott —to the philosophical aspect of literature has been frequently condemned, sometimes by those who happen to prefer a different philosophy, sometimes by those who assert that the literary critic has no business trafficking with philosophy at all. I wish to answer the latter charge.

The answer lies, I think, in a distinction between systematic and literary philosophy. By systematic philosophy I mean, of course, the kind of philosophy which is outlined in the histories of philosophy, the kind with which university departments of philosophy busy themselves. With philosophy in this sense the literary critic should seek friendship but not wedlock. In the equipment of a critic, as W. C. Brownell put it, "a tincture at least of philosophic training may be timidly prescribed. . . . Drenched in philosophy, the critical faculty is almost certain to drown." Perhaps it would be better to say that the more philosophy a critic can carry without altering his center of gravity, the sharper his criticism will be in its logical niceties, the tighter and richer in its intellectual texture. An excess of philosophy, however, may easily betray him into a rigid application of ideas to a field which is, after all, not amenable to philosophic standards. This is why the professional philosopher is so rarely a good literary critic. He is simply not at home. Despite all his training in thought, he is likely to manhandle thought in literary works. He is handicapped not merely because of his ineptness in the realm of the concrete and sensuous, but, far more seriously, because of his inclination to want a writer to look as firmly philosophic as possible and then to belabor him when he is literary, that is to say the greater part of the time. It is the very nature of literary philosophy to be loose, to be unsystematic, to be open not closed, to be generous not exclusive, to be suggestive not decisive. While the most articulate of the arts, literature does not aim at the specialized articulation of philosophy, the perfect web of abstract thought. Writers, like people in general, have a philosophy of life, not a formulated scheme such as professional philosophers require. The informal philosophies of our writers can be appropriately judged only by literary critics, who, being literary, share the writers' distrust of fixed systems, the writers' assumption that reason cannot exhaust the whole of reality, the conviction of a man like Plato, who was man of letters as well as philosopher, that logical explication must give way to symbol and myth when the highest truths are to be adumbrated.

---

philosophy.

Literature needs also, as Mr. Elliott is well aware, a humane society, a usable present, since writers absorb their age into their lives and work and are nourished by it.

Literature is not philosophy; it is, if I may quote what I have said elsewhere, "the record, in terms of beauty, of the striving of mankind to know and express itself." Blending its love of beauty with its love of truth, it aims at nothing more than a working philosophy, enough articulation to give it firmness. Its subject is, essentially, the inner nature of man; it offers a working philosophy of man, or that "philosophy of wisdom" of which Erasmus spoke. It is not a parasitic but an independent growth. It may feed upon the works of systematic thinkers, but somewhat casually, not strictly following their logic. It could, in fact, get along without them, for literature has its own philosophic life and would go on even if philosophy had never been or should cease to be. Writers are thinkers, unsystematic thinkers, for whom everything is grist: experience here and now, the traditions of literature and the arts, history, science, religion, philosophy, all the concerns of man.

This is equally true of literary critics. Their activity is that of the writers; they too achieve some sort of working philosophy, but with them the end aimed at is different since they are not makers but judges. For them a working philosophy is requisite, not for informing works of art with significance, but for evaluating the significance of works of art. And in order to evaluate, they must be a great deal more conscious of their working philosophy than the artist. To the artist a philosophy is ideally an ardent faith, something so profoundly felt that it no longer needs reflection, something given which only asks to be formed or made, so that he is free to bestow upon it his full attention as an artist. Sound, therefore, is the advice which Jacques Maritain addresses to the artist: "Do not *separate* your art from your faith. But leave *distinct* what is distinct. Do not try to blend by force what life unites so well. If you were to make your esthetic an article of faith, you would spoil your faith. If you were to make your devotion a rule of artistic operation, or turn the desire to edify into a method of your art, you would spoil your art." But this unanalyzed integrity which M. Maritain recommends to the artist is not for the critic as well. His task is not to shape a symbol but to separate elements, to distinguish, to explain, to classify, to compare and contrast, to weigh, to reach a palpable conclusion, and for this rational task he needs a rational control of his philosophy.

There are those, to be sure, who would have the literary critic set aside his philosophy if it happens to be different from that of the work he is criticizing. They would have him suppress his disbelief. For the time being he should be like a guileless child, willing to credit the fairy tale. This I think is often impossible, and in any case absurd. But not wholly absurd. Let me explain by describing how, it seems to me, a good critic will read a book new to him. He will read it in two ways, first one way and then the

other, or else in the two ways simultaneously. One way we may speak of
as "feeling the book," the other as "thinking the book." By feeling the book
I mean passively responding to the will of the author, securing the total impression aimed at. If the book accords with the critic's tastes and beliefs,
this will be easy; otherwise, he will have to attempt an abeyance of disbelief, a full acceptance of the work for the time being, in order to understand
it. But understanding is not criticism, and therefore he must read it another
way, "thinking the book," that is, analyzing closely the esthetic pattern and
the ethical burden, and reflecting upon these in terms of his criteria until he
is ready with a mature opinion of the book's value. If obliged to suspend
disbelief when reading the first way, he is now obliged to state and justify
his disbelief.

A good critic will read in this double fashion, I think, no matter what
his working philosophy may be. How much of extant literature a critic can
genuinely accept and admire will depend on his particular philosophy. To
the thoroughgoing naturalist of the present day, the great bulk of literature
from Homer to the middle nineteenth century is, on the ethical side, mis-
guided, dated, of antiquarian interest. To the humanist, on the other hand,
this same body of literature represents, on the ethical side, the "wisdom of
the ages" as opposed to the brief unwisdom of the romantics and the naturalists. Since the romantics pretended to high wisdom and the naturalists
have proclaimed their austere love of truth, the humanist deems it appropriate to meet them on their own ground and to try to demonstrate their
philosophic immaturity. Today, when a crude naturalism runs rampant
in literature and the arts, as well as in the realm of political thought and
action, the humanist conceives that he may be forgiven his comparative
indifference to the esthetic aspects of contemporary writings, may be permitted to dwell upon the subversiveness of their ethical significance, their
celebration of the indignity of man, their basic defeatism.

How much of the dignity of man of which we prate is symbolized in
our literature, the true mirror of our thoughts? Sometimes it is travestied by
the lingering formulas of romanticism, more often it is drably belied by
books and plays in which man is pictured as irrational and unfree, in ugly
bondage to heredity and environment. To the pale cast of our thought, what
a piece of nature is a man! How ignoble in rationalizing! How infinite in
blundering! Here is something to which the literary critic may well apply
a humane philosophy, bringing his literary judgment into relation with a
general or final judgment, if he would not be numbered among those "Irresponsibles" whom Archibald MacLeish has excoriated.

If the life of man is indeed as nasty and brutish as the most typical
literature of our time represents it, the victory of the organized, mechanized

evil which is now loose in the world will only confirm a disaster that has already taken place. As Walter Lippmann declared with unwonted fervor in an address to his Harvard Class, what has made possible the victories of this scientized evil is "the lazy, self-indulgent materialism, the amiable, lackadaisical, footless, confused complacency of the free nations of the world. They have dissipated, like wastrels and drunkards, the inheritance of freedom and order that came to them from hard-working, thrifty, faithful, believing, and brave men. The disaster in the midst of which we are living is a disaster in the character of men."

I think that Mr. Lippmann is right. Vast armaments alone will not save us. We must also rewin our all but lost inheritance of freedom and order, and with freedom and order that on which they depend, belief in the dignity of man. And this in turn can come only through a religious renewal of belief in man as a spiritual being, or if that is beyond our attainment, a humanistic renewal of belief in man as a rational and free animal, a belief still richly current in the time of Washington and Jefferson, a belief that comes down to us all the way from ancient Greece. We have had our "return to Nature"; it is time for another great historical return, the "return to Man."

If the literary critic has no concern with such problems, he might as well close up shop and let the tempest ride.

PRIMITIVISM AND DECADENCE

YVOR WINTERS

THE dichotomy of major and minor poetry is obviously unsatisfactory, nor is the reason for this the one so often given, that general descriptive terms have no meaning. They can at least be given meaning. If Ben Jonson is a major poet and Campion a minor poet, it is patently outrageous to apply either epithet to Byron; yet Byron for the present has a place in our literature, and, though it seems incredible that he should be read as long as Jonson or as Campion, it is probable that he will be read for a long time. Of Jonson and Campion we may say that both are masters; few men have lived to write as well; it is unlikely that many men have lived to appreciate them fully. Their difference is mainly a difference of scope; the achievement of Campion cannot be dimmed by comparison with the achievement of the greatest poets, for within its scope it is unimpeachable. The achievement of Byron, on the other hand, suffers by comparison with the work of any of the minor masters, even with that of Googe or Turberville; in a superficial sense he attempted as much as did Jonson, but he understood with precision nothing that he touched, and his art he understood least of all.

The more important poets might be placed in four groups: the second-rate, those whose gift for language is inadequate to their task, poets such as Byron, D. H. Lawrence, or Poe, and regardless of their other virtues or failings; the major, those who possess all of the virtues, both of form and of range; the primitive, those who utilize all of the means necessary to the most vigorous form, but whose range of material is limited; and the decadent, those who display a fine sensitivity to language and who may have a very wide scope, but whose work is incomplete formally (in the manner of the pseudo-referent and qualitative poets) or is somewhat but not too seriously weakened by a vice of feeling (in the manner of the better post-romantic ironist). The second type of decadent poets may differ from the second-rate only in degree of weakness. In this essay I shall endeavor to discover some of the implications of the terms *decadent* and *primitive* as used in this way. The nature of major poetry and of the second-rate should be reasonably obvious, even though there might be disagreement over examples.

It will be seen that most experimental poetry, particularly experimental poetry of the types developed in the late nineteenth and early twentieth centuries, appears to issue either in primitivism or in decadence, if it issues in nothing worse. The term *primitivism,* however, may be allowed to include traditional minor poetry as well.

If we compare *The Dance,* by Hart Crane, to one of the better poems of Jonson or of George Herbert, it is decadent in the sense in which I have just defined the term: it is incomplete poetry. Historically, however, Crane's poetry is related not only to Jonson, but to the romantics, especially to Whitman, much of whose doctrine Crane adopts. Whitman's doctrine is illusory: like all of the anti-rational doctrines of the past two centuries, it vanishes if pursued by definition. Whitman, as a second-rate poet, however, was equipped to write of it, after a fashion, without rendering its nature immediately evident. His poetic language was as vague as his expository; he had no capacity for any feeling save of the cloudiest and most general kind. Crane's poetic gift is finer than Whitman's, and the precision of his language forces one to recognize the inadequacy of his reference. If he

is decadent in comparison to Jonson, he yet marks an advance in relationship to Whitman. It would probably be easier to convince most readers at
present that something is wrong with Crane than that something is wrong
with Whitman. The reason for this is simple: one observes rather quickly
that something is wrong with Crane, because something is right, and
one is thus able to get one's bearings. From one point of view his language
is frequently that of a master. Nowhere in Whitman can one find such
splendor or even such precision of language as in *The Dance* or as in *The
River.* And if one proceeds from these to his most finished performances,
Repose of Rivers, Faustus and Helen II, and *Voyages II,* one has poems
in which the trace of decadence is scarcely discernible.[1] It would not have
been impossible, then, for Crane to decrease the amount of pseudo-reference
in his poems; as a decadent poet, he was not bound to deteriorate; nor does
his poetry indicate that contemporary literature is in a state of deterioration.

Mr. Pound's *Cantos* are decadent in relation to *Paradise Lost,* since
their structure is purely qualitative. But, historically, there is probably
another relationship to Whitman here, in which Mr. Pound shows not

---

[1] Of *Repose of Rivers* one may say that the individual images are miraculous,
but that their order is not invariably necessary; this fact, combined with the lack of
rhythmical conviction as the poet proceeds from one image to the next, results in a
frail, almost tentative structure. *Faustus and Helen II* is purely descriptive and hence
offers no temptations to sin; the fantastic subject matter, combined with the relative
safety of the approach, enabled Crane to utilize his entire talent for rhetorical ingenuity without risk of its betraying him. In *Voyages II,* which seems to me his greatest
poem, he disciplined this talent to meet a more dangerous and exacting theme, and
achieved greater solidity than in *Repose of Rivers.*

It will be observed that my selections do not coincide with those of Mr. Allen
Tate. Mr. Tate speaks of *The River* as Crane's "most complex and sustained performance, a masterpiece of aesthetic form," and of *Praise for an Urn* as "the finest elegy
in American poetry" (*Hound and Horn:* Summer, 1932). This seems to me sheer
nonsense. The latter poem is metrically a very stiff and inexpert free verse; except
for the two striking lines about the clock and half a dozen other passable lines, it is
sentimental and affected. "The slant moon on the slanting hill," "Delicate riders of
the storm," "The everlasting eyes of Pierrot/ and of Gargantua the laughter," are
sentimental clichés of the twenties, and their quality pervades the whole poem. As to
The River, it is as ineptly put together as any romantic poem I have read: the poem
should begin with the passage about the cannery works, and everything previous
should be discarded; about half the lines from the cannery works to the Pullman
breakfasters should be revised, the eyeless fish, the old gods of the rain, and much
of the rest of it being the shoddiest of decoration, not even skillful charlatanry; and
in the last part of the poem, which is the finest and which is very powerful, there are
still bad lines, for examples, "Throb past the city storied of three thrones," "All fades
but one thin skyline 'round . . . Ahead," and the two final lines of the poem: The
defects of *The River* are not due to the theme, but merely to carelessness, and could
easily have been revised away. The pantheism which wrecks *The Dance* appears in
The River in a fairly harmless form, and merely lends pathos to certain lines, particularly to those describing the end of Dan Midland.

decay but growth. It is not a relationship of theme, as in Crane's poetry, but one of form. Mr. Pound's long line is in part a refinement of Whitman's line; his progression from image to image resembles Whitman's in everything save Whitman's lack of skill. The *Cantos* are structurally Whitmanian songs, dealing with non-Whitmanian matter, and displaying at their best great suavity and beauty. As Crane shifts out of pseudo-reference into rational reference in *Voyages II,* so Mr. Pound in his versions of Propertius, using the same form as in the *Cantos,* produces coherent comment on formulable themes, or does so part of the time. The change may be due to the genius of Propertius, but it is possible in Mr. Pound's form. The form, however, would not permit of any very rapid or compact reasoning.

I have elsewhere suggested that post-romantic irony represents an advance over the uncritical emotionalism of such poets as Hugo or Shelley, in so far as it represents the first step in a diagnosis.

The primitive poet is the major poet on a smaller scale. The decadent poet is the major, or primitive, poet with some important faculty absent from the texture of all his work. Dr. Williams is a good example of the type of poet whom I should call the contemporary primitive. His best poems display no trace of the formal inadequacies which I have mentioned as the signs of decadence. Such poems as *The Widow's Lament* or *To Waken An Old Lady* are fully realized; the form is complete and perfect; the feeling is sound. Dr. Williams has a surer feeling for language than any other poet of his generation, save, perhaps, Stevens at his best. But he is wholly incapable of coherent thought and he had not the good fortune to receive a coherent system as his birthright. His expository writing is largely incomprehensible; his novel, *A Voyage to Pagany,* displays an almost ludicrous inability to motivate a long narrative. His experience is disconnected and fragmentary, but sometimes a fragment is wrought to great beauty. His widest range has been reached in a single piece of prose, *The Destruction of Tenochtitlan,* in which he found his material more or less ready for treatment in the form of history; in treating it, he achieved one of the few great prose styles of our time.[1]

Dr. Williams bears a certain resemblance to the best lyric poets of the thirteenth century; there is in both an extreme sophistication of style,

---

[1] In connection with the fragmentariness, the primitivism, of this piece, it is worth noting that the rhetoric, perhaps merely because of the perfection to which it raises traditional heroic prose, resembles closely that of Macaulay's *History,* the passage in Macaulay describing the formation and character of Cromwell's army, offering especially striking similarity. Macaulay *chose* to write a five volume work, one of the supreme English masterpieces, in this style. Dr. Williams happened to write a twelve-page masterpiece in the style, or so one is forced to conclude from the quality of most of his prose.

a naïve limitation of theme (Dr. Williams has a wider range than the early poets, however) and a fresh enthusiasm for the theme. It was out of such poetry as *Alisoun* that English poetry little by little grew. Sidney represents a resurgence of the same quality at a later date, but touched with Petrarchan decadence.[1] Decadent poetry, as I have defined it, would have been impossible in thirteenth century England: it requires a mature poetry as a background.

A decadent poet such as Crane may, as I have said, if considered historically, represent a gain and not a loss. As a matter of fact, he may embody the most economical method of recovery for an old and rich tradition in a state of collapse, for he offers all of the machinery of a mature and complicated poetry. Both decadent and primitive lack an understanding and correlation of their experience: the primitive accepts his limitations through wisdom or ignorance; the decadent endeavors to conceal them, or like some primitives, may never discover them; the primitive, however, treats of what he understands and the decadent of more than he understands. For either to achieve major poetry there is necessary an intellectual clarification of some kind. But to attain major poetry from the position of a primitive poet such as Dr. Williams might necessitate the creation of a good deal of technical machinery as well; whereas the pseudo-referent poet has most of his machinery made and already partly in action.

There is probably the same relationship between the Petrarchan rhetoric of the sixteenth century, with its decorative and more or less pseudo-referent conceit, and the best Metaphysical verse of the seventeenth century. In Shakespeare's sonnets the rhetoric is Petrarchan, yet the Petrarchan conceit is given a weight of meaning new to it; something similar occurs in the poetry of Fulke Greville. The gap between the sonnets of Shakespeare and the sonnets of Donne is not extremely great. Yet the best thirteenth century lyrics, like the best early Tudor lyrics, those by such men as Vaux, Googe, Gascoigne, and Turberville, are better poetry than the work of Daniel or of Drayton, in spite of the fact that they would have been less immediately useful in certain ways to Donne. So with our contemporaries: Dr. Williams is more consistently excellent than Crane, and at his best is possibly better. Crane's machinery, convenient as it might at any moment prove, remains, so long as it is not utilized, a source of confusion.

The decadent poetry of Mr. Pound does not appear to me to provide so many opportunities for filling out as does that of Crane, partly because

---

[1] In connection with this statement and others regarding the lyrics of the sixteenth century, see my review of the *Oxford Book of 16th Century Verse*, edited by E. K. Chambers, in the *Hound and Horn*, Volume VI, Number 4.

of the meter, which presents a problem too elaborate in itself for discussion here, and partly because all, or nearly all, superfluous machinery in the way of pseudo-referent forms has been avoided. That is, the difficulty of extending the usefulness of a convention may often bear a direct relationship to the perfection with which the convention accomplishes the aims for which it was created.

A perfect primitive poet is not of necessity better than a decadent poet, though he may be; in fact a decadent poet may seem of greater value than a poet whom one might call major. Some major poets are greater than others, and a poem by Mr. Stevens, technically decadent because tinged with his vice—*Of the Manner of Addressing Clouds,* for example—may suffer extremely little from its decadence and be in other respects a poem of tremendous power.

The poetry of Mr. Paul Valéry demonstrates that decadence may be a very economical mode of recovery. Mr. Valéry was formed in the influence of the Symbolists, poets decadent, frequently, in the same way as the Americans of the second and third decades of the twentieth century. The poet who illustrates this point more clearly than any other in English is Mr. T. Sturge Moore, who shares in a considerable measure the background of Mr. Valéry.

Mr. J. V. Cunningham, in the *Commonweal* for July 27, 1932, describes Mr. Moore's favorite theme as that "spiritual pride which would overreach natural limits . . . the effort to violate human relationships by imposing one's identity on others," together with criticism of such spiritual pride. Mr. Cunningham cites the excellent poem *On Four Poplars* as an instance of the subject matter, and other poems could be cited. The theme, however, is not limited to the ethical sphere in Mr. Moore, but has its religious counterpart, in a mysticism related to that of poets so diverse as Hart Crane and Robinson Jeffers, which leads to the attempt to violate our relationship with God, or with whatever myth we put in his place, even with Nothingness, and which leads concurrently to the minimizing of moral distinctions, that is, of the careful perception of strictly human experience. Mr. Moore differs from the Romantic mystics in defining this temptation without succumbing; in defining not only the temptation but its legitimate uses, and its dangers. His repeated poems on the subject of Silence, and his repeated references to Semele, are among the more obvious indications of his interest in the subject. His great lyric *To Silence* may be taken as an allegorical summary of this theme and of his own relationship to romantic tradition, the tradition of rejuvenation through immersion in pure feeling, or sensation, the immersion which is the mystical communion of the romantic, and which occurs in its most perfect literary examples

among the devotees of imitative form to be found in the French Symbolist
and American Experimental schools.

Mr. Moore's immersion has actually led to rejuvenation, to an in-
exhaustibly fascinating freshness of perception: the immersion of other
poets has too often led to disintegration. I quote the entire text of the
poem *To Silence:*

> O deep and clear as is the sky,
> A soul is as a bird in thee
> That travels on and on; so I,
> Like a snared linnet, now break free,
> Who sought thee once with leisured grace
> As hale youth seeks the sea's warm bays.
>
> And as a floating nereid sleeps
> In the deep-billowed ocean-stream;
> And by some goat-herd on lone rock
> Is thought a corpse, though she may dream
> And profit by both health and ease
> Nursed on those high green rolling seas,—
>
> Long once I drifted in thy tide,
> Appearing dead to those I passed;
> Yet lived in thee, and dreamed, and waked
> Twice what I had been. Now, I cast
> Me broken on thy buoyant deep
> And dreamless in thy calm would sleep.
>
> Silence, I almost now believe
> Thou art the speech on lips divine,
> Their greatest kindness to their child.
> Yet I, who for all wisdom pine,
> Seek thee but as a bather swims
> To refresh and not dissolve his limbs:—
>
> Though these be thine, who asked and had,
> And asked and had again, again,
> Yet always found they wanted more
> Till craving grew to be a pain;
> And they at last to silence fled,
> Glad to lose all for which they pled.
>
> O pure and wide as is the sky
> Heal me, yet give me back to life!
> Though thou foresee the day when I,
> Sated with failure, dead to strife,
> Shall seek in thee my being's end,
> Still be to my fond hope a friend.

The structure of the poem is logical and the reference is exact, but the feeling is very strange. There is a remarkable freshness of sensitivity, yet it is a different freshness from that of a primitive, such as Dr. Williams. It might almost be characterized as the hypersensitivity of convalescence: the poet is minutely sensitive to dangers and meanings past but imminent, to which Dr. Williams is not only insensitive but of the very existence of which he is unaware.

If we can imagine that human experience is portrayable geometrically as a continuous circle on which there are equally spaced points, A, C, E, and G, and that classical poetry has been written with these as its chief points of reference, we can then imagine a breakdown, a period of confusion, in which these points are lost, but after which a new set of points, B, D, F, and H, also spaced equally but not the same points, are established. These new points would give a comparable balance, or intelligence, perhaps, but an altered view of the detail, that is, an altered quality of perception, of feeling. Or it might be that the old points would merely be regained after the breakdown, the quality of the perception being then affected by the past experience of the breakdown.

It is as if we extended the allegory of the poem just quoted, thus; Silence is equal to pure quality, unclassified sensation (a purely hypothetical infinity, which, however, we can approach indefinitely),[1] and the immersion in sensation (or confusion) amounts to the dissolution of one's previous standards in order to obtain a fresh sensibility. This is what the romantic movement amounted to, the degree of dissolution varying with each poet, regardless of whether the dissolution was necessary. Mr. Moore states explicitly, however, in this poem and in others, not only the value of the immersion, but its peril, and the need of the return. This does not mean that Mr. Moore at any point in his career has performed experiments like those of Rimbaud or of Joyce; he has not done so publicly, and there is no reason to suppose that he has done so privately. But his sensibility was

---

[1] Cf. Morris Cohen, *Reason and Nature,* page 37: "Avenarius wishes to purify our world-view by returning to the natural view of experience as it existed before it was visited by the sophistications of thought (in the form of introjection). But the empiricist's uncritical use of the category of the *given,* and the nominalistic dogma that relations are created rather than discovered by thought, lead Avenarius to banish not only animism and other myths, but also the categories, substance, causality, etc., as inventions of the mind. In doing this he runs afoul of the great insight of Kant that without concepts or categories percepts are blind." Also Allen Tate, *The Fallacy of Humanism,* in *The Critique of Humanism* (Brewer and Warren: 1930): "Pure Quality is nature itself because it is the source of experience. . . . Pure Quality would be pure evil, and it is only through the means of our recovery from a lasting immersion in it . . . that any man survives the present hour; Pure Quality is pure disintegration."

profoundly affected by those who did perform them; he is a part of the tradition that had at an earlier point in its history subjected itself to the immersion: his private history as a poet begins at the point in the history of the tradition at which recovery has begun, and his talents enable him to bring that recovery to its highest pitch development; but he remembers and understands what preceded him, and his sensibility bears witness to the fact. He thus resembles Paul Valéry, though of the two poets his relationship to the Symbolist tradition is perhaps the more obvious. The feeling of strangeness and freshness is still upon Mr. Moore's poetry, as upon one who has just emerged from the sea. One should examine in particular the following poems: *To Silence, To Slow Music, From Titian's Bacchanal,* the first half of the double sonnet *Silence, Love's First Communion, An Aged Beauty's Prayer, The Deeper Desire,* the sonnets on Sappho, *Semele, Io, Suggested by the Representation on a Grecian Amphora, The Song of Chiron, Tragic Fates, To a Child Listening to a Repeater,* and among his longer works, *Daimonassa* (perhaps his greatest single achievement), *Mariamne, The Sea Is Kind, The Centaur's Booty,* and *The Rout of the Amazons.*

The term *decadence* is frequently used to denote or connote personal immorality, yet even in this sense the historical defense is sometimes effective. There is no doubt that Verlaine was personally childish, sentimental, and debauched. He was in some ways one of the most muddled souls of a muddled century: his life was pseudo-referent even though his poetry was frequently not, and, like his poetry, was too often governed wholly by mood. He was not, as Baudelaire was, morally intelligent among whatever sins he may have committed, and was never much the wiser for his sins or wrote better poetry because of them. The greater part of his life was simply confusion; yet a narrow margin of it he evaluated with precision; to that extent he was superior to such formless predecessors as Lamartine or de Musset, who smeared everything with a consistent texture of falsity. As a poet, Verlaine at his best was rather a primitive than a decadent, for his poetry is not ambitious; his best art was as natural and proper, if we consider his situation in time and space, and potentially as valuable to his successors, as was the art of the author of *Alisoun.*

I do not mean that Verlaine's limitations were inevitable, however. In offering an historical excuse for decadence, formal or personal, I do not mean to imply that there is ever an historical necessity for either, but merely that life is painful if one expects more than two or three men in a century to behave as rational animals, and that for a good many men there are mitigating circumstances. Baudelaire ran through romanticism early in his career, to achieve the most remarkable balance of powers in French literature after Racine; he had no need of several generations of graduated decadence; his recovery was accomplished at a bound. He was determined by his period only to this extent: that he dealt with the problem of evil in the terms in which he had met it, the terms of the romantic view of life; and it was because of these terms that he was able to embody the universal principles of evil in the experience of his own age and evaluate that experience.

Our own position may be similar. If we doubt the value of the romantic communion, if we cannot see that the poet who has survived it is a better poet for it, we may at least say this: that the communion, as we have experienced it historically, if not personally, has extended our knowledge of evil and so made us wiser; for the moral intelligence is merely the knowledge and evaluation of evil; and the moral intelligence is the measure of the man and of the poet alike. It may seem a hard thing to say of that troubled and magnificent spirit, Hart Crane, that we shall remember him chiefly for his having shown us a new mode of damnation, yet it is for this that we remember Orestes, and Crane has in addition the glory of being, if not his Aeschylus, perhaps, in some fragmentary manner, his own Euripides.

Again, we should remember that there is no certitude that several generations of graduated decadence will lead to recovery; they may lead merely to a general condition of hypochondria. Crane's first book was better than his second, and the work of his last few years displays utter collapse. T. S. Eliot abandoned Laforguian irony not to correct his feelings, but to remain satisfied with them: his career since has been largely a career of what one might call psychic impressionism, a formless curiosity concerning queer feelings which are related to odds and ends of more or less profound thought. There is current at present a very general opinion that it is impossible in our time to write good poetry in the mode, let us say, of Bridges, either because of the kind of poetry that has been written since ("the stylistic advances of Eliot and of Pound"), or because of social conditions ("the chaos of modern thought"), or because of both, or because of something else. I believe this to be a form of group hypochondria. The simple fact of the matter is, that it is harder to imitate Bridges than to imitate Pound or Eliot, as it is harder to appreciate him, because Bridges is a finer poet and a saner man; he knows more than they, and to meet him on his own ground we must know more than to meet them.

Many experimental poets, by limiting themselves to an abnormal convention, limit themselves in range or in approach: that is, become primitives or decadents of necessity; and they lack the energy or ability to break free of the elaborate and mechanical habits which they have, in perfecting, imposed upon themselves. Miss Moore, Dr. Williams, Gerard Hopkins, and Ezra Pound might all serve as examples. In other words, the selection of a convention is a very serious matter; and the poet who sets out to widen his tradition may often succeed only in narrowing or sterilizing himself. Crashaw's experimenting at its wildest gets wholly out of hand and becomes pseudo-referent decadence. Nevertheless, the experimenting of Donne and of Crashaw is subject to the check of a comprehensible philosophy, as the experimentalism of Pound and of Crane is not. The experimentalism of Milton was subject to such a check and was, I think one may say, necessitated by the unprecedented scope of his plan and by the unprecedented violence and magnificence of his mind, but this is not to say that he was the greatest of poets, though he was, of course, one of the greatest.

The relationship between experimentalism, decadence, and primitivism is thus seen to be intimate, though it would be rash to formulate many laws of the relationship.

Decadent poetry may be valuable as a point of departure, either to its authors or to others, exactly in so far as its deficiencies are recognized and are susceptible of correction. Not all types of decadent poetry need be equally valuable in this respect, though the understanding of one may equal in value the understanding of another as a form of moral knowledge. Unless the deficiencies of a decadent convention are recognized, there is little likelihood that the convention will be improved; there is great likelihood that it will deteriorate; for it is the nature of man to deteriorate unless he recognizes the tendency and the source of the deterioration and expends actual effort to reduce them.

6. *Aesthetics*

CRITICISM AS PURE SPECULATION

JOHN CROWE RANSOM

I

I WILL testify to the weight of responsibility felt by
the critic who enters a serial discussion with such other
lecturers as Mr. Wilson, Mr. Auden, and Mr. Foerster;
and delivers his opinion to an audience at Princeton, where live at least
two eminent critics, in Mr. Tate and Mr. Blackmur, and one eminent
esthetician, in Mr. Greene.

Indeed, Mr. Blackmur and Mr. Greene have recently published
books [1] which bear on this discussion. Mr. Blackmur's essays are probably
all that can be expected of a critic who has not explicitly submitted them
to the discipline of general esthetics; but with that limitation the best critic
in the world might expose himself to review and reproach. Mr. Greene's
esthetic studies, in turn, may have wonderful cogency as philosophical discourse; but if throughout them he should fail to maintain intimate contact
with the actual works of art he would invite damaging attentions from the
literary critics. I am far from suggesting such proceedings against them.
Mr. Blackmur has his native philosophical sense to keep his critical foundations from sliding into the sea. Mr. Greene is in a very strong position:
recognizing the usual weakness of formal esthetics, he tries a device to
secure his own studies against it; for when he needs them he uses reports
from reputable actual critics upon the practices in the several arts. A chasm,
perhaps an abyss, separates the critic and the esthetician ordinarily, if the
books in the library are evidence. But the authority of criticism depends on

"Criticism as Pure Speculation," by John Crowe Ransom, from *The Intent of
the Critic,* D. A. Stauffer, ed., reprinted by permission of Princeton University Press.

[1] *The Expense of Greatness,* by R. P. Blackmur, Arrow Editions, 1940; *The
Arts and the Art of Criticism,* by Theodore Meyer Greene, Princeton University
Press, 1940.

its coming to terms with esthetics, and the authority of literary esthetics depends on its coming to terms with criticism. Mr. Greene is an esthetician, and his department is philosophy, but he has subscribed in effect to this thesis. I am a sort of critic, and my department is English poetry, so that I am very much in Mr. Blackmur's position: and I subscribe to the thesis, and am altogether disposed to solicit Mr. Greene's philosophical services.

When we inquire into the "intent of the critic," we mean: the intent of the generalized critic, or critic as such. We will concede that any professional critic is familiar with the technical practices of poets so long as these are conventional, and is expert in judging when they perform them brilliantly and when only fairly, or badly. We expect a critical discourse to cover that much, but we know that more is required. The most famous poets of our own time, for example, make wide departures from conventional practices: how are they to be judged? Innovations in poetry, or even conventions when pressed to their logical limits, cause the ordinary critic to despair. They cause the good critic to review his esthetic principles; perhaps to re-formulate his esthetic principles. He tries the poem against his best philosophical conception of the peculiar character that a poem should have.

Mr. T. S. Eliot is an extraordinarily sensitive critic. But when he discusses the so-called "metaphysical" poetry, he surprises us by refusing to study the so-called "conceit" which is its reputed basis; he observes instead that the metaphysical poets of the seventeenth century are more like their immediate predecessors than the latter are like the eighteenth and nineteenth century poets, and then he goes into a very broad philosophical comparison between two whole "periods" or types of poetry. I think it has come to be understood that his comparison is unsound; it has not proved workable enough to assist critics who have otherwise borrowed liberally from his critical principles. (It contains the famous dictum about the "sensibility" of the earlier poets, it imputes to them a remarkable ability to "feel their thought," and to have a kind of "experience" in which the feeling cannot be differentiated from the thinking.) Now there is scarcely another critic equal to Eliot at distinguishing the practices of two poets who are closely related. He is supreme as a comparative critic when the relation in question is delicate and subtle; that is, when it is a matter of close perception and not a radical difference in kind. But this line of criticism never goes far enough. In Eliot's own range of criticism the line does not always answer. He is forced by discontinuities in the poetic tradition into sweeping theories that have to do with esthetics, the philosophy of poetry; and his own philosophy probably seems to us insufficient, the philosophy of the literary man.

The intent of the critic may well be, then, first to read his poem sensitively, and make comparative judgments about its technical practice, or, as we might say, to emulate Eliot. Beyond that, it is to read and remark the poem knowingly; that is, with an esthetician's understanding of what a poem generically "is."

Before I venture, with inadequate argument, to describe what I take to be the correct understanding of poetry, I would like to describe two other understandings which, though widely professed, seem to me misunderstandings. First, there is a smart and bellettristic theory of poetry which may be called "psychologistic." Then there is an altogether staid and commonplace theory which is moralistic. Of these in their order.

II

It could easily be argued about either of these untenable conceptions of poetry that it is an act of despair to which critics resort who cannot find for the discourse of poetry any precise differentia to remove it from the category of science. Psychologistic critics hold that poetry is addressed primarily to the feelings and motor impulses; they remind us frequently of its contrast with the coldness, the unemotionality, of science, which is supposed to address itself to the pure cognitive mind. Mr. Richards came out spectacularly for the doctrine, and furnished it with detail of the greatest ingenuity. He very nearly severed the dependence of poetic effect upon any standard of objective knowledge or belief. But the feelings and impulses which he represented as gratified by the poem were too tiny and numerous to be named. He never identified them; they seemed not so much psychological as infrapsychological. His was an esoteric poetic: it could not be disproved. But neither could it be proved, and I think it is safe at this distance to say that eventually his readers, and Richards himself, lost interest in it as being an improvisation, much too unrelated to the public sense of a poetic experience.

With other critics psychologism of some sort is an old story, and one that will probably never cease to be told. For, now that all of us know about psychology, there must always be persons on hand precisely conditioned to declare that poetry is an emotional discourse indulged in resentment and compensation for science, the bleak cognitive discourse in its purity. It becomes less a form of knowledge than a form of "expression." The critics are willing to surrender the honor of objectivity to science if they may have the luxury of subjectivity for poetry. Science will scarcely object. But one or two things have to be said about that. In every experience, even in science, there is feeling. No discourse can sustain itself without interest, which is feeling. The interest, or the feeling, is like an automatic index to the human value of the proceeding—which would not otherwise proceed. Mr. Eliseo Vivas is an esthetician who might be thought to reside in the camp of the enemy, for his affiliations are positivist; yet in a recent essay he writes about the "passion" which sustains the heroic labors of the scientist as one bigger and more intense than is given to most men.

I do not mean to differ with that judgment at all in remarking that we might very well let the passions and the feelings take care of themselves; it is precisely what we do in our pursuit of science. The thing to attend to is the object to which they attach. As between two similar musical phrases, or between two similar lines of poetry, we may often defy the most proficient psychologist to distinguish the one feeling—response from the other; unless we permit him to say at long last that one is the kind of response that would be made to the first line, and the other is the kind of response that would be made to the second line. But that is to do, after much wasted motion, what I have just suggested: to attend to the poetic object and let the feelings take care of themselves. It is their business to "respond." There may be a feeling correlative with the minutest alteration in an object, and adequate to it, but we shall hardly know. What we do know is that the feelings are grossly inarticulate if we try to abstract them and take their testimony in their own language. Since it is not the intent of the critic to be inarticulate, his discriminations must be among the objects. We understand this so well intuitively that the critic seems to us in possession of some esoteric knowledge, some magical insight, if he appears to be intelligent elsewhere and yet refers confidently to the "tone" or "quality" or "value" of the feeling he discovers in a given line. Probably he is bluffing. The distinctness resides in the cognitive or "semantical" objects denoted by the words. When Richards bewilders us by reporting affective and motor disturbances that are too tiny for definition, and other critics by reporting disturbances that are too massive and gross, we cannot fail to grow suspicious of this whole way of insight as incompetent.

Eliot has a special version of psychologistic theory which looks extremely fertile, though it is broad and nebulous as his psychologistic terms require it to be. He likes to regard the poem as a structure of emotion and feeling. But the emotion is singular, there being only one emotion per poem, or at least per passage: it is the central emotion or big emotion which attaches to the main theme or situation. The feeling is plural. The emotion combines with many feelings; these are our little responses to the single words and phrases, and he does not think of them as being parts of the central emotion or even related to it. The terminology is greatly at fault, or we should recognize at once, I think, a principle that might prove very valuable. I would not answer for the conduct of a technical philosopher in assessing this theory; he might throw it away, out of patience with its jargon. But a lay philosopher who respects his Eliot and reads with all his sympathy might salvage a good thing from it, though I have not heard of anyone doing so. He would try to escape from the affective terms, and translate Eliot into more intelligible language. Eliot would be saying in effect that a poem has a central logic or situation or "paraphrasable core" to which an appropriate interest doubtless attaches, and that in this respect the poem is like a discourse of science behind which lies the sufficient passion. But he would be saying at the same time, and this is the important thing, that the poem has also a context of lively local details to which other and independent interests attach; and that in this respect it is unlike the discourse of science. For the detail of scientific discourse intends never to be independent of the thesis (either objectively or affectively) but always functional, and subordinate to the realization of the thesis. To say that is to approach to a structural understanding of poetry, and to the kind of understanding that I wish presently to urge.

III

As for the moralistic understanding of poetry, it is sometimes the specific moralists, men with moral axes to grind, and incidentally men of unassailable public position, who cherish that; they have a "use" for poetry. But not exclusively, for we may find it held also by critics who are more spontaneous and innocent: apparently they fall back upon it because it attributes some special character to poetry, which otherwise refuses to yield up to them a character. The moral interest is so much more frequent in poetry than in science that they decide to offer its moralism as a differentia.

This conception of poetry is of the greatest antiquity—it antedates the evolution of close esthetic philosophy, and persists beside it too. Plato sometimes spoke of poetry in this light—perhaps because it was recommended to him in this light—but nearly always scornfully. In the *Gorgias,* and other dialogues, he represents the poets as moralizing, and that is only what he, in the person of Socrates, is doing at the very moment, and given to doing; but he considers the moralizing of poets as mere "rhetoric," or popular philosophy, and unworthy of the accomplished moralist who is the real or technical philosopher. Plato understood very well that the poet does not conduct a technical or an original discourse like that of the scientist—and the term includes here the moral philosopher—and that close and effective moralizing is scarcely to be had from him. It is not within the poet's power to offer that if his intention is to offer poetry; for the poetry and the morality are so far from being identical that they interfere a little with each other.

Few famous estheticians in the history of philosophy have cared to bother with the moralistic conception; many critics have, in all periods. Just now we have at least two schools of moralistic critics contending for the official possession of poetry. One is the Neo-Humanist, and Mr. Foerster has identified himself with that. The other is the Marxist, and I believe it is represented in some degree and shade by Mr. Wilson, possibly by Mr. Auden. I have myself taken profit from the discussions by both schools, but recently I have taken more—I suppose this is because I was brought up in a scholastic discipline rather like the Neo-Humanist—from the writings of the Marxist critics. One of the differences is that the Neo-Humanists believe in the "respectable" virtues, but the Marxists believe that respectability is the greatest of vices, and equate respectable with "genteel." That is a very striking difference, and I think it is also profound.

But I do not wish to be impertinent; I can respect both these moralities, and appropriate moral values from both. The thing I wish to argue is not the comparative merits of the different moralities by which poetry is judged, but their equal inadequacy to the reading of the poet's intention. The moralistic critics wish to isolate and discuss the "ideology" or theme or paraphrase of the poem and not the poem itself. But even to the practitioners themselves, if they are sophisticated, comes sometimes the apprehension that this is moral rather than literary criticism. I have not seen the papers of my colleagues in this discussion, for that was against the rules, but it is reported to me that both Mr. Wilson and Mr. Foerster concede in explicit words that criticism has both the moral and the esthetic branches; Mr. Wilson may call them the "social" and esthetic branches. And they would hold the critical profession responsible for both branches. Under these circumstances the critics cease to be mere moralists and become dualists; that is better. My feeling about such a position would be that the moral criticism we shall have with us always, and have had always, and that it is easy—comparatively speaking—and that what is hard, and needed, and indeed more and more urgent after all the failures of poetic understanding, is a better esthetic criticism. This is the branch which is all but invariably neglected by the wise but morally zealous critics; they tend to forget their dual responsibility. I think I should go so far as to think that, in strictness, the business of the literary critic is exclusively with an esthetic criticism. The business of the moralist will naturally, and properly, be with something else.

If we have the patience to read for a little while in the anthology, paying some respect to the varieties of substance actually in the poems, we cannot logically attribute ethical character by definition to poetry; for that character is not universal in the poems. And if we have any faith in a community of character among the several arts, we are stopped quickly from risking such a definition for art at large. To claim a moral content for most of sculpture, painting, music, or architecture, is to plan something dialectically very roundabout and subtle, or else to be so arbitrary as to invite instant exposure. I should think the former alternative is impractical, and the latter, if it is not stupid, is masochistic.

The moralistic critics are likely to retort upon their accusers by accusing them in turn of the vapid doctrine known as Art for Art's Sake. And with frequent justice; but again we are likely to receive the impression that it is first because Art for Art's Sake, the historic doctrine, proved empty, and availed them so little esthetically, like all the other doctrines that came into default, that they have fled to their moralism. Moralism does at least impute to poetry a positive substance, as Art for Art's Sake does not. It asserts an autonomy for art, which is excellent; but autonomy to do what? Only to be itself, and to reduce its interpreters to a tautology? With its English adherents in the 'nineties the doctrine seemed to make only a negative requirement of art, that is, that it should be anti-Victorian as we should say today, a little bit naughty and immoral perhaps, otherwise at least non-moral, or carefully squeezed dry of moral substance. An excellent example of how two doctrines, inadequate equally but in opposite senses, may keep themselves alive by abhorring each other's errors.

It is highly probable that the poem considers an ethical situation, and there is no reason why it should repel this from its consideration. But, if I may say so without being accused of verbal trifling, the poetic consideration of the ethical situation is not the same as the ethical consideration of it. The straight ethical consideration would be prose; it would be an act of interested science, or an act of practical will. The poetic consideration, according to Schopenhauer, is the objectification of this act of will; that is, it is our contemplation and not our exercise of will, and therefore qualitatively a very different experience; knowledge without desire. That doctrine also seems too negative and indeterminate. I will put the point as I see it in another way. It should be a comfort to the moralist that there is ordinarily a moral composure in the poem, as if the poet had long known good and evil, and made his moral choice between them once and for all. Art is post-ethical rather than unethical. In the poem there is an increment of meaning which is neither the ethical content nor opposed to the ethical content. The poetic experience would have to stop for the poet who is developing it, or for the reader who is following it, if the situation which is being poetically treated should turn back into a situation to be morally determined; if, for example, the situation were not a familiar one, and one to which we had habituated our moral wills; for it would rouse the moral will again to action, and make the poetic treatment impossible under its heat. Art is more cool than hot, and a moral fervor is as disastrous to it as a burst of passion itself. We have seen Marxists recently so revolted by Shakespeare's addiction to royal or noble personae that they cannot obtain esthetic experience from the plays; all they get is moral agitation. In another art, we know, and doubtless we approve, the scruple of the college authorities in not permitting the "department of fine arts" to direct the collegians in painting in the nude. Doctor Hanns Sachs, successor to Freud, in a recent number of his *American Imago,* gives a story from a French author as follows:

"He tells that one evening strolling along the streets of Paris he noticed a row of slot machines which for a small coin showed pictures of women in full or partial undress. He observed the leering interest with which men of all kind and description, well dressed and shabby, boys and old men, enjoyed the peep show. He remarked that they all avoided one of these machines, and wondering what uninteresting pictures it might show, he put his penny in the slot. To his great astonishment the generally shunned picture turned out to be the Venus of Medici. Now he begins to ponder: Why does nobody get excited about her? She is decidedly feminine and not less naked than the others which hold such strong fascination for everybody. Finally he finds a satisfactory answer: They fight shy of her because she is beautiful."

And Doctor Sachs, though in his own variety of jargon, makes a number of wise observations about the psychic conditions precedent to the difficult apprehension of beauty. The experience called beauty is beyond the powerful ethical will precisely as it is beyond the animal passion, and indeed these last two are competitive, and coordinate. Under the urgency of either we are incapable of appreciating the statue or understanding the poem.

IV

The ostensible substance of the poem may be anything at all which words may signify: an ethical situation, a passion, a train of thought, a flower or landscape, a thing. This substance receives its poetic increment. It might be safer to say it receives some subtle and mysterious alteration under poetic treatment, but I will risk the cruder formula: the ostensible substance is increased by an x, which is an increment. The poem actually continues to contain its ostensible substance, which is not fatally diminished from its prose state: that is its logical core or paraphrase. The rest of the poem is x, which we are to find.

We feel the working of this simple formula when we approach a poetry with our strictest logic, provided we can find deliverance from certain inhibiting philosophical prepossessions into which we have been conditioned by the critics we have had to read. Here is Lady Macbeth planning a murder with her husband:

> When Duncan is asleep—
> Whereto the rather shall his hard day's journey
> Soundly invite him—his two chamberlains
> Will I with wine and wassail so convince,
> That memory, the warder of the brain,
> Shall be a fume, and the receipt of reason
> A limbec only; when in swinish sleep
> Their drenched natures lie as in a death,
> What cannot you and I perform upon
> The unguarded Duncan? what not put upon
> His spongy officers, who shall bear the guilt
> Of our great quell?

It is easy to produce the prose argument or paraphase of this speech; it has one upon which we shall all agree. But the passage is more than its argument. Any detail, with this speaker, seems capable of being expanded in some direction which is not that of the argument. For example, Lady Macbeth says she will make the chamberlains drunk so that they will not remember their charge, nor keep their wits about them. But it is indifferent to this argument whether memory according to the old psychology is located at the gateway to the brain, whether it is to be disintegrated into fume as of alcohol, and whether the whole receptacle of the mind is to be turned into a still. These are additions to the argument both energetic and irrelevant—though they do not quite stop or obscure the argument. From the point of view of the philosopher they are excursions into particularity. They give, in spite of the argument, which would seem to be perfectly self-sufficient, a sense of the real density and contingency of the world in which arguments and plans have to be pursued. They bring out the private character which the items of an argument can really assume if we look at them. This character spreads out in planes at right angles to the course of the argument, and in effect gives to the discourse another dimension, not present in a perfectly logical prose. We are expected to have sufficient judgment not to let this local character take us too far or keep us too long from the argument.

All this would seem commonplace remark, I am convinced, but for those philosophically timid critics who are afraid to think that the poetic increment is local and irrelevant, and that poetry cannot achieve its own virtue and keep undiminished the virtues of prose at the same time. But I will go a little further in the hope of removing the sense of strangeness in the analysis. I will offer a figurative definition of a poem.

A poem is, so to speak, a democratic state, whereas a prose discourse —mathematic, scientific, ethical, or practical and vernacular—is a totalitarian state. The intention of a democratic state is to perform the work of state as effectively as it can perform it, subject to one reservation of conscience; that it will not despoil its members, the citizens, of the free exercise of their own private and independent characters. But the totalitarian state is interested solely in being effective, and regards the citizens as no citizens at all; that is, regards them as functional members whose existence is totally defined by their allotted contributions to its ends; it has no use for their private characters, and therefore no provision for them. I indicate of course the extreme or polar opposition between two polities, without denying that a polity may come to us rather mixed up.

In this trope the operation of the state as a whole represents of course the logical paraphrase or argument of the poem. The private character of the citizens represents the particularity asserted by the parts in the poem. And this last is our x.

For many years I had seen—as what serious observer has not—that a poem as a discourse differentiated itself from prose by its particularity, yet not to the point of sacrificing its logical cogency or universality. But I could get no further. I could not see how real particularity could get into a universal. The object of esthetic studies became for me a kind of discourse, or a kind of natural configuration, which like any other discourse or configuration claimed universality, but which consisted actually, and notoriously, of particularity. The poem was concrete, yet universal, and in spite of Hegel I could not see how the two properties could be identified as forming in a single unit the "concrete universal." It is usual, I believe, for persons at this stage to assert that somehow the apparent diffuseness or particularity in the poem gets itself taken up or "assimilated" into the logic, to produce a marvellous kind of unity called a "higher unity," to which ordinary discourse is not eligible. The belief is that the "idea" or theme proves itself in poetry to be even more dominating than in prose by overcoming much more energetic resistance than usual on the part of the materials, and the resistance, as attested in the local development of detail, is therefore set not to the debit but to the credit of the unifying power of the poetic spirit. A unity of that kind is one which philosophers less audacious and more factual than Hegel would be loath to claim. Critics incline to call it, rather esoterically, an "imaginative" rather than a logical unity, but one supposes they mean a mystical, an ineffable, unity. I for one could neither grasp it nor deny it. I believe that is not an uncommon situation for poetic analysts to find themselves in.

It occurred to me at last that the solution might be very easy if looked for without what the positivists call "metaphysical prepossessions." Suppose the logical substance remained there all the time, and was in no way specially remarkable, while the particularity came in by accretion, so that the poem turned out partly universal, and partly particular, but with respect to different parts. I began to remark the dimensions of a poem, or other work of art. The poem was not a mere moment in time, nor a mere point in space. It was sizeable, like a house. Apparently it had a "plan," or a central frame of logic, but it had also a huge wealth of local detail, which sometimes fitted the plan functionally or served it, and sometimes only subsisted comfortably under it; in either case the house stood up. But it was the political way of thinking which gave me the first analogy which seemed valid. The poem was like a democratic state, in action, and observed both macroscopically and microscopically.

The house occurred also, and provided what seems to be a more negotiable trope under which to construe the poem. A poem is a *logical structure* having a *local texture*. These terms have been actually though not systematically employed in literary criticism. To my imagination they are architectural. The walls of my room are obviously structural; the beams and boards have a function; so does the plaster, which is the visible aspect of the final wall. The plaster might have remained naked, aspiring to no character, and purely functional. But actually it has been painted, receiving color; or it has been papered, receiving color and design, though these have no structural value; and perhaps it has been hung with tapestry, or with paintings, for "decoration." The paint, the paper, the tapestry are texture. It is logically unrelated to structure. But I indicate only a few of the textural possibilities in architecture. There are not fewer of them in poetry.

The intent of the good critic becomes therefore to examine and define the poem with respect to its structure and its texture. If he has nothing to say about its texture he has nothing to say about it specifically as a poem, but is treating it only insofar as it is prose.

I do not mean to say that the good critic will necessarily employ my terms.

v

Many critics today are writing analytically and with close intelligence, in whatever terms, about the logical substance or structure of the poem, and its increment of irrelevant local substance or texture. I believe that the understanding of the ideal critic has to go even further than that. The final desideratum is an ontological insight, nothing less. I am committed by my title to representation of criticism as, in the last resort, a speculative exercise. But my secret committal was to speculative in the complete sense of —ontological.

There is nothing especially speculative or ontological in reciting, or even appraising, the logical substance of the poem. This is its prose core— its science perhaps, or its ethics if it seems to have an ideology. Speculative interest asserts itself principally when we ask why we want the logical substance to be compounded with the local substance, the good lean structure with a great volume of texture that does not function. It is the same thing as asking why we want the poem to be what it is.

It has been a rule, having the fewest exceptions, for estheticians and great philosophers to direct their speculations by the way of overstating and overvaluing the logical substance. They are impressed by the apparent obedience of material nature, whether in fact or in art, to definable form or "law" imposed upon it. They like to suppose that in poetry, as in chemistry, everything that figures in the discourse means to be functional, and that the poem is imperfect in the degree that it contains items, whether by accident or intention, which manifest a private independence. It is a bias with which we are entirely familiar, and reflects the extent to which our philosophy hitherto has been impressed by the successes of science in formulating laws which would "govern" their objects. Probably I am here reading the state of mind of yesterday rather than of today. Nevertheless we know it. The world-view which ultimately forms itself in the mind so biassed is that of a world which is rational and intelligible. The view is sanguine, and naïve. Hegel's world-view, I think it is agreed, was a subtle version of this, and if so, it was what determined his view of art. He seemed to make the handsomest concession to realism by offering to knowledge a kind of universal which was not restricted to the usual abstracted aspects of the material, but included all aspects, and was a concrete universal. The concreteness in Hegel's handling was not honestly, or at any rate not fairly, defended. It was always represented as being in process of pointing up and helping out the universality. He could look at a work of art and report all its substance as almost assimilated to a ruling "idea." But at least Hegel seemed to distinguish what looked like two ultimate sorts of substance there, and stated the central esthetic problem as the problem of relating them. And his writings about art are speculative in the sense that he regarded the work of art not as of great intrinsic value necessarily, but as an object-lesson or discipline in the understanding of the world-process, and as its symbol.

I think of two ways of construing poetry with respect to its ultimate purpose; of which the one is not very handsome nor speculatively interesting, and the other will appear somewhat severe.

The first construction would picture the poet as a sort of epicure, and the poem as something on the order of a Christmas pudding, stuffed with what dainties it will hold. The pastry alone, or it may be the cake, will not serve; the stuffing is wanted too. The values of the poem would be intrinsic, or immediate, and they would include not only the value of the structure but also the incidental values to be found in the texture. If we exchange the pudding for a house, they would include not only the value of the house itself but also the value of the furnishings. In saying intrinsic or immediate, I mean that the poet is fond of the precise objects denoted by the words, and writes the poem for the reason that he likes to dwell upon them. In talking about the main value and the incidental values I mean to recognize the fact that the latter engage the affections just as truly as the former. Poetic discourse therefore would be more agreeable than prose to the epicure or the literally acquisitive man; for prose has but a single value, being about one thing only; its parts have no values of their own, but only instrumental values, which might be reckoned as fractions of the single value proportionate to their contributions to it. The prose is one-valued and the poem is many-valued. Indeed, there will certainly be poems whose texture contains many precious objects, and aggregates a greater value than the structure.

So there would be a comfortable and apparently eligible view that poetry improves on prose because it is a richer diet. It causes five or six pleasures to appear, five or six good things, where one had been before; an alluring consideration for robustious, full-blooded, bourgeois souls. The view will account for much of the poem, if necessary. But it does not account for all of it, and sometimes it accounts for less than at other times.

The most impressive reason for the bolder view of art, the speculative one, is the existence of the "pure," or "abstractionist," or non-representational works of art; though these will probably occur to us in other arts than poetry. There is at least one art, music, whose works are all of this sort. Tones are not words, they have no direct semantical function, and by themselves they mean nothing. But they combine to make brilliant phrases, harmonies, and compositions. In these compositions it is probable that the distinction between structure or functional content, on the one hand, and texture or local variation and departure, on the other, is even more determinate than in an impure art like poetry. The world of tones seems perfectly inhuman and impracticable; there is no specific field of experience "about which" music is telling us. Yet we know that music is powerfully affective. I take my own musical feelings, and those attested by other audients, as the sufficient index to some overwhelming human importance which the musical object has for us. At the same time it would be useless to ask the feelings precisely what they felt; we must ask the critic. The safest policy is to take the simplest construction, and try to improvise as little fiction as possible. Music is not music, I think, until we grasp its effects both in structure and in texture. As we grow in musical understanding the structures become always more elaborate and sustained, and the texture which interrupts them and sometimes imperils them becomes more bold and unpredictable. We can agree in saying about the works of music that these are musical structures, and they are richly textured; we can identify these elements, and perhaps precisely. To what then do our feelings respond? To music as structural composition itself; to music as manifesting the structural principles of the world; to modes of structure which we feel to be ontologically possible, or even probable. Schopenhauer construed music very much in that sense. Probably it will occur to us that musical compositions bear close analogy therefore to operations in pure mathematics. The mathematicians confess that their constructions are "nonexistential"; meaning, as I take it, that the constructions testify with assurance only to the structural principles, in the light of which they are possible but may not be actual, or if they are actual may not be useful. This would define the mathematical operations as speculative; as motivated by an interest so generalized and so elemental that no word short of ontological will describe it.

But if music and mathematics have this much in common, they differ sharply in their respective world-views or ontological biasses. That of music, with its prodigious display of texture, seems the better informed about the nature of the world, the more realistic, the less naïve. Perhaps the difference is between two ontological educations. But I should be inclined to imagine it as rising back of that point; in two ontological temperaments.

There are also, operating a little less successfully so far as the indexical evidences would indicate, the abstractionist paintings, of many schools, and perhaps also works of sculpture; and there is architecture. These arts have tried to abandon direct representational intention almost as heroically as music. They exist in their own materials and indicate no other specific materials; structures of color, light, space, stone—the cheapest of materials. They too can symbolize nothing of value unless it is structure or composition itself. But that is precisely the act which denotes will and intelligence;

which becomes the act of fuller intelligence if it carefully accompanies its
structures with their material textures; for then it understands better the
ontological nature of materials.

Returning to the poetry. It is not all poems, and not even all "powerful" poems, having high index-ratings, whose semantical meanings contain
situations important in themselves or objects precious in themselves. There
may be little correlation between the single value of the poem and the
aggregate value of its contents—just as there is no such correlation whatever
in music. The "effect" of the poem may be astonishingly disproportionate
to our interest in its materials. It is true, of course, that there is no art employing materials of equal richness with poetry, and that it is beyond the
capacity of poetry to employ indifferent materials. The words used in poetry
are the words the race has already formed, and naturally they call attention
to things and events that have been thought to be worth attending to. But
I suggest that any poetry which is "technically" notable is in part a work
of abstractionist art, concentrating upon the structure and the texture, and
the structure-texture relation, out of a pure speculative interest.

At the end of *Love's Labour's Lost* occurs a little diversion which
seems proportionately far more effective than that laborious play as a
whole. The play is over, but Armado stops the principals before they
disperse to offer them a show:

> ARM. But, most esteemed greatness, will you hear the dialogue
> that the two learned men have compiled in praise of the owl and
> the cuckoo? It should have followed in the end of our show.
>
> KING. Call them forth quickly; we will do so.
>
> ARM. Holla! approach.
>
> *Re-enter Holofernes, etc.*
>
> This side is Hiems, Winter, this Ver, the Spring; the one main-
> tained by the owl, the other by the cuckoo. Ver, begin.

THE SONG

SPRING.
> When daisies pied and violets blue
> And lady-smocks all silver-white
> And cuckoo-buds of yellow hue
> Do paint the meadows with delight,
> The cuckoo then, on every tree,
> Mocks married men; for thus sings he,
>   Cuckoo;

Cuckoo, cuckoo: O word of fear,
Unpleasing to a married ear!

When shepherds pipe on oaten straws,
And merry larks are ploughmen's clocks,
When turtles tread, and rooks, and daws,
And maidens bleach their summer smocks,
The cuckoo then, on every tree,
Mocks married men; for thus sings he,
    Cuckoo;
Cuckoo, cuckoo: O word of fear,
Unpleasing to a married ear!

WINTER.

When icicles hang by the wall,
And Dick the shepherd blows his nail,
And Tom bears logs into the hall,
And milk comes frozen home in pail,
When blood is nipp'd and ways be foul,
Then nightly sings the staring owl,
    Tu-who;
Tu-whit, tu-who, a merry note,
While greasy Joan doth keel the pot.
When all aloud the wind doth blow,
And coughing drowns the parson's saw,
And birds sit brooding in the snow,
And Marian's nose looks red and raw,
When roasted crabs hiss in the bowl,
Then nightly sings the staring owl,
    Tu-who;
Tu-whit, tu-who, a merry note,
While greasy Joan doth keel the pot.

ARM. The words of Mercury are harsh after the
songs of Apollo. You that way,—we this way.
                  (Exeunt.)

The feeling-index registers such strong approval of this episode that
a critic with ambition is obliged to account for it. He can scarcely account
for it in terms of the weight of its contents severally.

At first glance Shakespeare has provided only a pleasant little caricature of the old-fashioned (to us, medieval) debate between personified characters. It is easygoing, like nonsense; no labor is lost here. Each party speaks two stanzas and concludes both stanzas with the refrain about his bird, the cuckoo or the owl. There is next to no generalized argument, or dialectic proper. Each argues by citing his characteristic exhibits. In the first stanza Spring cites some flowers; in the second stanza, some business by country persons, with interpolation of some birds that make love. Winter in both stanzas cites the country business of the season. In the refrain the cuckoo, Spring's symbol, is used to refer the love-making to more than the birds; and this repeats itself though it is naughty. The owl is only a nominal symbol for Winter, an "emblem" that is not very emblematic, but the refrain manages another reference to the kitchen, and repeats itself, as if Winter's pleasures focussed in the kitchen.

In this poem texture is not very brilliant, but it eclipses structure. The argument, we would say in academic language, is concerned with "the relative advantages of Spring and Winter." The only logical determinateness this structure has is the good coordination of the items cited by Spring as being really items peculiar to Spring, and of the Winter items as peculiar to Winter. The symbolic refrains look like summary or master items, but they seem to be a little more than summary and in fact to mean a little more than they say. The argument is trifling on the whole, and the texture from the point of view of felt human importance lacks decided energy; both which observations are to be made, and most precisely, of how many famous lyrics, especially those before that earnest and self-conscious nineteenth century! The value of the poem is greater than the value of its parts: that is what the critic is up against.

Unquestionably it is possible to assemble very fine structures out of ordinary materials. The good critic will study the poet's technique, in confidence that here the structural principles will be discovered at home. In this study he will find as much range for his activities as he desires.

Especially must he study the metrics, and their implications for structural composition. In this poem I think the critic ought to make good capital of the contrast between the amateurishness of the pleasant discourse as meaning and the hard determinate form of it phonetically. The meter on the whole is out of relation to the meaning of the poem or to anything else specifically; it is a musical material of low grade, but plastic and only slightly resistant material, and its presence in every poem is that of an abstractionist element that belongs to the art.

And here I will suggest another analogy, this one between Shakespeare's poem and some ordinary specimen of painting. It does not matter how old-fashioned or representational the painting is, we shall all, if we are instructed in the tradition of this art, require it to exhibit along with its represented object an abstract design in terms of pure physical balance or symmetry. We sense rather than measure the success of this design, but it is as if we had drawn a horizontal axis and a vertical axis through the center of the picture, and required the painted masses to balance with respect to each of these two axes. This is an over-simple statement of a structural requirement by which the same details function in two worlds that are different, and that do not correlate with each other. If the painting is of the Holy Family, we might say that this object has a drama, or an economy, of its own; but that the physical masses which compose it must enter also into another economy, that of abstract design; and that the value of any unit mass for the one economy bears no relation to its value for the other. The painting is of great ontological interest because it embodies this special dimension of abstract form. And turning to the poem we should find that its represented "meaning" is analogous to the represented object in the painting, while its meter is analogous to the pure design.

A number of fascinating speculative considerations must follow upon this discovery. They will have to do with the most fundamental laws of this world's structure. They will be profoundly ontological, though I do not mean that they must be ontological in some recondite sense; ontological in such a homely and compelling sense that perhaps a child might intuit the principles which the critic will arrive at analytically, and with much labor.

I must stop at this point, since I am desired not so much to anticipate the critic as to present him. In conclusion I will remark that the critic will doubtless work empirically, and set up his philosophy only as the drift of his findings will compel him. But ultimately he will be compelled. He will have to subscribe to an ontology. If he is a sound critic his ontology will be that of his poets; and what is that? I suggest that the poetic world-view is Aristotelian and "realistic" rather than Platonic and "idealistic." He cannot follow the poets and still conceive himself as inhabiting the rational or "tidy" universe that is supposed by the scientists.

PURE AND IMPURE POETRY

ROBERT PENN WARREN

CRITICS are rarely faithful to their labels and their special strategies. Usually the critic will confess that no one strategy—the psychological, the moralistic, the formalistic, the historical—or combination of strategies, will quite work the defeat of the poem. For the poem is like the monstrous Orillo in Boiardo's *Orlando Innamorato*. When the sword lops off any member of the monster, that member is immediately rejoined to the body, and the monster is as formidable as ever. But the poem is even more formidable than the monster, for Orillo's adversary finally gained a victory by an astonishing feat of dexterity: he slashed off both the monster's arms and quick as a wink seized them and flung them into the river. The critic who vaingloriously trusts his method to account for the poem, to exhaust the poem, is trying to emulate this dexterity: he thinks that he, too, can win by throwing the lopped-off arms into the river. But he is doomed to failure. Neither fire nor water will suffice to prevent the rejoining of the mutilated members to the monstrous torso. There is only one way to conquer the monster: you must eat it, bones, blood, skin, pelt, and gristle. And even then the monster is not dead, for it lives in you, is assimilated into you, and you are different, and somewhat monstrous yourself, for having eaten it.

So the monster will always win, and the critic knows this. He does not want to win. He knows that he must always play stooge to the monster. All he wants to do is to give the monster a chance to exhibit again its miraculous power.

With this fable, I shall begin by observing that poetry wants to be pure. And it always succeeds in this ambition. In so far as we have poetry at all, it is always pure poetry; that is, it is not non-poetry. The poetry of Shakespeare, the poetry of Pope, the poetry of Herrick, is pure, in so far as it is poetry at all. We call the poetry "higher" or "lower," we say "more powerful" or "less powerful" about it, and we are, no doubt, quite right in doing so. The souls that form the great rose of Paradise are seated in banks and tiers of ascending blessedness, but they are all saved, they are all perfectly happy; they are all "pure," for they have all been purged of mortal

"Pure and Impure Poetry" reprinted by permission of Robert Penn Warren and *The Kenyon Review*.

taint. This is not to say, however, that if we get poetry from one source, such a single source, say Shakespeare, should suffice us in as much as we can always appeal to it, or that, since all poetry is equally pure, we engage in a superfluous labor in trying to explore or create new sources of poetry. No, for we can remember that every soul in the great rose is precious in the eyes of God. No soul is the substitute for another.

Poetry wants to be pure, but poems do not. At least, most of them do not want to be too pure. The poems want to give us poetry, which is pure, and the elements of a poem, in so far as it is a good poem, will work together toward that end, but many of the elements, taken in themselves, may actually seem to contradict that end, or be neutral toward the achieving of that end. Are we then to conclude that, because neutral or recalcitrant elements appear in poems, even in poems called great, these elements are simply an index to human frailty, that in a perfect world there would be no dross in poems which would, then, be perfectly pure? No, it does not seem to be merely the fault of our world, for the poems include, deliberately, more of the so-called dross than would appear necessary. They are not even as pure as they might be in this imperfect world. They mar themselves with cacophonies, jagged rhythms, ugly words and ugly thoughts, colloquialisms, clichés, sterile technical terms, head work and argument, self-contradictions, clevernesses, irony, realism—all things which call us back to the world of prose and imperfection.

Sometimes a poet will reflect on this state of affairs, and grieve. He will decide that he, at least, will try to make one poem as pure as possible. So he writes:

> Now sleeps the crimson petal, now the white;
> Nor waves the cypress in the palace walk;
> Nor winks the gold fin in the porphyry font:
> The firefly wakens: waken thou with me.

We know the famous garden. We know how all nature conspires here to express the purity of the moment: how the milk-white peacock glimmers like a ghost, and how like a ghost the unnamed "she" glimmers on to her tryst; how earth lies "all Danaë to the stars," as the beloved's heart lies open to the lover; and how, in the end, the lily folds up her sweetness, "and slips into the bosom of the lake," as the lovers are lost in the sweet dissolution of love.

And we know another poet and another garden. Or perhaps it is the same garden, after all:

> I arise from dreams of thee
> In the first sweet sleep of night,
> When the winds are breathing low

And the stars are shining bright.
I arise from dreams of thee,
And a spirit in my feet
Hath led me—who knows how?
To thy chamber window, Sweet!

We remember how, again, all nature conspires, how the wandering airs "faint," how the Champak's odors "pine," how the nightingale's complaint "dies upon her heart," as the lover will die upon the beloved's heart. Nature here strains out of nature, it wants to be called by another name, it wants to spiritualize itself by calling itself another name. How does the lover get to the chamber window? He refuses to say how, in his semi-somnambulistic daze, he got there. He blames, he says, "a spirit in my feet," and hastens to disavow any knowledge of how that spirit operates. In any case, he arrives at the chamber window. Subsequent events and the lover's reaction toward them are somewhat hazy. We only know that the lover, who faints and fails at the opening of the last stanza, and who asks to be lifted from the grass by a more enterprising beloved, is in a condition of delectable passivity, in which distinctions blur out in the "purity" of the moment.

Let us turn to another garden: the place, Verona; the time, a summer night, with full moon. The lover speaks:

But soft! what light through yonder window breaks?
It is the east. . . .

But we know the rest, and know that this garden, in which nature for the moment conspires again with the lover, is the most famous of them all, for the scene is justly admired for its purity of effect, for giving us the very essence of young, untarnished love. Nature conspires beneficently here, but we may chance to remember that beyond the garden wall strolls Mercutio, who can celebrate Queen Mab, but who is always aware that nature has other names as well as the names the pure poets and pure lovers put upon her. And we remember that Mercutio outside the wall, has just said:

. . . 'twould anger him
To raise a spirit in his mistress's circle
Of some strange nature, letting it there stand
Till she had laid it and conjured it down.

Mercutio has made a joke, a bawdy joke. That is bad enough, but worse, he has made his joke witty and, worst of all, intellectually complicated in its form. Realism, wit, intellectual complication—these are the enemies of the garden purity.

But the poet has not only let us see Mercutio outside the garden wall.

Within the garden itself, when the lover invokes nature, when he spiritual-
izes and innocently trusts her, and says,

> Lady, by yonder blessed moon I swear,

the lady herself replies,

> O, swear not by the moon, the inconstant moon,
> That monthly changes in her circled orb.

The lady distrusts "pure" poems, nature spiritualized into forgetfulness.
She has, as it were, a rigorous taste in metaphor, too; she brings a logical
criticism to bear on the metaphor which is too easy; the metaphor must
prove itself to her, must be willing to subject itself to scrutiny beyond the
moment's enthusiasm. She injects the impurity of an intellectual style into
the lover's pure poem.

And we must not forget the voice of the nurse, who calls from within,
a voice which, we discover, is the voice of expediency, of half-measures,
of the view that circumstances alter cases—the voice of prose and imperfection.

It is time to ask ourselves if the celebrated poetry of this scene, which
as poetry is pure, exists despite the impurities of the total composition, if
the effect would be more purely poetic were the nurse and Mercutio absent
and the lady a more sympathetic critic of pure poems. I do not think so.
The effect might even be more vulnerable poetically if the impurities were
purged away. Mercutio, the lady, and the nurse are critics of the lover, who
believes in pure poems, but perhaps they are necessary. Perhaps the lover
can only be accepted in their context. The poet seems to say: "I know
the worst that can be said on this subject, and I am giving fair warning.
Read at your own risk." So the poetry arises from a recalcitrant and contradictory context; and finally involves that context.

Let us return to one of the other gardens, in which there is no Mercutio
or nurse, and in which the lady is more sympathetic. Let us mar its purity
by installing Mercutio in the shrubbery, from which the poet was so careful
to banish him. You can hear his comment when the lover says:

> And a spirit in my feet
> Hath led me—who knows how?
> To thy chamber window, Sweet!

And we can guess what the wicked tongue would have to say in response
to the last stanza.

It may be that the poet should have made his peace early with Mercutio, and have appealed to his better nature. For Mercutio seems to be
glad to cooperate with a poet. But he must be invited; otherwise, he is

apt to show a streak of merry vindictiveness about the finished product. Poems are vulnerable enough at best. Bright reason mocks them like sun from a wintry sky. They are easily left naked to laughter when leaves fall in the garden and the cold winds come. Therefore, they need all the friends they can get, and Mercutio, who is an ally of reason and who himself is given to mocking laughter, is a good friend for a poem to have.

On what terms does a poet make his peace with Mercutio? There are about as many sets of terms as there are good poets. I know that I have loaded the answer with the word *good* here, that I have implied a scale of excellence based, in part at least, on degree of complication. I shall return to this question. For the moment, however, let us examine a poem whose apparent innocence and simple lyric cry should earn it a place in any anthology of "pure poetry."

> Western wind, when wilt thou blow
>   That the small rain down can rain?
> Christ, that my love were in my arms
>   And I in my bed again!

The lover, grieving for the absent beloved, cries out for relief. Several kinds of relief are involved in the appeal to the wind. First there is the relief that would be had from the sympathetic manifestation of nature. The lover, in his perturbation of spirit, invokes the perturbations of nature. He exclaims,

> Western wind, when wilt thou blow

and Lear exclaims,

> Blow, winds, and crack your cheeks! rage! blow!

Second, there is the relief that would be had by the fulfillment of grief— the frost of grief, the drouth of grief broken, the full anguish expressed, then the violence allayed in the peace of tears. Third, there is the relief that would be had in the excitement and fulfillment of love itself. There seems to be a contrast between the first two types of relief and the third type; speaking loosely, we may say that the first two types are romantic and general, the third type realistic and specific. So much for the first two lines.

In the last two lines, the lover cries out for the specific solace of his case: reunion with his beloved. But there is a difference between the two lines. The first is general, and romantic. The phrase "in my arms" does not seem to mean exactly what it says. True, it has a literal meaning, if we can look close at the words, but it is hard to look close because of the romantic aura—the spiritualized mist about them.[1] But with the last line the perfectly literal meaning suddenly comes into sharp focus. The mist is rifted and we can look straight at the words, which, we discover with a slight shock of surprise, do mean exactly what they say. The last line is realistic and specific. It is not even content to say,

> And I in bed again!

It is, rather, more scrupulously specific, and says,

> And I in *my* bed again! [2]

All of this does not go to say that the realistic elements here are to be taken as cancelling, or negating, the romantic elements. There is no ironical leer. The poem is not a celebration of carnality. It is a faithful lover who speaks. He is faithful to the absent beloved, and he is also faithful to the full experience of love. That is, he does not abstract one aspect of the experience and call it the whole experience. He does not strain nature out of nature; he does not over-spiritualize nature. This nameless poet would never have said, in the happier days of his love, that he had been led to his Sweet's chamber window by a "spirit in my feet"; and he certainly would not have added the coy disavowal, "who knows how?" But because the nameless poet refused to over-spiritualize nature, we can accept the spirituality of the poem.

Another poem gives us another problem.

> Ah, what avails the sceptered race,
>   Ah, what the form divine!
> What every virtue, every grace!
>   Rose Aylmer, all were thine.
>
> Rose Aylmer, whom those wakeful eyes
>   May weep, but never see,
> A night of memories and of sighs
>   I consecrate to thee.

---

[1] It may be objected here that I am reading the phrase "in my arms" as a 20th Century reader. I confess the fact. Certainly, several centuries have passed since the composition of the little poem, and those centuries have thickened the romantic mist about the words, but it is scarcely to be believed that the 16th century was the clear, literal Eden dawn of poetry when words walked without the fig leaf.

[2] In connection with the word *my* in this line, we may also feel that it helps to set over the comfort and satisfaction there specified against the bad weather of the first two lines. We may also glance at the word *small* in the second line. It is the scrupulous word, the word that, realistically, makes us believe in the rain. But, too, it is broader in its function. The storm which the lover invokes will not rend the firmament, it will not end the world; it will simply bring down the "small" rain, a credible rain.

This is another poem about lost love: a "soft" subject. Now to one kind of poet the soft subject presents a sore temptation. Because it is soft in its natural state, he is inclined to feel that to get at its poetic essence he must make it softer still, that he must insist on its softness, that he must render it as "pure" as possible. At first glance, it may seem that Landor is trying to do just that. What he says seems to be emphatic, unqualified, and open. Not every power, grace, and virtue could avail to preserve his love. That statement insists on the pathetic contrast. And in the next stanza, wakefulness and tearfulness are mentioned quite unashamedly, along with memories and sighs. It is all blurted out, as pure as possible.

But only in the paraphrase is it "blurted." The actual quality of the first stanza is hard, not soft. It is a chiseled stanza, in which formality is insisted upon. We may observe the balance of the first and second lines; the balance of the first half with the second half of the third line, which recapitulates the structure of the first two lines; the balance of the two parts of the last line, though here the balance is merely a rhythmical and not a sense balance as in the preceding instances; the binders of discreet alliteration, repetition, and assonance. The stanza is built up, as it were, of units which are firmly defined and sharply separated, phrase by phrase, line by line. We have the formal control of the soft subject, ritual and not surrender.

But in the second stanza the rigor of this formality is somewhat abated, as the more general, speculative emphasis (why cannot pomp, virtue, and grace avail?) gives way to the personal emphasis, as though the repetition of the beloved's name had, momentarily, released the flood of feeling. The first line of the second stanza spills over into the second; the "wakeful eyes" as subject find their verb in the next line, "weep," and the *wake-weep* alliteration, along with the rest after *weep,* points up the disintegration of the line, just as it emphasizes the situation. Then with the phrase "but never see" falling away from the long thrust of the rhetorical structure to the pause after *weep,* the poem seems to go completely soft, the frame is broken. But, even as the poet insists on "memories and sighs" in the last two lines he restores the balance. Notice the understatement of "A night." It says: "I know that life is a fairly complicated affair, and that I am committed to it and to its complications. I intend to stand by my commitment, as a man of integrity, that is, to live despite the grief. Since life is complicated, I cannot, if I am to live, spare too much time for indulging grief. I can give *a* night, but not all nights." The lover, like the hero of Frost's poem "Stopping by Woods on a Winter Evening," tears himself from the temptation of staring into the treacherous, delicious blackness, for he, too, has "promises to keep." Or he resembles the Homeric heroes who, after the perilous passage is made, after their energy has saved their lives, and after they have beached their craft and eaten their meal, can then set aside an hour before sleep to mourn the comrades lost by the way—the heroes who, as Aldous Huxley says, understand realistically a whole truth as contrasted with a half-truth.

Is this a denial of the depth and sincerity of the grief? The soft reader, who wants the poem pure, may be inclined to say so. But let us look at the last line to see what it gives us in answer to this question. The answer seems to lie in the word *consecrate*. The meter thrusts this word at us; we observe that two of the three metrical accents in the line fall on syllables of this word forcing it beyond its prose emphasis. The word is important and the importance is justified, for the word tells us that the single night is not merely a lapse into weakness, a trivial event to be forgotten when the weakness is overcome. It is, rather, an event of the most extreme and focal importance, an event formally dedicated, "set apart for sacred uses," an event by which other events are to be measured. So the word *consecrate* formalizes, philosophizes, ritualizes the grief; it specifies what style in the first stanza has implied.

But here is another poem of grief, grief at the death of a child:

> There was such speed in her little body,
> And such lightness in her footfall,
> It is no wonder that her brown study
> Astonishes us all.
>
> Her wars were bruited in our high window.
> We looked among orchard trees and beyond
> Where she took arms against her shadow,
> Or harried unto the pond
>
> The lazy geese, like a snow cloud
> Dripping their snow on the green grass,
> Tricking and stopping, sleepy and proud,
> Who cried in goose, Alas,
>
> For the tireless heart within the little
> Lady with rod that made them rise
> From their noon apple dreams, and scuttle
> Goose-fashion under the skies!
>
> But now go the bells, and we are ready;
> In one house we are sternly stopped
> To say we are vexed at her brown study,
> Lying so primly propped.

Another soft subject, softer, if anything, than the subject of "Rose Aylmer," and it presents the same problem. But the problem is solved in a different way.

•

The first stanza is based on two time-honored clichés: first, "Heaven, won't that child ever be still, she is driving me distracted"; and second, "She was such an active, healthy-looking child, would you've ever thought she would just up and die?" In fact, the whole poem develops these clichés, and exploits, in a back-hand fashion, the ironies implicit in their inter-relation. And in this connection, we may note that the fact of the clichés, rather than more original or profound observations, at the root of the poem is important; there is in the poem the contrast between the staleness of the clichés and the shock of the reality. Further, we may note that the second cliché is an answer, savagely ironical in itself, to the first: the child you wished would be still *is* still, despite all that activity which your adult oc-cupations deplored.

But such a savage irony is not the game here. It is too desperate, too naked, in a word, too pure. And ultimately, it is, in a sense, a meaningless irony if left in its pure state, because it depends on a mechanical, accidental contrast in nature, void of moral content. The poem is concerned with modifications and modulations of this brute, basic irony, modulations and modifications contingent upon an attitude taken toward it by a responsible human being, the speaker of the poem. The savagery is masked, or ameliorated.

In this connection, we may observe, first, the phrase "brown study." It is not the "frosted flower," the "marmoreal immobility," or any one of a thousand such phrases which would aim for the pure effect. It is merely the brown study which astonishes—a phrase which denies, as it were, the finality of the situation, underplays the pathos, and merely reminds one of those moments of childish pensiveness into which the grown-up cannot penetrate. And the phrase itself is a cliché—the common now echoed in the uncommon.

Next, we may observe that stanzas two, three, and four simply docu-ment, with a busy yet wavering rhythm (one sentence runs through the three stanzas) the tireless naughtiness which was once the cause of rebuke, the naughtiness which disturbed the mature goings-on in the room with the "high window." But the naughtiness has been transmuted, by events just transpired, into a kind of fanciful story-book dream-world, in which geese are whiter than nature, and the grass greener, in which geese speak in goose language, saying "Alas," and have apple dreams. It is a drowsy, delicious world, in which the geese are bigger than life, and more important. It is an unreal (now unreal because lost), stylized world. Notice how the phrase "the little lady with rod" works: the detached, grown-up primness of "little lady"; the formal, stiff effect gained by the omission of the article before *rod;* the slightly unnatural use of the word *rod* itself, which sets some distance between us and the scene (perhaps with the hint of the fairy story, a magic wand, or a magic rod—not a common, every-day stick). But the stanzas tie back into the premises of the poem in other ways. The little girl, in her naughtiness, warred against her shadow. Is it crowding matters too hard to surmise that the shadow here achieves a sort of covert symbolic significance? The little girl lost her war against her "shadow," which was always with her. Certainly the phrase "tireless heart" has some rich connotations. And the geese which say "Alas!" conspire with the family to deplore the excessive activity of the child. (They do not conspire to express the present grief, only the past vexation—an inversion of the method of the pastoral elegy, or of the method of the first two garden poems.)

The business of the three stanzas, then, may be said to be two-fold. First, they make us believe more fully in the child and therefore in the fact of the grief itself. They "prove" the grief, and they show the deliciousness of the lost world which will never look the same from the high window. Second, and contrariwise, they "transcend" the grief, or at least give a hint of a means for transcending the immediate anguish: the lost world is, in one sense, redeemed out of time, it enters the pages of the picture book where geese speak, where the untrue is true, where the fleeting is fixed. What was had cannot, after all, be lost. (By way of comparison—a comparison which, because extreme, may be helpful—I cite the transcendence in *La Récherche du Temps Perdu*.) The three stanzas, then, to state it in another way, have validated the first stanza and have prepared for the last.

The three stanzas have made it possible for us to say, when the bell tolls, "we are ready." Some kind of terms, perhaps not the best terms possible but some kind, have been made with the savage underlying irony. But the terms arrived at do not prevent the occasion from being a "stern" one. The transcendence is not absolute, and in the end is possible only because of an exercise of will and self-control. Because we control ourselves, we can say "vexed" and not some big word. And the word itself picks up the first of the domestic clichés on which the poem is based—the outburst of impatience at the naughty child who, by dying, has performed her most serious piece of naughtiness. But now the word comes to us charged with the burden of the poem, and further, as re-echoed here by the phrase "brown study," charged by the sentence in which it occurs; we are gathered formally, ritualistically, sternly together to say the word *vexed*.[1] *Vexed* becomes the ritualistic, the summarizing word.

---

[1] It might be profitable, in contrast with this poem, to analyze "After the Burial," by James Russell Lowell, a poem which is identical in situation. But in Lowell's poem the savagery of the irony is unqualified. In fact, the whole poem insists, quite literally, that qualification is impossible: the scheme of the poem is to set up the brute fact

I have used the words *pure* and *impure* often in the foregoing pages, and I confess that I have used them rather loosely. But perhaps it has been evident that I have meant something like this: the pure poem tries to be pure by excluding, more or less rigidly, certain elements which might qualify or contradict its original impulse. In other words, the pure poems want to be, and desperately, all of a piece. It has also been evident, no doubt, that the kinds of impurity which are admitted or excluded by the various little anthology pieces which have been analyzed, are different in the different poems. This is only to be expected, for there is not one doctrine of "pure poetry"—not one definition of what constitutes impurity in poems—but many. And not all of the doctrines are recent. When, for example, one cites Poe as the father of *the* doctrine of pure poetry, one is in error; Poe simply fathered *a* particular doctrine of pure poetry. One can find other doctrines of purity long antedating Poe. When Sir Philip Sidney, for example, legislated against tragi-comedy, he was repeating a current doctrine of purity. When Ben Jonson told William Drummond that Donne, for not keeping of accent, deserved hanging, he was defending another kind of purity, and when Dryden spoke to save the ear of the fair sex from metaphysical perplexities in amorous poems, he was defending another kind of purity, just as he was defending another when he defined the nature of the heroic drama. The 18th Century had a doctrine of pure poetry, which may be summed up under the word *sublimity,* but which involved two corollary doctrines, one concerning diction and the other concerning imagery. But at the same time that this century, by means of these corollary doctrines, was tidying up and purifying, as Mr. Monk and Mr. Henn have indicated, the doctrine derived from Longinus, it was admitting into the drama certain impurities which the theorists of the heroic drama would not have admitted.[1]

But when we think of the modern doctrine of pure poetry, we usually think of Poe, as critic and poet, perhaps of Shelley, of the Symbolists, of the Abbé Brémond, perhaps of Pater, and certainly of George Moore and

---

of death against possible consolations. It insists on "tears," the "thin-worn locket," the "anguish of deathless hair," "the smallness of the child's grave," the "little shoe in the corner." It is a poem which, we might say, does not progress, but ends where it begins, resting in the savage irony from which it stems; or we might say that it is a poem without any "insides" for the hero of the poem is not attempting to do anything about the problem which confronts him—it is a poem without issue, without conflict, a poem of unconditional surrender. In other words, it tries to be a pure poem, pure grief, absolutely inconsolable. It is a strident poem, and strident in its rhythms. The fact that we know this poem to be an expression of a bereavement historically real makes it an embarrassing poem, as well. It is a naked poem.

[1] Samuel Holt Monk: *The Sublime: a Study of Critical Theories in XVIII-Century England,* and T. R. Henn: *Longinus and English Criticism.*

the Imagists. We know Poe's position: the long poem is "a flat contradiction in terms," because intense excitement, which is essential in poetry, cannot be long maintained; the moral sense and the intellect function more satisfactorily in prose than in poetry, and, in fact, "Truth" and the "Passions," which are for Poe associated with intellect and the moral sense, may actually be inimical to poetry; vagueness, suggestiveness, are central virtues, for poetry has for "its object an *indefinite* instead of a *definite* pleasure"; poetry is not supposed to undergo close inspection, only a cursory glance, for it, "above all things, is a beautiful painting whose tints, to minute inspection, are confusion worse confounded, but start out boldly to the cursory glance of the connoisseur"; poetry aspires toward music, since it is concerned with "indefinite sensations, to which music is an *essential,* since the comprehension of sweet sound is our most indefinite conception"; melancholy is the most poetical effect and enters into all the higher manifestations of beauty. We know, too, the Abbé Brémond's mystical interpretation, and the preface to George Moore's anthology, and the Imagist manifesto.

But these views are not identical. Shelley, for instance, delights in the imprecision praised and practiced by Poe, but he has an enormous appetite for "Truth" and the "Passions," which are, except for purposes of contrast, excluded by Poe. The Imagist manifesto, while excluding ideas, endorses precision rather than vagueness in rendering the image, and admits diction and objects which would have seemed impure to Poe and to many poets of the 19th Century, and does not take much stock in the importance of verbal music. George Moore emphasizes the objective aspect of his pure poetry, which he describes as "something which the poet creates outside his own personality," and this is opposed to the subjective emphasis in Poe and Shelley; but he shares with both an emphasis on verbal music, and with the former a distaste for ideas.

But more recently, the notion of poetic purity has emerged in other contexts, contexts which sometimes obscure the connection of the new theories with the older theories. For instance Max Eastman has a theory. "Pure poetry," he says in *The Literary Mind,* "is the pure effort to heighten consciousness." Mr. Eastman, we discover elsewhere in his book, would ban idea from poetry, but his motive is different from, say, the motive of Poe, and the difference is important: Poe would kick out the ideas because the ideas hurt the poetry, and Mr. Eastman would kick out the ideas because the poetry hurts the ideas. Only the scientist, he tells us, is entitled to have ideas on any subject, and the rest of the citizenry must wait to be told what attitude to take toward the ideas which they are not permitted to have except at secondhand. Literary truth, he says, is truth which is "uncertain or comparatively unimportant." But he assigns the poet a function—to heighten consciousness. But in the light of this context we would have to rewrite his original definition: pure poetry is the pure effort to heighten consciousness, but the consciousness which is heightened must not have any connection with ideas, must involve no attitude toward any ideas.

Furthermore, to assist the poet in fulfilling the assigned function, Mr. Eastman gives him a somewhat sketchy doctrine of "pure" poetic diction. For instance, the word *bloated* is not admissible into a poem because it is, as he testifies, "sacred to the memory of dead fish," and the word *tangy* is, though he knows not exactly how, "intrinsically poetic." The notion of a vocabulary which is intrinsically poetic seems, with Mr. Eastman, to mean a vocabulary which indicates agreeable or beautiful objects. So we might rewrite the original definition to read: pure poetry is the pure effort to heighten consciousness, but the consciousness which is heightened must be a consciousness exclusively of agreeable or beautiful objects—certainly not a consciousness of any ideas.

In a recent book, *The Idiom of Poetry,* Frederick Pottle has discussed the question of pure poetry. He distinguishes another type of pure poetry in addition to the types already mentioned. He calls it the "Elliptical," and would include in it symbolist and metaphysical poetry (old and new) and some work by poets such as Collins, Blake, and Browning. He observes— without any pejorative implication, for he is a critical relativist and scarcely permits himself the luxury of evaluative judgments—that the contemporary product differs from older examples of the elliptical type in that "the modern poet goes much farther in employing private experiences or ideas than would formerly have been thought legitimate." To the common reader, he says, "the prime characteristic of this kind of poetry is not the nature of its imagery but its obscurity: its urgent suggestion that you add something to the poem without telling you what that something is." This omitted "something" he interprets as the prose "frame," to use his word, the state-ment of the occasion, the logical or narrative transitions, the generalized application derived from the poem, etc. In other words, this type of pure poetry contends that "the effect would be more powerful if we could some-how manage to feel the images fully and accurately without having the effect diluted by any words put in to give us a 'meaning'—that is, if we could expel all the talk *about* the imaginative realization and have the pure realization itself." [1]

---

[1] F. W. Bateson, in *English Poetry and the English Language,* discusses the impulse in contemporary poetry. Tennyson, he points out in connection with "The Sailor Boy," dilutes his poetry by telling a story as well as writing a poem, and "a shorter poem would have spoilt his story." The claims of prose conquer the claims of

For the moment I shall pass the question of the accuracy of Mr. Pottle's description of the impulse of Elliptical Poetry and present the question which ultimately concerns him. How pure does poetry need to be in practice? That is the question which Mr. Pottle asks. He answers by saying that a great degree of impurity *may* be admitted, and cites our famous didactic poems, *The Faerie Queene, The Essay on Man, The Vanity of Human Wishes, The Excursion.* That is the only answer which the relativist, and nominalist, can give. Then he turns to what he calls the hardest question in the theory of poetry: what kind of prosaism is acceptable and what is not? His answer, which he advances very modestly, is this:

. . . the element of prose is innocent and even salutary when it appears as— take your choice of three metaphors—a background on which the images are projected, or a frame in which they are shown, or a thread on which they are strung. In short, when it serves a *structural* purpose. Prose in a poem seems offensive to me when . . . the prosaisms are sharp, obvious, individual, and ranked coordinately with the images.

At first glance this looks plausible, and the critic has used the sanctified word *structural*. But at second glance we may begin to wonder what the sanctified word means to the critic. It means something rather mechanical —background, frame, thread. The structure is a showcase, say a jeweler's showcase, in which the little jewels of poetry are exhibited, the images. The showcase shouldn't be ornamental itself ("sharp, obvious, individual," Mr. Pottle says), for it would then distract us from the jewels; it should be chastely designed, and the jewels should repose on black velvet and not on flowered chintz. But Mr. Pottle doesn't ask what the relation among the bright jewels should be. Apparently, not only does the showcase bear no relation to the jewels, but the jewels bear no relation to each other. Each one is a shining little focus of heightened consciousness, or pure realization, existing for itself alone. Or perhaps he should desire that they be arranged in some mechanical pattern, such a pattern, perhaps, as would make it easier for the eye to travel from one little jewel to the next when the time comes to move on. Structure becomes here simply a device of salesmanship, a well-arranged showcase.

It is all mechanical. And this means that Mr. Pottle, after all, is himself

---

poetry. Of the Victorians in general: "The dramatic and narrative framework of their poems, by circumventing the disconcerting plunges into *medias res* which are the essence of poetry, brings it down to a level of prose. The reader knows where he is; it serves the purpose of introduction and note." Such introduction and notes in the body of the poem itself are exactly what Mr. Pottle says is missing in Elliptical Poetry. Mr. Bateson agrees with Poe in accepting intensity as the criterion of the poetic effect, and in accepting the corollary that a poem should be short. But he, contradicting Poe, seems to admire precise and complicated incidental effects.

an exponent of pure poetry. He locates the poetry simply in the images, the nodes of "pure realization." This means that what he calls the "element of prose" includes definition of situation, movement of narrative, logical transition, factual description, generalization, ideas. Such things, for him do not participate in the poetic effect of the poem; in fact, they work against the poetic effect, and so, though necessary as a frame, should be kept from being "sharp, obvious, individual." [1]

I have referred to *The Idiom of Poetry,* first, because it is such an admirable and provocative book, sane, lucid, generous-spirited, and second, because, to my mind, it illustrates the insidiousness with which a doctrine of pure poetry can penetrate into the theory of a critic who is suspicious of such a doctrine. Furthermore, I have felt that Mr. Pottle's analysis might help me to define the common denominator of the various doctrines of pure poetry.

That common denominator seems to be the belief that poetry is an essence that is to be located at some particular place in a poem, or in some particular element. The exponent of pure poetry persuades himself that he has determined the particular something in which the poetry inheres, and then proceeds to decree that poems shall be composed, as nearly as possible, of that element and of nothing else. If we add up the things excluded by various critics and practitioners, we get a list about like this:

1. ideas, truths, generalizations, "meaning"
2. precise, complicated, "intellectual" images
3. unbeautiful, disagreeable, or neutral materials
4. situation, narrative, logical transition
5. realistic details, exact descriptions, realism in general
6. shifts in tone or mood
7. irony
8. metrical variation, dramatic adaptations of rhythm, cacophony, etc.

---

[1] Several other difficulties concerning Mr. Pottle's statement may suggest themselves. First, since he seems to infer that the poetic essence resides in the image, what view would he take of meter and rhythm? His statement, strictly construed, would mean that these factors do not participate in the poetic effect, but are simply part of the frame. Second, what view of dramatic poetry is implied? It seems again that a strict interpretation would mean that the story and the images bear no essential relation to each other, that the story is simply part of the frame. That is, the story, characters, rhythms, and ideas, are on one level and the images, in which the poetry inheres, are on another. But Miss Spurgeon, Mr. Knight, and other critics have given us some reason for holding that the images do bear some relation to the business of the other items. In fact, all of the items, as M. Maritain has said, "feelings, ideas, representations, are for the artist merely materials and means, still symbols." That is, they are all elements in a single expressive structure.

9. meter itself

10. subjective and personal elements

No one theory of pure poetry excludes all of these items, and, as a matter of fact, the items listed are not on the same level of importance. Nor do the items always bear the same interpretation. For example, if one item seems to be central to discussions of pure poetry, it is the first: "ideas," it is said, "are not involved in the poetic effect, and may even be inimical to it." But this view can be interpreted in a variety of ways. If it is interpreted as simply meaning that the paraphrase of a poem is not equivalent to the poem, that the poetic gist is not to be defined as the statement embodied in the poem with the sugar-coating as bait, then the view can be held by opponents as well as exponents of any theory of pure poetry. We might scale down from this interpretation to the other extreme interpretation that the poem should merely give the sharp image in isolation. But there are many complicated and confused variations possible between the two extremes. There is, for example, the interpretation that "ideas," though they are not involved in the poetic effect, must appear in poems to provide, as Mr. Pottle's prosaisms do, a kind of frame, or thread, for the poetry— a spine to support the poetic flesh or a Christmas tree on which the baubles of poetry are hung.[1] T. S. Eliot has said something of this sort:

> The chief use of the "meaning" of a poem, in the ordinary sense, may be (for here again I am speaking of some kinds of poetry and not all) to satisfy one habit of the reader, to keep his mind diverted and quiet, while the poem does its work upon him: much as the imaginary burglar is always provided with a bit of nice meat for the house-dog.

Here, it would seem, Mr. Eliot has simply inverted the old sugar-coated pill theory: the idea becomes the sugar-coating and the "poetry" becomes the medicine. This seems to say that the idea in a poem does not participate in the poetic effect, and seems to commit Mr. Eliot to a theory of pure poetry. But to do justice to the quotation, we should first observe that the parenthesis indicates that the writer is referring to some sort of provisional and superficial distinction and not to a fundamental one, and second observe that the passage is out of its context. In the context, Mr. Eliot goes on to say that some poets "become impatient of this 'meaning' [explicit statement of ideas in logical order] which seems superfluous, and perceive possibilities of intensity through its elimination." This may mean either of two things. It may mean that ideas do not participate in the poetic effect, or it

---

[1] Such an interpretation seems to find a parallel in E. M. Forster's treatment of plot in fiction. Plot in his theory becomes a mere spine and does not really participate, except in a narrow, formal sense, in the fictional effect. By his inversion of the Aristotelian principle, the plot becomes merely a necessary evil.

may mean, though they do participate in the poetic effect, they need not appear in the poem in an explicit and argued form. And this second reading would scarcely be a doctrine of pure poetry at all, for it would involve poetic casuistry and not poetic principle.

We might, however, illustrate the second interpretation by glancing at Marvell's "Horatian Ode" on Cromwell. Marvell does not give us narrative; he does not give us an account of the issues behind the Civil War; he does not state the two competing ideas which are dramatized in the poem, the idea of "sanction" and the idea of "efficiency." But the effect of the poem does involve these two factors; the special reserved, scarcely resolved, irony, which is realized in the historical situation, is an irony derived from unstated materials and ideas. It is, to use Mr. Pottle's term again, a pure poem in so far as it is elliptical in method, but it is anything but a pure poem if by purity we mean the exclusion of idea from participation in the poetic effect. And Mr. Eliot's own practice implies that he believes that ideas do participate in the poetic effect. Otherwise, why did he put the clues to his ideas in the notes at the end of the *Waste Land* after so carefully excluding any explicit statement of them from the body of the poem? If he is regarding those ideas as mere bait—the "bit of nice meat for the house-dog"—he has put the ideas in a peculiar place, in the back of the book—like giving the dog the meat on the way out of the house with the swag or giving the mouse the cheese after he is in the trap. All this would lead one to the speculation that Marvell and Mr. Eliot have purged away statement of ideas from their poems, not because they wanted the ideas to participate less in the poetry, but because they wanted them to participate more fully, intensely, and immediately. This impulse, then, would account for the characteristic type of image, types in which precision, complication, and complicated intellectual relation to the theme are exploited; in other words, they are trying—whatever may be their final success—to carry the movement of mind to the center of the process. On these grounds they are the exact opposite of poets who, presumably on grounds of purity, exclude the movement of mind from the center of the poetic process—from the internal structure of the poem—but pay their respect to it as a kind of footnote, or gloss, or application coming at the end. Marvell and Eliot, by their cutting away of frame, are trying to emphasize the participation of ideas in the poetic process. Then Elliptical Poetry is not, as Mr. Pottle says it is, a pure poetry at all if we regard intention; the elliptical poet is elliptical for the purposes of inclusion, not exclusion.

But waiving the question of Elliptical Poetry, no one of the other theories does—or could—exclude all the items on the list above. And that fact may instruct us. If all of these items were excluded, we might not have any poem at all. For instance, we know how some critics have pointed out that even in the strictest imagist poetry idea creeps in—when the image leaves its natural habitat and enters a poem it begins to "mean" something. The attempt to read ideas out of the poetic party violates the unity of our being and the unity of our experience. "For this reason," as Santayana puts it, "philosophy, when a poet is not mindless, enters inevitably into his poetry, since it has entered into his life; or rather, the detail of things and the detail of ideas pass equally into his verse, when both alike lie in the path that has led him to his ideal. To object to theory in poetry would be like objecting to words there; for words, too, are symbols without the sensuous character of the things they stand for; and yet it is only by the net of new connections which words throw over things, in recalling them, that poetry arises at all. Poetry is an attenuation, a rehandling, an echo of crude experience; it is itself a theoretic vision of things at arm's length." Does this not lead us to the conclusion that poetry does not inhere in any particular element but depends upon the set of relationships, the structure, which we call the poem?

Then the question arises: what elements cannot be used in such a structure? I should answer that nothing that is available in human experience is to be legislated out of poetry. This does not mean that anything can be used in *any* poem, or that some materials or elements may not prove more recalcitrant than others, or that it might not be easy to have too much of some things. But it does mean that, granted certain contexts, any sort of material, a chemical formula for instance, might appear functionally in a poem. It also may mean that, other things being equal, the greatness of a poet depends upon the extent of the area of experience which he can master poetically.

Can we make any generalizations about the nature of the poetic structure? First, it involves resistances, at various levels. There is the tension between the rhythm of the poem and the rhythm of speech (a tension which is very low at the extreme of free verse and at the extreme of verse such as that of "Ulalume," which verges toward a walloping doggerel); between the formality of the rhythm and the informality of the language; between the particular and the general, the concrete and the abstract; between the elements of even the simplest metaphor; between the beautiful and the ugly; between ideas (as in Marvell's poem); between the elements involved in irony (as in "Bells for John Whiteside's Daughter" or "Rose Aylmer"); between prosaisms and poeticisms (as in "Western Wind"). This list is not intended to be exhaustive; it is intended to be merely suggestive. But it may be taken to imply that the poet is like the jiujitsu expert; he wins by utilizing the resistance of his opponent—the materials of the poem. In other words, a poem, to be good, must earn itself. It is a motion toward a point of rest, but if it is not a resisted motion, it is motion of no consequence. For example, a poem which depends upon stock materials and stock responses is simply a toboggan slide, or a fall through space. And the good poem must, in some way, involve the resistances; it must carry something of the context of its own creation; it must come to terms with Mercutio. This is another way of saying that a good poem involves the participation of the reader; it must, as Coleridge puts it, make the reader into "an active creative being." Perhaps we can see this most readily in the case of tragedy: the definition of good or evil is not a "given" in tragedy, it is something to be earned in the process, and even the tragic villain must be "loved." We must kill him, as Brutus killed Caesar, not as butchers but as sacrificers. And all of this adds up to the fact that the structure is a dramatic structure, a movement through action toward rest, through complication toward simplicity of effect.

In the foregoing discussion, I have deliberately omitted reference to another type of pure poetry, a type which, in the context of the present war, may well become dominant. Perhaps the most sensible description of this type can be found in an essay by Herbert Muller:

If it is not the primary business of the poet to be eloquent about these matters [faith and ideals], it still does not follow that he has more dignity or wisdom than those who are, or that he should have more sophistication. At any rate the fact is that almost all poets of the past did freely make large, simple statements, and not in their prosy or lax moments.

Mr. Muller then goes on to illustrate by quoting three famous, large, simple statements:

> In la sua voluntade e nostra pace [1]

and

> We are such stuff
> As dreams are made on; and our little lives
> Are rounded with a sleep.

and

> The mind is its own place, and in itself
> Can make a heaven of hell, a hell of heaven.

Mr. Muller is here attacking the critical emphasis on ironic tension in poetry. His attack really involves two lines of argument. First, the poet is not wiser than the statesman, philosopher, or saint, people who are eloquent about faith and ideals and who say what they mean, without benefit of irony. This Platonic (or pseudo-Platonic) line of argument is, I think, off the point in the present context. Second, the poets of the past

---

[1] [In His will is our peace.]

have made large, simple affirmations that have said what they meant. This line of argument is very much on the point.

Poets *have* tried very hard, for thousands of years, to say what they mean. But they have not only tried to say what they mean, they have tried to prove what they mean. The saint proves his vision by stepping cheerfully into the fires. The poet, somewhat less spectacularly, proves his vision by submitting it to the fires of irony—to the drama of his structure—in the hope that the fires will refine it. In other words, the poet wishes to indicate that his vision has been earned, that it can survive reference to the complexities and contradictions of experience. And irony is one such device of reference.

In this connection let us look at the first of Mr. Muller's exhibits. The famous line occurs in Canto III of the *Paradiso*. It is spoken by Piccarda Donati, in answer to Dante's question as to why she does not desire to rise higher than her present sphere, the sphere of the moon. But it expresses, in unequivocal terms, a central theme of the *Commedia,* as of Christian experience. On the one hand, it may be a pious truism, fit for sampler work, and on the other hand, it may be a burning conviction, tested and earned. Dante, in his poem, sets out to show how it has been earned and tested. One set of ironic tensions, for instance, which centers about this theme concerns the opposition between the notion of human justice and the notion of divine justice. The story of Paolo and Francesca is so warm, appealing, and pathetic in its human terms and their punishment so savage and unrelenting, so incommensurable, it seems, with the fault, that Dante, torn by the conflict, falls down as a dead body falls. Or Farinata, the enemy of Dante's house, is presented by the poet in terms of his human grandeur, which now, in Hell, is transmuted into a super-human grandeur,

> com' avesse l'inferno in gran dispitto.[1]

Ulysses remains a hero, a hero who should draw special applause from Dante, who defined the temporal end of man as the conquest of knowledge. But Ulysses is damned, as the great Brutus is damned, who hangs from the jaws of the fiend in the lowest pit of traitors. So divine justice is set over against human pathos, human dignity, human grandeur, human intellect, human justice. And we recall how Virgil, more than once, reminds Dante that he must not apply human standards to the sights he sees. It is this long conflict, which appears in many forms, this ironic tension, which finally gives body to the simple eloquence of the line in question; the statement is meaningful, not for what it says, but for what has gone before. It is earned. It has been earned by the entire poem.

---

[1] [As if he held hell in great contempt.]

I do not want to misrepresent Mr. Muller. He does follow his quotations by the sentence: "If they are properly qualified in the work as a whole, they may still be taken straight, they *are* [he italicizes the word] taken so in recollection as in their immediate impact." But can this line be taken so in recollection, and was it taken so in its "immediate impact"? And if one does take it so, is he not violating, very definitely, the poet's meaning, for the poet means the *poem,* he doesn't mean the line.

It would be interesting to try to develop the contexts of the other passages which Mr. Muller quotes. But in any case, he was simply trying, in his essay, to guard against what he considered to be, rightly or wrongly, a too narrow description of poetry; he was not trying to legislate all poetry into the type of simple eloquence, the unqualified statement of "faith and ideas." But we have already witnessed certain, probably preliminary, attempts to legislate literature into becoming a simple, unqualified, "pure" statement of faith and ideal. We have seen the writers of the 1920's called the "irresponsibles." We have seen writers such as Proust, Eliot, Dreiser, and Faulkner, called writers of the "death drive." Why are these writers condemned? Because they have tried, within the limits of their gifts, to remain faithful to the complexities of the problems with which they were dealing, because they refused to take the easy statement as solution, because they tried to define the context in which, and the terms by which, faith and ideals could be earned. But this method will scarcely satisfy the mind which is hot for certainties; to that mind it will seem merely an index to lukewarmness, indecision, disunity, treason. The new theory of purity would purge out all complexities and all ironies and all self-criticism. And this theory will forget that the hand-me-down faith, the hand-me-down ideals, no matter what the professed content, is in the end not only meaningless but vicious. It is vicious because, as parody, it is the enemy of all faith.

TENSION IN POETRY

ALLEN TATE

I

MANY poems that we ordinarily think of as good poetry—and some, besides, that we neglect—have certain common features that will allow us to invent, for their sharper apprehension, the name of a single quality. I shall call that quality tension. In abstract language, a poetic work has distinct quality as the ultimate effect of the whole, and that whole is the "result" of a configuration of meaning which it is the duty of the critic to examine and evaluate. In setting forth this duty as my present procedure I am trying to amplify a critical approach that I have used on other occasions, without wholly giving up the earlier method, which I should describe as the analysis of the general ideas implicit in the poetic work.

Towards the end of this essay I shall cite examples of "tension," but I shall not say that they exemplify tension only, or that other qualities must be ignored. There are all kinds of poetry, as many as there are good poets, as many even as there are good poems, for poets may be expected to write more than one kind of poetry; and no single critical insight may impute an exclusive validity to any one kind. In all ages there are schools demanding that one sort only be written—their sort: political poetry for the sake of the cause; picturesque poetry for the sake of the home town; didactic poetry for the sake of the parish; even a generalized personal poetry for the sake of the reassurance and safety of numbers. This last I suppose is the most common variety, the anonymous lyricism in which the common personality exhibits its commonness, its obscure and standard eccentricity, in a language that seems always to be deteriorating; so that today many poets are driven to inventing private languages, or very narrow ones, because public speech has become heavily tainted with mass feeling.

Mass language is the medium of "communication," and its users are less interested in bringing to formal order what is today called the "affective state" than in arousing that state.

Once you have said that everything is One it is obvious that literature is the same as propaganda; once you have said that no truth can be known apart from the immediate dialectical process of history it is obvious that all contemporary artists must prepare the same fashionplate. It is clear too that the One is limited in space as well as time, and the no less Hegelian Fascists are right in saying that all art is patriotic.

What Mr. William Empson calls patriotic poetry sings not merely in behalf of the State; you will find it equally in a lady-like lyric and in much of the political poetry of our time. It is the poetry of the mass language, very different from the "language of the people" which interested the late W. B. Yeats. For example:

> What from the splendid dead
> We have inherited—
> Furrows sweet to the grain, and the weed subdued—
> See now the slug and the mildew plunder.
> Evil does overwhelm
> The larkspur and the corn;
> We have seen them go under.

From this stanza by Miss Millay we infer that her splendid ancestors made the earth a good place that has somehow gone bad—and you get the reason from the title: "Justice Denied in Massachusetts." How Massachusetts could cause a general dessication, why (as we are told in a footnote to the poem) the execution of Sacco and Vanzetti should have anything to do with the rotting of the crops, it is never made clear. These lines are mass language: they arouse an affective state in one set of terms, and suddenly an object quite unrelated to those terms gets the benefit of it; and this effect, which is usually achieved, as I think it is here, without conscious effort, is sentimentality. Miss Millay's poem was admired when it first appeared about ten years ago, and is no doubt still admired, by persons to whom it communicates certain feelings about social justice, by persons for whom the lines are the occasion of feeling shared by them and the poet. But if you do not share those feelings, as I happen not to share them in the images of dessicated nature, the lines and even the entire poem are impenetrably obscure.

I am attacking here the fallacy of communication in poetry. (I am not attacking social justice.) It is no less a fallacy in the writing of poetry than of critical theory. The critical doctrine fares ill the further back you apply it; I suppose one may say—if one wants a landmark—that it began to prosper after 1798; for on the whole nineteenth-century English verse is a poetry of communication. The poets were trying to use verse to convey ideas and feelings that they secretly thought could be better conveyed by science (consult Shelley's *Defense*), or by what today we call, in a significantly bad poetic phrase, the Social Sciences. Yet possibly because the poets believed the scientists to be tough, and the poets joined the scientists in thinking the poets tender, the poets stuck to verse. It may hardly be said that we change this tradition of poetic futility by giving it a new name, Social Poetry. May a poet hope to deal more adequately with sociology than with physics? If he seizes upon either at the level of scientific procedure, has he not abdicated his position as poet?

At a level of lower historical awareness than that exhibited by Mr. Edmund Wilson's later heroes of the Symbolist school, we find the kind of verse that I have been quoting, verse long ago intimidated by the pseudo-rationalism of the Social Sciences. This sentimental intimidation has been so complete that, however easy the verse looked on the page, it gave up all claim to sense. (I assume here what I cannot now demonstrate, that Miss Millay's poem is obscure but that Donne's "Second Anniversarie" is not.) As another example of this brand of obscurity I have selected at random a nineteenth-century lyric, "The Vine," by James Thomson:

> The wine of love is music,
>   And the feast of love is song:
> When love sits down to banquet,
>   Love sits long:
>
> Sits long and rises drunken,
>   But not with the feast and the wine;
> He reeleth with his own heart,
>   That great rich Vine.

The language here appeals to an existing affective state; it has no coherent meaning either literally or in terms of ambiguity or implication; it may be wholly replaced by any of its several paraphrases, which are already latent in our minds. One of these is the confused image of a self-intoxicating man-about-town. Now good poetry can bear the closest literal examination of every phrase, and is its own safeguard against our irony. But the more closely we examine this lyric, the more obscure it becomes; the more we trace the implications of the imagery, the denser the confusion. The imagery adds nothing to the general idea that it tries to sustain; it even deprives that idea of the dignity it has won at the hands of a long succession of better poets going back, I suppose, to Guinizelli:

> Al cor gentil ripara sempre Amore
> Come alla selva augello in la verdura . . .[1]

---

[1] [Within the gentle heart Love shelters him
As birds within the green shade of the grove.—D. G Rosetti (trans.)]

What I want to make clear is the particular kind of failure, not the degree, in a certain kind of poetry. Were we interested in degrees we might give comfort to the nineteenth century by citing lines from John Cleveland or Abraham Cowley, bad lyric verse no better than "The Vine," written in an age that produced some of the greatest English poetry. Here are some lines from Cowley's "Hymn: to light," a hundred-line inventory of some of the offices performed by the subject in a universe that still seems to be on the whole Ptolemaic; I should not care to guess the length the poem might have reached under the Copernican system. Here is one of the interesting duties of light:

> Nor amidst all these Triumphs does thou scorn
> The humble glow-worm to adorn,
> And with those living spangles gild,
> (O Greatness without Pride!) the Bushes of the Field.

Again:

> The Violet, springs little Infant, stands,
> Girt in thy purple Swadling-bands:
> On the fair Tulip thou dost dote;
> Thou cloath'st it in a gay and party-colour'd Coat.

This, doubtless, is metaphysical poetry; however bad the lines may be—they are pretty bad—they have no qualities, bad or good, in common with "The Vine." Mr. Ransom has given us, in a remarkable essay, "Shakespeare at Sonnets" (*The World's Body,* 1938), an excellent description of this kind of poetry: "The impulse to metaphysical poetry . . . consists in committing the feelings in the case . . . to their determination within the elected figure." That is to say, in metaphysical poetry the logical order is explicit; it must be coherent; the imagery by which it is sensuously embodied must have at least the appearance of logical determinism: perhaps the appearance only, because the varieties of ambiguity and contradiction possible beneath the logical surface are endless, as Mr. Empson has demonstrated in his elucidation of Marvell's "The Garden." Here it is enough to say that the development of imagery by extension, its logical determinants being an Ariadne's thread that the poet will not permit us to lose, is the leading feature of the poetry called metaphysical.

But to recognize it is not to evaluate it; and I take it that Mr. Ransom was giving us a true Aristotelian definition of a genus, in which the identification of a type does not compel us to discern the implied values. Logical extension of imagery is no doubt the key to the meaning of Donne's "Valediction: forbidding mourning"; it may equally initiate inquiry into the ludicrous failure of "Hymn: to light," to which I will now return.

While "The Vine" and "Hymn: to light" seem to me equally bad
poetry, Cowley's failure is somewhat to be preferred; its negative superiority lies in a firmer use of the language. There is no appeal to an affective
state; the leading statement can be made perfectly explicit: God is light,
and light is life. The poem is an analytical proposition exhibiting the properties inherent in the major term; that is, exhibiting as much of the universe
as Cowley could get around to before he wearied of logical extension. But
I think it is possible to infer that good poetry could have been written in
Cowley's language; and we know that it was. Every term, even the verbs
converted into nouns, denotes an object, and in the hands of a good poet
would be amenable to controlled distortions of literal representation. But
here the distortions are uncontrolled. Everything is in this language that a
poet needs except the poetry, or the imagination, or what I shall presently
illustrate under the idea of tension.

I have called "Hymn: to light" an analytical proposition. That is the
form in which the theme must have appeared to Cowley's mind; that is to
say, simple analysis of the term, *God,* gave him, as it gave everybody else
in Christendom, the proposition: God is light. (Perhaps, under neo-Platonic
influence, the prime Christian symbol, as Professor Fletcher and others
have shown in reducing to their sources the powers of the Three Blessed
Ladies of *The Divine Comedy.*) But in order to write his poem Cowley
had to develop the symbol by synthetic accretion, by adding to light properties not inherent in its simple analysis:

> The Violet, springs little Infant, stands,
>   Girt in thy purple Swadling-bands . . .

The image, such as it is, is an addition to the central figure of light, an assertion of a hitherto undetected relation among the objects, light, diapers, and
violets—a miscellany that I recommend to the consideration of Mr. E. E.
Cummings, who could get something out of it that Cowley did not intend
us to get. If you will think again of "The Vine," you will observe that
Thomson permits, in the opposite direction, an equal license with the
objects *de*noted by his imagery, with the unhappy results that we have
already seen.

"The Vine" is a failure in denotation. "Hymn: to light" is a failure in
connotation. The language of "The Vine" lacks objective content. Take
"music" and "song" in the first two lines; the context does not allow us
to apprehend the terms in extension; that is, there is no reference to objects
that we may distinguish as "music" and "song"; the wine of love could have
as well been song, its feast music. In "Hymn: to light," a reduction to their
connotations of the terms *violet, swadling-bands,* and *light* (the last being

represented by the pronoun *thou*) yields a clutter of images that may be unified only if we forget the firm denotations of the terms. If we are going to receive as valid the infancy of the violet, we have to ignore the metaphor that conveys it, for the metaphor renders the violet absurd; by ignoring the diaper, and the two terms associated with it, we cease to read the passage, and begin for ourselves the building up of acceptable denotations for the terms of the metaphor.

Absurd: but on what final ground I call these poems absurd I cannot state as a principle. I appeal to the reader's experience, and invite him to form a judgment of his own. It is easy enough to say, as I shall say in detail in a moment, that good poetry is a unity of all the meanings from the furthest extremes of intension and extension. Yet our recognition of the action of this unified meaning is the gift of experience, of culture, of, if you will, our humanism. Our powers of discrimination are not deductive powers, though they may be aided by them; they wait rather upon the cultivation of our total human powers, and they represent a special application of those powers to a single medium of experience—poetry.

I have referred to a certain kind of poetry as the embodiment of the fallacy of communication: it is a poetry that communicates the affective state, which (in terms of language) results from the irresponsible denotations of words. There is a vague grasp of the "real" world. The history of this fallacy, which is as old as poetry but which towards the end of the eighteenth century began to dominate not only poetry, but other arts as well—its history would probably show that the poets gave up the language of denotation to the scientists, and kept for themselves a continually thinning flux of peripheral connotations. The companion fallacy, to which I can give only the literal name, the fallacy of mere denotation, I have also illustrated from Cowley: this is the poetry which contradicts our most developed human insights in so far as it fails to use and direct the rich connotation with which language has been informed by experience.

II

We return to the inquiry set for this discussion: to find out whether there is not a more central achievement in poetry than that represented by either of the extreme examples that we have been considering. I proposed as descriptive of that achievement, the term *tension*. I am using the term not as a general metaphor, but as a special one, derived from lopping the prefixes off the logical terms *ex*tension and *in*tension. What I am saying, of course, is that the meaning of poetry is its "tension," the full organized body of all the extension and intension that we can find in it. The remotest

figurative significance that we can derive does not invalidate the extensions
of the literal statement. Or we may begin with the literal statement and
by stages develop the complications of metaphor: at every stage we may
pause to state the meaning so far apprehended, and at every stage the meaning will be coherent.

The meanings that we select at different points along the infinite line
between extreme intension and extreme extension will vary with our personal "drive," or "interest," or "approach": the Platonist will tend to stay
pretty close to the end of the line where extension, and simple abstraction
of the object into a universal, is easiest, for he will be a fanatic in morals
or some kind of works, and will insist upon the shortest way with what will
ever appear to him the dissenting ambiguities at the intensive end of the
scale. The Platonist (I do not say that his opponent is the Aristotelian)
might decide that Marvell's "To His Coy Mistress" recommends immoral
behavior to the young men, in whose behalf he would try to suppress the
poem. That, of course, would be one "true" meaning of "To His Coy
Mistress," but it is a meaning that the full tension of the poem will not
allow us to entertain exclusively. For we are compelled, since it is there,
to give equal weight to an intensive meaning so rich that, without contradicting the literal statement of the lover-mistress convention, it lifts that convention into an insight into one phase of the human predicament—the
conflict of sensuality and asceticism.

I should like to quote now, not from Marvell, but a stanza from Donne
that I hope will reinforce a little what I have just said and connect it with
some earlier remarks.

> Our two soules therefore, which are one,
> Though I must goe, endure not yet
> A breach, but an expansion,
> Like gold to aiery thinnesse beate.

Here Donne brings together the developing imagery of twenty lines
under the implicit proposition; the unity of two lovers' souls is a nonspatial entity, and is therefore indivisible. That, I believe, is what Mr. John
Crowe Ransom would call the logic of the passage: it is the abstract form of
its extensive meaning. Now the interesting feature here is the logical contradiction of embodying the unitary, nonspatial soul in a spatial image:
the malleable gold is a plane whose surface can always be extended mathe-
matically by one-half, towards infinity; the souls are this infinity. The finite
image of the gold, in extension, logically contradicts the intensive meaning
(infinity) which it conveys; but it does not invalidate that meaning. We
have seen that Cowley compelled us to ignore the denoted diaper in order

that we might take seriously the violet which it pretended to swathe. But in Donne's "Valediction: forbidding mourning" the clear denotation of the gold contains, by intension, the full meaning of the passage. If we reject the gold, we reject the meaning, for the meaning is wholly absorbed into the image of the gold. Intension and extension are here one, and they enrich each other.

Before I leave this beautiful object, I should like to notice two incidental features in further proof of Donne's mastery. "Expansion"—a term denoting an abstract property common to many objects, perhaps here one property of a gas: it expands visibly the quality of the beaten gold.

>   . . . endure not yet
>   a breach . . .

But if the lovers' souls are the formidable, inhuman entity that we have seen, are they not superior to the contingency of a breach? Yes and no: both answers are true answers; for by means of the sly "yet" Donne subtly guards himself against our irony, which would otherwise be quick to scrutinize the extreme metaphor. The lovers have not endured a breach, but they are simple, miserable human beings, and they may quarrel tomorrow.[1]

Now all this meaning and more, and it is all one meaning, is embedded in that stanza: I say more because I have not exhausted the small fraction of significance that my limited powers have permitted me to see. For example, I have not discussed the rhythm, which is of the essential meaning; I have violently isolated four lines from the meaning of the whole poem. Yet, fine as it is, I do not think the poem the greatest poetry; perhaps only very little of Donne makes that grade, or of anybody else. Donne offers many examples of tension in imagery, easier for the expositor than greater passages in Shakespeare.

But convenience of elucidation is not a canon of criticism. I wish now to introduce other kinds of instance, and to let them stand for us as a sort of Arnoldish touchstones to the perfection that poetic statement has occasionally reached. I do not know what bearing my comment has had, or my touchstones may have, upon the larger effects of poetry or upon long poems. The long poem is partly a different problem. I have of necessity confined both commentary and illustration to the slighter effects that seemed to me commensurate with certain immediate qualities of language. For, in the long run, whatever the poet's "philosophy," however wide may be the

---

[1] Mr. F. O. Matthiessen informs me that my interpretation here, which detaches the "yet" from the developing figure, is not the usual one. Mr. Matthiessen refers the phrase to the gold, for which in his view it prepares the way.

extension of his meaning—like Milton's Ptolemaic universe in which he didn't believe—by his language shall you know him; the quality of his language is the valid limit of what he has to say.

I have not searched out the quotations that follow: they at once form the documentation and imply the personal bias from which this inquiry has grown. Only a few of the lines will be identified with the metaphysical technique, or, in Mr. Ransom's fine phrase, the metaphysical strategy. Strategy would here indicate the point on the intensive-extensive scale at which the poet deploys his resources of meaning. The metaphysical poet as a rationalist begins at or near the extensive or denoting end of the line; the romantic or Symbolist poet at the other, intensive end; and each by a straining feat of the imagination tries to push his meanings as far as he can towards the opposite end, so as to occupy the entire scale. I have offered one good and one bad example of the metaphysical strategy, but only defective examples of the Symbolist, which I cited as fallacies of mass language: Thomson was using language at its mass level, unhappily ignorant of the need to embody his connotations in a rational order of thought. (I allude here also, and in a quite literal sense, to Thomson's personal unhappiness, as well as to the excessive pessimism and excessive optimism of other poets of his time.) The great Symbolist poets, from Rimbaud to Yeats, have heeded this necessity of reason. It would be a hard task to choose between the two strategies, the Symbolist and the metaphysical; both at their best are great, and both are incomplete.

These touchstones, I believe, are not poetry of the extremes, but poetry of the center: poetry of tension, in which the "strategy" is diffused into the unitary effect.

> Ask me no more whither doth hast
> The Nightingale when May is past:
> For in your sweet dividing throat
> She winters, and keeps warm her note.

. . . . .

> O thou Steeled Cognizance whose leap commits
> The agile precincts of the lark's return . . .

. . . . .

> That time of year thou mayst in me behold
> When yellow leaves, or none, or few do hang
> Upon those boughs which shake against the cold,
> Bare ruined choirs where late the sweet birds sang.

. . . . .

> Beauty is but a flower
> Which wrinkles will devour;

Brightness falls from the air,
Queens have died young and fair,
Dust hath closed Helen's eye.
I am sick, I must die.
Lord, have mercy upon us!

. . . . .

And then may chance thee to repent
The time that thou hast lost and spent
To cause thy lovers sigh and swoon;
Then shalt thou know beauty but lent,
And wish and want as I have done.

. . . . .

We have lingered in the chambers of the sea
By seagirls wreathed with seaweed red and brown
Till human voices wake us and we drown.

. . . . .

I am of Ireland
And the Holy Land of Ireland
And time runs on, cried she.
Come out of charity
And dance with me in Ireland.

. . . . .

And my poor fool is hanged! No, no, no life!
Why should a dog, a horse, a rat, have life
And thou no breath at all? Thou'lt come no more,
Never, never, never, never, never!—
Pray you undo this button; thank you, sir.—
Do you see this? Look on her,—look,—her lips,—
Look there, look there!

. . . . .

'Tis madness to resist or blame
The force of angry heavens flame:
And, if we would speak true,
Much to the Man is due,
Who, from his private Gardens, where
He liv'd reserved and austere,
As if his highest plot
To plant the Bergamot,
Could by industrious Valour climbe
To ruin the great Work of Time,
And cast the Kingdome old
Into another Mold.

. . . . .

Cover her face; mine eyes dazzle; she died young.

III

There are three more lines that I wish to look at: a tercet from the *Divine Comedy*. I know little of either Dante or his language; yet I have chosen as my final instance of tension—the instance itself will relieve me of the responsibility of the term—I have chosen not a great and difficult passage, but only a slight and perfect one. It is from a scene that has always been the delight of the amateur reader of Dante; we can know more about it with less knowledge than about any other, perhaps, in the poem. The damned of the Second Circle are equivocally damned: Paolo and Francesca were illicit lovers but their crime was incontinence, neither adultery nor pandering, the two crimes of sex for which Dante seems to find any real theological reprobation, for they are committed with the intent of injury.

You will remember that when Dante first sees the lovers they are whirling in a high wind, the symbol here of lust. When Francesca's conversation with the poet begins, the wind dies down, and she tells him where she was born, in these lines:

> Siede la terra dove nata fui
> Sulla marina dove il Po discende
> Per aver pace co' seguaci sui.

Mr. Courtney Landon renders the tercet:

> The town where I was born sits on the shore,
> Whither the Po descends to be at peace
> Together with the streams that follow him.

But it misses a good deal; it misses the force of *seguaci* by rendering it as a verb. Professor Grandgent translates the third line: "To have peace with its pursuers," and comments: "The tributaries are conceived as chasing the Po down to the sea." Precisely; for if the *seguaci* are merely followers, not pursuers, the wonderfully ordered density of this simple passage is sacrificed. For although Francesca has told Dante where she lives, in the most directly descriptive language possible, she has told him more than that. Without the least imposition of strain upon the firmly denoted natural setting, she fuses herself with the river Po near which she was born. By a subtle shift of focus we see the pursued river as Francesca in Hell: the pursuing tributaries are a new visual image for the pursuing winds of lust. A further glance yields even more: as the winds, so the tributaries at once pursue and become one with the pursued; that is to say, Francesca has completely absorbed the substance of her sin—she is the sin; as, I believe it is said, the damned of the Inferno are plenary incarnations of the sin

that has put them there. The tributaries of the Po are not only the winds
of lust by analogy of visual images; they become identified by means of
sound:

> . . . discende
> Per aver pace co' seguaci sui.

The sibilants dominate the line; they are the hissing of the wind. But in
the last line of the preceding tercet Francesca has been grateful that the
wind has subsided so that she can be heard—

> Mentre che il vento, come fa, si tace.

After the wind has abated, then, we hear in the silence, for the first time,
its hiss, in the susurration to the descending Po. The river is thus both a
visual and an auditory image, and since Francesca is her sin and her sin
is embodied in this image, we are entitled to say that it is a sin that we can
both hear and see.

7. History

THE HISTORICAL INTERPRETATION OF LITERATURE

EDMUND WILSON

I WANT to talk about the historical interpretation of
literature—that is, about the interpretation of literature in its social, economic and political aspects.

To begin with, it will be worth while to say something about the kind
of criticism which seems to be furthest removed from this. There is a kind
of comparative criticism which tends to be non-historical. The essays of
T. S. Eliot, which have had such an immense influence in our time, are,
for example, fundamentally non-historical. Eliot sees, or tries to see, the
whole of literature, so far as he is acquainted with it, spread out before him
under the aspect of eternity. He then compares the work of different periods
and countries, and tries to draw from it general conclusions about what

"The Historical Interpretation of Literature" from *The Triple Thinkers*, by
Edmund Wilson, Oxford University Press, 1948. Reprinted by permission of the
author and John Lehmann, Ltd.

literature ought to be. He understands, of course, that our point of view in connection with literature changes, and he has what seems to me a very sound conception of the whole body of writing of the past as something to which new works are continually being added, and which is not thereby merely increased in bulk but modified as a whole—so that Sophocles is no longer precisely what he was for Aristotle, or Shakespeare what he was for Ben Jonson or for Dryden or for Dr. Johnson, on account of all the later literature that has intervened between them and us. Yet at every point of this continual accretion, the whole field may be surveyed, as it were, spread out before the critic. The critic tries to see it as God might; he calls the books to a Day of Judgment. And, looking at things in this way, he may arrive at interesting and valuable conclusions which could hardly be reached by approaching them in any other way. Eliot was able to see, for example—what I believe had never been noticed before—that the French Symbolist poetry of the nineteenth century had certain fundamental resemblances to the English poetry of the age of Donne. Another kind of critic would draw certain historical conclusions from these purely aesthetic findings, as the Russian D. S. Mirsky did; but Eliot does not draw them.

Another example of this kind of non-historical criticism, in a somewhat different way and on a somewhat different plane, is the work of the late George Saintsbury. Saintsbury was a connoisseur of wines; he wrote an entertaining book on the subject. And his attitude toward literature, too, was that of the connoisseur. He tastes the authors and tells you about the vintages; he distinguishes the qualities of the various wines. His palate was as fine as could be, and he possessed the great qualification that he knew how to take each book on its own terms without expecting it to be some other book and was thus in a position to appreciate a great variety of kinds of writing. He was a man of strong social prejudices and peculiarly intransigent political views, but, so far as it is humanly possible, he kept them out of his literary criticism. The result is one of the most agreeable and most comprehensive commentaries on literature that have ever been written in English. Most scholars who have read as much as Saintsbury don't have Saintsbury's discriminating taste. Here is a critic who has covered the whole ground like any academic historian, yet whose account of it is not merely a chronology but a record of fastidious enjoyment. Since enjoyment is the only thing he is looking for, he does not need to know the causes of things, and the historical background of literature does not interest him very much.

There is, however, another tradition of criticism which dates from the beginning of the eighteenth century. In the year 1725, the Neapolitan philosopher Vico published *La Scienza Nuova,* a revolutionary work on the philosophy of history, in which he asserted for the first time that the social world was certainly the work of man, and attempted what is, so far as I know, the first social interpretation of a work of literature. This is what Vico says about Homer: "Homer composed the *Iliad* when Greece was young and consequently burning with sublime passions such as pride, anger and vengeance—passions which cannot allow dissimulation and which consort with generosity; so that she then admired Achilles, the hero of force. But, grown old, he composed the *Odyssey,* at a time when the passions of Greece were already somewhat cooled by reflection, which is the mother of prudence—so that she now admired Ulysses, the hero of wisdom. Thus also, in Homer's youth, the Greek people liked cruelty, abuse, savagery, fierceness, ferocity; whereas, when Homer was old, they were already enjoying the luxuries of Alcinoüs, the delights of Calypso, the pleasures of Circe, the songs of the sirens and the pastimes of the suitors, who went no further in aggression and combat than laying siege to the chaste Penelope —all of which practices would appear incompatible with the spirit of the earlier time. The divine Plato is so struck by this difficulty that, in order to solve it, he tells us that Homer had foreseen in inspired vision these dissolute, sickly and disgusting customs. But in this way he makes Homer out to have been but a foolish instructor for Greek civilization, since, however much he may condemn them he is displaying for imitation these corrupt and decadent habits which were not to be adopted till long after the foundation of the nations of Greece, and accelerating the natural course which human events would take by spurring the Greeks on to corruption. Thus it is plain that the Homer of the *Iliad* must have preceded by many years the Homer who wrote the *Odyssey;* and it is plain that the former must belong to the northeastern part of Greece, since he celebrates the Trojan War, which took place in his part of the country, whereas the latter belongs to the southeastern part, since he celebrates Ulysses, who reigned there."

You see that Vico has here explained Homer in terms both of historical period and of geographical origin. The idea that human arts and institutions were to be studied and elucidated as the products of the geographical and climatic conditions in which the people who created them lived, and of the phase of their social development through which they were passing at the moment, made great progress during the eighteenth century. There are traces of it even in Dr. Johnson, that most orthodox and classical of critics —as, for example, when he accounts for certain characteristics of Shakespeare by the relative barbarity of the age in which he lived, pointing out, just as Vico had done, that "nations, like individuals, have their infancy." And by the eighties of the eighteenth century Herder, in his *Ideas on the*

Philosophy of History, was writing of poetry that it was a kind of "Proteus among the people, which is always changing its form in response to the languages, manners, and habits, to the temperaments and climates, nay even to the accents of different nations." He said—what could still seem startling even so late as that—that "language was not a divine communication, but something men had produced themselves." In the lectures on the philosophy of history that Hegel delivered in Berlin in 1822–23, he discussed the national literatures as expressions of the societies which had produced them—societies which he conceived as great organisms continually transforming themselves under the influence of a succession of dominant ideas.

In the field of literary criticism, this historical point of view came to its first complete flower in the work of the French critic Taine, in the middle of the nineteenth century. The whole school of historian-critics to which Taine belonged—Michelet, Renan, Sainte-Beuve—had been occupied in interpreting books in terms of their historical origins. But Taine was the first of these to attempt to apply these principles systematically and on a large scale in a work devoted exclusively to literature. In the introduction to his *History of English Literature,* published in 1863, he made his famous pronouncement that works of literature were to be understood as the upshot of three interfusing factors: *the moment, the race and the milieu.* Taine thought he was a scientist and a mechanist, who was examining works of literature from the same point of view as the chemist in experimenting with chemical compounds. But the difference between the critic and the chemist is that the critic cannot first combine his elements and then watch to see what they will do; he can only examine phenomena which have already taken place. The procedure that Taine actually follows is to pretend to set the stage for the experiment by describing the moment, the race and the milieu, and then to say: "such a situation demands such and such a kind of writer." He now goes on to describe the kind of writer that the situation demands, and the reader finds himself at the end confronted with Shakespeare or Milton or Byron or whoever the great figure is—who turns out to prove the accuracy of Taine's prognosis by precisely living up to the description.

There was thus a certain element of imposture in Taine; but it was the rabbits he pulled out that saved him. If he had really been the mechanist that he thought he was, his work on literature would have had little value. The truth was that Taine loved literature for its own sake—he was at his best himself a brilliant artist—and he had very strong moral convictions which give his writing emotional power. His mind, to be sure, was an analytical one, and his analysis, though terribly oversimplified, does have an explanatory value. Yet his work was what we call creative. Whatever he may say about chemical experiments, it is evident when he writes of a great writer that the moment, the race and the milieu have combined, like the three sounds of the chord in Browning's poem about Abt Vogler, to produce not a fourth sound but a star.

To Taine's set of elements was added, dating from the middle of the century, a new element, the economic, which was introduced into the discussion of historical phenomena mainly by Marx and Engels. The non-Marxist critics themselves were at the time already taking into account the influence of the social classes. In his chapters on the Norman conquest of England, Taine shows that the difference between the literatures produced respectively by the Normans and by the Saxons was partly the difference between a ruling class, on the one hand, and a vanquished and oppressed class, on the other. And Michelet, in his volume on the Regency, which was finished the same year that the *History of English Literature* appeared, studies the *Manon Lescaut* of the Abbé Prévost as a document representing the point of view of the small gentry before the French Revolution. But Marx and Engels derived the social classes from the way that people made or got their livings—from what they called the *methods of production;* and they tended to regard these economic processes as fundamental to civilization.

The Dialectical Materialism of Marx and Engels was not really so materialistic as it sounds. There was in it a large element of the Hegelian idealism that Marx and Engels thought they had got rid of. At no time did these two famous materialists take so mechanistic a view of things as Taine began by professing; and their theory of the relation of works of literature to what they called the *economic base* was a good deal less simple than Taine's theory of the moment, the race and the milieu. They thought that art, politics, religion, philosophy and literature belonged to what they called the *superstructure* of human activity; but they saw that the practitioners of these various professions tended also to constitute social groups, and that they were always pulling away from the kind of solidarity based on economic classes in order to establish a professional solidarity of their own. Furthermore, the activities of the superstructure could influence one another, and they could influence the economic base. It may be said of Marx and Engels in general that, contrary to the popular impression, they were tentative, confused and modest when it came down to philosophical first principles, where a materialist like Taine was cocksure. Marx once made an attempt to explain why the poems of Homer were so good when the society that produced them was from his point of view—that is, from the point of view of its industrial development—so primitive; and this gave him a good deal of trouble. If we compare his discussion of this problem with Vico's discussion of Homer, we see that the explanation of literature in terms of a philosophy of social history is becoming, instead of simpler and easier, more difficult and more complex.

Marx and Engels were deeply imbued, moreover, with the German admiration for literature, which they had learned from the age of Goethe. It would never have occurred to either of them that *der Dichter* [1] was not one of the noblest and most beneficent of humankind. When Engels writes about Goethe, he presents him as a man equipped for "practical life," whose career was frustrated by the "misery" of the historical situation in Germany in his time, and reproaches him for allowing himself to lapse into the "cautious, smug and narrow" philistinism of the class from which he came; but Engels regrets this, because it interfered with the development of the "mocking, defiant, world-despising genius," "der geniale Dichter," "der gewaltige Poet," [2] of whom Engels would not even, he says, have asked that he should have been a political liberal if Goethe had not sacrificed to his bourgeois shrinkings his truer esthetic sense. And the great critics who were trained on Marx—Franz Mehring and Bernard Shaw—had all this reverence for the priesthood of literature. Shaw deplores the absence of political philosophy and what he regards as the middle-class snobbery in Shakespeare; but he celebrates Shakespeare's poetry and his dramatic imagination almost as enthusiastically as Swinburne did, describing even those potboiling comedies—*Twelfth Night* and *As You Like It*—the themes of which seem to him most trashy—as "the Crown Jewels of English dramatic poetry." Such a critic may do more for a writer by showing him as a real man dealing with a real world at a definite moment of time than the impressionist critic of Swinburne's type who flourished in the same period of the late nineteenth century. The purely impressionist critic approaches the whole literature as an exhibit of belletristic jewels, and he can only write a rhapsodic catalogue. But when Shaw turned his spotlight on Shakespeare as a figure in the Shavian drama of history, he invested him with a new interest as no other English critic had done.

The insistence that the man of letters should play a political role, the disparagement of works of art in comparison with political action, were thus originally no part of Marxism. They only became associated with it later. This happened by way of Russia, and it was due to special tendencies in that country that date from long before the Revolution or the promulga-

---

[1] [The poet.]

[2] [The ingenious poet, the powerful poet.]

tion of Marxism itself. In Russia there have been very good reasons why
the political implications of literature should particularly occupy the critics.
The art of Pushkin itself, with its marvelous power of implication, had
certainly been partly created by the censorship of Nicholas I, and Pushkin
set the tradition for most of the great Russian writers that followed him.
Every play, every poem, every story, must be a parable of which the moral
is *implied*. If it were stated, the censor would suppress the book as he
tried to do with Pushkin's *Bronze Horseman,* where it was merely a question of the packed implications protruding a little too plainly. Right down
through the writings of Chekhov and up almost to the Revolution, the
imaginative literature of Russia presents the peculiar paradox of an art
that is technically objective and yet charged with social messages. In Russia
under the Tsar, it was inevitable that social criticism should lead to political
conclusions, because the most urgent need from the point of view of any
kind of improvement was to get rid of the tsarist regime. Even the neo-
Christian moralist Tolstoy, who pretended to be non-political, was to exert
a subversive influence, because his independent preaching was bound to
embroil him with the Church, and the Church was an integral part of the
tsardom. Tolstoy's pamphlet called *What Is Art?,* in which he throws over-
board Shakespeare and a large part of modern literature, including his own
novels, in the interest of his intransigent morality, is the example which
is most familiar to us of the moralizing Russian criticism; but it was only
the most sensational expression of a kind of approach which had been
prevalent since Belinsky and Chernyshevsky in the early part of the century. The critics, who were usually journalists writing in exile or for a con-
traband press, were always tending to demand of the imaginative writers
that they should dramatize bolder morals.

Even after the Revolution had destroyed the tsarist government, this
state of things did not change. The old habits of censorship persisted in
the new socialist society of the Soviets, which was necessarily made up of
people who had been stamped by the die of the despotism. We meet here
the peculiar phenomenon of a series of literary groups that attempt, one
after the other, to obtain official recognition or to make themselves sufficiently powerful to establish themselves as arbiters of literature. Lenin and
Trotsky and Lunacharsky had the sense to oppose these attempts; the
comrade-dictators of Proletcult or Lev or Rapp would certainly have been
just as bad as the Count Benckendorff who made Pushkin miserable, and
when the Stalin bureaucracy, after the death of Gorky, got control of this
department as of everything else, they instituted a system of repression
that made Benckendorff and Nicholas I look like Lorenzo de' Medici. In
the meantime, Trotsky, who was Commissar of War but himself a great

political writer with an interest in belles-lettres, attempted, in 1924, apropos of one of these movements, to clarify the situation. He wrote a brilliant and valuable book called *Literature and Revolution,* in which he explained the aims of the government, analyzed the work of the Russian writers, and praised or rebuked the latter as they seemed to him in harmony or at odds with the former. Trotsky is intelligent, sympathetic; it is evident that he is really fond of literature and that he knows that a work of art does not fulfill its function in terms of the formulas of party propaganda. But Mayakovsky, the Soviet poet, whom Trotsky had praised with reservations, expressed himself in a famous joke when he was asked what he thought of Trotsky's book—a pun which implied that a Commissar turned critic was inevitably a Commissar still; [1] and what a foreigner cannot accept in Trotsky is his assumption that it is the duty of the government to take a hand in the direction of literature.

This point of view, indigenous to Russia, has been imported to other countries through the permeation of Communist influence. The Communist press and its literary followers have reflected the control of the Kremlin in all the phases through which it has passed, down to the wholesale imprisonment of Soviet writers which has been taking place since 1935. But it has never been a part of the American system that our Republican or Democratic administration should lay down a political line for the guidance of the national literature. A recent gesture in this direction on the part of Archibald MacLeish, who seemed a little carried away by his position as Librarian of Congress, was anything but cordially received by serious American writers. So long as the United States remains happily a non-totalitarian country, we can very well do without this aspect of the historical criticism of literature.

Another element of a different order has, however, since Marx's time been added to the historical study of the origins of works of literature. I mean the psychoanalysis of Freud. This appears as an extension of something which had already got well started before, which had figured even in Johnson's *Lives of the Poets,* and of which the great exponent had been Sainte-Beuve: the interpretation of works of literature in the light of the personalities behind them. But the Freudians made this interpretation more exact and more systematic. The great example of the psychoanalysis of an artist is Freud's own essay on Leonardo da Vinci; but this has little critical interest: it is an attempt to construct a case history. One of the best examples I know of the application of Freudian analysis to literature is in

---

[1] *The first pancake lies like a narkom* . . . (people's commissar)—a parody of the Russian saying, . . . *The first pancake lies like a lump.*

Van Wyck Brooks' book, *The Ordeal of Mark Twain,* in which Mr. Brooks uses an incident of Mark Twain's boyhood as a key to his whole career. Mr. Brooks has since repudiated the method he resorted to here, on the ground that no one but an analyst can ever know enough about a writer to make a valid psychoanalytic diagnosis. This is true, and it is true of the method that it has led to bad results where the critic has built a Freudian mechanism out of very slender evidence, and then given us merely a romance exploiting the supposed working of this mechanism, in place of an actual study that sticks close to the facts and the documents of the writer's life and work. But I believe that Van Wyck Brooks really had hold of something important when he fixed upon that childhood incident of which Mark Twain gave so vivid an account to his biographer—that scene at the deathbed of his father when his mother had made him promise that he would not break her heart. If it was not one of those crucial happenings that are supposed to determine the complexes of Freud, it has certainly a typical significance in relation to Mark Twain's whole psychology. The stories that people tell about their childhood are likely to be profoundly symbolic even when they have been partly or wholly made up in the light of later experience. And the attitudes, the compulsions, the emotional "patterns" that recur in the work of a writer are of great interest to the historical critic.

These attitudes and patterns are embedded in the community and the historical moment, and they may indicate its ideals and its diseases as the cell shows the condition of the tissue. The recent scientific experimentation in the combining of Freudian with Marxist method and of psychoanalysis with anthropology, has had its parallel development in criticism. And there is thus another element added to our equipment for analyzing literary works, and the problem grows still more complex.

The analyst, however, is of course not concerned with the comparative values of his patients any more than the surgeon is. He cannot tell you why the neurotic Dostoevsky produces work of immense value to his fellows while another man with the same neurotic pattern would become a public menace. Freud himself emphatically states in his study of Leonardo that his method can make no attempt to account for Leonardo's genius. The problems of comparative artistic value still remain after we have given attention to the Freudian psychological factor just as they do after we have given attention to the Marxist economic factor and to the racial and geographical factors. No matter how thoroughly and searchingly we may have scrutinized works of literature from the historical and biographical points of view, we must be ready to attempt to estimate, in some such way as Saintsbury and Eliot do, the relative degrees of success attained by the products of the various periods and the various personalities. We must be able to tell good from bad, the first-rate from the second-rate. We shall not otherwise write literary criticism at all, but merely social or political history as reflected in literary texts, or psychological case histories from past eras, or, to take the historical point of view in its simplest and most academic form, merely chronologies of books that have been published.

And now how, in these matters of literary art, do we tell the good art from the bad? Norman Kemp Smith, the Kantian philosopher, whose courses I was fortunate enough to take at Princeton twenty-five years ago, used to tell us that this recognition was based primarily on an emotional reaction. For purposes of practical criticism this is a safe assumption on which to proceed. It is possible to discriminate in a variety of ways the elements that in any given department go to make a successful work of literature. Different schools have at different times demanded different things of literature: *unity, symmetry, universality, originality, vision, inspiration, strangeness, suggestiveness, improving morality, socialist realism,* etc. But you could have any set of these qualities that any school of writing has called for and still not have a good play, a good novel, a good poem, a good history. If you identify the essence of good literature with any one of these elements or with any combination of them, you simply shift the emotional reaction to the recognition of the element or elements. Or if you add to your other demands the demand that the writer must have *talent,* you simply shift this recognition to the talent. Once people find some grounds of agreement in the coincidence of their emotional reactions to books, they may be able to discuss these elements profitably; but if they do not have this basic agreement, the discussion will make no sense.

But how, you may ask, can we identify this élite who know what they are talking about? Well, it can only be said of them that they are self-appointed and self-perpetuating, and that they will compel you to accept their authority. Impostors may try to put themselves over, but these quacks will not last. The implied position of the people who know about literature (as is also the case in every other art) is simply that they know what they know, and that they are determined to impose their opinions by main force of eloquence or assertion on the people who do not know. This is not a question, of course, of professional workers in literature—such as editors, professors and critics, who very often have no real understanding of the products with which they deal—but of readers of all kinds in all walks of life. There are moments when a first-rate writer, unrecognized or out of fashion with the official chalkers-up for the market, may find his support in the demand for his work of an appreciative cultivated public.

But what is the cause of this emotional reaction which is the critic's divining rod? This question has long been a subject of study by the branch of philosophy called esthetics, and it has recently been made a subject of scientific experimentation. Both these lines of inquiry are likely to be prejudiced in the eyes of the literary critic by the fact that the inquiries are sometimes conducted by persons who are obviously deficient in literary feeling or taste. Yet one should not deny the possibility that something of value might result from the speculations and explorations of men of acute minds who take as their given data the esthetic emotions of other men.

Almost everybody interested in literature has tried to explain to himself the nature of these emotions that register our approval of artistic works; and I of course have my own explanation.

In my view, all our intellectual activity, in whatever field it takes place, is an attempt to give a meaning to our experience—that is, to make life more practicable; for by understanding things we make it easier to survive and get around among them. The mathematician Euclid, working in a convention of abstractions, shows us relations between the distances of our unwieldy and cluttered-up environment upon which we are able to count. A drama of Sophocles also indicates relations between the various human impulses, which appear so confused and dangerous, and it brings out a certain justice of Fate—that is to say, of the way in which the interaction of these impulses is seen in the long run to work out—upon which we can also depend. The kinship, from this point of view, of the purposes of science and art appears very clearly in the case of the Greeks, because not only do both Euclid and Sophocles satisfy us by making patterns, but they make much the same kind of patterns. Euclid's *Elements* takes simple theorems and by a series of logical operations builds them up to a climax in the square on the hypotenuse. A typical drama of Sophocles develops in a similar way.

Some writers (as well as some scientists) have a different kind of explicit message beyond the reassurance implicit in the mere feat of understanding life or of moulding the harmony of artistic form. Not content with such an achievement as that of Sophocles—who has one of his choruses tell us that it is better not to be born, but who, by representing life as noble and based on law, makes its tragedy easier to bear—such writers attempt, like Plato, to think out and recommend a procedure for turning it into something better. But other departments of literature—lyric poetry such as Sappho's, for example—have *less* philosophical content than Sophocles. A lyric gives us nothing but a pattern imposed on the expression of a feeling; but this pattern of metrical quantities and of consonants and vowels that balance has the effect of reducing the feeling, however unruly or painful it may seem when we experience it in the course of our lives, to something orderly, symmetrical and pleasing; and it also relates this feeling to the more impressive scheme, works it into the larger texture, of the body of poetic art. The discord has been resolved, the anomaly subjected to discipline. And this control of his emotion by the poet has the effect at second-hand of making it easier for the reader to manage his own emotions. (Why certain sounds and rhythms gratify us more than others, and how they are connected with the themes and ideas that they are chosen as appropriate for conveying, are questions that may be passed on to the scientist.)

And this brings us back again to the historical point of view. The experience of mankind on the earth is always changing as man develops and has to deal with new combinations of elements; and the writer who is to be anything more than an echo of his predecessors must always find expression for something which has never yet been expressed, must master a new set of phenomena which has never yet been mastered. With each such victory of the human intellect, whether in history, in philosophy or in poetry, we experience a deep satisfaction: we have been cured of some ache of disorder, relieved of some oppressive burden of uncomprehended events.

This relief that brings the sense of power, and, with the sense of power, joy, is the positive emotion which tells us that we have encountered a first-rate piece of literature. But stay! you may at this point warn: are not people often solaced and exhilarated by literature of the trashiest kind? They are: crude and limited people do certainly feel some such emotion in connection with work that is limited and crude. The man who is more highly organized and has a wider intellectual range will feel it in connection with work that is finer and more complex. The difference between the emotion of the more highly organized man and the emotion of the less highly organized one is a matter of mere gradation. You sometimes discover books—the novels of John Steinbeck, for example—that seem to mark precisely the borderline between work that is definitely superior and work that is definitely bad. When I was speaking a little while back of the genuine connoisseurs who establish the standards of taste, I meant, of course, the people who can distinguish Grade A and who prefer it to the other grades.

THE SENSE OF THE PAST

LIONEL TRILLING

IN recent years the study of literature in our universities has again and again been called into question, chiefly on the ground that what is being studied is not so much literature itself as the history of literature. John Jay Chapman was perhaps the first to state the case against the literary scholars when in 1927 he denounced the "archaeological, quasi-scientific, and documentary study of the fine arts" because, as he said, it endeavored "to express the fluid universe of many emotions in terms drawn from the study of the physical sciences." And since Chapman wrote, the issue in the universities has been clearly drawn in the form of an opposition of "criticism" to "scholarship." Criticism has been the aggressor, and its assault upon scholarship has been successful almost in proportion to the spiritedness with which it has been made; at the present time, although the archaeological and quasi-scientific and documentary study of literature is still the dominant one in our universities, it is clear to everyone that scholarship is on the defensive and is ready to share the rule with its antagonist.

This revision of the academic polity can be regarded only with satisfaction. The world seems to become less and less responsive to literature; we can even observe that literature is becoming something like an object of suspicion, and it is possible to say of the historical study of literature that its very existence is an evidence of this mistrust. DeQuincey's categories of *knowledge* and *power* are most pertinent here; the traditional scholarship, insofar as it takes literature to be chiefly an object of knowledge, denies or obscures that active power by which literature is truly defined. All sorts of studies are properly ancillary to the study of literature. For example, the study of the intellectual conditions in which a work of literature was made is not only legitimate but sometimes even necessary to our perception of its power. Yet when Professor Lovejoy in his influential book, *The Great Chain of Being,* tells us that for the study of the history of ideas a really dead writer is better than one whose works are still enjoyed, we naturally pull up short and wonder if we are not in danger of becoming like the Edinburgh body-snatchers who *saw to it* that there were enough cadavers for study in the medical school.

Criticism made its attack on the historians of literature in the name of literature as power. The attack was the fiercer because literary history had all too faithfully followed the lead of social and political history, which, having given up its traditional connection with literature, had allied itself with the physical sciences of the nineteenth century and had adopted the assumption of these sciences that the world was reflected with perfect literalness in the will-less mind of the observer. The new history had many successes and it taught literary study what it had itself learned, that in an age of science prestige is to be gained by approximating the methods of science. Of these methods the most notable and most adaptable was the investigation of genesis, of how the work of art came into being. I am not concerned to show that the study of genesis is harmful to the right experience of the work of art: I do not believe it is. Indeed, I am inclined to suppose that whenever the genetic method is attacked we ought to suspect that special interests are being defended. So far is it from being true that the genetic method is in itself inimical to the work of art, that the very opposite is so; a work of art, or any human thing, studied in its genesis can take on an added value. Still, the genetic method can easily be vulgarized, and when it is used in its vulgar form, it can indeed reduce the value of a thing; in much genetic study the implication is clear that to the scholar the work of art is nothing but its conditions.

One of the attractions of the genetic study of art is that it seems to offer a high degree of certainty. Aristotle tells us that every study has its own degree of certainty and that the well-trained man accepts that degree and does not look for a greater one. We may add that there are different kinds as well as different degrees of certainty, and we can say that the great mistake of the scientific-historical scholarship is that it looks for a degree and kind of certainty that literature does not need and cannot allow.

The error which is made by literary scholars when they seek for a certainty analogous with the certainty of science has been so often remarked that at this date little more need be said of it. Up to a point the scientific study of art is legitimate and fruitful; the great thing is that we should recognize the terminal point and not try to push beyond it, that we should not expect that the scientific study of, say, literature will necessarily assure us of the experience of literature; and if we wish as teachers to help others to the experience of literature, we cannot do so by imparting the fruits of our scientific study. What the partisans of the so-called New Criticism revolted against was the scientific notion of the fact as transferred in a literal way to the study of literature. They wished to restore autonomy to the work of art, to see it as the agent of power rather than as the object of knowledge.

The faults of these critics we know. Perhaps their chief fault they share with the scientific-historical scholars themselves—they try too hard. No less than the scholars, the critics fall into an error that Chapman denounced, the great modern illusion "that anything whatever . . . can be discovered through hard intellectual work and concentration." We often feel of them that they make the elucidation of poetic ambiguity or irony a kind of intellectual calisthenic ritual. Still, we can forgive them their strenuousness, remembering that something has happened to our relation with language which seems to require that we make methodical and explicit what was once immediate and unformulated.

But there is another fault of the New Critics of which we must take notice. It is that in their reaction from the historical method they forget that the literary work is ineluctably an historical fact, and, what is more important, that its historicity is a fact in our aesthetic experience. Literature, we may say, must in some sense always be an historical study, for literature is an historical art. It is historical in three separate senses.

In the old days the poet was supposed to be himself an historian, a reliable chronicler of events. Thucydides said that he was likely to be an inaccurate historian, but Aristotle said that he was more accurate, because more general, than any mere annalist; and we, following Aristotle, suppose that a large part of literature is properly historical, the recording and interpreting of personal, national, and cosmological events.

Then literature is historical in the sense that it is necessarily aware of its own past. It is not always consciously aware of this past, but it is always practically aware of it. The work of any poet exists by reason of its connection with past work, both in continuation and in divergence, and what we call his originality is simply his special relation to tradition. The point has been fully developed by T. S. Eliot in his well-known essay, "Tradition and the Individual Talent." And Mr. Eliot reminds us how each poet's relation to tradition changes tradition itself, so that the history of literature is never quiet for long and is never merely an additive kind of growth. Each new age makes the pattern over again, forgetting what was once dominant, finding new affinities; we read any work within a kaleidoscope of historical elements.

And in one more sense literature is historical, and it is with this sense that I am here chiefly concerned. In the existence of every work of literature of the past, its historicity, its *pastness,* is a factor of great importance. In certain cultures the pastness of a work of art gives it an extra-aesthetic authority which is incorporated into its aesthetic power. But even in our own culture with its ambivalent feeling about tradition, there inheres in a work of art of the past a certain quality, an element of its aesthetic existence, which we can identify as its pastness. Side by side with the formal elements of the work, and modifying these elements, there is the element of history, which, in any complete aesthetic analysis, must be taken into account.

The New Critics exercised their early characteristic method almost exclusively upon lyric poetry, a genre in which the historical element, although of course present, is less obtrusive than in the long poem, the novel, and the drama. But even in the lyric poem the factor of historicity is part of the aesthetic experience; it is not merely a negative condition of the other elements, such as prosody or diction, which, if they are old enough, are likely to be insufficiently understood—it is itself a positive aesthetic factor with positive and pleasurable relations to the other aesthetic factors. It is a part of the *given* of the work, which we cannot help but respond to. The New Critics imply that this situation *should* not exist, but it cannot help existing, and we have to take it into account.

We are creatures of time, we are creatures of the historical sense, not only as men have always been but in a new way since the time of Walter Scott. Possibly this may be for the worse; we would perhaps be stronger if we believed that Now contained all things, and that we in our barbarian moment were all that had ever been. Without the sense of the past we might be more certain, less weighted down and apprehensive. We might also be less generous, and certainly we would be less aware. In any case, we have the sense of the past and must live with it, and by it.

And we must read our literature by it. Try as we will, we cannot be like Partridge at the play, wholly without the historical sense. The leap of the imagination which an audience makes when it responds to *Hamlet* is enormous, and it requires a comprehensive, although not necessarily a highly instructed, sense of the past. This sense does not, for most artistic purposes, need to be highly instructed; it can consist largely of the firm belief that there really is such a thing as the past.

In the New Critics' refusal to take critical account of the historicity of a work there is, one understands, the impulse to make the work of the past more immediate and more real, to deny that between Now and Then there is any essential difference, the spirit of man being one and continuous. But it is only if we are aware of the reality of the past as past that we can feel it as alive and present. If, for example, we try to make Shakespeare literally contemporaneous, we make him monstrous. He is contemporaneous only if we know how much a man of his own age he was; he is relevant to us only if we see his distance from us. Or to take a poet closer to us in

actual time, Wordsworth's Immortality Ode is acceptable to us only when
it is understood to have been written at a certain past moment; if it had
appeared much later than it did, if it were offered to us now as a contemporary work, we would not admire it; and the same is true of *The
Prelude,* which of all works of the romantic movement is closest to our
present interest. In the pastness of these works lies the assurance of their
validity and relevance.

The question is always arising, What is the real poem? Is it the poem
we now perceive? Is it the poem the author consciously intended? Is it the
poem the author intended and his first readers read? Well, it is all these
things, depending on the state of our knowledge. But in addition the poem
is the poem as it has existed in history, as it has lived its life from Then to
Now, as it is a thing which submits itself to one kind of perception in one
age and another kind of perception in another age, as it exerts in each age
a different kind of power. This makes it a thing we can never wholly understand—other things too, of course, help to make it that—and the mystery,
the unreachable part of the poem, is one of its aesthetic elements.

To suppose that we can think like men of another time is as much
of an illusion as to suppose that we can think in a wholly different way.
But it is the first illusion that is exemplified in the attitude of the anti-
historical critics. In the admirable poetry textbook of Mr. Cleanth Brooks
and Mr. Robert Penn Warren, the authors disclaim all historical intention.
Their purpose being what it is, they are right to do so, but I wonder if they
are right in never asking in their aesthetic analysis the question: What effect
is created by our knowledge that the language of a particular poem is not
such as would be uttered by a poet writing now? To read a poem of even
a hundred years ago requires as much translation of its historical circumstance as of its metaphors. This the trained and gifted critic is likely to
forget; his own historical sense is often so deeply ingrained that he is not
wholly conscious of it, and sometimes, for reasons of his own, he prefers
to keep it merely implicit. Yet whether or not it is made conscious and
explicit, the historical sense is one of the aesthetic and critical faculties.

What more apposite reminder of this can we have than the early impulse of the New Critics themselves to discover all poetic virtue in the poetry
of the seventeenth century, the impulse, only lately modified, to find the
essence of poetic error in the poetry of romanticism? Their having given
rein to this impulse is certainly not illegitimate. They were doing what we
all do, what we all must and even should do; they were involving their
aesthetics with certain cultural preferences, they were implying choices
in religion, metaphysics, politics, manners. And in so far as they were
doing this by showing a preference for a particular period of the past, which

they brought into comparison with the present, they were exercising their historical sense. We cannot question their preference itself; we can only question the mere implicitness of their historical sense, their attitude of making the historical sense irrelevant to their aesthetic.

But if the historical sense is always with us, it must, for just that reason, be refined and made more exact. We have, that is, to open our minds to the whole question of what we mean when we speak of causation in culture. Hume, who so shook our notions of causation in the physical sciences, raises some interesting questions of causation in culture. "There is no subject," he says, "in which we must proceed with more caution than in tracing the history of the arts and sciences; lest we assign causes which never existed and reduce what is merely contingent to stable and universal principles." The cultivators of the arts, he goes on to say, are always few in number and their minds are delicate and "easily perverted." "Chance, therefore, or secret and unknown causes must have great influence on the rise and progress of all refined arts." But there is one fact, he continues, which gives us the license to speculate—this is the fact that the choice spirits arise from and are related to the mass of the people of their time. "The question, therefore, is not altogether concerning the taste, genius and spirit of a few, but concerning those of a whole people; and may, therefore, be accounted for, in some measure, by general causes and principles." This gives us our charter to engage in cultural history and cultural criticism, but we must see that it is a charter to deal with a mystery.

The refinement of our historical sense chiefly means that we keep it properly complicated. History, like science and art, involves abstraction: we abstract certain events from others and we make this particular abstraction with an end in view, we make it to serve some purpose of our will. Try as we may, we cannot, as we write history, escape our purposiveness. Nor, indeed, should we try to escape, for purpose and meaning are the same thing. But in pursuing our purpose, in making our abstractions, we must be aware of what we are doing; we ought to have it fully in mind that our abstraction is not perfectly equivalent to the infinite complication of events from which we have abstracted. I should like to suggest a few ways in which those of us who are literary scholars can give to our notion of history an appropriate complication.

It ought to be for us a real question whether, and in what way, human nature is always the same. I do not mean that we ought to settle this question before we get to work, but only that we insist to ourselves that the question is a real one. What we certainly know has changed is the *expression* of human nature, and we must keep before our minds the problem of the relation which expression bears to feeling. Professor Stoll, the well-known

Shakespearean critic, has settled the matter out of hand by announcing the essential difference between what he calls "convention" and what he calls "life," and he insists that the two may have no truck with each other, that we cannot say of Shakespeare that he is psychologically or philosophically acute because these are terms we use of "life," whereas Shakespeare was dealing only with "convention." This has the virtue of suggesting how important is the relation of "convention" to "life," but it misses the point that "life" is always expressed through "convention" and in a sense always *is* "convention," and that convention has meaning only because of the intentions of life. Professor Stoll seems to go on the assumption that Shakespeare's audiences were conscious of convention; they were aware of it, but certainly not conscious of it; what they were conscious of was life, into which they made an instantaneous translation of all that took place on the stage. The problem of the interplay between the emotion and the convention which is available for it, and the reciprocal influence they exert on each other, is a very difficult one, and I scarcely even state its complexities, let alone pretend to solve them. But the problem with its difficulties should be admitted, and simplicity of solution should always be regarded as a sign of failure.

A very important step forward in the complication of our sense of the past was made when Professor Whitehead and after him Professor Lovejoy taught us to look not for the expressed but the assumed ideas of an age, what Whitehead describes as the "assumptions which appear so obvious that people do not know that they are assuming them because no other way of putting things has ever occurred to them."

But a regression was made when Professor Lovejoy, in that influential book of his, assured us that "the ideas in serious reflective literature are, of course, in great part philosophical ideas in dilution." To go fully into the error of this common belief would need more time than we have now at our disposal. It is part of our suspiciousness of literature that we undertake thus to make it a dependent art. Certainly we must question the assumption which gives the priority in ideas to the philosopher and sees the movement of thought as always from the systematic thinker, who thinks up the ideas, in, presumably, a cultural vacuum, to the poet who "uses" the ideas "in dilution." We must question this even if it means a reconstruction of what we mean by "ideas."

And this leads to another matter about which we may not be simple, the relation of the poet to his environment. The poet, it is true, is an effect of environment, but we must remember that he is no less a cause. He may be used as the barometer, but let us not forget that he is also part of the weather. We have been too easily satisfied by a merely elementary meaning of environment; we have been content with a simple quantitative implication of the word, taking a large and literally environing thing to be always the environment of a smaller thing. In a concert room the audience and its attitude are of course the environment of the performer, but also the performer and his music make the environment of the audience. In a family the parents are no doubt the chief factors in the environment of the child; but also the child is a factor in the environment of the parents and himself conditions the actions of his parents toward him.

Corollary to this question of environment is the question of influence, the influence which one writer is said to have had on another. In its historical meaning, from which we take our present use, *influence* was a word intended to express a mystery. It means a flowing-in, but not as a tributary river flows into the main stream at a certain observable point; historically the image is an astrological one and the meanings which the Oxford Dictionary gives all suggest "producing effects by *insensible* or *invisible* means" —"the infusion of any kind of divine, spiritual, moral, immaterial or *secret* power or principle." Before the idea of influence we ought to be far more puzzled than we are; if we find it hard to be puzzled enough, we may contrive to induce the proper state of uncertainty by turning the word upon ourselves, asking, "What have been the influences that made me the person I am, and to whom would I entrust the task of truly discovering what they were?"

Yet another thing that we have not understood with sufficient complication is the nature of ideas in their relation to the conditions of their development and in relation to their transmission. Too often we conceive of an idea as being like the baton that is handed from runner to runner in a relay race. But an idea as a transmissible thing is rather like the sentence that, in the parlor game, is whispered about in a circle; the point of the game is the amusement that comes when the last version is compared with the original. As for the origin of ideas, we ought to remember that an idea is the formulation of a response to a situation; so, too, is the modification of an existing idea. Since the situations in which people or cultures find themselves are limited in number, and since the possible responses are also limited, ideas certainly do have a tendency to recur, and because people think habitually ideas also have a tendency to persist when the situation which called them forth is no longer present; so that ideas do have a certain limited autonomy, and sometimes the appearance of a complete autonomy. From this there has grown up the belief in the actual perfect autonomy of ideas. It is supposed that ideas think themselves, create themselves and their descendants, have a life independent of the thinker and the situation. And from this we are often led to conclude that ideas, systematic ideas, are directly responsible for events.

A similar feeling is prevalent among our intellectual classes in relation to words. Semantics is not now the lively concern that it was a few years ago, but the mythology of what we may call political semantics has become established in our intellectual life, the belief that we are betrayed by words, that words push us around against our will. "The tyranny of words" became a popular phrase and is still in use, and the semanticists offer us an easier world and freedom from war if only we assert our independence from words. But nearly a century ago Dickens said that he was tired of hearing about "the tyranny of words" (he used that phrase); he was, he said, less concerned with the way words abuse us than with the way we abuse words. It is not words that make our troubles, but our own wills. Words cannot control us unless we desire to be controlled by them. And the same is true of the control of systematic ideas. We have come to believe that some ideas can betray us, others save us. The educated classes are learning to blame ideas for our troubles, rather than blaming, what is a very different thing— our own bad thinking. This is the great vice of academicism, that it is concerned with ideas rather than with thinking, and nowadays the errors of academicism do not stay in the academy; they make their way into the world, and what begins as a failure of perception among intellectual specialists finds its fulfillment in policy and action.

In time of war, when two different cultures, or two extreme modifications of the same culture, confront each other with force, this belief in the autonomy of ideas becomes especially strong and therefore especially clear. In any modern war there is likely to be involved a conflict of ideas which is in part factitious but which is largely genuine. But this conflict of ideas, genuine as it may be, suggests to both sides the necessity of believing in the fixed, immutable nature of the ideas to which each side owes allegiance. What gods were to the ancients at war, ideas are to us. Thus, in the last war, an eminent American professor of philosophy won wide praise for demonstrating that Nazism was to be understood as the inevitable outcome of the ideas of Schopenhauer and Nietzsche, while the virtues of American democracy were to be explained by tracing a direct line of descent from Plato and the Athenian polity. Or consider a few sentences from a biography of Byron, written when, not so long ago, the culture of Nazism was at its height. The author, a truly admirable English biographer, is making an estimate of the effect of the romantic movement upon our time. He concludes that the romantic movement failed. Well, we have all heard that before, and perhaps it is true, although I for one know less and less what it means. Indeed, I know less and less what is meant by the ascription of failure to any movement in literature. All movements fail, and perhaps the romantic movement failed more than most because it attempted more than most; possibly it attempted too much. To say that a literary movement failed seems to suggest a peculiar view of both literature and history; it implies that literature ought to settle something for good and all, that life ought to be progressively completed. But according to our author, not only did the romantic movement fail—it left a terrible legacy.

Nationalism was essentially a Romantic movement, and from nationalism springs the half-baked racial theorist with his romantic belief in the superiority of "Aryan" blood and his romantic distrust of the use of reason. So far-reaching were the effects of the Romantic Revival that they still persist in shapes under which they are no longer recognized. . . . For Romantic literature appeals to that strain of anarchism which inhabits a dark corner of every human mind and is continually advancing the charms of extinction against the claims of life —the beauty of all that is fragmentary and youthful and half-formed as opposed to the compact achievement of adult genius.

It is of course easy enough to reduce the argument to absurdity— we have only to ask why Germany and not ourselves responded so fiercely to the romantic ideas which, if they be indeed the romantic ideas, were certainly available to everybody. The failure of logic is not, however, what concerns us, but rather what the logic is intended to serve: the belief that ideas generate events, that they have an autonomous existence, and that they can seize upon the minds of some men and control their actions independently of circumstance and will.

Needless to say, these violations of historical principle require a violation of historical fact. The Schopenhauer and the Nietzsche of the first explanation have no real reference to two nineteenth-century philosophers of the same name; the Plato is imaginary, the Athens out of a storybook, and no attempt is made to reconcile this fanciful Athens with the opinion of the real Athens held by the real Plato. As for the second explanation, how are we to connect anarchism, and hostility to the claims of life, and the fragmentary, and the immature, and the half-formed, with Kant, or Goethe, or Wordsworth, or Beethoven, or Berlioz, or Delacroix? And how from these men, who *are* romanticism, dare we derive the iron rigidity and the desperate centralization which the New Order of the Nazis involved, or the systematic cruelty, or the elaborate scientism with which the racial doctrine was implicated?

The two books to which I refer are of course in themselves harmless and I don't wish to put upon them a weight which they should not properly be made to bear. But they do suggest something of the low estate into which history has fallen among our educated classes, and they are of a piece with the depreciation of the claims of history which a good many literary people nowadays make, a depreciation which has had the effect of leading young students of literature, particularly the more gifted ones, to incline more and more to resist historical considerations, justifying themselves, as it is natural they should, by pointing to the dulness and deadness and falsifications which have resulted from the historical study of literature. Our resistance to history is no doubt ultimately to be accounted for by nothing less than the whole nature of our life today. It was said by Nietzsche—the real one, not the lay figure of cultural propaganda—that the historical sense was an actual faculty of the mind, "a sixth sense," and that the credit for the recognition of its status must go to the nineteenth century. What was uniquely esteemed by the nineteenth century is not likely to stand in high favor with us: our coldness to historical thought may in part be explained by our feeling that it is precisely the past that caused all our troubles, the nineteenth century being the most blameworthy of all the culpable centuries. Karl Marx, for whom history was indeed a sixth sense, expressed what has come to be the secret hope of our time, that man's life in politics, which is to say, man's life in history, shall come to an end. History, as we now understand it, envisions its own extinction—that is really what we nowadays mean by "progress"—and with all the passion of a desire kept secret even from ourselves, we yearn to elect a way of life which shall be satisfactory once and for all, time without end, and we do not want to be reminded by the past of the considerable possibility that our present is but perpetuating mistakes and failures, and instituting new troubles.

And yet, when we come to think about it, the chances are all in favor of our having to go on making our choices and so of making our mistakes. History, in its meaning of a continuum of events, is not really likely to come to an end. There may therefore be some value in bringing explicitly to mind what part in culture is played by history in its other meaning of an ordering and understanding of the continuum of events. There is no one who is better able to inform us on this point than Nietzsche. We can perhaps listen to him with the more patience because he himself would have had considerable sympathy for our impatience with history, for although he thought that the historical sense brought certain virtues, making men "unpretentious, unselfish, modest, brave, habituated to self-control and self-renunciation," he also thought that it prevented them from having the ability to respond to the very highest and noblest developments of culture, making them suspicious of what is wholly completed and fully matured. This ambivalent view of the historical sense gives him a certain authority when he defines what the historical sense is and does. It is, he said, "the capacity for divining quickly the order of the rank of the valuations according to which a people, a community, or an individual has lived." In the case of a people or of a community, the valuations are those which are expressed not only by the gross institutional facts of their life, what Nietzsche called "the operating forces," but also and more significantly by their morals and manners, by their philosophy and art. And the historical sense, he goes on to say is "the 'divining instinct' for the relationships of these valuations, for the relation of the valuations to the operating forces." The historical sense, that is, is to be understood as the critical sense, as the sense which life uses to test itself. And since there never was a time when the instinct for divining—and "quickly"!—the order of rank of cultural expressions was so much needed, our growing estrangement from history must be understood as the sign of our desperation.

Nietzsche's own capacity for quickly divining the order of rank of cultural things was, when he was at his best, more acute than that of any other man of his time, or since. If we look for the explanation of his acuity, we find it in the fact that it never occurred to him to separate his historical sense from his sense of art. They were not two senses, but one. And the merit of his definition of the historical sense, especially when it is taken in conjunction with the example of himself, is that it speaks to the historian and to the student of art as if they were one person. To that person Nietzsche's definition prescribes that culture be studied and judged as life's continuous evaluation of itself, the evaluation being understood as never finding full expression in the "operating forces" of a culture, but as never finding expression at all without reference to these gross, institutional facts.

8. Psychology

ARCHETYPAL PATTERNS IN TRAGIC POETRY

MAUD BODKIN

I

In an article, "On the Relation of Analytical Psychology to Poetic Art," [1] Dr. C. G. Jung has set forth an hypothesis in regard to the psychological significance of poetry. The special emotional significance possessed by certain poems— a significance going beyond any definite meaning conveyed—he attributes to the stirring in the reader's mind, within or beneath his conscious response, of unconscious forces which he terms "primordial images," or archetypes. These archetypes he describes as "psychic residua of numberless experiences of the same type," experiences which have happened not to the individual but to his ancestors, and of which the results are inherited in the structure of the brain, *a priori* determinants of individual experience.

It is the aim of the present writer to examine this hypothesis, testing it in regard to examples where we can bring together the recorded experience and reflection of minds approaching the matter from different standpoints. It is hoped that, in this way, something may be done towards enriching the formulated theory of the systematic psychologist through the insight of more intuitive thinkers, while at the same time the intuitive thinker's results may receive somewhat more exact definition.

My first illustration I shall take from an essay by Professor Gilbert Murray,[2] where the effect of great poetic drama is described in language somewhat similar to that of Jung. Gilbert Murray has been comparing the

---

"Archetypal Patterns in Tragic Poetry" from *Archetypal Patterns in Poetry* by Maud Bodkin, reprinted by permission of Oxford University Press.

[1] Included in *Contributions to Analytical Psychology,* trans. H. G. and C. F. Baynes (Kegan Paul, 1928).

[2] *"Hamlet* and *Orestes,"* in *The Classical Tradition in Poetry* (Oxford, 1927).

tragedies of *Hamlet* and of *Orestes,* noting the curious similarities between them, and how the theme that underlies them seems to have shown an "almost eternal durability." When such themes as stirred the interest of primitive man move us now, he says, "they will tend to do so in ways which we recognize as particularly profound and poetical" (p. 238). Gilbert Murray apologizes for the metaphor of which he cannot keep clear when he says that such stories and situations are "deeply implanted in the memory of the race, stamped as it were upon our physical organism." We say that such themes "are strange to us. Yet there is that within us which leaps at the sight of them, a cry of the blood which tells us we have known them always" (p. 239). And again: "In plays like *Hamlet* or the *Agamemnon* or the *Electra* we have certainly fine and flexible character-study, a varied and well-wrought story, a full command of the technical instruments of the poet and the dramatist; but we have also, I suspect, a strange, unanalysed vibration below the surface, an undercurrent of desires and fears and passions, long slumbering yet eternally familiar, which have for thousands of years lain near the root of our most intimate emotions and been wrought into the fabric of our most magical dreams. How far into past ages this stream may reach back, I dare not even surmise; but it seems as if the power of stirring it or moving with it were one of the last secrets of genius" (pp. 239–240).

We have here an expression, itself somewhat imaginative and poetical, of an experience in presence of poetry which we may submit to closer examination—and this in two ways. We may study the themes that show this persistence within the life of a community or race, and may compare the different forms which they assume; also we may study analytically in different individuals the inner experience of responding to such themes.

The inquiry is plainly of subtlety and complexity apt to discourage at the outset those who prefer to avoid all questions that cannot be investigated in accordance with a strict technique. There is little possibility here for experiment, since the kind of emotional experience which it is desired to investigate cannot be commanded at will under test conditions. A profound response to great poetic themes can be secured only by living with such themes, dwelling and brooding upon them, choosing those moments when the mind seems spontaneously to open itself to their influence. We must take where we can find it the recorded experience of those who have such acquaintance with poetry.

To the present writer it appears, however, that it is by the study of such deeper experience that psychology at the present time particularly needs enrichment. We might almost say that academic psychologists have been routed by the attack of those medical writers who claim access to the deeper layers of the mind, just because the demand for exact verifiable results has held academic psychologists to the mere outworks or surface of the mind they set out to study. If inexactness of thought or one-sided emphasis has characterized the medical writers, this can be established only by following them along the obscure paths they have opened into the concrete human psyche, and bringing to bear, if possible, a wider ranging interest and a more exact and cautious scrutiny.

The student who seeks to explore the imaginative response of present-day minds to the great themes of poetry may profit by considering the work not only of the medical psychologists, but also of the anthropologists who have attempted to study scientifically the reactions of more primitive minds. In studying the reception by a people of new cultural elements anthropologists have made use of the term "cultural pattern" to designate the pre-existing "configuration," or order of arrangement, of tendencies which determine the response of members of the group to the new element. In discussing the value for our "conceptual explorations" of "the culture pattern concept," Goldenweiser [1] has noted its relation to the concept of form and system in the arts and cultural disciplines; and L. L. Bernard, in the same work, has undertaken a classification of different kinds of environment, distinguishing the psycho-social environment, which includes such systems of symbols as are preserved in books, and in which he says "psychic processes reach the highest type of their objectified development." Such stored symbolic content can at any time become effective in activating the corresponding patterns in the minds of members of the group whose collective product and possession the symbols are.

It is within the general field of anthropology or social psychology that I conceive the inquiry to lie which I am here attempting to pursue. I shall use the term "archetypal pattern" to refer to that within us which, in Gilbert Murray's phrase, leaps in response to the effective presentation in poetry of an ancient theme. The hypothesis to be examined is that in poetry—and here we are to consider in particular tragic poetry—we may identify themes having a particular form or pattern which persists amid variation from age to age, and which corresponds to a pattern or configuration of emotional tendencies in the minds of those who are stirred by the theme.

In Jung's formulation of the hypothesis, and in the more tentative metaphorical statement of Gilbert Murray, it is asserted that these patterns are "stamped upon the physical organism," "inherited in the structure of the brain"; but of this statement no evidence can be considered here. Jung believes himself to have evidence of the spontaneous production of ancient

---

[1] *The Social Sciences and Their Interrelations,* edited by W. F. Ogburn and Alexander A. Goldenweiser (Allen & Unwin, 1928).

patterns in the dreams and fantasies of individuals who had no discoverable access to cultural material in which the patterns were embodied. This evidence is, however, hard to evaluate; especially in view of the way in which certain surprising reproductions, in trance states, of old material, have been subsequently traced to forgotten impressions of sense in the lifetime of the individual.

Of more force in the present state of our knowledge is the general argument that where forms are assimilated from the environment upon slight contact only, predisposing factors must be present in mind and brain. Whoever has experienced and reflected upon the attempt to convey an idea, especially an idea of intimate and emotional character, to a mind unprepared to receive it, will have realized that it is not mere contact with an idea's expression that secures its assimilation. Some inner factor must co-operate. When it is lacking, the experienced futility of attempted communication is the most convincing proof that it is, as Mr. F. C. Bartlett has said, "not fanciful to hold" that for the capture of objects complete, by the assimilative imagination, there must stir within us "larger systems of feeling, of memory, of ideas, of aspirations." Such systems may be cultural patterns confined to a particular group at a certain time, or may characterize a particular individual; but there are others of much wider range. Our question is whether there are some whose "almost eternal durability," in Gilbert Murray's phrase, justifies us in applying to them the term archetypal, and renders them of special interest and importance to the student of psychology and of literature.

II

We come nearer to our particular subject in raising the question: What is the distinctive advantage of having recourse to poetry for the study of these patterns?

Such a theme as that discussed by Gilbert Murray existed as a traditional story in ancient Greece before Aeschylus, and in Northern Europe before Shakespeare handled it. In that form it was already, as A. C. Bradley says of another traditional theme, "an inchoate poem": "such a subject, as it exists in the general imagination, has some aesthetic value before the poet touches it"; "it is already in some degree organized and formed." [1] Enriched by the poet's touch, the traditional story lives on in our imagination, a memory with aesthetic value, but fading into formlessness, when, as perhaps now in the mind of the reader, the reference to Orestes or to Ham-

---

[1] *Oxford Lectures on Poetry* (Macmillan, 1909), pp. 11–12.

let excites only a faint recollection of what was once a vivid poetic experience. When, therefore, we desire to examine psychologically the emotional pattern corresponding to a poetic theme, we may sometimes avail ourselves of references to the mere tales recalled in outline, but for closer examination there is need that the actual poetic experience be recovered, since it is in the imaginative experience actually communicated by great poetry that we shall find our fullest opportunity of studying the patterns that we seek—and this from the very nature of poetic experience.

In the writings of Professor Spearman, which have had so much influence in the determining of psychological method, there are references to imagination—one particularly to imagination as exercise in poetry [1]—in which he asserts that imagination in its intellectual aspect does not differ essentially from any other logical process in which new content may also be said to be generated, as when, from a given term, say "good," and a knowledge of the nature of verbal opposition, we pass to the term, "bad." Such a treatment of imagination illustrates the kind of abstraction that makes psychology, to some thinkers, appear so unreal and empty a study. A student who is interested in imaginative activity as exercised in poetry cannot accept the view that its intellectual aspect can be separated from its emotional nature and covered by any such logical formula as Spearman proposes.

Of the three laws of cognition which Professor Spearman formulates it would seem to be the first which most nearly concerns the poetic imagination. This law is stated: "Any lived experience tends to evoke immediately a knowing of its characters and experiences." A note adds: "The word 'immediately' means here the absence of any mediating process." [2] It is perhaps within this mediating process, denied by Spearman, that we may find a distinctive place for imagination as exercised in poetry.

When psychologists have raised the question: How does lived experience come to awareness? they have usually been content to assert that it happens through introspection, and to leave to philosophers any further investigation of the question. It is here that difficulty has arisen between the academic and the medical psychologists; since the latter believe themselves to have discovered large ranges of lived experience, of conative character, of which introspection can give no account—a discovery that seems surprising to those who believe that in introspection we have direct access to the nature of our desires.

---

[1] *The Nature of Intelligence and the Principles of Cognition* (Macmillan, 1927), pp. 334–336.

[2] *Op. cit.*, p. 48.

Professor S. Alexander,[1] examining the question as a philosopher, concludes that lived experience, which is of conative character—as distinct from sensations and images, the objects of the mind—can only be "enjoyed"; it cannot be contemplated. Introspection, he says, is "enjoyment" lived through, together with "a whole apparatus of elaborated speech" (p. 18), which causes the elements of the experience enjoyed to stand out in "subtly dissected form" (p. 19). "It is small wonder," he adds, "that we should regard our introspection as turning our minds into objects, seeing how largely the language which expresses our mental state has been elaborated in pursuit of practical interests and in contact with physical objects."

If this view is accepted, we see that the mediating process necessary before lived experience can come to awareness is the linking of such experience with actions and objects that affect the senses and can be contemplated, and with words that recall these objects in all their variety of human perspective. It is in the process of fantasy that the contemplated characters of things are broken from their historical setting and made available to express the needs and impulses of the experiencing mind. The recent study of dreams appears to have made it certain that the bewildering sequence of the images thrown up by the sleeping mind is due to processes of interaction between emotional dispositions lacking the customary control. In individual waking fantasy, and in myth and legend, we have other sequences of images which emotional patterns determine, and which seem to us strange as dreams, when, repeating them in the words used also for the results of logical reflection, we are led to contrast these incompatible renderings of experience.

When a great poet uses the stories that have taken shape in the fantasy of the community, it is not his individual sensibility alone that he objectifies. Responding with unusual sensitiveness to the words and images which already express the emotional experience of the community, the poet arranges these so as to utilize to the full their evocative power. Thus he attains for himself vision and possession of the experience engendered between his own soul and the life around him, and communicates that experience, at once individual and collective, to others, so far as they can respond adequately to the words and images he uses.

We see, then, why, if we wish to contemplate the emotional patterns hidden in our individual lives, we may study them in the mirror of our spontaneous actions, so far as we can recall them, or in dreams and in the flow of waking fantasy; but if we would contemplate the archetypal patterns that we have in common with men of past generations, we do well to study

---

[1] *Space, Time, and Deity* (Macmillan, 1920).

them in the experience communicated by the great poetry that has continued to stir emotional response from age to age. In studying such poetry
here, we are not asking what was in the mind of Aeschylus or of Shakespeare when he fashioned the figure of Orestes or of Hamlet, nor do we
ask how these figures affected a Greek or an Elizabethan audience. The
question is between the writer and the reader of this book: what do the
figures of Orestes and Hamlet stand for in the experience communicated to
us, as we see, read, or vividly recall the Greek or Shakespearian tragedy?

III

A preliminary difficulty, already touched on, must be considered in
more detail. How can we secure that the experience communicated by a
great play shall be present to us with such completeness and intensity that
we can make adequate study of it?

A parallel question has been discussed by Percy Lubbock [1] in regard
to the study of the form of a novel. Critical perception, he says, is of no
use to us if we cannot retain the image of a book, and the book reaches us
as a passage of experience never present in its completeness. The task of
the reader, before he can criticize, is to refashion the novel out of the march
of experience as it passed. The procession "must be marshalled and concentrated somewhere" (p. 15).

In watching a play adequately interpreted upon the stage, we find, perhaps more readily than in the silent reading of a novel, that the procession
of experience is marshalled and concentrated at certain points; so that, recalling the images of these, we can look back upon the whole play as a living
unity. The powerful emotional impression thus attained may persist while
the play is read and recurred to again and again, and the individual impression clarified by comparison with the reflective results of critics and
scholars. Central passages, while the play is thus lived with, grow ever
richer in meaning, becoming intertwined with the emotional experience of
one's own life.

Some such experience of *Hamlet* I must presume in the reader, since
I cannot afford space to recall the play at all fully. I will venture, however,
to refer to that passage in which for me the significance of the whole play
seems most concentrated.

From the experience of seeing *Hamlet* performed some thirty years
ago, there has remained with me the memory of the strange exaltation and
wonder of beauty that attended the words of the dying Hamlet to Horatio:

---

[1] *The Craft of Fiction* (The Travellers' Library, 1926).

> If thou didst ever hold me in thy heart,
> Absent thee from felicity awhile,
> And in this harsh world draw thy breath in pain,
> To tell my story.

This is one of the passages chosen by Matthew Arnold [1] as "touch-stones" for poetry—passages possessing both in style and substance supreme poetic quality, the Aristotelian high truth and seriousness, beyond that of history or ordinary speech. I would suggest that this "high truth" of which Matthew Arnold speaks—like that character attributed by Lascelles Abercrombie to great poetry, "a confluence of all kinds of life into a single flame of consciousness"—belongs to the lines not as isolated, but as grown familiar in their setting—the unified experience of the play converging upon them and the incantation of their music carrying them ever deeper into the secret places of the mind that loves them.

One may make some attempt to analyse that "incantation," [2] or enchantment in which rhythm and sound of words evidently play a part. It seems to me that the enchantment of the line, "Absent thee from felicity awhile," is heightened by the later echoing of its sounds in the lines spoken by Horatio:

> Good night, sweet prince,
> And flights of angels sing thee to thy rest!

Against this music of heaven we feel more poignantly the contrast of the words, "in this harsh world draw thy breath in pain," that move, labouring, toward their goal in the words, "to tell my story." Through their power of incantation these words, as they fall in their place, seem to gather up all the significance of that struggle of a powerful impulse to action against an obscure barrier, all the impotent anger and perplexity, and longing for justification and release, that make up the story of Hamlet as Shakespeare tells it, and make also of Hamlet, and of these lines, a symbol for whatever such struggle and longing has tortured the mind that is responding to Hamlet's words.

IV

Before attempting to compare, with reference to underlying emotional pattern, *Hamlet* and the plays concerned with Orestes, we may consider briefly the study made of *Hamlet* by Dr. Ernest Jones. [3]

---

[1] "The Study of Poetry," *Essays in Criticism*, 2nd series, 1889.

[2] Cf. Lascelles Abercrombie, *The Idea of Great Poetry*, 1925, p. 19.

[3] "A Psycho-Analytic Study of *Hamlet*," included in *Essays in Applied Psychoanalysis*, 1923.

Dr. Jones, in exploring the nature of Hamlet's conflict, has to some extent followed the same line of inquiry that I am pursuing here. For what is it that the critic is actually doing when he traces the motives of a character in a play?

In projecting the figure of a man of a certain disposition and analysing the forces behind his behaviour, the critic is inevitably using the emotional experience which he himself undergoes in living through the play. Having experienced, as communicated by the speeches of Hamlet, a certain psychological movement in which a strong impulse to action is aroused, and again and again sinks back into apathy and despair—a movement which, while imaginatively experiencing it, the reader imputes to the fictitious speaker—afterwards, in reviewing the total impression so received, with analysis and synthesis of its successive movements, the critic discerns, so far as his thought does not deceive him, within the fictitious personality of Hamlet, the reflected pattern of the emotional forces that have operated within his own imaginative activity.

To Dr. Jones the conflict of Hamlet appears an example of the working of the Oedipus complex. Hamlet cannot whole-heartedly will the slaying of his uncle, because "his uncle incorporates the deepest and most buried part of his own personality." The repressed desire for the death of his father and the sexual enjoyment of his mother, persisting unconsciously from infancy, has produced an unwitting identification by Hamlet of himself and his guilty uncle, so that only at the point of death, "when he has made the final sacrifice . . . is he free . . . to slay his other self" (p. 57).

This psychological hypothesis, contributed by Freud and elaborated by Dr. Jones, has been welcomed by certain literary critics. Herbert Read, referring to the view of J. M. Robertson, that *Hamlet* is "not finally an intelligible drama as it stands"—that Shakespeare could not make a psychologically consistent play out of his barbaric plot and supersubtle hero— urges that however baffling to critics the play may have proved, nevertheless in experiencing it we are aware of a personal intensity of expression, a *consistent* intensity, giving the play a unity which the older academic critics lacked means to explore.[1] Dr. Jones's hypothesis, he considers, does serve to explain this acceptance by our feeling of any difficulties and incoherence which our thought may find. Using the terms I have suggested, we might say that the hypothesis of the Oedipus complex—i.e. of a persistent unconscious wish, hostile to the father and dishonouring to the mother, in conflict with the sentiment of filial love and loyalty—offers to

---

[1] Herbert Read, *Reason and Romanticism* (Faber & Gwyer), p. 101.

our thought an emotional pattern which does correspond to the play of feeling stimulated during a full imaginative participation in the drama. Professor Bradley has spoken of *Hamlet* as deserving the title of "tragedy of moral idealism," [1] because of the intensity, both of idealizing love and of horror at betrayal of love, that we feel in Hamlet's speeches. He dwells upon the shock to such a moral sensibility as Hamlet's of witnessing the faithlessness of his mother and uncle; yet there seems a discrepancy between the horror and disgust that a sensitive mind might naturally feel at such faithlessness in others and the overwhelming disgust that Hamlet feels, at himself, his whole world and his attempted action, unless we realize that he feels the treachery of his mother and uncle echo within himself, and within the sentiment of loyal love to his father that is his strongest conscious motive. If, in reviewing the experience communicated by the play, we conceive a loyal love undermined, as it were, by a bewildered sense of treachery within as well as without, we must, I think, agree that the Freudian hypothesis does throw some light upon that intimate immediate experience which is the final touchstone of critical theory.

v

Perhaps the most important contribution that has been made by the Freudian theory of dream interpretation to the understanding of the emotional symbolism of poetic themes is that concerned with the "splitting" of type figures. In comparing the Hamlet story with the story of Oedipus, Dr. Jones asserts that both are variants of the same *motif,* but in one the father figure remains single, while in the other it is "split into two"—the father loved and revered, and the hated tyrannical usurper.

This assertion involves two elements of hypothesis:

1. The fundamental assumption—implied also in the statements of Jung and Gilbert Murray, with which this discussion opened—that these ancient stories owe their persistence, as traditional material of art, to their power of expressing or symbolizing, and so relieving, typical human emotions.

2. That the emotion relieved is in this case the two-sided—ambivalent—attitude of the son towards the father. Let us examine this latter hypothesis more closely.

It appears to be characteristic of the relation between father and son that the father should excite in the son both feelings of admiration, love, and loyalty, and also impulses of anger, jealousy, and self-assertion. The

---

[1] *Shakespearian Tragedy* (Macmillan, 1912), p. 113.

more the son learns to "idolize" his father, developing what **Shand has**
called the "conscience of the sentiment," so that any muttering of jealousy
or hostile criticism is suppressed as disloyal, the more acute will become
the tension of the inner attitude. It is such an attitude that can find relief
in imaginative activity wherein both the love and the repressed hostility
have play. In the story of Oedipus, according to the Freudian hypothesis,
a repressed persistent impulse to supplant the father and enjoy the mother
finds expression in the first part of the action; then in the latter part, in
the hero's remorse and suffering, appears the expression of the sentiment of
respect and loyalty. In the Hamlet legend—as it appears, e.g. in the Amleth
Saga—combined fear and hostile self-assertion against the father find expression through all the incidents of simulated stupidity, and secret bitter
word-play, and at last in the achievement of the plotted slaying of the
usurper; while at the same time the sentiment of love and loyalty is trium-
phantly expressed in that same act of filial vengeance. It is Shakespeare
only who appears to have brought into the rendering of the ancient story
the subtle factor of the division and paralysis of the will of the hero, by
the intuitive apprehension that the impulse that drove his uncle against his
father was one with that present in himself.

The story of Orestes may be considered as another example of the
imaginative expression of the ambivalent attitude of child toward parent.
In this story, as presented by the three great Attic tragedians, there is a
wealth of material illustrating the manner in which inner forces of emotion
may, through shapes created by imagination, become palpable to sense.
But we must be content here to consider briefly only the outline of the
story.

Considered as a variant of the Hamlet theme, its distinctive note is
that the usurper upon whom the son's fierce self-assertion and craving for
vengeance strike is not alone the male kinsman, but also the queen-mother,
who has betrayed, and with her own hands murdered the father. Therefore the moment of triumphant self-assertion, when the son has proved
his manhood, and vindicated his loyalty upon his father's enemies, is also
the moment when there awakens the palpable, pursuing horror of the
outraged filial relation—since this enemy was also a parent, the mother
of the slayer.

The conflict presented in the Orestes dramas is plainly concerned
not directly with sex, but with combined love and hate of either son or
daughter converging upon a parent figure which may be either father or
mother. It is the enduring conflict between the generations which continues to find expression in the story, when more temporary questions—
such as that between patriarchy and mother-right, which may have been

present in Athenian minds—are no longer urgent. That this theme of conflict between the generations had great significance within the sensibility that found expression in Shakespeare's plays, is evident from the tragedy of *King Lear*.

In this drama the emotional conflict between the generations is communicated from the standpoint of the old man, the father who encounters in separate embodiment in his natural successors, the extremes of bestial self-seeking, and of filial devotion. Bradley has noted how the play illustrates "the tendency of imagination to analyse and subtract, to decompose human nature into its constituent factors." [1] This mode of thought, he suggests,[2] is responsible for "the incessant references to the lower animals" which occur throughout the play. Thus Goneril is likened to a kite, a serpent, a boar, a dog, a wolf, a tiger. This analysing work of the imagination, separating the bestial and the angelic in human nature and giving them distinct embodiment, in the wicked daughters and Cordelia (and again in Edmund and Edgar, the cruel and the loyal sons of Gloucester), presents another instance of what we have already observed in the "splitting" of the father figure. The splitting in this play is from the point of view of the parent; as, in the Orestes or Hamlet story, it is from the point of view of the child. As, to the feeling of the child, the parent may be both loved protector and unjustly obstructing tyrant, and these two aspects find their emotional symbolism in separate figures in the play; so, to the feeling of the parent, the child may be both loving support of age and ruthless usurper and rival, and these two aspects find expression in separate figures, such as the tender and the wicked daughters of Lear.

VI

We have considered, so far, the emotional pattern corresponding to a particular theme—the conflict between the generations—which, though a recurring one, is by no means co-extensive with the realm of tragic drama. Can we identify an archetypal pattern corresponding to tragedy itself—its universal idea or form?

Gilbert Murray, taking the "essential tragic idea" to be that of "climax followed by decline, or pride by judgement," and attempting a closer analysis of this sequence, maintains that what is "really characteristic" of the tragic conflict is "an element of mystery derived ultimately from the ancient

---

[1] *Shakespearian Tragedy*, p. 264.
[2] *Ibid.*, p. 266.

religious concepts of *katharsis* and atonement." [1] The death or fall of the tragic hero has in some sense the character of a purifying or atoning sacrifice.

In considering this conception we may first remedy an inadequacy that the reader has probably noticed in the previous discussion of the dramas of Hamlet and Lear, Orestes and Oedipus. We have so far ignored the royal status of the father and son concerned in the tragic conflict. Yet the kingly status has great significance for the feeling expressed in the play.

Consider, for instance, the tragedy of *King Lear*. "The master movement of the play," says Granville-Barker, is Lear's passing "from personal grievance to the taking upon him, as great natures may, of the imagined burden of the whole world's sorrow." [2] It is Lear's royal status that helps to make this movement possible. King Lear is at once "a poor, infirm, weak, and despised old man"—a father broken to tears and madness by his daughters' cruelty, and also in his sufferings a superhuman figure—one who can bid the "all shaking thunder strike flat the thick rotundity of the world" in vengeance for his wrongs. It is in part the associations with which history, and pre-history, has invested the name and image of king that make it possible for us, under the spell of Shakespeare's verse, to accept the figure of Lear as in this way exalted in his agony beyond human stature. His madness, his pitiful humanity, appear, according to that comment which Shakespeare puts into the mouth of an attendant, on behalf of all onlookers, "a sight . . . past speaking in a king." The word "king" is here, through its position in the play, loaded with a significance for the sources of which we must go far back in the story of the race and of the individual.

It is probably because, to the mind of the young child, the father appears of unlimited power that in the life-history of the individual imagination the figures of father and king tend to coalesce. Legends and fairy stories that reflect the feelings of more primitive people towards their king are interpreted by the child in the light of his own earlier feeling towards his father. In the case both of the child and of the primitive individual the same process seems to take place—an emerging of the consciousness of self from out a matrix of less differentiated awareness, which may be called collective or group-consciousness. The figures of both father and king tend to retain within those deeper levels of the mind to which poetry may penetrate, something of the *mana* that invested the first representative of a power akin to, but vastly beyond, that of the individual emerging into self-consciousness.

It is this supernatural aspect which the father-king of tragic drama

---

[1] *Op. cit.*, "Drama," p. 66.
[2] H. Granville-Barker, *Prefaces to Shakespeare* (1927), 1st series, p. 171.

has for the kindled imagination that is of importance when we try to understand the element of religious mystery which is characteristic of tragedy—plainly in the past, and, as Gilbert Murray holds, in some subtler fashion still in our experience to-day.

Upon this character of tragedy and the tragic hero it is possible, I think, to gain a certain fresh light from a consideration of the conclusions at which Dr. Jung has arrived through his study of fantasy figures appearing in personal analysis.

In *The Psychology of the Unconscious,* in the chapter entitled "The Sacrifice," he examines the symbol of the dying hero as it appears in individual fantasy, representing, according to his interpretation, an inflated infantile personality—a childish self that must be sacrificed, if the libido is to move forward into active life—and in a later work he discusses, under the title of the "Mana Personality," [1] a hero figure which he finds appearing with a richer content at late stages of analysis.

It is especially at times when barriers of personal repression are removed and images of "cosmic" character are arising freely, that the fantasy figure may appear of some great prophet or hero who tends to assume control of the personality.[2] If the conscious or practical personality is poorly developed there is the greater likelihood that it will be overwhelmed when such powerful images rise from the unconscious.

As a literary example of such a case, parallel to actual ones within his experience, Jung accepts H. G. Wells's story of Preemby,[3] "a small, irrelevant, fledgling of a personality," to whom is presented in dream and fantasy the figure of Sargon, King of Kings, in such compelling fashion that he is led to identify himself with it. Jung observes that here "the author depicts a really classical type of compensation," [4] and we may compare it with the type of compensation which occurs in connexion with what we have already considered as the ambivalent attitude towards a parent.

If, within the conscious life, in relation to a parent, only reactions of admiration and affection are recognized, while other reactions, of hostile character, excited within the brain, are repressed, it is these latter that tend to present in dreams a parent figure as object of violence or contempt. Simi-

---

[1] *Two Essays on Analytical Psychology,* 1928, trans. by H. G. and C. F. Baynes, Essay II, ch. iv.

[2] An interesting autobiographical account of this condition may be found in the writings of E. Maitland (*The Story of Anna Kingsford and Edward Maitland and of the New Gospel of Interpretation,* 1st ed., 1893). See especially the passage where he describes the first arrival of the authoritative "presence," and the voice distinctly heard: "at last I have found a man through whom I can speak."

[3] *Christina Alberta's Father,* 1925.

[4] *Op. cit.,* p. 193.

larly, if within the conscious life the personal self comes to be known only as "an onlooker, an ineffective speechless man," utterly insignificant; while yet, within the life that animates that particular brain, strong reactions are excited of sympathetic exultation and delight at imaginative representations of human achievement—as the little Preemby of Wells thrilled at "the mystery of Atlantis and of the measurements of the Pyramids"—then there may arise, as compensatory to the belittled self, the figure of a hero-self, or *mana* personality, fashioned, as it were, from the stuff of these imaginative reactions; just as the figure of the hated father was fashioned from the energy of the repressed hostility, in compensation for the over-idealizing love.

The Preemby of Wells's story is saved from his delusion, after many sufferings, by learning to think of his vision as of the spirit of man and its achievements—an inheritance belonging no more to him personally than to every other man. In the same manner every individual in whose fantasy such mighty ghosts arise, with their superhuman claims and relationships, must learn to distinguish such claims from those of the personal self; while yet the personal self may be enriched through the conscious experience of its relation to the great forces which such figures represent.

In this way, according to the view of Jung—by interpreting and giving conscious direction to the "pure nature-process" [1] of fantasy in which compensatory images arise—such fantasy can become instrumental to the purging of the individual will and its reconciliation with itself. Is it in some such fashion as this that tragic drama, deeply experienced, now or in the past, exercises the function of purgation or atonement in relation to the passions of the spectator? With this question in view, we may examine a little further the nature of the emotional experience of tragic art, still using the examples of *Hamlet* and of *King Lear*.

Professor Bradley, in examining the experience of tragedy, cites these dramas as examples of tragedies at whose close we feel pain mingled with something like exultation. There is present, he declares, "a glory in the greatness of the soul," and awareness of an "ultimate power" which is "no mere fate," but spiritual, and to which the hero "was never so near . . . as in the moment when it required his life." [2]

I quote these statements of Bradley, not, of course, as universally acceptable, but as the attempt of one eminent critic to render his own deeply pondered experience of tragic drama. The experience is rendered in terms rather of philosophy or religion than of psychology. Can we translate it into any more psychological terms? What is this spiritual power, akin

---

[1] *Op. cit.,* p. 258.
[2] *Oxford Lectures on Poetry,* p. 84.

to the characters, and, in some sense, a whole of which they are "parts, expressions, products"? [1] I would propose (following the view set forth by F. M. Cornford) the psychological hypothesis that this power is the common nature lived and immediately experienced by the members of a group or community—"the collective emotion and activity of the group." [2] This common nature can, in Alexander's phrase, be enjoyed, but never directly contemplated. As unfathomable to introspection, it is termed by Jung the Collective Unconscious—the life-energy that in its spontaneous movement toward expression generates alike the hero figures of myth and legend and the similar figures that, appearing in individual fantasy, may overwhelm the personal consciousness.

According to Bradley, the tragic exultation that we feel at the close of *Hamlet* is connected with our sense that the spiritual power of which Hamlet is in some manner the expression or product, is receiving him to itself. It would be this same sense that, as Bradley observes,[3] demands, and is satisfied by, the words of Horatio, introducing, against Shakespeare's custom, the reference to another life: "flights of angels sing thee to thy rest." If, as I suggest, the spiritual power, which the philosopher analysing his poetic experience is constrained to represent, be conceived psychologically as the awakened sense of our common nature in its active emotional phase, then our exultation in the death of Hamlet is related in direct line of descent to the religious exultation felt by the primitive group that made sacrifice of the divine king or sacred animal, the representative of the tribal life, and, by the communion of its shed blood, felt that life strengthened and renewed. Hamlet, though he dies, is immortal, because he is the representative and creature of the immortal life of the race. He lives, as he desired to live, in the story with which he charged Horatio—and us who, having participated in that story, descend from the poetic ecstasy to draw breath again in the harsh world of our straitened separate personalities.

The insight of Nietzsche, who knew at once the intoxication of the artist and the analytic urge of the philosopher, discerned the essential nature of tragedy as a vision generated by a dance.[4] The dance of rhythmical speech, like the dance of the ancient chorus, excites the Dionysian ecstasy wherein arises, serene and clear, the Apollonian vision of the imaged meanings the dancing words convey.

The painful images within the vision are at once intimately known and felt, and also "distanced" like the objects in a far stretching landscape,

[1] *Shakespearian Tragedy,* p. 37.

[2] F. M. Cornford, *From Religion to Philosophy* (Arnold, 1912), p. 78.

[3] *Op. cit.,* p. 147.

[4] See *The Birth of Tragedy,* Section 8.

"estranged by beauty." So far as the memory material used by the imaginative activity comes from personal experience, it has undergone "separation . . . from the concrete personality of the experiencer" and "extrusion of its personal aspects"; [1] but experience is also used which has never been connected with the personal self—as when, in *King Lear,* Shakespeare causes the actor to "impersonate Lear and the storm together," [2] and in the storm "it is the powers of the tormented soul that we hear and see." [3] Here, dramatist, actor, and spectator are using experience which was never personal, but shaped through previous apprehension of physical storms into which was imaginatively projected that same impersonal emotional energy from which the daemonic figure of the hero is now fashioned.

To the impersonal, "distanced," vision corresponds, in Schopenhauer's phrase, "a Will-free subject," one indifferent to the aims and fears of the ego—not held to its private perspective. [4]

This felt release, and Dionysian union with a larger whole, would seem to constitute that element of religious mystery—of purgation and atonement—traditionally connected with the idea of tragedy.

VII

If now, summing up our results, we recur to the question: what determining emotional pattern corresponds to the form of tragedy? we may answer first, in accordance with our earlier discussion, that the pattern consists of emotional tendencies of opposite character which are liable to be excited by the same object or situation, and, thus conflicting, produce an inner tension that seeks relief in the activity either of fantasy, or of poetic imagination, either originally or receptively creative. The nature of the opposed tendencies that find relief through diverse renderings of the essential tragic theme, the death or fall of a hero, it is not easy to describe at once with conciseness and adequacy. But we may attempt this through the concept of an ambivalent attitude toward the self.

---

[1] E. Bullough, "Distance as an Aesthetic Principle," *Brit. J. of Psychol.* v. part 2, p. 116.

[2] Granville-Barker, *Prefaces to Shakespeare,* p. 142.

[3] A. C. Bradley, *Shakespearian Tragedy,* p. 270.

[4] This character of the aesthetic experience is vividly expressed, in imaginative form, in the lines of De la Mare:

> When music sounds, all that I was I am
> Ere to this haunt of brooding dust I came.

Here we have the felt contrast between the subject of the aesthetic experience—"all that I was I am"—and the self that is bounded in space and time by the bodily organism—"this haunt of brooding dust."

In the gradual fashioning and transforming, through the experience of life, of an idea of the self, every individual must in some degree experience the contrast between a personal self—a limited ego, one among many—and a self that is free to range imaginatively through all human achievement. In infancy and in the later years of those who remain childish, a comparatively feeble imaginative activity together with an undisciplined instinct of self-assertion may present a fantasy self—the image of an infantile personality—in conflict with the chastened image which social contacts, arousing the instinct of submission, tend to enforce. In the more mature mind that has soberly taken the measure of the personal self as revealed in practical life, there remains the contrast between this and the self revealed in imaginative thought—well-nigh limitless in sympathy and aspiration.

Within what McDougall calls the self-regarding sentiment these contrasting images, and the impulses that sustain and respond to them, may bring about persistent tension. The experience of tragic drama both gives in the figure of the hero an objective form to the self of imaginative aspiration, or to the power-craving, and also, through the hero's death, satisfies the counter movement of feeling toward the surrender of personal claims and the merging of the ego within a greater power—the "community consciousness."

Thus the archetypal pattern corresponding to tragedy may be said to be a certain organization of the tendencies of self-assertion and submission. The self which is asserted is magnified by that same collective force to which finally submission is made; and from the tension of the two impulses and their reaction upon each other, under the conditions of poetic exaltation, the distinctive tragic attitude and emotion appears to arise.

The theme of the conflict between the generations—considered earlier, in relation to Hamlet and Orestes, as corresponding to an ambivalent attitude toward a parent figure—is plainly related to this more general theme and pattern; since, as we saw, the same underlying emotional associations cling to the images of father and of king. In experiencing imaginatively the conflict of the generations, the spectator is identified with the hero both as son, in his felt solidarity with the father and revolt against him, and again, when, making reparation for the "injustice" against his predecessor, he gives place to a successor, and is reunited with that whole of life whence he emerged.[1]

One or two points in regard to the argument may be briefly reviewed. The question is sometimes asked whether the creative activity of the

---

[1] Cf. the mystic saying of Anaximander, concerning the cycle of birth and death, wherein things "give reparation to one another and pay the penalty of their injustice," and the discussion of it by F. M. Cornford, *op. cit.* See especially pp. 8, 147, 176.

poet and the imaginative response of the reader are sufficiently alike, psychologically, to be considered together. Here I have been concerned primarily with imaginative response, and have not attempted to consider the distinctive activity of original composition. In so far, however, as the poet's work, e.g. a play of Shakespeare, does reveal his imaginative response to material communicated to him by others and by him to us, I have of course been concerned with the poet's experience.

The concept of racial experience enters the present essay in two ways: (1) all those systems or tendencies which appear to be inherited in the constitution of mind and brain may be said to be due to racial experience in the past. It is not necessary for our purpose to determine exactly the method of this "biological inheritance" from our ancestors. Of more importance for our purpose is the question concerning (2) the racial experience which we may "enjoy" in responding to that "social inheritance" of meanings stored in language which also comes to us from our ancestors, and wakens into activity the potentialities of our inherited nature. In such racial or collective experience as we have discussed in relation to tragic poetry, so far as there is reference to an experiencer, this seems to be not an individual, but rather that larger whole from which what we know as the individual, or personal, self has been differentiated, and which remains with us as the sense, either latent or active, of a greater power.

In the present paper it is maintained that racial experience in this sense is an important factor in the total experience of tragic drama, at the present day, as in the ritual dance from which drama arose. In regard to this question further examination of the imaginative experience can alone be decisive.

III

The Practice of
Criticism

---

1. POETRY
2. FICTION
3. DRAMA

Introduction

THE most distinguishing feature of modern criticism has been its focus upon a particular work, or works, of literature. As stated in the introduction to the preceding section, textual analysis grew out of a dissatisfaction with scholarly techniques and the inadequate "impressionism" of the popular reviews. The exponents of textual criticism—or close reading—believed that a reader could best gain an appreciation through an understanding of the specific text. As Ezra Pound wrote: the teaching or evaluation of literature in general terms or in terms not directly related to the work itself is "inexcusable after the era of 'Agassiz and the fish'—by which I mean now that general education is in a position to profit by the parallels of biological study based on examination and comparison of particular specimens." In part, no doubt, this tendency resulted from a feeling that scientific methods should be employed in the study of an art based upon language, as was the case with I. A. Richards and his followers. In another respect, it was the application of a method already in practice among the French—*explication de texte*. In any case, criticism since 1920 has minimized the value of a concern with the author's life or his social milieu, emphasizing instead the search for literary standards by which excellence might be determined.

Undoubtedly this emphasis has occasionally been carried to an extreme. The charge most frequently made against modern critics is that they have become so antagonistic to the methods of scholarship that they have become unscholarly; that is, with an increasing confidence in their own methods, they have refused to take advantage of the disciplines of scholarship; or they have, in their zeal to interpret a specific text, gone beyond any possible intention of the author of the work and have, therefore, applied criteria inappropriate to the work.

These are serious charges, but they are, perhaps, best refuted by the example of the works themselves—such works as appear on the following pages of this anthology. In addition, however, we might ask: "Who are the scholars?" If they are men who have been trained in traditional graduate colleges, then approximately one half the critics represented in this section are "scholars" in the strictest and most conventional sense. The term "literary critic" applied to them is an indication of interest and has nothing to do with their regard for historic or linguistic accuracy. To say that modern criticism is in rebellion against genuine scholarship is completely to misunderstand (or willfully to misstate) the problem. It is in rebellion against the positivistic kind of scholarship which American and British universities inherited from Germany early in the nineteenth century, a scholarship which saw in the biographical details of an author's life or in the sociological details of his background the pertinent clues to the meaning of his work. By the beginning of the present century such study had deteriorated in the majority of cases to a thoroughly piecemeal preoccupation with isolated details of an author's life or with the minutiae of his social background. When applied to the teaching of literature, such an approach resulted in two significant errors: (1) the student was taught more about the author's life than about his works; (2) when the works were considered, they were seen more as monuments of a past time than as examples of living literature in pertinent relationship to the students' own moral and aesthetic sensibilities. In its most pernicious form, such scholarship acquired so great a devotion for factual information concerning biography, bibliography, and the classification of texts that it failed to concern itself with the more important aims of criticism: understanding and evaluation.

However, it is not only as a rebellion against scholarship (the recovering of a lost focus) that modern critical practice justifies itself. Recent criticism has been greatly concerned with the problem of getting at the "intention" of a work of literature. Do the acknowledged intentions of the author (even when they are available) represent a trustworthy guide to the full meaning of the work? If not, how does the reader discover the true meaning—the real "intention" inherent in a poem, a novel, or a play? This question was discussed in detail in the preceding section (see Wimsatt and Beardsley, "The Intentional Fallacy"), but there is another approach by which it may be examined—an approach which discloses it to be not so much a question as the expression of a special need of our age. The application of this method depends upon the assumption that our age is the victim of what has been called a "dissociation of sensibility"; that is, in its simplest sense, that the background myth or established moral order within which writers of other ages have worked is almost totally (certainly relatively) lacking in our time. In more stable times the writer was able to present his work against a recognized moral background, so that any variation from the commonly held view represented an immediate clue to the intentions of the work. Such variations usually indicated either a redefinition of the myth or a subtle and artistic revelation of an additional, previously unsuspected content. Lacking this communal awareness, we have been forced to rely upon the private sensibility of the artist himself. Hence the responsibility of the critic to educate himself in every possible technique for the discovery and examination of the "private," often even "unconscious," intention. Yet even without carrying this view to such an extreme, we do find a kind of general agreement among modern authors that the moral basis for society (which is usually expressed through religious forms or community myth) has become so fragmentary as to interfere with easy communication between the writer and his readers. Thus, perhaps more than at any time in history, it has become the responsibility of the critic to apply all possible criteria (the techniques of science, scholarship, morality, and aesthetics) to extract and clarify the total meaning of a work of literature.

The earliest exegetical studies, naturally enough, concentrated upon poetry, most often upon poetry in its shortest forms. This was partly the result of circumstance. A short work appears most easily grasped by the memory and the imagination, at least in its structural form. Again, however, the seeming neglect of the longer forms represented no more than a reflection of the dominant interests of our early critics, most of whom were themselves engaged in writing lyric verse (Pound, Eliot, Ransom, Tate), most of whom had been attracted to the achievements of the French symbolist poets (Baudelaire, Laforgue, Mallarmé, Verlaine, Rimbaud), and a few of whom had been attracted by the revival of interest in the so-called metaphysical poets of the English seventeenth century (Donne, Herbert, Marvell). Criticism of the shorter form did not, necessarily, indicate a lack of appreciation for the longer forms. Poet-critics such as Pound and Eliot themselves soon became interested in writing within the longer forms of epic and dramatic verse, and all modern criticism has come increasingly to respect and to consider, not only longer works such as the productions of Dryden, Pope, and Milton, but also the productions of an entire career, such as that of Pope, or of Wordsworth. What is important to remember here is that modern criticism is not a system imposed upon literature by any person or group of persons; it is an approach to literature, the outgrowth of a slow development covering most of the first half of our century.

The situation in the criticism of fiction is similar to that in poetry, but of slower growth. Ability to deal with fictional problems came only after considerable activity in the criticism of poetry. The earliest studies grew out of an increased interest in the works of Henry James, and they were based, in great part, upon critical insights enunciated by him, particularly in the prefaces to the New York edition of his works. The first significant work was that performed by Percy Lubbock in *The Craft of Fiction* (1929) and by various critics in the James issue of *Hound & Horn* (1934).

Brooks and Warren issued *Understanding Fiction* in 1943, based upon the practice of close textual examination and the principles of "formalistic" analysis. F. R. Leavis's *The Great Tradition* (1948) considered the works of such novelists as Austen, Eliot, James, Conrad, and Lawrence, while (in the same year) William Van O'Connor edited a collection of articles into a volume titled *Forms of Modern Fiction*. *The Art of Modern Fiction* (West and Stallman, 1949) combined critical analyses with discussions of particular technical problems of the short story, the short novel, and the novel. During 1950 alone, at least three critical anthologies of fiction appeared. Yet despite these books, and others by more conservative writers (for which see the list of recent books at the end of this volume, under Daiches, Geismar, Kazin, and Muller), it is undoubtedly true that modern criticism has not yet done full justice to such novelists as Tolstoy, Turgeniev, Balzac, Zola, or Dreiser. This is a deficiency which time will, no doubt, appropriately eliminate.

In drama there has been less significant work done than in either poetry or fiction. The cause of this, no doubt, is the impoverishment of the theater in England and America between 1900 and 1950, a situation discussed by Eric R. Bentley in his "The Drama at Ebb." Since Mr. Bentley wrote his article there has been a flurry of excitement at the revival of verse drama, which revives the hope also that contemporary criticism will not always be forced to concern itself only with past works. The important point is that until we have a significant modern theater, we cannot have important dramatic criticism. Certainly such a book as Francis Fergusson's recent *The Idea of a Theater* is much more exciting because it discusses dramas from the Greeks to *Murder in the Cathedral* in terms of an "idea of a theater" which would have validity for us today in a theatrical as well as a literary sense.

1. Poetry

WHAT DOES POETRY COMMUNICATE?

CLEANTH BROOKS

The question of what poetry communicates, if anything, has been largely forced upon us by the advent of "modern" poetry. Some of that poetry is admittedly highly difficult—a very great deal of it is bound to *appear* difficult to the reader of conventional reading habits, even in spite of the fact—actually, in many cases, *because* of the fact—that he is a professor of literature.

For this reason, the difficult moderns are often represented as untraditional and generally irresponsible. (The War, incidentally, has encouraged the tendency: critics who ought to know better lend themselves to the popular plea that we should go back to the good old days when a poet meant what he said and there was no nonsense about it.)

The question, however, allows only one honest answer: modern poetry (if it is really poetry, and, at its best, it is really poetry) communicates whatever any other poetry communicates. The fact is that the question is badly asked. What does traditional poetry communicate? What does a poem like Herrick's "Corinna's going a-Maying" communicate? The example is a fair one: the poem has been long praised, and it is not noted for its difficulty.

The textbook answer is easy: the poem is a statement of the *carpe diem* theme. So it is, of course. But what does the poem do with the theme —specifically: Does the poet accept the theme? How seriously does he accept it? Within what context? etc., etc. These are questions of the first importance, a point that becomes obvious when we come to deal with such a matter as the following: after describing the joys of the May-day celebration, the poet prefaces his final invitation to Corinna to accept these joys by referring to them as "the harmlesse follie of the time." Unless we are absentmindedly dictating a stock answer to an indifferent freshman, we shall certainly feel constrained to go further in describing what the poem "says."

Well, let us try again. Herrick's poem says that the celebration of nature is a beautiful but harmless folly, and his invitation to Corinna, thus, is merely playful, not serious. The Anglican parson is merely pretending for the moment that he is Catullus and that his Corinna is a pagan nymph. The poem is a pretense, a masquerade.

But there are the closing lines of the poem:

> Our life is short; and our dayes run
> As fast away as do's the Sunne:
> And as a vapour, or a drop of raine
> Once lost, can ne'er be found againe:
> So when or you or I are made
> A fable, song, or fleeting shade;
> All love, all liking, all delight
> Lies drown'd with us in endlesse night.
> Then while time serves, and we are but decaying;
> Come, my Corinna, come, let's goe a-Maying.

Obviously, there is a sense in which the invitation is thoroughly serious.

Confronted with this apparent contradiction, we can conclude, if we like, that Herrick is confused; or softening the censure, we can explain that he was concerned only with providing some sort of framework for a description of the Devonshire spring. But if Herrick is confused about what he is saying in the poem, he behaves very strangely for a man in that plight. Far from being unconscious of the contradictory elements in the poem, he quite obviously has them in mind. Indeed, he actually takes pains to stress the clash between the Christian and pagan world views; or, rather, while celebrating the pagan view, he refuses to suppress references to the Christian. For instance, for all the dew-besprinkled description of the morning, he makes the ominous, unpagan word "sin" run throughout the poem. While the flowers are rejoicing and the birds are singing their hymns of praise, it is a "sin" and a "profanation" for Corinna to remain within doors. In the second stanza, the clash between paganism and Christianity becomes quite explicit: Corinna is to be "briefe in praying:/Few Beads are best" on this morning which is dedicated to the worship of the nature god. And in the third stanza, paganism becomes frankly triumphant. Corinna is to

> . . . sin no more, as we have done, by staying. . . .

Moreover, a great deal that is usually glossed over as decoration or atmosphere in this poem is actually used by the poet to point up this same conflict. Herrick persists (with a shrewdness worthy of Sir James Frazer) in seeing the May-day rites as religious rites, though, of course, those of a pagan religion. The flowers, like worshipers, bow to the east; the birds sing "Mattens" and "Hymnes"; and the village itself, bedecked with greenery, becomes a cluster of pagan temples:

> Devotion gives each House a Bough,
> Or Branch: Each Porch, each doore, ere this,
> An Arke a Tabernacle is. . . .

The religious terms—"devotion," "ark," "tabernacle"—appear insistently. Corinna is actually being reproached for being late to church—the church of nature. The village itself has become a grove, subject to the laws of nature. One remembers that the original sense of "pagan" was "country-dweller" because the worship of the old gods and goddesses persisted longest there. On this May morning, the country has come into the village to claim it, at least on this one day, for its own. Symbolically, the town has disappeared and its mores are superseded.

I cannot see how we can avoid admitting that all this is communicated by the poem. Here it is in the poem. And its repercussions on the theme (if we still want to view the poem as a communication of a theme) are important. Among other things, they qualify the theme thus: the poem is obviously not a brief for the acceptance of the pagan ethic so much as it is a statement that the claims of the pagan ethic—however much they may be overlaid—exist, and on occasion emerge, as on this day.

The description of Corinna herself supplies another important qualification of the theme. The poet suggests that she properly falls under the dominion of nature as do the flowers and birds and trees. Notice the opening of the second stanza:

> Rise; and put on your Foliage. . . .

And this suggestion that she is a part of nature, like a plant, is reinforced throughout the poem. The trees drenched in dew will shake down dew-drops on her hair, accepting her as a companion and equal. Her human companions, the boys and girls of the village, likewise are plants—

> There's not a budding Boy, or Girle, this day,
> But is got up, and gone to bring in May.

Indeed, as we go through the first three stanzas of the poem, the old relationships gradually dissolve: the street itself turns into a park, and the boys and girls returning with their arms loaded with branches of whitethorn, merge into the plants themselves. Corinna, like them, is subject to nature, and to the claims of nature; and the season of springtime cannot, and ought not, to be denied. Not to respond is to "sin" against nature itself.

All this is "communicated" by the poem, and must be taken into account when we attempt to state what the poem "says." No theory of communication can deny that this is part of what the poem communicates, however awkwardly a theory of communication may be put to it to handle the problem.

We have still not attempted to resolve the conflict between the Christian and pagan attitudes in the poem, though the qualification of each of them, as Herrick qualifies each in the poem, may make it easier to discover possible resolutions which would have appealed to Herrick the Anglican parson who lived so much of his life in Devonshire and apparently took so much interest, not only in the pagan literature of Rome and Greece, but in the native English survivals of the old fertility cults.

Something of the nature of the poet's reconcilement of the conflicting claims of paganism and Christianity—and this, again, is part of what the poem communicates—is foreshadowed in the fourth stanza. The paganism with which the poem is concerned is clearly not an abstract and doctrinaire paganism. It comes to terms with the authoritative Christian mores, casually and without undue thought about the conflict—at least the paganism in action does: the village boys and the girls with their grass-stained gowns, coming to the priest to receive the blessing of the church.

> And some have wept, and woo'd, and plighted Troth,
> And chose their Priest, ere we can cast off sloth. . . .

After the poet's teasing play between attitudes in the first three stanzas, we are apparently approaching some kind of viable relation between them in this most realistic stanza of the poem with its

> Many a jest told of the Keyes betraying
> This night, and Locks pickt. . . . .

The explicit resolution, of course, is achieved, with a change of tone, in the last stanza, with its

> Come, let us goe, while we are in our prime;
> And take the harmlesse follie of the time.
> We shall grow old apace, and die . . .

I shall not try to indicate in detail what the resolution is. Here one must refer the reader to the poem itself. Yet one can venture to suggest the tone. The tone would be something like this: All right, let's be serious. Dismiss my pagan argument as folly. Still, in a sense, we are a part of nature, and are subject to its claims, and participate in its beauty. Whatever may be true in reality of the life of the soul, the body does decay, and unless we make haste to catch some part of that joy and beauty, that beauty—whatever else may be true—is lost.

If my clumsy paraphrase possesses any part of the truth, then this is still another thing which the poem communicates, though I shall hardly be able to "prove" it. As a matter of fact, I do not care to insist upon this or any other paraphrase. Indeed it is just because I am suspicious of such necessarily abstract paraphrases that I think our initial question, "What does the poem communicate?" is badly asked. It is not that the poem communicates nothing. Precisely the contrary. The poem communicates so much and communicates it so richly and with such delicate qualifications that the thing communicated is mauled and distorted if we attempt to convey it by any vehicle less subtle than that of the poem itself.

This general point is reinforced if we consider the function of particular words and phrases within the poem. For instance, consider

> Our life is short; and our dayes run
> As fast away as do's the Sunne:
> And as a vapour, or a drop of raine
> Once lost, can ne'er be found againe. . . .

Why does the rain-drop metaphor work so powerfully? It is hardly because the metaphor is startlingly novel. Surely one important reason for its power is the fact that the poet has filled the first two stanzas of his poem with references to the dew. And the drops of dew have come to stand as a symbol of the spring and early dawn and of the youth of the lovers themselves. The dew-drops are the free gift of nature, spangling every herb and tree; they sparkle in the early light like something precious, like gems; they are the appropriate decoration for the girl; but they will not last—Corinna must hasten to enjoy them if she is to enjoy them at all. Thus, in the context of the poem they become a symbol heavily charged with meanings which no dictionary can be expected to give. When the symbol is revived at the end of the poem, even though in somewhat different guise, the effort is powerful; for the poet has made the little globule of moisture come to stand for the brief beauty of youth. And this too is part of what the poem says, though it is said indirectly, and the dull or lazy reader will not realize that it has been said at all.

The principle of rich indirection applies even to the individual word. Consider

> Then while time serves, and we are but decaying;
> Come, my Corinna, come, let's goe a-Maying.

"While time serves" means loosely "while there is yet time," but in the full context of the poem it also means "while time serves us," while time is still servant, not master—before we are mastered by time. Again, mere recourse to the dictionary will not give us this powerful second meaning. The poet is exploiting the potentialities of language—indeed, as all poets must do, he is remaking language.

To sum up: our examination of the poem has not resulted in our locating an idea or set of ideas which the poet has communicated with certain appropriate decorations. Rather, our examination has carried us further and further into the poem itself in a process of exploration. As we have made this exploration, it has become more and more clear that the poem is not only the linguistic vehicle which conveys the thing communicated most "poetically," but that it is also the sole linguistic vehicle which conveys the things communicated accurately. In fact, if we are to speak exactly, the poem itself is the *only* medium that communicates the particular "what" that is communicated. The conventional theories of communication offer no easy solution to our problem of meanings: we emerge with nothing more enlightening than this graceless bit of tautology: the poem says what the poem says.

There is a further point that comes out of our examination: our examination tends to suggest that not only our reading of the poem is a process of exploration, but that Herrick's process of making the poem was probably a process of exploration too. To say that Herrick "communicates" certain matters to the reader tends to falsify the real situation. The old description of the poet was better and less dangerous: the poet is a maker, not a communicator. He explores, consolidates, and "forms" the total experience that is the poem. I do not mean that he fashions a replica of his particular experience of a certain May morning like a detective making a moulage of a footprint in wet clay. But rather, out of the experiences of many May mornings, and out of his experience of Catullus, and possibly out of a hundred other experiences, he fashions, probably through a process akin to exploration, the total experience which is the poem.

This experience is *communicable,* partially so, at least. If we are willing to use imaginative understanding, we can come to know the poem as an object—we can share in the experience. But the poet is most truthfully described as a *poietes* or maker, not as an expositor or communicator. I do not mean to split hairs. It is doubtless possible to elaborate a theory of communication which will adequately cover these points. I believe that I. A. Richards, if I understand him correctly, has attempted to qualify his theory in precisely this way. At any rate, the net effect of his criticism has been to emphasize the need of a more careful reading of poetry and to regard the poem as an organic thing.

But most proponents of poetry as communication have been less discerning, and have used this view of poetry to damn the modern poets. I refer to such typical critics as Max Eastman and F. L. Lucas. But perhaps the most hard-bitten and vindictive of all the adherents of the theory is a man to whom the phrase "theory of communication" may seem novel and unfamiliar: I mean the average English professor. In one form or another, whether in a conception which makes poetry a romantic raid on the absolute or in a conception of more didactic persuasion which makes poetry an instrument of edification, some form of the theory of communication is to be found deeply embedded in the average teacher's doctrine of poetry. In many contexts it does little or no harm; but it can emerge to becloud the issues thoroughly when one confronts poetry which is unfamiliar or difficult.

Much modern poetry is difficult. Some of it may be difficult because the poet is snobbish and definitely wants to restrict his audience, though this is a strange vanity and much rarer than Mr. Eastman would have us think. Some modern poetry is difficult because it is bad—the total experience remains chaotic and incoherent because the poet could not master his material and give it a form. Some modern poetry is difficult because of the special problems of our civilization. But a great deal of modern poetry is difficult for the reader simply because so few people, relatively speaking, are accustomed to reading *poetry as poetry*. The theory of communication throws the burden of proof upon the poet, overwhelmingly and at once. The reader says to the poet: Here I am; it's your job to "get it across" to me—when he ought to be assuming the burden of proof himself.

Now the modern poet has, for better or worse, thrown the weight of the responsibility upon the reader. The reader must be on the alert for shifts of tone, for ironic statement, for suggestion rather than direct statement. He must be prepared to accept a method of indirection. He is further expected to be reasonably well acquainted with the general tradition—literary, political, philosophical, for he is reading a poet who comes at the end of a long tradition and who can hardly be expected to write honestly and with full integrity and yet ignore this fact. But the difficulties are not insuperable, and most of them can be justified in principle as the natural results of the poet's employment of his characteristic methods. For example, surely there can be no objection to the poet's placing emphasis on methods characteristic of poetry—the use of symbol rather than abstraction, of suggestion rather than explicit pronouncement, of metaphor rather than direct statement.

In stressing such methods, it is true, the modern poet has not produced a poetry which easily yields manageable abstractions in the way that some of the older poetry seems to do. But this is scarcely a conclusion that is flattering to the antagonists of modern poetry. What does an "older poem" like "Corinna's going a-Maying" say? What does this poem communicate?

If we are content with the answer that the poem says that we should enjoy youth before youth fades, and if we are willing to write off everything else in the poem as "decoration," then we can properly censure Eliot or Auden or Tate for not making poems so easily tagged. But in that case we are not interested in poetry; we are interested in tags. Actually, in a few years, when time has wrought its softening changes, and familiarity has subdued the modern poet's frightful mien, and when the tags have been obligingly supplied, we may even come to terms with our difficult moderns.

Postscript:

In a recent essay, Arthur Mizener connects the reference to "the god unshorn" in the first lines of Herrick's poem with a comparable passage in Spenser.

> At last the golden Orientall gate
>   Of greatest heauen gan to open faire,
>   And Phoebus fresh, a bridegrome to his mate,
>   Came dauncing forth, shaking his deawie haire:
>   And hurled his glistring beames through gloomy aire.
>   Which when the wakeful Elf perceiu'd streight way
>   He started vp, and did his selfe arraye:
>   In svn-bright armes, and battailovs array:
> For with that Pagan proud he combat will that day.

"There is," Mizener comments, "a nice fusion, if, to our tastes, not a complete ordering of Pagan and Christian elements here. Phoebus, fresh as the Psalmist's bridegroom, comes dancing (with, I suppose, both a pagan grace and the rejoicing of a strong man to run a race) from the gate of a heaven which is actually felt simultaneously in terms of the clear and lovely classical fantasy on nature and in terms of a Christian vision of the metaphysical source of the meaning of life." And a little later in the essay Mizener goes on to say: "Certainly the Red Cross Knight's 'sunbright armes' ('the armour of a Christian man') are intended to be compared to the 'glistring beames' with which Apollo attacks the darkness, as the virtuous and enlightened Elf is about to attack the darkly evil Pagan. And it is tempting to suppose that since the strength of Holiness is that of the sun, of 'the god unshorn,' the references to Apollo's hair and to the bridegroom's energy are also significant."

Later still in his essay, Mizener quotes the following passage from *Paradise Lost:*

> . . . nor appear'd
> Less than Arch Angel ruin'd, and th' excess
> Of Glory obscur'd: As when the Sun new ris'n
> Looks through the Horizontal misty Air
> Shorn of his Beams, or from behind the Moon

In dim Eclipse disastrous twilight sheds
On half the Nations, and with fear of change
Perplexes Monarchs.

"By the first of these sun comparisons," Mizener points out, "the archangel ruined is the sun deprived of its power to dispel with its beams the foul mists of winter and make the earth fruitful once more; the fallen angel is Apollo, shorn. . . . Nor is it easy to believe the epithet insignificant here; with all his learning Milton must certainly have known how common a symbol of virility the hair was among the Greeks. Herrick, a much less learned man, knew this, as his use of it in 'Corinna's going a-Maying' clearly shows:

Get up, get up, for shame, the Blooming Morn
Upon her wings presents the god unshorne."

It is unfair, of course, to quote from Mizener's essay without reference to his general thesis, and to quote only those bits of it which bear directly upon the dawn passage in Herrick's poem. (The essay, by the way, should be read in entirety and for its own sake: "Some Notes on the Nature of English Poetry," *The Sewanee Review,* Winter, 1943.) Even so, the passage quoted may be of value in demonstrating to the skeptical reader, suspicious that too much is being "read into" Herrick's innocent poem, how other poets of the same general period used the sun figure.

In Herrick's poem, "the god unshorne" is obviously the prepotent bridegroom of nature, the fertility god himself, toward whom the plants bow in adoration and whose day is now to be celebrated.

MARVELL'S GARDEN

THE IDEAL SIMPLICITY APPROACHED BY RESOLVING CONTRADICTIONS

WILLIAM EMPSON

THE chief point of the poem is to contrast and reconcile conscious and unconscious states, intuitive and intellectual modes of apprehension; and yet that distinction is never made, perhaps could not have been made; his thought is

"Marvell's Garden" from *Some Versions of Pastoral* by William Empson. Reprinted by permission of New Directions, and Chatto and Windus.

implied by his metaphors. There is something very Far-Eastern about this; I was set to work on the poem by Dr. Richards' recent discussion of a philosophical argument in Mencius. The Oxford edition notes bring out a crucial double meaning (so that this at least is not my own fancy) in the most analytical statement of the poem, about the Mind—

> Annihilating all that's made
> To a green thought in a green shade.

"Either 'reducing the whole material world to nothing material, i.e. to a green thought,' or 'considering the material world as of no value compared to a green thought' "; either contemplating everything or shutting everything out. This combines the idea of the conscious mind, including everything because understanding it, and that of the unconscious animal nature, including everything because in harmony with it. Evidently the object of such a fundamental contradiction (seen in the etymology: turning all *ad nihil,* to nothing, and *to* a thought) is to deny its reality; the point is not that these two are essentially different but that they must cease to be different so far as either is to be known. So far as he has achieved his state of ecstasy he combines them, he is "neither conscious nor not conscious," like the seventh Buddhist state of enlightenment. This gives its point, I think, to the other ambiguity, clear from the context, as to whether the *all* considered was *made* in the mind of the author or the Creator; to so peculiarly "creative" a knower there is little difference between the two. Here as usual with "profound" remarks the strength of the thing is to combine unusually intellectual with unusually primitive ideas; thought about the conditions of knowledge with a magical idea that the adept controls the external world by thought.

The vehemence of the couplet, and this hint of physical power in thought itself (in the same way as the next line gives it colour), may hint at an idea that one would like to feel was present, as otherwise it is the only main idea about Nature that the poem leaves out; that of the *Hymn to David* and *The Ancient Mariner,* the Orpheus idea, that by delight in Nature when terrible man gains strength to control it. This grand theme too has a root in magic; it is an important version of the idea of the man powerful because he has included everything in himself, is still strong, one would think, among the mountain climbers and often the scientists, and deserves a few examples here. I call it the idea of the *Hymn to David,* though being hidden behind the religious one it is nowhere overtly stated, except perhaps in the line

> Praise above all, for praise prevails.

David is a case of Orpheus-like behaviour because his music restrained the madness of Saul.

> His furious foes no more maligned
> When he such melody divined,
> And sense and soul detained;

By *divining*—intuiting—the harmony behind the universe he "makes it divine," rather as to discover a law of nature is to "give nature laws," and this restrains the madman who embodies the unruled forces of nature from killing him. The main argument of the verses describing nature (or nature as described by David) is that the violence of Nature is an expression of her adoration of God, and therefore that the man of prayer who also adores God delights in it and can control it.

> Strong the gier eagle on his sail
> Strong against tide, th' enormous whale ·
> Emerges, as he goes.

> But stronger still, in earth or air
> Or in the sea, the man of prayer,
> And far beneath the tide.

The feeling is chiefly carried by the sound; long Latin words are packed into the short lines against a short one-syllable rhyming word full of consonants; it is like dancing in heavy skirts; he juggles with the whole cumbrous complexity of the world. The *Mariner* makes a more conscious and direct use of the theme, but in some degree runs away from it at the end. The reason it was a magical crime for a sailor to kill the albatross is that it both occurs among terrible scenes of Nature and symbolises man's power to extract life from them, so ought doubly to be delighted in. So long as the Mariner is horrified by the creatures of the calm he is their slave; he is set free to act, in the supreme verses of the poem, as soon as he delights in them. The final moral is

> He prayeth best, that loveth best
> All things both great and small.

But that copybook maxim is fine only if you can hold it firmly together with such verses as this, which Coleridge later omitted:

> The very deeps did rot; oh Christ
> That such a thing could be;
> Yea, slimy things did crawl with legs
> Upon the slimy sea.

And it was these creatures, as he insisted in the margin by giving the same name to both, that the Mariner blessed unaware when he discovered their beauty. This is what Coleridge meant by alternately saying that the poem has too much of the moral and too little; knowing what the conventional phrases of modern Christianity ought to mean he thought he could shift to a conventional moral that needs to be based upon the real one. Byron's nature-poetry gives more obvious examples of the theme; he likes to compare a storm on the Jura or what not to a woman whom, we are to feel, only Byron could dominate. Poe was startled and liberated by it into a symbol of his own achievement; the sailor in *The Maelstrom* is so horrified as to be frozen, through a trick of neurosis, into idle curiosity, and this becomes a scientific interest in the portent which shows him the way to escape from it.

Nature when terrible is no theme of Marvell's, and he gets this note of triumph rather from using nature when peaceful to control the world of man.

> How safe, methinks, and strong, behind
> These Trees have I encamp'd my Mind;
> Where Beauty, aiming at the Heart,
> Bends in some Tree its useless Dart;
> And where the World no certain Shot
> Can make, or me it toucheth not.
> But I on it securely play
> And gaul its Horsemen all the day.

The masculine energy of the last couplet is balanced immediately by an acceptance of Nature more masochist than passive, in which he becomes Christ with both the nails and the thorns. (*Appleton House,* lxxvi.)

> Bind me ye *Woodbines* in your 'twines,
> Curle me about ye gadding *Vines,*
> And Oh so close your Circles lace,
> That I may never leave this Place:
> But, lest your Fetters prove too weak,
> Ere I your Silken Bondage break,
> Do you, O *Brambles,* chain me too,
> And courteous *Briars* nail me through.

He does not deify himself more actively, and in any case the theme of the *Garden* is a repose.

> How vainly men themselves amaze
> To win the Palm, or Oke, or Bayes;
> And their uncessant Labours see
> Crown'd from some single Herb or Tree.
> Whose short and narrow verged Shade
> Does prudently their Toyles upbraid;
> While all Flow'rs and all Trees do close
> To weave the Garlands of repose.

This first verse comes nearest to stating what seems the essential distinction, with that between powers inherent and powers worked out in practice, being a general and feeling one could be; in this ideal case, so the wit of the thing claims, the power to have been a general is already satisfied in the garden. "Unemployment" is too painful and normal even in the fullest life for such a theme to be trivial. But self-knowledge is possible in such a state so far as the unruly impulses are digested, ordered, made transparent, not by their being known, at the time, as unruly. Consciousness no longer makes an important distinction; the impulses, since they must be balanced already, neither need it to put them right nor are put wrong by the way it forces across their boundaries. They let themselves be known because they are not altered by being known, because their principle of indeterminacy no longer acts. This idea is important for all the versions of pastoral, for the pastoral figure is always ready to be the critic; he not only includes everything but may in some unexpected way know it.

Another range of his knowledge might be mentioned here. I am not sure what arrangement of flower-beds is described in the last verse, but it seems clear that the sun goes through the "zodiac" of flowers in one day, and that the bees too, in going from one bed to another, reminding us of the labours of the first verse, pass all summer in a day. They compute their time as well as we in that though their lives are shorter they too contract all experience into it, and this makes the poet watch over large periods of time as well as space. So far he becomes Nature, he becomes permanent. It is a graceful finale to the all-in-one theme, but not, I think, very important; the crisis of the poem is in the middle.

Once you accept the Oxford edition's note you may as well apply it to the whole verse.

> Meanwhile the Mind, from pleasure less,
> Withdraws into its happiness;
> The Mind, that Ocean where each kind
> Does streight its own resemblance find;
> Yet it creates, transcending these,
> Far other worlds, and other Seas,
> Annihilating . . .

From pleasure less. Either "from the lessening of pleasure"—"we are quiet in the country, but our dullness gives a sober and self-knowing happiness, more intellectual than that of the overstimulated pleasures of the town" or "made less by this pleasure"—"The pleasures of the country give a repose and intellectual release which make me less intellectual, make my mind less worrying and introspective." This is the same puzzle as to the consciousness of the thought; the ambiguity gives two meanings to pleasure, corresponding to his Puritan ambivalence about it, and to the opposition between pleasure and happiness. *Happiness,* again, names a conscious state, and yet involves the idea of things falling right, happening so, not being ordered by an anxiety of the conscious reason. (So that as a rule it is a weak word; it is by seeming to look at it hard and bring out its implications that the verse here makes it act as a strong one.)

The same doubt gives all their grandeur to the next lines. The sea if calm reflects everything near it; the mind as knower is a conscious mirror. Somewhere in the sea are sea-lions and -horses and everything else, though they are different from land ones; the unconsciousness is unplumbed and pathless, and there is no instinct so strange among the beasts that it lacks its fantastic echo in the mind. In the first version thoughts are shadows, in the second (like the *green thought*) they are as solid as what they image; and yet they still correspond to something in the outer world, so that the poet's intuition is comparable to pure knowledge. This metaphor may reflect back so that *withdraws* means the tide going down; the *mind* is *less* now, but will return, and it is now that one can see the rock-pools. On the Freudian view of an Ocean, *withdraws* would make this repose in Nature a return to the womb; anyway it may mean either "withdraws into self-contemplation" or "withdraws altogether, into its mysterious processes of digestion." *Streight* may mean "packed together," in the microcosm, or "at once"; the beasts see their reflection (perhaps the root idea of the metaphor) as soon as they look for it; the calm of Nature gives the poet an immediate self-knowledge. But we have already had two entrancingly witty verses about the sublimation of sexual desire into a taste for Nature (I should not say that this theme was the main emotional drive behind the poem, but it takes up a large part of its overt thought), and the *kinds* look for their *resemblance,* in practice, out of a desire for *creation;* in the mind, at this fertile time for the poet, they can *find* it "at once," being "packed together." The transition from the beast and its reflection to the two pairing beasts implies a transition from the correspondences of thought with fact to those of thought with thought, to find which is to be creative; there is necessarily here a suggestion of rising from one "level" of thought to another; and in the next couplet not only does the mind transcend the world it mirrors, but a sea, to which it is parallel, transcends both land and sea too, which implies self-consciousness and all the antinomies of philosophy. Whether or not you give *transcendent* the technical sense "predicable of all categories" makes no great difference; in including everything in itself the mind includes as a detail itself and all its inclusions. And it is true that the sea reflects the *other worlds* of the stars; Donne's metaphor of the globe is in the background. Yet even here the double meaning is not lost; all land-beasts have their sea-beasts, but the sea also has the kraken; in the depths as well as the transcendence of the mind are things stranger than all the kinds of the world.

Miss M. C. Bradbrook has pointed out to me that the next verse, while less triumphant, gives the process a more firmly religious interpretation.

> Here at the Fountains sliding foot,
> Or by some Fruit-trees mossy root,
> Casting the Bodies Vest aside,
> My Soul into the boughs does glide;
> There like a Bird it sits, and sings,
> Then whets, and combs its silver Wings;
> And, till prepar'd for longer flight,
> Waves in its Plumes the various Light.

The bird is the dove of the Holy Spirit and carries a suggestion of the rainbow of the covenant. By becoming inherent in everything he becomes a soul not pantheist but clearly above and apart from the world even while still living in it. Yet the paradoxes are still firmly maintained here, and the soul is as solid as the green thought. The next verse returns naturally and still with exultation to the jokes in favour of solitude against women.

Green takes on great weight here, as Miss Sackville West pointed out, because it has been a pet word of Marvell's before. To list the uses before the satires may seem an affectation of pedantry, but shows how often the word was used; and they are pleasant things to look up. In the Oxford text: pages 12, 1.23; 17, 1.18; 25, 1.11; 27, 1.4; 38, 1.3; 45, 1.3; 46, 1.25; 48, 1.18; 49, 1.48; 70, 1.376; 71, 1.390; 74, 1.510; 122, 1.2. Less rich uses: 15, 1.18; 21, 1.44; 30, 1.55; 42, 1.14; 69, 1.339; 74, 11.484, 496; 78, 1.628; 85, 1.82; 89, 1.94; 108, 1.196. It is connected here with grass, buds, children, an as yet virginal prospect of sexuality, and the peasant stock from which the great families emerge. The "unfathomable" grass makes the soil fertile and shows it to be so; it is the humble, permanent, undeveloped nature which sustains everything, and to which everything must return. No doubt D. H. Lawrence was right when he spoke up for *Leaves of Grass* against Whitman and said they felt themselves to be very aristocratic, but that too is eminently a pastoral fancy. Children are connected with this both as buds, and because of their contact with Nature (as in Wordsworth), and unique fitness for Heaven (as in the Gospels).

> The tawny mowers enter next,
> Who seem like Israelites to be,
> Walking on foot through a green sea.

connects greenness with oceans and gives it a magical security;

> And in the greenness of the grass
> Did see my hopes as in a glass

connects greenness with mirrors and the partial knowledge of the mind. The complex of ideas he concentrates into this passage, in fact, had been worked out already, and in a context that shows how firmly these ideas about Nature were connected with direct pastoral. The poem indeed comes immediately after a pastoral series about the mower of grass.

> I am the Mower Damon, known
> Through all the Meadows I have mown;
> On me the Morn her dew distills
> Before her darling Daffodils

In these meadows he feels he has left his mark on a great territory, if not on everything, and as a typical figure he has mown all the meadows of the world; in either case Nature gives him regal and magical honours, and I suppose he is not only the ruler but the executioner of the daffodils—the Clown as Death.

> Only for him no Cure is found,
> Whom Juliana's Eyes do wound.
> 'Tis death alone that this must do:
> For Death thou art a Mower too.

He provides indeed more conscious and comic mixtures of heroic and pastoral:

> every Mower's wholesome heat
> Smelled like an Alexander's sweat.

It is his grand attack on gardens which introduces both the connection through wit between the love of woman and of nature, which is handled so firmly in the *Garden:*

> No white nor red was ever seen
> So am'rous as this lovely green:

—and the belief that the fruitful attitude to Nature is the passive one:

> His [the gardener's] green Seraglio has its Eunuchs too;
> Lest any Tyrant him outdoe.
> And in the Cherry he does Nature vex,
> To procreate without a Sex.
> 'Tis all enforced; the Fountain and the Grot;
> While the sweet Fields do lye forgot;
> Where willing Nature does to all dispence
> A wild and fragrant Innocence:
> And *Fauns* and *Faryes* do the Meadows till,
> More by their presence than their skill.

It is Marvell himself who tills the Garden by these magical and contemplative powers.

Grass indeed comes to be taken for granted as the symbol of pastoral humility:

> Unhappy Birds! what does it boot
> To build below the Grasses' Root;
> When Lowness is unsafe as Hight,
> And Chance o'ertakes what scapeth Spight?

It is a humility of Nature from which she is still higher than man, so that the grasshoppers preach to him from their pinnacles:

> And now to the Abyss I pass
> Of that unfathomable Grass,
> Where men like Grashoppers appear,
> But Grashoppers are Gyants there;
> They, in there squeking Laugh, contemn
> Us as we walk more low than them:
> And, from the Precipices tall
> Of the green spire's, to us do call.

It seems also to be an obscure merit of grass that it produces "hay," which was the name of a country dance, so that the humility is gaiety.

> With this the golden fleece I shear
> Of all these Closes ev'ry Year,
> And though in Wool more poor than they,
> Yet I am richer far in Hay.

To nineteenth-century taste the only really poetical verse of the poem is the central fifth of the nine; I have been discussing the sixth, whose dramatic position is an illustration of its very penetrating theory. The first four are a crescendo of wit, on the themes "success or failure is not important, only the repose that follows the exercise of one's powers" and "women, I am pleased to say, are no longer interesting to me, because nature is more beautiful." One effect of the wit is to admit, and so make charming, the impertinence of the second of these, which indeed the first puts in its place; it is only for a time, and after effort among human beings, that he can enjoy solitude. The value of these moments made it fitting to pretend they were eternal; and yet the lightness of his expression of their sense of power is more intelligent, and so more convincing, than Wordsworth's solemnity on the same theme, because it does not forget the opposing forces.

> When we have run our Passions heat,
> Love hither makes his best retreat.
> The *Gods,* that mortal beauty chase,

> Still in a Tree did end their race.
> *Apollo* hunted *Daphne* so,
> Only that she might Laurel grow,
> And *Pan* did after *Syrinx* speed,
> Not as a Nymph, but for a Reed.

The energy and delight of the conceit has been sharpened or keyed up here till it seems to burst and transform itself; it dissolves in the next verse into the style of Keats. So his observation of the garden might mount to an ecstasy which disregarded it; he seems in this next verse to imitate the process he has described, to enjoy in a receptive state the exhilaration which an exercise of wit has achieved. But striking as the change of style is, it is unfair to empty the verse of thought and treat it as random description; what happens is that he steps back from overt classical conceits to a rich and intuitive use of Christian imagery. When people treat it as the one good "bit" of the poem one does not know whether they have recognised that the Alpha and Omega of the verse are the apple and the Fall.

> What wond'rous Life in this I lead!
> Ripe Apples drop about my head;
> The Luscious Clusters of the Vine
> Upon my Mouth do crush their Wine;
> The Nectaren, and curious Peach,
> Into my hands themselves do reach;
> Stumbling on Melons, as I pass,
> Insnar'd with Flow'rs, I fall on Grass.

Melon, again, is the Greek for apple; "all flesh is *grass,*" and its own *flowers* here are the snakes in it that stopped Eurydice. Mere grapes are at once the primitive and the innocent wine; the nectar of Eden, and yet the blood of sacrifice. *Curious* could mean "rich and strange" (nature), "improved by care" (art) or "inquisitive" (feeling toward me, since nature is a mirror, as I do toward her). All these eatable beauties give themselves so as to lose themselves, like a lover, with a forceful generosity; like a lover they *ensnare* him. It is the triumph of the attempt to impose a sexual interest upon nature; there need be no more Puritanism in this use of sacrificial ideas than is already inherent in the praise of solitude; and it is because his repose in the orchard hints at such a variety of emotions that he is contemplating *all that's made.* Sensibility here repeats what wit said in the verse before; he tosses into the fantastic treasure-chest of the poem's thought all the pathos and dignity that Milton was to feel in his more celebrated Garden; and it is while this is going on, we are told in the next verse, that the mind performs its ambiguous and memorable *withdrawal.* For each of the three central verses he gives a twist to the screw of the microscope and is living in another world.

I must go back to the *annihilating* lines, whose method is less uncommon. Similar ideas and tricks of language are used in Donne's *Exstasie*, where various puns impose on us the idea that an adequate success in love is a kind of knowledge which transcends the barriers of the ordinary kind. There is again some doubt how far the author knew what he was doing.

> As our blood labours to beget
> Spirits, as like souls as it can, . . .
> So must pure louers' soules descend . . .

To the modern reader this is a pun on the senses' "subtle material essence" (e.g. "spirits of salt") and "nonmaterial unit of life"; it seems used with as much "wit" as the other puns, to trick us into feeling that soul and body may be interfused. The Oxford edition notes make clear that to Donne this was neither a pun nor a sophistry; "The spirits . . . are the thin and active part of the blood, and are of a kind of middle nature, between soul and body" (Sermons); one view of them was that there was a hierarchy of more and more spiritual ones. It is curious how the change in the word leaves the poetry unaffected; by Swift's time the two senses were an absurd accident from which one could get ironies against materialism. No doubt in some important senses Donne was right, but however supported by Cambridge Platonism it is a genuine primitive use of the word. Whereas he would certainly have known there was a pun on "sense" even if he took it for granted. "Our bodies why do we forbeare?" . . .

> We owe them thanks, because they thus,
> Did us, to us, at first convey,
> Yielded their forces, sense, to us,
> Nor are dross to us, but allay.

The antithesis for *allay* makes it mean "alloy," a less valuable substance put into their gold to strengthen it for practical use; *allay* could mean "keeping the spiritual pleasure from being too great, more than our strength could bear," which goes with "alloy," then, behind that, "relief to the pain of desire," which makes the flesh less unimportant. This is reinforced by the special meaning of sense ("the wanton stings and motions of the s"). That rich word confuses the pleasure and the knowledge given by the senses (Donne wants to imply they are mutually dependent) and suggests that soul and body are in a healthy intuitive relation—"plenty of sense." The use of *sense* for sensibleness became stronger later in the century, but it is already clearly an element in the word—for example in saying "there is no sense" in a statement when it has meaning but is not sensible. "We could not know each other at all without sensations, therefore cannot know each other fully without sensuality, nor would it be sensible to try to do so."

The poem uses the word again later, and there the sexual meaning is clear.

> So must pure louers' soules descend
> To affections, and to faculties,
> Which sense may reach and apprehend,
> Else a great Prince in Prison lies,
> To our bodies turn we then. . . .

Affections are "loves," "weaknesses," and in the philosophical sense "physical effects." *Apprehend* means "know" and by derivation "clutch," and *reach* would go with either, which gives *sense* a sort of bridge between its meanings.

It is possible that Donne means to throw in a pun on "know," as in "Adam knew his wife."

> Wee then, who are this new soule, know,
> Of what we are compos'd, and made,
> For, the atomies of which we grow,
> Are soules, which no change can invade.

Know is isolated by the comma ("know each other"), and *of* may then take a step towards "by means of." Then, with Donne's usual leap in pretending to give a reason, he makes each soul entirely immaterial; "the intellectual knowledge has, for us, all the advantages of the physical one, even granted that they are distinguishable." If he did this it would have to be done consciously and wilfully.

One should not of course take such poetry as only a clever game. This truth-seeking idea seems fundamental to the European convention of love-poetry; love is always idealised as a source of knowledge not only of the other party but of oneself and of the world.

This Exstasie doth unperplex

because it makes the disparate impulses of the human creature not merely open to the prying of the mind but prepared for its intrusion. It is along these lines, I think, that D. H. Lawrence's hatred of the whole conception might be answered, or rather that he answered it himself. On the other hand, I think Donne felt quite casual about these particular tricks; the juggle with *sense* has the same graceful impudence as his frankly absurd arguments. M. Legouis may be right in saying that he set out merely to dramatise the process of seduction; it is only clear that he found the argument fascinating and believed that it had some truth in some cases. He did not think it so false as to depend on his puns, even where he recognised them; he may well have understood what the puns themselves depend upon. They insist on relics of primitive thought in civilised language, and thereby force the languages to break down its later distinctions and return to ideas natural to the human mind. Dr. Richards' account of romantic nature poetry in *Coleridge on Imagination* is a very good example; the personalised Nature is treated both as external to man and as created by an instinct of the mind, and by tricks of language these are made to seem the same. But if they were simply called the same we would not so easily be satisfied by the tricks. What we feel is that though they are essentially unlike they are practically unlike in different degrees at different times; a supreme condition can therefore be imagined, though not attained, in which they are essentially like. (To put it like this is no doubt to evade a philosophic issue.) A hint of the supreme condition is thus found in the actual one (this makes the actual one include everything in itself), but this apparently exalted claim is essentially joined to humility; it is effective only through the admission that it is only a hint. Something of the tone of pastoral is therefore inherent in the claim; the fault of the Wordsworthian method seems to be that it does not show this.

I shall add here a pun from *As You Like It,* which shows how the same issue may be raised by a casual joke. The pun in its context makes a contradiction, and this is felt to show an intuitive grasp of some of the puzzles of the context. Fortunately there is no doubt that a pun is meant because the text insists upon it; the N.E.D. shows that the modern spellings, though used loosely, already made the distinction. Apart from facsimiles no edition that I have seen has yet printed the text. The point of the two spellings is to show that the two senses are at work; it is none the less fair to take the senses the other way round. (This is from the Folio; there is no Quarto.)

CLOWN. . . . truly, I would the Gods hadde made thee poeticall.

AUDREY. I do not know what Poetical is: is it honest in word and deed: is it a true thing?

CLOWN. No trulie: for the truest poetrie is the most faining, and Louers are given to Poetrie; and what they sweare in Poetrie, may be said as Louers, they do feigne.

AUDREY. Do you wish then that the Gods had made me Poetical?

CLOWN. I do truly: for thou swear'est to me thou art honest: Now if thou wert a Poet, I might haue some hope thou didst feigne.

"A material fool" is the pleased judgment of the listening Jaques; he feels that there is a complete copy of the human world among fools, as of beasts among sea-beasts. This indeed is one of the assumptions of pastoral, that you can say everything about complex people by a complete consideration of simple people. The jokes are mainly carried on by puns on "honest"—chastity in women, truth in speech, simplicity in clowns, and the hearty sense "generous because free from hypocrisy"; my point is the pun on "fain" (*desiring*) and "feign" (*pretend; in lovers pretend honest desire*). The doubt of the poet's honesty is referred to the broader doubt of his self-knowledge, just as *honest* itself shifts from "truth-telling" to "sincere in his own mind." The pun itself is common, though I think it is only here, where it enriches the thought so much, that Shakespeare spelt it out for the reader.

> EGEUS. Thou hast by moonlight at her window sang
> With faining voice, verses of faining love,
> And Stolne the impression of her fantasie.

He feigns true love because he would fain possess her; the word love itself may be used of a desire not permanent or generous; Egeus would call that a feigning love even if Nature deceives both of them, and the man thinks himself sincere. The easy but capacious mind of Spenser takes this for granted (F.Q.,V.xii.36; Hymn to Love, 216); nobody pretends without purpose, so it is a useful trick of language. Touchstone's use of it about poetry is more searching.

The root of the joke is that a physical desire drives the human creature to a spiritual one. The best poetry is the most genuinely passionate (fain) but there may be two pretences (feign), that the desire felt for this woman is spiritual and that any woman is the object of so spiritual a desire. "To write poetry is not the quickest way to satisfy desire; there must be some other impulse behind the convention of love-poetry; something feigned in the choice of topic; some other thing of which they are fain." As for the distinction between their rôles as poets and lovers, both senses may apply to them in both, also to *swearing,* since "go to hell" is spontaneous, not meant, not meant to deceive, and a sort of feigning in which you are fain of what you feign. For that matter they are wooing the reader even if they are not trying to seduce a mistress; the process at its simplest involves desire and detachment, nature and sophistication; levels mysteriously interrelated which a sane man separates only for a joke. Touchstone's pretence of acidity allows of a real plea for his own case because it implies that the most refined desires are inherent in the plainest, and would be false if they weren't; he shows a staircase by giving the two lowest steps, lust and cheating. In the Marvell and Donne examples it is the top of a staircase that is in question, but the same method is used to define it. Two ideas are united which in normal use are contradictory, and our machinery of interpretation so acts that we feel there is a series of senses in which they could be more and more truly combined. This is clearest in what Mr. James Smith defined as metaphysical conceits, those that genuinely sum up a metaphysical problem. The top and next steps in the Aristotelian staircase about form and matter, for example, would be pure form and material, already form, which it informs. Donne is using this when he calls each lover's soul the body of the other's; the fact that we do not believe that the lovers are in this condition does not keep us from a feeling of belief in the conceit, because we believe in the staircase which it defines; the lovers appear as conscious of the staircase and higher up on it than most. Nor for that matter do we believe that the clown is at the bottom of his staircase; his understanding of it acts as a proof that he isn't. A good case of a poem with some doubt about the staircase it requires is provided by Shakespeare's *Phoenix and Turtle;* it depends on the same ideas as Donne's *First Anniversary,* but gets very different feelings out of them. The entire flatness of the use of the convention makes it seem first an engagingly simple-minded piece of "idealism" and then, since the union of the birds is likely after all to be of a simple kind, an expression of cultivated and good-humoured sensuality; this does not by any means destroy the pathetic dignity of the close. There is a suggestion that the author finds the convention fascinating but absurd, which he shows mainly by his sound-effects. This seems to me intentional, very delightful, and not a thing that Chapman (who has been suggested as the author) could possibly have done. It is clear here that once you cease to impose a staircase the thing shifts from heroic to mock-pastoral. Some such idea needs to be added to Mr. James Smith's account (perhaps he would call it obvious) because otherwise there seems no way of putting in a judgment of value; on his account a metaphysical conceit is essentially a vivid statement of a puzzle, and in practice it is more.

I should say that this process is at work in much poetry that does not seem ambiguous at all, and shall pursue the question into Homer as the fountainhead of simplicity. This may also throw some light on the obscure connection between heroic and pastoral; the fact seems to be that both rely on a "complex in simple" formula.

One idea essential to a primitive epic style is that the good is not separable (anyway at first level judgments) from a life of straightforward worldly success in which you keep certain rules; the plain satisfactions are good in themselves and make great the men who enjoy them. From this comes the "sense of glory" and of controlling nature by delight in it. It is absurd to call this a "premoralistic" view, since the rules may demand great sacrifices and it is shameful not to keep them; there is merely a naïve view of the nature of good. (Both a limitation of the things that are good and a partial failure to separate the idea of good from the idea of those things.) The naïve view is so often more true than the sophisticated ones that this comes in later ages to take on an air of massive grandeur; it gives a feeling of freedom from humbug which is undoubtedly noble, and the Homeric heroes support this by the far from savage trait of questioning the beliefs they still die for. Stock epithets about "the good wine" or "the well-built gates" imply "so one always rightly feels"; such a thing essentially has virtue in it, *is* a piece of virtue; a later reader feels this to be symbolic, a process of packing all the sorts of good into a simple one. Material things are taken as part of a moral admiration, and to a later reader (with less pride, for example, in the fact that his culture uses iron) this seems an inspiriting moral paradox like those of pastoral—"to one who knows how to live the ideal is easily reached." It is assumed that Ajax is still enormously grand when he cooks his dinner; the later reader feels he must really be very grand not to lose his dignity, whereas at the time it was a thing of some splendour to have so much dinner to cook or such implements to do it with. This comes to have the same effect as a pretence of pastoral humility in the author. Also the heroic individual has an enormous effect on everything in sight, gods and men, and yet finds everything of manageable dimensions; the later reader feels that this belongs to a village society rather than a large-town one. Certainly the heroes are not grand merely because they are brave; they can run away like other people, and say so more frankly. Indeed a great part of their dignity comes from the naïve freshness with which they can jump from one level of argument to another, and this leaves room for the effects I am considering.

Thus the puzzles become more obvious later, but this is not to say they were not used at the start. The heroes are given a directly moral grandeur by the perpetual clashes between free-will and necessity, symbolised by their relations with the gods, out of which they construct their speeches; they fight on when certain of failure and kill each other with the apology that they too are fated, and such fore-knowledge as they have makes them half divine. It is very curious that what is supposed to be another branch of the same race, when it arrived in India, had none of this interest in the problems of free-will; the dignity of the heroes in the Mahabarata is based on puzzles about the One and the Many. Nor did it develop later; the Buddha was once actually faced with the problem of free-will raised so starkly by his system, and brushed it aside on grounds of morality; I understand that all Buddhist theologians have ignored the issue. Whereas all new ideas in Europe, Christianity and the sciences in turn, have been

taken as new problems about necessity and free-will. Thus the reason why
the Homeric *but* where one expects "and" has so much poetic force is that
it implies some argument, such as all the characters are happy with, and
the argument would lead you to other levels of thought. (This acts as a feeling that the two things put together are vividly different in themselves.) "He
spoke, and held still his hand upon the silvery hilt, and thrust back the great
sword into the scabbard, nor did he disobey the order of Minerva; but she
had gone to Olympus, to the mansions of aegis-bearing Jove, amongst the
other deities." *But* makes her already indifferent; the puzzle about how far
men are free and how far the gods are only forces in their minds is thrust
upon your attention. Also there is a strong feeling in the epic that the heroes
are too great to kill each other for detested Helen and the unnecessary recovery of corpses ("Nor do I fear so much about the dead body of
Patroclus, which will quickly satiate the dogs and birds of the Trojans, as
much as I fear for my own head, lest it suffer anything, and for thine") and
yet that only this would display their greatness; a rich contradiction on
which to build a hierarchy of value. I began by saying that such writing was
based on a naïve idea of the nature of good, but in fact other ideas of good
are implicit in it; Shakespeare's *Troilus and Cressida* is often taken as a
sort of parody of the *Iliad,* but there is little in it that Homer did not imply.
What becomes strange to a more sophisticated society is the order in which
the ideas can be built up; in such a society everybody has been told some
refined ideas about good (or what not) and wants them put in at once; to
take a simple thing and imply a hierarchy in it can then only be done in a
strange world like that of Milton's Adam or a convention like that of
pastoral. To say this is to echo what many of Homer's critics, including
Milton himself, have said about the peculiar advantage he got from his date,
and I am only trying to show that it fits in with my theory.

I have not been able to say what machinery erects a staircase on a
contradiction, but then the only essential for the poet is to give the reader
a chance to build an interesting one; there are continual opportunities in
the most normal uses of language. Any statement of identity between terms
already defined ("God is love") is a contradiction because you already
know they are not identical; you have to ignore senses that would be unimportant ("the first cause was a creative impulse") and there are likely
to be degrees in which the two may be called identical which lead to different important senses. That the process is not simple is obvious when you
turn them round; "love is God" would be quite different. "Might is Right"
and "Right is Might" were felt to be clear and opposite statements of
ethical theory, and it is not clear how this was possible. It is no good to
read them as "if a man has might, then he has right," etc.; a supporter of

this opinion would say that if a man has no might he has no right, and the two sentences are still identical. The same applies to the similar interpretations "Might is a member of the class Right," etc.; it would be the only member of its class. I think these are at work; the analogy of the second word to an adjective in this version shows how the first is felt to be the more solid and unchangeable. But the second word is in fact belittled rather than made inclusive. Yet you cannot read them simply as substitutions; "always say might instead of right; there is no reason for not making a full use of power" and "never calculate chances; to be in the right is the only thing to be considered." These are present and seem to control the senses from the back, but the subdued word is still there and is not negated. *Right* in the first is some sort of justification and *might* in the second some sort of hope or claim. "A great and crowded nation has the right to expand"; "because we have right on our side we are certain to win." A vague sense that "is" has other uses than the expression of identity makes us ready to find meanings in such sentences; this may well have been the historical reason why it was too convenient to be simplified. But the principle of language that makes the two different is simply a traffic rule; the two words are felt to cover some of the same ground and in some cases of conflict the first has the right of way.

It might I think also be argued that any contradiction implies a regress, though not one definite one. To say that it is always an example of the supreme process of seeing the Many as One is to ignore the differences in the feelings aroused by different examples; but there may always be a less ambitious process at work that uses similar machinery. The pretence that two words are identical acts as a hint that they have been fitted into some system, in which each key word is dependent on the others, like the parts of an organism; admittedly the words are not the same but they have been "unified." One characteristic of an organism is that you can only change it (as a whole and without killing it) by a process like edging up a chimney in rock-climbing; one element must be changed to the small extent that the elasticity of the system allows and then the others must be changed to fit it. So to find your way into the interpretation seems essentially a process of shifting the words again and again. This at least describes the sense of richness (readiness for argument not pursued) in such language and the fact that one ambiguity, even though obtained in several parallel words, is not enough for it.

That this talk about a hierarchy of "levels" is vague I can cheerfully admit; the idea is generally vague in the authors who use it, and none the less powerful for being left in a suggestive form. But the three central verses of the Marvell poem are at least a definite example; in the course of suggesting various interlocking hierarchies (knowing that you know that you know, reconciling the remaining unconscious with the increasing conscious-ness, uniting in various degrees perception and creation, the one and the many), it does in fact rise through a hierarchy of three sharply contrasted styles and with them give a more and more inclusive account of the mind's relation to Nature. Only a metaphysical poet with so perfect a sense of form and so complete a control over the tricks of the style, at the end of its de-velopment, could actually dramatise these hints as he gave them.

DRYDEN: ODE ON ANNE KILLIGREW 1686

E. M. W. TILLYARD

HENRYSON's *Testament of Cresseid* is a beautiful and moving poem of one good minor poet; Davies's *Or-chestra* a beautiful and exhilarating poem of another. Dryden's *Ode on Anne Killigrew* is a masterpiece of a major poet. We need not like it best, but, if we do compare, it makes the other two look a little amateurish. One reason for this is the high proportion of our attention which, at first sight, the purely formal qualities of the *Ode* usurp. Henry-son's tragic story, the setting of *Orchestra* and the world picture and the politics set forth in it, count for more than the purely prose content of the *Ode*. Dryden does indeed tell us things about Anne Killigrew: that she was virtuous and gifted; that she wrote verse and painted landscapes and royal portraits; and that she died of smallpox. But the two hundred lines spent in saying this are, as information, nearly all padding, while what astonishes and delights is the wealth of imaginative invention and the glory of the verbal music. Here, if anywhere, Arnold's attribution of the prosaic to Augustan verse is refuted, while the raptures into which his contemporaries fell over one kind of musical verse are perfectly appropriate to the excel-lence if not to the kind of Dryden's.

The form of the *Ode* is inherited directly from Cowley, but further ancestry included Spenser's *Epithalamion* and Ben Jonson, while the accent of majesty owes much to Milton and particularly to his short pieces *On*

"Dryden: Ode On Anne Killegrew 1686" from *Five Poems* by E. M. W. Tillyard. Reprinted by permission of The Macmillan Company, and Chatto and Windus.

Time, Upon the Circumcision, and *At a Solemn Music.* Compare for instance this from Dryden's *Ode*

> Hear then a mortal Muse thy praise rehearse
> In no ignoble verse

with this from *On Time*

> Then long Eternity shall greet our bliss
> With an individual kiss.

The invention and music are not equally brilliant throughout, but I cannot agree with Mark Van Doren that the *Ode* is "sadly uneven" and that apart from three great stanzas the rest are at the most equal to Cowley. In general the tone of solemn rapture is sustained, and the ebbings form the preparations, necessary in a long lyric, for the full flood of music. There may however be isolated lapses. It is hard to feel warmly about the political metaphor in stanza six: the idea that through the descriptive passages in her poetry she had staked out claims in the adjacent province of painting, as an ambitious ruler forms seditious groups in the country he means to invade.

> To the next realm she stretched her sway,
> For Painture near adjoining lay,
> A plenteous province and alluring prey.
> A Chamber of Dependences was framed
> (As conquerors will never want pretence,
> When armed, to justify the offence),
> And the whole fief in right of Poetry she claimed.

And at the end of stanza seven the line

> What next she had designed, Heaven only knows

is not impressive in sound even if we can forget the absurdity which a modern does, and a contemporary did not, find in it.[1]

After the music the construction calls for admiration. The poem is an elegy on a poetess and like the Dido poem in Spenser's *Shepherd's Calendar,* like *Lycidas,* and like *Adonais* it presupposes the happy fate of the deceased. It is built on the two themes of earth and heaven, which themselves are linked by the commonplace that earthly poetry partakes of the divine; and it evolves as follows. The first stanza gives the three main themes: poetry, for Anne Killigrew is even now singing; heaven and earth,

---

[1] *Heaven only knows* means in the context that heaven, having heard her songs there, does know, as mortals cannot, what her next artistic efforts would have been, had she survived.

for she sings in some heavenly region, while her earthly songs served as prelude and probation for the heavenly music. The second stanza has the same mixture of theme but with the emphasis on earth and her pre-natal poetical antecedents. By immediate heredity she comes of poetical stock, by re-incarnation from Sappho. The stanza ends with heaven. Anne Killigrew's is too pure a soul to suffer further incarnation: when she has ceased listening to the poem now addressed to her she must return to the quire of heavenly singers. The third stanza again contains all three themes but with the emphasis on Heaven, which celebrated her birth with joy. This pure heavenly rejoicing suggests its contrary in stanza four, the general impurity of contemporary poetry; and the pessimistic satirical and urgent tone contrasts finely with the serene static tone of the first three stanzas. It comes to rest on Anne Killigrew and the thought that she was both an exception and an atonement. In so doing it introduces the body of the ode, stanzas five to eight, which deal with the lady's attainments on earth. Heaven is kept in the background, and we hear of her successes in poetry and in painting and of her untimely death. Death leads to mourning, and in stanza nine her brother's sorrow when he learns the news is conjectured. But he is at sea and has no news. Only, if sailorlike he scans the stars, he might notice a new bright member of the Pleiades—the star which is his sister's soul. This mention of the stars is the return of the theme of heaven; and it leads to the last stanza, where poetry heaven and earth are brought together in the description of the opening graves and the Last Judgement with Anne Killigrew leading the poets, the first souls to join their resurrected bodies, to their heavenly mansion. The poem's evolution is perfect, and it is the greatest pity that in the *Oxford Book of English Verse,* the chief recent means of access, it should have been truncated.

So far I have dealt with matters of forms, and it may now be asked of what feelings, opinions, or states of mind are the poem's music and formal perfection the index.

The states of mind poems express stand at varying distances from the subjects these poems purport to treat. Dryden's subject, Anne Killigrew's premature death, has no close connection with the things he was really saying. He must have known that her poems and pictures were the indifferent stuff which posterity has decided them to be. Nevertheless he used the conventional grief and extravagant adulation to convey certain strongly held opinions and feelings.

One of these is a heartfelt enthusiasm for the arts, the same enthusiasm that animates Dryden's literary criticism. When he praises Anne Killigrew's accomplishment, he is speaking not for her but for poetry and painting in their entirety; and when at the end he makes the earth lie more lightly on the poets than on other men, he is paying a sincere tribute to the poetic sensibility: a tribute not less sincere for the outrageous assertion that Anne Killigrew will lead the poetic throng to heaven. There is no piety in his references to heavenly music, yet through them he demonstrates how sincerely he prizes the practice of the arts on this earth.

Next, by attributing to Anne Killigrew many excellences which she did not possess and by putting that attribution into a shapely form Dryden expressed his belief in manners and decorum. Decorum is connected with what should be, not with what is. We regulate the opening and the end of our letters on that principle. And Dryden attributed to the object of his elegy the qualities it was proper for her to have, whether or not she did in fact have them.

Both the above beliefs belong to a more general one which we can call a belief in civilisation and which includes the beliefs in solid craft against empty ingenuity, in reason against fanaticism, in order against disorder, in monarchy against mob-rule, in established religion against arbitrary and undisciplined nonconformity. Some of these beliefs could be substantiated from the details of the poem. For instance the single line in stanza five

> Each test and every light her Muse will bear

testifies to the belief in solid craft. But the most powerful expression is of the general principle, and it is given by the very movement and composition of the poem: by the controlled yet enthusiastic movement, by the masterly formal and logical shape, and by the nobly pompous circumlocutions.

> Born to the spacious empire of the Nine—

the accent of that implies social and political order.

If even a portion of the above claims is accepted the *Ode* is found to possess a substance that answers worthily to those formal and musical qualities that first strike us. It takes its rank among the major elaborate lyrics such as the opening odes in the third book of Horace.

II

Most of the matters just enumerated have a direct bearing on the general thought of the age. I therefore can now pass easily from speaking of Dryden's *Ode* as a work of art to the ideas which it embodies.

(a)

THE WORLD PICTURE

Many of the things which I said Dryden stood for would have been accepted by other ages. Certainly, Henryson and Davies believed in order and decorum. What then distinguishes Dryden's belief from theirs? It is not a question of mere knowledge. Dryden knows all about order and degree and the "vast chain of being"; he still inherits the medieval scheme of the universe. His account of the various regions of the eternal heavens where the soul of Anne Killigrew might inhabit is as precise as anything in *Orchestra*. She has left the regions of mutability below the moon; she may be in a planet (comparatively close to the earth); she may be in the region of the fixed stars and circle with the great host of heaven; or she may be called to "more superior bliss," farther from earth and nearer to God, in the empyrean. Similarly with the stars: he knows about their conjunctions and horoscopes. He uses the technical term *in trine* when he says that the more malicious stars (like Saturn and Mars) were in a benign mood at Anne Killigrew's birth. Along with this correctness is the orthodoxy of the last stanza. Anne Killigrew, now in heaven, will reassume her body on the Day of Judgement and reascend to her final heavenly home. It looks as if the old material were there; and yet the emphasis has altered, being now on man and off the rest of creation in a new way. In other words the humanism of the Renaissance, which in Davies was still truly combined with the inherited world picture, has been carried much further and has destroyed the old proportions. Dryden really believes in the social virtues of human civilisation, but he does not really believe in astrology (as the "advanced" men of his age did not believe in it) nor in the angels. In fact he uses both stars and angels primarily as ornaments. The address of Anne Killigrew as a "young probationer and candidate of heaven" is charming, even impressive, in its context but it is an ornamental conceit not a conceit containing the genuine belief that she was in the act of ascending the ladder of creation into the angelic state. Walton in his biography of Hooker describes him on his deathbed

meditating the number and nature of the angels and their blest obedience and order, without which peace would not be in heaven; and oh that it might so on earth.

Of course Hooker was a divine, but even so he lived in a different world from Dryden's. His vision of cosmic order is a grander if stranger imagining than Dryden's eminently human principle of ornamental decorum. Then

take the lower end of the chain of being: the animals and inanimate nature.
One of Anne Killigrew's pictures takes these in.

> The sylvan scenes of herds and flocks
> And fruitful plains and barren rocks;
> Of shallow brooks that flowed so clear,
> The bottom did the top appear;
> Of deeper too and ampler floods,
> Which as in mirrors show'd the woods;
> Of lofty trees, with sacred shades
> And perspectives of pleasant glades,
> Where nymphs of brightest form appear
> And shaggy satyrs standing near,
> Which them at once admire and fear.

This is purely descriptive and ornamental. There is not the least sense of
any of the things pictured being a part of a cosmic as against a decorative
scene. Nymphs and satyrs are simple classical ornament, they are not the
classical equivalent of "real" supernatural beings with their necessary place
in the chain. The same is true of the herds and flocks. Nor is there any sense
of the landscape being emblematic or of corresponding to any other cosmic
plane. Anything that is not purely pictorial is realistic, looking forward to
the nature-poetry of Thomson, to the age of science and away from the age
of theology.

It could not be otherwise. The doubts about the world order, present
yet pending in the age of Elizabeth, had been realised. The heavens had
proved to be not immutable, the earth was no longer the centre of creation,
and the political stability of the Tudors, which had done so much to con-
serve the framework of the old order, had given way to a less popular house
and to civil war. With the beginnings of science it was the facts and not the
supposed perfect organisation of the physical world that excited men's
imaginations. And the exploitation of those facts was man's affair and not
God's. A new adjustment was necessary, and it was at the expense of the
two extremes of the chain of being.

The theological effects of this change in the scale came out in the next
century. Dryden's age was one of great nominal piety. In believing less in
the angels it did not intend to believe less in God. But by believing more
exclusively in man it did prepare for a theological change. When there was
a continuous chain of existence up to the foot of God's throne, God, though
inconceivably remote, was directly linked with man. When the intervening
links were snapped, there might remain other means of access, yet the
suggestion arose that God was somehow less concerned with his creation
than before. Those who had no very lively sense of the single soul's direct
communication with its God would tend to sever communication altogether.

Hence the Deism of the eighteenth century with its idea of a God, perfectly benevolent indeed, but who had created once and for all a world so satisfactory that further interference by him was unnecessary. Dryden would have repudiated such heresy, but by his accent when he writes of the angels and the lower creation he was really preparing the way for it.

(b)

DECORUM

Dryden's *Ode* implies a strong agreement with the contemporary estimation of manners and decorum. It offers a splendid pompous façade and in so doing protests that a good outward show is self-valuable. In stanza seven the king and queen are described in terms of what ideally they should be, not as they were, and Dryden has perfect assurance that he is right to speak thus. We may perceive this assurance the better, if, in contrast, we speculate on the state of mind of the *Times* reporter who in describing the coronation of Edward VII wrote quite blatantly and in cool prose that the noblest looking figure in the Abbey was the King. It was surely very different from Dryden's when he wrote

In beauty foremost, as in rank, the queen.

Given the times he lived in, Dryden really had no choice but to write like that: anything else, in a formal ode, would be scandalously ill-mannered. Any compulsion the *Times* reporter experienced was a smaller and more commercial matter; and we can hope that as he wrote he felt a sinking of the heart or a touch of nausea. For a second example of decorum take the landscape in stanza six. Though it may be vivid and though some of the details may recall actual nature, it is above all what a landscape should be: a staged piece after the manner of Claude; decorous above everything.

It is worth comparing this sense of decorum with the incident of changing the tapestries mentioned above (p. 28). There too decorum entered in, but more profoundly. The medieval sense of decorum was of course partly superstitious—it would be unlucky to make peace in a place hung with warlike tapestries—but it went beyond mere human manners to the whole nature of the world. The Augustan sense of decorum concerned human manners and social life, and did not go beyond these.

This emphasis on manners must have gained strength from the recent contacts with France. The French have felt and still do feel more strongly than the Anglo-Saxons about the value of manners irrespectively of what they express or conceal. The contrasted tempers are well brought out in Henry James's *American* in the episode where the hero's French friend is hanging between life and death after a duel. The preparations, physical, sentimental and spiritual, for death have been made with perfect completeness and propriety, and a second Frenchman is made to remark that with everything so well arranged it would be a pity if death did not ensue. Henry James's American does not sympathise, but a contemporary of Dryden would have understood. The American thought the Frenchman insincere and heartless, the Frenchman thought the American barbaric. Similarly modern readers dislike Restoration literature for being merely formal, a façade with no true feeling behind it, while Restoration readers were shocked by any display of naked feeling. Such displays were found in the Miracle Plays and in the medieval ballad and were thought uncivilised or, as they put it, Gothic. It should be possible to admit the claims of both habits of mind: to admire both the emotional sincerity of *Clerk Saunders* and the genuine moral discipline which any high standard of decorum cannot fail to imply.

There is another form of decorum. When Dryden says he is praising the reception of Anne Killigrew to heaven "in no ignoble verse," he implies the doctrine of decorum governing the different literary kinds. There was an appropriate style for the various subjects. The heavenly theme must be answered by a high manner. It is a principle that explains why Milton used so rough a metre in writing on Hobson and why in *Paradise Lost* he cultivated a sustained manner of writing remote from the chatter of fireside or marketplace. The whole principle is well illustrated by Dryden's last paragraph of his preface to *Religio Laici,* in which he explains why he writes in the style he has chosen.

The expression of a poem designed purely for instruction ought to be plain and natural and yet majestic; for here the poet is presumed to be a kind of lawgiver, and those three qualities I have named are proper to the legislative style. The florid elevated and figurative way is for the passions.

The same notion of decorum extended to the portrayal of character. Just as Dryden's queen *must* be the most beautiful lady present at the coronation, so any person represented must bear the ideal qualities of his station or profession. Rymer in his *Tragedies of the Last Age* attacked Evadne in Beaumont and Fletcher's *Maid's Tragedy* for her immodesty. The play was a tragedy and it is decorous that all women in tragedy, whatever their conduct, should be naturally modest.

Tragedy cannot represent a woman without modesty as natural and essential to her. If a woman has got any accidental historical impudence, if, documented in the school of Nanna or Heloisa, she is furnished with some stock of acquired impudence, she is not longer to stalk in tragedy on her high shoes but must rub off and pack down with the carriers into the province of comedy, there to be kicked about and exposed to laughter.

Similarly in his *Short View of Tragedy* Rymer attacked Shakespeare's Iago.

But what is most intolerable is Iago. He is no blackamoor soldier, so we may be sure he should be like other soldiers of our acquaintance. Yet never in tragedy, nor in comedy, nor in nature, was a soldier with his character. Take it in the author's own words:

> EMILIA. . . . some eternal villain,
> Some busy and insinuating rogue,
> Some cogging, cozening slave, to get some office.

Horace describes a soldier otherwise:

> Impiger, iracundus, inexorabilis, acer.[1]

Shakespeare knew his character of Iago was inconsistent . . . but to entertain the audience with something new and surprising, against common sense and nature, he would pass upon us a close, dissembling, false, insinuating rascal instead of an open-hearted frank, plain-dealing soldier, a character constantly worn by them for some thousands of years in the world.

Rymer was an extremist, but the things he pushed to extremes were the things the whole age accepted.

(c)

CLASSICISM

Dryden's poem is highly civilised in a certain way, and it was natural for his contemporaries to look for support to those epochs of history which seemed to be civilised in the same way and to turn against those which seemed hardly civilised at all. In Athens between the times of Pericles and Aristotle and especially in the Rome of Caesar and Augustus human nature and society seemed to be properly prized, superstition properly suppressed, and decorum properly observed, while in the Middle Ages human nature was twisted by asceticism, superstition was rampant, and a fanatical enthusiasm made decorum impossible. Dryden's age knew very much less history than our own. It judged the Periclean and Augustan ages by the acts and opinions of a tiny minority, and it knew nothing of the turn towards humanism about the twelfth century. This ignorance was not all loss, for it enabled the educated class to master a limited area of literature and to get the pleasure that comes from such mastery. This class attained an enviable coherence and uniformity of culture through the assurance that a limited body of knowledge was genuinely common property. Dryden knew that, when in the first stanza of his *Ode* he speculated on the heavenly region where Anne Killigrew's soul might inhabit, every educated reader would know that he was recalling, though in Christian terms, Virgil's speculations

---

[1] [Energetic, irascible, inexorable, brave.]

at the beginning of the *Georgics* on where the apotheosised Augustus would have his heavenly seat. And it is partly because he is so sure he will be understood that Dryden can take this most daring flight with such steady nerves.

The same passage fulfils too an actual obligation to imitate the classical authors. It was necessary to seek ratification in classical precedent. When Ben Jonson, the first neo-classic critic in England, enjoined *imitation* he meant by it the borrowing and then the moulding of a classical prototype to your own use: in fact what Pope did later in his imitations of Horace. Dryden not only obeys the injunction in the passage just mentioned but by a single touch shows how entirely he approves of it. At the beginning of stanza five he discusses the relation of art and nature in Anne Killigrew's verse.

> Art she had none, yet wanted none,
> For Nature did that want supply;
> So rich in treasures of her own
> She might our boasted stores defy.
> Such noble vigour did her verse adorn
> That it seemed borrowed, where 'twas only born.

Anne Killigrew's originality, far from being a virtue, needed Dryden's defence. She should have been derivative but luckily she had such native energy that she gave the impression of having borrowed from the classics. The passage is a rough parallel to Pope's elegant fiction in his *Essay on Criticism* of "Young Maro" or Virgil having so strong a native genius as to rely on nature alone. He then turns to Homer (whom he should have copied deliberately) and finds that he has produced something which after all has the appearance of being derived from Homer—and all is well in the end.

(d)

THE STATUS OF THE ARTS

When in the last stanza Dryden speaks of the poets being the first to leave their graves at the Day of Judgement and calls them sacred, he does so in an accent of serene assurance: an assurance lacking in similar pronouncements on the sanctity of poets in Shelley's *Defence of Poetry* and Carlyle's section on the Hero as Poet. Shelley's and Carlyle's protests have the shrillness induced by the knowledge of powerful opposition; Dryden is confident that his words will pass. In an age when scientific truth was threatening the realms of the imagination it is strange that the status of the arts was so high. Yet there is no question that it was so and that it remained so for some years after Dryden's death. One manifestation was the superlative status of the epic among human activities and of epic poets among mortal men. The Earl of Mulgrave in his *Essay upon Poetry,* a poem in couplets published in 1682, was doing nothing unusual when he called Heroic Poems the "chief effort of human sense," and Heroic Poets "gigantic souls" as far above other human beings as an ordinary man is above a changeling. Earlier in the century (1641) in *Reason of Church Government* Milton had said that poetic abilities

are the inspired gift of God rarely bestowed but yet to some in every nation; and are of power, beside the office of a pulpit, to inbreed and cherish in a great people the seeds of virtue and public civility, to allay the perturbations of the mind and set the affections in right tune:

and Dryden's contemporaries would not have gainsaid him. To recognise that the status of poetry remained high beyond the age of Dryden one can read the list of subscribers prefixed to the first edition of Pope's *Iliad* and recall the stories of people pointing him out to their children as the great poet.

How such a state of things was possible is not difficult to perceive. In the Middle Ages poetry had its place either as the handmaiden of religion or as legitimate amusement, but when the hold of the Church over all departments of life was relaxed, some of the awe and glamour possessed by the Church was transferred elsewhere. A part went to the monarchy, a part went to the arts. What had been a craft turned into a fine art; and a craftsman turned into an inspired artist. The process continued into the age of science and actually reached its height in spite of the birth and spread of ideas which, unchecked, would be fatal to the arts. Taken by themselves the ideas animating the newly founded Royal Society were hostile to poetry. Yet Dryden could let his poetic imagination expatiate in his *Ode on Anne Killigrew,* while approving the new scientific activities of the age; a situation not unlike Davies's when he cheerfully included in *Orchestra* his stanza on the Copernican theory, a theory which was destined to destroy the main tenets of the poem.

(e)

THE HEROIC CONVENTION

The principles hitherto discussed went beyond the Restoration period, but there is another that applies to it alone. The gigantic proportions to which Dryden inflates Anne Killigrew is one of many examples of the gigantic inflation of human nature common at the time. In the Heroic Plays the characters are all excessive and the sentiments extreme. Lovers are violently amorous, young soldiers excessively audacious, duty pitilessly exacting and certain to conflict with the claims of love. In *Annus Mirabilis* the English naval commanders show a more than human stature and courage:

> Our dreaded admiral from far they threat,
> Whose batter'd rigging their whole war receives;
> All bare, like some old oak which tempests beat,
> He stands, and sees below his scatter'd leaves.
>
> Heroes of old, when wounded, shelter sought;
> But he, who meets all danger with disdain,
> Ev'n in their face his ship to anchor brought
> And steeple-high stood propt upon the main.
>
> At this excess of courage all amaz'd,
> The foremost of his foes a while withdraw;
> With such respect in enter'd Rome they gaz'd
> Who on high chairs the godlike fathers saw.

In the *Conquest of Granada* Almanzor is a character excessive in courage, contempt of death and power of command. The comment on him after the first episode of the play is

> How much of virtue lies in one great soul,
> Whose single force can multitudes control.

Near the end of his life in the story of Sigismonda and Guiscardo, included in the *Fables,* Dryden gave his finest picture of heroic characters, a picture so convincing that we forget the convention to which they belong. These are Tancred, Duke of Salerno, and his daughter Sigismonda. Tancred discovers his daughter's secret marriage with a man of lower rank, Guiscardo, and in the ensuing quarrel between father and daughter neither will yield in the least to the other. They are towering uncompromising characters: the father wilful and tyrannical, the daughter calculatingly passionate and entirely certain of herself. We are reminded less of Dryden's earlier heroic characters than of York and Queen Margaret in the third part of Shakespeare's *Henry VI.* A second magnificent transformation of the heroic principle is in Congreve's *Way of the World,* where Mirabel and Millamant are great characters, sharply distinguished from the smaller folk that surround them. And in nothing does Congreve show greater art than in masking this sharp distinction during the actual experience of the play. As we watch, Mirabel and Millamant are two of a number of comic characters; it is only on later reflection that we recall their heroic proportions.

Sigismonda and Guiscardo and the *Way of the World* are exceptional.

What we are now considering is a habit of mind so wide-spread at this time that it must mean something. Part of the meaning is the belief in decorum, mentioned above. Appearances were at the time unusually important. Even if the reality behind the appearance is defective, the appearance is better than nothing and must be maintained. Hence convention agreed to portray commanders as coming up to an ideal and superhuman standard of audacity. But decorum does not account for a thrasonical tone peculiar to the Restoration heroes. There had been heroes of other ages, whose deeds were as exaggerated as any Almanzor's; and it is instructive to compare them in other respects. Malory's Launcelot is excessive in knightly prowess but he is anything but a boastful self-sufficient man. When in a specific test he had proved himself the greatest knight in the world, he "wept as he had been a child that had been beaten." Compare this with Almanzor's protest:

> But know that I alone am king of me.

The Elizabethans had their boasters and their arrogantly self-sufficient men, Tamburlaine and Bussy, but though they were attracted they condemned them. Christian humility, not stoical self-sufficiency, was still believed in. But the narrower humanism of Dryden's day and the Baconian arrogance of the new science inflated the human pretensions; and to these the practice of the heroic convention was partly due. But the peculiar thrasonical tone of this convention arose, I conjecture, not from a belief in this more exclusive humanism but in the doubts that beset it. Was man really up to these pretensions? Did the English political record really correspond to the sublime characters given to the royal rulers? Yet these pretensions were persisted in, and the very stridency of tone in which they were made expressed the uneasy conscience that lay behind them. The next century asked the same questions and gave a different answer. Pope has a very different version of human nature and he can be bitterly satirical on the qualities and exploits of an English king. And, as a whole, the eighteenth century, while believing in the unaided human reason, was modest in its claims for humanity.

Luckily Dryden's *Ode on Anne Killigrew* escapes the offensiveness of some heroic writing. Dryden's claims for his heroine are so patently ridiculous that we do not take them seriously, and they are conventionally extravagant rather than thrasonical. They thus turn our minds to those general matters of faith in which Dryden sincerely believed and of whose value no reasonable person can have any doubt: to the faith in the value of good manners and of an ordered way of life.

THE MASK OF POPE

AUSTIN WARREN

NEOCLASSICAL theory of poetry and neoclassical
poetry imperfectly agree. This discrepancy is most
simply accounted for by remembering that the period
called, in literary and aesthetic history, "neoclassical" is, in philosophical
and cultural history, the age of the Enlightenment—the age, that is, of rationalism.

Some bold spirits, impatient of adjustment, were willing to enter
heaven at the loss of an eye: in the celebrated quarrel over the relative
merits of the Ancients and the Moderns, the Modernists firmly took their
stand on the achievements of the natural sciences and on social progress,
regarding much of ancient literature, notably Homer, as obsolete, childish
stuff, compounded of immoral gods, absurd miracles, and primitive manners. The classicists—likely to be either men of letters or churchmen—were
necessarily less neat in their position, for they shared with their contemporaries the desire to be sensible, enlightened, and modern, though at the
same time they genuinely admired the achievements of ages unlike their
own. Hence their creed often formalizes past moments in literary history,
while their practice is very much of their own time.

Thus, while the Enlightenment reinforces the impetus of the *Georgics*
and the Horatian epistles towards literature as instruction, the orthodox
neoclassical creed still runs: the Epic and the Tragedy are the highest
genres. Dryden praises the *Georgics* for showing what virtuosity can do in
making poetry out of the most unpromising stuff (*opus superabat mate-
riam*); [1] but in his own work, he distinguishes between the *sermo pedestris* [2]
of such ratiocinative essays as *Religio Laici* and his "poetry," a distinction
not invalidated by the customary real superiority of his "lower" over his
"higher" style. When Pope says, "I stoop to truth and moralize my song,"
he is not wholly ironic.

Neoclassical poems are likely to conform to Cartesian criteria for truth

---

"Alexander Pope" from *Rage for Order* by Austin Warren. Reprinted by
permission of the author and The University of Chicago Press.

[1] [The workmanship was more beautiful than the material.]
[2] [An ordinary or plain style.]

—clarity and distinctness; and the poet is likely to be a well-educated, methodical and elegant expositor of accepted ethical generalizations. But neoclassical criticism continues to employ a terminology important parts of which are ultimately referable to Plato: words like "invention" (creative imagination), "inspiration," "fire," and "poetic fury." Like Enlightened Christians who retain the orthodox word "revelation" but are centrally concerned to show that theirs is a reasonable religion, the poet-critics use language difficult to reconcile with their performance, or thin down and rationalize the old terms. Thus Johnson dismissed, as mere commonplace, Young's conjectural exhortation to literary originality; Pope's preface to Homer exalts "invention" and "fire" above all the strategies of literary intelligence; yet neoclassical poetry lacks that large boldness it praises. It praises what it cannot really imitate.

The poets and critics were partially aware of this situation. Unlike the simpler Modernists, they found a characteristic adjustment in a double standard of loss and gain, progress and decadence, an advance in refinement, a diminution of vigor. "Our numbers were in their nonage till Waller and Denham" has to be reconciled with the acknowledgement that the great Elizabethans were "giant wits before the Flood." Walsh's famous advice to Pope must not be taken too simply: it really means, the great things are done; the age of myth-making is over; what remains to be done is to achieve that "correctness," that nicety of detail, which bolder writers and bolder ages perforce neglect.

Attempting to reconcile Homer and Shakespeare with Hobbes and Locke, the poets found themselves handicapped. The dramatists— Wycherly, Congreve, Dryden (in *All for Love,* which, and not *Cato,* gives us a conception of good neoclassical tragedy)—fared best, though neoclassicism suffers for the want of a tragic genius comparable to Racine's. Milton's epic is not easy to locate in literary history; but, written by a poet versed in the Italian and French critics, praised as well as "tagged" by Dryden, demonstrated by Addison to be a "regular" epic, admired by Pope as well as Dennis and Gildon, *Paradise Lost* may be regarded as England's neoclassical epic. After *Paradise Lost,* however, epic poetry loses virtue in both France and England, though it is still to be essayed by the ambitions of Blackmore, Glover, and Voltaire. As Pope's ironic recipe for writing an epic implies, a series of technical devices drawn by generalization from the accredited masterpieces is inadequate unless there is an epic spirit— perhaps he would have added, if properly questioned, and an heroic age.

The idea of the Great Poem, of the Great Genius, of the (often correlated) Grand Style intimidated many Augustan poets; "froze the genial current" of their souls. Only, it seems, if they could say to themselves,

"This is of course not poetry, or not *really great* poetry," could they have a fair chance of writing it. Thus Prior, though himself proud of his epic-didactic *Solomon,* his certification that he is a "major" poet, is really sure of his tone, really poetic only in his fables and songs and mock-didactic *Alma.* "Rural elegance: An Ode" and its companion odes and elegies are negligible exercises; but let Shenstone suppose himself to be writing "Levites" and he moves toward poetry. Intending a burlesque of Spenser he is free to write imaginatively of his childhood. More violent ways of emancipating oneself from the censorship of reason were those of Chatterton and Macpherson, both of whom found pseudonymous personalities through which to express their censorable selves. Chatterton, whose public self held the atheist and republican views of a "man of reason" and wrote able satire ("Kew Gardens"), created for his more imaginative self the *persona* of the fifteenth-century Catholic priest. The two kinds of verse written by Christopher Smart in and out of his mind instance a more violent split.

The most successful reconciliation of classicism and rationalism, or poetry and philosophy, or the incorrect, great past and the neater, thinner present, took place in terms of burlesque. Burlesque is often mask, often humility. The mock-epic is not mockery of the epic but elegantly affectionate homage, offered by a writer who finds it irrelevant to his age. As its signal advantage, burlesque (with its allied forms, satire and irony) allows a self-conscious writer to attend to objects, causes, and persons in which he is deeply interested yet of which, in part or with some part of him, he disapproves. *Interest* is a category which subsumes love and hate, approval and disapproval; very often it is an unequal, an unsteady mixture. Burlesque covers a multitude of adjustments; and each specimen requires to be separately scrutinized and defined.

Gay's *Shepherd's Week* is one of the clearer cases. Written at Pope's request, it was intended to exhibit the disgustingly crude manners and speech of genuine rustics and so, by reverse, to vindicate Pope's "Vergilian" pastorals against Philip's wobblingly "natural" ones. Actually, however, it exhibits the unsteadiness of Gay's own feelings. We have Johnson's testimony that contemporary readers felt, like us, that most of Gay's shots had hit an unintended target. Without meaning to betray Pope's cause—indeed imagining that he had endorsed it, he discovered in the writing the division of his emotional loyalties, and discovered, in that division, his attachment to folkways and rural pieties.

In the mock-genres (as well as in the satire and the epistle) it was possible to escape the stylistic restrictions of Great Poetry—its avoidance of "low" terms, its aim at consistent dignity and elegance. It was possible to shift, honorably, from the Beautiful to the Characteristic.

Pope's development followed, in general, this line—from the elegantly decorative to the richly—even the grotesquely—expressive. His poetry is not so homogeneous as its virtual confinement to couplets has often suggested. We should differentiate the *Pastorals,* the Homer, *Eloisa* (which is not only an Ovidian "heroic epistle" but a soliloquy from tragedy, in the manner of Racine), the *Essay on Criticism* and the *Essay on Man,* the Satires and Epistles, and the Mock-Epics. Pope's contemporaries did not confuse them, or like them equally. Joseph Warton was not the only reader to think that in *Eloisa* and the *Elegy* Pope showed himself capable of the Pathetic and to regret his turning from this mode to satire. Nor did Coleridge, in the next "age," fail to distinguish between the Homer (to which he assigned the chief responsibility for the poetic diction of the eighteenth century) and the satires (composed in such words as a Lake Reformer might have used).

The two pieces, early and late, which give the measure of Pope's development are the *Pastorals,* written before he was eighteen, and the *Dunciad,* which appeared in its enlarged and final form the year before his death.

The *Pastorals* once seemed a monument to poetic "progress." In testimony to his admirer Spence, Pope judged them "the most correct in the versification and musical in the numbers" of all his works; and Warton, in an estimate echoed by Johnson, finds their merit in their "correct and musical versification, musical to a degree of which rhyme could hardly be thought capable, and in [their] giving the first specimen of that harmony in English verse which is now become indispensably necessary. . . ." These are technical estimates, specifically of prosody. The *Pastorals* offer evidence of other care and contrivance; they combine as many traditional motifs as possible (*e.g.,* the elegy, the singing match); they profess—in contraction and enrichment of Spenser's precedent—to traverse the four seasons, the four times of day, the four ages of man. Demonstrably superior to Philips's rival pieces—now turgidly elegant, now rustically English, now plain childish—Pope's stylized pastorals consistently exclude realism.

> See what delight in sylvan scenes appear!
> Descending Gods have found Elysium here.
> In woods bright Venus with Adonis strayed,
> And chaste Diana haunts the forest-shade.

In an early letter, Pope explains his prosodic aims in terms suggestive of a "pure" poetry. The principle of delightful variation is conceived of syllabically and as one might conceive of it if one were writing a string quartet. Indeed Pope's initial aim amounts to a precise working within strict quasi-musical forms. Characteristic canons concern the artful shifting of the caesura, the prohibition of the Alexandrine and the triplet rhyme—indulgences which weaken, by relaxing, the triumph of variation within the confines of twenty syllables. The rules sound mechanical; but the poet who wrote them trusted, confidently, to his ear: "One must," he said to Spence, "tune each line over in one's head to try whether they go right or not."

That the "great rule of verse is to be musical" Pope would never deny —assuming, however, that there are more kinds of music than the sweetness of pastoral verse and the majesty of heroic; he could even distinguish "softness" from "sweetness." Whether in blame or praise, eighteenth-century critics often tagged Pope as "sweet" or "smooth," or "melodious," as though his work were all of a texture. But Pope claimed: "I have followed the significance of the numbers, and the adapting them to the sense, much more even than Dryden; and much oftener than any one minds it" —that is, not only in the set pieces. He liked to recollect a showy couplet from his juvenile and discarded epic:

> Shields, helms, and swords all jangle as they hang
> And sound formidinous with angry clang.

Such an instance, however, makes Pope's notion of "representative harmony" appear limited to the stunt-effects of Poe's "Bells" or Lindsay's "Congo" or his own and Dryden's Cecilian correlations of poetry and music. Nor is Pope helpful to a subtle cause in the *Essay on Criticism,* where his four specimens appear to restrict the phonetic expressiveness of verse to the categories of the loud-harsh, the smooth-soft, the slow, and the rapid. For it is not onomatopoeia exclusively or primarily which he is commending; in modern terminology, he wants to say that the meaning of a poem is inclusive of its sound as well as its paraphrasable statement. The "echoes to the sense" are both rhythmical (accelerating or prolonging the line, interrupting it into staccato effect, or letting it flow in a legato) or they are phonative (euphonic or cacophonous—according to ease or difficulty of articulation); often these devises work together;

> Behold yon Isle, by Palmers, Pilgrims trod,
> *Men bearded, bald, cowled, uncowled, shod, unshod,*
> Peeled, patched, and pie-bald, linsey-woolsey brothers,
> Grave mummers! sleeveless some, and shirtless others.

Except for allowing himself the extra syllable in the feminine rhyme, Pope restricts himself to his decasyllabics; but though neoclassical doctrine allows for no further metrical variation than an occasional trochaic substitution, Pope's ear evades the rule by counting, as unstressed, syllables which any intelligent reading (including his own) must certainly have stressed, so permitting himself such a seven-stress line as has been cited. The excess of stressed syllables slows up the lines; the serried syntax gives an irregular, staccato movement; the dominance of plosives helps, with abruptness, in the total intended tone or "meaning" of grotesqueness.

The neoclassical theory of serious diction called for a thinly honorific vocabulary, for adjectives which singled out an obvious attribute implicit in the noun—the *verdant* meadow, the *blue* violet—or served as loosely decorative epithets—the *pleasing* shades, the *grateful* clusters, the *fair* fields: all examples from the *Pastorals*. The inhibitions, imposed upon the joint authority of Philosophy and the Ancients, are stringent. Words must not be ambiguous or multiple-meaninged (for then they become puns, and puns are forms of verbal wit, and verbal wit is "false wit"); they must not be homely or technical (since poetry addresses men *as such,* gentlemen, not specialists in science or laborers); they must be lucid (for poetry owes its kinship to philosophy, with its consequent dignity, to its universality).

These inhibitions are removed or greatly mitigated, however, when the poet does not profess Poetry but only an epistle or a burlesque imitation. The difference is notable in the *Moral Essays,* the *Rape,* the *Dunciad.*

> But hark! the chiming clocks to dinner call;
> A hundred footsteps *scrape* the Marble Hall;
> The rich buffet well-covered serpents grace,
> And *gaping* Tritons *spew* to wash your face.
>
> . . . . . .
>
> Whether the nymph shall break Diana's law,
> Or some frail China jar receive a flaw;
> Or stain her honor, or her new brocade;
> Forget her prayers, or miss a masquerade;
> Or lose her heart, or necklace, at a ball . . .

Zeugma, the joining of two unlike objects governed by a single verb, is of course a form of pun; yet this verbal play constitutes one of Pope's most poetic resources in the *Rape:* it is this device, one might say, which gives the tone to the whole.

Burlesque are both Pope's masterpieces, *The Rape* and the *Dunciad.* Of the mock-epic, we may provisionally say that it plays form against matter, a lofty and elaborate form against a trivial situation or set of persons or theme: it is a study in "perspective by incongruity." But "form against matter" is too simple a naming. The real failure of the post-Miltonic epic lay, surely, in the supposition that the heroic poem could be written in an unheroic age; that a poem which, generically, involved the interrelation of the human and the divine, the natural and the super-natural, could be written in an age when "thinking people" had grown too prudent for heroism, too sophisticated for religion. John Dennis, whose taste, among the ancients was for Homer, Pindar, and Sophocles, and among the moderns for Milton, was not unsound in his critical contention that great poetry, like that of his favorites, must be religious. So we might restate the incongruity as between heroic things and refined, between an age of faith and an age of reason. The mock-epic reminds an unheroic age of its own nature; by historical reference, it defines the "civilized" present.

Is Pope, then, satirizing Belinda's world? Scarcely, or but lightly. His intent is rather to counterpoint contrasting modes than to decide how far his aristocracy has gained by its elegance, how far lost by its safe distance from war, politics, poverty, and sin. The poem is in nothing more dexterous than in its controlled juxtaposition of worlds. In another context we should find ominous those brilliant lines which couple by incongruity the worlds of the bourgeoisie and the proletariat with that of the leisure class:

> The hungry Judges soon the sentence sign
> And wretches hang that jury-men may dine;
> The merchant from the Exchange returns in peace,
> And the long labors of the Toilet cease.

The Rape owes its richness and resonance to its over-structure of powerful, dangerous motifs, the calculated ministration of shocks. What keeps it from being that filigree artifice, as which the romantics saw (and praised) it is playing with fire—especially the fires of sex and religion. Though himself scarcely a "good Catholic," Pope's parents were, and he is writing of an "old Catholic" society; and many of his effects involve the suggestion of blasphemous parallels: the linking of English folklore and the Lives of the Saints, and of both to his gentle mythology of urbane "machines." He links the nurse's moonlit elves and fairy ring and the priest's tales of "virgins visited by Angel-powers" (the visions of the Cave of Spleen are "Dreadful as hermit's dreams in haunted shades,/Or bright as visions of expiring maids,") which may or may not be reducible to physiological disturbances; the Baron and Belinda have their altars to Pride and Love, their real religions as well as their professed.

What, for religion, is got by parody parallel is, for sexual morality, managed by *insinuendo*. Though it is admitted that nymphs may break Diana's law, we see none do so; the titular *Rape* is only of a lock. The opening of Canto III (a preview for the *School for Scandal*), shows the chorus at work ("At every word a reputation dies"); but we do not hear the death. A characteristic passage of *double entendre* retails the difficulty of preserving a *"melting* maid's" purity in such a time and place of temptation as the midnight masquerade, while assuring us that her male companions' Honor, or her sylph, preserves her virtue.

There can be no doubt that the specific ambiguities of the poem— its perspectives through parody, irony, and other incongruity—are purposed. But open to doubt is whether these effects are not local and episodic, unsubject to central design and all-governing tone; for, though silly things have been said about Pope's work of composition (as if "closed couplets" must all be equally discrete and unreconciled), he was, of course, so intent on making every verse exciting and finished as to make it difficult for the whole to subordinate them. In the case of *The Rape* he is often in danger but, I think, unvanquished. What organizes the poem is not exclusively the narrative, with its chronological and dramatic sequence of scenes (including two battles); it is yet more its tone—the steadiness with which it holds, against heroic and religious perspectives, to its serio-comic view of a little elegant society.

Not to the manor born, Pope makes the drawing room seem an achievement. He so treats a woman's day, says Johnson, that "though nothing is disguised, everything is striking; and we feel all the appetite of curiosity for that from which we have a thousand times turned fastidiously away." Pope had not turned fastidiously away; like Proust, another "outsider," he was fascinated by the ritual which gave—or signified, as may be—the aristocratic status. He has practised, on other matter, the Wordsworthian formula of giving to the unmarvelous the light of wonder. Society is a wonder, we are made to feel; convention a triumph of happy contrivance; coffee a luxury; a card game a crisis. This effect is in large measure the result of the "machinery" of sylphs, who not only contrast with Homer's and Milton's "machines" but parallel Pope's women—those coquettes, termagants, dociles, and prudes whose natures they abstract and stylize.

The burlesque of *The Rape* provides, then, an elaborate stratification of attitudes and effects: amusement at trifles taken seriously; delight at elegance; recollections of earlier literature (Homer and Spenser) in counterpoint against the current literary mode; juxtaposition of corresponding worlds (Achilles's shield; the great petticoat); reminders of the economic and political structures which make possible this leisure class comedy, of the moral and religious structures which make possible a society at all.

In the *Dunciad,* the mock-heroic framework is relaxed, intermittent. There are frequent local parodies of passages from Homer, Virgil, and Milton; there are classical devices like the Homeric games, the descent into the lower world, the pre-view of future history from the mount of vision; but there is no plot, no "fable." The loose organization is expressively loose. The poem tenders some recent episodes in a long contest between stupidity and intelligence, anarchy and culture, barbarism and civilization. In this long contest, stupidity and its allies win out, not because of their superior plans, designs, or purposes—for there is no real war of opposed strategies; but because of their sheer multitudinous mass, their dead weight. The poem, a kind of antimasque, is a series of ritual tableaux and pageants and processions, chiefly sluggish of movement and visually dusky. There are occasional light reliefs, like the episode of the dilettanti, fresh from the Grand Tour where (in lines which, for satiric effect, return to Pope's old Pastoral "sweetness") one looks

> To happy Convents, bosomed deep in vines,
> Where slumber Abbots, purple as their wines:
> To Isles of fragrance, lily-silvered vales,
> Diffusing languor in the panting gales.

But the general tone, prefigured in the brilliant IVth Canto of *The Rape,* is sombre and grotesque.

Time has assisted rather than damaged the poem. Though Pope's friends warned him against keeping alive his lampooned enemies, the warning was futile. Outside of literary circles, even in Pope's own time, most of the names must have been meaningless. And today it is certainly not the case that one need master footnotes to understand the poem Pope wrote; for the context provides the categories, which are permanent, while the proper names are annually replaceable. If one is confused by the blur of names, that too serves the purpose: these are not the names of the few masters but the many applicants. As for the applicants: Pope is satirizing not bad men or poor men "as such" but bad poets and commercial publishers and undiscriminating patrons and pedantic professors. To relax one's critical standards is to be literarily immoral.

The finale is seriously epic by virtue of Pope's belief in the diabolical power of stupidity. In the myth of Book IV, civilization dies. According to Pope's view of history, brief episodes of enlightenment had all along alternated with far longer sequences of darkness: the primitive Golden Age gave way to barbarism; Roman civilization yielded to Gothic monkery and mummery; the Renaissance of Leo and Raphael and the Enlightenment of Newton and Locke and Bolingbroke were not threatened by extinction. What there is of the mythic and the dramatic in Pope comes from this sense. He felt the precariousness of civilization.

If this is a comic poem, it is comic only as Volpone is comic, by virtue of a grim extravagance, a grim grotesqueness; for it is not without reminder of the *Inferno* with its moral categories, its wry jokes, and its smoky lighting. The method involves not only "representative Harmony" but visual imagery of a correspondent sort: the clumsiness and ugliness of the dull, the filthy foulness of their games, in which moral horror turns physical.

> Slow rose a form, in majesty of Mud;
> Shaking the horrors of his sable brows,
> And each ferocious feature grim with ooze.

Pope was not a metaphysician; and it is unlikely that in another age he would have attempted to be, though he might well have been something else—a "metaphysical poet." His "views" are flat and tiresome when he expresses them in general terms, when (as in his letters) he undertakes to moralize like a noble Roman. If he could turn a maxim memorably, it was not this which made him, and keeps him, a poet but his power to see and hear what he felt, to find correlatives for his feelings toward people and doctrines. He images Hervey as a bug, a spaniel, a puppet, a toad; the scholars as grubs preserved in amber; the bad poet as a spider; the virtuosi as "locusts blackening all the land"; he sees Chaos regain its dominion.

> Light dies before Thy uncreating world;
> Thy hand, great Anarch! lets the curtain fall,
> And Universal Darkness buries all.

The extent of Pope's work, its unfailing literary scrupulosity, its contemporary fame—all have disposed readers to reject or accept it as a totality, and to do this too simply in action or reaction. This is unjust. Like Virgil and Milton (not to mention greater names), Pope can survive the scrutiny of more than one critical system. But he survives, of course, by selection and redaction. There are pieces, and aspects of pieces, for romantic taste, for imagist taste, for didactic, for our own (which we are not yet choosing to name). That Pope was everywhere alert, careful, experimental seems clear; but criticism must assign his "false lights" and his "true," distinguish his triumphs from his interesting failures.

The historical situation to which I have assigned Pope's triumphs is not merely historical: it has its recurrent parallels. The idea of Poetry, without which we are helpless to judge poetry, has persistent power to intimidate. Poetry is always turning into a vested interest, an academic institution, guarding the taste of the "last age" and hostile to prophetic and aesthetic renovation. The heresies of "poetic diction" and the "poetic subject" require periodic exorcism. Like religion, poetry cannot be merely repetitive, merely traditional; "Ye have heard it said of old time . . . but I say unto you . . ."

Poetry as Past Poetry intimidates. So may the ideas of Great Poetry and of the Major Poet. Critics cannot dispense with the concepts, though even they may (as Eliot says of Arnold) skimp adequate concern for *genuineness* in their zeal to begin awarding First and Second Honors. But poets—at least since the seventeenth century—have not been helped by these Longinian incitations: How would Homer have done this? Has my work high seriousness? Am I a major poet? Should I not be writing in the larger forms? Has my poetry the grandeur of generality? These are all false, even dangerous, forms of self-examination.

Yet, unless the modern poet is a "primitive," if he would be a poet after the age of twenty-five, he must have read his great predecessors with some sense of the literary history to which he presumes to add. To be a poet at all (instead of an honest businessman or a modestly straightforward prose-man) is a pretension likely either to give one delusions of infallibility or to cripple one by the fear of not measuring up to The Poets or justifying one's existence to a society not in known need of poets. Meanwhile the wrong kinds of consciousness make the writing of poetry impossible, permit only of falsetto substitutionary production, cerebral or verbalistic manufacture.

No more than Pope can the modern poet assume the singing-rôles of Spenser or Tennyson. He cannot allow the identification of himself with the "I" of the poems, which is a *persona,* a mask: Crispin, Prufrock, Crazy Jane. He cannot write with innocent, unprotected seriousness; he must be permitted his alibi of irony, his strategy of stratification. "Light verse can be serious." *The Oxford Book of Light Verse,* a creative anthology, brilliantly illustrates Auden's dictum; so does Auden's own practice. Let me be playful and grotesque, our poet says; thus, and thus only, can I do my work. Let me put on my mask and I will chant the truth.

WORDSWORTH

F. R. LEAVIS

Wordsworth's greatness and its nature seem to be, in a general way, pretty justly recognized in current acceptance, the established habit of many years. Clear critical recognition, however, explicit in critical statement, is another matter, and those who really read him to-day—who read him as they read contemporary literature—will agree that, in spite of the number of distin-

"Wordsworth" from *Revaluation* by F. R. Leavis, reprinted by permission of George W. Stewart, Publisher, Inc., and Chatto and Windus.

guished critics who have written on him, satisfactory statement is still something to be attempted. And to attempt it with any measure of success would be to revalue Wordsworth, to achieve a clearer insight and a fresh realization.

There is—a time-honoured critical blur or indecision—the question of Wordsworth's "thought." "I think Wordsworth possessed more of the genius of a great philosophic poet than any man I ever knew, or, as I believe, has existed in England since Milton," said Coleridge. With this pronouncement, standing by itself, no one need be concerned to quarrel; most Wordsworthians probably see in it something for positive acclaim. But under the same date [1] in *Table Talk*, Coleridge has already been more explicit: "Then the plan laid out and, I believe, partly suggested by me, was, that Wordsworth should assume the station of a man in mental repose, one whose principles were made up, and so prepared to deliver upon authority a system of philosophy. . . . It is in substance what I have been all my life doing in my system of philosophy." "System of philosophy," it might still be contended (in spite, perhaps, of the concluding reference to Coleridge's own system), is an expression susceptible of more than one value, but it is generally agreed that Coleridge here proposes for Wordsworth an ambition that proved unmistakably to be far beyond Wordsworth's powers. If the great design fell so far short of realization, that was not for lack of time or will. This there is no need to argue. What does seem worth insisting on is the felicitous accuracy (unconscious, no doubt) of Arnold's word when he says that the "philosophy" is an "illusion."

For Wordsworth's "philosophy" certainly appears, as such, to invite discussion, and there is a general belief that we all know, or could know by re-reading *The Prelude,* what his doctrines concerning the growth of the mind and relation of Man to Nature are. His philosophic verse has a convincingly expository tone and manner, and it is difficult not to believe, after reading, say, Book II of *The Prelude,* that one has been reading a paraphrasable argument—difficult not to believe, though the paraphrase, if resolutely attempted, would turn out to be impossible. Few readers, it would seem, have ever made the attempt, and, in fact, to make it resolutely is the real difficulty—if "difficulty" can describe the effect of a subtle, pervasive and almost irresistible dissuasion from effort.

This, at any rate, describes fairly the working of Wordsworth's philosophic verse. His triumph is to command the kind of attention he requires and to permit no other. To demonstrate this conclusively is much easier in spoken discussion before an open text than in writing: one really needs to

---

[1] 21st July 1832.

go through some hundreds of line of *The Prelude,* Book II, analysing and commenting. Here a few illustrations must suffice, as indeed, to point the attention effectively, they should: that once done, the demonstration is the reading, as any one who cares to open his Wordsworth may see; the facts, to the adverted eye, are obvious.

Consider, to start with, a representative improvement as revealed in Professor de Selincourt's admirable edition of *The Prelude.* A key passage runs, in the version of 1805–6 (ll. 238–266):

> Bless'd the infant Babe,
> (For with my best conjectures I would trace
> The progress of our Being) blest the Babe,
> Nurs'd in his Mother's arms, the Babe who sleeps
> Upon his Mother's breast, who, when his soul
> Claims manifest kindred with an earthly soul,
> Doth gather passion from his Mother's eye!
> Such feelings pass into his torpid life
> Like an awakening breeze, and hence his mind
> Even [in the first trial of its powers]
> Is prompt and watchful, eager to combine
> In one appearance, all the elements
> And parts of the same object, else detach'd
> And loth to coalesce. Thus day by day,
> Subjected to the discipline of love,
> His organs and recipient faculties
> Are quicken'd, are more vigorous, his mind spreads,
> Tenacious of the forms which it receives.
> In one beloved presence, nay and more,
> In that most apprehensive habitude
> And those sensations which have been deriv'd
> From this beloved Presence, there exists
> A virtue which irradiates and exalts
> All objects through all intercourse of sense.
> No outcast he, bewilder'd and depress'd:
> Along his infant veins are interfus'd
> The gravitation and the filial bond
> Of nature, that connect him with the world.
> Emphatically such a Being lives
> An inmate of this *active* universe.

In the version of 1850 we read (ll. 233–254):

> Blest the infant Babe,
> (For with my best conjecture I would trace
> Our Being's earthly progress) blest the Babe,
> Nursed in his Mother's arms, who sinks to sleep
> Rocked on his Mother's breast; who with his soul
> Drinks in the feelings of his Mother's eye!

> For him, in one dear Presence, there exists
> A virtue which irradiates and exalts
> Objects through widest intercourse of sense.
> No outcast he, bewildered and depressed:
> Along his infant veins are interfused
> The gravitation and the filial bond
> Of nature that connect him with the world.
> Is there a flower, to which he points with hand
> Too weak to gather it, already love
> Drawn from love's purest earthly fount for him
> Hath beautified that flower; already shades
> Of pity cast from inward tenderness
> Do fall around him upon aught that bears
> Unsightly marks of violence or harm.
> Emphatically such a Being lives
> Frail creature as he is, helpless as frail,
> An inmate of this active universe . . .

No one is likely to dispute that the later version is decidedly the more satisfactory. But it is worth asking in what way. The earlier, it will be noticed, is by very much the more explicit. More important, it calls for a different kind of attention—the kind of attention one gives to a philosophical or psychological argument.

> . . . eager to combine
> In one appearance, all the elements
> And parts of the same object, else detach'd
> And loth to coalesce.
>
> In one beloved presence, nay and more,
> In that most apprehensive habitude
> And those sensations which have been deriv'd
> From this beloved Presence . . .

—The phraseology is technical, and we are reminded of that close study of Hartley, and of Wordsworth's belief (as a philosopher) that associationism explained his own experience. (That belief itself suggests pretty forcibly how external in Wordsworth was the relation between systematic philosopher and poet; and a comment on his debt to Hartley is the exasperating classification, on Hartleian principles, of the collected Poems.) Actually, the earlier version does not explain anything any more satisfactorily than the later: the parts afterwards omitted merely incite to an attention that the argument will not bear. Not that Wordsworth is likely to have given himself this reason for the change; guided by his poet's touch, he was reducing recalcitrant elements to the general mode in which the best parts of *The Prelude* are written.

That mode is one examined by Mr. Empson (from his own special approach) in an analysis of the central passage of *Tintern Abbey:* (see *Seven Types of Ambiguity,* pp. 191–194). His analysis, though he misquotes and seriously mispunctuates, is in general effect sound enough: he is exhibiting in a particular instance, which could be very easily matched, what many readers of Wordsworth besides the present one must have known as an essential Wordsworthian habit. Wordsworth in such passages as are in question produces the mood, feeling or experience and at the same time appears to be giving an explanation of it. The expository effect sorts well with—blends into—the characteristic meditative gravity of the emotional presentment ("emotion recollected in tranquillity"), and in the key passages, where significance seems specially to reside, the convincing success of the poetry covers the argument: it is only by the most resolute and sustained effort (once it occurs to one that effort is needed) that one can pay to the argument, as such, the attention it appears to have invited and satisfied. And when one does pay the necessary attention one always finds the kind of thing illustrated in Mr. Empson's analysis.

How difficult it is to attend to the argument Mr. Empson, earlier in his book, perhaps illustrates unwittingly: "Wordsworth frankly had no inspiration other than his use, when a boy, of the mountains as a totem or father-substitute . . ." (*Ambiguity,* p. 26). Mr. Empson, of course, may be able to give some good reason for his remark, and one can think of passages he might cite. But the principal document is Book II of *The Prelude,* and Wordsworth there stresses the mother: he explicitly and at length relates the mode of experience celebrated in the famous central passage of *Tintern Abbey* (that analysed by Mr. Empson) to the experience of the child in its mother's arms.[1]

In the passage quoted above (in both versions) it is plain enough. Yet I myself must confess to having been long familiar, if that is the word, with Book II before I really took note of what the passage was about—realized its relation to the passage in *Tintern Abbey.* Then reading it one day (in the earlier version) I found myself halting at:

> In one beloved presence, nay and more,
> In that most apprehensive habitude
> And those sensations which have been deriv'd
> From this beloved Presence, there exists
> A virtue which irradiates and exalts
> All objects through all intercourse of sense.

---

[1] Mr. Empson has replied that there is, he thinks, both the father and the mother in Wordsworth's Nature.

Partly it was that "Presence" (the mother's), recalling the common Wordsworthian use of the word—"A Presence which is not to be put by"—"A presence that disturbs me with the joy of elevated thoughts." But more still it was the feeling that the full stop came too soon—that a final phrase was missing. And then the phrase offered itself:

> And rolls through all things.

Plainly, what had arrested me was the suggestion of the lines in *Tintern Abbey:*

> A motion and a spirit, that impels
> All thinking things, all objects of all thought,
> And rolls through all things.

For the first time I recognized with full attention and complete realization what is quite explicit: that Wordsworth here is explaining how he comes to have the kind of experience he describes in *Tintern Abbey*. Or, lest I should be misunderstood, let me say that for the first time it occurred to me to put it in this way, for the meaning must be in some sense clear at first reading. So hard is it (for I have established by experiment and inquiry that I am not, in this matter, exceptionally obtuse) to read Wordsworth with the kind of attention that the argument, if it were what it appears to be, would demand. Actually, of course, no real explaining is done in either version, and in the later Wordsworth removes all incitement to the inquiry whether or not what he offers would be accepted as an explanation if it were rendered in prose. The poetry, uninterrupted in the amended version, is complete and satisfactory; it defines convincingly—presents in such a way that no further explanation seems necessary—the sense of "belonging" in the universe, of a kinship known inwardly through the rising springs of life and consciousness and outwardly in an interplay of recognition and response:

> No outcast he, bewilder'd and depress'd;
> Along his infant veins are interfus'd
> The gravitation and the filial bond
> Of nature, that connect him with the world.

—"Thank God I am not free, any more than a rooted tree is free." The play of varied metaphorical implications (the imagery is complex—"interfus'd," "gravitation," "filial bond") does what a Hartleian commentary can only weaken.

Even if there were not so much poetry to hold the mind in a subtly incompatible mode of attention, it would still be difficult to continue attending to the philosophic argument, because of the way in which the verse, evenly meditative in tone and movement, goes on and on, without dialectical suspense and crisis or rise and fall. By an innocently insidious trick Wordsworth, in this calm ruminative progression, will appear to be preoccupied with a scrupulous nicety of statement, with a judicial weighing of alternative possibilities, while actually making it more difficult to check the argument from which he will emerge, as it were inevitably, with a far from inevitable conclusion. Examine, for instance, what leads up to the "Thus" of line 415 in Book II (1805–6; l. 396 in the 1850 version):

> Nor should this, perchance,
> Pass unrecorded, that I still had lov'd
> The exercise and produce of a toil
> Than analytic industry to me
> More pleasing, and whose character I deem
> Is more poetic as resembling more
> Creative agency. I mean to speak
> Of that interminable building rear'd
> By observation of affinities
> In objects where no brotherhood exists
> To common minds. My seventeenth year was come
> And, whether from this habit, rooted now
> So deeply in my mind, or from excess
> Of the great social principle of life,
> Coercing all things into sympathy,
> To unorganic natures I transferr'd
> My own enjoyments, or, the power of truth
> Coming in revelation, I convers'd
> With things that really are, I, at this time
> Saw blessings spread around me like a sea.
> 415   Thus did my days pass on, and now at length
> From Nature and her overflowing soul
> I had receiv'd so much that all my thoughts
> Were steep'd in feeling . . .

Nowhere does *The Prelude* yield a more satisfactory presentment of the "thought," though the orthodox doctrinal passages of *The Excursion* —at the beginning of Book IV, for instance—are plain enough.

Yet the burden of *The Prelude* is, nevertheless, not essentially ambiguous, and Wordsworth's didactic offer was not mere empty self-delusion. It was not for nothing that men like Mill and Leslie Stephen could count Wordsworth an influence in their lives, and there was more to be derived from him than mere emotional refreshment—

> He laid us, as we lay at birth,
> On the cool flowery lap of earth.

He had, if not a philosophy, a wisdom to communicate. The mistake encouraged by Coleridge is understandable, and we can see how *The Recluse* should have come to be projected—see, too, that the petering out of the enterprise in that long life does not prove essential failure (though it proves the enterprise misconceived). It may be said, fairly, that Wordsworth went on tinkering with *The Prelude* through his life instead of completing the great "philosophic poem" because, as he had in the end tacitly to recognize, his resources weren't adequate to the ambition—he very obviously hadn't enough material. But it must also be said that in letting the ambition lapse he was equally recognizing its superfluity: his real business was achieved. His wisdom is sufficiently presented in the body of his living work.

What he had for presentment was a type and a standard of human normality, a way of life; his preoccupation with sanity and spontaneity working at a level and in a spirit that it seems appropriate to call religious. His philosophizing (in the sense of the Hartleian studies and applications) had not the value he meant it to have; but it is an expression of his intense moral seriousness and a mode of the essential discipline of contemplation that gave consistency and stability to his experience. Wordsworth, we know, is the "poet of Nature," and the associations of the term "Nature" here are unfortunate, suggesting as it does a vaguely pantheistic religion-substitute. If this is all Wordsworth has to offer, or if, as Mr. Empson, expressing (apparently) very much this notion of him, states, he "had no inspiration other than his use when a boy of the mountains as a totem or father-substitute," then (the world being what it is) one may save one's irony for other things than his supersession, as the presiding genius of Lakeland, by Mr. Hugh Walpole. But Wordsworth himself, in the famous passage that, "taken from the conclusion of the first book of *The Recluse,*" he offers "as a kind of *Prospectus* of the design and scope of the whole Poem," proposes something decidedly different when he stresses "the Mind of Man" as

> My haunt, and the main region of my song.

And Wordsworth here, as a matter of fact, is critically justified. Creative power in him, as in most great poets, was accompanied by a high degree of critical consciousness in the use of it. His critical writings give a good view of his creative preoccupations; and both his main preoccupation and his achievement are fairly intimated by this passage from the *Letter to John Wilson:*

> You have given me praise for having reflected faithfully in my Poems the feelings of human nature. I would fain hope that I have done so. But a great

Poet ought to do more than this; he ought, to a certain degree, to rectify men's feelings, to give them new compositions of feelings, to render their feelings more sane, pure, and permanent, in short, more consonant to nature, that is, to eternal nature, and the great moving spirit of things. He ought to travel before men occasionally as well as at their sides.

"Nature" in the phase "poet of Nature" can hardly be made to take on the force suggested here; that is why the description is so unacceptable. Wordsworth's preoccupation was with a distinctively human naturalness, with sanity and spiritual health, and his interest in mountains was subsidiary. His mode of preoccupation, it is true, was that of a mind intent always upon ultimate sanctions, and upon the living connexions between man and the extra-human universe; it was, that is, in the same sense as Lawrence's was, religious.

If the association of Wordsworth's name with Lawrence's seems incongruous, as it may reasonably do, the following passage, nevertheless, is very well known:

> For I must tread on shadowy ground, must sink
> Deep—and, aloft ascending, breathe in worlds
> To which the heaven of heavens is but a veil.
> All strength—all terror, single or in bands,
> That ever was put forth in personal form—
> Jehovah—with his thunder, and the choir
> Of shouting Angels, and the empyreal thrones—
> I pass them unalarmed. Not Chaos, not
> The darkest pit of lowest Erebus,
> Nor aught of blinder vacancy, scooped out
> By help of dreams—can breed such fear and awe
> As fall upon us often when we look
> Into our Minds, into the Mind of Man—
> My haunt, and the main region of my song.

This, perhaps, may not extravagantly be allowed to recall Lawrence's preoccupation with the deep levels, the springs, of life, the illimitable mystery that wells up into consciousness (cf. "This is the innermost symbol of man: alone in the darkness of the cavern of himself, listening to the soundlessness of inflowing fate"). It is possible, at any rate, to rest too easily satisfied with the sense one commonly has of Wordsworth as of a tranquil surface reflecting the sky. How little a "wise passiveness" (the purpose of which being in Lawrence's words—and there is point in applying words of Lawrence here—"so that that which is perfectly ourselves can take place in us") is mere passiveness the lines quoted above from *The Recluse* sufficiently convey.

[But the main effect of bringing Wordsworth and Lawrence together must, of course, be contrast. And the contrast that is proposed by Law-

rence's notoriety is a violent one. His preoccupation with sex is vulgarly
both misconceived and overemphasized; nevertheless, no one would dispute
that it is an essential characteristic. Wordsworth's poetry, on the other
hand, is remarkable for exhibiting the very opposite of such a preoccupation—for that is perhaps the best way of putting the case, which may be
very easily misrepresented or misapprehended. Shelley, for instance, in
Peter Bell the Third, says:

> But from the first 'twas Peter's drift
> To be a kind of moral eunuch;
> He touched the hem of Nature's shift,
> Felt faint—and never dared uplift
> The closest, all-concealing tunic.

Peter Bell the Third contains some very good criticism of Wordsworth,
but this stanza tells us more about Shelley—it is of him that that kind of
"feeling faint" is characteristic. Shelley, indeed, is unwittingly illustrating
the difference between himself and Wordsworth that he intends to be commenting on.]

It is the difference constituting so large an element in the contrast
felt, at a glance, when passages of Wordsworth and Shelley are juxtaposed.
There is an obvious contrast in movement; or rather, of Shelley's eager,
breathless hurry—his verse always seems to lean forward, so that it must
run in order not to fall—with Wordsworth's static contemplation ("I gazed
and gazed . . ."). But the immediately relevant prompting is to description in terms of temperature: if Wordsworth, as Shelley says, is "cold"
(which is truer in suggestion than "felt faint," and hardly congruous with
it), Shelley himself seems fevered. And the effect of warmth derives very
largely from the pervasiveness in Shelley's verse of caressing, cherishing,
fondling, and, in general, sensuously tender suggestions, explicit and implicit, more and less subtle. To bring these under the general head of the
"erotic" may seem arbitrary, yet an examination of Shelley's work will
show the relation between the "gentle odours" of this first stanza of *The
Question* and the subsequent image of embracing, so significantly inappropriate, to be representative:

> I dreamed that, as I wandered by the way,
>   Bare Winter suddenly was changed to Spring,
> And gentle odours led my steps astray,
>   Mixed with a sound of waters murmuring
> Along a shelving bank of turf, which lay
>   Under a copse, and hardly dared to fling
> Its green arms round the bosom of the stream,
> But kissed it and then fled, as thou mightest in dream.

At any rate, one of the most remarkable facts about Wordsworth's poetry is the virtual absence from it of this whole set of associations and suggestions, and it is this absence that Shelley, when he calls Wordsworth "cold," is remarking upon; this is the fact, however perceived, that evokes that "moral eunuch"—"A solemn and unsexual man," says Shelley, later in the poem. The nature of the fact neither Shelley nor, in his psychoanalytics about Wordsworth's poetic decline, Mr. Herbert Read recognizes. The pathological efficacy that Mr. Read ascribes to the episode of Annette Vallon is discredited by the peculiarity just noted: such an absence of the erotic element hardly suggests repression. It suggests that, whatever reason Wordsworth may have had for choosing not to deal in "animated description of the pleasures of love," he had no need of subconscious relief and covert outlets.

[There are, in fact, no signs of morbid repression anywhere in Wordsworth's poetry. And his various prose remarks about love plainly come from a mind that is completely free from timidity or uneasiness.] The phrase just quoted may be found in the *Letter to John Wilson* (1800). Discussing there the limiting bents and prepossessions that disqualify different readers, "some," says Wordsworth, "cannot tolerate a poem with a ghost or any supernatural agency in it; others would shrink from an animated description of the pleasures of love, as from a thing carnal and libidinous; some cannot bear to see delicate and refined feelings ascribed to men in low conditions of society. . . ." To take an illustration from a later period of his life, in the *Letter to a Friend of Robert Burns* he pronounces: "The poet, trusting to primary instincts, luxuriates among the felicities of love and wine; nor does he shrink from the company of the passion of love, though immoderate. . . ."

[Sex, nevertheless, in spite of this pronouncement, is virtually absent from Wordsworth's poetry. The absence no doubt constitutes a limitation, a restriction of interest; but it constitutes at the same time an aspect of Wordsworth's importance.] The point of this remark depends on another striking difference between Wordsworth and both Lawrence and Shelley; on the characteristic of his own poetry that Wordsworth indicates here: "I have said that poetry is the spontaneous overflow of powerful feelings: it takes its origin from emotion recollected in tranquillity. . . ." Wordsworth here describes the withdrawn, contemplative collectedness of his poetry—"Thus devoted, concentrated in purpose," and the double description has been elucidated earlier in the *Preface:*

Not that I always began to write with a distinct purpose formally conceived; but habits of meditation have, I trust, so prompted and regulated my feelings, that my descriptions of such objects as strongly excite those feelings, will be found to carry along with them a *purpose*. If this opinion be erroneous, I can have little right to the name of a Poet. For all good poetry is the spontaneous overflow of powerful feelings: and though this be true, Poems to which any value can be attached were never produced on any variety of subjects but by a man who, being possessed of more than usual organic sensibility, had also thought long and deeply. For our continued influxes of feeling are modified and directed by our thoughts, which are indeed the representatives of all our past feelings; and, as by contemplating the relation of these general representatives to each other, we discover what is really important to men, so . . . [*etc.*]

Spontaneity, that is, as Wordsworth seeks it, involves no cult of the instinctive and primitive at the expense of the rationalized and civilized; it is the spontaneity supervening upon complex development, a spontaneity engaging an advanced and delicate organization. He stands for a distinctly human naturalness; one, that is, consummating a discipline, moral and other. A poet who can bring home to us the possibility of such a naturalness should to-day be found important. In Wordsworth's poetry the possibility is offered us realized—realized in a mode central and compelling enough to enforce the bearing of poetry upon life, the significance of this poetry for actual living. The absence both of the specifically sexual in any recognizable form and of any sign of repression serves to emphasize this significance, the significance of this achieved naturalness, spontaneous, and yet the expression of an order and the product of an emotional and moral training.

No one should, after what has been said, find it necessary to impute to the critic at this point, or to suppose him to be applauding in Wordsworth, a puritanic warp. Wordsworth was, on the showing of his poetry and everything else, normally and robustly human. The selectiveness and the habit of decorum involved in "recollection in tranquillity" were normal and, in a wholly laudatory sense of the word, conventional; that is, so endorsed by common usage as to be natural. The poetic process engaged an organization that had, by his own account, been determined by an upbringing in a congenial social environment, with its wholesome simple pieties and the traditional sanity of its moral culture, which to him were nature. He may have been a "Romantic," but it would be misleading to think of him as an individualist. The implicit social and moral preoccupation of his self-communings in solitude, his recollecting in tranquillity, is fairly suggested by this, from the *Letter to John Wilson:*

I return then to the question, please whom? or what? I answer, human nature as it has been and ever will be. But, where are we to find the best measure of this? I answer, from within; by stripping our own hearts naked, and by looking out of ourselves towards men who lead the simplest lives, and most according to nature; men who have never known false refinements, wayward and artificial desires, false criticisms, effeminate habits of thinking and feeling, or who having known these things have outgrown them. This latter class is the most to be depended upon, but it is very small in number.

This, of course, is in a sense commonplace about Wordsworth. Yet it would appear to be very easy, in a confusion of anecdotage and criticism, biography and poetry, to slip into giving the observation that he was self-centred a wholly uncritical and misleading effect.

> He had as much imagination
> As a pint-pot;—he never could
> Fancy another situation
> From which to dart his contemplation
> Than that wherein he stood.

Shelley here again notes a striking difference between himself and Wordsworth. He could hardly be expected to note—what is not the commonplace it ought to be—that the self-projecting and ardently altruistic Shelley is, in the comparison, the narrowly limited and the egoist (which term, it may be added, applies with less injustice to Milton than to Wordsworth). Wordsworth, it is true, has no dramatic gift, and compared with Shakespeare's, the range of interests he exhibits is narrow. But he exhibits also in his poetry, as an essential characteristic, an impersonality unknown to Shelley.

This characteristic (consider the capacity and the habit it implies) is closely associated with the social-moral centrality insisted on above. The insistence will no doubt be challenged; it is at any rate time to take account of the aspect of Wordsworth stressed by Dr. Bradley in his well-known essay (see *Oxford Lectures on Poetry*). Wordsworth is often spoken of as a "mystic," and the current valuation would appear to rest his greatness largely upon the "visionary moments" and "spots of time." Wordsworth himself undoubtedly valued the "visionary" element in his experience very highly, and it is important to determine what significance he attributes to it. In this passage from Book II of *The Prelude* he is as explicit as he ever is:

> and, at that time,
> Have felt whate'er there is of power in sound
> To breath an elevated mood, by form
> Or image unprofaned; and I would stand,
> Beneath some rock, listening to sounds that are
> The ghostly language of the ancient earth,
> Or make their dim abode in distant winds.
> Thence did I drink the visionary power.
> I deem not profitless these fleeting moods
> Of shadowy exultation: not for this,
> That they are kindred to our purer mind

> And intellectual life; but that the soul,
> Remembering how she felt, but what she felt
> Remembering not, retains an obscure sense
> Of possible sublimity, to which,
> With growing faculties she doth aspire,
> With faculties still growing, feeling still
> That whatsoever point they gain, they still
> Have something to pursue.

It would be difficult to suggest anything more elusive than this possibility which the soul glimpses in "visionary" moments and,

> Remembering how she felt, but what she felt
> Remembering not,

retains an "obscure sense" of.[1] Perhaps it will be agreed that, though Wordsworth no doubt was right in feeling that he had something to pursue, the critic here is in a different case. If these "moments" have any significance for the critic (whose business it is to define the significance of Wordsworth's poetry), it will be established, not by dwelling upon or in them, in the hope of exploring something that lies hidden in or behind their vagueness, but by holding firmly on to that sober verse in which they are presented.

How strong are the eighteenth-century affinities of this verse Mr. Nichol Smith brings out when, in his introduction to *The Oxford Book of Eighteenth Century Verse,* he quotes a piece of Akenside and suggests rightly that it might have passed for Wordsworth. Wordsworth's roots were deep in the eighteenth century. To say this is to lay the stress again—where it ought to rest—on his essential sanity and normality.

But though he is so surely and centrally poised, the sureness had nothing of complacency about it. It rests consciously over unsounded depths and among mysteries, itself a mystery. This recognition has its value in the greater validity of the poise—in a kind of sanction resulting. So, too, Wordsworth's firm hold upon the world of common perception is the more notable in one who knows of "fallings from us, vanishings, blank misgivings"

---

[1] Cf. . . . . in such strength
    Of usurpation, when the light of sense
    Goes out, but with a flash that has revealed
    The invisible world, doth greatness make abode,
    There harbours; whether we be young or old,
    Our destiny, our being's heart and home,
    Is with infinitude, and only there;
    With hope it is, hope that can never die,
    Effort, and expectation, and desire,
    And something evermore about to be.

        The Prelude, Book VI, ll. 599–608 (1805–6).

("when the light of sense goes out"), and is capable of recording such moments as when

> That I had bodily eyes, I forgot, and what I saw
> Appear'd like something in myself, a dream,
> A prospect in my mind.[1]

The point of stressing Wordsworth's normality and sanity in dealing with such passages as this comes out when we turn from it to, say, Shelley's *Mont Blanc* or compare *Mont Blanc* with Wordsworth's *Simplon Pass*.

If any one demands a more positive valuation of the "visionary moments" in Wordsworth (disputing, perhaps, the complete representativeness of the "shadowy" passage quoted above), it may be granted that they sometimes clearly signify a revitalizing relaxation of purpose, of moral and intellectual effort, in a surrender to

> The gravitation and the filial bond
> Of nature, that connect him with the world.

For if Wordsworth was too inveterately human and moral for the "Dark Gods" (how incongruous a phrase in connexion with him!) to be invoked here, he none the less drew strength from his sense of communion with the non-human universe.

.   .   .   .   .

"Dark Gods," some readers will have commented, is indeed an incongruous phrase in connexion with Wordsworth. And it is now time to qualify the present account of him, as it stands now, by taking note of criticisms that it will have provoked from a quarter opposite to that saluted in the last paragraph. Does not, for instance, the formula, "recollection in tranquillity," apply to Wordsworth's poetry with a limiting effect that has as yet not been recognized? Is the tranquillity of this wisdom really at all close to any "spontaneous overflow of powerful feelings?" Are the feelings, as recollected, so very powerful?

It has to be admitted that the present of this poetry is, for the most part, decidedly tranquil and that the emotion—anything in the nature of strong excitement or disturbance—seems to belong decidedly to the past. If, as might be said, the strength of the poetry is that it brings maturity and youth into relation, the weakness is that the experience from which it draws life is confined mainly to youth, and lies at a distance. What, an intelligent contemporary reader might have asked at the creative period, will happen as youth recedes? What did happen we know, in any case, and the fact of

---

[1] *The Prelude*, Book II, ll. 342–352 (1805–6).

the decline may reasonably be held to have a bearing on the due estimate of Wordsworth's wisdom.

In the discussion above of the distinctive characteristics of his poetry "poise" has received some emphasis; further inquiry is necessary in the direction that the term suggests. There is, relevant to this inquiry, a significant passage in Book I of *The Excursion:*

> From his native hills
> He wandered far; much did he see of men,
> Their manners, their enjoyments, and pursuits,
> Their passions and their feelings; chiefly those
> Essential and eternal in the heart,
> That, 'mid the simpler forms of rural life,
> Exist more simple in their elements,
> And speak a plainer language. In the woods,
> A lone Enthusiast, and among the fields,
> Itinerant in this labour, he had passed
> The better portion of his time; and there
> Spontaneously had his affections thriven
> Amid the bounties of the year, the peace
> And liberty of nature; there he kept
> In solitude and solitary thought
> His mind in a just equipoise of love.
> Serene it was, unclouded by the cares
> Of ordinary life; unvexed, unwarped
> By partial bondage. In his steady course,
> No piteous revolutions had he felt,
> No wild varieties of joy and grief.
> Unoccupied by sorrow of its own,
> His heart lay open; and by nature tuned
> And constant disposition of his thoughts
> To sympathy with man, he was alive
> To all that was enjoyed where'er he went,
> And all that was endured; for in himself
> Happy, and quiet in his cheerfulness,
> He had no painful pressure from without
> That made him turn aside from wretchedness
> With coward fears. He could *afford* to suffer
> With those whom he saw suffer.

The Wanderer as described here would seem to be very much what the intelligent reader imagined above might have expected Wordsworth to become. Indeed, the description is, fairly obviously, very much in the nature of an idealized self-portrait. If Wordsworth, even when well embarked on *The Excursion,* was not quite this, this clearly is what he would have liked to be. That he should have wished to be this is significant. That he should have needed to wish it is the great difference between himself and the Wanderer. For Wordsworth's course had not been steady; he sought the Wanderer's "equipoise" just because of the "piteous revolutions" and the "wild varieties of joy and grief" that he had so disturbingly known. The Wanderer could not have written Wordsworth's poetry; it emerges out of Wordsworth's urgent personal problem; it is the answer to the question: "How, in a world that has shown itself to be like this, is it possible to go on living?"

Behind, then, the impersonality of Wordsworth's wisdom there is an immediately personal urgency. Impelling him back to childhood and youth —to their recovery in a present of tranquil seclusion—there are the emotional storms and disasters of the intervening period, and these are also implicitly remembered, if not "recollected," in the tranquillity of his best poetry. In so far as his eyes may fairly be said to "avert their ken from half of human fate," extremely painful awareness of this half is his excuse. For if his problem was personal, it was not selfishly so, not merely self-regarding; and it is also a general one: if (and how shall they not?) the sensitive and imaginative freely let their "hearts lie open" to the suffering of the world, how are they to retain any health or faith for living? Conflicting duties seem to be imposed (for it is no mere blind instinct of self-preservation that is in question). Wordsworth is not one of the few great tragic artists, but probably not many readers will care to censure him for weakness or cowardice. His heart was far from "unoccupied by sorrow of its own," and his sense of responsibility for human distress and his generously active sympathies had involved him in emotional disasters that threatened his hold on life. A disciplined limiting of contemplation to the endurable, and, consequently, a withdrawal to a reassuring environment, became terrible necessities for him.

It is significant that (whatever reason Wordsworth may have had for putting it there) the story of Margaret should also, following, as it does, close upon the description of the Wanderer, appear in Book I of *The Excursion*. It seems to me the finest thing that Wordsworth wrote, and it is certainly the most disturbingly poignant. The poignancy assures us with great force that the Wanderer, for all his familiarity with the Preface to the *Lyrical Ballads,* is not Wordsworth—not, at any rate, the poet; and it clearly bears a significant relation to the early date of composition: Wordsworth began *Margaret; or, The Ruined Cottage*—the substance of this part of Book I of *The Excursion* in 1795 and finished in 1797. At this period he was, we have reason to believe, striving towards his "equipoise" with great difficulty; striving, because of his great need.

The difficulty does not merely appear in the poignancy of the poetry, which contrasts so with the surrounding verse; it gets its implicit comment in the by-play between Wordsworth and the Wanderer. At a painful point in the story "the Wanderer paused" (1.592):

> Why should we thus, with an untoward mind,
> And in the weakness of humanity,
> From natural wisdom turn our hearts away;
> To natural comfort shut our eyes and ears;
> And, feeding on disquiet, thus disturb
> The calm of nature with our restless thoughts?

Wordsworth gladly acquiesced:

> That simple tale
> Passed from my mind like a forgotten sound.

But it refused to be dismissed; it rose insistently up through the distracting idle talk:

> In my own despite
> I thought of that poor Woman as of one
> Whom I had known and loved.

No doubt the particular memory of Annette asserts itself here, but that recognition (or guess) makes it all the more important to give due weight to the corrective hint thrown out by the Wanderer a little later:

> " 'Tis a common tale,
> An ordinary sorrow of man's life . . ."

—Wordsworth at this date cannot easily afford to suffer with those whom he sees suffer.

That is very apparent in the way "that Woman's sufferings" (which had "seemed present") are, at the end of the story, distanced. Wordsworth, "in the impotence of grief," turns to trace, around the Cottage, the "secret spirit of humanity" that "still survives"

> 'mid the calm oblivious tendencies
> Of nature, 'mid her plants, and weeds, and flowers
> And silent overgrowings . . .

The "old Man," with consummate poetic skill, endorses those tendencies:

> Why then should we read
> The forms of things with an unworthy eye?
> She sleeps in the calm earth, and peace is here.
> I well remember that those very plumes,
> Those weeds, and the high spear-grass on that wall,
> By mist and silent rain-drops silvered o'er,
> As once I passed, into my heart conveyed
> So still an image of tranquillity,

> So calm and still, and looked so beautiful
> Amid the uneasy thoughts which filled my mind,
> That what we feel of sorrow and despair
> From ruin and from change, and all the grief
> That passing shows of Being leave behind,
> Appeared an idle dream . . .

Michael was written in 1800—three years later. Wordsworth here has no need to withdraw his mind from the theme to a present "image of tranquillity." The things of which he speaks never "seem present" in this story; they are seen always as belonging, in their moving dignity, to the past. "Recollection" holds them at such a distance that serenity, for all the pathos, never falters; and an idealizing process, making subtle use of the mountain background, gives to "human suffering" a reconciling grandeur. *Michael,* of course, is only one poem (and an exceptionally fine one), but the implied representative significance of this comparison with *Margaret* is justly implied. When in the characteristic good poetry of Wordsworth painful things are dealt with, we find them presented in modes, more and less subtle, that are fairly intimated by his own phrase (the context [1] of which is very relevant):

> Remov'd and to a distance that was fit.

In *Michael* Wordsworth is very much more like the Wanderer. What, the contemporary reader already invoked may be imagined as asking, will be the next phase in the development? What will happen as youth, where lie the emotional sources of his poetry—"the hiding-places of my power"—and young manhood, which, in the way suggested, provides the creative pressure and incitement, recede further and further into the past, and the "equipoise" becomes a settled habit? The answer appears plainly enough in the description of the Wanderer—in that complacent "partial bondage" and in that curiously italicized *"afford":* one may come to afford too easily. The equipoise settles towards inertness:

> I long for a repose that ever is the same.

The *Ode to Duty* (1805) from which this line comes would, of course, be cited by many as going with the patriotic sonnets of these years to prove that Wordsworth, so far from subsiding in the way suggested, had acquired a new "inspiration," a new source of energy. The Ode, no doubt, is an impressive performance; but it may be ventured that few to whom Wordsworth matters would grieve much if some very inferior bard were proved to have written it. As for the sonnets, their quality is a comment on the value to the poet of his new inspiration: the worst of them (look, for in-

---

[1] *The Prelude,* Book VIII, l. 305.

stance, at "It is not to be thought of . . .") are lamentable claptrap, and the best, even if they are distinguished declamation, are hardly distinguished poetry. And the association in general of these patriotic moral habits with a settled addiction to Miltonizing has to be noted as (in the poet of the *Lyrical Ballads*) significant.

It is not that these new attitudes, and the process by which he settled into them, are not wholly respectable. There was never anything incompatible between the "natural piety" that his poetry cherishes and celebrates and the immemorial pieties and loyalties centering in the village church (see his reference to the "Village Steeple" in Book X of *The Prelude,* 1805–6; 1.268). The transition was easy. But when he made it his days ceased to be "bound each to each" back to childhood. No longer could he say:

> The days gone by
> Come back upon me from the dawn almost
> Of life: the hiding-places of my power
> Seem open . . .

The Wordsworth who in the *Ode to Duty* spoke of the "genial sense of youth" as something he happily surrendered had seen the hiding-places of his power close. The "equipoise" had lost its vitality; the exquisitely fine and sensitive organization of the poet no longer informed and controlled his pen. The energy of the new patriotic moral interests, far from bringing the poet new life, took the place of creative sensibility, and confirmed and ensured its loss.

In fact, the new power belongs, it might be said, not to the "hiding-places"—it has no connexion with them—but to the public platform (a metaphor applying obviously to the patriotic development, with which, it should be noted, the religious is not accidentally associated): the public voice is a substitute for the inner voice, and engenders an insensitiveness to this—to its remembered (or, at least, to its recorded) burden and tone. For the sentiments and attitudes of the patriotic and Anglican Wordsworth do not come as the intimately and particularly realized experience of an unusually and finely conscious individual; they are external, general and conventional; their quality is that of the medium they are proffered in, which is insensitively Miltonic, a medium not felt into from within as something at the nerve-tips, but handled from outside. This is to question, not their sincerity, but their value and interest; their representativeness is not of the important kind. Their relation to poetry may be gathered from the process to which, at their dictation, Wordsworth subjected *The Prelude:* in the pursuit of formal orthodoxy he freely falsified and blunted the record of experience.

This process is forecast in the *Immortality Ode,* the essential purpose of which is to justify it. Criticism of Stanza VIII ("Mighty Prophet! Seer blest!") has been permissible, even correct, since Coleridge's time. But the empty grandiosity apparent there is merely the local manifestation of a general strain, a general factitiousness. The Ode (1803–6) belongs to the transition at its critical phase and contains decided elements of the living. But these do not lessen the dissatisfaction that one feels with the movement—the movement that makes the piece an ode in the Grand Style; for, as one reads, it is in terms of the movement that the strain, the falsity, first asserts itself. The manipulations by which the changes of mood are indicated have, by the end of the third stanza, produced an effect that, in protest, one describes as rhythmic vulgarity (for Dryden to do this kind of thing is quite another matter). The effort towards the formal ode is, clearly, the effort towards the formal attitude (Wordsworth himself being the public in view), and the strain revealed in technique has an obvious significance. What this is it hardly needs Stanza VI to proclaim:

> . . . even with something of a Mother's mind
> And no unworthy aim,
> The homely Nurse doth all she can
> To make her Foster-child, her Inmate Man,
> Forget the glories he hath known,
> And that imperial palace whence he came.

There is no suggestion of "that imperial palace" in the relevant parts of *The Prelude,* and "Foster-child" patently falsifies the feeling towards "Earth" ("the gravitation and the filial bond") recorded there.

SYMBOLIC ACTION IN A POEM BY KEATS

KENNETH BURKE

We are here set to analyze the "Ode on a Grecian Urn" as a viaticum that leads, by a series of transformations, into the oracle, "Beauty is truth, truth beauty." We shall analyze the Ode "dramatistically," in terms of symbolic action.

"Symbolic Action In a Poem by Keats" from *A Grammar of Motives* by Kenneth Burke. Prentice-Hall, Inc., 1945. The material originally appeared in the Appendix, pages 447–463. Reprinted by permission of author and publisher.

To consider language as a means of *information* or *knowledge* is to consider it epistemologically, semantically, in terms of "science." To consider it as a mode of *action* is to consider it in terms of "poetry." For a poem is an act, the symbolic act of the poet who made it—an act of such a nature that, in surviving as a structure or object, it enables us as readers to re-enact it.

"Truth" being the essential word of knowledge (science) and "beauty" being the essential word of art or poetry, we might substitute accordingly. The oracle would then assert, "Poetry is science, science poetry." It would be particularly exhilarating to proclaim them one if there were a strong suspicion that they were at odds (as the assertion that "God's in his heaven, all's right with the world" is really a *counter*-assertion to doubts about God's existence and suspicions that much is wrong). It was the dialectical opposition between the "aesthetic" and the "practical," with "poetry" on one side and utility (business and applied science) on the other that was being ecstatically denied. The *relief* in this denial was grounded in the romantic philosophy itself, a philosophy which gave strong recognition to precisely the *contrast* between "beauty" and "truth."

Perhaps we might put it this way: If the oracle were to have been uttered in the first stanza of the poem rather than the last, its phrasing proper to that place would have been: "Beauty is *not* truth, truth *not* beauty." The five stanzas of successive transformation were necessary for the romantic philosophy of a romantic poet to transcend itself (raising its romanticism to a new order, or new dimension). An abolishing of romanticism through romanticism! (To transcend romanticism through romanticism is, when all is over, to restore in one way what is removed in another.)

But to the poem, step by step through the five stanzas.

As a "way in," we begin with the sweeping periodic sentence that, before the stanza is over, has swiftly but imperceptibly been transmuted in quality from the periodic to the breathless, a cross between interrogation and exclamation:

> Thou still unravish'd bride of quietness,
>   Thou foster-child of silence and slow time,
> Sylvan historian, who canst thus express
>   A flowery tale more sweetly than our rhyme:
> What leaf-fring'd legend haunts about thy shape
>   Of deities or mortals, or of both,
>   In Tempe or the dales of Arcady?
> What men or gods are these? What maidens loth?
> What mad pursuit? What struggle to escape?
>   What pipes and timbrels? What wild ecstasy?

Even the last quick outcries retain somewhat the quality of the periodic structure with which the stanza began. The final line introduces the subject of "pipes and timbrels," which is developed and then surpassed in Stanza II:

> Heard melodies are sweet, but those unheard
>   Are sweeter; therefore, ye soft pipes, play on;
> Not to the sensual ear, but, more endear'd,
>   Pipe to the spirit ditties of no tone:
> Fair youth, beneath the trees, thou canst not leave
>   Thy song, nor ever can those trees be bare;
>   Bold Lover, never, never canst thou kiss,
> Though winning near the goal—yet, do not grieve;
>   She cannot fade, though thou hast not thy bliss,
>   Forever wilt thou love, and she be fair!

If we had only the first stanza of this Ode, and were speculating upon it from the standpoint of motivation, we could detect there tentative indications of two motivational levels. For the lines express a doubt whether the figures on the urn are "deities or mortals"—and the motives of gods are of a different order from the motives of men. This bare hint of such a possibility emerges with something of certainty in the second stanza's development of the "pipes and timbrels" theme. For we explicitly consider a contrast between body and mind (in the contrast between "heard melodies," addressed "to the sensual ear," and "ditties of no tone," addressed "to the spirit").

Also, of course, the notion of inaudible sound brings us into the region of the mystic oxymoron (the term in rhetoric for "the figure in which an epithet of a contrary significance is added to a word: e.g., *cruel kindness; laborious idleness*"). And it clearly suggests a concern with the level of motives-behind-motives, as with the paradox of the prime mover that is itself at rest, being the unmoved ground of all motion and action. Here the poet whose sounds are the richest in our language is meditating upon *absolute* sound, the *essence* of sound, which would be soundless as the prime mover is motionless, or as the "principle" of sweetness would not be sweet, having transcended sweetness, or as the sub-atomic particles of the sun are each, in their isolate purity, said to be devoid of temperature.

Contrast Keats's unheard melodies with those of Shelley:

> Music, when soft voices die,
> Vibrates in the memory—
> Odours, when sweet violets sicken,
> Live within the sense they quicken.

> Rose leaves, when the rose is dead,
> Are heaped for the beloved's bed;
> And so thy thoughts, when thou art gone,
> Love itself shall slumber on.

Here the futuristic Shelley is anticipating retrospection; he is looking forward to looking back. The form of thought is naturalistic and temporalistic in terms of *past* and *future*. But the form of thought in Keats is mystical, in terms of an *eternal present*. The Ode is striving to move beyond the region of becoming into the realm of *being*. (This is another way of saying that we are here concerned with two levels of motivation.)

In the last four lines of the second stanza, the state of immediacy is conveyed by a development peculiarly Keatsian. I refer not simply to translation into terms of the erotic, but rather to a quality of *suspension* in the erotic imagery, defining an eternal prolongation of the state just prior to fulfilment—not exactly arrested ecstasy, but rather an arrested pre-ecstasy.[1]

Suppose that we had but this one poem by Keats, and knew nothing of its author or its period, so that we could treat it only in itself, as a series of internal transformations to be studied in their development from a certain point, and without reference to any motives outside the Ode. Under such conditions, I think, we should require no further observations to characterize (from the standpoint of symbolic action) the main argument in the second stanza. We might go on to make an infinity of observations about the details of the stanza; but as regards major deployments we should deem it enough to note that the theme of "pipes and timbrels" is developed by the use of mystic oxymoron, and then surpassed (or given a development-atop-the-development) by the stressing of erotic imagery (that had been ambiguously adumbrated in the reference to "maidens loth" and "mad pursuit" of Stanza I). And we could note the quality of *incipience* in this imagery, its state of arrest not at fulfilment, but at the point just prior to fulfilment.

Add, now, our knowledge of the poem's place as an enactment in a particular cultural scene, and we likewise note in this second stanza a variant of the identification between death and sexual love that was so typical of 19th-century romanticism and was to attain its musical monument in the Wagnerian *Liebestod*. On a purely dialectical basis, to die in

---

[1] Mr. G. Wilson Knight, in *The Starlit Dome,* refers to "that recurring tendency in Keats to image a poised form, a stillness suggesting motion, what might be called a 'tiptoe' effect."

love would be to be born to love (the lovers dying as individual identities
that they might be transformed into a common identity). Adding historical
factors, one can note the part that capitalist individualism plays in sharpen-
ing this consummation (since a property structure that heightens the sense
of individual identity would thus make it more imperiously a "death" for
the individual to take on the new identity made by a union of two). We
can thus see why the love-death equation would be particularly representative of a romanticism that was the reflex of business.

Fortunately, the relation between private property and the love-death
equation is attested on unimpeachable authority, concerning the effect of
consumption and consummation in a "mutual flame":

> So between them love did shine,
> That the turtle saw his right
> Flaming in the phoenix' sight;
> Either was the other's mine.
>
> Property was thus appall'd,
> That the self was not the same;
> Single nature's double name
> Neither two nor one was called.

The addition of fire to the equation, with its pun on sexual burning,
moves us from purely dialectical considerations into psychological ones.
In the lines of Shakespeare, fire is the third term, the ground term for the
other two (the synthesis that ends the lovers' roles as thesis and antithesis).
Less obviously, the same movement from the purely dialectical to the
psychological is implicit in any imagery of a *dying* or a *falling* in common,
which when woven with sexual imagery signalizes a "transcendent" sexual
consummation. The figure appears in a lover's compliment when Keats
writes to Fanny Brawne, thus:

I never knew before, what such a love as you have made me feel, was;
I did not believe in it; my Fancy was afraid of it lest it should burn me up. But
if you will fully love me, though there may be some fire, 'twill not be more
than we can bear when moistened and bedewed with pleasures.

Our primary concern is to follow the transformations of the poem itself.
But to understand its full nature as a symbolic act, we should use whatever knowledge is available. In the case of Keats, not only do we know
the place of this poem in his work and its time, but also we have material
to guide our speculations as regards correlations between poem and poet.
I grant that such speculations interfere with the symmetry of criticism as
a game. (Criticism as a game is best to watch, I guess, when one confines

himself to the single unit, and reports on its movements like a radio commentator broadcasting the blow-by-blow description of a prizefight.) But
linguistic analysis has opened up new possibilities in the correlating of
producer and product—and these concerns have such important bearing
upon matters of culture and conduct in general that no sheer conventions
or ideals of criticism should be allowed to interfere with their development.

From what we know of Keats's illness, with the peculiar inclination to
erotic imaginings that accompany its fever (as with the writings of D. H.
Lawrence) we can glimpse a particular bodily motive expanding and in-
tensifying the lyric state in Keats's case. Whatever the intense *activity* of
his thoughts, there was the material *pathos* of his physical condition. Whatever transformations of mind or body he experienced, his illness was there
as a kind of constitutional substrate, whereby all aspects of the illness
would be imbued with their derivation from a common ground (the
phthisic fever thus being at one with the phthisic chill, for whatever the
clear contract between fever and chill, they are but modes of the same
illness, the common underlying substances).

The correlation between the state of agitation in the poems and the
physical condition of the poet is made quite clear in the poignant letters
Keats wrote during his last illness. In 1819 he complains that he is "scarcely
content to write the best verses for the fever they leave behind." And he
continues: "I want to compose without this fever." But a few months
later he confesses, "I am recommended not even to read poetry, much less
write it." Or: "I must say that for 6 Months before I was taken ill I had
not passed a tranquil day. Either that gloom overspre[a]d me or I was
suffering under some passionate feeling, or if I turn'd to versify that exacer-
bated the poison of either sensation." Keats was "like a sick eagle looking
at the sky," as he wrote of his mortality in a kindred poem, "On Seeing
the Elgin Marbles."

But though the poet's body was a *patient,* the poet's mind was an
agent. Thus, as a practitioner of poetry, he could *use* his fever, even perhaps encouraging, though not deliberately, esthetic habits that, in making
for the perfection of his lines, would exact payment in the ravages of his
body (somewhat as Hart Crane could write poetry only by modes of living that made for the cessation of his poetry and so led to his dissolution).

Speaking of agents, patients, and action here, we might pause to
glance back over the centuries thus: in the Aristotelian grammar of motives, action has its reciprocal in passion, hence *passion* is the property
of a *patient.* But by the Christian paradox (which made the martyr's
action identical with his passion, as the accounts of the martyrs were
called both Acts and Passionals), *patience* is the property of a *moral*

agent. And this Christian view, as secularized in the philosophy of romanticism, with its stress upon creativeness, leads us to the possibility of a bodily suffering redeemed by a poetic act.

In the third stanza, the central stanza of the Ode (hence properly the fulcrum of its swing) we see the two motives, the action and the passion, in the process of being separated. The possibility raised in the first stanza (which was dubious whether the level of motives was to be human or divine), and developed in the second stanza (which contrasts the "sensual" and the "spirit"), becomes definitive in Stanza III:

> Ah, happy, happy boughs! that cannot shed
> Your leaves, nor ever bid the Spring adieu;
> And happy melodist, unwearied,
> For ever piping songs for ever new;
> More happy love! more happy, happy love!
> For ever warm and still to be enjoy'd,
> For ever panting, and for ever young;
> All breathing human passion far above,
> That leaves a heart high-sorrowful and cloy'd.
> A burning forehead, and a parching tongue.

The poem as a whole makes permanent, or fixes in a state of arrest, a peculiar agitation. But within this fixity, by the nature of poetry as a progressive medium, there must be development. Hence, the agitation that is maintained throughout (as a mood absolutized so that it fills the entire universe of discourse) will at the same time undergo internal transformations. In the third stanza, these are manifested as a clear division into two distinct and contrasted realms. There is a transcendental fever, which is felicitous, divinely above "all breathing human passion." And this "leaves" the other level, the level of earthly fever, "a burning forehead and a parching tongue." From the bodily fever, which is a passion, and malign, there has split off a spiritual activity, a wholly benign aspect of the total agitation.

Clearly, a movement has been finished. The poem must, if it is well-formed, take a new direction, growing out of and surpassing the curve that has by now been clearly established by the successive stages from "Is there the possibility of two motivational levels?" through "there are two motivational levels" to "the 'active' motivational level 'leaves' the 'passive' level."

Prophesying, with the inestimable advantage that goes with having looked ahead, what should we expect the new direction to be? First, let us survey the situation. Originally, before the two strands of the fever had been definitely drawn apart, the bodily passion could serve as the scene or ground of the spiritual action. But at the end of the third stanza, we abandon the level of bodily passion. The action is "far above" the passion, it "leaves" the fever. What then would this transcendent act require, to complete it?

It would require a scene of the same quality as itself. An act and a scene belong together. The nature of the one must be a fit with the nature of the other. (I like to call this the "scene-act ratio," or "dramatic ratio.") Hence, the act having now transcended its bodily setting, it will require, as its new setting, a transcendent scene. Hence, prophesying *post eventum,* we should ask that, in Stanza IV, the poem *embody* the transcendental act by endowing it with an appropriate scene.

The scene-act ratio involves a law of dramatic consistency whereby the quality of the act shares the quality of the scene in which it is enacted (the synecdochic relation of container and thing contained). Its grandest variant was in supernatural cosmogonies wherein mankind took on the attributes of gods by acting in cosmic scenes that were themselves imbued with the presence of godhead.[1]

Or we may discern the logic of the scene-act ratio behind the old controversy as to whether "God willed the good because it is good," or "the good is good because God willed it." This strictly theological controversy had political implications. But our primary concern here is with the *dramatistic* aspects of this controversy. For you will note that the whole issue centers in the problem of the *grounds* of God's creative act.

Since, from the purely dramatic point of view, every act requires a scene in which it takes place, we may note that one of the doctrines (that "God willed the good because it is good") is more symmetrical than the other. For by it, God's initial act of creation is itself given a ground, or scene (the objective existence of goodness, which was so real that God himself did not simply make it up, but acted in conformity with its nature when willing it to be the law of his creation). In the scholastic formulas taken over from Aristotle, God was defined as "pure act" (though this pure act was in turn the ultimate ground or *scene* of human acting and willing). And from the stand-point of purely dramatic symmetry, it would be desirable to have some kind of "scene" even for God. This requirement is met, we are suggesting, in the doctrine that "God willed the good *because* it is good." For this word, "because," in assigning a reason for

---

[1] In an article by Leo Spitzer, *"Milieu and Ambiance:* An Essay in Historical Semantics" (September and December 1942 numbers of *Philosophy and Phenomenological Research*), one will find a wealth of material that can be read as illustrative of "dramatic ratio."

God's willing, gives us in principle a kind of scene, as we may discern in the pun of our word, "ground," itself, which indeterminately applies to either "place" or "cause."

If even theology thus responded to the pressure for dramatic symmetry by endowing God, as the transcendent act, with a transcendent scene of like quality, we should certainly expect to find analogous tactics in this Ode. For as we have noted that the romantic passion is the secular equivalent of the Christian passion, so we may recall Coleridge's notion that poetic action itself is a "dim analogue of Creation." Keats in his way confronting the same dramatistic requirement that the theologians confronted in theirs, when he has arrived at his transcendent act at the end of Stanza III (that is, when the benign fever has split away from the malign bodily counterpart, as a divorcing of spiritual action from sensual passion), he is ready in the next stanza for the imagining of a scene that would correspond in quality to the quality of the action as so transformed. His fourth stanza will concretize, or "materialize," the act, by dwelling upon its appropriate ground.

> Who are these coming to the sacrifice?
>   To what green altar, O mysterious priest,
> Lead'st thou that heifer lowing at the skies,
>   And all her silken flanks with garlands drest?
> What little town, by river or sea shore,
>   Or mountain built with peaceful citadel,
>   Is emptied of this folk, this pious morn?
> And, little town, thy streets for evermore
>   Will silent be; and not a soul to tell
>   Why thou art desolate, can e'er return.

It is a vision, as you prefer, of "death" or of "immortality." "Immortality," we might say, is the "good" word for "death," and must necessarily be conceived in terms of death (the necessity that Donne touches upon where he writes, ". . . but thinke that I/ Am, by being dead, immortall"). This is why, when discussing the second stanza, I felt justified in speaking of the variations of the love-death equation, though the poem spoke not of love and *death,* but of love *for ever.* We have a deathy-deathless scene as the corresponding ground of our transcendent act. The Urn itself, as with the scene upon it, is not merely an immortal act in our present mortal scene; it was originally an immortal act in a mortal scene quite different. The imagery, of sacrifice, piety, silence, desolation, is that of communication with the immortal or the dead.[1]

---

[1] In imagery there is no negation, or disjunction. Logically, we can say, "this *or* that," "this, *not* that." In imagery we can but say "this *and* that," "this *with* that,"

This use of the love-death equation is as startlingly paralleled in a letter to Fanny Brawne:

I have two luxuries to brood over in my walks, your loveliness and the hour of my death. O that I could take possession of them both in the same moment.

Incidentally, we might note that the return to the use of rhetorical questions in the fourth stanza serves well, on a purely technical level, to keep our contact with the mood of the opening stanza, a music that now but vibrates in the memory. Indeed, one even gets the impression that the form of the rhetorical question had never been abandoned; that the poet's questings had been couched as questions throughout. This is tonal felicity at its best, and something much like unheard tonal felicity. For the actual persistence of the rhetorical questions through these stanzas would have been wearisome, whereas their return now gives us an inaudible variation, by making us feel that the exclamations in the second and third stanzas had been questions, as the questions in the first stanza had been exclamations.

But though a lyric greatly profits by so strong a sense of continuousness, or perpetuity, I am trying to stress the fact that in the fourth stanza we *come upon* something. Indeed, this fourth stanza is related to the three foregoing stanzas quite as the sestet is related to the octave in Keats's sonnet, "On First Looking Into Chapman's Homer":

> Much have I travell'd in the realms of gold,
> And many goodly states and kingdoms seen;
> Round many western islands have I been
> Which bards in fealty to Apollo hold.
> Oft of one wide expanse had I been told
> That deep-brow'd Homer ruled as his demesne;
> Yet did I never breathe its pure serene
> Till I heard Chapman speak out loud and bold;
>
> Then felt I like some watcher of the skies
> When a new planet swims into his ken;
> Or like stout Cortez when with eagle eyes

"this-that," etc. Thus, imagistically considered, a commandment cannot be simply a proscription, but is also latently a provocation (a state of affairs that figures in the kind of stylistic scrupulosity and/or curiosity to which Gide's heroes have been particularly sensitive, as "thou shalt not . . ." becomes imaginatively transformed into "what would happen if . . ."). In the light of what we have said about the deathiness of immortality, and the relation between the erotic and the thought of a "dying," perhaps we might be justified in reading the last line of the great "Bright Star!" sonnet as naming states not simply alternative but also synonymous:

And so live ever—or else swoon to death.

> He stared at the Pacific—and all his men
> Look'd at each other with a wild surmise—
> Silent, upon a peak in Darien.

I am suggesting that, just as the sestet in this sonnet, *comes upon a scene,*
so it is with the fourth stanza of the Ode. In both likewise we end on the
theme of silence; and is not the Ode's reference to the thing that "not a
soul can tell" quite the same in quality as the sonnet's reference to a
"wild surmise"?

Thus, with the Urn as viaticum (or rather, with the *poem* as viaticum,
and *in the name* of the Urn), having symbolically enacted a kind of act
that trancends our mortality, we round out the process by coming to dwell
upon the transcendental ground of this act. The dead world of ancient
Greece, as immortalized on an Urn surviving from that period, is the vessel
of this deathy-deathless ambiguity. And we have gone dialectically from
the "human" to the "divine" and thence to the "ground of the divine"
(here tracing in poetic imagery the kind of "dramatistic" course we have
considered, on the purely conceptual plane, in the theological speculations
about the "grounds" for God's creative act). Necessarily, there must be
certain inadequacies in the conception of this ground, precisely because
of the fact that immortality can only be conceived in terms of death. Hence
the reference to the "desolate" in a scene otherwise possessing the be-
nignity of the eternal.

The imagery of pious sacrifice, besides its fitness for such thoughts
of departure as when the spiritual act splits from the sensual pathos, suggests also a bond of communication between the levels (because of its
immortal character in a mortal scene). And finally, the poem, in the
name of the Urn, or under the aegis of the Urn, is such a bond. For we
readers, but re-enacting it in the reading, use it as a viaticum to transport
us into the quality of the scene which it depicts on its face (the scene
containing as a fixity what the poem as act extends into a process). The
scene *on* the Urn is really the scene *behind* the Urn; the Urn is literally the
ground of this scene, but transcendentally the scene is the ground of the
Urn. The Urn contains the scene out of which it arose.

We turn now to the closing stanza:

> O Attic shape! Fair attitude! with brede
> Of marble men and maidens overwrought,
> With forest branches and the trodden weed;
> Thou, silent form, dost tease us out of thought
> As doth eternity: Cold Pastoral!
> When old age shall this generation waste,

Thou shalt remain, in midst of other woe
Than ours, a friend to man, to whom thou say'st,
Beauty is truth, truth beauty,—that is all
Ye know on earth, and all ye need to know.

In the third stanza we were at a moment of heat, emphatically sharing an imagery of loves "panting" and "for ever warm" that was, in the transcendental order, companionate to "a burning forehead, and a parching tongue" in the order of the passions. But in the last stanza, as signalized in the marmorean utterance, "Cold Pastoral!" we have gone from transcendental fever to transcendental chill. Perhaps, were we to complete our exegesis, we should need reference to some physical step from phthisic fever to phthisic chill, that we might detect here a final correlation between bodily passion and mental action. In any event we may note that, the mental action having departed from the bodily passion, the change from fever to chill is not a sufferance. For, as only the *benign* aspects of the fever had been left after the split, so it is a wholly benign chill on which the poem ends.[1]

I wonder whether anyone can read the reference to "brede of marble men and maidens overwrought" without thinking of "breed" for "brede" and "excited" for "overwrought." (Both expressions would thus merge notions of sexuality and craftsmanship, the erotic and the poetic.) As for the designating of the Urn as an "Attitude," it fits in admirably with our stress upon symbolic action. For an attitude is an arrested, or incipient *act*—not just an *object,* or *thing.*

Yeats, in *A Vision,* speaks of "the diagrams in Law's *Boehme,* where one lifts a paper to discover both the human entrails and the starry heavens." This equating of the deeply without and the deeply within (as also with Kant's famous remark) might well be remembered when we think of the sky that the "watcher" saw in Keats's sonnet. It is an internal sky, attained through meditations induced by the reading of a book. And so the oracle, whereby truth and beauty are proclaimed as one, would seem to derive from a profound inwardness.

Otherwise, without these introductory mysteries, "truth" and "beauty" were at odds. For whereas "beauty" had its fulfilment in romantic poetry, "truth" was coming to have its fulfilment in science, technological accuracy,

---

[1] In a letter to Fanny Brawne, Keats touches upon the fever-chill contrast in a passage that also touches upon the love-death equation, though here the chill figures in an untransfigured state:

I fear that I am too prudent for a dying kind of Lover. Yet, there is a great difference between going off in warm blood like Romeo; and making one's exit like a frog in a frost.

accountancy, statistics, actuarial tables, and the like. Hence, without benefit of the rites which one enacts in a sympathetic reading of the Ode (rites that remove the discussion to a difference level), the enjoyment of "beauty" would involve an esthetic kind of awareness radically in conflict with the kind of awareness deriving from the practical "truth." And as regards the tactics of the poem, this conflict would seem to be solved by "estheticizing" the true rather than by "verifying" the beautiful.

Earlier in our essay, we suggested reading "poetry" for "beauty" and "science" for "truth," with the oracle deriving its *liberating* quality from the fact that it is uttered at a time when the poem has taken us to a level where earthly contradictions do not operate. But we might also, in purely conceptual terms, attain a level where "poetry" and "science" cease to be at odds; namely: by translating the two terms into the "grammar" that lies behind them. That is: we could generalize the term "poetry" by widening it to the point where we could substitute for it the term "act." And we could widen "science" to the point where we could substitute "scene." Thus we have:

"beauty"	equals	"poetry"	equals	"act"
"truth"	equals	"science"	equals	"scene"

We would equate "beauty" with "act," because it is not merely a decorative thing, but an assertion, an affirmative, a creation, hence in the fullest sense an act. And we would equate "truth" or "science" with the "scenic" because science is a knowledge of *what is*—and *all that is* comprises the over-all universal *scene*. Our corresponding transcendence, then, got by "translation" into purely grammatical terms, would be: "Act is scene, scene act." We have got to this point by a kind of purely conceptual transformation that would correspond, I think, to the transformations of imagery leading to the oracle in the Ode.

"Act is scene, scene act." Unfortunately, I must break the symmetry a little. For poetry, as conceived in idealism (romanticism) could not quite be equated with *act,* but rather with *attitude.* For idealistic philosophies, with their stress upon the subjective, place primary stress upon the *agent* (the individual, the ego, the will, etc.). It was medieval scholasticism that placed primary stress upon the *act.* And in the Ode the Urn (which is the vessel or representative of poetry) is called an "attitude," which is not outright an act, but an incipient or arrested act, a *state of mind,* the property of an *agent.* Keats, in calling the Urn an attitude, is *personifying* it. Or we might use the italicizing resources of dialectic by saying that for Keats, beauty (poetry) was not so much "the *act* of an agent" as it was "the act of an *agent.*"

Perhaps we can re-enforce this interpretation by examining kindred strategies in Yeats, whose poetry similarly derives from idealistic, romantic sources. Indeed, as we have noted elsewhere,[1] Yeats's vision of immortality in his Byzantium poems but carries one step further the Keatsian identification with the Grecian Urn:

> Once out of nature I shall never take
> My bodily form from any natural thing,
> But such a form as Grecian goldsmiths make
> Of hammered gold and gold enamelling . . .

Here certainly the poet envisions immortality as "esthetically" as Keats. For he will have immortality as a golden bird, a fabricated thing, a work of Grecian goldsmiths. Here we go in the same direction as the "overwrought" Urn, but farther along in that direction.

The ending of Yeats's poem, "Among School Children," helps us to make still clearer the idealistic stress upon agent:

> Labour is blossoming or dancing where
> The body is not bruised to pleasure soul,
> Nor beauty torn out of its own despair,
> Nor blear-eyed wisdom out of midnight oil.
> O chestnut tree, great rooted blossomer,
> Are you the leaf, the blossom or the bole?
> O body swayed to music, O brightening glance,
> How can we know the dancer from the dance?

Here the chestnut tree (as personified agent) is the ground of unity or continuity for all its scenic manifestations; and with the agent (dancer) is merged the act (dance). True, we seem to have here a commingling of act, scene, and agent, all three. Yet it is the *agent* that is "foremost among the equals." Both Yeats and Keats, of course, were much more "dramatistic" in their thinking than romantic poets generally, who usually center their efforts upon the translation of *scene* into terms of *agent* (as the materialistic science that was the dialectical counterpart of romantic idealism preferred conversely to translate *agent* into terms of *scene,* or in other words, to treat "consciousness" in terms of "matter," the "mental" in terms of the "physical," "people" in terms of "environment").

To review briefly: The poem begins with an ambiguous fever which in the course of the further development is "separated out," splitting into a bodily fever and a spiritual counterpart. The bodily passion is the malign aspect of the fever, the mental action its benign aspect. In the course of

---

[1] "On Motivation in Yeats" (*The Southern Review,* Winter 1942).

the development, the malign passion is transcended and the benign active partner, the intellectual exhilaration, takes over. At the beginning, where the two aspects were ambiguously one, the bodily passion would be the "scene" of the mental action (the "objective symptoms" of the body would be paralleled by the "subjective symptoms" of the mind, the bodily state thus being the other or ground of the mental state). But as the two become separated out, the mental action transcends the bodily passion. It becomes an act in its own right, making discoveries and assertions not grounded in the bodily passion. And this quality of action, in transcending the merely physical symptoms of the fever, would thus require a different ground or scene, one more suited in quality to the quality of the transcendent act.

The transcendent act is concretized, or "materialized," in the vision of the "immortal" scene, the reference in Stanza IV to the original scene of the Urn, the "heavenly" scene of a dead, or immortal, Greece (the scene in which the Urn was originally enacted and which is also fixed on its face). To indicate the internality of this vision, we referred to a passage in Yeats relating the "depths" of the sky without to the depths of the mind within; and we showed a similar pattern in Keats's account of the vision that followed his reading of Chapman's Homer. We suggested that the poet is here coming upon a new internal sky, through identification with the Urn as act, the same sky that he came upon through identification with the enactments of Chapman's translation.

This transcendent scene is the level at which the earthly laws of contradiction no longer prevail. Hence, in the terms of this scene, he can proclaim the unity of truth and beauty (of science and art), a proclamation which he needs to make precisely because here was the basic split responsible for the romantic agitation (in both poetic and philosophic idealism). That is, it was gratifying to have the oracle proclaim the unity of poetry and science because the values of technology and business were causing them to be at odds. And from the perspective of a "higher level" (the perspective of a dead or immortal scene transcending the world of temporal contradictions) the split could be proclaimed once more a unity.

At this point, at this stage of exaltation, the fever has been replaced by chill. But the bodily passion has completely dropped out of account. All is now mental action. Hence, the chill (as in the ecstatic exclamation, "Cold Pastoral!") is proclaimed only in its benign aspect.

We may contrast this discussion with explanations such as a materialist of the Kretschmer school might offer. I refer to accounts of motivation that might treat disease as cause and poem as effect. In such accounts, the disease would not be "passive," but wholly active; and what we have called the mental action would be wholly passive, hardly more than an epiphenomenon, a mere symptom of the disease quite as are the fever and the chill themselves. Such accounts would give us no conception of the essential matter here, the intense linguistic activity.

WALLACE STEVENS
AND THE IMAGE OF MAN

MORTON DAUWEN ZABEL

STEVENS' poetry is distinguished by a mastery of two qualities in which he remains largely unrivalled among his contemporaries—the richness of his imagery and the sustained authority of his rhetoric. The two elements are mutually dependent; one supports and substances the other; in an age generally hostile to the values they represent he has given them an emphasis and an authenticity that makes his distinction isolated even beyond the independent integrity his career describes.

The sensory and symbolic properties of his verse—what Hopkins would have called its "keepings"—show an opulence and wit that doubtless appear suspect and extravagant in these later days of poetic realism and strenuous fact-facing. Even in his first decade of publication, during the heyday of Imagism, his luxuriance of metaphor and allegory surpassed the rhetorical fancies and colors in which Miss Lowell's disciples and the popular lyricists were trading. When set against the austerity of Frost and Robinson or the spectral scenes in Eliot and the midwestern school, he displayed an exoticism that made his art a case apart from the critical and anti-romantic motives then dominating the literary scene. Stevens was accordingly labeled a "dandy," a "connoisseur," a confecter of extravagant fictions, and a sophisticated defender of those romantic indulgences from which it had taken the severest possible discipline to wean the American taste. One early critic set him down as a conjuror, another as a "poetic Harlequin," the Humanists fell on even so concentrated a poem as "Anecdote of the Jar" as recklessly irresponsible in its meaning, as recently as September 1940 a young English critic (Julian Symons) has said that most of the poems in *Harmonium* "contain a slightly tittery joke" and that "The Comedian as the Letter C" "remains a piece of virtuosity, a

"Wallace Stevens and the Image of Man," by Morton Dauwen Zabel, originally published in *The Harvard Advocate* in 1940. Reprinted by permission of the author.

literary curio." No defender of Stevens' art will deny flatly the characterization implied in these criticisms; their prejudice helps fix his poetic character almost as accurately as the most enthusiastic favor. They also make it clear why Stevens was quick in winning a place among those poets—few in any age and rare in ours—who transport their readers to an unmistakable milieu of the imagination, to a characteristic atmosphere in which the special cast of the artist's taste, sympathies, and temperament is recognized. His work carries a radical stamp of personality that is able, merely by the references and figurative devices in which it deals, to win half the battle of words and meaning.

A poet's imagery is the individuating medium of his sensibility. So, of course, are his rhythm, his tonal quality, his particular vision and the idea or intuition it embodies. But the range of these in poetry is both limited and difficult to fix; they lack the atmospheric and dramatic force of imagery; they may be, for practical purposes at least, indistinguishable in large numbers of poets, sometimes even in poets of sharply contrasting temperaments and purposes. We find the clues to Baudelaire's world in his imagery of cats, clocks, courtesans, rich rooms, ships, islands, and stark Parisian streets; we are inducted into Mallarmé's researches by his symbolism of fans, fauns, tombs, stones, bibelots, and hieratic masks and emblems; we enter the conscious and the secret parts of Hopkins' spirit through his metaphors of sensory miracle and shock, of "skeined, stained, veined variety" in nature, of the intimate sublimity and stupendous particles of Creation upon which he fastened for its meaning; Eliot depicted the history of the contemporary spirit in his *mise-en-scène* of vacant lots, cheap hotels, rat-infested alleys, refuse-choked rivers, stale-aired boarding-houses, and purgatorial drawing-rooms whose squalor and desolation, already emphasized by contrasts of past splendor or fallen glory, prepared the way for the devotional symbols of *Ash Wednesday* and the analytical patterns of "Burnt Norton" and "East Coker." The types represented by Hardy, Yeats, Rilke, and Valéry are similarly indexed; Sandburg, Cummings and Auden are unmistakably though more derivatively marked; the serious poet who never finds this personal medium for his imagination is as likely to fall into indistinguishable anonymity as men of minor and indeterminate talent.

Among modern poets who show marked originality in this line two orders of imagery predominate. They may be defined by the examples of Mallarmé and Hopkins. Mallarmé's imagism is absolute in its claims, irreducible and exhaustive in its tendency, refined and specialized in subtlety to the point of discovering the positive identity of its underlying concepts; it implies a final perfection in its correspondence with idea; it resists rational sublimation except in terms of a total intuitive synthesis (Mallarmé translated "symbolism" as "synthesis") of concept and object. To both the concept and its analogy a special initiation is required in the reader, and this initiation only the poem can realize. "The world has become, in Mallarmé's own expression, 'transfusible en du songe,'" says Charles Mauron, and it is only by participating in the dream and at the same time submitting to the cold control of the penetrating sensibility of the poet that we enter into the processes of Mallarmé's intuition. The general fault of poets who accept Mallarmé's example is that their symbols surpass his in boldness and singularity but fail to establish that continuity of effect and reference, of pervading and realizing intelligence, which reduces the arbitrariness of his usage to a logical order. They either subtilize the image out of recognition or depend on a framework of reference outside poetry itself—upon correspondences or arguments never fundamentally integrated by the poetic experience. To imitate Mallarmé is usually to risk the defeat of expression. He represents a standard of "purity" almost inhuman in its demands, and many of his own poems succeed in their purpose only by falling short of it.

Hopkins' imagery, on the contrary, is realistic in its basis—as exhaustively but consistently realistic as the threading of a psychological maze in James. Sometimes it is an almost baffling complex of meaning that Hopkins attempts to elucidate, as in the day-and-night figure at the close of "Spelt from Sibyl's Leaves"; often he seized his insight under an impulse deliberately violent and reckless, as in "The Windhover"; but his effect is dramatic and immediate, not analytical and attenuated. His imagery is concrete in spite of its exorbitant sharpness of perception and detail; it confesses the inadequacy of metaphor or allegory to cope with intuition or idea; yet it remains capable of realistic sublimation and the reader's reward comes when he finds the patience to join Hopkins in his supreme exercise of the instinctive and scrutinizing faculties. Hopkins had his reasons for shrinking from the structural rationality of Aquinas and finding greater satisfaction in the pages of Augustine and Duns Scotus. Mallarmé, despite the allegory of the poet's defeat implied in the "Faune," maintains his sense of severe control, of persistent and fathoming lucidity, of a concentrating rigor that must finally arrive at perfect focus and penetration. Hopkins conveys a sense of restive agony and search of man as "law's indifference," of a passion for certitude frustrated by human limitation and doubt, of a rebellious failure to penetrate to his desired meaning except in momentary and miraculous flashes of intense lyric intuition. Mallarmé's is the imagery of intuitive intellection. Hopkins' is the imagery of experience. The two poets surpass their imitators by the intensity and scrupulous sincerity they brought to their radically different modes of elucidating the purpose and responsibility of poetry.

Stevens arrived at a harmonizing of their methods beyond what we get in most modern poets. His images have succeeded in balancing the intellectual and realistic implications of metaphor, and the limitations of his poetry, when compared with that of Eliot, Crane, and Tate, have been repaired by an exceptional felicity and fluent charm of imagistic artistry which those poets, whatever their superior capacities in thought and judgment, have not arrived at—have, indeed, often left to stand at the level of experimental or tentative mastery.

He arrived at this success by a remarkable amenity and confidence of imagination, apparent in the continuous exhilaration of early poems like "Ploughing on Sunday," "Disillusionment of Ten O'Clock," "The Emperor of Ice Cream," and "The Plot against the Giant." This sometimes has dwindled to sleight-of-hand meretriciousness in "Thirteen Ways of Looking at a Blackbird" and "New England Verses," or to the baroque decoration of "Anecdote of the Prince of Peacocks," "Tea at the Palaz of Hoon," and "Frogs Eat Butterflies," in which the imputation of a "tittery joke" is inescapable; sometimes it flowers into rootless blooms of sheer fantasy; but it shows at all times an easy, aristocratic self-assurance in grasping symbolic values and ultimately it made it possible for him with no stretching of phrases, straining of style, or forced intellection, to cover his astonishing amount of ground with an effect of fluent authority, as in the successive stanzas of "Sunday Morning" and "The Comedian." No recent poet has surpassed the effects of verbal luxuriance in these works; they describe an inexhaustible festival of the senses; their imagery of tropical splendor, aesthetic fastidiousness, and eccentric tastes spills on the page. It is a world of fat living and indulgent grossness, of surfeiting abundance, of Bakstian gorgeousness and barbaric pomp peculiarly symptomatic of the decadence and moral starvation of the pre-war years out of which this poetry grew. Melon-flowers, flaming birds, marguerites, coquelicots, roses, peacocks, parakeets, bananas, barbaric glass, rosy chocolate and gilt umbrellas, water-lights and fountains, forms, flames, and the flakes of flames come thick, and with these comes another order of richness—the effète elegance of privileged lives as indicated by rich furniture, yacht voyages, Florida winters, and superb houses, all of them indications, as Mr. Munson once said, of the passionate American drive toward comfort. That drive figures in Stevens' special animus as a poet, as Marianne Moore took hers from her passionate enthusiasm for scientific text-books, social histories, and natural phenomena, and Eliot his from his immersion in the phrases and figures of classical literatures. It is a world of

> visible, voluble delugings,
> which yet found means to set his simmering mind
> Spinning and hissing with oracular
> Notations of the wild, the ruinous waste.

But that waste hems this world in. Chaos, confusion, and decadence are its threats. The mindless disorder of nature surrounds the indulgent mind as it surrounds the jar in Tennessee. "The droning of the surf," "the disturbing vastness of ocean," the mystery of foam and cloud wherein "sultry moon-monsters are dissolving" set their mysterious dangers against any hope of passive content. The dim forms of primitive passion and terrifying fetish hover above the life of ease and privileged self-indulgence as they weigh upon the Sunday morning luxury of the emancipated woman; they make Crispin's journey a restive search for a way to live and to justify intelligence by. As the jar, imposed upon the wilderness, describes its principle of form and order, so the mind, eternally at odds with the vagaries of imagination, imposes its principle of reason, purpose, and law.

> The imagination, here, could not evade
> In poems of plums, the strict austerity
> Of one vast, subjugating, final tone.

Sanity and the discipline of reason thus assert their authority over "our bawdiness unpurged by epitaph" (*i.e.,* by the meaning of death) and also over that "imagination which is the will of things." "The arrant spices of the sun" demand control if they are to yield "an image that is sure." That image is for Stevens the ultimate object of a poet's search.

He sought it first in the vitality of the imagination; then, in the name of intelligence, among the mysteries of the sensory and subconscious life; he has finally come to extend his search in the direction of humane and political values in his effort to rescue from "this hoard of destruction, a picture of ourselves, now, an image of our society," that law of life and spirit which it is the duty of the artist (the man with the blue guitar) to pluck from the calamities and disorder of experience. Thus Stevens has condensed into his poems the history of human privilege, aggression, luxury, and social wealth, and the struggle of men to find—in religion, in art, in moral and ethical disciplines, in philosophic order—the law of intelligence by which man may be rescued from his damnation. The overpowering vitality of nature is opposed by the rigor of taste, of order, and of the moral principle. Abundance is opposed by the desperate anxiety of man's uncertain and dispossessed spirit. Surfeit is subjected to analysis. The massive splendor of nature and the reckless life of the senses are corrected by the inexorable and imperative demands of integrity and reason. The motive of *Harmonium* was once expressed in the sentence:

> Lend no part to any humanity that suffuses
> you in its own light,

but now that humanity is seen in its own desperate struggle against confusion, violence, and moral debilitation, the field of the poems has widened. The whole agony of society is accepted as a protest against the tyrannical theories and civilized confusions that threaten to defeat the purpose and dignity of man.

Stevens' poetry (the distinction is not peculiar to him; great poetry usually shows it and much of serious modern verse strongly emphasizes it) rests on a conscious antithesis of forces: of man against nature, of animal existence against intelligence, of mind against passion and appetite, of order against chaos, and it has been his task to concentrate these oppositions in "the image that is pure" against the confusions of man's phenomenal experience. The antithesis is capable of, and in a serious poet demands, wide application, and Stevens' latest extension of its meaning has taken the form of setting the autonomous values of art against the conditions of modern ordeal, where personality disintegrates into community, man into mass, intelligence into the heat of struggle and sympathy, aesthetic and intellectual judgment into the passions of social conflict. Yet the arc described by Stevens' development is not a mere "up and down between two elements," and he has not surrendered to "the malady of the quotidian." Where once he aimed to define the uses of privilege and the pleasures of art, he has now compelled art out of its superiority by demanding that its intelligence and value be conferred on the chaos of society. The idea of order is made vulnerable to the tests and proof of human necessity. The richness of Stevens' early images was saved from triviality and enervation by the balance of his taste and judgment—by his urbanity, wit, ironic humor, and by a quality of compassion which even his excessive sophistication never wholly concealed. Thus the heat and extravagance of sensory experience were corrected, not by Hopkins' rule of conscience and spiritual rigor, but by an ethic of prudence operating through the instruments of a civilized sense of human dignity and a scrupulous diffidence of temper. This prudence was not artificially induced; it was motivated by a sense of honor, a habit of intellectual search and analysis. The method of Mallarmé becomes here not so much a mode of discovering philosophical essences as a means of refining the values of taste and pride in order that they may become available to humanity. Aesthetic absolutes are compelled out of abstraction and made to come to terms with the real conditions of human existence.

Thus luxury met its test in spiritual necessity; opulence was checked by the needs of conscience. The universe itself was always, for Stevens, an intimate and confidential thing. Whether vast and ominous or concentrated to minute particulars, it has yielded its wealth and mystery to his perceptions. It was humanity that was abstract, complex, and elusive —an oddity, an enigma, and a minuscule. To make of man himself the instrument of knowledge and the medium of universal values became his task as a poet, and on that task he is still engaged. He pursues it with the great advantage of having seen man in his highest endowments of wit, pride, and imagination—an image waiting to realize its highest potentialities, an homunculus fit to contain the whole meaning of creation. As his absurdity begins to fall from him, his confusion to wane, and purpose in the universe to come clear, the doll begins to possess more than mere brain, taste, and humor; he emerges as an image of redeemed humanity. To make him that is Stevens' purpose as a poet, and he has brought to it one of the wittiest, most humane, and most original talents of our time.

MODERN POETRY

HERBERT READ

> "A warlike, various, and a tropical age is best to *write of,* but worst to write in."—COWLEY

FINALLY, we come to the modern phase. It might be asked, Is there a modern phase? Everything in the contemporary scene is so confused, tendencies seem so contradictory, there seem to be no fixed points to which we can relate the beginning or the end of a phase. I must admit, therefore, that there is a certain presumption in what I am going to say in this lecture, but I hope that presumption is one of historical method, not of contemporary prejudice.

The phases through which we have traced the development of Eng-

"Modern Poetry" from *Phases of English Poetry* by Herbert Read. Reprinted by permission of New Directions and Faber and Faber, Ltd.

lish poetry might be illustrated by a series of diagrams: in the first the
poet coincides with his circle; in the second he is a point within the circle;
in the third he is a point on the circumference; and finally he is a point
outside the circle. These are respectively the positions of the anonymous
creator of ballad poetry, the humanist poet (with whom, for this purpose,
we might associate the poets of love and sentiment), the religious poet, and
the romantic poet. The ballad poet is identical with the world he lives in.
The humanist poet is the nucleus of his world, the focus of intelligence and
intellectual progress. The religious poet lives at the periphery of his world
—at the point where his world is in contact with the infinite universe. The
romantic poet is his own universe; the world for him is either rejected
as unreal in favour of some phantom world, or is identified with the poet's
own feelings. The four phases complete a cycle, beginning with the world
as poet and ending with the poet as world. My presumption is that the
typical modern poet is aware of the completion of this cycle, and as a consequence either despairs of his function, or is desperately anxious to find
a way out of the state of eccentricity.

It is part of my general thesis that each of these phases of English
poetry can be related to a social background. It might be difficult to trace
a parallel development in poetry and history, since some phases of history
are without literary significance. The Industrial Revolution, for example,
though it profoundly affected the economy of daily life, has no corresponding phase in literature and art. It has transformed the diffusion of literature, but the more essential changes were due to the Social Revolution
which preceded, and the Scientific Movement which followed, this purely
economic catastrophe. It is not, however, any part of my purpose to investigate the social foundations of literature, because I believe that in general it is a fallacious mode of approach for the literary critic. Art transcends
the conditions that create it, and cannot therefore be explained by those
conditions. A condition of fear, it is said, created the first religion:

Primus in orbe Deos fecit timor. . . .[1]

But fear does not explain the nature of the gods that were created. Similarly, the rise of the novel may have been conditioned by the growth of
social democracy, but no analysis in economic terms will explain the evolution of the novel as a literary form. History and criticism are separate sciences; it is possible to throw bridges from one to the other, and a good
deal of enlightenment may pass across that way; but it is vain to imagine
that the two systems of knowledge can be completely fused and correlated.

---

[1] [Fear first made gods in the world.—STATIUS, *Theb.*, 3, 661.]

Nevertheless, when either history or literature fails us, then we can call in the knowledge of one as the basis of an hypothesis for the nature of the other. Our knowledge of Athenian society, for example, is to a great extent deduced from Greek literature—I do not mean in the obvious sense that Greek literature has supplied us with many of the details of Greek life, but in the general sense that the form and type of Greek literature correspond in ways which the historian must intuitively divine with the social habits of the people. I want now to suggest that we can gain some inkling of what is significant in modern poetry by the opposite process— by asking ourselves what form and type of literature might be expected to develop from the social conditions under which we live. Having formed some hypothesis by this method, it would then be simple to look for correspondences in the poetry of to-day.

It is not easy, of course, to describe our own society. It presents very different features to the London banker, the Welsh miner, the French peasant, and the American mechanic. But the problem is simplified for us because we are only concerned with the poet's point of view. The world is a sad place for a poet at any time. He is by nature abnormally sensitive. He is a point of intensest feeling thrown out like an antenna by the social body to test the amorphous limits of existence, the nature of "becoming." He is the advance-guard of experience. His reward is that the social body reacts to his sensitive register and adapts itself accordingly. The poet is then the representative man, the acknowledged type of his race. But to-day (I refer particularly to English conditions) the poet makes his signals to a numb and indifferent body. He is ignored. There has surely never been a period in our literary history when poetry was so little read and the poet so little recognised. There are poets who find a fickle or ephemeral public, but they generally suffer that worst pain and ignominy of *living* to see their work neglected and finally ignored. The last poet not to be regarded by the people at large as a social anomaly was Tennyson, and that was largely for reasons that had nothing to do with poetry.

There are two possible explanations: either society has surpassed the poet, and can now dispense with him; or the poet has developed his art beyond the limits of social usefulness. Both explanations imply a failure in the poet, and both are in a measure true. Tennyson's effort to write in the manner and with the energy of a national poet was on the whole a noble one, and is to be respected. His failure to achieve an epic tone—I would like to say an epic *tenor*—was simply that there was no epic to write within the categories of traditional poetry. Epics are never based on esoteric legend or any bookman's lore; they emerge from action, and take shape whilst the deeds they celebrate are still a lively reality to the general public.

The deeds that are celebrated must at least arouse some vibration in the complex recesses of national glory and self-awareness, King Arthur and his Knights are too remote, and Milton was wiser than Tennyson in rejecting this theme.

An epic is intimately related to the aspirations of its age, and almost every age has its epic, though we do not always recognise them as such. The *Prelude* is the last English epic; it is the epic of the man of feeling. When the modern epic comes to be written it will embody the aspirations of the age, though probably in a most unexpected manner. It will be unexpected because an age never recognizes its own portrait. Browning is the only nineteenth-century poet who in any way suggests an unexpected manner, though a contemporary poet has in part achieved one.

It was Browning's distinction to generalise and humanise the romantic individualism of Shelley and Wordsworth. He realised that the old poetic categories had become a store of musty and moth-eaten stage-properties. He was still a romantic, but he passed from the romantic naturalism of *Pippa Passes* to the romantic humanism of *Parleyings*. And yet it was a humanism very different from that of Chaucer and Spenser. The significant thing about Browning is that he invaded still another province in the interests of poetry; he showed that the psychological analysis of the motives underlying human conduct was full of dramatic possibilities, and because the atmosphere of such an analysis could not be conveyed by the accepted poetic diction, he invented a new poetic diction of his own. I am not sure that the originality of Browning's diction has yet been fully recognized, but it has been studied to some effect by modern poets, and though not many of them will be found to acknowledge their debt (in literature the son is always ashamed of his parents), there is nevertheless no denying certain premonitions of modernity in such lines as these:

> Tell him—I know not wherefore the true word
> Should fade and fall unuttered to the last—
> It was the name of him I sprang to meet
> When came the knock, the summons and the end.
> "My great heart, my strong hand are back again!"
> I would have sprung to these, beckoning across
> Murder and hell gigantic and distinct
> O' the threshold, posted to exclude me heaven:
> He is ordained to call and I to come!
> Do not the dead wear flowers when dressed for God?
> Say,—I am all in flowers from head to foot!
> Say,—not one flower of all he said and did,
> Might seem to flit unnoticed, fade unknown,
> But dropped a seed, has grown a balsam-tree

Whereof the blossoming perfumes the place
At this supreme of moments! . . .
The Ring and the Book, VII

What, then the long day dies at last? Abrupt.
The sun that seemed, in stooping, sure to melt
Our mountain ridge, is mastered: black the belt
Of westward crags, his gold could not corrupt,
Barriers again the valley, lest the flow
Of lavish glory waste itself away
—Whither? For new climes, fresh eyes, breaks the day!
Night was not to be baffled. If the glow
Were all that's gone from us! Did clouds, afloat
So filmily but now, discard no rose,
Sombre throughout the fleeciness that grows
A sullen uniformity. I note
Rather displeasure—in the overspread
Change from the swim of gold to one pale lead
Oppressive to malevolence—than late
Those amorous yearnings when the aggregate
Of cloudlets pressed that each and all might sate
Its passion and partake in relics red
Of day's bequeathment: now, a frown instead
Estranges, and affrights who needs must fare
On and on till his journey ends: but where?
Caucasus? Lost now in the night. Away
And far enough lies that Arcadia.
The human heroes tread the world's dark way
No longer. Yet I dimly see almost—
Yes, for my last adventure! 'Tis a ghost.
So drops away the beauty! There he stands
Voiceless, scare strives with deprecating hands.
                    Gerard de Lairesse

Many things have happened since Browning's heyday. Though it is
possible that his diction may have had some influence on modern poetry,
it is quite certain that his philosophy has had none. I myself now attach
more importance to Browning's philosophy than I did in the first edition
of this book; compared with Tennyson's, for example, it shows a wider
range of intelligence, and a mind less given to convention and prejudice.
His essay on the theory of poetry is a turgid document, but that is because
he did not know how to write prose. Nevertheless, his distinction between
the poet as "fashioner" (the objective poet) and the poet as "seer" (the
subjective poet) is a valid one. He surely regarded himself as a seer rather
than a fashioner, and writes of the subjective poet as one who "digs where
he stands," preferring to seek absolute truth in his own soul because he

regards his soul as "the nearest reflex of that absolute mind, according to the intuitions of which he desires to perceive and speak."

The modern poet is still a subjective poet, but he has been disillusioned. The last thing he is sure about is that his soul is a reflex of the absolute mind. So long as he remains a poet he must believe in an absolute truth, for what is his art but an attempt at absolute truth. But he now struggles without hope, or with the knowledge that the truth as he sees it is a private reality of his own. It might interest other people, and some might even be found to believe in it. But that position would savour too much of deception for the poet; he does not want other people to believe in his ideals, because ideals have made the world a waste land; and why should his ideals be more efficacious than those of other times?

This is not a pose in the modern poet. The modern poet is before all things honest. He does not write for fame, nor for money—he would be disappointed if he did. He merely writes to vent his own spleen, his own bitterness, his own sense of the disparity between the ugliness of the world that is and the beauty of the world that might be. He is trapped in a mechanical civilisation. Everywhere about him are steel cages, and the grinning futile faces of slaves. There is no beauty in the characteristic product of the age—machinery; that is a sentimental notion. There is no beauty in anything rational—only, at the best, the harmony of numbers. Beauty emerges from the unknown, often from the inane; it may be a combination of objective facts, but it is generally an irrational, an unforeseen combination. It may inhabit the sphere of intelligence, but it controls intelligence. It is the pattern of intelligence, but not intelligence itself.

The poet is not a direct product of civilisation. It cannot be maintained that the greater the civilisation, the greater will be its poets. The Roman civilisation was greater in scope and organisation and in general culture than the Greek civilisation, but no one but a bigoted Latinist would hold that the Latin poets were superior to the Greek. But a good civilisation gives the poet opportunities; it gives him security and leisure and all the conditions necessary for a life of contemplation, and gives him these without denying him the advantages of civilisation. Today the poet could only gain the conditions of contemplation by renouncing civilisation —by retiring to a hermitage or a desert island. To be part of our civilisation is to be part of its ugliness and haste and economic barbarism. It is to be a butterfly on the wheel.

But a poet is born. He is born in spite of the civilisation. When, therefore, he is born into his apathetic and hostile civilisation, he will react in the only possible way. He will become the poet of his own spleen, the victim of his own frustrated sense of beauty, the prophet of despair.

These are the characteristics which we might expect of modern poetry, starting merely from an objective consideration of the conditions under which the modern poet lives. And these are, in fact, the characteristics of that type of modern poetry which seems to me to be the only *typical* modern poetry.

In formal characteristics, modern poetry is a further development of Wordsworth's theory of poetic diction, as modified and corrected by Coleridge. Wordsworth's drift was all in the direction of sincerity of expression, and if his passion for sincerity drove him to such an exaggeration as that "there neither is nor can be any essential difference between the language of prose and metrical composition," it really only remained for Coleridge to point out that there were two kinds of sincerity, the one proceeding from impassioned meditation and possessing the rhythm and originality of creative expression, the other proceeding from rational observation, and possessing the evenness and clarity of logical and informative expression. Wordsworth was right in spirit, and his influence was fundamental and revolutionary; it is impossible to conceive the development of English poetry during the last century without Wordsworth. The implications of his theory are only now in the process of being worked out; Browning was a progress in one direction; the direction of flexibility, of making diction follow the subtleties of an unusual imaginative vision. But only within the last few years has the doctrine of sincerity in poetic diction been resumed with all Wordsworth's insistence.

Sincerity is only a word, a word of banal associations. But it is sometimes necessary to resort to such words, for in spite of their triteness, they often express profound truths which cannot very easily be conveyed in a more indirect manner. "To thine own self be true . . ." is more than a birthday sentiment or a New Year's resolution: it is the only fundamental principle of literature and of life. In life the lack or otherwise of this guiding principle divides all kinds of impostors—above all, those who impose on themselves—from real men, men whose word is apt to be their act, and whose actions are fair, free, and consistent. In literature this maxim is a universal criterion; it governs every kind of genuine expression, from the extreme of romantic naturalism to the extreme of impersonal classicism. Equally, whether describing the state of his own soul (the confused complex of his own feelings) or the exact lineaments of an object dispassionately observed, the writer, so long as he maintains the validity of his art, holds close to the description of his own immediate mental processes, and is in no sense influenced by considerations which have nothing to do with his immediate activity. He describes as he sees, and he thinks as he feels. (This is not to say, however, that he thinks *when* he feels; that would be to subordinate thought to feeling. I mean that thought, which has its own logical processes, pursues a path that always runs parallel to the process of feeling. Thought can at any moment be tested by reference to its accompanying state of sensibility. And, *vice versa,* a state of sensibility can always be tested by reference to its accompanying process of thought. Sensibility unaccompanied by thought is sentimentality.)

Wordsworth's sincerity effected a revolution in English poetic diction. Modern poetry has carried that revolution a step further. Wordsworth, in his effort to reach a perfectly natural and sincere mode of expression, rejected the artificial poetic diction of the eighteenth century and attempted to equate poetic diction with the natural diction of everyday speech. In this way he rejected too much: the language of poetry differs legitimately from the language of everyday speech, because it is the language of a heightened state of sensibility and, above all, because it is the language of a creative state of being. As we have seen, Coleridge corrected Wordsworth on this point, and the modern poet accepts Coleridge's position. But while Wordsworth rejected the artificial language of the old poetic convention, he somewhat inconsistently accepted the metrical conventions. It is true that his preference was for the simpler metrical schemes, and that he never thought of writing *The Prelude* in rhymed couplets. In a poem like *The Prelude* there is, in spite of the metre, a large amount of rhythmical composition which runs counter to the metrical scheme and is independent of it. For example:

> Ere we retired
> The cock had crowed, and now the eastern sky
> Was kindling, not unseen, from humble copse
> And open field, through which the pathway wound,
> And homeward led my steps. Magnificent
> The morning rose, in memorable pomp,
> Glorious as e'er I had beheld—in front,
> The sea lay laughing at a distance; near,
> The solid mountains shone, bright as the clouds,
> Grain-tinctured, drenched in empyrean light;
> And in the meadows and the lower grounds
> Was all the sweetness of a common dawn—
> Dews, vapours, and the melody of birds,
> And labourers going forth to till the fields.

It is perhaps no more than the old question of the scansion of blank verse, but my contention is that blank verse always tends to scan irregularly, and, generally speaking, that the more impassioned and poetic the verse becomes, the more irregular or "free" becomes the metre.

The modern poet has no uncompromising theory of metrical composition. His theory, if any, is that it is sufficient to be a poet and to be honest with one's self, and that the rest follows naturally. To be an extremist on the question of metre would be to repeat the mistake of Wordsworth on the question of language. The modern poet does not deny the right of regular verse to exist, or to be poetic. He merely affirms that poetry is sincerity, and has no essential alliance with regular schemes of any sort. He reserves the right to adapt his rhythm to his mood, to modulate his metre as he progresses. He may go further and maintain that this is what every great poet has done. It amuses him to see the academic scholar growing grey in the effort to explain away the irregularities of Shakespeare's blank verse. He knows that in its greatest moments there is no regularity in Shakespeare's verse, but only a tremendous sincerity, and a rhythm that is the rhythm of the emotional mood expressed, and not the rhythm of a regular scheme. Such lines as these, far from seeming inexplicable, are for him, in spite of their irregularity, the very perfection of poetic diction:

> ISABELLA. What says my brother?
> CLAUDIO. Death is a fearful thing.
> ISABELLA. And shamed life a hateful.
> CLAUDIO. Ay, but to die, and go we know not where;
> To lie in cold obstruction, and to rot:
> This sensible warm motion to become
> A kneaded clod; and the delighted spirit
> To bathe in fiery floods, or to reside
> In thrilling regions of thick-ribbed ice;
> To be imprison'd in the viewless winds,
> And blow with restless violence round about
> The pendent world; or to be worse than worst •
> Of those, that lawless and incertain thoughts
> Imagine howling!—'tis too horrible!
> The weariest and most loathed worldly life,
> That age, ache, penury, and imprisonment
> Can lay on nature, is a paradise
> To what we fear of death.
> ISABELLA. Alas, alas!
> CLAUDIO. Sweet sister, let me live:
> What sin you do to save a brother's life,
> Nature dispenses with the deed so far,
> That it becomes a virtue.
> ISABELLA. O, you beast!
> O faithless coward! O dishonest wretch!
> Wilt thou be made a man out of my vice?
> Is't not a kind of incest, to take life
> From thine own sister's shame? What should I think?
> Heaven shield, my mother play'd my father fair!

For such a warped slip of wilderness
Ne'er issued from his blood. Take my defiance:
Die; perish! might but my bending down
Reprieve thee from thy fate, it should proceed:
I'll pray a thousand prayers for thy death,
No word to save thee.
   CLAUDIO. Nay, hear me, Isabel.
   ISABELLA. O, fie, fie, fie!
Thy sin's not accidental, but a trade:
Mercy to thee would prove itself a bawd:
'Tis best that thou diest quickly.
   CLAUDIO. O, hear me, Isabella!
          Measure for Measure, III, 1

  Apart from the large number of irregular lines in this passage, there
is a wild irregularity of rhythm which quite submerges the ostensible blank-
verse form. With lines like these it is only necessary to compare examples
of authentic modern poetry to recognise an essential similarity, which is
their common sincerity:

A word then (for I will conquer it),
The word final, superior to all,
 Subtle, sent up—what is it?—I listen;
Are you whispering it, and have been all the time, you sea-waves?
Is that it from your liquid rims and wet sands?
Whereto answering, the sea,
Delaying not, hurrying not,
Whisper'd me through the night, and very plainly before daybreak,
Lisped to me the low and delicious word death,
And again, death, death, death, death,
Hissing melodious, neither like the bird nor like my arous'd child's heart,
But edging near as privately for me rustling at my feet,
Creeping thence steadily up to my ears and laving me softly all over,
Death, death, death, death, death.
      WALT WHITMAN

No, now I wish the sunshine would stop,
and the white shining houses, and the gay red flowers on the balconies
and the bluish mountains beyond, would be crushed out
between two valves of darkness;
the darkness falling, the darkness rising, with muffled sound
obliterating everything.
I wish that whatever props up the walls of light
would fall, and darkness would come hurling heavily down,
and it would be thick black dark for ever.
Not sleep which is grey with dreams,
nor death, which quivers with birth,
but heavy sealing darkness, silence, all immovable.
What is sleep?

It goes over me, like a shadow over a hill,
but it does not alter me, nor help me.
And death would ache still, I am sure;
it would be lambent, uneasy.
I wish it would be completely dark everywhere,
inside me, and out, heavily dark
utterly.

D. H. LAWRENCE

Eyes I dare not meet in dreams
In death's dream kingdom
There do not appear:
There, the eyes are
Sunlight on a broken column
There, is a tree swinging
And voices are
In the winds singing
More distant and more solemn
Than a fading star.

Let me be no nearer
In death's dream kingdom
Let me also wear
Such deliberate disguises
Rat's coat, crowskin, crossed staves
In a field
Behaving as the wind behaves
No nearer—
Not that final meeting
In the twilight kingdom.

T. S. ELIOT

What I have so far said about the principles of modern poetry may give the impression that it is or ought to be simple and artless in nature, the spontaneous expression of untrammelled minds. It might be so if nature and life were simple. Actually they are very complicated, and in his effort to render his feelings exactly the poet may be driven to a complicated utterance. It is a charge against much modern poetry that it is obscure. The answer to this charge is that it is not always possible to make a light out of darkness. By definition a poet is a being of abnormal sensibility, and the reactions of such a being to the complex problems of existence, both personal and universal, are sure to be of a complexity quite beyond the normal limits of expression. Where he cannot see clearly, the poet will be driven to divine intuitively, and to express himself analogically, by means of metaphor, symbol, and allegory. It would be possible to say, were the word not so debased, that he resorted to mysticism. In modern poetry, rather accidentally, the word "symbolism" has become associated with this mode of expression, and as a convenient label it will do as well as any other. It is more particularly associated, of course, with modern French poetry, and Stephane Mallarmé, and his disciple Paul Valéry, are typical representatives of this mode of poetic expression. We have seen in the last chapter how this school of poets has become associated with quite another question, the question of pure poetry. Valéry protested against this association; he preferred to be associated with mathematics, Leonardo da Vinci, and a portable typewriter. I suspect that his cynicism on this point hid a profounder conviction——a conviction, perhaps, that poetry has more to do with metaphysics than with abstract music. But I must not diverge into any further discussion of this quarrel, which is only remotely concerned with English poetry. I only wish to make the point that obscurity is not the same things as ignorance, and that indeed the obligation of sincerity to one's self does not stop at the limits of rational understanding, but pursues truth with all the resources of the human intelligence.

I do not pretend that sincerity can be attained without technical skill. Far otherwise. The technical demands of modern poetry are greater than those of traditional poetry. What, for example, are the problems which face the writer of a sonnet of the conventional form? He has a verse of a definite size: fourteen lines, each line of a definite number of feet. In addition, he has a scheme of rhymes. The form must be neatly filled; there must be no padding. He must begin with an arresting line, and his concluding couplet must clinch the movement and meaning of the whole poem. It is not easy; it is not every emotion or subject that will fit perfectly into the given form. But the true poet may be supposed to recognise intuitively the appropriateness of subject to form; and no doubt, especially in the matter of rhymes, he will find the given form inspiring him to happy elaborations of the theme.

Compare the situation of the modern poet. He rejects the sonnet and all other purely conventional forms, because he is convinced that he can give more exact expression to his subject without them; he distrusts the *arbitrariness* induced by the requisites of a fixed form. Far from seeking freedom and irresponsibility (implied by the unfortunate term *free verse*), he seeks a stricter discipline, which is the discipline of the exact concord to thought and feeling, the discipline of sincerity.

He himself knows when he has achieved this authenticity of expression, and every true appreciator of poetry knows it too. Modern poetry cannot have the superficial correctness of conventional poetry, and it is therefore more difficult to fill the conventional *rôle*. But the practice of free verse leaves room for a sufficient number of charlatans, and since they cannot be tested by a rule-of-thumb method, it is to be feared that they often enjoy an easy success with that large proportion of the readers of poetry who pay a superficial homage to the art. The appreciation of modern poetry demands a more than usual amount of attention and discrimination. You must test the modern poet as you would test your friends: by faith and familiarity and a perfect knowledge.

It would be arrogant to attempt to illustrate the insincerity of much modern poetry. I have already given specimens of the authentic kind, such as it reveals itself to my own sensibility. That should suffice. It is for each of us to follow the dictates of his own instincts and taste.

We are left with only one more question. It is this: How can the modern poet, in face of a hostile world, and with his doctrine of sincerity, find a means of reconciling his world and his art? How can he once more resume his function as the explorer and the educator of human sensibility?

It seems that there is only one ideal solution: it is that the poet should enter again into the first phase of the historical development of poetry, and become the insidious inspirer of a fresh communal poetry. There is no possibility of assuming the *rôle* of the humanist poet, who is the germinating point or nucleus of a renaissant world: the world of the poet is no longer in a state of cultural germination. Nor can he assume the *rôle* of the religious poet; his world is no longer religious in any profound or accepted sense. Nor can he assume the *rôle* of the idealistic or transcendental poet, for to renounce the world and aspire to unity with the spirit of nature or of the universe seems to him to be the vanity of vanities. How can he with any more hope expect to resume the original *rôle* of the poet, the *rôle* of the ballad-maker?

Not, at any rate, in the obvious way. The poet who nowadays aspires to write for the masses, to write poetry with the intention that it shall be read and adopted by the people at large, will find himself in the falsest of positions. Coppée or Jammes in France, Whitman and Sandburg in America, Edward Carpenter and Rudyard Kipling in England—these are our would-be popular poets. But how much does the populace care for them? Their poems sell well, no doubt, especially in the case of Coppée, Whitman, and Kipling. But the market is middle-class or bourgeois—students, teachers, and all the half-educated and palpitating devourers of tendencious literature. The real populace—the populace that sings "Tipperary" or "Keep the home fires burning," or "Roll out the barrel," or "Lili Marlene"—this populace ignores its self-appointed bards.

The only literature that is at the same time vital and popular is the literature of the music-hall, in which, of course, I include the broadcast variety.

I am not going to suggest that such literature as it at present exists is in any sense poetry. That would be a perverse and snobbish attitude. There is no poetry in "Tipperary" and "Keep the home fires burning"—there is only sentimentality. But it is just a possibility—and no more than a possibility —that the music-hall song and its allied forms—music-hall patter and revue libretto—contain the germ of a new popular poetry. (It is significant that the two poets who have been most influential in our time, T. S. Eliot and W. H. Auden, have both experimented with a poetry of this kind.) The danger of such a poetry is that it should be too derivative from the art which it should transcend—a criticism which I do not apply to Mr. Eliot's poems, which are surely a sardonic comment on the whole situation. I do not mean, however, that the poetry I am envisaging should take the elements of something which already exists in an immature state and give them the form and polish of a preconceived culture. That is quite the wrong method. The poet must instead divine the group-feeling or emotional complex out of which the music-hall song proceeds and which the music-hall song imperfectly satisfies (imperfectly because only temporarily). He must then create a poetry which not only satisfies the immediate emotional needs of the populace, but which also possesses those universal elements of thought and feeling that ensure permanency. It will not be an easy victory for any poet: it means a surrender of every personal standpoint, and a sacrifice of all pride of knowledge and exclusiveness of sensibility. And at present our very conceptions of the poet and the poet's activity presuppose a condition of pride and of isolation. Inwardly I feel that this life of the intelligence is the only reality, and that the art of poetry is the difficult art of defining the nature of mind and emotion—a veiled activity, leading the poet deep into the obscurities of the human heart. But this is my personal attitude; more dispassionately I recognise that poetry can never again become a popular art until this research is abandoned and the poet gives himself wholly to "the cadence of consenting feet."

2. *Fiction*

PATTERN AND RHYTHM

E. M. FORSTER

Oᴜʀ interludes, gay and grave, are over, and we return to the general scheme of the course. We began with the story, and having considered human beings, we proceeded to the plot which springs out of the story. Now we must consider something which springs mainly out of the plot, and to which the characters and any other element present also contribute. For this new aspect there appears to be no literary word—indeed the more the arts develop the more they depend on each other for definition. We will borrow from painting first and call it the pattern. Later we will borrow from music and call it rhythm. Unfortunately both these words are vague—when people apply rhythm or pattern to literature they are apt not to say what they mean and not to finish their sentences: it is, "Oh, but surely the rhythm . . ." or "Oh, but if you call that pattern . . ."

Before I discuss what pattern entails, and what qualities a reader must bring to its appreciation; I will give two examples of books with patterns so definite that a pictorial image sums them up: a book the shape of an hour-glass and a book the shape of a grand chain in that old-time dance, the Lancers.

Thais, by Anatole France, is the shape of an hour-glass.

There are two chief characters, Paphnuce the ascetic, Thais the courtesan. Paphnuce lives in the desert, he is saved and happy when the book starts. Thais leads a life of sin in Alexandria, and it is his duty to save her. In the central scene of the book they approach, he succeeds; she goes into a monastery and gains salvation, because she has met him, but he, because he has met her, is damned. The two characters converge, cross, and recede with mathematical precision, and part of the pleasure we get from

---

the book is due to this. Such is the pattern of *Thais*—so simple that it makes a good starting-point for a difficult survey. It is the same as the story of *Thais,* when events unroll in their time-sequence, and the same as the plot of *Thais,* when we see the two characters bound by their previous actions and taking fatal steps whose consequence they do not see. But whereas the story appeals to our curiosity and the plot to our intelligence, the pattern appeals to our aesthetic sense, it causes us to see the book as a whole. We do not see it as an hour-glass—that is the hard jargon of the lecture room which must never be taken literally at this advanced stage of our enquiry. We just have a pleasure without knowing why, and when the pleasure is past, as it is now, and our minds are left free to explain it, a geometrical simile such as an hour-glass will be found helpful. If it was not for this hour-glass the story, the plot, and the characters of Thais and Paphnuce would none of them exert their full force, they would none of them breathe as they do. "Pattern," which seems so rigid, is connected with atmosphere, which seems so fluid.

Now for the book that is shaped like the grand chain: *Roman Pictures* by Percy Lubbock.

Roman Pictures is a social comedy. The narrator is a tourist in Rome; he there meets a kindly and shoddy friend of his, Deering, who rebukes him superciliously for staring at churches and sets him out to explore society. This he does, demurely obedient; one person hands him on to another; café, studio, Vatican and Quirinal purlieus are all reached, until finally, at the extreme end of his career he thinks, in a most aristocratic and dilapidated palazzo, whom should he meet but the second-rate Deering; Deering is his hostess's nephew, but had concealed it owing to some backfire of snobbery. The circle is complete, the original partners have rejoined, and greet one another with mutual confusion which turns to mild laughter.

What is so good in *Roman Pictures* is not the presence of the "grand chain" pattern—any one can organize a grand chain—but the suitability of the pattern to the author's mood. Lubbock works all through by administering a series of little shocks, and by extending to his characters an elaborate charity which causes them to appear in a rather worse light than if no charity was wasted on them at all. It is the comic atmosphere, but sub-acid, meticulously benign. And at the end we discover to our delight that the atmosphere has been externalized, and that the partners, as they click together in the marchesa's drawing-room, have done the exact thing which the book requires, which it required from the start, and have bound the scattered incidents together with a thread woven out of their own substance.

Thais and *Roman Pictures* provide easy examples of pattern; it is not often that one can compare a book to a pictorial object with any accuracy, though curves, etc., are freely spoken of by critics who do not quite know what they want to say. We can only say (so far) that pattern is an aesthetic aspect of the novel, and that though it may be nourished by anything in the novel—any character, scene, word—it draws most of its nourishment from the plot. We noted, when discussing the plot, that it added to itself the quality of beauty; beauty a little surprised at her own arrival: that upon its neat carpentry there could be seen, by those who cared to see, the figure of the Muse; that Logic, at the moment of finishing its own house, laid the foundation of a new one. Here, here is the point where the aspect called pattern is most closely in touch with its material; here is our starting point. It springs mainly from the plot, accompanies it like a light in the clouds, and remains visible after it has departed. Beauty is sometimes the shape of the book, the book as a whole, the unity, and our examination would be easier if it was always this. But sometimes it is not. When it is not I shall call it rhythm. For the moment we are concerned with pattern only.

Let us examine at some length another book of the rigid type, a book with a unity, and in this sense an easy book, although it is by Henry James. We shall see in it pattern triumphant, and we shall also be able to see the sacrifices an author must make if he wants his pattern and nothing else to triumph.

The Ambassadors, like *Thais,* is the shape of an hour-glass. Strether and Chad, like Paphnuce and Thais, change places, and it is the realization of this that makes the book so satisfying at the close. The plot is elaborate and subtle, and proceeds by action or conversation or meditation through every paragraph. Everything is planned, everything fits; none of the minor characters are just decorative like the talkative Alexandrians at Nicias' banquet; they elaborate on the main theme, they work. The final effect is pre-arranged, dawns gradually on the reader, and is completely successful when it comes. Details of intrigue, of the various missions from America, may be forgotten, but the symmetry they have created is enduring.

Let us trace the growth of this symmetry.[1]

Strether, a sensitive middle-aged American, is commissioned by his old friend, Mrs. Newsome, whom he hopes to marry, to go to Paris and rescue her son Chad, who has gone to the bad in that appropriate city. The Newsomes are sound commercial people, who have made money over manufacturing a small article of domestic utility. Henry James never tells

---

[1] There is a masterly analysis of *The Ambassadors* from another standpoint in *The Craft of Fiction.*

us what the small article is, and in a moment we shall understand why. Wells spits it out in *Tono Bungay,* Meredith reels it out in *Evan Harrington,* Trollope prescribes it freely for Miss Dunstable, but for James to indicate how his characters made their pile—it would not do. The article is somewhat ignoble and ludicrous—that is enough. If you choose to be coarse and daring and visualize it for yourself as, say, a button-hook, you can, but you do so at your own risk; the author remains uninvolved.

Well, whatever it is, Chad Newsome ought to come back and help make it, and Strether undertakes to fetch him. He has to be rescued from a life which is both immoral and unremunerative.

Strether is a typical James character—he recurs in nearly all the books and is an essential part of their construction. He is the observer who tries to influence the action, and who through his failure to do so gains extra opportunities for observation. And the other characters are such as an observer like Strether is capable of observing—through lenses procured from a rather too first-class oculist. Everything is adjusted to his vision, yet he is not a quietist—no, that is the strength of the device; he takes us along with him, we move as well as look on.

When he lands in England (and a landing is an exalted and enduring experience for James, it is as vital as Newgate for Defoe; poetry and life crowd round a landing): when Strether lands, though it is only old England, he begins to have doubts of his mission, which increase when he gets to Paris. For Chad Newsome, far from going to the bad, has improved; he is distinguished, he is so sure of himself that he can be kind and cordial to the man who has orders to fetch him away; his friends are exquisite, and as for "women in the case" whom his mother anticipated, there is no sign of them whatever. It is Paris that has enlarged and redeemed him—and how well Strether himself understands this!

His greatest uneasiness seemed to peep at him out of the possible impression that almost any acceptance of Paris might give one's authority away. It hung before him this morning, the vast bright Babylon, like some huge iridescent object, a jewel brilliant and hard, in which parts were not to be discriminated nor differences comfortably marked. It twinkled and trembled and melted together; and what seemed all surface one moment seemed all depth the next. It was a place of which, unmistakably, Chad was fond; wherefore, if he, Strether, should like it too much, what on earth, with such a bond, would become of either of them?

Thus, exquisitely and firmly, James sets his atmosphere—Paris irradiates the book from end to end, it is an actor though always unembodied, it is a scale by which human sensibility can be measured, and when we

have finished the novel and allow its incidents to blur that we may see
the pattern plainer, it is Paris that gleams at the centre of the hour-glass
shape—Paris—nothing so crude as good or evil. Strether sees this soon,
and sees that Chad realizes it better than he himself can; and when he
has reached this stage of initiation the novel takes a turn: there is, after
all, a woman in the case; behind Paris, interpreting it for Chad, is the
adorable and exalted figure of Mme. de Vionnet. It is now impossible for
Strether to proceed. All that is noble and refined in life concentrates in
Mme. de Vionnet and is reinforced by her pathos. She asks him not to
take Chad away. He promises—without reluctance, for his own heart has
already shown him as much—and he remains in Paris not to fight it but
to fight for it.

For the second batch of ambassadors now arrives from the New
World. Mrs. Newsome, incensed and puzzled by the unseemly delay, has
despatched Chad's sister, his brother-in-law, and Mamie, the girl whom
he is supposed to marry. The novel now becomes, within its ordained
limits, most amusing. There is a superb set-to between Chad's sister and
Mme. de Vionnet, while as for Mamie—here is disastrous Mamie, seen
as we see all things, through Strether's eyes.

As a child, as a "bud," and then again as a flower of expansion, Mamie
had bloomed for him, freely, in the almost incessantly open doorway of home;
where he remembered her at first very forward, as then very backward—for
he had carried on at one period, in Mrs. Newsome's parlours, a course of
English literature reinforced by exams and teas—and once more, finally, as
very much in advance. But he had kept no great sense of points of contact; it
not being in the nature of things at Woollett that the freshest of the buds should
find herself in the same basket with the most withered of the winter apples.
. . . He none the less felt now, as he sat with the charming girl, the signal
growth of a confidence. For she *was* charming, when all was said, and none the
less so for the visible habit and practice of freedom and fluency. She was
charming, he was aware, in spite of the fact that if he hadn't found her so he
would have found her something he should have been in peril of expressing
as "funny." Yes, she was funny, wonderful Mamie, and without dreaming it;
she was bland, she was bridal—with never, that he could make out as yet, a
bridegroom to support it; she was handsome and portly, and easy and chatty,
soft and sweet and almost disconcertingly reassuring. She was dressed, if we
might so far discriminate, less as a young lady than as an old one—had an
old one been supposable to Strether as so committed to vanity; the complexities
of her hair missed moreover also the looseness of youth; and she had a mature
manner of bending a little, as to encourage and reward, while she held neatly
in front of her a pair of strikingly polished hands: the combination of all of
which kept up about her the glamour of her "receiving," placed her again perpetually between the windows and within sound of the ice cream plates, suggested the enumeration of all the names, gregarious specimens of a single type,
she was happy to "meet."

Mamie! She is another Henry James type; nearly every novel contains a Mamie—Mrs. Gereth in *The Spoils of Poynton* for instance, or Henrietta Stackpole in *The Portrait of a Lady*. He is so good at indicating instantaneously and constantly that a character is second rate, deficient in sensitiveness, abounding in the wrong sort of worldliness; he gives such a character so much vitality that its absurdity is delightful.

So Strether changes sides and loses all hope of marrying Mrs. Newsome. Paris is winning—and then he catches sight of something new. Is not Chad, as regards any fineness in him, played out? Is not Chad's Paris after all just a place for a spree? This fear is confirmed. He goes for a solitary country walk, and at the end of the day he comes across Chad and Mme. de Vionnet. They are in a boat, they pretend not to see him, because their relation is at bottom an ordinary liaison, and they are ashamed. They were hoping for a secret week-end at an inn while their passion survived; for it will not survive, Chad will tire of the exquisite Frenchwoman, she is part of his fling; he will go back to his mother and make the little domestic article and marry Mamie. They know all this, and it is revealed to Strether though they try to hide it; they lie, they are vulgar—even Mme. de Vionnet, even her pathos, once so exquisite, is stained with commonness.

It was like a chill in the air to him, it was almost appalling, that a creature so fine could be, by mysterious forces, a creature so exploited. For, at the end of all things, they *were* mysterious; she had but made Chad what he was—so why could she think she had made him infinite? She had made him better, she had made him best, she had made him anything one would; but it came to our friend with supreme queerness that he was none the less only Chad. The work, however admirable, was nevertheless of the strict human order, and in short it was marvellous that the companion of mere earthly joys, of comforts, aberrations—however one classed them—within the common experience, should be so transcendently prized.

She was older for him tonight, visibly less exempt from the touch of time; but she was as much as ever the finest and subtlest creature, the happiest apparition, it had been given him, in all his years, to meet; and yet he could see her there as vulgarly troubled, in very truth, as a maidservant crying for a young man. The only thing was that she judged herself as the maidservant wouldn't; the weakness of which wisdom too, the dishonour of which judgment, seemed but to sink her lower.

So Strether loses them too. As he says: "I have lost everything—it is my only logic." It is not that they have gone back. It is that he has gone on. The Paris they revealed to him—he could reveal it to them now, if they had eyes to see, for it is something finer than they could ever notice for themselves, and his imagination has more spiritual value than their youth. The pattern of the hour-glass is complete; he and Chad have changed places, with more subtle steps than Thais and Paphnuce, and the light in the clouds proceeds not from the well-lit Alexandria, but from the jewel which "twinkled and trembled and melted together, and what seemed all surface one moment seemed all depth the next."

The beauty that suffuses *The Ambassadors* is the reward due to a fine artist for hard work. James knew exactly what he wanted, he pursued the narrow path of aesthetic duty, and success to the full extent of his possibilities has crowned him. The pattern has woven itself with modulation and reservations Anatole France will never attain. Woven itself wonderfully. But at what sacrifice!

So enormous is the sacrifice that many readers cannot get interested in James, although they can follow what he says (his difficulty has been much exaggerated), and can appreciate his effects. They cannot grant his premise, which is that most of human life has to disappear before he can do us a novel.

He has, in the first place, a very short list of characters. I have already mentioned two—the observer who tries to influence the action, and the second-rate outsider (to whom, for example, all the brilliant opening of *What Maisie Knew* is entrusted). Then there is the sympathetic foil—very lively and frequently female—in *The Ambassadors;* Maria Gostrey plays this part. There is the wonderful rare heroine, whom Mme. de Vionnet approached and who is consummated by Milly in *The Wings of the Dove:* there is sometimes a villain, sometimes a young artist with generous impulses; and that is about all. For so fine a novelist it is a poor show.

In the second place, the characters, beside being few in number, are constructed on very stingy lines. They are incapable of fun, of rapid motion, of carnality, and of nine-tenths of heroism. Their clothes will not take off, the diseases that ravage them are anonymous, like the sources of their income, their servants are noiseless or resemble themselves, no social explanation of the world we know is possible for them, for there are no stupid people in their world, no barriers of language, and no poor. Even their sensations are limited. They can land in Europe and look at works of art and at each other, but that is all. Maimed creatures can alone breathe in Henry James's pages—maimed yet specialized. They remind one of the exquisite deformities who haunted Egyptian art in the reign of Akhenaton—huge heads and tiny legs, but nevertheless charming. In the following reign they disappear.

Now this drastic curtailment, both of the numbers of human beings and of their attributes, is in the interest of the pattern. The longer James worked, the more convinced he grew that a novel should be a whole—

not necessarily geometric like *The Ambassadors,* but it should accrete round a single topic, situation, gesture, which should occupy the characters and provide a plot, and should also fasten up the novel on the outside —catch its scattered statements in a net, make them cohere like a planet, and swing through the skies of memory. A pattern must emerge, and anything that emerged from the pattern must be pruned off as wanton distraction. Who so wanton as human beings? Put Tom Jones or Emma or even Mr. Casaubon into a Henry James book, and the book will burn to ashes, whereas we could put them into one another's books and only cause local inflammation. Only a Henry James character will suit, and though they are not dead—certain selected recesses of experience he explores very well —they are gutted of the common stuff that fills characters in other books, and ourselves. And this castrating is not in the interests of the Kingdom of Heaven, there is no philosophy in the novels, no religion (except an occasional touch of superstition), no prophecy, no benefit for the superhuman at all. It is for the sake of a particular aesthetic effect which is certainly gained, but at this heavy price.

H. G. Wells has been amusing on this point, and perhaps profound. In *Boon*—one of his liveliest works—he had Henry James much upon his mind, and wrote a superb parody of him.

James begins by taking it for granted that a novel is a work of art that must be judged by its oneness. Some one gave him that idea in the beginning of things and he has never found it out. He doesn't find things out. He doesn't even seem to want to find things out. He accepts very readily and then—elaborates. . . . The only living human motives left in his novels are a certain avidity and an entirely superficial curiosity. . . . His people nose out suspicions, hint by hint, link by link. Have you ever known living human beings do that? The thing his novel is *about* is always there. It is like a church lit but with no congregation to distract you, with every light and line focussed on the high altar. And on the altar, very reverently placed, intensely there, is a dead kitten, an egg shell, a piece of string . . . Like his *Altar of the Dead* with nothing to the dead at all. . . . For if there was, they couldn't all be candles, and the effect would vanish.

Wells sent *Boon* as a present to James, apparently thinking the master would be as much pleased by such heartiness and honesty as was he himself. The master was far from pleased, and a most interesting correspondence ensued.[1] Each of the eminent men becomes more and more himself as it proceeds. James is polite, reminiscent, bewildered, and exceedingly formidable; he admits that the parody has not "filled him with a fond elation," and regrets in conclusion that he can sign himself "only yours

---

[1] See the *Letters of H. James,* Vol. II.

faithfully, Henry James." Wells is bewildered too, but in a different way; he cannot understand why the man should be upset. And, beyond the personal comedy, there is the great literary importance of the issue. It is this question of the rigid pattern: hour-glass or grand chain or converging lines of the cathedral or diverging lines of the Catherine wheel, or bed of Procrustes—whatever image you like as long as it implies unity. Can it be combined with the immense richness of material which life provides? Wells and James would agree it cannot, Wells would go on to say that life should be given the preference, and must not be whittled or distended for a pattern's sake. My own prejudices are with Wells. The James novels are a unique possession and the reader who cannot accept his premises misses some valuable and exquisite sensations. But I do not want more of his novels, especially when they are written by some one else, just as I do not want the art of Akhenton to extend into the reign of Tutankhamen.

That then is the disadvantage of a rigid pattern. It may externalize the atmosphere, spring naturally from the plot, but it shuts the doors on life and leaves the novelist doing exercises, generally in the drawing-room. Beauty has arrived, but in too tyrannous a guise. In plays—the plays of Racine, for instance—she may be justified because beauty can be a great empress on the stage, and reconcile us to the loss of the men we knew. But in the novel, her tyranny as it grows powerful grows petty, and generates regrets which sometimes take the form of books like *Boon*. To put it in other words, the novel is not capable of as much artistic development as the drama: its humanity or the grossness of its material hinder it (use whichever phrase you like). To most readers of fiction the sensation from a pattern is not intense enough to justify the sacrifices that made it, and their verdict is "Beautifully done, but not worth doing."

Still this is not the end of our quest. We will not give up the hope of beauty yet. Cannot it be introduced into fiction by some other method than the pattern? Let us edge rather nervously towards the idea of "rhythm."

Rhythm is sometimes quite easy. Beethoven's Fifth Symphony, for instance, starts with the rhythm "diddidy dum," which we can all hear and tap to. But the symphony as a whole has also a rhythm—due mainly to the relation between its movements—which some people can hear but no one can tap to. This second sort of rhythm is difficult, and whether it is substantially the same as the first sort only a musician could tell us. What a literary man wants to say though is that the first kind of rhythm, the diddidy dum, can be found in certain novels and may give them beauty. And the other rhythm, the difficult one—the rhythm of the Fifth Symphony as a whole—I cannot quote you any parallels for that in fiction, yet it may be present.

Rhythm in the easy sense, is illustrated by the work of Marcel Proust.[1]

Proust's conclusion has not been published yet, and his admirers say that when it comes everything will fall into its place, times past will be recaptured and fixed, we shall have a perfect whole. I do not believe this. The work seems to me a progressive rather than an aesthetic confession, and with the elaboration of Albertine the author was getting tired. Bits of news may await us, but it will be surprising if we have to revise our opinion of the whole book. The book is chaotic, ill constructed, it has and will have no external shape; and yet it hangs together because it is stitched internally, because it contains rhythms.

There are several examples (the photographing of the grandmother is one of them) but the most important from the binding point of view is his use of the "little phrase" in the music of Vinteuil. It does more than anything else—more even than the jealousy which successively destroys Swann, the hero, and Charlus—to make us feel that we are in a homogeneous world. We first hear Vinteuil's name in hideous circumstances. The musician is dead—an obscure little country organist, unknown to fame —and his daughter is defiling his memory. The horrible scene is to radiate in several directions, but it passes, we forget about it.

Then we are at a Paris salon. A violin sonata is performed and a little phrase from its andante catches the ear of Swann and steals into his life. It is always a living being, but takes various forms. For a time it attends his love for Odette. The love affair goes wrong, the phrase is forgotten, we forget it. Then it breaks out again when he is ravaged by jealousy, and now it attends his misery and past happiness at once, without losing its own divine character. Who wrote the sonata? On hearing it is Vinteuil, Swann says, "I once knew a wretched little organist of that name—it couldn't be by him." But it is, and Vinteuil's daughter and her friend transcribed and published it.

That seems all. The little phrase crosses the book again and again, but as an echo, a memory; we like to encounter it, but it has no binding power. Then, hundreds and hundreds of pages on, when Vinteuil has become a national possession, and there is talk of raising a statue to him in the town where he has been so wretched and so obscure, another work of his is performed—a posthumous sextet. The hero listens—he is in an unknown rather terrible universe while a sinister dawn reddens the sea. Suddenly

---

[1] The first three books of *A la recherche du temps perdu* have been excellently translated by C. K. Scott Moncrieff under the title of *Remembrance of Things Past*. (A. & C. Boni.) [*Remembrance of Things Past* has, of course, now appeared in its entirety in English.]

for him and for the reader too, the little phrase of the sonata recurs—half heard, changed, but giving complete orientation, so that he is back in the country of his childhood with the knowledge that it belongs to the unknown.

We are not obliged to agree with Proust's actual musical descriptions (they are too pictorial for my own taste): but what we must admire is his use of rhythm in literature, and his use of something which is akin by nature to the effect it has to produce—namely a musical phrase. Heard by various people—first by Swann, then by the hero—the phrase of Vinteuil is not tethered; it is not a banner such as we find George Meredith using— a double-blossomed cherry tree to accompany Clara Middleton, a yacht in smooth waters for Cecilia Halkett. A banner can only reappear, rhythm can develop, and the little phrase has a life of its own, unconnected with the lives of its auditors, as with the life of the man who composed it. It is almost an actor, but not quite, and that "not quite" means that its power has gone towards stitching Proust's book together from the inside, and towards the establishment of beauty and the ravishing of the reader's memory. There are times when the little phrase—from its gloomy inception, through the Sonata into the sextet—means everything to the reader. There are times when it means nothing and is forgotten, and this seems to me the function of rhythm in fiction; not to be there all the time like a pattern, but by its lovely waxing and waning to fill us with surprise and freshness and hope.

Done badly, rhythm is most boring, it hardens into a symbol and instead of carrying us on it trips us up. With exasperation we find that Galsworthy's spaniel John, or whatever it is, lies under the feet again; and even Meredith's cherry trees and yachts, graceful as they are, only open the windows into poetry. I doubt that it can be achieved by the writers who plan their books beforehand, it has to depend on a local impulse when the right interval is reached. But the effect can be exquisite, it can be obtained without mutilating the characters, and it lessens our need of an external form.

That must suffice on the subject of easy rhythm in fiction: which may be defined as repetition plus variation, and which can be illustrated by examples. Now for the more difficult question. Is there any effect in novels comparable to the effect of the Fifth Symphony as a whole, where, when the orchestra stops, we hear something that has never actually been played? The opening movement, the andante, and the trio-scherzo-trio-finale-trio-finale that composes the third block, all enter the mind at once, and extend one another into a common entity. This common entity, this new thing, is the symphony as a whole, and it has been achieved mainly (though not entirely) by the relation between the three big blocks of sound which the orchestra has been playing. I am calling this relation "rhythmic." If the correct musical term is something else, that does not matter; what we have now to ask ourselves is whether there is any analogy to it in fiction.

I cannot find any analogy. Yet there may be one; in music fiction is likely to find its nearest parallel.

The position of the drama is different. The drama may look towards the pictorial arts, it may allow Aristotle to discipline it, for it is not so deeply committed to the claims of human beings. Human beings have their great chance in the novel. They say to the novelist: "Recreate us if you like, but we must come in," and the novelist's problem, as we have seen all along, is to give them a good run and to achieve something else at the same time. Whither shall he turn? not indeed for help but for analogy. Music, though it does not employ human beings, though it is governed by intricate laws, nevertheless does offer in its final expression a type of beauty which fiction might achieve in its own way. Expansion. That is the idea the novelist must cling to. Not completion. Not rounding off but opening out. When the symphony is over we feel that the notes and tunes composing it have been liberated, they have found in the rhythm of the whole their individual freedom. Cannot the novel be like that? Is not there something of it in *War and Peace?*—the book with which we began and in which we must end. Such an untidy book. Yet, as we read it, do not great chords begin to sound behind us, and when we have finished does not every item—even the catalogue of strategies—lead a larger existence than was possible at the time?

MADAME BOVARY

PERCY LUBBOCK

IF Flaubert allows himself the liberty of telling his story in various ways—with a method, that is to say, which is often modified as he proceeds—it is likely that he has good cause to do so. Weighing every word and calculating every effect so patiently, he could not have been casual and careless over

"Madame Bovary" from *Craft of Fiction,* by Percy Lubbock. Reprinted by permission of Peter Smith, publisher.

his method; he would not take one way rather than another because it saved him trouble, or because he failed to notice that there were other ways, or because they all seemed to him much the same. And yet at first it does seem that his manner of arriving at his subject—if his subject is Emma Bovary —is considerably casual. He begins with Charles, of all people—Charles, her husband, the stupid soul who falls heavily in love with her prettiness and never has the glimmer of an understanding of what she is; and he begins with the early history of Charles, and his upbringing, and the irrelevant first marriage that his mother forces upon him, and his widowhood; and then it happens that Charles has a professional visit to pay to a certain farm, the farmer's daughter happens to be Emma, and so we finally stumble upon the subject of the book. Is that the neatest possible mode of striking it? But Flaubert seems to be very sure of himself, and it is not uninteresting to ask exactly what he means.

As for his subject, it is of course Emma Bovary in the first place; the book is the portrait of a foolish woman, romantically inclined, in small and prosaic conditions. She is in the centre of it all, certainly; there is no doubt of her position in the book. But *why* is she there? The true subject of the novel is not given, as we saw, by a mere summary of the course which is taken by the story. She may be there for her own sake, simply, or for the sake of the predicament in which she stands; she may be presented as a curious scrap of character, fit to be studied; or Flaubert may have been struck by her as the instrument, the victim, the occasion, of a particular train of events. Perhaps she is a creature portrayed because he thinks her typical and picturesque; perhaps she is a disturbing little force let loose among the lives that surround her; perhaps, on the other hand, she is a hapless sufferer in the clash between her aspirations and her fate. Given Emma and what she is by nature, given her environment and the facts of her story, there are dozens of different subjects, I daresay, latent in the case. The woman, the men, all they say and do, the whole scene behind them— none of it gives any clue to the right manner of treating them. The one irreducible idea out of which the book, as Flaubert wrote it, unfolds—this it is that must be sought.

Now if Emma was devised for her own sake, solely because a nature and a temper like hers seemed to Flaubert an amusing study—if his one aim was to make the portrait of a woman of that kind—then the rest of the matter falls into line, we shall know how to regard it. These conditions in which Emma finds herself will have been chosen by the author because they appeared to throw light on her, to call out her natural qualities, to give her the best opportunity of disclosing what she is. Her stupid husband and her fascinating lovers will enter the scene in order that she may become what-

ever she has it in her to be. Flaubert elects to place her in a certain provincial town, full of odd characters; he gives the town and its folk an extraordinary actuality; it is not a town *quelconque,*[1] not a generalized town,
but as individual and recognizable as he can make it. None the less—always
supposing that Emma by herself is the whole of his subject—he must have
lit on this particular town simply because it seemed to explain and expound her better than another. If he had thought that a woman of her sort,
rather meanly ambitious, rather fatuously romantic, would have revealed
her quality more intensely in a different world—in success, freedom, wealth
—he would have placed her otherwise; Charles and Rodolphe and Homard
and the rest of them would have vanished, the more illuminating set of circumstances (whatever they might be) would have appeared instead. Emma's world as it is at present, in the book that Flaubert wrote, would have
to be regarded accordingly, as all a *consequence* of Emma, invented to do
her a service, described in order that they may make the description of
her. Her world, that is to say, would belong to the treatment of the story;
none of it, not her husband, not the life of the market-town, would be a
part of the author's postulate, the groundwork of his fable; it would be
possible to imagine a different setting, better, it might be, than that which
Flaubert has chosen. All this—*if* the subject of the book is nothing but the
portrait of such a woman.

But of course it is not so; one glance at our remembrance of the book
is enough to show it. Emma's world could not be other than it is, she could
not be shifted into richer and larger conditions, without destroying the whole
point and purpose of Flaubert's novel. She by herself is not the subject of
his book. What he proposes to exhibit is the history of a woman like her in
just such a world as hers, a foolish woman in narrow circumstances; so
that the provincial scene, acting upon her, making her what she becomes,
is as essential as she is herself. Not a portrait, therefore, not a study of character for its own sake, but something in the nature of a drama, where the
two chief players are a woman on one side and her whole environment on
the other—that is Madame Bovary. There is a conflict, a trial of strength,
and a doubtful issue. Emma is not much of a force, no doubt; her impulses
are wild, her emotions are thin and poor, she has no power of passion with
which to fight the world. All she has is her romantic dream and her plain,
primitive appetite; but these can be effective arms, after all, and she may
yet succeed in getting her way and making her own terms. On the other
hand the limitations of her life are very blank and uncompromising indeed;
they close all round her, hampering her flights, restricting her opportuni-

---

[1] [Just any (town).]

ties. The drama is set, at any rate, whatever may come of it; Emma marries her husband, is established at Yonville and faced with the poverty of her situation. Something will result, the issue will announce itself. It is the mark of a dramatic case that it contains an opposition of some kind, a pair of wills that collide, an action that pulls in two directions; and so far Madame Bovary has the look of a drama. Flaubert might work on the book from that point of view and throw the emphasis on the issue. The middle of his subject would then be found in the struggle between Emma and all that constitutes her life, between her romantic dreams and her besetting facts. The question is what will happen.

But then again—that is not exactly the question in this book. Obviously the emphasis is not upon the commonplace little events of Emma's career. They might, no doubt, be the steps in a dramatic tale, but they are nothing of the kind as Flaubert handles them. He makes it perfectly clear that his view is not centred upon the actual outcome of Emma's predicament, whether it will issue this way or that; *what* she does or fails to do is of very small moment. Her passages with Rodolphe and with Leon are pictures that pass; they solve nothing, they lead to no climax. Rodolphe's final rejection of her, for example, is no scene of drama, deciding a question that has been held in suspense; it is one of Emma's various mischances, with its own marked effect with *her,* but it does not stand out in the book as a turning-point in the action. She goes her way and acts out her history; but of whatever suspense, whatever dramatic value, there might be in it Flaubert makes nothing, he evidently considers it of no account. Who, in recalling the book, thinks of the chain of incident that runs through it, compared with the long and living impression of a few of the people in it and of the place in which they are set? None of the events really matter for their own sake; they might have happened differently, not one of them is indispensable as it is. Emma must certainly have made what she could of her opportunities of romance, but they need not necessarily have appeared in the shape of Leon or Rodolphe; she would have found others if these had not been at hand. The *events,* therefore, Emma's excursions to Rouen, her forest-rides, her one or two memorable adventures in the world, all these are only Flaubert's way of telling his subject, of making it count to the eye. They are not in themselves what he has to say, they simply illustrate it.

What it comes to, I take it, is that though Madame Bovary, the novel, is a kind of drama—since there is the interaction of this woman confronted by these facts—it is a drama chosen for the sake of the picture in it, for the impression it gives of the manner in which certain lives are lived. It might have another force of its own; it might be a strife of the characters

and wills, in which the men and women would take the matter into their
own hands and make all the interest by their action; it might be a drama,
say, as Jane Eyre is a drama, where another obscure little woman has a
part to play, but where the question is how she plays it, what she achieves
or misses in particular. To Flaubert the situation out of which he made his
novel appeared in another light. It was not as dramatic as it was pictorial;
there was not the stuff in Emma, more especially that could make her the
main figure of a drama; she is small and futile, she could not well uphold
an interest that would depend directly on her behaviour. But for a picture, where the interest depends only on what she *is*—that is quite different. Her futility is then a real value; it can be made amusing and vivid
to the last degree, so long as no other weight is thrown on it; she can
make a perfect impression of life, though she cannot create much of a story.
Let Emma and her plight, therefore, appear as a picture; let her be shown
in the act of living her life, entangled as it is with her past and her present;
that is how the final fact at the heart of Flauberts' subject will be best
displayed.

Here is the clue, it seems, to his treatment of the theme. It is pictorial, and its object is to make Emma's existence as intelligible and visible
as may be. We who read the book are to share her sense of life, till no
uncertainty is left in it; and we are to see and understand her experience,
and see *her* while she enjoys or endures it; we are to be placed within her
world, to get the immediate taste of it, and outside her world as well, to get
the full effect, more of it than she herself could see. Flaubert's subject
demands no less, if the picture is to be complete. She herself must be
known thoroughly—that is his first care; the movement of her mind is to
be watched at work in all the ardour and the poverty of her imagination.
How she creates her makeshift romances, how she feeds on them, how
they fail her—it is all part of the picture. And then there is the dull and
limited world in which her appetite is somehow to be satisfied, the small
town that shuts her in and cuts her off; this, too, is to be rendered, and in
order to make it clearly tell beside the figure of Emma it must be as distinct and individual, as thoroughly characterized as she is. It is more than
a setting for Emma and her intrigue; it belongs to the book integrally,
much more so than the accidental lovers who fall in Emma's way. They
are mere occasions and attractions for her fancy; the town and the *curé*
and the apothecary and the other indigenous gossips need a sharper definition. And accordingly Flaubert treats the scenery of his book, Yonville
and its odd types, as intensely as he treats his heroine; he broods over it
with concentration and give it all the salience he can. The town with its
life is not behind his heroine, subdued in tone to make a background; it

is *with* her, no less fully to the front; its value in the picture is as strong as her own.

Such is the picture that Flaubert's book is to present. And what, then, of the point of view towards which it is to be directed? If it is to have that unity which it needs to produce its right effect there can be no uncertainty here, no arbitrary shifting of the place from which an onlooker faces it. And in the tale of Madame Bovary the question of the right point of view might be considerably perplexing. Where is Flaubert to find his centre of vision?—from what point, within the book or without, will the unfolding of the subject be commanded most effectively? The difficulty is this—that while one aspect of his matter can only be seen from within, through the eyes of the woman, another must inevitably be seen from without, through nobody's eyes but the author's own. Part of his subject is Emma's sense of her world; we must see how it impresses her and what she makes of it, how it thwarts her and how her imagination contrives to get a kind of sustenance out of it. The book is not really written at all unless it shows her view of things, as the woman she was, in that place, in those conditions. For this reason it is essential to pass into her consciousness, to make her *subjective;* and Flaubert takes care to do so and to make her so, as soon as she enters the book. But it is also enjoined by the story, as we found, that her place and conditions should be seen for what they are and known as intimately as herself. For this matter Emma's capacity fails.

Her intelligence is much too feeble and fitful to give a sufficient account of her world. The town of Yonville would be very poorly revealed to us if Flaubert had to keep within the measure of *her* perceptions; it would be thin and blank, it would be barely more than a dull background for the beautiful apparition of the men she desires. What were her neighbours to her? They existed in her consciousness only as tiresome interruptions and drawbacks, except now and then when she had occasion to make use of them. But to us, to the onlooker, they belong to her portrait, they represent the dead weight of provincial life which is the outstanding fact in her case. Emma's rudimentary idea of them is entirely inadequate; she has not a vestige of the humour and irony that is needed to give them shape. Moreover they affect her far more forcibly and more variously than she could even suspect; a sharper wit than hers must evidently intervene, helping out the primitive workings of her mind. Her pair of eyes is not enough; the picture beheld through them is a poor thing in itself, for she can see no more than her mind can grasp; and it does her no justice either, since she herself is so largely the creation of her surroundings.

It is a dilemma that appears in any story, wherever the matter to be represented is the experience of a simple soul or a dull intelligence. If it is the experience and the actual taste of it that is to be imparted, the story must be viewed as the poor creature saw it; and yet the poor creature cannot tell the story in full. A shift of the vision is necessary. And in Madame Bovary, it is to be noted, there is no one else within the book who is in a position to take up the tale when Emma fails. There is no other personage upon the scene who sees and understands any more than she; perception and discrimination are not to be found in Yonville at all—it is an essential point. The author's wit, therefore, and none other, must supply what is wanting. This necessity, to a writer of Flaubert's acute sense of effect, is one that demands a good deal of caution. The transition must be made without awkwardness, without calling attention to it. Flaubert is not the kind of storyteller who will leave it undisguised; he will not begin by "going behind" Emma, giving her view, and then openly, confessedly, revert to his own character and use his own standards. There is nothing more disconcerting in a novel than to *see* the writer changing his part in this way—throwing off the character into which he has been projecting himself and taking a new stand outside and away from the story.

Perhaps it is only Thackeray, among the great, who seems to find a positively wilful pleasure in damaging his own story by open maltreatment of this kind; there are times when Thackery will even boast of his own independence, insisting in so many words on his freedom to say what he pleases about his men and woman and to make them behave as he will. But without using Thackeray's licence a novelist may still do his story an ill turn by leaving too naked a contrast between the subject we picture of what passes through Emma's mind—Emma's or Becky's, as it may be—and the objective rendering of what he sees for himself, between the experience that is mirrored in another thought and that which is shaped in his own. When one has lived *into* the experience of somebody in the story and received the full sense of it, to be wrenched out of the story and stationed at a distance is a shock that needs to be softened and muffled in some fashion. Otherwise it may weaken whatever was true and valid in the experience; for here is a new view of it, external and detached, and another mind at work, the author's—and that sense of having shared the life of the person in the story seems suddenly unreal.

Flaubert's way of disguising the inconsistency is not a peculiar art of his own, I dare say. Even in him it was probably quite unconscious, well as he was aware of most of the refinements of his craft; and perhaps it is only a sleight of hand that might come naturally to any good story-teller. But it is interesting to follow Flaubert's method to the very end, for it holds out so consummately; and I think it is possible to define it here. I should say, then, that he deals with the difficulty I have described by keeping Emma always at a certain distance, even when he appears to be entering her mind most freely. He makes her subjective, places us so that we see her through her eyes—yes; but he does so with an air of aloofness that forbids us ever to become entirely identified with her. This is how she thought and felt, he seems to say; look and you will understand; such is the soul of this foolish woman. A hint of irony is always perceptible, and it is enough to prevent us from being lost in her consciousness, immersed in it beyond easy recall. The woman's life is very real, perfectly felt; but the reader is made to accept his participation in it as a pleasing experiment, the kind of thing that appeals to a fastidious curiosity—there is no question of its ever being more than this. The *fact* of Emma is taken with entire seriousness, of course; she is there to be studied and explored, and no means of understanding her point of view will be neglected. But her value is another matter; as to that Flaubert never has an instant's illusion, he always knows her to be worthless.

He knows it without asserting it, needless to say; his valuation of her is only implied; it is in his tone—never in his words, which invariably respect her own estimate of herself. His irony, none the less, is close at hand and indispensable; he has a definite use for this resource and he could not forego it. His irony gives him perfect freedom to supersede Emma's limited vision whenever he pleases, to abandon her manner of looking at the world, and to pass immediately to his own more enlightened, more commanding height. Her manner was utterly convincing while she exhibited it; but we always knew that a finer mind was watching her display with a touch of disdain. From time to time it leaves her and begins to create the world of Homard and Binet and Lheureux and the rest, in a fashion far beyond any possible conception of hers. Yet there is no dislocation here, no awkward substitution of one set of values for another; very discreetly the same standard has reigned throughout. That is the way in which Flaubert's impersonality, so called, artfully operates.

And now another difficulty; there is still more that is needed and that is not yet provided for. Emma must be placed in her world and fitted into it securely. Some glimpse of her appearance in the sight of those about her—this, too, we look for, to make the whole account of her compact and complete. Her relation to her husband, for instance, is from her side expressed very clearly in her view of him, which we possess; but there are advantages in seeing it from his side too. What did *he* really think of her, how did she appear to him? Light on this question not only makes a more solid figure of her for the reader, but it also brings her once for all into the company of the people round her, establishes her in the circle of their experience. Emma from within we have seen, and Yonville from the author's point of vantage; and now here is Emma from a point by her very side, when the seeing eye becomes that of her husband. Flaubert manages this ingeniously, making his procedure serve a further purpose at the same time. For he has to remember that his story does not end with the death of Emma; it is rounded off, not by her death, but by her husband's discovery of her long faithlessness, when in the first days of his mourning he lights upon the packet of letters that betrays her. The end of the story is in the final stroke of irony which gives the man this far-reaching glance into the past, and reveals thereby the mental and emotional confusion of his being—since his only response is a sort of stupefied perplexity. Charles must be held in readiness, so to speak, for these last pages; his inner mind, and his point of view, must be created in advance and kept in reserve, so that the force of the climax, when it is reached, may be instantly felt. And so we have the early episodes of Charles's youth and his first marriage, all his history up to the time when he falls in Emma's way; and Flaubert's questionable manner of working round to his subject is explained. Charles will be needed at the end, and Charles is here firmly set on his feet; the impression of Emma on those who encounter her is also needed, and here it is; and the whole book, mainly the affair of Emma herself, is effectively framed in this other affair, that of Charles, in which it opens and closes. Madame Bovary is a well-made book —so we have always been told, and so we find it to be, pulling it to pieces and putting it together again. It never is unrepaying to do so once more.

And it is a book that with its variety of method, and with its careful restriction of that variety to its bare needs, and with its scrupulous use of its resources—it is a book, altogether, that gives a good point of departure for an examination of the methods of fiction. The leading notions that are to be followed are clearly laid down in it, and I shall have nothing more to say that is not in some sense an extension and an amplification of hints to be found in Madame Bovary. For that reason I have lingered in detail over the treatment of a story about which, in other connections, a critic might draw different conclusions. I remember again how Flaubert vilified his subject while he was at work on it; his love of strong colours and flavours was disgusted by the drab prose of such a story—so he thought and said. But as the years went by and he fought his way from one chapter to another, did he begin to feel that it was not much of a subject after all, even of its kind? It is not clear; but after yet another re-reading of the book one wonders afresh. It is not a fertile subject—it is not; it does not strain and struggle for development, it only submits to it. But that aspect is not *my* subject, and Madame Bovary, a beautifully finished piece of work, is for my purpose singularly fertile.

THE PAINTER'S SPONGE AND VARNISH BOTTLE

F. O. MATTHIESSEN

I

ONE sign of how little technical analysis James has received is the virtual neglect of his revisions. Beyond Theodora Bosanquet's sensitive remarks in "Henry James at Work" and an occasional citation to annotate the elaborations of his later manner, they have been passed by. The only detailed exception is an essay on *Roderick Hudson* wherein the writer held that James' additions had largely served to spoil the clean outlines of its style.[1] Yet James made these revisions at the plenitude of his powers, and they constituted a re-*seeing* of the problems of his craft. He knew that it would be folly to try to recast the structure of any of his works. In the first preface that he wrote, that to *Roderick Hudson,* he developed an analogy for his aims in the way his fellow-craftsman on canvas went about to freshen his surfaces, to restore faded values, to bring out "buried secrets." He undertook, in particular, a minute verbal reconsideration of the three early novels that he chose to republish.

My reason for singling out *The Portrait of a Lady* is that it is a much richer book than either of the two others. *Roderick Hudson* is full of interest for James' development, since the two halves of his nature, the creator and the critic, are in a sense projected in Roderick and Rowland. Moreover, he there first tried out his device of having his narrative interpreted by the detached observer. But the book as a whole remains apprentice work. The revision of *The American*—the most extensive of all—might tell us, among other things, how James tried to repair what he had himself come to consider the falsely romantic aspects of his denouement.

"The Painter's Sponge and Varnish Bottle" from *Henry James: The Major Phase* by F. O. Matthiessen. Copyright, 1944, by Oxford University Press, Inc.

[1] Hélène Harvitt, "How Henry James Revised *Roderick Hudson:* A Study in Style"; *PMLA* (March 1924), 203–27.

But *The Portrait of a Lady* is his first unquestioned masterpiece. By considering all the issues that the revisions raise, we may see it with renewed clarity.[1]

Larger changes are very few. A page of conversation between Ralph Touchett and Lord Warburton (at the very end of Chapter XXVII) was recast in a way that shows James' more mature sense of a dramatic scene. What had been two pages of psychological scrutiny of Osmond just before his proposal to Isabel (Chapter XXIX) were felt by James to be otiose, and were cut to ten lines—an item of interest for the conventional view that the older James always worked the other way. But, with two important exceptions later to be looked into, we are to be concerned here with the tiniest brush strokes. What must be kept constantly in mind, therefore, is the design of the canvas as a whole. If that is done, we may have the intimate profit of watching the artist at his easel and of gaining insight into his principles of composition.

The writer's equivalent for the single flake of pigment is the individual word; and two words which James felt to be in need of consistent readjustment—"picturesque" and "romantic"—form in themselves an index to his aims. He had begun the book in Florence and had finished it in Venice. He had been at the time still strongly under the spell of Italian art, which, as he wrote William, had first taught him "what the picturesque is." He had consequently used the word freely as a kind of aesthetic catch-all, too loosely as he came to feel, for he struck it out in almost every case. He had applied it to Gardencourt, to Isabel's grandmother's house in Albany, to Osmond's *objets d'art;* he changed it in the first case to "pictorial," in the others to "romantic." [2] Some of its many other occurrences must have made the later James wince, especially where he had said that

---

[1] James had developed early the habit of touching up his texts wherever possible; and he even made a few slight alterations in the *Portrait* between its appearance in *The Atlantic Monthly* (November 1880–December 1881) and in volume form. For instance, Madame Merle's first name was changed from Geraldine to Serena. But the changes that can instruct us in the evolution of his technique are naturally those he introduced when returning to the book after more than a quarter of a century.

James' copies of both *The American* and *The Portrait of a Lady,* containing his innumerable revisions in longhand on the margins and in inserted pages of typescript, are now in the Houghton Library at Harvard.

I want to thank again the group of Harvard and Radcliffe students with whom I read through Henry James in the winter of 1943, since they did most of the spade work for this essay.

[2] I have included all the detailed references to both editions in the version of this essay that appeared in *The American Bookman* (Winter 1944). To avoid spotting these pages with unnecessary footnotes, I refer to that periodical any reader who is interested in following out the comparison for himself.

Madame Merle had "a picturesque smile." That was altered to "amused."
It is significant that when the word was retained, it was qualified by the
speaker, by Isabel, who says that she would be a little on both sides of a
revolution, that she would admire the Tories since they would have "a
chance to behave so exquisitely. I mean so picturesquely." "So exquisitely"
was added in the revision, and it is no accident that where, in the earlier
version, Lord Warburton had remarked that Isabel found the British "picturesque," he was later made to say " 'quaint.' " That putting into quotation marks underscores Isabel's attitude, as, indeed, do several instances
where James introduced "romantic" not merely as a substitute for "picturesque." Isabel's first judgment of Caspar as "not especially good-
looking" becomes "he was not romantically, rather obscurely handsome";
and her initial response to Warburton as "one of the most delectable persons she had met" is made much firmer—she judges him, "though quite
without luridity—as a hero of romance." And when we find that she
doesn't tell her sister about either his or Osmond's proposal, not simply
because "it entertained her to say nothing" but because "it was more romantic," and she delighted in "drinking deep, in secret, of romance,"
we have the clue to what James is building up through his greatly increased
use of this adjective and noun. He is bound to sharpen the reader's impression of how incorrigibly romantic Isabel's approach to life is, an important issue when we come to judge the effect of the book's conclusion.

Another word that shows the drift of James' later concern is "vulgar." One of James' most limiting weaknesses, characteristic of his whole
phase of American culture, was dread of vulgarity, a dread that inhibited
any free approach to natural human coarseness. But here the increased intrusion of the word does no great damage. When "the public at large"
becomes "a vulgar world," or when Henrietta Stackpole asserts that our
exaggerated American stress on brain power isn't a "vulgar fault" (she
had originally pronounced it a "glorious" one), or when Isabel adds to
her accruing reflections that Osmond had married her, "like a vulgar
adventurer," for her money, we simply see more sharply the negative
pole of James' vision.

His positive values come out in a whole cluster of words affecting the
inner life of his characters, words in which we may read all the chief
attributes of Jamesian sensibility. Ralph's "delights of observation" become "joys of contemplation." Warburton's sisters' "want of vivacity" is
sharpened to "want of play of mind" just as Isabel's "fine freedom of composition" becomes "free play of intelligence." On the other hand, Warburton, in Ralph's description, is toned down from "a man of imagination"
to "a man of a good deal of charming taste," in accordance with the high

demands that James came to put upon the imagination as the discerner of truth. It is equally characteristic that Isabel's "feelings" become her "consciousness," and that her "absorbing happiness" in her first impressions of England becomes "her fine, full consciousness." She no longer feels that she is "being entertained" by Osmond's conversation; rather she has "what always gave her a very private thrill, the consciousness of a new relation." Relations, intelligence, contemplation, consciousness—we are accumulating the words that define the Jamesian drama. No wonder that James came to feel that it had been flat to say that Isabel was fond "of psychological problems." As he rewrote it, she became fond, as he was, "ever, of the question of character and quality, of sounding, as who should say, the deep personal mystery."

II

To progress from single words to questions of style, we note at once the pervasive colloquialization. The younger James had used the conventional forms, "cannot" and "she would"; in his revised conversation these always appear as "can't" and "she'd." Of more interest is his handling of the "he said—she said" problem, upon which the older James could well take pride for his ingenuity. Isabel "answered, smiling" becomes Isabel "smiled in return" or Isabel "gaily engaged." Osmond "hesitated a moment" becomes that Jamesian favorite, Osmond "just hung fire." And for one more out of a dozen other evasions of the obvious, the Countess Gemini no longer "cried . . . with a laugh"; her sound and manner are condensed into one word, "piped."

James' humor has often been lost sight of in discussion of the solemnities of his mandarin style. But he didn't lose it himself. His original thumb-nail characterization of Isabel's sister was descriptive: "Lily knew nothing about Boston; her imagin tion was confined within the limits of Manhattan." A graphic twist brings that to life with a laugh: "her imagination was all bounded on the east by Madison Avenue."

The later James was more concrete. He had also learned what a source of life inheres in verbal movement. "Their multifarious colloquies" is heavily abstract, whereas "their plunge . . . into the deeps of talk" takes us right into the action. So too with the diverse ways in which James launched his characters into motion, as when Henrietta "was very well dressed" became "she rustled, she shimmered"; or when the Countess, instead of entering the room "with a great deal of expression," did it "with a flutter through the air." Such movement means that James was envisaging his scenes more dramatically; and, in the passage where Isabel has just been introduced to Osmond, we can see how natural it had become for the novelist to heighten any theatrical detail. Where he had formerly written that Isabel sat listening to Osmond and Madame Merle "as an impartial auditor of their brilliant discourse," he now substituted "as if she had been at the play and had paid even a large sum for her place." And as this scene advances, instead of saying that Madame Merle "referred everything" to Isabel, James wrote that she "appealed to her as if she had been on the stage, but she could ignore any learnt cue without spoiling the scene."

Operating more pervasively, here as always, upon James' imagination, were analogies with pictures rather than with the stage. When he wanted to enrich his bare statement that the Countess "delivered herself of a hundred remarks from which I offer the reader but a brief selection," he said that she "began to talk very much as if, seated brush in hand before an easel, she were applying a series of considered touches to a composition of figures already sketched in." A phrase that shows us James' very process is when Isabel, instead of "examining the idea" (of Warburton's "being a personage"), is made to examine "the image so conveyed." The growth from ideas to images is what James had been fumbling for in his earlier preoccupation with the picturesque. The word might now embarrass him, but not the secret he had learned through it. He had originally opened the first of the chapters to be laid in Osmond's villa by remarking that "a picturesque little group" was gathered there. What he meant to imply was made much more explicit in the revision: "a small group that might have been described by a painter as composing well."

That concern with composition grew from the conviction which he voiced in the preface to *Roderick Hudson,* that the novelist's subject, no less than the painter's, consisted ever in "the related state, to each other, of certain figures and things." And characters, he came to believe, could be best put into such relations when they were realized as visually, as lambently, as possible. This belief led him into one of his most recurrent types of revision, into endowing his *dramatis personae* with characterizing images. He had concluded his initial account of Ralph's ill health by remarking, "The truth was that he had simply accepted the situation." In place of that James was to introduce the poignancy that is Ralph's special note: "His serenity was but the array of wild flowers niched in his ruin." In comparable fashion, James added to his first description of Osmond, with no parallel in the original, an image that embodies the complex nature we are to find in him: "He suggested, fine gold coin as he was, no stamp nor emblem of the common mintage that provides for general circulation; he was the elegant complicated medal struck off for a special occasion."

Such elaborate images, more than any other aspect of James' later style, show his delight in virtuosity. Occasionally they seem to have been added purely because his eye fell on a dull patch of canvas, and he set out to brighten it up. Warburton's dim sisters don't contribute much in the original beyond "the kindest eyes in the world." But, in revising, James let himself go: their eyes are now "like the balanced basins, the circles of 'ornamental water,' set, in parterres, among the geraniums." In that image any functional intention may seem lost in the rococo flourish; but such was not usually the case. Take one very typical instance in the first detailed description of Caspar Goodwood—and it is significant of James' matured intentions that he introduced characterizing images of his chief figures at such important points. We are told in the first version that Caspar had undergone the usual gentleman athlete's education at Harvard, but that "later, he had become reconciled to culture." In the revision James conveyed much more of Caspar's energetic drive by means of a muscular image: "later on he had learned that the finer intelligence too could vault and pull and strain."

The full effect that James was trying for in such images might be instanced by the chapter which introduces Henrietta. Here we might follow James in the process of enlivening his sketch by a dozen fresh touches. The most interesting of these bring out Henrietta's character by the device of interrelating her appearance with her career. He did not rest content with saying that "she was scrupulously, fastidiously neat. From top to toe she carried not an ink stain." He changed this into: "she was as crisp and new and comprehensive as a first issue before the folding. From top to toe she had probably no misprint." In spite of the loudness of her voice (which caused James to alter Henrietta "murmured" to Henrietta "rang out"), Ralph was originally surprised to find that she was not "an abundant talker." But in the revision the detailed glance at her profession is sustained, and he finds her not "in the large type, the type of horrid 'head-lines.'" Yet she still remains fairly terrifying to Ralph, and, a few pages farther on, James emphasized that by another kind of image. To point up the fact that "she was brave," he added, "she went into cages, she flourished lashes, like a spangled lion-tamer." With that as a springboard James could rise to the final sentence of this chapter. Originally Ralph had concluded, "Henrietta, however, is fragrant—Henrietta is decidedly fragrant!" But this became a punch line: "Henrietta, however, does smell of the Future—it almost knocks one down!"

James remarked in his preface that he had given the reader "indubitably too much" of Henrietta—a thing that could be said of most of his *ficelles;* but in retouching he had at least done what he could to brighten every inch. In relation to her we may note another phase of his revision, his addition of epithets to characterize the world of which she is part. In Rome she is struck by the analogy between the ancient chariot ruts and "the iron grooves which mark the course of the American horse-car." These become more up to date: "the overjangled iron grooves which express the intensity of American life." Where James had written "the nineteenth century," he was later to call it "the age of advertisement"; and glancing, not at America but at Europe, he named it "an overcivilized age." But it was Henrietta's realm he was thinking of again when, instead of having Madame Merle remark that "it's scandalous, how little I know about the land of my birth," he had her call it rather, in his most revelatory addition of this type: "that splendid, dreadful, funny country—surely the greatest and drollest of them all."

III

So far I have avoided the question that is usually raised first about James' revisions: Didn't he sometimes overwrite to no purpose as a mere occupational disease? Occasionally, without doubt, it is the older James talking instead of a character, as when Pansy, instead of saying, "I have no voice—just a little thread," is made to transform this into ". . . just a small sound like the squeak of a slatepencil making flourishes." But look at another sample where at first it would appear as though James had taken twice as many words to say the same thing, where "Marriage meant that a woman should abide with her husband" became "Marriage meant that a woman should cleave to the man with whom, uttering tremendous vows, she had stood at the altar." In its context we can at least see what James was after. This passage is part of Isabel's reflections, and both its fuller rhythm and density are meant to increase its *inner* relevance. The best way, therefore, to judge the final value of James' rewriting is to relate it in each case to the character involved, an obligatory proceeding in dealing with the writer who asked, in *The Art of Fiction:* "What is a picture or a novel that is *not* of character?"

The diverse types of revision demanded by the different characters may also remind us that we have in this book the most interestingly variegated group that James ever created. The center of attention is always Isabel, and the changes devoted to her may be read as a brief outline of the interpretation which James hoped we should give to his heroine. A few involve her looks. Whereas acquaintances of the Archer girls used to refer to her as "the thin one," James' tenderness for her was later to make this sound less invidious: "the willowy one." From his initial description of her in the house at Albany, he wanted to emphasize that she was less mistress of her fate than she fondly believed. He pointed this up by changing "young girl" to "creature of conditions." He also, as a past master of what could be gained by the specific notation, changed the conditioning of her taste from "a glimpse of contemporary aesthetics" to "the music of Gounod, the poetry of Browning, the prose of George Eliot" —a change which recalls that these were also Minny Temple's tastes.

But James' chief interest in his heroine is revealed through another type of change. Warburton's belief that she is "a thoroughly interesting woman" is made more intimate—"a really interesting little figure." And a few lines below, when Ralph concludes that a character like hers "is the finest thing in nature," he says more precisely what he means by adding, in the revision, that she is "a real little passionate force." James devoted many of his later brush strokes to bringing her out as exactly that. Instead of passively wanting "to be delighted," she now wants "to hurl herself into the fray." It is equally symptomatic of her conduct that she refuses Warburton, not because such a marriage fails "to correspond to any vision of happiness that she had hitherto entertained," but because it fails "to support any enlightened prejudice in favour of the free exploration of life." The Isabel whom the later James saw with so much lucidity is a daughter of the transcendental afterglow, far less concerned about happiness than about enlightenment and freedom.

Another addition indicates that what is most required to make her respond is "a bait to her imagination." That is exactly why she is caught by Osmond. Mrs. Touchett originally said that Isabel was capable of marrying him "for his opinions"; but she heightens this with more of the girl's romanticism in saying "for the beauty of his opinions or for his autograph of Michael Angelo." And that is how we see Isabel reacting to him. His "things of a deep interest" become "objects, subjects, contacts . . . of a rich association." She reads into them also, in a favorite phrase of the later James, "histories within histories." When she defends him to Ralph, the revision makes her grounds much more explicit by adding to her question, "What do you know against him?"—"What's the matter with Mr. Osmond's type, if it be one? His being so independent, so individual, is what *I* most see in him." And again, instead of saying "Mr. Osmond is simply a man—he is not a proprietor," she expands this with her feeling, "Mr. Osmond's simply a very lonely, a very cultivated and a very honest man—he's not a prodigious proprietor."

This is the Isabel of whom James felt it no longer adequate just to say, "she was an excitable creature, and now she was much excited." He transformed that into an image: "Vibration was easy to her, was in fact too constant with her, and she found herself now humming like a smitten harp." Such vibrations are intrinsic to the rhythm of her thought. She no longer reflects merely that "she had loved him," but extends that reflection with "she had so anxiously and yet so ardently given herself." It is not padding, therefore, when, upon discovering how wrong she has been about Osmond, she does not conclude, "There was only one way to repair it—to accept it," but adds ". . . just immensely (oh, with the highest grandeur!) to accept it."

The revisions affecting Osmond are of a very different sort. Far more of them relate to his appearance, to the polished, elegant and slightly ambiguous surface which James wants the reader to study more fully. His "sharply-cut face" becomes "extremely modelled and composed." James' description of his eyes is far more careful. They are no longer "luminous" and "intelligent" expressing "both softness and keenness," but "conscious, curious eyes . . . at once vague and penetrating, intelligent and hard." This is quite in keeping with his smile, which is now his "cool" smile, and with his voice, of which it is now said that, though fine, it "somehow wasn't sweet." He does not speak "with feeling" but "beautifully"; and his laugh, instead of being "not ill-natured," has now "a finer patience." James has done an expert job of heightening Osmond's thoroughly studied effect. He underscores the fact that Osmond's taste was his only law by saying, not that he lived "in a serene, impersonal way," but "in a sorted, sifted, arranged world," where his "superior qualities" become "standards and touchstones other than the vulgar."

Osmond is entirely devoted to forms, and to accent this trait, James introduces one of his most interesting later devices: he interrelates Osmond's character with his surroundings in a way that shows again how much the novelist had learned from the plastic arts.[1] On the first occasion that Osmond entertains Isabel, James wants her to be impressed with the rare distinction of the collector's villa. Osmond's footboy is now made deliberately picturesque: instead of remaining merely "the shabby footboy," he becomes "tarnished as to livery and quaint as to type," and, with a fine added flourish, James tells us that he might "have issued from some stray sketch of old-time manners, been 'put in' by the brush of a Longhi or a Goya." James also added in the revision that Osmond was marked for Isabel "as by one of those signs of the highly curious that he was showing her on the underside of old plates and in the corner of sixteenth-century drawings." As Isabel thinks over this visit afterwards, she reflects that his care for beauty "had been the main occupation of a lifetime of

---

[1] I have given further instances from his earlier works in "Henry James and the Plastic Arts," *The Kenyon Review* (Autumn 1943).

which the arid places were watered with the sweet sense of a quaint, half-anxious, half-helpless fatherhood." In the revision these thoughts rise from her impression of how she had seen him: his preoccupation with beauty made his life "stretch beneath it in the disposed vistas and with the ranges of steps and terraces and fountains of a formal Italian garden —allowing only for arid places freshened by the natural dews," and so on.

In building up the reasons why she took her romantic view of him, James also embarked on an extended flight:

> What continued to please this young lady was his extraordinary subtlety. There was such a fine intellectual intention in what he said, and the movement of his wit was like that of a quick-flashing blade.
> What continued to please this young woman was that while he talked so for amusement he didn't talk, as she had heard people, for "effect." He uttered his ideas as if, odd as they often appeared, he were used to them and had lived with them; old polished knobs and heads and handles, of precious substance, that could be fitted if necessary to new walking-sticks—not switches plucked in destitution from the common tree and then too elegantly waved about.

The new passage stresses, if in oblique ways and with some needless verbiage, Osmond's utter dependence on art rather than on nature. The "old polished knobs," like the "complicated medal" to which he is compared, make him indisseverable from his collector's items. It is not surprising that such a deliberately shaped work of art as he is "mystified" Isabel. (In the first version he had merely "puzzled" her.) It is fitting too that, as she comes under his fascination, she should feel not merely "a good deal older than she had done a year before," but also "as if she were 'worth more' for it, like some curious piece in an antiquary's collection." For, in ways that her inexperience cannot possibly fathom, that is precisely how Osmond proposes to treat her. She appeals to him, not for being "as bright and soft as an April cloud," but in one of James' most functional revisions, "as smooth to his general need of her as handled ivory to the palm."

The mystification is only Isabel's, the ambiguity is all in what Osmond concealed, not in any doubts that James entertained about him. The revision increases his "lost" quality. His "peculiarities" are called his "perversities," and where it was remarked that he consulted his taste alone, James now adds "as a sick man consciously incurable consults at last only his lawyer." The reader accepts entirely Ralph's judgment of Osmond as a sterile dilettante; but his quality is deepened when Ralph recognizes the futility of trying to persuade Isabel, not that the man is "a humbug," but rather that there is something "sordid or sinister" in him. With that deepening even Osmond becomes poignant: his "keen, expressive, emphatic" face becomes "firm, refined, slightly ravaged"—a far more telling portrait.

The character in this book around whom ambiguity gathers most is Madame Merle, since she has to play a double rôle throughout. James' changes involving her are chiefly of two sorts. He decided, for one thing, that her surface should be less transparent to Isabel. And so it is when Isabel asks her if she has not suffered that her "picturesque smile" is elaborated into "the amused smile of a person seated at a game of guesses." She is also called "smooth" instead of "plump." When Madame Merle introduced her to Osmond, Isabel wondered about "the nature of the tie that united them. She was inclined to imagine that Madame Merle's ties were peculiar." As James looked over that, it seemed to strike too close to the actual liaison, which he didn't want Isabel to suspect for a long time yet. So he toned it up to "the nature of the tie binding these superior spirits. She felt that Madame Merle's ties always somehow had histories."

But in the other type of change for Madame Merle, James felt, as he did with Osmond, that he must make her character unmistakable to the reader. So he no longer endowed her with "a certain nobleness," but with a "certain courage"; not with "geniality" but with "grace." Even in changing the music that Isabel overheard her playing from "something of Beethoven's" to "something of Schubert's," James must have felt that he was bringing it more within Madame Merle's emotional compass. When Isabel finally comes to know her secret, the girl reflects, not just that her friend was "false," but "even deeply false . . . deeply, deeply, deeply." And Madame Merle's guilt is spoken of, not in terms "of vivid proof," but "of ugly evidence . . . of grim things produced in court."

Such details—of which there are many more—are important in allaying the usual suspicion that James' ambiguity is unintentional, the obscurantism of a man who couldn't make up his own mind. When the writing becomes denser, as it frequently does in the revision, this is owing rather to James' gradual development of one of his special gifts, the ability so to handle a conversation that he keeps in the air not merely what is said, but what isn't—the passage of thoughts without words. The situation here which challenged most this skill of the later James was when Warburton turned up again after Isabel's marriage. What she had to decide was whether, despite his honorable pretensions, he was still in love with her. Their interplay is made more subtle. To judge the value of this kind of rewriting you must follow the whole chapter, but one series of slight changes may show what James was about.

As they met again, in the first version, Isabel "hardly knew whether she were glad or not." Warburton, however, "was plainly very well pleased." In the revision his feelings are not given to us so explicitly: he "was plainly quite sure of his own sense of the matter." Only as the conversation advances do Isabel—and the reader—gain the evidence she is after. In a moment or two, he remarks how charming a place she has to live in. In the original he said this, "brightly, looking about him." But this became: "with a look, round him, at her established home, in which she might have caught the dim ghost of his old ruefulness." That reveals to Isabel nearly all she needs, and her impression is clinched, when, instead of turning upon her "an eye that gradually became more serious," he gives her, in addition, "the deeper, the deepest consciousness of his look." From that moment Isabel knows how unwise it would be for him to marry her stepdaughter Pansy, no matter how much Osmond wants the match.

If such a situation caused James thus to weave the texture of his style more complexly, the changes that relate to Pansy and to Ralph, though equally slight, may reveal another significant quality. In the scale of emotional vibrations James is more impressive in striking the note of tenderness than that of passion. We can observe this in the way he heightened some of his most moving passages. How utterly Pansy is at the mercy of her father's will is underlined by several details. Consider, for instance, her smile, in connection with which we can note again James' extraordinary care to bring out every revelatory phase of his characters' looks. At the moment of Pansy's first appearance in the narrative, James remarked that her "natural and usual expression seemed to be a smile of perfect sweetness." But the point about Pansy is that she has had so little chance to be natural or spontaneous, and so James revised this: her face was "painted with a fixed and intensely sweet smile." So too with the characterizing image that he created for her. Instead of saying that Pansy entertained Isabel "like a little lady," James wrote that she "rose to the occasion as the small, winged fairy in the pantomime soars by the aid of the dissimulated wire." Thus Pansy's trapped state is suggested to us from the outset, and on the occasion when Isabel tells her that she is going to marry her father, James made two additions that show how he had learned to handle irony. Originally Isabel had said, "My good little Pansy, I shall be very kind to you." But to that James added: "A vague, inconsequent vision of her coming in some odd way to need it had intervened with the effect of a chill." And when Pansy answered, "Very well then; I have nothing to fear," James no longer had her declare that "lightly," but "with her note of prepared promptitude." And he also added, as part of Isabel's reflection: "What teaching she had had, it seemed to suggest—or what penalties for non-performance she dreaded!"

We can read, in these extensions, the same thing that we have observed in the major characters, James' deepening of emotional tones. The most affecting passage in the book is the death of Ralph, for there James is expressing the tenderness of pure devotion, disencumbered of any worldly aims. The characterizing image noted above was designed to increase our sense of Ralph's precarious holds on life. To increase also our sense of his devotion to Isabel, "his cousin" was twice changed to "the person in the world in whom he was most interested." The scene between these two, as he lies dying, is very short, and the only significant change is in Ralph's last speech. In the original this read: " 'And remember this,' he continued, 'that if you have been hated, you have also been loved.' " To that James added: " 'Ah, but, Isabel—*adored!*' he just audibly and lingeringly breathed." There it may become a debatable matter of taste whether the simple form is not more moving; but the later James felt impelled to a more high-keyed emotional register. Both Ralph and Isabel, instead of "murmuring" or "adding softly" are made to "wail." [1] It is difficult to keep such tones from becoming sentimental, but how little James was inclined to sentimentalize can be seen in his handling of Ralph's funeral. Originally James pronounced it "not a disagreeable one"; but he made his later statement stronger: it was "neither a harsh nor a heavy one."

IV

The two most extensive passages of rewriting are yet to be looked at. One relates to the Countess Gemini, and the other to Caspar Goodwood. Both can give us insight into how James conceived dramatic structure, and how he also felt that the climax of this book needed strengthening.

In comparing the two versions, it is notable that the sequence of chapters which James pronounced, in the preface, as being the best in the book—the sequence that extends from Isabel's glimpse of the two together, with Osmond seated while Madame Merle is standing, through the long vigil in which Isabel gradually pieces together her situation—that these three chapters (XL–XLII), with their important issues, were left substantially unchanged. So too with the fateful interview between Osmond and Isabel (Chapter XLVI) which shows how hopelessly far apart they

---

[1] This is also true in the other most directly emotional scene, the death of Ralph's father:

" 'My father died an hour ago.'
'Ah, my poor Ralph!' the girl murmured, putting out her hand to him."

" 'My dear father died an hour ago.'
'Ah, my poor Ralph!' she gently wailed, putting out her two hands to him."

have grown. But the scene with the Countess (Chapter LI), in which Isabel's suspicions are first given explicit names, was greatly recast. Some of the reasons for this are suggested by what James wrote in his notebook at the time when the novel had begun to appear in *The Atlantic* and he was trying to see his way clear to his conclusion: "After Isabel's marriage there are five more instalments, and the success of the whole story greatly depends upon this portion being well conducted or not. Let me then make the most of it—let me imagine the best. There has been a want of action in the earlier part, and it may be made up here. The elements that remain are in themselves, I think, very interesting, and they are only to be strongly and happily combined. The weakness of the whole story is that it is too exclusively psychological—that it depends too little on incident; but the complete unfolding of the situation that is established by Isabel's marriage may nonetheless be quite sufficiently dramatic. The idea of the whole thing is that the poor girl, who has dreamed of freedom and nobleness, who has done, as she believes, a generous, natural, clear-sighted thing, finds herself in reality ground in the very mill of the conventional. After a year or two of marriage the antagonism between her nature and Osmond's comes out—the open opposition of a noble character and a narrow one. There is a great deal to do here in a small compass; every word, therefore, must tell—every touch must count. If the last five parts of the story appear crowded, this will be rather a good defect in consideration of the perhaps too great diffuseness of the earlier portion."

As James went on outlining his intentions, he was still undecided whether the revelation of Pansy's parentage should come through Madame Merle herself or through the Countess: "Better on many grounds that it should be the latter; and yet in that way I lose the 'great scene' between Madame Merle and Isabel." Twenty-five years later he was still bothered by what he had lost. In the passage of deadly quietness between Isabel and Osmond, and, subsequently, between Isabel and Madame Merle, he seems to have felt that his drama was too inward, that he needed a more emotional scene. And so he rewrote nearly all the lines in which the Countess told Isabel of the liaison.

He had already given considerable attention to making the Countess' character a more lively mixture. Ralph's first description of her was changed from "rather wicked" to "rather impossible"; and in her own disarming self-characterization, instead of saying, "I am only rather light," she pronounced herself "only rather an idiot and a bore." James had originally said that her expression was "by no means disagreeable"; but here he particularized: it was made up of "various intensities of emphasis and wonder, of horror and joy." Also, to a quite astonishing degree, by recurring to a bird-image for her, he sustained her in a whir. For example, in her first meeting with Isabel, she delivered her remarks "with a variety of little jerks and glances." But the bird-motif gave these the momentum of "little jerks and pecks, of roulades of shrillness," with the result that James was stimulated to a further flight of his own, and added that her accent was "as some fond recall of good English, or rather of good American, in adversity."

This kind of a character had dramatic possibilities, and, in his revision, James exploited them to the full. He did everything he could to make her revelations to Isabel into the "great scene" he had missed. Isabel is alone, thinking of what will happen if, in defiance of Osmond's wishes, she goes to England to see Ralph before he dies. Then, suddenly, the Countess "stood before her." Thus the original, but in the rewriting the Countess "hovered before her." And to give us an intimation that something is coming, James added that the Countess "lived assuredly, it might be said, at the window of her spirit, but now she was leaning far out." As Lawrence Leighton, who first drew my attention to the importance of this scene for James' structure, remarked, this is like "an extra blast from the trumpets" to announce the herald. It occurs to Isabel for the first time that her sister-in-law might say something, not "important," but "really human."

In what follows much subtle attention was paid to the Countess' diction. James endowed her with a more characteristic colloquial patter, with such epithets as "poverina" and "cara mia." Instead of saying that Madame Merle had wanted "to save her reputation," she says, "to save her skin"; and, in her view, Isabel has not merely "such a pure mind"—she calls it "beastly pure," as such a woman would. Her speeches are considerably increased in length, one of them by almost a page. There is hardly any addition to her ideas, but as Mr. Leighton also observed, "James wanted a good harangue, the sort of speech an actress could get her teeth into." Her quality is melodramatic, but it is effectively more baleful than in the first version.

James has also built up the contrast between her and Isabel. The Countess expected—and hoped—that the girl would burst out with a denunciation of Osmond. But instead she is filled with pity for Madame Merle. She thinks even of Osmond's first wife, that "he must have been false" to her—"and so very soon!" That last phrase is an addition that emphasizes Isabel's incurable innocence, despite all the experience through which she is passing. It glances ironically also at her own situation. When she goes on to reflect that at least Osmond has been faithful to her, the Countess says it depends on what you call faithful: "When he married you he was no longer the lover of another woman—*such* a lover as he had been, *cara mia,* between their risks and their precautions, while the thing lasted!" Everything after the dash is added, and we can hear the Countess smacking her lips over such details, while Isabel recoils into herself. Where the first version had remarked that she "hesitated, though there was a question in her eyes," the utter cleavage between her and her gossipy interlocutress is now brought out: she "hesitated as if she had not heard; as if her question— though it was sufficiently there in her eyes—were all for herself." When, a moment or two later, Isabel wondered why Madame Merle never wanted to marry Osmond, the Countess had originally contented herself with saying that Madame Merle "had grown more ambitious." But to that James added: " 'besides, she has never had, about him,' the Countess went on, leaving Isabel to wince for it so tragically afterwards—'she *had* never had, what you might call any illusions of *intelligence*.' " The Countess is happy to get in a dig at her brother, but for Isabel and for the reader there is the irony that Isabel herself had been fooled by just such illusions. That gives the final twist to the knife.

After this scene there remain only four chapters. There is the brief final encounter with Madame Merle, who sees in an instant that Isabel now knows everything. Isabel then says good-bye to Pansy, but promises that she won't desert her. The rest of the book is taken up with Isabel's trip to England, with her farewell to Ralph, and with Caspar's return to her. The last chapter is largely her struggle with him, and James' significant additions are led up to by the emphases that he has given to Caspar's character earlier in the book. He has introduced many details that sharpen the impression of Caspar's indomitable energy. When Isabel first compares him with Warburton, she feels that there is "something too forcible, something oppressive and restrictive" about him. But this was made more concrete: "a disagreeably strong push, a kind of hardness of presence." A revelatory image was introduced to contrast Isabel's feeling about Warburton: instead of refusing to "lend a receptive ear" to his suit, she now "resists conquest" at his "large quiet hands." But Caspar is "a kind of fate," now, indeed, "a kind of grim fate." He himself gives fuller expression to the tension between them when he has first pursued her to London. Instead of saying, "Apparently it was disagreeable to you even to write," he makes it "repugnant." And he remarks bitterly, not that his insistence on his suit "displeases" her, but that it "disgusts." As the best means of characterizing him, James developed a recurrent image of armour. In his first account he had merely remarked that Caspar was "the strongest man" Isabel had ever known; but to this he added: "she saw the different fitted parts of him as she had seen, in museums and portraits, the different fitted parts of armoured warriors—in plates of steel handsomely inlaid with gold." Later on, his eyes, instead of wearing "an expression of ardent remonstrance," seemed "to shine through the vizard of a helmet." And when Isabel tries to measure his possible suffering, she no longer reflects that "he had a sound constitution," but that "he was naturally plated and steeled, armed essentially for aggression."

He follows her to Italy to object strenuously to her engagement to Osmond: "Where does he come from? Where does he belong?" That second question was added in the revision, as was also Isabel's thought, "She had never been so little pleased with the way he said 'belawng.' " But, in spite of everything, Isabel cannot escape feeling Caspar's power; and in rewriting their final scene, James made an incisive analysis of his mixed repulsion and attraction for her. She is alone under the trees at Gardencourt, when Caspar suddenly appears—just as Warburton had surprised her there once before. In what follows we are made to feel her overpowering sensation of his physical presence, from the moment that James adds that he was "beside her on the bench and pressingly turned to her." As he insists that her husband is "the deadliest of fiends," and that he, Caspar, is determined to prevent her from the "horror" of returning to him (both "deadliest" and "horror" were additions), Isabel realizes that "she had never been loved before." To that realization the original had added: "It wrapped her about; it lifted her off her feet." But now James wrote: "She had believed it, but this was different; this was the hot wind of the desert, at the approach of which the others dropped dead, like mere sweet airs of the garden. It wrapped her about; it lifted her off her feet, while the very taste of it, as of something potent, acrid, and strange, forced open her set teeth."

That image takes her as far away from her surroundings and the gentlemanly devotion of a Warburton as it does from the decadent egotism of an Osmond. For a moment she is completely overpowered. Caspar's voice, saying, "Be mine, as I'm yours," comes to her, not merely "through a confusion of sound," but "harsh and terrible, through a confusion of vaguer sounds." He takes her in his arms, and in the first version, the climax is reached with: "His kiss was like a flash of lightning; when it was dark again she was free." But now James felt it necessary to say far more: "His kiss was like white lightning, a flash that spread and spread again, and stayed; and it was extraordinary as if, while she took it, she felt each thing in his hard manhood that had least pleased her, each aggressive fact of his face, his figure, his presence, justified of its intense identity and made one with this act of possession. So had she heard of those wrecked and under water following a train of images before they sink. But when darkness returned she was free."

That conveys James' awareness of how Isabel, in spite of her marriage, has remained essentially virginal, and of how her resistance and her flight from Caspar are partly fear of sexual possession. But the fierce attraction she also feels in this passage would inevitably operate likewise for a girl of her temperament, in making her do what she conceived to be her duty, and sending her back to her husband.

v

That brings us to the ending of the book, which has seldom been rightly interpreted. The difference between the two versions is one of the few of James' revisions that is generally known. Henrietta has told Caspar that Isabel has gone back to Rome:

"Look here, Mr. Goodwood," she said; "just you wait." On which he looked up at her.

Thus the final lines in the original. But to these James added:

—but only to guess, from her face, with a revulsion, that she simply meant he was young. She stood shining at him with that cheap comfort, and it added, on the spot, thirty years to his life. She walked him away with her, however, as if she had given him now the key to patience.

Many critics have held this difference to mean that James had changed his mind, that in the original he had given Caspar more hope. But he seems rather to have made unmistakably explicit what he had always intended to imply. He had said in his notebook outline that Isabel was to be greatly moved by Caspar's "passionate outbreak": "she feels the full force of his devotion—to which she has never done justice; but she refuses. She starts again for Italy—and her departure is the climax and termination of the story."

James had also observed there that Henrietta was to have "the last word," to utter "a characteristic characterization of Isabel." But he must have felt in revising that he had been too brief, that he had failed to drive home to the reader that what was being expressed was no sure promise about Isabel, but rather Henrietta's optimism, which refuses to accept defeat.

The end of Isabel's career is not yet in sight. That fact raises a critical issue about James' way of rounding off his narratives. He was keenly aware of what his method involved. As he wrote in his notebook, upon concluding his detailed project: "With strong handling it seems to me that it may all be very true, very powerful, very touching. The obvious criticism of course will be that it is not finished—that it has not seen the heroine to the end of her situation—that I have left her *en l'air*. This is both true and false.

The *whole* of anything is never told; you can only take what groups together. What I have done has that unity—it groups together. It is complete in itself—and the rest may be taken up or not, later."

This throws a great deal of light—perhaps more than any single passage of his published work—on how James conceived of structure. He recounted in the preface to the *Portrait* how Turgenieff had encouraged him in his belief that the important thing to start with was not an air-tight plot, but rather a character or group of characters who are so living that the main question becomes to "invent and select" the complications that such characters "would be most likely to produce and to feel."

Years before the *Portrait,* William James had commented on the effect of such a method, as it struck him in *A Most Extraordinary Case* (1868), one of the first half dozen stories that Henry had printed. William felt that here he understood for the first time what Henry was aiming for: "to give an impression like that we often get of people in life: Their orbits come out of space and lay themselves for a short time along of ours, and then off they whirl again into the unknown, leaving us with little more than an impression of their reality and a feeling of baffled curiosity as to the mystery of the beginning and the end of their being." William thought such a method difficult to make succeed, but "with a deep justification in nature." He was to grow somewhat less sure of its efficacy, as can be read in his tone about *The Tragic Muse:* "the final winding up is, as usual with you, rather a losing of the story in the sand, yet that is the way in which things lose themselves in real life." Henry, on the other hand, grew steadily to have more confidence in what he was doing, until he declared, in the preface to *Roderick Hudson:* "Really, universally, relations stop nowhere, and the exquisite problem of the artist is eternally but to draw, by a geometry of his own, the circle within which they shall happily *appear* to do so." That gives his essential conception of the kind of wholeness that form imposes.

He had been particularly concerned in the *Portrait* with launching Isabel Archer into action, with presenting her so vividly that his narrative would compose itself around the primary question, "Well, what will she *do?*" It has recently been assumed that James believed entirely in the rightness of his heroine's conduct, and that since our age no longer feels as he —and she—did about the strictness of the marriage vow, we can no longer respond to the book except as to a period piece. But that is to misread not merely the ending, but all of James' own "characteristic characterization" of Isabel. He could hardly have made a more lucid summary of the weaknesses that she exposed to Europe: "her meagre knowledge, her inflated ideals, her confidence at once innocent and dogmatic, her temper at once exacting and indulgent"—that whole passage of analysis on the evening after her arrival at Gardencourt, a passage untouched in the revision, is meant to have our closest scrutiny.

As Isabel embarks on her "free exploration" of life, Henrietta is outspoken in declaring that she is drifting rather to "some great mistake," that she is not enough "in contact with reality," with the "toiling, striving" world. Ralph tells her that she has "too much conscience"—a peculiarly American complication in the romantic temperament. Although all her diverse friends are united in their disapproval of Osmond, she proceeds to do the wrong thing for the right reasons. She has a special pride in marrying him, since she feels that she is not only "taking," but also "giving"; she feels too the release of transferring some of the burden of her inheritance to another's conscience—James' way of commenting on how harm was done to her by her money. But once she discerns what Osmond is really like, and how he has trapped her, she is by no means supine in his toils. She stands up to him with dignity, she even asks Pansy, "Will you come away with me now?" Yet Isabel knows that is impossible; she knows, even as she leaves, that she will have to return to Rome for Pansy's sake.

But much more is involved than that—James' whole conception of the discipline of suffering. It is notable that his kinship here to Hawthorne becomes far more palpable in the final version. Take the instance when, at the time of Ralph's death, Isabel realizes how Mrs. Touchett has missed the essence of life by her inability to feel. It seemed to Isabel that Ralph's mother "would find it a blessing today to be able to indulge a regret. She wondered whether Mrs. Touchett were not trying, whether she had not a desire for the recreation of grief." James made this much fuller, particularly the latter portion. Isabel wondered if Mrs. Touchett "were not even missing those enrichments of consciousness and privately trying—reaching out for some after taste of life, dregs of the banquet; the testimony of pain or the cold recreation of remorse." The view of suffering adumbrated there, even the phrasing, recalls Hawthorne's *The Christmas Banquet,* where the most miserable fate is that of the man whose inability to feel bars him out even from the common bond of woe.

The common bond of sin, so central to Hawthorne's thought, was also accentuated through James' retouching. When Madame Merle finally foresees what is ahead, she says to Osmond in the original, "How do bad people end? You have made me bad." But James extended this with a new italicized emphasis, "How do bad people end?—*especially as to their common* crimes. You have made me as bad as yourself." Isabel's link with humanity, if not through sin—unless her willful spirit counts as such—is through her acceptance of suffering. The inevitability of her lot is made more binding in the revision. Her reflection that "she should not escape, she should last," becomes "she should never escape, she should last to the end." She takes on heightened stature when James no longer says that, while she sat with Ralph, "her spirit rose," but that "her ache for herself became somehow her ache for *him*." The pathos of her situation is also intensified in proportion to her greater knowledge of what is involved. "She reflected that things change but little, while people change so much" is far less affecting than "she envied the security of valuable 'pieces' which change by no hair's breadth, only grow in value, while their owners lose inch by inch, youth, happiness, beauty."

In both the original and the revision Isabel lays the most scrupulous emphasis upon the sacredness of a promise. Despite all her eagerness for culture, hers is no speculative spirit. Osmond comes to despise her for having "the moral horizon" of a Unitarian minister—"poor Isabel, who had never been able to understand Unitarianism!" But whether she understands it or not, she is a firm granddaughter of the Puritans, not in her thought but in her moral integrity. In portraying her character and her fate, James was also writing an essay on the interplay of free will and determinism. Isabel's own view is that she was "perfectly free," that she married Osmond of her most deliberate choice, and that, however miserable one may be, one must accept the consequences of one's acts. James knew how little she was free, other than to follow to an impulsive extreme everything she had been made by her environment and background.

Thus he leaves her to confront her future, and is satisfied if he has endowed his characters with so much "felt life" that the reader must weigh for himself what is likely to lie ahead in her relation with Osmond. It may be that, as Isabel herself conjectures, he may finally "take her money and let her go." It may be that once she has found a husband for Pansy, she will feel that she no longer has to remain in Rome. James believed that the arbitrary circle of art should stimulate such speculations beyond its confines, and thus create also the illusion of wider life. He had about Isabel a tragic sense, but he did not write a tragedy, as he was to do in *The Wings of the Dove,* since this earlier drama was lacking in the finality of purgation and judgment. But his view of his material was not at all ambiguous. He knew how romantic Isabel was, how little experienced she was in mature social behavior. He had shown that she was completely mistaken in believing that "the world lay before her—she could do whatever she chose." But James also knew the meaning and the value of renunciation. The American life of his day, in its reckless plunge to outer expansiveness and inner defeat, had taught him that as his leading spiritual theme. Through Isabel Archer he gave one of his fullest and freshest expressions of inner reliance in the face of adversity. It is no wonder that, after enumerating her weaknesses, he had concluded: "she would be an easy victim of scientific criticism if she were not intended to awaken on the reader's part an impulse more tender . . ."

CRIME AND PUNISHMENT

A STUDY OF DOSTOEVSKY'S NOVEL

R. P. BLACKMUR

Crime and punishment has upon most readers an impact as immediate and obvious and full as the news of murder next door; one *almost* participates in the crime, and the trivial details become obsessively important. It has besides a secondary impact, by which, as one feels it, one discovers that one has been permanently involved in the nature of the crime: one has somehow contributed to the clarification of the true residual nature of crime in general through having contributed to the enactment of this crime in particular. It is the feeling of this impact that leads us to say our powers of attention have been exhausted. But there is a third and gradual impact, which comes not only at the end but almost from the beginning to the end, creating in us new and inexhaustible powers of attention. This is the impact of what Dostoevsky meant by punishment. The three impacts are united by the art of the novelist, and they are felt simultaneously. It is only that we are not aware at the time of the triple significance, and must, when it does transpire, rebuild it analytically. Thus we may come to estimate what it is that we know—what it is that has been clarified in the history of Raskolnikov which we had known all along in ourselves without being aware of it: we estimate our own guilt.

A crime is above all an act against the institutions of human law, custom, or religion; and there is a sense in which any act may be understood as criminal, for if the institution cannot be found against which it is committed, then it may be called an anarchic act—against some institution that has not yet come to exist, but which will exist because of the crime. This notion comes from putting Rousseau's dusty vision in reverse. If, as

"Crime and Punishment; a Study of Dostoevsky's Novel," reprinted by permission of the author.

Rousseau thought for one inspired moment, the evils of living come mostly from human institutions, it is as likely true, though not as inspired that our institutions arise out of the evil that we do. It is Laforgue who has said it best, and without any but poetic logic to blister his cry:

> *Allez, sterile ritournelles!*
> *La Vie est vraie et crimminelle!* [1]

This cry of Laforgue represents the lyric sense that must inhabit every criminal who truly imagines his crime, if only for a flash, *before* he commits it to act. What the criminal imagines afterwards is another thing and we shall come to it. Here it is the crime only that has been imagined, and the promise of liberation in the cry within.

So it is with Raskolnikov. If we feel his case in terms of the Laforgue lines we can understand both the motivation of his crime and the external logic of most of his conduct afterwards. It is the story of *Crime and Punishment* at the level of its immediate impact. We are very near it; it is the murder that only by some saving accident we did not ourselves commit— as we did not make a million, win a race, or conquer Europe, all the things it is still not impossible to do, and which, because we have not done them, may yet tempt us to murder. Between temptation and deed there is no distance at all in symbolic meaning. With that symbolic strength in mind, the story of Raskolnikov becomes not only possible but probable, and, as we attend it, not only probable but proved. Let us look and see.

How easy it is to believe that this young, handsome, proud, and sensitive boy might be drawn *first of all* to the possibility of murder as the way out of an intolerable situation. It is the situation of poverty, debt, starvation, shabbiness, sickness, loneliness; for Raskolnikov has reached such a stage of privation that even thought has become a luxury—a kind of luxurious hallucinated hysteria; an extremity in which only the rashest dream seems a normal activity. It is the situation of the sponge, too, for Raskolnikov has come to depend on his mother and sister for help they can not afford to give, for help they can give only by prostituting themselves in marriage and servile relationships. The sponge who is aware that he is a sponge is in an awkward situation; the pride of his awareness deprives him of the use of the exactions he makes; and that is how it is with Raskolnikov, as he lies in his attic committing symbolic murder. He deceives himself, proudly, that he has conceived murder to symbolize his mother's and sister's freedom as well as his own. He lends his dark motive the external colour of a good deed, and then identifies the colour with the motive, and forgets what the murder, dark within him, really is. But to starve and be a

---

[1] [Go, sterile repetitions! Life is real and criminal!]

sponge, that is not all Raskolnikov has to put up with in his pride; he is in the situation, too, of the proud man of intellect who has as yet done nothing and who is afraid that there will be nothing for him to do unless he invents it. Not only can he do nothing for his poverty or for his family, he is in the terrible position of being unable to do anything for himself. Such is his pride, that none of the ordinary things men do will be enough; and such is his pride, too, that none of the things ordinary people—his mother, his sister, his forgotten friends,—can do for him are tolerable to him; he is the man for whom no one can do anything. Deeper still, he is that part of all men which cannot be touched, but which must create an image of itself in some extraordinary deed, some act against ordinary people and against the ordinary part of himself. The extraordinary wells within him and inundates the ordinary self with its fever. And in that fever, which never leaves him while we know him, the possibility of murder becomes the necessity of murder.

What is fully imagined as necessary has goodness and freedom at the very heart of its horror, a sentiment which may be interpreted in different ways, having to do either with the tearing down of order or with the envelopment of disorder, or, finally, with the balancing of several disorders so as to form an order. At the level of immediate impact, Raskolnikov's story is concerned with the tearing down of order; that is the melodrama which carries us along and exhausts our attention. What Dostoevsky does to that story, the immense clarification of secret life and intimate impulse which he brings to it, composes the secondary impact of the story, and brings us to the second stage where the disorder brought about in the first stage is enveloped by the created personality of Raskolnikov. Actually, the two processes go on at once, in the sense that no matter how far into the second stage Dostoevsky leads us, the first stage is never left behind, but is rather always present, a frame of action and image, to carry the significance of the second stage. This is to say that Dostoevsky never fails of the primary task of the novelist; if his story seems for the moment to have been left behind, it is only that in reality it has got ahead of us, and when we catch up we see how much has been done without our noticing it. The story of the Crime is blended with the clarification of the Punishment; the actor creates the role which expresses the nature and significance of his deed; Raskolnikov, in the end, becomes the product of his crime, but still depends on it to command our attention.

That is how Dostoevsky envelopes the disorder consequent upon Raskolnikov's attempt at the destruction of order. With the third possibility, whereby the imagination not only envelops disorder—our substantial chaos —in a created personality, but proceeds to balance the sense of several disorders—the tensions of chaos—against each other so as to form a new order; with this possibility Dostoevsky has little to do. It is not that he was necessarily unequal to the task, but that the nature, source, and direction of his insights did not lead him to undertake it. His view of necessity was simpler, and his sense of possibility more simplified, than the task would require; his vision was that of the primitive Christian, and that vision was so powerful within him that it blinded him to everything else. To him the edge of the abyss of sin was the horizon of salvation by faith, and suffering was the condition of vision. Sin was the Crime, and the suffering created by faith was the punishment.

If we push the operation of this insight one step further, it becomes evident that the act of life itself is the Crime, and that to submit, by faith, to the suffering of life at the expense of the act is to achieve salvation—or, if you like a less theological phrase, it is to achieve integration or wholeness of personality. It is only dramatically true that the greater the sin the greater the salvation, and it is only arbitrarily true that any one act is sinful more than another act or than all acts. The crime of Raskolnikov, and its punishment in created suffering, could have been as great if he had never stirred from his room, if only the novelist's imagination could have conceived them. But the imagination requires images, as vision requires fables and thought requires formulas, before conceptions can be realised; which is to say that the faculties of men are not equal to their needs except by the intervention of symbols which they discover rather than create, and which they discover best of all in stories of violence, or of the sense of violence, or of the promise of violence.

So we watch, with the immediate attention which discovers meaning, the process of Raskolnikov trying to make a hero—a complete man—of himself by committing a foul and frivolous murder. Any animal might strike another down without need when the odour of blood is thick, and it means nothing. But we are shown how much this murder of an old and malevolent pawnbroker, ripe for death, as Raskolnikov says, ripe as a louse, is not meaningless but huge with meaning. The meaning begins with the stench of Petersburg, the stench of the detailed plans, the stench of pothouses, the pervading sense of the filthy possibilities of the human heart, and the glittering eyes of the victim peering through the slit of the door. The meaning grows more meaningful, irretrievably meaningful, when in the second chapter we are exposed to Marmeladov in the stinking tavern and hear his confession of drunken humiliation and of what it has brought upon Katerina his wife in the way of sickness and shame and anger and hair-pulling, and brought upon his daughter too, in her glad submissive acceptance of the humiliation of prostitution. It is impossible to *say* how this adds

to the richness of Raskolnikov's motive, but like the general images of
stench and violence, and drunkenness, it is impossible not to *know* and
very precisely, how much it does add. Let us say that, it exposes Raskolnikov, and through him the reader, to a kind of dead-level human degradation in terms of images which revolt him as he assents to them.

At any rate they fit him—for the purposes of the story—they fit him
to see as further degradation the events which his mother's letter reports to
him. Before he opens the letter we see his cluttered mind in his sleazy room
trying to work around the idea of a "fortune all at once"; and in the letter
he reads how indeed that is precisely what Douania his sister is about to
get by selling herself to Luzhin. Douania has permitted herself or has been
driven to do just the practical, ordinary thing which Raskolnikov, the
extraordinary man, is unable to do, and which—as it is being done for *him*
—is the more intolerably humiliating to him. Her marriage is like the
prostitution of Sonia. Thinking of it, Hamlet-like, the idea of the murder
rediscovers itself most naturally in his mind, and he finds that he had *felt
beforehand* that it would come back; it has begun to acquire a kind of
reality quite independent of him except that it requires to be completed.

Your ordinary novelist might well have now proceeded to the completion of the deed, but Dostoevsky saw deeper into the nature of the deed
and knew that it required further preparation, so that it might be as ripe as
the victim. Raskolnikov goes out for a breath of air and to escape the
pressure of his dilemma. But there is no escape, except from one level of
intensity to a deeper level. Walking on the boulevard the double pressure
of Sonia and of Douania springs upon him in the shape of the drunken
young girl, with the torn dress, and indecorous posture, evidently just
seduced and then discarded, who is being pursued by the plump gentleman.
In his shabby and dishevelled pride, and with his uprooted and irresolute
mind he first attempts to save the girl and then gives it up as a bad job;
he revolts against his revulsion, reminding himself of the percentage theory
of vice whereby "a certain number" are bound to go that way, and resolves
forthwith to go see Razumihin, that simpleton of a man who takes things
as they are. But again he changes his mind; he cannot see Razumihin till
after "It." The image of the debauched girl has set the murder to pursuing
him still more closely. He contrives for himself, as he thinks, an escape in
the green islands of the Neva, where there is no stench, no drunkenness, no
human filth. The human filth is stronger. He first buys himself a glass of
Vodka, and then walks out exhausted, turning aside on the way home and
falls asleep in the bushes, where a dream assaults him with a fresh image of
the little sorrel horse beaten to death because it cannot pull all humanity. In
the dream he rushes to kiss the bleeding face of the horse as it dies, and

at that moment wakes. The moment of waking is the nearest he comes to renouncing his crime before committing it, and it is the nearest, too, that he comes to realising its nature before the event. "It was as though an abscess that had been forming for a month past in his heart had suddenly broken. Freedom, freedom! He was free from that spell, that sorcery, that obsession!" He had reached the point which Shakespeare, in his own play of Crime and Punishment, *Measure for Measure,* calls the point where the two prayers cross, where, in the human heart, good and evil are created in the one gesture.

It was coincidence, you will remember, that decided the event. Raskolnikov happened to hear, on his way home, that the old pawnbroker would be left alone at seven the following evening, and he heard it at precisely the moment that he had given up the idea of the murder, when he had, in fact, begun again to use his reason and will. But the other thing had grown in him like a disease, and feeding on the coincidence, was able to destroy his will and reason, that is to say his sense of propriety in the social order. It may be observed, for those who carp at the use of coincidence as belittling the probabilities, that on the contrary the use of coincidence in art, like the sense of it in life, heightens the sense of inevitability; for coincidence is the artist's way of representing those forces in us not ourselves. Coincidence, properly dealt with, creates our sense of that other self within us whom we neither can ever quite escape nor quite meet up with.

In this case it is the perfected chain of coincidence, upon which Dostoevsky lavishes so many pages, that builds up the murder so that it is a kind of separate being existing between Raskolnikov and his victim. As he climbs the stairs, he feels that Alyona Ivanovna ought to be ready for him, ready to be murdered, for he feels that the murder is somewhere between them, other than either, but equally accessible to both. It was in the nature of Dostoevsky's insight to see always that the actor and the patient are both implicated in the deed, and that they are joined by it. The actor, in this case, has more consciousness than the patient of the implication; in *The Idiot* it is the other way round, and Myshkin, the patient, is shown as more conscious, or more representative, of the deeds that are done to him than the doers of the deeds can possibly be. In *Crime and Punishment,* it is Sonia who is perhaps the counterpart of Myshkin, for to her all deeds happen whether the doers realize it or not, and they happen, moreover, completely. It is perhaps because Raskolnikov is the other sort, the sort who requires of a deed that before it is credible or fully significant he must do it himself. He does not believe in the murder until he has done it, and not altogether even then. Constantly it slips away, a thing he realizes that he has forgotten, or a thing he has to re-enact, to emphasize, and so a thing that tends to lose its meaning except as he identifies himself with it; whereas to Sonia, once she has learned of it, once she has submitted herself to the idea of it in him, she has no doubts about it and it is entirely meaningful. Nothing herself, Sonia is able to contain everything; while Raskolnikov, who must be everything himself, can contain nothing for long. Dante would have known how to punish him, looking for a mirror through an eternal hell; but Dostoevsky has rather to transform him in order to save him, or more accurately to show him as about to be saved in Sonia's eyes.

But he is not transformed for a long time, never permanently in the book; never can he leave the murder which fixed him, nor the images of which it was made: the images of stench, poverty, drunkenness, vanity, sick-hunger, lechery and intellectual debauchery, through which the murder comes to be a deed in being, with the double power of invocation and growth. At first, indeed, he forgets it for the images and the sickness which went with it, and when he wakes to it he finds that instead of feeling it behind him it has somehow got ahead of him and he is driven to catch up to it. Instead of freedom, power, completeness, he is more at loss than ever, and more incoherent, there are only "scraps and shreds of thought," suspicions, excitements, alarms, and fresh temptations to extraordinary declarations of himself. This is, of course, the first phase of the Punishment for the Crime, that having striven by the crime to reach a complete solution of his incomplete life, he should find himself not only less complete than ever and more wayward but actually perilously incoherent, with a personality on the verge of dissipation. He lives in a haunted vertigo, into which for the time he can invoke only the shrieking phantoms of rage and dread. He is in the position, so humiliating to his continuing pride, where he is completely powerless as the perfectly good man, as powerless as Sonia. There is nothing he can yet see to do for himself, and nothing any longer that he can do for others. When the police send for him about his IOU which his landlady had sold, he feels himself possessed by "a gloomy sensation of agonising, everlasting solitude and remoteness," and knows that it will never be possible for him to appeal to anyone in any circumstance of life. There is a sense in which Dostoevsky might have stopped at this point, for he had put Raskolnikov on the path at the end of which lay the meaning of his Crime as Punishment. For as in the Christian psychology no man may complete himself in deed, so the meaning of a deed can never be completed within the history of the man who enacts it. Only the judgment completes either the man, or his deed, or his meaning.

But both the deed and the meaning can continue in their course of meaningfulness. The growth of meaning is infinite. At the moment he feels his agonising solitude form consciously within him he hears the police discuss the murder; that is, it is given to him from outside for the first time, and as not his murder, but as an object in no one's possession; at once he is driven to confess, to seize it for his own, but a combination of the fumes of paint and the pang of creation cause him to faint. When he comes to, he goes out leaving a strange impression and a potent silence behind him.

Out of that strangeness and silence grows the pursuit-game which occupies the rest of the book, for Raskolnikov having decided that suspicions may have been roused about him from his peculiar conduct, begins playing a complicated and eccentric game, or rather a set of games. He pursues the police, eggs the police on to pursue him, and himself both pursues the murder, the acknowledgment of it, and denies it whenever he comes face to face with it. The result of all this rash, tortuous, and vain activity is that he creates such an image of the murder that at last it overwhelms him. He plays his hands so that others play to him. In the event, there is nothing for anyone to believe about him except the extraordinary reality of the murder. He could not have made more certain of his arrest and imprisonment had that been his entire object. Only he delayed it, played with it, encouraged it to develop, in order to get the full savour of it and of himself.

First he rouses unconscious suspicions in Razumihin, then in Zossim —of the doctor in whom the suspicions may have been quite conscious, for he looked at Raskolnikov "curiously" whenever there was opportunity, and especially after that scene where Raskolnikov himself first realises the murder in a parallel and arbitrary image which brims and trembles as you look at it. It is that image which comes when Raskolnikov lies abed listening to the doctor and Razumihin talk of the murder, and how a housepainter has been mixed up in it. Nastasya, who is present, bursts out that Lizaveta was murdered, too.

"Lizaveta," murmured Raskolnikov hardly audibly.
"Lizaveta, who sold old clothes. Didn't you know her? She used to come here. She mended a shirt for you, too."
Raskolnikov turned to the wall where in the dirty, yellow paper he picked out one clumsy, white flower with brown lines on it and began examining how many petals there were in it, how many scallops in the petals and how many lines on them. He felt his arms and legs as lifeless as though they had been cut off. He did not attempt to move, but stared obstinately at the flower.

It is so that the murder is brought home by the housemaid's first mention of the other and incidental murder of Lizaveta. We feel what passed in Raskolnikov's mind, and feel it as if it passed in his face, and in his hands, too: quite as if he had plucked the scalloped petals of the clumsy white flower off the wallpaper. Razumihin, who was simple, may have seen nothing, but the doctor, looking at this dissenting soul, surely saw what Raskolnikov saw in the flower even if he could not then have named it. The blankest or the most conventional image is, as Dostoevsky knew, the best to hold the deepest symbol if only there is enough tension present when it is named. It is only another instance of this device that when Raskolnikov is about to go into the bar where he meets and gives himself away to Zametov, he first sees a good many drunken women, some of forty and some of seventeen, almost all of whom "had blackened eyes." Raskolnikov, who had gone out to end *this,* as he put it to himself, reflects upon this bevy with blackened eyes and pocked cheeks, that even the worst life is precious.

"Only to live, to live and live! Life, whatever it may be! . . . How true it is! Good God, how true! Man is a vile creature! . . . And vile is he who calls him vile for that," he added a moment later.

Whereupon he proceeds to risk his life, to make it precious, by playing like Hamlet on Rosencrantz and Guildenstern, upon the suspicious nerves of Zametov the police clerk as he drank tea in a restaurant. This scene, like the two great scenes with Porfiry, and like the last scene with Svidrigailov, show Raskolnikov clinging with a kind of ultimate shuddering tenacity to his original proud role of the extraordinary man, the role of Napoleon within the little man, and clinging the more desperately because in the act of playing it he sees the role is false, the role of the condemned man whose life is thereby sweet.

What else happens at the same time, the history of the growth of the Punishment along with the realisation of the Crime, is of course present in these scenes, but it has been instigated in other scenes—those with his mother and sister and Luzhin and Razumihin and the Marmeladovs; and it is perfected in other scenes still, those with Sonia especially, though these scenes might well be lifeless and pointless without their counterparts with Porfiry and Svidrigailov. There is a synergy—a working together and back and forth—between these counterparts much as there is a synergy between the two parts, the proud, self-willed part and the meek, submissive part of Raskolnikov's character. This working together takes place, and the resultant unity is seen, not because there is any logical or organic connection between the parts, but because, quite to the contrary, the conflicting elements are dramatised in association, in parallels that, as they say, never actually meet except as opposites. The more nearly they seem to be forced into meeting, the more disparate they actually show themselves to be. The fusion, if it can be called a fusion, is in the dramatic *product* of the conflicting elements, not of the elements themselves.

It is something along these lines, I think, that the theory of the "doubles" in Dostoevsky must be approached, and this whether we think of single characters or of whole books and the doubleness of the conflicts within either. Let us look at Raskolnikov, who is usually thought of as a typical Dostoevsky Double. He is self-willed and well-less, he is proud and he becomes humiliated, he loves Sonia and hates her at the same moment, he is fond of Razumihin and cannot tolerate him, he is both on the edge of confession and of anathema all along, he is good to the point of giving all that he has and evil to the point of taking life; and in short there is neither certainty nor limit to any of his moods or acts; any role is dominant for the moment to another role that may at once take its place because it has been really dominant underneath. But he is not these roles in turn, he is the product of all their playing taken together. In any pair, the one may be taken as the idea of the other, and the other the reality of the idea, and the only alternation is as to which, at a given moment, is idea and which reality. The relation is rather like that between the idea of murder and the image of the white flower on the wallpaper, where we can reverse it and say it is the relation between the idea of the flower and the image of the murder. What we get is a kind of steady state precariously maintained between the conflicting elements. The balance tips, but it recovers in the act of tipping. We should feel it as we feel similar physiological states in the body—only as the disturbance and forward drive of life—were it not that the language itself and Dostoevsky's taste for seeing the opposite to every presented element have together a tendency to formularise pure types, and then to ignore for the moment what does not exemplify the type. What happens is, by language and its dialectic mode, that Dostoevsky's imagination arrests, for the maximum possible amount of attention, the moments when the balance does tip from love to hate, from pride to humiliation, from idea to deed, from image to tension, and by the arrest, by the attention which is bent upon the moment of arrest, we see how the one in each case fecundates the other. We seem to see deeply what they make together by seeing wilfully what they are apart.

By a little progress of this notion, we can say that Raskolnikov is balanced in turn against the other characters in this novel, and that the other characters and their stories make something with Raskolnikov which is quite different from anything found in them as types, though there would be no product of their whole conflict if there was not a great deal that was living within each type, from Razumihin to Porfiry to Svidrigailov to Sonia, and all the rest. As illustration, let us take first the Marmeladov family, and consider by what astonishing luck it was that Dostoevsky thought of putting them into the history of Raskolnikov and the punishment of his crime. They were to have been, the whole little crowd of them, a novel all to themselves called "The Drunkards," a novel showing, no doubt, all the ills and humiliations that can come from the head of a poor family who has given over to heavy drinking. The luck is that Dostoevsky had them all going, with past and present and future, when Raskolnikov happened to meet old Marmeladov in the tavern and heard his humiliating confession with such apparently inexplicable sympathy. The truth is that he has something deeply in common with him, and again that Marmeladov has something which he has not yet but which he must have. What they have in common comes out when Marmeladov says that he has *nowhere to turn* except to his sick and somewhat crazy wife. Raskolnikov sees that it is not Marmeladov the good-natured drunk that turns, but Marmeladov humiliated, on hands and knees, with his hair pulled, Marmeladov in the mud which he Raskolnikov has not yet reached, but will reach in good time. Man grows used to everything, the scoundrel, says Raskolnikov, and adds: But what if he is not a scoundrel?

The scene is something like the great scenes in Dickens, caricature by direst observation, with the difference that Dostoevsky—and this is perhaps the way Dostoevsky himself read Dickens—replaces zest of observation for its own sake with the severity of attention that is based upon zeal, and replaces the anguish of social consciousness with the dignity of religion. Marmeladov, like Micawber, is able to represent much beyond himself because he is something of a buffoon; he can talk and act for talking and acting's sake; and he can be honest, and let himself go, just to see what will happen; he can see himself at his worst in order to be at his best. And so he does; he produces, to show himself at his utmost, and for the sake of Raskolnikov, for the sake of this new strange novel in which he unconsciously finds himself, the character and personality of Sonia, whom Raskolnikov needs as complement and salvation, and whom the novel needs for mechanics and plot. And not Sonia only, he also produces, by just the agency of his being, scenes in which all manner of things which bear on the novel can take place. His death, his funeral, the lyric insanity of Katerina his wife and her death-dance in the streets, all these are provided with new and enriched context by the accidental meeting in the tavern of the *distrait* Raskolnikov and the drunken buffoon Marmeladov. And not only Marmeladov himself, but each of his family, as he precipitates their fates through his drunkenness and buffoonery, add to the context of Raskolnikov's growing fate.

Together they furnish him with his own opposite. As he is the person who above all must act, they are the persons who must be acted upon. He is the criminal, and they are the victims, victims generally and all the way through in much the same way that the old pawnbroker was in Raskolnikov's eyes "ripe" to be murdered. No degradation is too great for the old drunkard who has nowhere to turn; you have only to put fresh degradation in his way and he will take it up with gusto. Katerina, too, eager to find insult in everyone's speech, in his absence or in his presence, imagines insult and injury upon herself at every opportunity. The children, even, with their illness and their rags cannot be treated except with brutality. And as for Sonia, she is not only eager and willing, she fairly demands further humiliation. By prostituting herself, this thin, bird-like creature, almost without a body, shows herself as inviting at best further depravity; for surely no one not depraved, no one not desiring to sack the *last* citadel of integrity, would have any use for her. Sonia had to come from such a family, for only out of the experience of such utter humiliation could her own perfect humility grow. As they are damned so she is blessed, by the enormous shift in significance caused by the shift of a single syllable. It is Gide, who knew Dostoevsky well, who observed that where humility opened the gates of heaven, humiliation opened those of hell. Sonia's blessedness is built upon the bottomlessness of their hell. She accepts, and makes into inner strength, a worse stage of the experience which tore them apart.

Thus, as Raskolnikov comes into contact with Marmeladov and his wife, as he probes them with his intellect, they absorb his sense of himself into a kind of private hell, an abyss beyond soundings, quite off the continental shelf of consciousness which his intellect, however demoniac, can reach. But Sonia, and this is the secret of her personality, can no more be penetrated by Raskolnikov's intellect than her soul can be ravished through the degradation of her body. That is her attraction as a prostitute: that she cannot be prostituted in anything that she has to offer; and that is her power over Raskolnikov, the power of perfect submissiveness which in another place Dostoevsky calls the greatest power in the world: it is the power that he cannot attain by any deed, but that can be attained by imitation, by suffering what she has suffered. It is the power of her suffering, the happiness of it, that not so much overcomes him as it infects or fecundates him. For he is not overcome, though it is promised that he will be; he fights back, the very feeling of her goodness, his very sense of the stigma of her faith, aggravates his pride and the intellectual structure upon which his pride is built, so that when he goes to her for comfort and strength he finds that he has to torture her, and to repel her at every level. The love he feels for her is also and simultaneously hate, and there is no difference between the emotions as he feels them, only as he intellectually knows what they are. And this is an example of the profound psychological rightness of Dostoevsky's judgment, for surely it takes only a pause for judgment to see that as hate or pride is the burden Raskolnikov carries so love or humility is the *burden* of Sonia's life. If she feels his burden as love and accepts it as of nature, he must feel the burden of her love as intolerable. He is indeed a kind of Prodigal Son who finds the love with which he is welcomed the very burden from which he ran away in the first place. It was not of Sonia that he made the following remark but thinking of her and just before seeing her, so it fits all the more: "Oh, if only I were alone and no one loved me and I too had never loved anyone! *Nothing of all this would have happened.*"

It will be remembered that earlier in the book Razumihin has explained to Douania that her brother is perhaps a person incapable of love. Razumihin may have meant only that Raskolnikov is a lonely fellow, but he was literally right as well; no one can be said to love who does not feel as acceptable the burden of love in return, and who does not feel, too, that in loving someone positively, he is imposing the most difficult of human burdens. Sonia knows this in herself, by intuition directed inwards as well as outwards, as a condition of her being, and it is to that double burden that she submits.

Like the crime which existed *between* the old pawnbroker, so between Sonia and Raskolnikov there exists her intuition of love, which she feels so strongly that he *must* know, that gradually by a contagion from her understanding he does know it. It is a love, this unassailable love of the unsmirchable prostitute, that has nothing to do with sex. Not that it might not have been sexual, and even might have taken the means of a kind of ultimate lechery of the spirit, and still have been within the Christian insight, but that Dostoevsky was unable ever to create a character or a mood which showed more than the most superficial aspects of sexual awareness. His people were not eunuchs or in any way deprived of sex but they were born without it. It is love *manqué* [1] that Dostoevsky deals with, love *malgré-lui;* [2] and it is for this reason perhaps that Dostoevsky is able to show love as pure spiritual renunciation. That is why, too, in what was to others the romantic fancy of purity in a prostitute, he sees a kind of exorbitant and omnivorous reality: a true dramatic enactment of the idea of purity. This is why, again, he so often concerns his characters with the idea of debauching young girls, girls before puberty, in whom sex as anyone else would have understood it would not have ripened, so that the debauchery would be of the actor alone.

If these remarks help explain the character and power of Sonia who is of the character of the saint, they help with the others as well, most particularly with the riddle of Svidrigailov, to whom we shall come in a moment for his own sake, but whom now we shall consider in his relation with the

[1] [defective love.]
[2] [despite itself.]

character of Douania, Raskolnikov's sister. This young lady is painted as all abloom with normality; she and her mother belong in Dostoevsky's long gallery of simple, intelligent, sincere, generous, impulsive, and dependably decent women, young and old, of whom there are samples in almost every one of his novels—as, to give but one example, Mme. Epanchin and her daughter Alglaia in *The Idiot*. Always they serve the same purpose, to act as foils or background for the extraordinary actions of distorted or driven individuals, such as Raskolnikov and Myshkin. They preserve their identity and their normal responsiveness through every form of violence and disorder; it is their normality which, by contrast, promotes the meaningfulness of the good and bad angels, the light and the dark angels, whose actions make the stories. Nothing in themselves but attractive types, they come to life in terms of the protagonists.

In *Crime and Punishment* they represent the normal conduct from which Raskolnikov departs; they represent the order of society which he tears down and envelops; it is them, their lives, to whom he gives meaning. In the same way Luzhin, the bourgeois on the make, and Lebetziatnikov the nihilist reformer, are caricatures, the one malicious and the other kindly, of normal types of eccentricity within the ordered society which produces at its extremes the super-egotist Raskolnikov and the super-reformer Sonia. But these figures gather part of their meaning from the driven, demoniac, "secret" character of Svidrigailov, the lecher of women and debaucher of souls: the mysterious figure whose evil is concentrated in what is asserted to be, but never shown, his intense and overweening sexuality. As an example of sexual behavior, Svidrigailov is incredible. Sex is Dostoevsky's symbol for a diabolic, destructive power, which he can sense but cannot measure, and which he cannot otherwise name. This aspect of the Svidrigailov type of figure is Dostoevsky's attempt to explain, to dramatise and invoke, a force which he does not seem ever to have understood but which he knows must exist. It is a lonely, awkward, proud sort of power, hovering always on the brink of suicide; it is haunted and haunting; it is the power of the "Other" thing, the other self, the dark side of the self, the substance and drive of that secret world in us which the devil creates, the power which in conventional life—the life which we mostly live—we successfully ignore, so that we tend to estimate its presence in others rather than in ourselves—as if others were our othermost selves. Thus Douania's soul had been imperilled by Svidrigailov's attempt to seduce her, and imperilled precisely by Svidrigailov's technique, which he outlines to Raskolnikov, of assaulting her through purity. He has caused her purity, not her baser emotions but her purity, somehow to desire him, and she had been rescued, in the first instance, in the nick of time: by the confusion, in

Marfa Petrovna's eyes, of her purity with her lust. Raskolnikov understands well enough what the risk is—that his sister may be contaminated, that her decency may somehow come to absorb the temptation which Svidrigailov affords her in the new terms of his generosity. What he does not understand is the means by which the contamination, the trespass, will take place, which is by the frustration of violence on Douania's part when in the lonely room with the locked door, she tries so hard to shoot him. She is left by the desperate effort—by the fruitless tumescence of her spirit—in a very ambiguous state, which the story of Raskolnikov's Crime and Punishment did not have time to develop. One is not sure whether in that scene Douania has absorbed something from Svidrigailov, or whether Svidrigailov has absorbed what he wanted from Douania. Something has passed between them, at any rate, which leaves Svidrigailov either done for or contented, either vastated or fully occupied. In either case his remaining hours are justified—his visit to his little girl fiancee and his farewell present, the advance in the hotel-room, the mouse in the bed, the five year-old girl whose smile turns in his dream to a harlot's grin, the dream of the flood, which is to say the coming of judgment, and the suicide at dawn. We feel that the enigma of Svidrigailov has either been solved beyond our understanding or that it did not really exist—quite the problem of the devil. At any rate, his function has been fulfilled for everyone but Raskolnikov.

His relations to Raskolnikov have gone beyond those with the others, both in scope and intent, however much they may depend for their actuality upon the others. For Svidrigailov is a foil for the whole story. He comes before the crime, in a way induces the crime to come into being, is the first to perceive the crime, and in a way *finishes* the crime without (since he does not have Raskolnikov's luck in finding Sonia) reaching the punishment. He *is* Raskolnikov in simpler perspective, he is Raskolnikov's other self, a mirror of being into which Raskolnikov never quite dares to look. He is the mystery of Raskolnikov's other self. The sense of him is symbolic, as it always is with mystery. Because he is a mystery beforehand, and exhibits himself mysteriously and providentially, he gathers meaning as he goes along, but not too clearly. He has the advantage of being not well understood, the figure grasped at but not caught, whom we are always about to understand. In fact we have frequently the sense of understanding him perfectly until we stop to query what it is we understand, when we find only that he represents precisely that secret life within us which drives us into incomprehensible actions. Like the character of Stavrogin in *The Possessed,* of whom Dostoevsky says in his notes that he was not *meant* to be understood, but was meant rather to be a reservoir of the portentous, the possible, the mysterious, he is the symbolic clarification of that which cannot be expressed other than symbolically. He is the promise upon which we lean, knowing that it cannot be kept. He recedes like the horizon that follows us, only when we look.

Perhaps we may say that Svidrigailov envelops the disorder brought about by Raskolnikov's crime by imaging a kind of order which we cannot reach but which is always about to overwhelm us. He is a symbol of the mystery of the abyss, and it is a great witness to the depth of Dostoevsky's imagination that he is able to create in the flesh, with eyes too blue and flesh too youthful, such figures at will.

It is no less a test of Dostoevsky's skill—not his depth but his skill—that he is able to employ the one remaining major character in the book without, as it were, creating him at all. I mean, of course, that thirty-five year old roly-poly of the disengaged intellect called Porfiry, that man whose life, as he insists to Raskolnikov, is already finished, who has no other life to live, and nothing to do with what remains to him but probe and prance intellectually. Porfiry is so much a victim of moral fatigue that he is beneath every level of being but that of intellectual buffoonery. He represents order; he understands desire, ambition, all forms of conduct, but he knows nothing of the sources and ends of conduct, except that he can catch at them, in the midst of the game of the drowning man which he plays so long and so skilfully, like so many straws that only just elude his dancing fingers. But he is unreal, except as an agency of the plot, something to make the wheels go round; he is a fancy of the pursuing intellect whom Raskolnikov must have invented had he not turned up of his own accord. As Svidrigailov and Sonia between them represent the under-part, and the conflict in the under-part, of Raskolnikov's secret self, so Porfiry represents the maximum possible perfection of the artificial, intellectual self under whose ministrations Raskolnikov *reasons* himself into committing his crime, and who therefore is the appropriate instrument for driving him to the point of confessing it. It is Porfiry, who has no morals and no faith, who is all the proud game of intellect, who whenever he comes to sack Raskolnikov leaves him in a state of collapse, just as it is either Svidrigailov or Sonia who gives him strength. Porfiry knows what he must do, and can point it out to him in the example of the peasant who came forward to take the suffering of the crime upon his guiltless shoulders, he knows all the intellect can know, and perhaps knows that it must collapse, but he cannot push Raskolnikov over the brink, because he knows it only conventionally, by rote. He understands the Crime, because he represents that against which it was committed, and knows with what it was committed, but he cannot touch the Punishment, the completion of the Crime, because it must take place in a region of the soul beyond his grasp, the region which reason, argument, all the armament of order only clutter up and from which they must be swept, the region where the assumption of guilt by all that is innocent within the self takes place through the submission of the sinful, acting self to the faithful, waiting self, which waits, in Dostoevsky's primitive Christian insight, only to be created.

I think we have touched both upon the elements that go to make up the obvious and immediate impact of Raskolnikov's crime and its consequences in action, and upon the elements which as we understand them as exhibited in the various characters leave us all—not Russians, not fanatics of humiliation, not the distorted shadowy figures of Dostoevsky's novel alone, but all of us without exception deeply implicated in the nature of the Crime. A word remains with which to fasten upon the nature of the Crime an indication of the nature of the Punishment. I do not know that there is a word ready to hand, for we have fallen quite out of the way of thinking in insights and images with the simple, direct intensity which was Dostoevsky's second nature. We lack the anterior conviction, the conviction before we begin to think, with which Dostoevsky mastered the relationship of man to God. But at least in saying that, we state Dostoevsky's major and abiding theme. To punish Raskolnikov, to bring him to retribution, to atonement, Dostoevsky had only to create his relationship to God, and to show at the same time how that relationship sprang from the nature of man as a creature of God quite apart from the structure of human society as an institution of men's minds. Dostoevsky believed that as Christ the innocent one took upon himself the suffering of all the innocent ones in the world, and so redeemed them along with the guilty, so the individual man has in him an innocent part which must take on the suffering caused by the guilty part. As he saw it, in our crime we create our guilt. Perhaps the commonplace example of false arrest will begin to make an analogue for what he meant. Which of us, falsely arrested would not at once begin to assess his guilt, even for the crime which brought about the false arrest? And you would assess this guilt the more clearly because you were aware of the haphazard, the hazarded, character of your innocence. Similarly, the depth of your guilt would be measured by the depth of your faith, which would then, if you had imagination enough, transform you.

It should be emphasized that it was transformation, not reformation, that Dostoevsky envisaged. Reformation would have dealt with the mere guilty act against society. Transformation, through suffering, is alone able to purge the guilt of being.

Finally, we may draw some comparisons, in this search for means of clarifying the nature of Dostoevsky's notion of punishment, from recent history in our own country. When Mooney was released from his generation of false imprisonment, it soon turned out that he had no symbolic dignity, but represented rather a mere miscarriage of institutional justice; and so with the Scottsboro boys; so, too, with Dreyfus in the last century, for Dreyfus had no dignity. But if we think of Sacco and Vanzetti, does there not arise within us at once a sense that their great and terrifying symbolic dignity is due to Vanzetti having assumed, with profound humility, the whole devastating guilt of the industrial society which killed him? Whether Vanzetti was innocent or guilty in law has become an irrelevant question. But the guilt which his last words and letters, his last conduct, somehow expiated, which was our guilt, remains permanently in question; for Vanzetti, like Raskolnikov, showed himself in the humiliation of his punishment, in humble relation to God.

THE FOUNTAIN AND THE THIRST

AN INTERPRETATION OF ANDRÉ GIDE

WALLACE FOWLIE

I

THE multiple aspects of André Gide's sensitivity and intelligence have been countless times enumerated and analysed. His restlessness, his endless quest and curiosity have led him through philosophies, experiences, and genres until his very extensive work stands out to-day as the major source for our contemporary aesthetic and moral problems. He has been publishing continuously for fifty-three years. But during this period, between 1891, when his first book, *Les Cahiers d'André Walter,* appeared, and 1944, when his *Journal, 1939–1942* was published in New York, Gide has maintained, despite the diversity of his thought, a central role of extraordinary unity. In fact, no other role could represent such oneness of purpose and attitude, because it is that of Narcissus.

Gide no longer appears to us as the diversifier or the wearer of many masks. Both contemplator and contemplative, he is the man of our age who has looked most religiously and most lovingly at himself and at the mirrored

"The Fountain and the Thirst: an Interpretation of André Gide" reprinted by permission of Wallace Fowlie.

features of the universe. Great books, those of our age and of other ages, renew the myths of mankind. Those of Gide renew the myth of Narcissus, of that being who questions himself by means of his sight and the steady searching of his eyes. To know the form of his very soul was the objective of the youth who bent down over the waters of the fountain and excluded from his sight and from his passion all that was not he himself.

We are familiar with the story of the myth, but we are usually unaware of its resurgence among us. We remember Narcissus as that youth for whom a kiss was impossible because the lips he desired were his own. He was the boy held not by the world, but by the appearance of the world as it outlined itself in the colourless water. Centred in this mirrored appearance of the world was his own form with which Narcissus strove to unite himself. Here the Greek myth reveals the universal quest of man: union with one's first self, union with reality and the pure part of one's created being.

As one book has succeeded another, the written words of Gide have become increasingly transparent and revelatory. His books are like crystal works of art, like the mirror-fountain of Narcissus, that catch partial reflections of the world and of himself. The steady gaze of Narcissus into the clear water is the myth of man, whereas the works of the artist are the sacrifice he makes to the world, of himself and of his self-contemplation. In each book Gide tries to recompose his features. Each book is a forcing of himself toward that form which has been lost in the universe. They are a series of mirrors, whose beauty lies not so much in the reflected traits as in the seriousness of the contemplation and the fervent search to unite with the original self.

At the very inception of his career, Gide wrote a brief tract on Narcissus (*Traité du Narcisse*). It was published in the same year that his first book appeared. To-day, in the perspective of many years, the interpretation of Narcissus seems more centrally relevant to Gide's work than his André Walter. The influence of Mallarmé and the symbolists is strong in both of these early pieces. Sterility and hamletism characterize Gide's first hero, André Walter, in his incapacity to meet life with action or equate his dream with reality. But in his statement on the problems of Narcissus, Gide alters the symbolist pose of immobility enacted by Baudelaire's albatross and Mallarmé's swan. The sailors who have imprisoned the albatross on the deck of the boat, and the lake which was frozen over the white wings of the swan, are symbols of the world opposing the necessary freedom of the artist's spirit. But the attraction which Narcissus feels in the calm water of the fountain has not been imposed upon him by any outside force. He is free in his self-love and wills this strange solitary contemplation. There is a vast difference between the detrimental weight of the world making impossible any soaring of the spirit and the long gaze of his eyes which Narcissus directs downward to the tranquil waters of a fountain. In each pose —in the incarcerated pose of the symbolist and in the self-willed and hypnotic pose of Narcissus—the artist is alone. But the reason for the pose is different in each case.

The experience of the romantic or the symbolist seeking to release himself from the bonds of society and the material world is less metaphysical than the experience of Narcissus seeking to attach himself to the profoundest part of his own being. The symbolist seeks release in order to create a new part of himself in a new freedom. Narcissus seeks attachment in order to discover the oldest and most permanent part of himself. One moves toward an unconceived form; the other toward a lost form. Narcissus is therefore religious in his striving to unite with what he feels to be a lost primitive reality, and the symbolist is still romantic in his striving to be what is unreal and imaginary.

Through his renewal of the Narcissus myth, André Gide has separated himself from the romantic trend which, more than any other, has characterized Western literature of the past 150 years. After his initial treatment of the subject in 1891, he has continued to recast the same problem in all of his major books. Not consciously has Gide recreated the myth in his writings. But the problem of Narcissus is Gide's, and the fervour of its application is religious.

II

The first important book of André Gide, *Les Neurritures Terrestres,* was published in 1897, but was not read until several years later. This work is a song of love, and especially a song on the thirst of love. Like Narcissus, the singer in *Les Neurritures Terrestres* is contemplating water in the desert of his desire, or that source which might satisfy his thirst.

Echo and the other nymphs who are abandoned by Narcissus are, in the personal experience of Gide, his early puritanism and timidity, Europe, and the life of intellection. Africa is both oasis and desert, both fertility and thirst, where the new Narcissus can forget much of his early heritage and lose himself in a new search for his being.

Les Neurritures Terrestres is the second major attack in French letters on the nineteenth century and on the exaggerated roles of science, bourgeoisism, and of the nation. The first attack was written in the century itself, in 1873, by a boy of nineteen, Arthur Rimbaud. *Une Saison en Enfer* announces a flight to Africa, where by joining the race of the negroes, Rimbaud might plunge into a pre-Christian period and forget the morality imposed upon him by his Catholic baptism and the bourgeois conventions of his age. Unlike Gide, Rimbaud was the artist of violence. He renewed, in his flights of self-annihilation, another myth, fully as ancient as that of Narcissus, in the history of man: the myth of the phoenix. The work of Rimbaud is a self-immolation. He had to destroy himself utterly in order to rise up again from his own ashes.

These two works are songs of love. Rimbaud's relates the love of violence and self-destruction, and Gide's relates the love of contemplation and of self. Rimbaud, in *Une Saison en Enfer,* portrays himself as the hyena, the convict, and the sinner who, Samson-like, causes to crash down upon his own head the world he despised and refused to obey. Gide, in *Les Nourritures Terrestres,* portrays himself as the sensualist who knows the universe through his senses, who feels directly the touch of the earth, of plants, the taste of wine, the longing of thirst and desire, the air of nights and dawns, the ecstasy of sleep. Rimbaud, in his phoenix reincarnation, denounced his century by destroying the artist in himself and by resurrecting himself in Ethiopia as a gun-runner for King Menelok. Gide, in his Narcissus reincarnation, denounced the same century by wilfully creating, from a background of bourgeois Calvinism, the artist in himself. The sands, the oasis springs, and the suppleness of young Arabs which he contemplated in North Africa were the reflections of himself, of the self he willed to become, of that part of him most distant from the earlier Paris self.

He tells us explicitly in *Les Nourritures Terrestres* that the characters he names never existed. Ménalque, who seems to be the teacher of this new fervor, and Nathanaël, who is the disciple being taught, are the two roles of Narcissus: the one who looks and the one who is seen. No characters in the book, and yet it is a book on love. The central dogma in this new religion of love is that of vision. Gide tells us countless times that the act of seeing is more significant than the thing seen. It is the desire which counts and enriches the soul, and not the possession of the thing desired.

This is perhaps the fullest definition we can give of the Gidian term "fervour." Fervour seems to imply an attainment to the bareness of being, to the first elemental part of a man, and also to the fullness of emotion, to the amplitude which precedes any satisfaction or collapse of emotion. Two words, *"attentes"* and *"fièvre,"* recur so persistently throughout the text of Gide that they can be taken as synonyms of his fervour in which one being is all beings. To wait, in a state of fever, describes the love of Narcissus. Nathanaël is the soul of Gide to which he speaks in his desert thirst and love, as the fountain is the reflection of Narcissus into which he directs his gaze.

Gide's own soul is his first and his last disciple. When he refers to an imaginary disciple, he relates his efforts to lead the disciple away from all things dissimilar to him: his family, his room, his books, his past. This same kind of seduction was related by Lautréament and by Rimbaud. With Gide it is less violent because he has the tenderness of Narcissus who fears to breathe lest the surface of the water be troubled. Narcissus learns to judge his own being by its ability to receive light, and Gide judges all beings thus. The extreme degree of luminous receptivity is the measure of love any being is capable of. Light refracted from his face is the joy of Narcissus.

No one exists in *Les Nourritures Terrestres*. Even Gide himself is just vision (*et même moi, je n'y suis rien que Vision.* p. 151).[1] And Narcissus also changes his being into vision. That is why in the ancient myth and in its modern version of *Les Nourritures Terrestres* there is no place for the theme of solitude. Because there is no experience of solitude in the usual romantic sense. To be alone *in* oneself, in the deepest part of oneself, is vastly different from being alone *with* oneself. When Narcissus is alone in himself, he ceases being a single person. *Je suis peuplé,*[2] writes Gide (p. 177) when he becomes aware of the multiple selves of his being. Hidden and moving within him are all men, all races, and all moments. The hypnotized quiet of Narcissus is necessary for Gide to feel inhabited.

The pose of Gide in *Les Nourritures Terrestres* is absence from the world. Yet all the world is present in him. He is not alone in his absence, because his solitary existence has become quietly and fervently all existence. Narcissus of the myth thus becomes the artist reincarnated in our age, to an extraordinarily pure degree, by André Gide. The love expressed in *Les Nourritures Terrestres* is the love of the artist: prepared and protracted and fortified by a very special kind of vision of the world. Little wonder that young men, gifted in the art of creative work and thought, have been moved and tormented by this book. It is about their problem which is a new kind of love evolved by the nineteenth and twentieth centuries.

The modern artist has become Narcissus, and *Les Neurritures Terrestres* is his epithalamium. It is a marriage song celebrating the union of the artist with the world. But the union is consummated by vision and not by participation. The artist is the man who sings of the world without acting in the world. He is chained before the picture of the world, and his sole relationship with it is his dangerous and exquisite power of sight.

The silences of the modern artist are as regular as his speech. When night blots out the picture of the world, his words are interrupted, his work arrested. Between the visible beauty of the world and the hidden depths of the artist's being, a creative relationship exists. But this is broken off and suspended during each period of night when he can no longer see.

---

[1] [And even I, I am nothing except vision.]
[2] [I am populous.]

Narcissus needed the light of the sun, as the modern artist does, in order to pursue his seeing inquest.

As Narcissus is the myth of the love which is generated solely by sight, so *Les Nourritures Terrestres* is the love of the ancient myth regenerated by an ever-deepening self-examination. Each instant brings a newer and more visible awareness of oneself. Each instant is therefore different from all other instants. The unpredictable newness of the coming instant under-lies the principle of narcissistic love. Because of it, the past is constantly being destroyed for Narcissus; as for Nathanaël, books, after they are read, are rejected and burned.

The desire for love is more real than love. To love, in the ordinary sense, implies the making of a choice. But Nathanaël has learned that he must choose nothing less than everything. And everything is nothing more than what he sees. God is totally in any one part of His universe. Since God is everywhere, any one being can reveal Him to us. And especially the being which is ourself.

III

The concept itself of God provides the transition between Gide's first important book, *Les Nourritures Terrestres,* and his second important book, *La Porte Entroite,* published twelve years later, in 1909.

In between these two books, *L'Immoraliste* appeared in 1902. This "récit" is a narrative version of *Les Nourritures Terrestres.* The protagonist Michel is a combination of Nathanaël and his teacher. Michel teaches him-self, cures himself, and watches himself throughout the story. His return to health in Africa is equivalent to a new awareness of himself and of deeply hidden desires within his being. He watches the Arab boy Mektir steal a pair of scissors and sees himself liberated from conventional morality. Out of the earlier song of desire and thirst, Gide fashioned in *L'Immoraliste* a circumstantial tale of narcissistic love.

La Porte Etroite is the same narcissistic dilemma, but raised to a Christian level. The title itself, "Straight is the gate," of Biblical origin, gives a clue to our interpretation. This narrow door is comparable to a mirror or a fountain or any reduced area on which one has to live by means of an extraordinary concentration of power. Alissa, in this novel, seeks to learn how to pass alone, without Jérôme, through the narrow door, as Narcissus, in the myth, seeks to inhabit his own solitude and pierce in the reflection on the water the continuous vision of himself.

One-fifth of the book is made up of extracts from Alissa's journal. This form of writing, used so consistently by Gide in almost every one of his books, is narcissistic in serving as a steadying mirror of one's thoughts and features. The narrative part of the story is both explicated and surpassed by Alissa's journal. There the themes become luminous and poignant because there they are really seen for the first time.

The persuasive quality of narcissism in *La Porte Etroite* is apparent not only in the title and in the journal form of writing, but also in the use of the garden setting, particularly on hot summer evenings, where many of the scenes take place and where the dilemma grows to its highest pitch of intensity. The garden in *La Porte Etroite* is comparable to the desert in *Les Nourritures Terrestres* and to the fountain in *Narcissus*. These three settings really serve as reflections of the same psychological state. They are limited and reduced, because they are needed to contain the form of only one individual, of that unique self which is André Gide.

Finally, to this list of narcissistic traits, to the title, to the journal, to the garden, in *La Porte Etroite,* we can add the close blood relationship of Alissa and Jérôme. The fact that Alissa is Jérôme's cousin makes for a kind of family reflection of himself, another self in whom the same traits are either reduced or enlarged. They experience the same inner feelings even when they are separated by large distances, as if they were the same person. And Alissa always more intensively than Jérôme, as if she were Narcissus and Jérôme were her reflection.

Even when Alissa and her sister Juliette were children, Jérôme knew that Alissa was the girl he wanted to watch and contemplate, and that her sister was the girl he wanted to play with. At the moment when, as a young boy, he saw Alissa's face covered with tears, he realized that his life vocation had been decided. He knew then that he was destined to watch and wait patiently and ineffectually throughout his life. His sentence, *Moi, je ne te quitterai jamais* (p. 41),[1] is stated at the beginning of a poem on the form of love in which no action takes place.

The roles of Jérôme and Alissa are easily reversible. Gide is in both of them, but more persistently in Alissa. Jérôme waits. He is Narcissus in the physical quietness of his body. But Alissa looks steadily at the thoughts and experiences of Jérôme, and at the garden site of her solitude. (*Ici rien n'est changé dans le jardin,* p. 127.)[2] She says that she sees everything through him (*je regarde à travers toi chaque chose,* p. 129),[3] and this she continues to do even more fully and more amorously when Jérôme is travelling. The narcissistic theme becomes most pronounced when Alissa confesses that her love is more perfect when Jérôme is at a great distance

---

1 [I shall never leave you.]
2 [Here nothing is changed in the garden.]
3 [I see everything through your eyes.]

from her (*de loin je t'aimais davantage,* p. 156).[1] Her solitude in the garden fashions for Alissa a love, not real, but which seems perfect, and turns her into a solipsist, which appears to be a modern term synonymous with narcissist.

The word "happiness" is often on the lips of Alissa. The meaning she attaches to it is difficult to ascertain, and yet in this meaning lies the key to her dilemma and her desires. We can understand best what happiness is not for Alissa. It is nothing which can be saved or guarded; it is nothing to which she wishes or hopes to attain quickly. It is exactly opposed to the happiness which Emma Bovary desires and believes she can have. Fundamentally, Emma is guided by a bourgeois morality of possession, whereas Alissa is guided by a morality of sacrifice.

Happiness for Emma depends on an obscure confusion of herself with some other being, and happiness for Alissa seems to depend on an infinite and continuous approach to God. Emma tries to save her life and therefore loses it. Alissa tries to lose her life by avoiding the world and Jérôme and all facile happiness. Constantly she narrows the physical sphere of her world. She eliminates her family, her books, Jérôme, and finally the garden itself. This is the action of Narcissus, of Nathanaël in *Les Neurritures Terrestres,* of Michel in *L'Immoraliste,* of the prodigal son in *Le Retour de l'Enfant Prodigue* (1907). It is Gide's personal interpretation of renouncement which equates salvation. To save oneself is to renounce everything and attain the ultimate state of unencumberedness which Gide defines as *"disponsibilité."*

Her journal is proof enough that Alissa was not happy in her regimen of renouncement. Michel in *L'Immoraliste* represents immoderate avidity, and Alissa in *La Porte Etroite* represents immoderate virtue. Both destroy their lives. Gratuitous ardour on a hedonistic level, as in *Les Neurritures Terrestres* and in *L'Immoraliste,* can become confused with ascetic severity on a puritanical level, as in *La Porte Etroite.* The religious experience in Gide, whether it be Pagan or Protestant, appears always in the form of search. The usual religious experience implies some direct knowledge of God, some awareness of the absolute. But Gide's experience is exclusively a quest. There is a vague sadness at the end of Michel's quest, and profound sadness at the end of Alissa's.

For Narcissus, the fate of continuously seeing attaches him to the fountain site of a garden. Alissa appears attached to the same site for the same intent purpose. She sees herself throughout the years grow dim and unlovely. In her the myth of world-renouncement and self-love become

---

[1] [Afar, I loved you more.]

the pathos of solipsism. Had she attained to a religious experience, her solitude would have been happiness. When woman is only Narcissus, she sees not her beauty and her principle as the adolescent boy did, but her vanishing beauty and her losing life.

IV

It was not until 1925, at the age of fifty-six, that Gide published what he called his first novel, *Les Faux-Monnayeurs*. Thus he comes to the form of the novel only after using other genres: the "treatise" on *Narcisse,* the dithyrambic utterances of *Les Nourritures Terrestres,* the sober tales of *L'Immoraliste* and *La Porte Etroite*. Mauriac has written that the novel begins where solipsism leaves off. But no single definition of the form is applicable to all novels. Mauriac's definition applies to his own writings, but Gide's novel is largely solipsistic, or, as we prefer to call it, "narcissistic."

The central character Edouard is the novelist, who is Gide, and who is also Narcissus. Edouard both acts in the drama and comments on it. He is therefore both protagonist and chorus. He is both Narcissus and the reflection. Perhaps the analogy with Narcissus is not quite so accurate as it would be with the Neptunian: the single man who is two. But the Neptunian, or the dual character, is a variation of Narcissus.

Edouard the novelist is alone, standing midway between two worlds. On one side of him is the world of the young: inhabited especially by Bernard and Olivier. And on the other side of him is the world of adults: composed especially of parents, of ministers, of teachers. The artist finds himself between the world of the rebels and the uninitiate and the world of the moralists who stand for security and law. He is the man outside of life, who suffers from his apartness from normal living, and yet who, because of this suffering, is able to contemplate life more steadily, more amorously, and more heroically than other men who are daily destroyed by life. Tonie Kröger in Thomas Mann's story admirably states this predicament when he says: "I am sick to death of depicting humanity without having any part or lot in it." Edouard is the artist incapable of any facile kind of happiness in terms of human relationships. In the same way, Alissa stands apart from her sister and from Jérôme. And the singer in *Les Nourritures Terrestres* stands apart from Nathanaël and Ménalque.

In *Les Faux-Monnayeurs* the Neptunian character of Edouard is involved in all the various dramas of the novel, and yet he remains aloof from them all. The drama closest to him, and therefore the central drama of the work, is his relationship to Bernard and Olivier. Edouard is unable to hold Bernard, but he does hold Olivier. The experience with Olivier, one which would be condemned by society, is transposed and spiritualized in the novel. By this experience Edouard reveals himself a Neptunian in playing simultaneously the roles of sinner and artist. He is both held by the earth and drawn to heaven. This is no case of schizophrenia, because Edouard remains at all times relentlessly lucid and determined. By being the artist, he wills to attract others different from himself.

The very title of the work, the "counterfeiters," proves that the subject is not schizophrenia but neptunianism. It is a novel about a man who behaves in one way in the eyes of the world, and who all the time is making plans for another behaviour. The artist, the teacher, and the priest, whose vocations demand a fairly fixed pattern of living, are most easily Neptunian. They can lead dual and simultaneous existences of good and evil. They can most easily appear one character and be another. Edouard is one man when he is seen by others in the novel, and another man when he sees himself in his own journal. Good and evil seem to be equal forces in *Les Faux-Monnayeurs,* and it is with considerable reason that the doctrine of manicheism has been exhumed from its pages. The endless dialogue which Edouard (or Gide) carries on with himself is much more than introspection; it is a dialogue between two different characters who are the same man.

Previous to Gide's work, the novel concerned itself largely with the role of fate, with the conflict between good and evil, with social forces, with the struggle between opposing passions. But it never concerned itself solely with the essence of a single being. This is what Gide tries to do in *Les Faux-Monnayeurs*. In Edouard's temptation to stay with Olivier, to influence him deliberately, and even to make him his secretary, lies the desire to see his own essence more bare. When at this point in the novel, Edouard decides to avoid the temptation and go to London, it is simply a case of Narcissus becoming Huguenot. He is attempting to know a way more difficult than that of his own nature. *Partir parce que l'on a trop grande envie de rester!* (p. 161.) [1]

In order to mark his break with Olivier at this time, Edouard buys a new notebook for his journal. The new format and the fresh clean pages, which help him to consummate a painful separation and begin a new chapter in his life, are a facile symbol for another fountain over whose waters the same thirst will be renewed. Edouard (or Gide) always remains the artist who lives by his thirst, and never becomes the protagonist who is defeated by passion or by events in a tragedy or in a novel.

---

[1] [To leave because one is too anxious to stay.]

This explains the final sentence of the book: *Je suis bien curieux de connaitre Caloub.*[1] There is no end or even climax to the narcissistic pose of Edouard. Events and dramas and sentiments affect him deeply, but they only interrupt momentarily the mirroring of himself in the universe and in the faces of those around him. The last pages of the novel relate the tragic suicide of the boy Boris in his classroom. The pistol shot which kills him is like a stone being thrown into the fountain. For a moment the reflection is shattered. Edouard can no longer see himself in the unpredictable death of a schoolboy. But gradually the waters resume their evenness and the gaze returns. There was not sufficient motivation in this suicide to satisfy the novelist and the analyst Edouard. He refuses to incorporate it in his *Faux-Monnayeurs* and his gaze continues to be directed toward that part of the universe which he can still fathom, and which is himself, so different from an ill-considered and brutal suicide. Like Narcissus, Gide is not concerned with progress in morality, but with something which is at once more particularized and more universalized than morality: with progress in man's sincerity.

In 1935, Gide published *Les Nouvelles Nourritures,* which is a recast of *Les Nourritures Terrestres* following an interlude of thirty-eight years. The style is more sober and chaste than that of the earlier book. Gide now seems more intent on formulating conclusions about sensory experience than on describing the experience itself. Yet underneath these more meditative and even philosophical passages continue the same fervent quest and excitement, the same *frémissement,* the same eager self-examination. And there seems to be a larger number of narcissistic images. Gide talks about the white page of his notebook as something which shines in front of him (*la page blanche luit devant moi,* p. 20); [2] he describes his pose of bending down and looking beyond the present (*je me penche par-delà le présent* p. 21); [3] he has learned to realize from the "moment" the quietness of "eternity" (*je sais à présent goûter la quiète éternité dans l'instant,* p. 27).[4] These are all exercises of Narcissus on his absorption with the universe.

Especially, in *Les Nouvelles Nourritures,* the innumerable sentences on the concept of God reveal the use which Gide has made of the term and his increasing personal enlightenment about what the name of God has meant to him in the past. We remember the opening sentence in *Les Nourritures Terrestres* of 1897: *Ne souhaite pas, Nathanaël, trouver Dieu ailleurs que partout.* ("Do not hope to find God elsewhere than everywhere.")

---

[1] [I am highly curious to make the acquaintance of Caleub.]
[2] [The white page gleams before me.]
[3] [I lean beyond the present.]
[4] [I know now how to taste calm eternity in an instant.]

In the new pages of 1935, God is described as being diffused throughout His creation, both hidden and lost in it, continually discovering Himself in it, to the point of confusing Himself with His own creation (*cf*. p. 76). The meaning which Gide might have attached to the concept of God during his lifetime has always been obscured by the facility and the frequency with which he uses the term. The meaning of God has always been replaced by the poetic invocation to the word "God." All the concepts in Gide's mind which are the most vaguely outlined and the most difficult to comprehend—namely, all these concepts which he enjoys the most—have been poured into the general concept of God as if it were a vase of endlessly changing proportions capable of contraction or expansion. The word "God" has been synonymous for Gide with all kinds of notions and sentiments, of questions and answers. It is the word reflecting all other words which has become "gidian" in its diversity and constancy. In the *Traité du Narcisse* it was "contemplation"; in *Les Nourritures Terrestres* it was "fervour"; in *La Porte Etroite* it was "renouncement"; in *Les Faux Monnayeurs* it was "detachment." These four words when given a religious connotation, designate the attitude of Narcissus in the profoundest meaning of its self-exploration. The confusions of Gide can never be solved as long as he remains Narcissus. He is looking not at God but at himself, and not even at himself but at a reflection of himself.

The parables which recur the most continuously in the writings of Gide substantiate two of his cardinal beliefs: (1) that a single individual is more interesting than all men; (2) that the only valid adventure for an individual is that one which is most dangerous for him to undertake. This is the meaning Gide attaches to the stories of the lost sheep and the prodigal son, and to the verse: "Whosoever loseth his life shall save it." These three lessons from the Gospels could easily be construed as Christian interpretations of the Narcissus myth. Each one seems to be built around the doctrinal admonition to leave the familiar world in order to engage oneself with the unknown.

In calling nature God, Gide joins himself with the great romantics, and especially with Rousseau who sought to merge himself with unfathomed and chaotic nature. Romanticism is the major protest man has made against civilization and against reason. The romantic tries first to establish his uniqueness (Narcissus, the dandy, the artist), and then to experience a quasi-mystical union with nature. But by calling nature God, the romantic does not thereby convert nature into God. The romantic union is one between man and the chaos of nature and sentiment. Gide, as we tried to point out at the beginning of this study, is the most recent of the romantic artists and one who subsumes and even transcends the move-

ment by the extraordinary fervour he brings to the role of Narcissus. He
tracks down his being, arrests all his movements, and then from the deepest part of his spirit conjures up a mythical past.

JAMES JOYCE: TWO KEYS

HARRY LEVIN

THE publication of *Ulysses* was heralded by a lecture,
in which Valéry Larbaud confided to the public the
main intentions of the book, very much as Joyce had
confided them to him. In particular, he pointed out that the title was a
key, that the contours of the story would be clear to readers who kept the
Odyssey in mind, and that an epic conception would impress its form upon
the confusing substance of modern life. Other commentators found, however, that not all of Joyce's latent meanings were to be so easily unlocked.
Readers who did not happen to be Dubliners felt that Thom's Dublin
Directory would make a better guide than Homer. For their benefit, as
A Key to the "Ulysses" of James Joyce, Paul Jordan Smith reprinted a
map of Dublin. Between these two schools of interpretation there is little
room for disagreement; they supplement each other and assist us to comprehend the work as a whole. A single broken phrase, emerging from the
last indistinct murmurs of *Finnegans Wake,* is almost an appeal for help:
"The keys to." We grasp at both keys to *Ulysses*—the map and the myth.

Joyce's Odysseus, an advertising canvasser, exercises his professional
wiles in devising a trade-mark for the firm of Alexander J. Keyes. He hits
upon Saint Peter's symbol, a pair of crossed keys, also the insignia of the
Isle of Man, and thus—if we are willing to follow the implications of a
second pun—twin emblems of human isolation. Together they stand for
the cross-purposes of the book, its epic symbolism and its naturalistic
atmosphere. The one releases the myth-making fantasy of literary tradition; the other reveals a literal-minded itinerary of daily business. We see
Stephen Dedalus compelled in a scuffle at the Westland Row Station to
give up his key to the Martello tower, the abandoned fortification at Sandycove where he has been lodging with Buck Mulligan—and Dr. Gogarty
would have us know that the actual key was a foot and a half long. We

"James Joyce: Two Keys" from *James Joyce, A Critical Introduction* by Harry
Levin. Reprinted by permission of New Directions, and Faber and Faber, Ltd.

see the canvasser, Leopold Bloom, promoted in his drunken wish-dream to the high estate of Lord Mayor of Dublin, and presented with the key to the city. And afterwards when, in sad sobriety, he invited Stephen to his home, we note as final evidence of Bloom's ineffectuality that he has forgotten his latch-key, and must introduce his guest through the area-way.

The primary object of *Ulysses* is to bring these two inglorious heroes together, after each has lost his respective key, and to see whether they have anything to say to each other. All of Joyce's books, like Thomas Mann's, fit into the broadening dialectical pattern of *Künstler* versus *Bürger*. In the critical terminology of Stephen Dedalus, *Ulysses* signalizes a shift from the personal to the epic; it leads the artist away from himself toward an exploration of the mind of the bourgeois. The form progresses, as Stephen has foretold, until the center of emotional gravity is equidistant between himself and the new hero, Mr. Bloom. But the latter is not a newcomer to Joyce's mind. As far back as 1906, Joyce had thought of setting down a full account of the uneventful day of an ineffectual Mr. Hunter. He first thought of unifying the series of disjointed sketches, on which he was then engaged, by the title *Ulysses at Dublin,* instead of *Dubliners.* Meanwhile, he was composing his autobiographical novel, and when he had half completed the original design for *A Portrait of the Artist as a Young Man,* it occurred to him that Mr. Hunter's day in Dublin could provide the occasion for a sequel.

Thus *Ulysses* puts the introspective *Portrait of the Artist* against the exterior background of *Dubliners.* It might be described as a desperate effort to reintroduce the artist to his native city. But it also endeavors to subject the city-dweller to a process of artistic transfiguration. At the beginning of the Irish revival John Eglinton, in Thoreauistic revolt against the culture of cities, had raised the question of a new heroic literature. The difficulty, he suggested in *Pebbles from a Brook,* lay in the unheroic nature of the citizen: ". . . a shell, his power gone from him, civilization like a robe whirled down the stream out of his reach, in eddies of London and Paris, the truth no longer the ichor of his being but a cloudy, evaporated mass of problems over his head—this is he, homo sapiens, poor, naked, neurotic, undeceived, ribless wretch—make what you can of him, ye bards!" Joyce could not take up this challenge at once, for he was a schoolboy at the time. For the time, when his English master assigned an essay on "Your Favorite Hero," he chose to write about Ulysses. Years later, when he was planning his great work, he chose Ulysses for the title role, and rediscovered in ancient myth an archetype for modern man.

His favorite story was still the *Odyssey,* Joyce told a friend, in reaffirming his choice. "It embodies everything." The man of many devices, who has known so many men and so many cities, is an all-embracing figure, a composite of the pettiest stratagems and the broadest sympathies in human nature. What a piece of work is a man—the apparition of Ulysses at Dublin prompts us to wonder—ambiguously a ribless wretch exalted to Homeric stature, and a legendary hero fallen upon evil days.

Out of these contradictions Joyce's characters derive their special irony and pathos. His epic title, like Galsworthy's *Forsyte Saga,* expresses his reservations. Most of the paladins of realistic fiction, ever since Cervantes made it the literary expression of middle-class culture, have been mock-heroes. Don Quixote's tilts with windmills may, in some Pickwickian sense, have been battles with giants; in the same sense, the traderoute of an Irish canvasser may be the pilgrimage of a contemporary Ulysses. Irish heroes are famous for their long pedigrees. But narrow-minded realism excludes those Mediterranean vistas from the thoroughfares of Dublin, and insists upon scaling a decade of prodigious adventure down to the dimensions of an ordinary day—"the dailiest day possible," in Arnold Bennett's phrase.

On that day, June 16, 1904, the Gold Cup races were run off at Ascot. At New York, when the *General Slocum* exploded in the East River, five hundred lives were lost. From the Orient came news of Russo-Japanese conflict over Port Arthur. Nothing in particular happened in Ireland; Dublin remained the center of paralysis. The weather was fair, and warmer in the afternoon, with thunder in the evening, and showers at night. At the Gaiety Theatre Mrs. Bandman Palmer was appearing in *Leah.* At the Queen's the Elster-Grimes Opera Company was performing *The Lily of Killarney.* Handbills, floating about the city, announced the coming of an American evangelist, J. Alexander Dowie. Clery's was advertising a summer sale; sandwich-men, bearing the more or less consecutive letters of H.E.L.Y.S., filed through the streets. In schools and churches, libraries and newspaper offices, shops and concert-halls, public-houses and houses of prostitution, there was business as usual.

In the morning, at Glasnevin Cemetery, the body of one Patrick Dignam is buried. At midnight, in the maternity hospital on Holles Street, a child is born to a Mrs. Mina Purefoy. Leopold Bloom is a passive spectator at both these events. He plays an even less active part in the event which takes place that afternoon in his own home at 7 Eccles Street, when his wife, the singer, Mme. Marion Tweedy Bloom, commits adultery with her concert-manager, Hugh E. ("Blazes") Boylan. Nor is the day a much more eventful one in the life of Stephen Dedalus. His six months of exile in Paris abruptly terminated with five momentous words: "Mother dying come home father." Now he is living in the Martello tower, and teaching in the private school of Mr. Garret Deasy at Dalkey. After his quarrel with Mulligan, he decides not to return to Sandycove; he tells an unemployed stranger that there will be a job at Dalkey next day, and walks homeward with Mr. Bloom. But he soon leaves his new friend and goes his own way. The decision of this indecisive day is for each of them to continue— Stephen as an exile, Bloom as a Dubliner.

Such intermingling of private lives and public routines does not often ask for heroic treatment. To amplify the subject of the city, as Balzac discovered, is to dwarf its inhabitants: he made the metropolis his actual hero, or rather villain, by investing Louis-Philippe's Paris with the sinister glamor of Haroun-al-Raschid's Bagdad or Dante's *Inferno*. Dickens and Dostoevsky were more concerned with penetrating into humble existences, by listening through partitions and looking down skylights in tenements and lodging-houses, but neither could dispense with the treacherous aid of melodrama. Joyce was somewhat susceptible to melodrama, but he managed to sublimate it—in the psychological crises of both Stephen and Bloom—to a highly subjective plane. He would not even use history, as Hugo and Tolstoy had done, to lend epic magnitude to an urban theme: they threw their heroes into bold relief, by allowing Jean Valjean to carry Marius through the foul sewers of Paris, or Pierre Bezuhov to rescue a scrofulous child from the smoking ruins of Moscow. In contrast to these gigantic protagonists, Mr. Bloom, extricating Stephen from a brawl with two British privates and hurrying him off to a cabman's shelter for a cup of coffee and rolls, is inconspicuous and pitiable.

Always evasive when confronted by action, Joyce shuns heroics. The relation of the *Odyssey* to *Ulysses* is that of parallels that never meet. The Homeric over-tones do contribute their note of universality, their range of tradition, to what might well be a trivial and colorless tale. But in so doing, they convert a realistic novel into a mock-epic. The present is treated as a travesty of the past; richness furnishes an ironic comment on reality. So, in Mr. Eliot's mock-epic of latter-day London, the spectacle of Queen Elizabeth in her barge of state is obscured by the smoke of the coal barges on a later and murkier Thames. Life is not less real, to Joyce, for being completely divorced from storied splendor. Heroic deeds are one thing, and daily chores are another, and he is careful to keep them in different spheres. The sphere of the city is the habitual and the commonplace. Perhaps this assumption will do more than anything else to date Joyce's work. Few imaginative writers since Flaubert, as Edmund Wilson demonstrates, have been willing to concede a sense of glory to their own times. But times change, and the established routines of city life are interrupted by air-raid sirens.

The occasion of the *Odyssey,* though it remains a matter of dark reminiscence, is the fall of a city. It is a story of exile and, after a long circuit of misadventures, homecoming. It is a vital, though belated, part of the most recurrent cycle of European legend: many nations trace their ancestry to the sons of Priam, and Neo-Platonic criticism viewed the peregrinations of Odysseus as an allegory of the soul. Stephen's temporary employer, Mr. Deasy, viewed the role of Kitty O'Shea in the fall of Parnell as that which Helen had played in the fall of Troy. The pastime of finding classical precedents for modern instances held its attraction for Joyce, and after a fashion he carries out Mulligan's glib scheme for Hellenizing Ireland. The closeness of the correspondences between his Irish characters and their Hellenic prototypes is a point that can be, and has been, heavily labored. Not everything in *Ulysses* has its avatar in the *Odyssey,* needless to say, nor have the sequence and emphasis of the ancient epic been preserved. The reader of Joyce who turns back to Homer is more struck by divergences than by analogies.

The principal adventures of the wily Odysseus are narrated retrospectively, and the interest is concentrated upon the drama of his return to his island kingdom. Four introductory books described the efforts of the son, Telemachus, to seek out his father. Only with the next four do we see Odysseus *en voyage,* from Ogygia where he has been staying for seven years with the nymph Calypso, to Phaeacia where he recounts his wanderings to the credulous ears of the court of Nausicaa's father. This indirect narration of his most spectacular exploits occupies only four books more. The last twelve, which comprise the second half of the *Odyssey,* are devoted to the arrival at Ithaca and the reunion with Penelope. The most offhand comparison of the successive women in the lives of Odysseus and Bloom will illustrate how freely Joyce has handled this material. Calypso is not Molly Bloom, though Bloom naturally rises from her bed; she is the invisible Martha Clifford, a typist with whom he is carrying on a surreptitious correspondence. The encounter with Nausicaa, otherwise Gerty MacDowell, comes late in the day and carries all too little consequence. The encounter with Circe, *alias* Bella Cohen, instead of being part of a shadowy flashback, is the climax of the book. And Molly is the faithful Penelope with a difference that is one of the most fertile sources of Joyce's irony.

Joyce's irony—he never lets us forget—is two-edged, and is constantly cutting back to the sources of his pathos. The immediate effect of this method, we have seen, is to reduce his characters to mock-heroic absurdity. A further and quite contradictory effect is to magnify them, to treat their little habits as profound rituals, to attach a universal significance

to the most minute particulars. "The business of the poet or novelist,"
Thomas Hardy noted, "is to show the sorriness of the grandest things and
the grandeur of the sorriest things." Joyce's use of detail is the concrete
link between naturalism and symbolism, the end-product of a twofold
process of reproduction and selection, which supplies the book with both
local color and ulterior meaning. Stephen is still watching for a sign, a
shading, an unexpected epiphany: "Signatures of all things I am here to
read . . ." They may be the merest *minutiae;* within the limited range
of history they may seem ephemeral and slight; but in the wider orbit of
nature they have their appointed function. The humblest object or crudest
incident is a microcosm that may contain a key to the secrets of that wider
universe.

> —History, Stephen said, is a nightmare from which I am trying to awake.
> From the playfield the boys raised a shout. A whirring whistle: goal.
> What if that nightmare gave you a back kick?
> —The ways of the Creator are not our ways, Mr Deasy said. All history
> moves towards one great goal, the manifestation of God.
> Stephen jerked his thumb towards the window, saying:
> —That is God.
> Hooray! Ay! Whrrwhee!
> —What? Mr Deasy asked.
> —A shout in the street, Stephen answered, shrugging his shoulders.

The student who demands a philosophy from Joyce will be put off
with an inarticulate noise and a skeptical shrug. *"Du sagst nichts und ver-
rätst nichts, O Ulysses, aber du wirkst!"* [1] exclaims Dr. Jung. A novel is
tested by its reality, and not by its message. Association, not logic, is the
motive power of Joyce's mentality; he plays with ideas as with words.
When Mrs. Bloom worries her husband with polysyllabic mysteries of
"metempsychosis," or when Stephen conceives the notion of an umbilical
telephone line to Edenville, they are simply asserting their sense of the
past, of the recurrence and continuity of human experience. Joyce does
not preach, any more than Donne, the transmigration of souls. His readers,
like Donne's, must be ready to distinguish between occult beliefs and metaphysical conceits. They must know the difference between doctrines and
attitudes. Any given system of ideas—even the eclectic make-believe of
Yeats' *Vision*—would have cramped Joyce. He was anxious to take all
knowledge for his playground.
Scholiasts, those who have taken Joyce for their playground, push

---

[1] [You say nothing and betray nothing. O Ulysses, but you have your effect
(your work).]

their game to an Alexandrian extreme. Joyce, no doubt, has given them every temptation and encouragement. Yet, when Stuart Gilbert informs us that each episode of *Ulysses* has not only its Homeric antecedent, but also its own organ of the body, its characteristic color, and a plethora of other symbols, we find ourselves approaching it gingerly, like Charlie Chaplin chewing a pudding in which a coin has been embedded. We are pleased with ourselves and Joyce and Mr. Gilbert, if Bloom broils an explicit kidney for breakfast or "green thought in a green shade" tinctures Stephen's seaside meditations. If the symbols are more extrinsic, we are less pleased; and if they are entirely out of sight, we seldom miss them. They are not there for us, but for Joyce. They are not evidences of esoteric philosophy, but of intricate technique. Utterly unshackled from the usual conventions, Joyce hedged himself in with far more complicated conditions and far more rigorous restrictions than any school of criticism would ever dare to exact.

It is not difficult to imagine the licensed premises of Barney Kiernan as a kind of Cyclops' cave; it is enlightening to regard the enraged Sinn Feiner who attacks our hero as a Polyphemus *de nos jours;* and it is entertaining to learn, from the authorized insight of Mr. Gilbert, that there are glimmerings of the olive-wood club of Odysseus in the fiery tip of Mr. Bloom's "knockmedown cigar." In some respects, the Homeric parallel is a useful contrivance for the reader. By giving him something to take for granted and showing him something to look for, by helping him to control an overwhelming flux of impressions, it justifies its existence. In other respects, it seems more important to Joyce than it could possibly be to any reader. Mr. Deasy's preoccupation with the foot-and-mouth disease, it seems, alludes to one of Joyce's journalistic ventures, as well as to Nestor's sacrifice of a heifer. The myth may well have served as a scaffolding, while Joyce constructed his work. Before it was printed, he tacitly removed the Homeric chapter headings that appear in the manuscript.

Since they resolve the book into such a transparent outline, in Joyce's own terms, it is convenient to reprint them here. They reveal, more graphically than further discussion or second-hand summary, how the myth of the *Odyssey* is superimposed upon the map of Dublin, how the retelling of an old fable is absorbed into the cross-section of a contemporary city. Joyce has rearranged the twenty-four books of Homer in three parts, subdivided into eighteen episodes of increasing length and elaboration. The first three constitute a prologue, more or less equivalent to the first four books of the *Odyssey,* the so-called *Telemachia.* In Joyce's personal epic, they effect the transition between the *Portrait of the Artist* and

Ulysses. Stephen is now identified with Telemachus: his new name signifies "away from war," and his continuing quest is for a father who was in the battle.

I.   1. *Telemachus.* 8 A.M. Breakfast at the Martello tower.
     2. *Nestor.* 10 A.M. A history lesson at Mr. Deasy's school.
     3. *Proteus.* 11 A.M. A walk along the beach at Sandymount.

The body of the book consists of the twelve subsequent episodes, always expanding and often reversing the eight books into which Homer has concentrated the wanderings of Odysseus. The emphasis has shifted back from the return, which is necessarily attenuated in Joyce's version, to the exile. The first public engagement, the funeral procession to Glasnevin Cemetery, reproduces the trip to Hades, which was one of the last incidents on the voyage of the wily Greek. Mr. Bloom's erratic route, from breakfast until midnight, manages to find some local landmark for every one of his predecessor's stopping-places in the cradle of civilization. When his fatigued imagination, at the end of the day, conjures up a chorus of daughters of Erin, their litany is a recital of his negligible exploits, and a running commentary on the central episodes of the book.

II.   1. *Calypso.* 8 A.M. Breakfast at 7 Eccles Street.
      Kidney of Bloom, pray for us.
      2. *Lotus Eaters.* 10 A.M. The public baths (and a phallic symbol).
      Flower of the Bath, pray for us.
      3. *Hades.* 11 A.M. At the funeral (with an eminent solicitor).
      Mentor of Menton, pray for us.
      4. *Aeolus.* Noon. At the office of his newspaper.
      Canvasser for the Freeman, pray for us.
      5. *Lestrygonians.* 1 P.M. Lunch at Davy Byrne's pub.
      Charitable Mason, pray for us.
      6. *Scylla and Charybdis.* 2 P.M. Bloom in library (soap in pocket).
      Wandering Soap, pray for us.
      7. *Wandering Rocks.* 3 P.M. The streets and the bookstall.
      Sweets of Sin, pray for us.
      8. *Sirens.* 4 P.M. Barmaids at the Ormond Hotel.
      Music without Words, pray for us.
      9. *Cyclops.* 5 P.M. Humiliation at Barney Kiernan's.
      Reprover of the Citizen, pray for us.
      10. *Nausicaa.* 8 P.M. Flirtation with Gerty MacDowell.
      Friend of all Frillies, pray for us.
      11. *Oxen of the Sun.* 10 P.M. The maternity hospital.
      Midwife Most Merciful, pray for us.
      12. *Circe.* Midnight. Bella Cohen's brothel (Bloom's amulet).
      Potato Preservative against Plague and Pestilence, pray for us.

Insofar as the story is Bloom's, this time-table is reliable. A notable exception is the library scene, where he cuts a dim and transient figure while Stephen holds the floor. Stephen, for the most part, is conspicuous by his absence until the evening episodes. The third section serves as an epilogue, corresponding to the *Nostos,* or homecoming, in the last twelve books of the *Odyssey.* Though it includes the long-awaited dialogue between Bloom and Stephen, the predominating figure is finally Molly Bloom. This is her part of the book, as the first is Stephen's, and the second Bloom's.

III. 1. *Eumaeus.* 1 A.M. The cabman's shelter.
     2. *Ithaca.* 2 A.M. 7 Eccles Street: the kitchen.
     3. *Penelope.* 2.45 A.M. 7 Eccles Street: the bedroom.

The architectural framework, which Joyce reconstructed from Homer, is most impressive when we contemplate the work as a whole and try to visualize the relation of its parts. When we turn from the structure to the texture, we are more easily persuaded to think of musical forms. The sonata, Ezra Pound insists, is a clearer model than the epic. Its introductory theme would be Stephen, its main theme Bloom; each, after a preliminary exposition, undergoes his own development, then a treatment in combination, and at last a recapitulation. Since the first three episodes of the first section are cleverly synchronized with the first three of the second, Bloom and Stephen do not begin to cross each other's paths until mid-day. At eight-forty-five precisely, the same little cloud hides the sun from Stephen in his tower and from Bloom on his walk home from the butcher-shop. Their morning hours are presented in isolation, and they are again isolated by the morning hours of the next day.

The two years that have elapsed since the conclusion of the *Portrait of the Artist* have done much to sharpen Stephen's mind, but nothing to change it. The savor of the Latin Quarter and the disintegration of his family seem to confirm his original decision. So long as he must remain in Dublin, the rebellious archangel continues to loom before his mind's eye: "Allbright he falls, proud lightning of the intellect." We follow Stephen's ramblings with a growing conviction that this is not homecoming, but an interruption of exile. True, he has tried his wings; he sometimes feels that he has fallen into the sea; frequently he dwells upon the sea-changed images of death by water. He is preoccupied with the lapwing, the emblematic bird that safeguards its children by crying away from its nest. If he is still Icarus, who, where, is Daedalus? When John Eglinton suggests that the name may have some bearing on his "fantastical humour," Stephen is touched by a pang of reminiscence:

Fabulous artificer, the hawklike man. You flew. Whereto? Newhaven-Dieppe, steerage passenger. Paris and back. Lapwing. Icarus. *Pater, ait.* Sea-bedabbled, fallen, weltering. Lapwing you are. Lapwing he.

Misunderstanding has become tragedy with the death of his mother. Throughout the day, from the early moment when Mulligan addresses the sea in Hellenic phrase as "our mighty mother," Stephen is haunted by the vision of her wasted body in its grave-clothes, and the odor of wax and rosewood and wetted ashes. The prayer which stuck in his throat at her death-bed, with its radiant evocation of the welcoming hosts of heaven, repeats itself over and over: *Liliata rutilantium te confessorum turma circumdet: iubilantium te virginum chorus excipiat.*[1] Self-reproach takes the quaint form of a Middle English expression for remorse of conscience, "Agenbite of Inwit": again and again, within his mind, we feel its mordant impact. At school he perplexes his pupils with the declension of *amor matris.*[2] All occasions inform against him; all reflection is darkly tinged with repressed accusations that materialize among the bitter ghosts of midnight.

Though Stephen's nature has not radically altered, Joyce's characterization throws new light upon it, and examines it for the first time "in mediate relation to others." A freer orientation, transcending the narrow limits of egotism, has enabled him to paint a more objective self-portrait. As his own youth receded, he was able to take a long-range view of "the artist as a young man," for better or for worse, with maturity and even humor. When Stephen seems as priggish to the reader as to the bumptious Mulligan, and when Mulligan seems more of a good fellow to the reader than to Stephen, we must acknowledge that Joyce has gone a long way toward detachment. There are still certain adverbial distinctions between Stephen's innate refinement and the vulgarity of the rest of the world; his speeches are spoken "coldly," Mulligan's "coarsely." This, perhaps, is the conscious outcome of self-dramatization. When Mulligan apologizes for a coarse remark, "O, it's only Dedalus whose mother is beastly dead," Stephen replies, coldly:

> —I am not thinking of the offence to my mother.
> —Of what, then? Buck Mulligan asked.
> —Of the offence to me, Stephen answered.
> Buck Mulligan swung round on his heel.
> —O, an impossible person! he exclaimed.

---

[1] [Let the band of bleeding martyrs made as white as lilies surround you; let the chorus of rejoicing virgins receive you.]

[2] [Love of the mother.]

The *Portrait of the Artist* has already familiarized us with the cast of Stephen's mind. A chance phrase of the newspaper editor, Myles Crawford, "I see it in your face," reminds him—as it reminds us—of the indelible words of Father Dolan and the old *traumata* of Clongowes Wood: "See it in your eye. Lazy idle little schemer." Among the later confusions of the brothel, the prefect of studies, armed with his pandybat, emerges like a jack-in-the-box from the pianola. Afterwards, as Mr. Bloom guides Stephen's faltering steps past Baird's stone-cutting works, we recall those private associations between various quarters of Dublin and Stephen's literary enthusiasms, and we think of Ibsen. So, in spite of his intoxication, does Stephen. Bloom's mind is a brighter mirror of the world around them. It reflects sense impressions concretely, whereas Stephen is continually refracting them through speculation and introspection. At Sandymount, as each of them covers the same ground, contrasting soliloquies balance "the intellectual imagination" of Stephen in the morning against the carnal susceptibilities of Bloom in the evening. The latter is so mobile, so suggestible, so easily distracted, that his thought is hard to dissociate from his terrain. He can claim, with Tennyson's *Ulysses,* "I am a part of all that I have met."

As we take our leave of Telemachus, sauntering along the strand with his ashplant, and catch our earliest glimpse of Ulysses, getting his wife's breakfast and putting out milk for the cat, we pass from the intransigent intellectual to the *homme moyen sensuel.*[1] Stephen, if not all spirit, is bent upon humbling his flesh. Bloom's first recorded reaction is his obvious physical relish for "the inner organs of beasts and fowls." His consistent earthiness, which does not spare us the intimacies of the stool or the bath, makes *Ulysses* one of the few books that attaches to animal functions the same importance that they have in life. Not that Bloom lacks intelligence, for he is shrewd and sensitive. "There's a touch of the artist about old Bloom," Lenehan says to M'Coy. There is just enough of the frustrated artist to draw him to Stephen, and Stephen in turn is drawn to Bloom by these very frustrations, since Bloom has accepted so much that he has rejected. He is seeking a father; Bloom has lost a son. They are complementary figures, and each is one-sided and maladjusted so long as he abides alone. Yet the attraction of opposites is not enough to produce a synthesis.

An Irish Jew, indeed, is a walking antithesis. Mr. Deasy has paved the way for Bloom's entrance with his little joke: Ireland is the one coun-

---

[1] [Man of average sensibility.]

try that has never persecuted the Jews, because she never let them in. England is dying, in the opinion of Mr. Deasy, an Orangeman, because she is in their hands. "And they are the signs of a nation's decay." And Stephen, listening, seems to see the dark eyes and eager gestures of patient wanderers in the ghettos and on the stock-exchanges of Europe. The question of why Joyce chose a Jew for his hero—which Valéry Larbaud raised, but did not answer—has answered itself. From Proust's Swann to Mann's Joseph, Jewish figures have received a disproportionate amount of consideration from contemporary novelists. The influence, variously manifested, of Marx in politics, Bergson in philosophy, Freud in the humane sciences, and Einstein in the mathematical sciences, has lent a semblance of plausibility to the argument of those critics of modern culture who would convict it of a non-Aryan taint. Whether the Jews be chosen people or bearers of the curse, they have a special affinity with an Irish author who dates his book from *"Trieste—Zurich—Paris."* Besides Mr. Hunter of Dublin, who must have been an Anglo-Irishman, we hear of other models for Mr. Bloom—a Greek in Trieste, a Hungarian in Zurich, the Austro-Italian writer Italo Svevo, and possibly members of an Italian Jewish household in which Joyce had lived. In any case, his hero would be a metropolitan type, neither a native nor a foreigner, a denizen of the megalopolis, a wanderer of the diaspora, equally at home and ill at ease in any city of the world. Mulligan calls Bloom the wandering Jew. "I fear thee, ancient mariner." Professor Lowes had confirmed this identification, by discerning the features of the same restless pilgrim in the garb of Coleridge's bright-eyed sea-farer. "Ahasuerus I call him," snarls the Sinn Feiner. "Cursed by God." Joyce, by accepting Victor Bérard's theory of the Semitic origins of the *Odyssey,* identifies Bloom with an even more ancient mariner, and links Homer with the Bible.

Bloom is an exile in Dublin, as Stephen is a Dubliner in exile. Before breakfast, musing on the attrition and corruption of the cities of the plain, he walks to the porkbutcher's, where surprisingly he picks up a prospectus for a Zionistic settlement. This stimulates him, from time to time, to escape from the waste land about him into tropical reveries of the promised land. The address of the project, Bleibtreustrasse, Berlin, carries its ironic reprimand, for he has not remained true to the religion of his fathers. He has not continued to observe the protestant religion of his mother, into which he has been baptised. He has gone, like Stephen, into spiritual exile. In Babylon he remembers Zion. When he brings back his pork kidney, he notices there is a letter to his wife from Boylan, and realises that there will be an informal rehearsal of "Love's Old Sweet Song" at his home that afternoon. This *leit-motif* of his wife's infidelity cuts him off from his family, just as relentlessly as Stephen is cut off by his mother's death-bed prayer.

Isolated together, Joyce sets his personification of the city alongside of his portrait of the artist. Neither is complete without the other, he knew very well, but he also knew that both are usually incomplete. He succeeded in uniting them by a literary *tour de force,* by crossing the two keys of topography and mythology. Bloom, however, is unaware of his symbolic role, just as Stephen is out of touch with his municipal environment. Stephen starts as an individual and becomes a type; Bloom starts as a type and becomes an individual. One by critical precept, the other by awful example, mark the distance between culture and philistinism. Matthew Arnold, though painfully conscious of this distance, might not have recognized them as unhonored prophets of Hellenism and Hebraism. The strains and stresses of middle-class life have alienated Stephen and vulgarized Bloom, have introverted the Hellene and extraverted the Hebrew. Still, somewhere between Stephen's esthetic feeling and Bloom's civic sense, between individual expression and social morality, lies our only hope for the good life. "Hebraism and Hellenism," Arnold has written, "—between these two points of influence moves our world. At one time it feels more powerfully the attraction of one of them, at another time of the other; and it ought to be, though it never is, evenly and happily balanced between them."

WILLIAM FAULKNER'S
LEGEND OF THE SOUTH

MALCOLM COWLEY

WILLIAM FAULKNER is one of the writers who reward and even in a sense demand a second reading. When you return to one of his books years after its publication, the passages that had puzzled you are easier to understand and each of them takes its proper place in the picture. Moreover, you lose very little by knowing the plot in advance. Faulkner's stories are not the sort that unwind in celluloid ribbons until the last inch of them has been reflected on a flat screen, with nothing to imagine and nothing more to see except the newsreel, the animated cartoon and the Coming Re-pulsions; instead his books are sculptural, as if you could walk round them for different views of the same solid object. But it is not merely a statue that he presented: rather it is a whole monument or, let us say, a city buried in the jungle, to which the author wishes to guide us, but not at once or by following a single path. We start out along one road, wind-ing between walls of jungle growth in the humid afternoon, and it is not long until we catch a glimpse of our destination. Just beyond us, however, is a swamp filled with snakes, and the guide makes us turn back. We take another road; we gain a clearer picture of the city; but this time there are other dangers in front of us, quicksands or precipices, and again the guide makes us return. By whatever road we travel, we always catch sight of our goal, always learn more about it and are always forced back; till at last we find the proper path and reach the heart of the city just as it is about to be overwhelmed by fire or earthquake. . . . Reading the same book a second time is like soaring over the jungle in a plane, with every section of the landscape falling into its proper perspective.

And there is another respect in which our judgment of the author changes when we return to not one but several of his novels in succession. On a first reading what had chiefly impressed us may have been their violence, which sometimes seemed to have no justification in art or na-ture. We had remembered incidents and figures like the violating of Temple Drake, in *Sanctuary;* like the pursuit and castration of Joe Christmas, in *Light in August;* like the idiot boy who fell in love and eloped with a cow, in *The Hamlet;* and like the nameless woman, in *The Wild Palms,* who bore her child unaided in the midst of a Mississippi River flood, on an Indian mound where all the snakes in the Delta had taken refuge. After a second reading, most of these nightmares retain their power to shock, but at the same time they merge a little into the background, as if they were the almost natural product of the long un-bearable Mississippi summers; as if they were thunder showers brewed in the windless heat. We pay less attention to the horrors as such, and more to the old situation out of which they developed and the new disasters it seems to foreshadow.

The situation itself, and not the violence to which it leads, is Faulk-ner's real subject. It is, moreover, the same situation in all his books—or, let us say, in all the novels and stories belonging to his Yocknapatawpha County series. Briefly it is the destruction of the old Southern order, by war and military occupation and still more by finance capitalism that tempts and destroys it from within. "Tell about the South," says Quentin Comp-son's roommate at Harvard, who comes from Edmonton, Alberta, and is curious about the unknown region beyond the Ohio. "What's it like there?" Shreve McCannon goes on to ask. "What do they do there? Why do they live there? Why do they live at all?" And Quentin, whose background is a little like that of the author and who often seems to speak for him— Quentin answers, "You can't understand it. You would have to be born there." Nevertheless, he tells a long and violent story that he regards as the essence of the Deep South, which is not so much a region as it is, in Quentin's mind, an incomplete and frustrated nation trying to recover its own identity, trying to relive its legendary past.

There was a boy, Quentin says—I am giving the plot of *Absalom, Absalom!*—a mountain boy named Thomas Sutpen whose family drifted into the Virginia Tidewater. There his father found odd jobs on a plantation. One day the father sent him with a message to the big house, but he was turned away at the door by a black man in livery. The mountain boy, puzzled and humiliated, was seized upon by the ambition to which he would afterwards refer as "the design." He would own a plantation, with slaves and a livery butler; he would build a mansion as big as any of those in the Tidewater; and he would have a son to inherit his wealth.

A dozen years later, Sutpen appeared in the frontier town of Jefferson, Mississippi, and, by some transaction the nature of which is never explained—though it certainly wasn't by honest purchase—he obtained a hundred square miles of land from the Chickasaws. He disappeared again, and this time he returned with twenty wild Negroes from the jungle and a French architect. On the day of his reappearance, he set about building the largest house in northern Mississippi, with timbers from the forest and bricks that his Negroes molded and baked on the spot; it was as if his mansion, Sutpen's Hundred, had been literally torn from the soil. Only one man in Jefferson—he was Quentin's grandfather, General Compson—ever learned how and where Sutpen had acquired his slaves. He had shipped to Haiti from Virginia, worked as an overseer on a sugar plantation and married the rich planter's daughter, who had borne him a son. Then, finding that his wife had Negro blood, he had simply put her away, with her child and her fortune, while keeping the twenty slaves as a sort of indemnity. He explained to General Compson in the stilted speech he had taught himself that she could not be "adjunctive to the forwarding of the design."

"Jesus, the South is fine, isn't it," says Shreve McCannon, listening while Quentin talks, half to himself. "It's better than the theatre, isn't it. It's better than Ben Hur, isn't it. No wonder you have to come away now and then, isn't it."

Sutpen married again, Quentin continues. This time his wife belonged to a pious family of the neighborhood, and she bore him two children, Henry and Judith. He became the biggest landowner and cotton planter in the county, and it seemed that his "design" had already been fulfilled. At this moment, however—it was Christmas in 1859—Henry came home from the University of Mississippi with an older and worldlier new friend, Charles Bon, who was in reality Sutpen's son by his first marriage. Charles became engaged to Judith. Sutpen learned his identity and without making a sign of recognition, ordered him to leave the house. Henry, who refused to believe that Charles was his half-brother, renounced his birthright and followed him to New Orleans. In 1861 all the male Sutpens went off to war, and all of them survived four years of fighting. Then, in the spring of 1865, Charles suddenly decided to marry Judith, even though he was certain by now that she was his half-sister. Henry rode beside him all the way back to Sutpen's Hundred, but tried to stop him at the gate, killed him when he insisted on going ahead with his plan, told Judith what he had done, and disappeared.

"The South," Shreve McCannon says as he listens to the story. "The South. Jesus. No wonder you folks all outlive yourselves by years and years." And Quentin says, remembering his own sister with whom he was in love—just as Charles Bon, and Henry too, were in love with Judith—"I am older at twenty than a lot of people who have died."

But Quentin's story of the Deep South does not end with the war. Colonel Sutpen came home, he says, to find his wife dead, his son a fugitive, his slaves dispersed (they had run away even before they were freed by the Union army) and most of his land about to be seized for debt. But still determined to carry out "the design," he did not even pause for breath before undertaking to restore his house and plantation as nearly as possible to what they had been. The effort failed; he lost most of his land and was reduced to keeping a crossroads store. Now in his sixties, he tried again to beget a son; but his wife's younger sister, Miss Rosa Coldfield, was outraged by his proposal ("Let's try it," he had said, "and if it's a boy we'll get married."); and later poor Milly Jones, with whom he had an affair, gave birth to a baby girl. At that Sutpen abandoned hope and provoked Milly's grandfather into killing him. Judith survived her father for a time, as did the half-caste son of Charles Bon by a New Orleans octoroon. After the death of these two by yellow fever, the great house was haunted rather than inhabited by an ancient mulatto woman, Sutpen's daughter by one of his slaves. The fugitive Henry Sutpen came home to die; the townspeople heard of his illness and sent an ambulance after him; but old Clytie thought they were arresting him for murder and set fire to Sutpen's Hundred. The only survivor of the conflagration was

Jim Bond, a half-witted, saddle-colored creature who was Charles Bon's grandson.

"Do you know what I think?" says Shreve McCannon after the story has ended. "I think that in time the Jim Bonds are going to conquer the western hemisphere. Of course it won't be quite in our time and of course as they spread toward the poles they will bleach out again like the rabbits and the birds do, so they won't show up so sharp against the snow. But it will still be Jim Bond; and so in a few thousand years, I who regard you will also have sprung from the loins of African kings. Now I want you to tell me just one thing more. Why do you hate the South?"

"I don't hate it," Quentin says quickly, at once. "I don't hate it," he repeats, speaking for the author as well as himself. *I don't hate it,* he thinks, panting in the cold air, the iron New England dark; *I don't. I don't! I don't hate it! I don't hate it!*

The reader cannot help wondering why this sombre and, at moments, plainly incredible story had so seized upon Quentin's mind that he trembled with excitement when telling it and felt that it revealed the essence of the Deep South. It seems to belong in the realm of Gothic romances, with Sutpen's Hundred taking the place of the haunted castle on the Rhine, with Colonel Sutpen as Faust and Charles Bon as Manfred. Then slowly it dawns on you that most of the characters and incidents have a double meaning; that besides their place in the story, they also serve as symbols or metaphors with a general application. Sutpen's great design, the land he stole from the Indians, the French architect, who built his house with the help of wild Negroes from the jungle, the woman of mixed blood whom he married and disowned, the unacknowledged son who ruined him, the poor white whom he wronged and who killed him in anger, the final destruction of the mansion like the downfall of a social order: all these might belong to a tragic fable of Southern history. With a little cleverness, the whole novel might be explained as a connected and logical allegory, but this, I think, would be going beyond the author's intention. First of all he was writing a story, and one that affected him deeply, but he was also brooding over a social situation. More or less unconsciously, the incidents in the story came to represent the forces and elements in the social situation, since the mind naturally works in terms of symbols and parallels. In Faulkner's case, this form of parallelism is not confined to *Absalom, Absalom!* It can be found in the whole fictional framework that he has been elaborating in novel after novel, until his work has become a myth or legend of the South.

I call it a legend because it is obviously no more intended as a historical account of the country south of the Ohio than *The Scarlet Letter* is intended as a history of Massachusetts or *Paradise Lost* as a factual description of the Fall. Briefly stated, the legend might run something like this: The Deep South was settled partly by aristocrats like the Sartoris clan and partly by new men like Colonel Sutpen. Both types of planters were determined to establish a lasting social order on the land they had seized from the Indians (that is, to leave sons behind them). They had the virtue of living single-mindedly by a fixed code; but there was also an inherent guilt in their "design," their way of life, that put a curse on the land and brought about the Civil War. After the War was lost, partly as a result of their own mad heroism (for who else but men as brave as Jackson and Stuart could have frightened the Yankee into standing together and fighting back?) they tried to restore "the design" by other methods. But they no longer had the strength to achieve more than a partial success, even after they had freed their land from the carpetbaggers who followed the Northern armies. As time passed, moreover, the men of the old order found that they had Southern enemies too: they had to fight against a new exploiting class descended from the landless whites of slavery days. In this struggle between the clan of Sartoris and the unscrupulous tribe of Snopes, the Sartorises were defeated in advance by a traditional code that prevented them from using the weapons of the enemy. But the Snopeses as price of their victory had to serve the mechanized civilization of the North, which was morally impotent in itself, but which, with the aid of its Southern retainers, ended by corrupting the Southern nation. In our own day, the problems of the South are still unsolved, the racial conflict is becoming more acute; and Faulkner's characters in their despairing moments foresee or forebode some catastrophe of which Jim Bond and his like will be the only survivors.

II

This legend of Faulkner's, if I have stated it correctly, is clearly not a scientific interpretation of Southern history (if such a thing exists); but neither is it the familiar plantation legend that has been embodied in hundreds of romantic novels. Faulkner presents the virtues of the old order as being moral rather than material. There is no baronial pomp in his novels; no profusion of silk and silver, mahogany and moonlight and champagne. The big house on Mr. Hubert Beauchamp's plantation (in *Go Down, Moses*) had a rotted floorboard in the back gallery that Mr. Hubert never got round to having fixed. Visitors used to find him sitting in the spring-house with his boots off and his feet in the water while he drank a morning toddy, which he invited them to share. Visitors to Sutpen's Hundred were offered champagne: it was the best, doubtless, and yet it was "crudely dispensed out of the burlesqued pantomime elegance of Negro butlers who (and likewise the drinkers who gulped it down like neat whiskey between flowery and unsubtle toasts) would have treated lemonade the same way." All the planters lived comfortably, with plenty of servants, but Faulkner never lets us forget that they were living on what had recently been the frontier. What he admires about them is not their wealth or their manners or their fine houses, but rather their unquestioning acceptance of a moral code that taught them "courage and honor and pride, and pity and love of justice and of liberty." Living with single hearts, they were, says Quentin Compson's father:

. . . . people too as we are, and victims too as we are, but victims of a different circumstance, simpler and therefore, integer for integer, larger, more heroic and the figures therefore more heroic too, not dwarfed and involved but distinct, uncomplex, who had the gift of living once or dying once instead of being diffused and scattered creatures drawn blindly limb from limb from a grab bag and assembled, author and victim too of a thousand homicides and a thousand copulations and divorcements.

The old order was a moral order: briefly that was its strength and the secret lost by its heirs. I don't wish to give the impression that Faulkner is the only Southern writer to advance this principle. During the last few years, it has been stated or suggested in a considerable body of Southern fiction and poetry, including the work of Allen Tate, Robert Penn Warren, Caroline Gordon and several others. The fact is that most of the ideas embodied in Faulkner's legend are held in common by many Southern writers of the new generation; what Faulkner has done is to express them in a whole series of novels written with his own emotional intensity and technical resourcefulness. But his version of the legend also has features that set it apart: most notably its emphasis on the idea that the Southern nation (like most of his own fictional heroes) was defeated from within.

In Faulkner's reading, the old order not only had its virtues of dignity and courage and love of justice; it also bore the moral burden of a guilt so great that the War and even Reconstruction were in some sense a merited punishment. There is madness, but there is a metaphorical meaning too, in Miss Rosa Coldfield's belief that Sutpen was a demon and that his sins were the real reason ". . . . why God let us lose the War: that only through the blood of our men and the tears of our women could He stay this demon and efface his name and lineage from the earth." Quentin's father is quite sane, in his sober moments, and yet he expresses almost the same idea about Sutpen's guilt and its consequences. He is telling the story of the Sutpens when he remarks that the Civil War was

". . . . a stupid and bloody aberration in the high (and impossible) destiny of the United States, maybe instigated by that family fatality which possessed, along with all circumstances, that curious lack of economy between cause and effect which is always a characteristic of fate when reduced to using human materials."

Colonel Sutpen himself has a feeling, not exactly of guilt, since he has never questioned the rightness of his design, but rather of amazement that so many misfortunes have fallen on him. Sitting in General Compson's office, he goes back over his career, trying to see where he had made his "mistake," for that is what he calls it. Sometimes the author seems to be implying that the sin for which Sutpen and his class are being punished is simply the act of cohabiting with Negroes. But before the end of *Absalom, Absalom!* we learn that miscegenation is only part of it. When Charles Bon's curious actions are explained, we find that he was taking revenge on his father for having refused to recognize him by so much as a single glance. Thus, heartlessness was the "mistake" that had ruined Sutpen, not the taking of a partly Negro wife and Negro concubines. And the point becomes clearer in a long story called "The Bear" (in *Go Down, Moses*), probably the best single piece that Faulkner has written. When Isaac McCaslin is twenty-one, he insists on relinquishing the big plantation that is his by inheritance; he thinks that the land is cursed. It is cursed in his eyes by the deeds of his grandfather: "that evil and unregenerate old man who could summon, because she was his property, a human being because she was old enough and female, to his widower's house and get a child on her and then dismiss her because she was of an inferior race, and then bequeath a thousand dollars to the infant because he would be dead then and wouldn't have to pay it." It follows that the land was cursed—and the War was part of the curse—because its owners had treated human beings as instruments; in a word, it was cursed by slavery.

All through his boyhood, Faulkner must have dreamed of fighting in the Civil War. It was a Sartoris war and not a Snopes war, like the one in which he afterwards risked his life in a foreign army. And yet his sympathies did not wholly lie with the slaveholding clan of Sartoris, even though it was his own clan. The men he most admired and must have pictured himself as resembling were the Southern soldiers—after all, they were the vast majority—who owned no slaves themselves and suffered from the institution of slavery. The men he would praise in his novels were those "who had fought for four years and lost . . . . not because they were opposed to freedom as freedom, but for the old reasons for which man (not the generals and politicians but man) has always fought and died in wars: to preserve a status quo or to establish a better future one to endure for his children." You might define his position as that of an anti-slavery Southern nationalist.

His attitude toward Negroes will seem surprising only to Northerners. It seems to have developed from the attitude of the slaveholders, which was often inhuman but never impersonal—that is, the slave might be treated as a domestic animal, but not as a machine or the servant of a machine. Apparently the slaveholding class had little or no feeling of racial animosity. Frederick Law Olmstead, a sharp and by no means a friendly observer, was struck by what he called "the close cohabitation and association of black and white." In his *Journey in the Seaboard Slave States,* the record of his travels in 1853–54, he said: "Negro women are carrying black and white babies together in their arms; black and white children are playing together (not going to school together); black and white faces are constantly thrust together out of the doors, to see the train go by." He described the relation between masters and servants as having a "familiarity and closeness of intimacy that would have been noticed with astonishment, if not with manifest displeasure, in almost any chance company at the North." In Faulkner's historical novels, we find this closeness of intimacy compounded with closeness of blood, for the servants are very often the illegitimate half-brothers or sisters of their white companions—not only more often than in life, a mild way of putting it, but also more often than in any Abolitionist tract. He describes the old South as inhabited by two races that lived essentially the same life on their different levels. Thus, he says in *Absalom, Absalom!* that the young planters were

. . . only in the surface matter of food and clothing and daily occupation any different from the Negro slaves who supported them—the same sweat, the only difference being that on the one hand it went for labor in the fields where on the other it went as the price of the spartan and meagre pleasures which were available to them because they did not have to sweat in the fields: the hard violent hunting and riding; the same pleasures: the one, gambling for worn knives and brass jewelry and twists of tobacco and buttons and garments because they happened to be easiest and quickest to hand; on the other for the money and horses, the guns and watches, and for the same reason; the same parties: the identical music from the identical instruments, crude fiddles and guitars, now in the big house with candles and silk dresses and champagne, now in dirt-floored cabins with smoking pine knots and calico and water sweetened with molasses.

"They will endure. They are better than we are," Ike McCaslin says of the Negroes, although he finds it more painful to utter this heresy than it is to surrender his plantation. "Stronger than we are," he continues. "Their vices are vices aped from white men or that white men and bondage have taught them: improvidence and intemperance and evasion—not laziness . . . and their virtues are their own: endurance and pity and tolerance and forbearance and fidelity and love of children, whether their own or not or black or not." In Faulkner's novels, the Negroes are an element of stability and endurance, just as the octoroons (like Charles Bon and Joe Christmas) are an element of tragic instability. His favorite characters are the Negro cooks and matriarchs who hold a white family together: Elnora and Dilsey and Clytie and Aunt Mollie Beauchamp. After the Compson family has gone to pieces (in *The Sound and the Fury*), it is Dilsey the cook who endures and is left behind to mourn. Looking up at the square, unpainted house with its rotting portico, she thinks, "Ise seed de first en de last"; and later in the kitchen, looking at the cold stove, "I seed de first en de last."

The increasing hatred between two races is explained in Faulkner's novels partly by the heritage of slavery and Reconstruction; partly by the coming into power of a new class which, so far as it consists of families with landless and slaveless ancestors, has a tradition of hostility to the Negroes. But Faulkner also likes to think that the lynch mobs were often led by the descendants of his old enemies, the carpetbaggers—

. . . that race threefold in one and alien even among themselves save for a single fierce will for rapine and pillage, composed of the sons of middle-aged Quartermaster lieutenants and Army sutlers and contractors in military blankets and shoes and transport mules, who followed the battles they themselves had not fought and inherited the conquest they themselves had not helped to gain . . . and left their bones and in another generation would be engaged in a fierce economic competition of small sloven farms with the black men they were supposed to have freed and the white descendants of fathers who had owned no slaves anyway whom they were supposed to have disinherited, and in the third generation would be back once more in the little lost county seats as barbers and garage mechanics and deputy sheriffs and mill and gin hands and power-plant firemen, leading, first in mufti then later in an actual formalized regalia of hooded sheets and passwords and fiery Christian symbols, lynching mobs against the race their ancestors had come to save.

III

Faulkner's novels of contemporary Southern life continue the legend into a period that he regards as one of moral confusion and social decay. He is continually seeking in them for violent images to convey his sense of despair. *Sanctuary* is the most violent of all his novels; it is also the most popular and by no means the least important (in spite of Faulkner's comment that it was "a cheap idea . . . deliberately conceived to make money"). The story of Popeye and Temple Drake has more meaning than appears on a first hasty reading—the only reading that most of the critics have been willing to grant it. George Marion O'Donnell went over the novel more carefully and decided that it formed a coherent allegory. Writing in *The Kenyon Review* (Autumn, 1939), he said that the pattern of the allegory was something like this:

Southern Womanhood Corrupted but Undefiled (Temple Drake), in the company of the Corrupted Tradition (Gowan Stevens, a professional Virginian), falls into the clutches of amoral Modernism (Popeye), which is itself impotent, but which with the aid of its strong ally Natural Lust ("Red") rapes Southern Womanhood unnaturally and then seduces her so satisfactorily that her corruption is total, and she becomes the tacit ally of Modernism. Meanwhile Pore White Trash (Goodwin) has been accused of the crime which he, with the aid of the Naif Faithful (Tawmmy), actually tried to prevent. The Formalized Tradition (Horace Benbow), perceiving the true state of affairs, tries vainly to defend Pore White Trash. However, Southern Womanhood is so hopelessly corrupted that she willfully sees Pore White Trash convicted and lynched; she is then carried off by Wealth (Judge Drake) to meaningless escape in European luxury. Modernism, carrying in it from birth its own impotence and doom, submits with masochistic pleasure to its own destruction for the one crime that it has not yet committed—Revolutionary Destruction of Order (the murder of the Alabama policeman, for which the innocent Popeye is executed).

Mr. O'Donnell deserves very great credit as the first critic to discuss Faulkner as a moralist, the first to compare him in passing with Hawthorne, and almost the first to see that he is engaged in creating Southern myths. In his comments on *Sanctuary,* however, he has been entirely too ingenious. There is no doubt that his allegorical scheme can be read into the novel, but it hardly seems possible that the author intended to put it there. Faulkner tells us that *Sanctuary* was written "in about three weeks." It was completely rewritten two years later, in the effort "to make out of it something which would not shame *The Sound and the Fury* and *As I Lay Dying* too much"; but I doubt that Faulkner had or took the time to give every character a double meaning. Lee Goodwin, for example, is not Pore White Trash, capitalized, but a tough, frightened moonshiner dishonorably discharged from the Army. Tawmmy is not the Naif Faithful, capitalized; he is simply faithful and stupid. If Temple Drake has any symbolic value, she represents the South as a whole, or the younger generation in the South, rather than Southern Womanhood (a phrase that makes Faulkner wince); but it is also quite possible that she represents nothing but a rather silly co-ed. Popeye, however, is another question; and at this point Mr. O'Donnell's reading is not only ingenious but comes very close to Faulkner's conscious or unconscious intention.

Popeye is one of several characters in Faulkner's novels who stand for something that might be called "amoral Modernism," considering that they are creatures of the time and have no social morality whatever; but it might also be called—more accurately, I think—the mechanical civilization that has invaded and partly conquered the South. Popeye is always described in mechanical terms: his eyes "looked like rubber knobs"; his face "just went awry, like the face of a wax doll set too near a hot fire and forgotten"; his tight suit and stiff hat were "all angles, like a modernistic lampshade"; and in general he had "that vicious depthless quality of stamped tin." He was the son of a professional strikebreaker, from whom he inherited syphilis, and the grandson of a pyromaniac. Like two other villains in Faulkner's novels, Joe Christmas and Januarius Jones, he had spent most of his childhood in an institution. He was the man "who made money and had nothing he could do with it, spend it for, since he knew that alcohol would kill him like poison, who had no friends and had never known a woman"—in other words, he was the compendium of all the hateful qualities that Faulkner assigns to finance capitalism. *Sanctuary* is not the connected allegory that Mr. O'Donnell presents in outline (he doesn't approve of allegorical writing by novelists), but neither is it the accumulation of pointless horrors as which it has been dismissed by other critics. It is an example of the Freudian method turned backwards, being full of sexual nightmares that are in reality social symbols. In the author's mind, the novel is somehow connected with what he regards as the rape and corruption of the South.

And the descendants of the old ruling caste, in Faulkner's novels, have the wish but not the courage or the strength of will to prevent this new disaster. They are defeated by Popeye (like Horace Benbow), or they run away from him (like Gowan Stevens, who had gone to school at Virginia and learned to drink like a gentleman, but not to fight for his principles), or they are robbed and replaced in their positions of influence by the Snopeses (like old Bayard Sartoris, the president of the bank), or they drug themselves with eloquence and alcohol (like Mr. Compson), or they retire into the illusion of being inviolable Southern ladies (like Mrs. Compson, who says, "It can't be simply to flout and hurt me. Whoever God is, He would not permit that. I'm a lady."), or they dwell so much on the past that they are incapable of facing the present (like Reverend Hightower, of *Light in August,* who loses his wife and his church through living in a dream world), or they run from danger to danger (like young Bayard Sartoris) frantically seeking their own destruction. Faulkner's novels are full of well-meaning and even admirable people, not only the grandsons of the cotton aristocracy, but also pine-hill farmers and storekeepers and sewing-machine agents and Negro cooks and sharecroppers; but they are almost all of them defeated by circumstances and they carry with them a sense of their own doom.

They also carry, whether heroes or villains, a curious sense of submission to their fate. "There is not one of Faulkner's characters," says André Gide in his dialogue on "The New American Novelists," "who, properly speaking, has a soul"; and I think he means that not one of them exercises the faculty of conscious choice between good and evil. They are haunted, obsessed, driven forward by some inner necessity. Like Miss Rosa Coldfield (in *Absalom, Absalom!*), they exist in "that dream state in which you run without moving from a terror in which you cannot believe, toward a safety in which you have no faith." Or like the slaves freed by General Sherman's army (in *The Unvanquished*), they follow the roads toward any river, believing that it will be their Jordan:

They were singing, walking along the road singing, not even looking to either side. The dust didn't even settle for two days, because all that night they still passed; we sat up listening to them, and the next morning every few yards along the road would be the old ones who couldn't keep up any more, sitting or lying down and even crawling along, calling to the others to help them; and the others—the young ones—not stopping, not even looking at them. "Going to Jordan," they told me. "Going to cross Jordan."

All Faulkner's characters, black and white, are a little like that. They dig for gold frenziedly after they have lost their hope of finding it (like Henry Armstid in *The Hamlet* and Lucas Beauchamp in *Go Down, Moses*); or they battle against and survive a Mississippi flood for the one privilege of returning to the state prison farm (like the tall convict in *The Wild Palms*); or, a whole family together, they carry a body through flood and fire and corruption to bury it in the cemetery at Jefferson (like the Bundrens in *As I Lay Dying*); or they tramp the roads week after week in search of men who had promised to marry them (like Lena Grove, the pregnant woman of *Light in August*); or, pursued by a mob, they turn at the end to meet and accept death (like Joe Christmas in the same novel). Even when they seem to be guided by a conscious design, like Colonel Sutpen, it is not something they have chosen by an act of will, but something that has taken possession of them: ". . . . not what he wanted to do but what he just had to do, had to do it whether he wanted to or not, because if he did not do it he knew that he could never live with himself for the rest of his life." In the same way, Faulkner himself writes, not what he wants to, but what he just has to write whether he wants to or not. And the effect produced on us by all these haunted characters, described in hypnagogic prose, is that of myths or fairy tales or dreams, where again the people act under compulsion, toward fatally predetermined ends.

In addition to being a fatalist, Faulkner is also an idealist, more strongly so than any other American writer of our time. The idealism disguises itself as its own opposite, but that is because he is deeply impressed by and tends to exaggerate the contrast between the life around him and the ideal picture in his mind. No other American writer makes such a use of negative turns of speech: his stories abound in words like "paintless," "lightless," "windowless," "not-feeling," "unvisioned." He speaks of "that *roadless* and even *pathless* waste of *unfenced* fallow and wilderness jungle —*no* barn, *no* stable, *not so much as* a hen-coop; just a log cabin built by hand and *no* clever hand either, a meagre pile of clumsily cut firewood sufficient for about one day and *not even* a gaunt hound to come bellowing out from under the house when he rode up." In the same story ("The Bear"), he speaks of ". . . the empty fields without plow or seed to work them, fenceless against the stock which did not exist within or without the walled stable which likewise was not there." He speaks of faces watching "without alarm, without recognition, without hope," and he speaks of the South under Reconstruction as "a lightless and gutted and empty land." Always in his mind he has an ideal picture of how the land and the people should be—a picture of painted, many-windowed houses, fenced fields, overflowing barns, eyes lighting up with recognition; and always, being honest, he measures that picture against the land and people he has seen. And both pictures are not only physical but moral; for always in the background of his novels is a sense of moral standards and a feeling of outrage at their being violated or simply pushed aside. Seeing little hope in the future, he turns to the past, where he hopes to discover a legendary and recurrent pattern that will illuminate and lend dignity to the world about him. So it is that Reverend Hightower, dying in the dingy ruin of his plans, sees a vision of Bedford Forrest's troopers, who lived without question by a single and universally accepted code:

He hears above his heart the thunder increase, myriad and drumming. Like a long sighing of wind in trees it begins, then they sweep into sight, borne now upon a cloud of phantom dust. They rush past, forwardleaning in the saddles, with brandished arms, beneath whipping ribbons from slanted and eager lances; with tumult and soundless yelling they sweep past like a tide whose crest is jagged with the wild heads of horses and the brandished arms of men like the crater of the world in explosion. They rush past, are gone; the dust swirls skyward sucking, fades away into the night which has fully come. Yet, leaning forward in the window . . . it seems to him that he still hears them: the wild bugles and the clashing sabres and the dying thunder of hooves.

3. *Drama*

HAMLET AND HIS PROBLEMS

T. S. ELIOT

Few critics have even admitted that *Hamlet* the play is the primary problem, and Hamlet the character only secondary. And Hamlet the character has had an especial temptation for that most dangerous type of critic; the critic with a mind which is naturally of the creative order, but which through some weakness in creative power exercises itself in criticism instead. These minds often find in Hamlet a vicarious existence for their own artistic realization. Such a mind had Goethe, who made of Hamlet a Werther; and such had Coleridge, who made of Hamlet a Coleridge; and probably neither of these men in writing about Hamlet remembered that his first business was to study a work of art. The kind of criticism that Goethe and Coleridge produced, in writing of Hamlet, is the most misleading kind possible. For they both possessed unquestionable critical insight, and both make their critical aberrations the more plausible by the substitution—of their own Hamlet for Shakespeare's—which their creative gift effects. We should be thankful that Walter Pater did not fix his attention on this play.

Two writers of our own time, Mr. J. M. Robertson and Professor Stoll of the University of Minnesota, have issued small books which can be praised for moving in the other direction. Mr. Stoll performs a service in recalling to our attention the labours of the critics of the seventeenth and eighteenth centuries,[1] observing that

they knew less about psychology than more recent Hamlet critics, but they were nearer in spirit to Shakespeare's art; and as they insisted on the importance

---

[1] I have never, by the way, seen a cogent refutation of Thomas Rymer's objections to *Othello*.

of the effect of the whole rather than on the importance of the leading character, they were nearer, in their old-fashioned way, to the secret of dramatic art in general.

Qua work of art, the work of art cannot be interpreted; there is nothing to interpret; we can only criticize it according to standards, in comparison to other works of art; and for "interpretation" the chief task is the presentation of relevant historical facts which the reader is not assumed to know. Mr. Robertson points out, very pertinently, how critics have failed in their "interpretation" of *Hamlet* by ignoring what ought be very obvious; that *Hamlet* is a stratification, that it represents the efforts of a series of men, each making what he could out of the work of his predecessors. The *Hamlet* of Shakespeare will appear to us very differently if, instead of treating the whole action of the play as due to Shakespeare's design, we perceive his *Hamlet* to be superposed upon much cruder material which persists even in the final form.

We know that there was an older play by Thomas Kyd, that extraordinary dramatic (if not poetic) genius who was in all probability the author of two plays so dissimilar as *The Spanish Tragedy* and *Arden of Feversham;* and what this play was like we can guess from three clues: from *The Spanish Tragedy* itself, from the tale of Belleforest upon which Kyd's *Hamlet* must have been based, and from a version acted in Germany in Shakespeare's lifetime which bears strong evidence of having been adapted from the earlier, not from the later, play. From these three sources it is clear that in the earlier play the motive was a revenge-motive simply; that the action or delay is caused, as in *The Spanish Tragedy,* solely by the difficulty of assassinating a monarch surrounded by guards; and that the "madness" of Hamlet was feigned in order to escape suspicion, and successfully. In the final play of Shakespeare, on the other hand, there is a motive which is more important than that of revenge, and which explicitly "blunts" the latter; the delay in revenge is unexplained on grounds of necessity or expediency; and the effect of the "madness" is not to lull but to arouse the king's suspicion. The alteration is not complete enough, however, to be convincing. Furthermore, there are verbal parallels so close to *The Spanish Tragedy* as to leave no doubt that in places Shakespeare was merely *revising* the text of Kyd. And finally there are unexplained scenes— the Polonius-Laertes and the Polonius-Reynaldo scenes—for which there is little excuse; these scenes are not in the verse style of Kyd, and not beyond doubt in the style of Shakespeare. These Mr. Robertson believes to be scenes in the original play of Kyd reworked by a third hand, perhaps Chapman, before Shakespeare touched the play. And he concludes, with very strong show of reason, that the original play of Kyd was, like certain other revenge plays, in two parts of five acts each. The upshot of Mr. Robertson's examination is, we believe, irrefragable: that Shakespeare's *Hamlet,* so far as it is Shakespeare's, is a play dealing with the effect of a mother's guilt upon her son, and that Shakespeare was unable to impose this motive successfully upon the "intractable" material of the old play.

Of the intractability there can be no doubt. So far from being Shakespeare's masterpiece, the play is most certainly an artistic failure. In several ways the play is puzzling, and disquieting as is none of the others. Of all the plays it is the longest and is possibly the one on which Shakespeare spent most pains; and yet he has left in it superfluous and inconsistent scenes which even hasty revision should have noticed. The versification is variable. Lines like

> Look, the morn, in russet mantle clad,
> Walks o'er the dew of yon high eastern hill.

are of the Shakespeare of *Romeo and Juliet.* The lines in Act V. sc. ii,

> Sir, in my heart there was a kind of fighting
> That would not let me sleep . . .
> Up from my cabin,
> My sea-gown scarf'd about me, in the dark
> Grop'd I to find out them: had my desire;
> Finger'd their packet;

are of his quite mature period. Both workmanship and thought are in an unstable position. We are surely justified in attributing the play, with that other profoundly interesting play of "intractable" material and astonishing versification, *Measure for Measure,* to a period of crisis, after which follow the tragic successes which culminate in *Coriolanus. Coriolanus* may be not as "interesting" as *Hamlet,* but it is, with *Antony and Cleopatra,* Shakespeare's most assured artistic success. And probably more people have thought *Hamlet* a work of art because they found it interesting, than have found it interesting because it is a work of art. It is the "Mona Lisa" of literature.

The grounds of *Hamlet's* failure are not immediately obvious. Mr. Robertson is undoubtedly correct in concluding that the essential emotion of the play is the feeling of a son towards a guilty mother:

(Hamlet's) tone is that of one who has suffered tortures on the score of his mother's degradation. . . . The guilt of a mother is an almost intolerable motive for drama, but it had to be maintained and emphasized to supply a psychological solution, or rather a hint of one.

This, however, is by no means the whole story. It is not merely the "guilt of a mother" that cannot be handled as Shakespeare handled the suspicion of Othello, the infatuation of Antony, or the pride of Coriolanus. The subject might conceivably have expanded into a tragedy like these, intelligible, self-complete, in the sunlight. *Hamlet,* like the sonnets, is full of some stuff that the writer could not drag to light, contemplate, or manipulate into art. And when we search for this feeling, we find it, as in the sonnets, very difficult to localize. You cannot point to it in the speeches; indeed, if you examine the two famous soliloquies you see the versification of Shakespeare, but a content which might be claimed by another, perhaps by the author of the *Revenge of Bussy d'Ambois,* Act V, sc. i. We find Shakespeare's Hamlet not in the action, not in any quotations that we might select, so much as in an unmistakable tone which is unmistakably not in the earlier play.

The only way of expressing emotion in the form of art is by finding an "objective correlative"; in other words, a set of objects, a situation, a chain of events which shall be the formula of that *particular* emotion; such that when the external facts, which must terminate in sensory experience, are given, the emotion is immediately evoked. If you examine any of Shakespeare's more successful tragedies, you will find this exact equivalence; you will find that the state of mind of Lady Macbeth walking in her sleep has been communicated to you by a skilful accumulation of imagined sensory impressions; the words of Macbeth on hearing of his wife's death strike us as if, given the sequence of events, these words were automatically released by the last events in the series. The artistic "inevitability" lies in this complete adequacy of the external to the emotion; and this is precisely what is deficient in *Hamlet.* Hamlet (the man) is dominated by an emotion which is inexpressible, because it is in *excess* of the facts as they appear. And the supposed identity of Hamlet with his author is genuine to this point: that Hamlet's bafflement at the absence of objective equivalent to his feelings is a prolongation of the bafflement of his creator in the face of his artistic problem. Hamlet is up against the difficulty that his disgust is occasioned by his mother, but that his mother is not an adequate equivalent for it; his disgust envelops and exceeds her. It is thus a feeling which he cannot understand; he cannot objectify it, and it therefore remains to poison life and obstruct action. None of the possible actions can satisfy it; and nothing that Shakespeare can do with the plot can express Hamlet for him. And it must be noticed that the very nature of the *données* of the problem precludes objective equivalence. To have heightened the criminality of Gertrude would have been to provide the formula for a totally different emotion in Hamlet; it is just *because* her character is so negative and insignificant that she arouses in Hamlet the feeling which she is incapable of representing.

The "madness" of Hamlet lay to Shakespeare's hand; in the earlier play a simple ruse, and to the end, we may presume, understood as a ruse by the audience. For Shakespeare it is less than madness and more than feigned. The levity of Hamlet, his repetition of phrase, his puns, are not part of a deliberate plan of dissimulation, but a form of emotional relief. In the character Hamlet it is the buffoonery of an emotion which can find no outlet in action; in the dramatist it is the buffoonery of an emotion which he cannot express in art. The intense feeling, ecstatic or terrible, without an object or exceeding its object, is something which every person of sensibility has known; it is doubtless a subject of study for pathologists. It often occurs in adolescence: the ordinary person puts these feelings to sleep, or trims down his feelings to fit the business world; the artist keeps them alive by his ability to intensify the world to his emotions. The Hamlet of Laforgue is an adolescent; the Hamlet of Shakespeare is not, he has not that explanation and excuse. We must simply admit that here Shakespeare tackled a problem which proved too much for him. Why he attempted it at all is an insoluble puzzle; under compulsion of what experience he attempted to express the inexpressibly horrible, we cannot ever know. We need a great many facts in his biography; and we should like to know whether, and when, and after or at the same time as what personal experience, he read Montaigne, II. xii, *Apologie de Raimond Sebond.* We should have, finally, to know something which is by hypothesis unknowable, for we assume it to be an experience which, in the manner indicated, exceeded the facts. We should have to understand things which Shakespeare did not understand himself.

RESTORATION COMEDY:
THE REALITY AND THE MYTH

L. C. KNIGHTS

I

H ENRY JAMES—whose "social comedy" may be allowed to provide a standard of maturity—once remarked that he found Congreve "insufferable," [1] and
perhaps the first thing to say of Restoration drama—tragedy as well as
comedy—is that the bulk of it is insufferably dull. There are long stretches
of boredom to be found in the lower ranges of Elizabethan drama, but
there is nothing comparable to the unmitigated fatigue that awaits the
reader of *Love in a Tub, Sir Martin Mar-all, Mr. Limberham, The Relapse,
or The Mourning Bride.* And who returns to Dryden's heroic plays with
renewed zest? The superiority of the common runs of plays in the first period
to that of the second is, at all events, a commonplace. It should be equally
commonplace that the strength of the Elizabethan drama lies partly in the
kind and scope—the quality and variety—of the interests that the playwrights were able to enlist, partly in the idiom that they had at their command: the drama drew on a vigorous non-dramatic literature, and literature
in general was in close relation with non-literary interests and a rich common language. That is not the whole story, but it is an important part of it,
and it seems profitable in a discussion of Restoration comedy, to keep these
facts in mind for comparison. Ever since Collier published *A Short View of
the Profaneness and Immorality of the English Stage* opponents of Restoration comedy have conducted their case almost entirely in moral terms, and
it has been easy for recent critics, rightly discarding Lamb's obvious subter-
fuge, to turn the moral argument upside down, to find freedom of manners
where Macaulay found licentiousness. "Morals" are, in the long run, decidedly relevant—but only in the long run: literary criticism has prior claims.
If, to start with, we try to see the comedy of manners in relation to its con-

---

"Restoration Comedy: The Reality and the Myth" from *Explorations* by L. C.
Knights, reprinted by permission of the author, Chatto and Windus, and George W.
Stewart, Publisher, Inc.

[1] *Letters,* Vol. I, p. 140.

temporary non-dramatic literature—to take its bearings in the general culture of the time—we may at least make possible a free and critical approach.

During the forty years that followed the Restoration, English literature, English culture, was "upper-class" to an extent that it had never been before, and was not, after Addison, to be again. "Now if they ask me," said Dryden, "whence it is that our conversation is so much refined? I must freely and without flattery, ascribe it to the court," and his insistence, as a writer, on "the benefit of converse" with his courtly patrons was not merely dedicatory fulsomeness; the influence of the current conception of "the gentleman" is shown plainly enough by the urbane ease of his critical prefaces; and Dryden's non-dramatic prose is fairly representative of the new age.[1]

It is this that explains why, if one comes to Restoration literature after some familiarity with the Elizabethans, the first impression made by the language is likely to be a sense of what has been lost; the disintegration of the old cultural unity has plainly resulted in impoverishment. The speech of the educated is now remote from the speech of the people (Bunyan's huge sales were, until the eighteenth century, outside "the circumference of wit"), and idiomatic vigour and evocative power seem to have gone out of the literary medium. But there was gain as well as loss. The common mode of Restoration prose—for there is now a common mode, a norm— was not evolved merely in the interests of good form and polite intercourse; it had behind it a more serious pressure. When, in 1667, Sprat attacked "this vicious abundance of phrase . . . this volubility of tongue, which makes so great a noise in the world," he had in mind the needs of scientific inquiry and rational discussion. "They have therefore," he said of the Royal Society, "been most rigorous in putting in execution the only remedy that can be found for this *extravagance,* and that has been a constant resolution to reject all amplifications, digressions, and swellings of style; to return back to the primitive purity and shortness, when men delivered so many *things* almost in an equal number of *words.* They have exacted from all their members a close, naked, natural way of speaking, positive expressions, clear senses, a native easiness, bringing all things as near the mathematical plainness as they can."[2] For the first time the English language was made—and to some extent made consciously—an instrument for rational dissection.

---

[1] On "the last and greatest advantage of our writing, which proceeds from *conversation,*" see in particular the *Defence of the Epilogue.* And the dialogue form in which Dryden cast the *Essay of Dramatic Poesy* was not unrecognizably far from actuality.

[2] *The History of the Royal Society of London: Spingarn, Critical Essays of the Seventeenth Century,* Vol. II, pp. 112 ff.

When once the aversion to bear uneasiness taketh place in a man's mind, it doth so check all the passions, that they are dampt into a kind of indifference; they grow faint and languishing, and come to be subordinate to that fundamental maxim, of not purchasing any thing at the price of a difficulty. This made that he had as little eagerness to oblige, as he had to hurt men; the motive of his giving bounties was rather to make men less uneasy to him, than more easy to themselves; and yet no ill-nature all this while. He would slide from an asking face, and could guess very well. It was throwing a man off from his shoulders, that leaned upon them with his whole weight; so that the party was not gladder to receive, than he was to give.

This is from Halifax's *Character of Charles II,* and the even tone, the sinuous ease of movement and the clarity of the analysis mark the passage as unmistakably post-Restoration. Halifax, of course, is in some ways an unusually handsome representative of his age; he is racy (the apt adjective is supplied by his editor, H. C. Foxcroft) as well as polite. But the achievement represented by his style was far from being a merely individual achievement. The shrewd and subtle portrait of Charles II is unlike anything that had appeared in English before his time, and it could only have appeared when it did.

Now an upper-class culture that produced *Absalom and Achitophel, The Character of a Trimmer,* Dryden's critical prefaces and Locke's *Second Treatise of Government,* may have been limited, but it was not altogether decadent. If the drama is inferior it is not because it represents—by Elizabethan standards—a limited culture, but because it represents contemporary culture so inadequately; it has no significant relation with the best thought of the time. Heroic tragedy is decadent because it is factitious; it substitutes violent emotionalism for emotion, the purple patch for poetry, and its rhetoric, unlike Elizabethan dramatic rhetoric, has no connexion with the congenial non-dramatic modes of the age; it is artificial in a completely damaging sense, *and by contemporary standards.* If we look for an early illustration of the bad mid-eighteenth-century conception of poetry as something applied from the outside [1] we find it in Dryden's verse plays, where he adopts canons of style that he would not have dreamed of applying—apart from his Odes—in his non-dramatic verse. Tragedy, he said, "is naturally pompous and magnificent." Nothing in English literature is more surprising—if we stop to consider—than the complete discrepancy between the sinewy ease of Dryden's satires and the stiff opaqueness of his dramatic verse; and "the lofty style," since it cannot modulate, is always coming down with a bump.

---

[1] ". . . enriching every subject (otherwise dry and barren) with a pomp of diction and luxuriant harmony of numbers."—Gray's note to *The Progress of Poesy,* 1754.

> I'm pleased and pained, since first her eyes I saw,
> As I were stung with some tarantula.
> Arms, and the dusty field, I less admire,
> And soften strangely in some new desire;
> Honor burns in me not so fiercely bright,
> But pales as fires when mastered by the light:
> Even while I speak and look, I change yet more,
> And now am nothing that I was before.
> I'm numbed, and fixed, and scarce my eyeballs move;
> I fear it is the lethargy of love! [1]

It is only in the easy strength of occasional lines ("A good, luxurious, palatable faith") that we hear his natural voice. In the plays as a whole —each made up of a succession of "great" moments and heroic postures —the "nature" that is "wrought up to a higher pitch" [2] bears little resemblance to the Nature that was to figure so largely in the Augustan code.

This, or a similar account, would probably be accepted by all critics of the Restoration heroic play. What is not commonly recognized (it is, at all events, not said) is that the comedy of manners exhibits a parallel attenuation and enfeeblement of what the age, taken as a whole, had to offer. I am not, for the moment, referring to the moral or social code expressed. The observation to start from is that the prose in which Restoration comedy is written—select which dramatist you like—is poor and inexpressive in comparison with the staple non-dramatic prose.

Congreve is usually accepted as the most brilliant stylist of the five or six comic dramatists who count. But place beside the extract quoted from Halifax a passage or two from *Love for Love* or *The Way of the World* (it makes no difference whether the speaker is Scandal or Mirabell), and Congreve's style shows as nerveless in the comparison:

A mender of reputations! ay, just as he is a keeper of secrets, another virtue that he sets up for in the same manner. For the rogue will speak aloud in the posture of a whisper; and deny a woman's name, while he gives you the marks of her person: he will forswear receiving a letter from her, and at the same time show you her hand in the superscription; and yet perhaps he has counterfeited the hand too, and sworn to a truth; but he hopes not to be believed; and refuses the reputation of a lady's favour, as a doctor says *No* to a bishopric, only that it may be granted him. In short, he is a public professor of secrecy, and makes proclamation that he holds private intelligence.

A. To give t'other his due, he has something of good nature, and does not always want wit.

---

[1] *The Conquest of Granada,* Part I, III, i.

[2] ". . . the nature of a serious play; this last is indeed the representation of nature, but 'tis nature wroght up to a higher pitch."—*Of Dramatic Poesy.* The final paragraph of the Preface to *Religio Laici* has some interesting remarks in this connexion; e.g. "The florid, elevated, and figurative way is for the passions."

B. Not always: but as often as his memory fails him, and his common-place of comparisons. He is a fool with a good memory, and some few scraps of other folks' wit. He is one whose conversation can never be approved, yet it is now and then to be endured. He had indeed one good quality, he is not exceptious; for he so passionately affects the reputation of understanding raillery, that he will construe an affront into a jest; and call down-right rudeness and ill language, satire and fire.

This reminds me of Arnold's definition of Macaulayese, "The external characteristic being a hard metallic movement with nothing of the soft play of life, and the internal characteristic being a perpetual semblance of hitting the right nail on the head without the reality." Both construction and movement are so far from being expressive *of* anything in particular that the main function of some words is, it seems, to complete an antithesis or to display a riddling wit.[1] The verbal pattern appears at times to be completely unrelated to a mode of perceiving. The passages quoted have an air of preening themselves on their acute discriminations, but the antitheses are mechanical, and the pattern is monotonously repeated: "She has beauty enough to make any man think she has wit; and complaisance enough not to contradict him who should tell her so"—the common form soon loses the sting of surprise. Burnet can write in an antithetical style which also penetrates:

> And tho' he desired to become absolute, and to overturn both our religion and our laws, yet he would neither run the risk, nor give himself the trouble, which so great a design required. He had an appearance of gentleness in his outward deportment: but he seemed to have no bowels nor tenderness in his nature: and in the end of his life he became cruel.[2]

The nearest approach to subtlety that Congreve's style allows is represented by such things as this:

> FAINALL. You are a gallant man, Mirabell; and though you may have cruelty enough not to satisfy a lady's longing, you have too much generosity not to be tender of her honour. Yet you speak with an indifference which seems to be affected, and confesses you are conscious of a negligence.
>
> MIRABELL. You pursue the argument with a distrust that seems to be unaffected, and confess you are conscious of a concern for which the lady is more indebted to you than is your wife.

It isn't really, very subtle. As for the "wit," when it isn't merely verbal and

---

[1] *The Old Bachelor* shows the riddles in the process of manufacture. *Bellmour:* He is the drum to his own praise—the only implement of a soldier he resembles; like that, being full of blustering noise and emptiness. *Sharper:* And like that, of no use but to be beaten, etc.

[2] Quote from Professor Nichol Smith's excellent anthology, *Characters from the Histories and Memoirs of the Seventeenth Century* (Clarendon Press).

obvious ("Fruitful, the head fruitful;—that bodes horns; the fruit of the head is horns," etc.) it is hopelessly dependent on convention.

> She that marries a fool, Sir Sampson, forfeits the reputation of her honesty or understanding: and she that marries a very witty man is a slave to the severity and insolent conduct of her husband. I should like a man of wit for a lover, because I would have such a man in my power; but I would no more be his wife than his enemy. For his malice is not a more terrible consequence of his aversion than his jealousy is of his love.

An intelligent husband, you see, must be jealous; take away that entertaining assumption and the point is blunted. Halifax is a witty writer, but his wit springs naturally from the situation he is concerned with and illuminates it. "A partner in government is so unnatural a thing that it is a squint-eyed allegiance which must be paid to such a double-bottomed monarchy." [1] Congreve's wit is entirely self-regarding.

If there were space to discuss the manner of Wycherley, Etherege and Vanbrugh, it is a similar account that would have to be given. I am not suggesting that they write in a completely indistinguishable common mode (though they all have passages that might come from any play); but in essentials—in the way in which they use their similes and antitheses, in the conception of "style" and "wit" that they exhibit—they all stand together. Not one of them has achieved a genuinely sensitive and individual mode of expression; and in each the pattern of the prose inhibits any but the narrowest—and the most devastatingly *expected*—response. That, I should claim, is the judgment to which an analysis of their prose inevitably leads. The trouble is not that the Restoration comic writers deal with a limited number of themes, but that they bring to bear a miserably limited set of attitudes. And these, in turn, are factitious to exactly the same degree as the prose is artificial and non-representative of the current non-dramatic medium.

II

Apart from the presentation of incidental and unrelated "wit" (which soon becomes as tiring as the epigrams of the "good talker"), Restoration comedy has two main interests—the behaviour of the polite and of pretenders to politeness, and some aspects of sexual relationships. Critics have made out a case for finding in one or other of these themes a unifying principle and a serious base for the comedy of manners. According to Miss Lynch, the "thoroughly conventionalized social mode" of the courtly

---

[1] Also from *The Character of a Trimmer:*—". . . the indecent courtship of some silken divines, who, one would think, did practise to bow at the altar, only to learn to make the better legs at Court."

circle "was discovered to have manifestly comic aspects, both when awkwardly misinterpreted, and when completely fulfilled through personalities to which, however, it could not give complete expression," [1] and both these discrepancies were exploited by Etherege and his successors. Bonamy Dobrée, attributing to the comic dramatists "a deep curiosity, and a desire to try new ways of living," finds that "the distinguishing characteristic of Restoration comedy down to Congreve is that it is concerned with the attempt to rationalize sexual relationships. It is this that makes it different from any other comedy that has ever been written. . . . It said in effect, 'Here is life lived upon certain assumptions; see what it becomes.' It also dealt, as no other comedy has ever done, with a subject that arose directly out of this, namely sex-antagonism, a consequence of the experimental freedom allowed to women, which gave matter for some of its most brilliant scenes." [2]

These accounts, as developed, certainly look impressive, and if Restoration comedy really answered to them—if it had something fresh and penetrating to say on sex and social relations—there would be no need to complain, even if one found the "solutions" distasteful. But Miss Lynch's case, at all events, depends on a vigorous reading into the plays of values which are not there, values which could not possibly be expressed, in fact, in the prose of any of the dramatists. (The candid reader can turn up the passages selected by Miss Lynch in support of her argument, and see if they are not all in the factitious, superficial mode that I have described.)

We may consider, by way of illustration, Etherege's *The Man of Mode*. When the play opens, Dorimant ("the finest of all fine gentlemen in Restoration comedy") is trying to rid himself of an old mistress, Mrs. Loveit, before taking up with a new, Bellinda, whilst Young Bellair, in love with Emilia, is trying to find some way out of marrying Harriet, an heiress whom his father has brought to town for him. The entertainment is made up of these two sets of complications, together with an exhibition of the would-be modishness of Sir Fopling Flutter. Events move fast. After a night spent in various sociabilities Dorimant keeps an appointment with Bellinda at 5 A.M. Letting her out of his lodgings an hour or so later, and swearing to be discreet "By all the Joys I have had, and those you keep in store," he is surprised by his companions, and in the resulting confusion Bellinda finds herself paying an unwilling visit to Mrs. Loveit. Dorimant appears and is rated by the women before he "flings off." Meanwhile Young Bellair and Emilia have secretly married. Dorimant, his equanimity recovered, turns up for the exposé, followed by his mistresses. The lovers

[1] K. M. Lynch, *The Social Mode of Restoration Comedy*, p. 216.
[2] Bonamy Dobrée, *Restoration Comedy*, pp. 22–23.

are forgiven, the mistresses are huddled off the stage, and it is decided that Dorimant, who, the previous day, had ingratiated himself with Harriet's mother, and whose "soul has quite given up her liberty," shall be allowed to pay court to the heiress.

It seems to me that what the play provides—apart from the briskly handled intrigue—is a demonstration of the physical stamina of Dorimant. But Miss Lynch sees further. For her, Dorimant is "the fine flowering of Restoration culture." Illustrating her theory of the double standard, she remarks: "We laugh at Sir Fopling Flutter because he so clumsily parodies social fashions which Dorimant interprets with unfailing grace and distinction. We laugh at Dorimant because his assumed affectation admits of so poor and incomplete an expression of an attractive and vigorous personality." [1] The "unfailing grace and distinction" are perhaps not much in evidence in Dorimant's spiteful treatment of Mrs. Loveit; [2] but even if we ignore those brutish scenes we are forced to ask, How do we know that there *is* this "attractive and vigorous personality" beneath the conventional forms? Dorimant's intrigues are of no more human significance than those of a barn-yard cock, and as for what Miss Lynch calls "his really serious affair with Harriet" (I feel this deserves a *sic*), it is purely theatrical, and the "pangs of love" are expressed in nothing but the conventional formulae: "She's gone, but she has left a pleasing Image of herself behind that wanders in my Soul." The answer to the question posed is that Miss Lynch's account is a mere assumption. Nothing that Dorimant actually *says* will warrant it—and nothing in the whole of Restoration comedy —in the words actually spoken—allows us a glimpse of those other "personalities" to which the conventional social modes "could not give complete expression." The "real values" [3] simply are not there.

A minor point can be made in passing. It is just possible to claim that Restoration comedy contains "social criticism" in its handling of "the vulgar." "Come Mr. Sharper," says Congreve's Belinda, "you and I will

----

[1] *The Social Mode of Restoration Comedy,* p. 181.

[2] See II, ii, and V, i, where Dorimant, trying to force a quarrel with Mrs. Loveit, attributes to her a fondness for Sir Fopling. The first of these scenes was too much for Etherege, and he makes Bellinda say:

> He's given me the proof which I desired of his love,
> But 'tis a proof of his ill nature too.
> I wish I had not seen him use her so.

But this is soon forgotten, and we are not, of course, called on to register an unfavourable judgment of Dorimant.

[3] "The love affairs of Courtal and Ariana, Freeman and Gatty [in *She Wou'd if She Cou'd*] are similarly embarrassed by social convention. . . . The conduct of these polite lovers acquires comic vitality through the continually suggested opposition of artificial and real values."—*Op. cit.,* p. 152.

take a turn, and laugh at the vulgar; both the great vulgar and the small," and Etherege's Lady Townley expresses the common attitude of the polite towards the social nuisances: "We should love wit, but for variety be able to divert ourselves with the extravagancies of those who want it." The butts, unfortunately, are only shown as fools by the discrepancy between their ambitions and their achievements, not because their ambitions are puerile. The subject is hardly worth discussing, since it is obviously nothing but an easily satisfied sense of superiority that is diverted by the "variety" of a constant succession of Dapperwits, Froths and Fopling Flutters. "When a humour takes in London," Tom Brown remarked, "they ride it to death ere they leave it. The primitive Christians were not persecuted with half that variety as the poor unthinking beaus are tormented with upon the theatre . . . A huge great muff, and a gaudy ribbon hanging at a bully's backside, is an excellent jest, and new-invented curses, as, Stap my vitals, damn my diaphragm, slit my wind pipe, sink me ten thousand fathom deep, rig up a new beau, though in the main 'tis but the same everlasting coxcomb." [1]

III

In the matter of sexual relations Restoration comedy is entirely dominated by a narrow set of conventions. The objection that it is only certain characters, not the dramatists themselves, who accept them can be more freely encountered when the assumptions that are expressed most frequently have been briefly illustrated.

The first convention is, of course, that constancy in love, especially in marriage, is a bore. Vanbrugh, who was the most uneasy if not the most honest of the comic dramatists (I think that in *The Provok'd Wife* he shows as unusually honest), unambiguously attributes this attitude to Sir John Brute:

What cloying meat is love—when matrimony's the sauce to it! Two years marriage has debauch'd my five senses. . . . No boy was ever so weary of his tutor, no girl of her bib, no nun of doing penance, or old maid of being chaste, as I am of being married. Sure there's a secret curse entail'd upon the very name of wife!

The woman's well enough; she has no vice that I know of, but she's a wife, and—damn a wife! [2]

What Vanbrugh saw as a fit sentiment for Sir John had by that

---

[1] Tom Brown, Works, Vol. III, *Amusements Comical and Serious,* "At the Playhouse," p. 39.
[2] *The Provok'd Wife,* I, i, II, i.

time (1697) served the Restoration stage—without change—for thirty years. In *She Wou'd if She Cou'd* Etherege had exhibited Sir Oliver Cockwood in an identical vein: "A pox of this tying man and woman together, for better, for worse." "To have a mistress love thee entirely " is "a damn'd trouble." "There are sots that would think themselves happy in such a Lady; but to a true bred Gentleman all lawful solace is abomination." [1] If Sir Oliver is a fool it is only because he is a trifle gross in his expression. "If you did but know, Madam," says the polite Freeman, "what an odious thing it is to be thought to love a Wife in good Company." [2] And the convention is constantly turning up in Congreve. "There is no creature perfectly civil but a husband," explains Mrs. Frail, "for in a little time he grows only rude to his wife, and that is the highest good breeding, for it begets his civility to other people." [3] "Marry her! Marry her!" Fainall advises Mirabell, "Be half as well acquainted with her charms, as you are with her defects, and my life on't, you are your own man again." [4] And Witwoud: "A wit should not more be sincere than a woman constant; one argues a decay of parts, as t'other of beauty." [5] Appetite, it seems (and this is the second assumption), needs perpetually fresh stimulus. This is the faith of Rhodophil in *Marriage à la Mode* and of Constant in *The Provok'd Wife,* as well as of Wycherley's old procuress, Mrs. Joyner. "If our wives would suffer us but now and then to make excursions," Rhodophil explains to Palamede, "the benefit of our variety would be theirs; instead of one continued, lazy, tired love, they would, in their turns, have twenty vigorous, fresh, and active lovers." [6] "Would anything but a madman complain of uncertainty?" asks Congreve's Angelica, for "security is an insipid thing, and the overtaking and possessing of a wish, discovers the folly of the chase." [7] And Fainall, in *The Way of the World,* speaks for a large class when he hints at a liking for sauce—a little gentleman's relish—to his seductions: "I'd no more play with a man that slighted his ill fortune than I'd make love to a woman who under-valued the loss of her reputation." [8] Fainall, of course, is what he is, but the attitude that makes sexual pleasure "the bliss," that makes woman "delicious"—some-

---

[1] *She Wou'd if She Cou'd,* I, i; III, iii.

[2] *Ibid.,* III, iii.

[3] *Love for Love,* I, ii.

[4] *The Way of the World,* I, ii.

[5] *Ibid.*

[6] *Marriage à la Mode,* II, i, Cf. *The Provok'd Wife,* III, i: *Constant,* "There's a poor sordid slavery in marriage, that turns the flowing tide of honour, and sinks us to the lowest ebb of infamy. 'Tis a corrupted soil: Ill-nature, sloth, cowardice, and dirt, are all its product."

[7] *Love for Love,* IV, iii.

[8] *The Way of the World,* I, 1.

thing to be savoured—as well as "damned" and "destructive," demands, for its support, "the pleasure of a chase." [1]

> Would you long preserve your lover?
> Would you still his goddess reign?
> Never let him all discover,
> Never let him much obtain. [2]

Restoration comedy used to be considered outrageously outspoken, but such stuff as this, far from being "outspoken," hovers on the outskirts of sexual relations, and sees nothing but the titillation of appetite (" 'Tis not the success," Collier observed, "but the manner of gaining it which is all in all"). [3] Sex is a hook baited with tempting morsels; [4] it is a thirst quencher; [5] it is a cordial; [6] it is a dish to feed on; [7] it is a bunch of grapes; [8] it is anything but sex. (This, of course, explains why some people can combine a delighted approval of Restoration comedy with an unbalanced repugnance for such modern literature as deals sincerely and realistically with sexual relationships.)

Now the objection referred to above was that sentiments such as these are not offered for straightforward acceptance. Many of them are attributed to characters plainly marked as Wicked (Maskwell, for example, is the black-à-vised villain of melodrama), or, more frequently, as trivial, and the dramatist can therefore dissociate himself. He may even be engaged in showing his audience the explicit, logical consequences of the half-conscious premises on which they base their own lives, saying, as Mr. Dobrée has it, "Here is life lived upon certain assumptions; see what it

---

[1] *The Old Bachelor,* I, i; III, ii ("O thou delicious, damned, dear destructive woman!"); IV, ii.

[2] *Ibid.,* II, ii.

[3] *A Short View of the Profaneness and Immorality of the English Stage,* Fifth Edition, 1738, p. 116.

[4] " 'Tis true you are so eager in pursuit of the temptation, that you save the devil the trouble of leading you into it: nor is it out of discretion that you don't swallow the very hook yourselves have baited, but . . . what you meant for a whet turns the edge of your puny stomachs."—*The Old Bachelor,* I, i. "Strike Heartwell home, before the bait's worn off the hook. Age will come. He nibbled fairly yesterday, and no doubt will be eager enough to-day to swallow the temptation."—*Ibid.,* III, i.

[5] "What was my pleasure is become my duty: and I have as little stomach to her now as if I were her husband. . . . Pox on't! that a man can't drink without quenching his thirst."—*The Double Dealer,* III, i.

[6] You must get you a mistress, Rhodophil. That, indeed, is living upon cordials; but as fast as one fails, you must supply it with another."—*Marriage à la Mode,* I, i.

[7] "Because our husbands cannot feed on one dish, therefore we must be starved."—*Ibid.,* III, i.

[8] "The only way to keep us new to one another, is never to enjoy, as they keep grapes, by hanging them upon a line; they must touch nothing, if you would preserve them fresh."—*Ibid.,* V, i.

becomes." To this there are several answers. The first is that reflexions of the kind that I have quoted are indistinguishable in tone and style from the general epigrammatic stock-in-trade (the audience was not altogether to be blamed if, as Congreve complained, they could not at first "distinguish betwixt the character of a Witwoud and a Lovewit"); and they are largely "exhibited," just as all the self-conscious witticisms are exhibited, for the sake of their immediate "comic" effect. One has only to note the laughter of a contemporary audience at a revival, and the places where the splutters occur, to realize how much of the fun provides a rather gross example of tendency wit.[1] The same attitudes, moreover, are manipulated again and again, turning up with the state monotony of jokes on postcards, and the play that is made with them demands only the easiest, the most superficial, response. But it is, after all, useless to argue about the degree of detachment, the angle at which these attitudes and assumptions are presented. As soon as one selects a particular comedy for that exercise one realizes that all is equally grist to the mill and that the dramatist (there is no need, here, to make distinctions) has no coherent attitude of his own. A consistent artistic purpose would not be content to express itself in a style that allows so limited, so local an effect.

But it is the triviality that one comes back to. In Dryden's *Marriage à la Mode* the characters accept the usual conventions: constancy is dull, and love only thrives on variety.

> PALAMEDE. O, now I have found it! you dislike her for no other reason but because she's your wife.
> RHODOPHIL. And is not that enough? All that I know of her perfections now, is only by memory . . . At last we arrived at that point, that there was nothing left in us to make us new to one another . . .
> PALAMEDE. The truth is, your disease is very desperate; but, though you cannot be cured, you may be patched up a little; you must get you a mistress, Rhodophil. That, indeed, is living upon cordials; but, as fast as one fails, you must supply it with another.

The mistress that Rhodophil selects is Melanthra, whom Palamede is to marry; Palamede falls in love with Doralice, Rhodophil's wife, and the

---

[1] The Freudian "censor" is at times projected in the form of the stage puritan. The plays written soon after the Commonwealth period appealed to Royalist prejudice by satirizing the "seemingly precise"; and even later, when "the bonfires of devotion," "the bellows of zeal," were forgotten, a good deal of the self-conscious swagger of indecency seems to have been directed against "our protestant husbands," city merchants, aldermen and the like; the "daring" effect was intensified by postulating a shockable audience somewhere—not necessarily in the theatre. Not that the really obscene jokes were merely bravado: Collier quite rightly remarked that "the modern poets seem to use smut as the old ones did Machines, to relieve a fainting situation." —*A Short View,* Fifth Edition, p. 4.

ensuing complications provide sufficient entertainment (the grotto scene, III, ii, is really funny). Mr. Dobrée, however, regards the play as a witty exposure of the impossibility of rationalizing sex relations, as Palamede and Rhodophil attempt to rationalize them. Dryden "laughs morality back into its rightful place, as the scheme which ultimately makes life most comfortable." [1] But what Dryden actually does is to *use* the conventions for the amusement they afford, not to examine them. The level at which the play works is fairly indicated by the opening song:

> Why should a foolish marriage vow,
>   Which long ago was made,
> Oblige us to each other now,
>   When passion is decayed?
> We loved, and we loved, as long as we could,
>   'Till our love was loved out in us both;
> But our marriage is dead, when the pleasure is fled:
>   'Twas pleasure first made it an oath.
>
> If I have pleasures for a friend
>   And further love in store,
> What wrong has he, whose jobs did end,
>   And who could give no more?
> 'Tis a madness that he should be jealous of me,
>   Or that I should bar him of another:
> For all we can gain, is to give ourselves pain,
>   When neither can hinder the other.

The lovers make no attempt to "rationalize sex" for the simple reason that genuine sexual feelings no more enter into the play as a whole than feelings of any kind enter into the song. (The obviously faked emotions of the heroic plot are, after all, relevant—and betraying.) And according to Mr. Dobrée, "In one sense the whole idea of Restoration comedy is summed up in the opening scene of *Marriage à la Mode*.[2]

In a sense, too, Mr. Dobrée is right. Restoration comedy nowhere provides us with much more of the essential stuff of human experience than we have there. Even Congreve, by common account the best of the comic writers, is no exception. I have said that his verbal pattern often seems to be quite unrelated to an individual mode of perceiving. At best it registers a very limited mode. Restoration prose is all "social" in its tone, implications and general tenor, but Congreve's observation is *merely* of the public surface. And Congreve's, too, relies on the conventional assumptions. In *The Way of the World,* it is true, they are mainly given to the bad and the foolish to express: it is Fainall who discourses on the pleasures

---

[1] *Restoration Comedy,* p. 133.
[2] *Ibid.,* p. 106.

of disliking one's wife, and Witwoud who maintains that only old age and ugliness ensure constancy. And Mirabell, who is explicitly opposed to some aspects of contemporary manners, goes through the common forms in a tone of rather weary aloofness: "I wonder, Fainall, that you who are married, and of consequence should be discreet, will suffer your wife to be of such a party." But Congreve himself is not above raising a cheap snigger;[1] and, above all, the characters with some life in them have nothing to fall back on—nothing, that is, except the conventional, and conventionally limited, pleasures of sex. Millamant, who says she loathes the country and hates the town, expects to draw vitality from the excitement of incessant solicitation:

> I'll be solicited to the very last, nay, and afterwards . . . I should think I was poor and had nothing to bestow, if I were reduced to an inglorious ease, and freed from the agreeable fatigues of solicitation. . . . Oh, I hate a lover that can dare to think he draws a moment's air, independent of the bounty of his mistress. There is not so impudent a thing in nature, as the saucy look of an assured man, confident of success. The pedantic arrogance of a very husband has not so pragmatical an air.

Everyone seems to have found Millamant intelligent and attractive, but her attitude is not far removed from that expressed in

> Would you long preserve your lover?
> Would you still his goddess reign?

and she shares with characters who are decidedly not attractive a disproportionate belief in "the pleasure of a chase." Which is not surprising in view of her other occupations and resources; visiting, writing and receiving letters, tea-parties and small talk make up a round that is never for a moment enlivened by the play of genuine intelligence.[2] And although Congreve recognizes, at times, the triviality of his characters,[3] it is to the world whose confines were the Court, the drawing-room, the play-house and the park—a world completely lacking the real sophistication and self-

---

[1]   Ay there's my grief; that's the sad change of life,
To lose my title, and yet keep my wife.
                The Way of the World, II, ii.

[2] As Lady Brute remarks. "After all, a woman's life would be a dull business, if it were not for the men . . . We shou'd never blame Fate for the shortness of our days; our time would hang wretchedly upon our hands."—*The Provok'd Wife*, III, iii.

[3] *Mirabell:* You had the leisure to entertain a herd of fools; things who visit you from their excessive idleness; bestowing on your easiness that time which is the encumbrance of their lives. How can you find delight in such society?—*The Way of the World*, II, i.

knowledge that might, in some measure, have redeemed it—that he limits his appeal.

It is, indeed, hard to resist the conclusion that "society"—the smart town society that sought entertainment at the theatres—was fundamentally bored.[1] In *The Man of Mode* Emilia remarks of Medley, "I love to hear him talk o' the intrigues, let 'em be never so dull in themselves, he'll make 'em pleasant i' the relation," and the idiotic conversation that follows (ii, i), affording us a glimpse of what Miss Lynch calls "the most brilliant society which Restoration comedy has to offer," [2] suggests in more than one way how badly society *needed* to be entertained. It is the boredom—the constant need for titillation—that helps to explain not only the heroic "heightening" of emotion, but the various scenic effects, the devices of staging and costume that became popular at this period. (Charles II "almost died of laughing" at Nell Gwynn's enormous hat.) The conventions—of sexual pursuit, and so on—were an attempt to make life interesting—an impossible job for those who were aware of so limited a range of human potentialities.

The dominating mood of Restoration comedy is, by common account, a cynical one. But one cannot even say that there is here, in contrast to naïve Romantic fervours, the tough strength of disillusion. If—recognizing that there is a place in the educational process for, say, La Rochefoucauld—one finds the "cynicism" of the plays distasteful, it is because it is easy and superficial; the attitudes that we are presented with are based on so meagre an amount of observation and experience. Thus, "Elle retrouvait dans l'adultère toutes les platitudes du mariage" [3] has, superficially, much the same meaning as, "I find now, by sad experience, that a mistress is much more changeable than a wife, and after a little time too, grows full as dull and insignificant." But whereas the first sentence has behind it the whole of *Madame Bovary,* the second comes from *Sir Martin Mar-all,* which (although Dryden shares the honours with the Duke of Newcastle) is perhaps the stupidest play I have ever read, and the context is imbecility.

But the superficiality is betrayed at every turn—by the obvious rhythms of the interspersed songs, as well as by the artificial elegance of the prose. And the cynicism is closely allied with—merges into—senti-

---

[1] The constitution, habits and demands of the theatre audience are admirably illustrated by Alexandre Beljame in that neglected classic of scholarship, *Le Public et les Hommes de Lettres en Angleterre au Dix-Huitième Siècle, 1660–1740.* See also C. V. Deane, *Dramatic Theory and the Rhymed Heroic Play,* Chapter I, Section 6.

[2] *The Social Mode of Restoration Comedy,* p. 177.

[3] [She found in adultery all the platitudes of marriage. From Flaubert's *Madame Bovary.*]

mentality. One thinks of the sentimentally conceived Fidelia in the resolutely "tough" *Plain Dealer;* and there is no doubt that the audience was meant to respond sympathetically when, at the end of *Love for Love,* Angelica declared her love for Valentine: "Had I the world to give you, it could not make me worthy of so generous a passion; here's my hand, my heart was always yours, and struggled very hard to make this utmost trial of your virtue." There is, of course, a good deal of loose emotion in the heroic plays, written—it is useful to remember—for the same audience:

> I'm numbed, and fixed, and scarce my eyeballs move;
> I fear it is the lethargy of love!
> 'Tis he; I feel him now in every part:
> Like a new lord he vaunts about my heart;
> Surveys, in state, each corner of my breast,
> While poor fierce I, that was, am dispossessed.[1]

> A secret pleasure trickles through my veins:
> It works about the inlets of my soul,
> To feel thy touch, and pity tempts the pass:
> But the tough metal of my heart resists;
> 'Tis warmed with the soft fire, not melted down.[2]

"Feeling," in Dryden's serious plays, is fairly represented by such passages as these, and Dryden, we know, was not alone in admiring the Fletcherian "pathos." But it is the lyric verse of the period that provides the strongest confirmatory evidence of the kind of bad taste that is in question. It is not merely that in Etherege, Sedley and Dorset the feelings comes from much nearer the surface than in the Metaphysical and the Caroline poets, intellectual "wit" no longer strengthens and controls the feeling. Conventional attitudes are rigged out in a conventional vocabulary and conventional images. (The stock outfit—the "fair eyes" that "wound," the "pleasing pains," the "sighs and tears," the "bleeding hearts" and "flaming darts"— can be studied in any anthology.[3] There is, in consequence, a pervasive strain of sentimental vulgarity.

> Farewell, ungrateful traitor!
> Farewell, my perjured swain
> Let never injured creature
> Believe a man again.

---

[1] *The Conquest of Granada,* Part I, III, i.

[2] *Don Sebastian,* III, i.

[3] See, for example, Aphra Behn's "Love in fantastic triumph sate," Buckingham's *To His Mistress* ("Phyllis, though your all powerful charms"), Dryden's "Ask not the cause why sullen spring," and "Ah, how sweet it is to love," and Sedley's *To Chloris*—all in *The Oxford Book of English Verse,* or Ault's *Seventeenth Century Lyrics.*

> The pleasure of possessing
> Surpasses all expressing,
> But 'Tis too short a blessing,
> And love too long a pain.
>
> . . . . .
>
> The passion you pretended,
>   Was only to obtain;
> But when the charm is ended,
>   The charmer you disdain.
> Your love by ours we measure
> Till we have lost our treasure,
> But dying is a pleasure
> When living is a pain.

This piece of music-hall sentiment comes from Dryden's *The Spanish Friar,* and it does not stand alone. The mode that was to produce, among other things of equal merit, "When lovely woman stoops to folly," had its origin in the lyrics of the Restoration period. Most of these were written by the group connected with the theatres, and they serve to underline the essential criticism of the plays. The criticism that defenders of Restoration comedy need to answer is not that the comedies are "immoral," but that they are trivial, gross and dull.

"GHOSTS" AND THE THEATER OF MODERN REALISM

FRANCIS FERGUSSON

I

Ghosts is not Ibsen's best play, but it serves my purpose, which is to study the foundations of modern realism, just because of its imperfections. Its power, and the poetry of some of its effects, are evident; yet a contemporary audience may be bored with its old-fashioned iconoclasm and offended by the clatter of its too-obviously well-made plot. On the surface it is a *drame à thèse,*[1] of the kind Brieux was to develop to its logical conclusion twenty

"*Ghosts* and *The Cherry Orchard:* The Theater of Modern Realism" from *The Idea of a Theater* by Francis Fergusson. Reprinted by permission of the author and Princeton University Press.

[1] [Thesis drama.]

years later: it proves the hollowness of the conventional bourgeois marriage. At the same time it is a thriller with all the tricks of the Boulevard entertainment: Ibsen was a student of Scribe in his middle period. But underneath this superficial form of thesis-thriller—the play which Ibsen started to write, the angry diatribe as he first conceived it—there is another form, the shape of the underlying action, which Ibsen gradually made out in the course of his two-years' labor upon the play, in obedience to his scruple of truthfulness, his profound attention to the reality of his fictive characters' lives. The form of the play is understood according to two conceptions of plot, which Ibsen himself did not at this point clearly distinguish: the rationalized concatenation of events with a univocal moral, and the plot as the "soul" or first actualization of the directly perceived action.

Halvdahn Khot, in his excellent study *Henrik Ibsen,* has explained the circumstances under which *Ghosts* was written. It was first planned as an attack upon marriage, in answer to the critics of *A Doll's House.* The story of the play is perfectly coherent as the demonstration and illustration of this thesis. When the play opens, Captain Alving has just died, his son Oswald is back from Paris where he has been studying painting, and his wife is straightening out the estate. The Captain had been accepted locally as a pillar of society but was in secret a drunkard and debauchee. He had seduced his wife's maid, and had a child by her; and this child, Regina, is now in her turn Mrs. Alving's maid. Mrs. Alving had concealed all this for something like twenty years. She was following the advice of the conventional Pastor Manders and endeavoring to save Oswald from the horrors of the household: it was for this reason she had sent him away to school. But now, with her husband's death, she proposes to get rid of the Alving heritage in all its forms, in order to free herself and Oswald for the innocent, unconventional "joy of life." She wants to endow an orphanage with the Captain's money, both to quiet any rumors there may be of his sinful life and to get rid of the remains of his power over her. She encounters this power, however, in many forms, through the Pastor's timidity and through the attempt by Engstrand (a local carpenter who was bribed to pretend to be Regina's father) to blackmail her. Oswald wants to marry Regina and has to be told the whole story. At last he reveals that he has inherited syphilis from his father—the dead hand of the past in its most sensationally ugly form—and when his brain softens at the end, Mrs. Alving's whole plan collapses in unrelieved horror. It is "proved" that she should have left home twenty years before, like Nora in *A Doll's House;* and that conventional marriage is therefore an evil tyranny.

In accordance with the principles of the thesis play, *Ghosts* is plotted as a series of debates on conventional morality, between Mrs. Alving and the Pastor, the Pastor and Oswald, and Oswald and his mother. It may also be read as a perfect well-made thriller. The story is presented with immediate clarity, with mounting and controlled suspense; each act ends with an exciting curtain which reaffirms the issues and promises important new developments. In this play, as in so many others, one may observe that the conception of dramatic form underlying the thesis play and the machine-made Boulevard entertainment is the same: the logically concatenated series of events (intriguing thesis or logical intrigue) which the characters and their relationships merely illustrate. And it was this view of *Ghosts* which made it an immediate scandal and success.

But Ibsen himself protested that he was not a reformer but a poet. He was often led to write by anger and he compared the process of composition to his pet scorpion's emptying of poison; Ibsen kept a piece of soft fruit in his cage for the scorpion to sting when the spirit moved him. But Ibsen's own spirit was not satisfied by the mere discharge of venom; and one may see, in *Ghosts,* behind the surfaces of the savage story, a partially realized tragic form of really poetic scope, the result of Ibsen's more serious and disinterested brooding upon the human condition in general, where it underlies the myopic rebellions and empty clichés of the time.

In order to see the tragedy behind the thesis, it is necessary to return to the distinction between plot and action, and to the distinction between the plot as the rationalized series of events, and the plot as "the soul of the tragedy." The action of the play is "to control the Alving heritage for my own life." Most of the characters want some material or social advantage from it—Engstrand money, for instance, and the Pastor the security of conventional respectability. But Mrs. Alving is seeking a true and free human life itself—for her son, and through him, for herself. Mrs. Alving sometimes puts this quest in terms of the iconoclasms of the time, but her spiritual life, as Ibsen gradually discovered it, is at a deeper level; she tests everything—Oswald, the Pastor, Regina, her own moves—in the light of her extremely strict if unsophisticated moral sensibility: by direct perception and not by ideas at all. She is tragically seeking; she suffers a series of pathoses and new insights in the course of the play; and this rhythm of will, feeling, and insight underneath the machinery of the plot is the form of the life of the play, the soul of the tragedy.

The similarity between *Ghosts* and Greek tragedy, with its single fated action moving to an unmistakable catastrophe, has been felt by many critics of Ibsen. Mrs. Alving, like Oedipus, is engaged in a quest for her true human condition; and Ibsen, like Sophocles, shows on-stage only the end of this quest, when the past is being brought up in the light of the present action and its fated outcome. From this point of view Ibsen is a plot-maker in the first sense: by means of his selection and arrangement of incidents he defines an action underlying many particular events and realized in various modes of intelligible purpose, of suffering, and of new insight. What Mrs. Alving sees changes in the course of the play, just as what Oedipus sees changes as one veil after another is removed from the past and the present. The underlying form of *Ghosts* is that of the tragic rhythm as one finds it in *Oedipus Rex*.

But this judgment needs to be qualified in several respects: because of the theater for which Ibsen wrote, the tragic form which Sophocles could develop to the full, and with every theatrical resource, is hidden beneath the clichés of plot and the surfaces "evident to the most commonplace mind." At the end of the play the tragic rhythm of Mrs. Alving's quest is not so much completed as brutally truncated, in obedience to the requirements of the thesis and the thriller. Oswald's collapse, before our eyes, with his mother's screaming, makes the intrigue end with a bang, and hammers home the thesis. But from the point of view of Mrs. Alving's tragic quest as we have seen it develop through the rest of the play, this conclusion concludes nothing: it is merely sensational.

The exciting intrigue and the brilliantly, the violently clear surface of *Ghosts* are likely to obscure completely its real life and underlying form. The tragic rhythm, which Ibsen rediscovered by his long and loving attention to the reality of his fictive lives, is evident only to the histrionic sensibility. As Henry James put it, Ibsen's characters "have the extraordinary, the brilliant property of becoming when represented at once more abstract and more living": i.e., both their lives and the life of . the play, the spiritual content and the form of the whole, are revealed in this medium. A Nazimova, a Duse, could show it to us on the stage. Lacking such a performance, the reader must endeavor to respond imaginatively and directly himself if he is to see the hidden poetry of *Ghosts*.

II

As Ibsen was fighting to present his poetic vision within the narrow theater admitted by modern realism, so his protagonist Mrs. Alving is fighting to realize her sense of human life in the blank photograph of her own stuffy parlor. She discovers there no means, no terms, and no nourishment; that is the truncated tragedy which underlies the savage thesis of the play. But she does find her son Oswald, and she makes of him the symbol of all she is seeking: freedom, innocence, joy, and truth. At the level of the life of the play, when Ibsen warms his characters into extraordinary human reality, they all have moral and emotional meanings for each other; and the pattern of their related actions, their partially blind struggle for the Alving heritage, is consistent and very complex. In this structure, Mrs. Alving's changing relation to Oswald is only one strand, though an important one. I wish to consider it as a sample of Ibsen's rediscovery, through modern realism, of the tragic rhythm.

Oswald is of course not only a symbol for his mother, but a person in his own right, with his own quest for freedom and release, and his own anomalous stake in the Alving heritage. He is also a symbol for Pastor Manders of what he wants from Captain Alving's estate: the stability and continuity of the Bourgeois conventions. In the economy of the play as a whole, Oswald is the hidden reality of the whole situation, like Oedipus' actual status as son-husband: the hidden fatality which, revealed in a series of tragic and ironic steps, brings the final peripety of the action. To see how this works, the reader is asked to consider Oswald's role in Act I and the beginning of Act II.

The main part of Act I (after a prologue between Regina and Engstrand) is a debate, or rather agon, between Mrs. Alving and the Pastor. The Pastor has come to settle the details of Mrs. Alving's bequest of her husband's money to the orphanage. They at once disagree about the purpose and handling of the bequest; and this disagreement soon broadens into the whole issue of Mrs. Alving's emancipation versus the Pastor's conventionality. The question of Oswald is at the center. The Pastor wants to think of him, and to make of him, a pillar of society such as the Captain was supposed to have been, while Mrs. Alving wants him to be her masterpiece of liberation. At this point Oswald himself wanders in, the actual but still mysterious truth underlying the dispute between his mother and the Pastor. His appearance produces what the Greeks would have called a complex recognition scene, with an implied peripety for both Mrs. Alving and the Pastor, which will not be realized by them until the end of the act. But this tragic development is written to be acted; it is to be found, not so much in the actual words of the characters, as in their moral-emotional responses and changing relationships to one another.

The pastor has not seen Oswald since he grew up; and seeing him now he is startled as though by a real ghost; he recognizes him as the very reincarnation of his father; the same physique, the same mannerisms, even the same kind of pipe. Mrs. Alving with equal confidence recognizes him as her own son, and she notes that his mouth-mannerism is like the Pastor's. (She had been in love with the Pastor during the early years of

her marriage, when she wanted to leave the Captain.) As for Oswald himself, the mention of the pipe gives him a Proustian intermittence of the
heart: he suddenly recalls a childhood scene when his father had given
him his own pipe to smoke. He feels again the nausea and the cold sweat,
and hears the Captain's hearty laughter. Thus in effect he recognizes himself as his father's in the sense of his father's *victim;* a premonition of the
ugly scene at the end of the play. But at this point no one is prepared to accept the full import of these insights. The whole scene is, on the surface,
light and conventional, an accurate report of a passage of provincial politeness. Oswald wanders off for a walk before dinner, and the Pastor and
his mother are left to bring their struggle more into the open.

Oswald's brief scene marks the end of the first round of the fight, and
serves as prologue for the second round, much as the intervention of the
chorus in the agon between Oedipus and Tiresias punctuates their struggle, and hints at an unexpected outcome on a new level of awareness.
As soon as Oswald has gone, the Pastor launches an attack in form upon
Mrs. Alving's entire emancipated way of life, with the question of Oswald,
his role in the community, his upbringing and his future, always at the
center of the attack. Mrs. Alving replies with her whole rebellious philosophy, illustrated by a detailed account of her tormented life with the
Captain, none of which the Pastor had known (or been willing to recognize) before. Mrs. Alving proves on the basis of this evidence that her
new freedom is right; that her long secret rebellion was justified; and that
she is now about to complete Oswald's emancipation, and thereby her
own, from the swarming ghosts of the past. If the issue were merely on
this rationalistic level, and between her and the Pastor, she would triumph
at this point. But the real truth of her situation (as Oswald's appearance
led us to suppose) does not fit either her rationalization or the Pastor's.

Oswald passes through the parlor again on his way to the dining
room to get a drink before dinner, and his mother watches him in pride
and pleasure. But from behind the door we hear the affected squealing of
Regina. It is now Mrs. Alving's turn for an intermittence of the heart: it
is as though she heard again her husband with Regina's mother. The insight which she had rejected before now reaches her in full strength,
bringing the promised pathos and peripety; she sees Oswald, not as her
masterpiece of liberation, but as the sinister, tyrannical, and continuing life
of the past itself. The basis of her rationalization is gone; she suffers the
breakdown of the moral being which she had built upon her now exploded
view of Oswald.

At this point Ibsen brings down the curtain in obedience to the principles of the well-made play. The effect is to raise the suspense by stimulating

our curiosity about the facts of the rest of the story. What will Mrs. Alving do now? What will the Pastor do—for Oswald and Regina are half-brother and sister; can we prevent the scandal from coming out? So the suspense is raised, but the attention of the audience is diverted from Mrs. Alving's tragic quest to the most literal, newspaper version of the facts.

The second act (which occurs immediately after dinner) is ostensibly concerned only with these gossipy facts. The Pastor and Mrs. Alving debate ways of handling the threatened scandal. But this is only the literal surface: Ibsen has his eye upon Mrs. Alving's shaken psyche, and the actual dramatic form of this scene, under the discussion which Mrs. Alving keeps up, is her pathos which the Act I curtain broke off. Mrs. Alving is suffering the blow in courage and faith; and she is rewarded with her deepest insight: "I am half inclined to think we are all ghosts, Mr. Manders. It is not only what we have inherited from our fathers and mothers that exists again in us, but all sorts of dead ideas and all kinds of old dead beliefs and things of that kind. They are not actually alive in us; but they are dormant all the same, and we can never be rid of them. Whenever I take up a newspaper and read it, I fancy I see ghosts creeping between the lines. There must be ghosts all over the world. They must be as countless as the grains of sand, it seems to me. And we are so miserably afraid of the light, all of us." [1] This passage, in the fumbling phrases of Ibsen's provincial lady, and in William Archer's translation, is not by itself the poetry of the great dramatic poets. It does not have the verbal music of Racine, nor the freedom and sophistication of Hamlet, nor the scope of the Sophoclean chorus, with its use of the full complement of poetic and musical and theatrical resources. But in the total situation in the Alving parlor which Ibsen has so carefully established, and in terms of Mrs. Alving's uninstructed but profoundly developing awareness, it has its own hidden poetry: a poetry not of words but of the theater, a poetry of the histrionic sensibility. From the point of view of the underlying form of the play—the form as "the soul" of the tragedy—this scene completes the sequence which began with the debate in Act I: it is the pathos-and-epiphany following that agon.

It is evident, I think, that insofar as Ibsen was able to obey his realistic scruple, his need for the disinterested perception of human life beneath the clichés of custom and rationalization, he rediscovered the perennial basis of tragedy. The poetry of *Ghosts* is under the words, in the detail of action, where Ibsen accurately sensed the tragic rhythm of human life in a thousand small figures. And these little "movements of the psyche"

---

[1] *Ghosts,* by Henrik Ibsen. Translated by William Archer.

are composed in a complex rhythm like music, a formal development sustained (beneath the sensational story and the angry thesis) until the very end. But the action is not completed: Mrs. Alving is left screaming with the raw impact of the calamity. The music is broken off, the dissonance unresolved—or, in more properly dramatic terms, the acceptance of the catastrophe, leading to the final vision or epiphany which should correspond to the insight Mrs. Alving gains in Act II, is lacking. The action of the play is neither completed nor placed in the wider context of meanings which the disinterested or contemplative purposes of poetry demand.

The unsatisfactory end of *Ghosts* may be understood in several ways. Thinking of the relation between Mrs. Alving and Oswald, one might say that she had romantically loaded more symbolic values upon her son than a human being can carry; hence his collapse proves too much—more than Mrs. Alving or the audience can digest. One may say that, at the end, Ibsen himself could not quite dissociate himself from his rebellious protagonist and see her action in the round, and so broke off in anger, losing his tragic vision in the satisfaction of reducing the bourgeois parlor to a nightmare, and proving the hollowness of a society which sees human life in such myopic and dishonest terms. As a thesis play, *Ghosts* is an ancestor of many related genres: Brieux's arguments for social reform, propaganda plays like those of the Marxists, or parables *à la* Andreev, or even Shaw's more generalized plays of the play-of-thought about social questions. But this use of the theater of modern realism for promoting or discussing political and social ideas never appealed to Ibsen. It did not solve his real problem, which was to use the publicly accepted theater of his time for poetic purposes. The most general way to understand the unsatisfactory end of *Ghosts* is to say that Ibsen could not find a way to represent the action of his protagonist, with all its moral and intellectual depth, within the terms of modern realism. In the attempt he truncated this action, and revealed as in a brilliant light the limitations of the bourgeois parlor as the scene of human life.

III

Oswald is the chief symbol of what Mrs. Alving is seeking, and his collapse ends her quest in a horrifying catastrophe. But in the complex life of the play, all of the persons and things acquire emotional and moral significance for Mrs. Alving; and at the end, to throw as much light as possible upon the catastrophe, Ibsen brings all of the elements of his composition together in their highest symbolic valency. The orphanage has burned to the ground; the Pastor has promised Engstrand money for his "Sailor's Home" which he plans as a brothel; Regina departs, to follow her mother in the search for pleasure and money. In these eventualities the conventional morality of the Alving heritage is revealed as lewdness and dishonesty, quickly consumed in the fires of lust and greed, as Oswald himself (the central symbol) was consumed even before his birth. But what does this wreckage mean? Where are we to place it in human experience? Ibsen can only place it in the literal parlor, with lamplight giving place to daylight, and sunrise on the empty, stimulating, virginal snow-peaks out the window. The emotional force of this complicated effect is very great; it has the searching intimacy of nightmare. But it is also as disquieting as a nightmare from which we are suddenly awakened; it is incomplete, and the contradiction between the inner power of dream and the literal appearances of the daylight world is unresolved. The spirit that moved Ibsen to write the play, and which moved his protagonist through her tragic progress, is lost to sight, disembodied, imperceptible in any form unless the dreary exaltation of the inhuman mountain scene conveys it in feeling.

Henry James felt very acutely the contradiction between the deep and strict spirit of Ibsen and his superb craftsmanship on one side, and the little scene he tried to use—the parlor in its surrounding void—on the other. "If the spirit is a lamp within us, glowing through what the world and the flesh make of us as through a ground-glass shade, then such pictures as Little Eyolf and John Gabriel are each a chassez-croisez of lamps burning, as in tasteless parlors, with the flame practically exposed," he wrote in *London Notes*.[1] "There is a positive odor of spiritual paraffin. The author nevertheless arrives at the dramatist's great goal—he arrives for all his meagerness at intensity. The meagerness, which is after all but an unconscious, an admirable economy, never interferes with that: it plays straight into the hands of his rare mastery of form. The contrast between this form—so difficult to have reached, so 'evolved,' so civilized—and the bareness and bleakness of his little northern democracy is the source of half the hard frugal charm he puts forth."

James had rejected very early in his career his own little northern democracy, that of General Grant's America, with its ugly parlor, its dead conventions, its enthusiastic materialism, and its "non-conducting atmosphere." At the same time he shared Ibsen's ethical preoccupation, and his strict sense of form. His comments on Ibsen are at once the most sympathetic and the most objective that have been written. But James's own solution was to try to find a better parlor for the theater of human life; to present the quest of his American pilgrim of culture on the wider "stage

---

[1] Jan.–Aug., 1897.

of Europe" as this might still be felt and suggested in the manners of the leisured classes in England and France. James would have nothing to do with the prophetic and revolutionary spirit which was driving the great continental authors, Ibsen among them. In his artistry and his moral exactitude Ibsen is akin to James; but this is not his whole story, and if one is to understand the spirit he tried to realize in Mrs. Alving, one must think of Kierkegaard, who had a great influence on Ibsen in the beginning of his career.

Kierkegaard (in *For Self-Examination*) has this to say of the disembodied and insatiable spirit of the time: ". . . thou wilt scarcely find anyone who does not believe in—let us say, for example, the spirit of the age, the *Zeitgeist*. Even he who has taken leave of higher things and is rendered blissful by mediocrity, yea, even he who toils slavishly for paltry ends or in the contemptible servitude of ill-gotten gains, even he believes, firmly and fully too, in the spirit of the age. Well, that is natural enough, it is by no means anything very lofty he believes in, for the spirit of the age is after all no higher than the age, it keeps close to the ground, so that it is the sort of spirit which is most like will-o'-the-wisp; but yet he believes in spirit. Or he believes in the world-spirit (*Weltgeist*) that strong spirit (for allurements, yes), that ingenious spirit (for deceits, yes); that spirit which Christianity calls an evil spirit—so that, in consideration of this, it is by no means anything very lofty he believes in when he believes in the world-spirit; but yet he believes in spirit. Or he believes in 'the spirit of humanity,' not spirit in the individual, but in the race, that spirit which, when it is god-forsaken for having forsaken God, is again, according to Christianity's teaching, an evil spirit—so that in view of this it is by no means anything very lofty he believes in when he believes in this spirit; but yet he believes in spirit.

"On the other hand, as soon as the talk is about a holy spirit—how many, dost thou think believe in it? Or when the talk is about an evil spirit which is to be renounced—how many, dost thou think, believe in such a thing?" [1]

This description seems to me to throw some light upon Mrs. Alving's quest, upon Ibsen's modern-realistic scene, and upon the theater which his audience would accept. The other face of nineteenth century positivism is romantic aspiration. And Ibsen's realistic scene presents both of these aspects of the human condition: the photographically accurate parlor, in

---

[1] Kierkegaard, *For Self Examination and Judge for Yourselves* (Princeton University Press, 1944), p. 94.

the foreground, satisfies the requirements of positivism, while the empty but stimulating scene out the window—Europe as a moral void, an un-inhabited wilderness—offers as it were a blank check to the insatiate spirit. Ibsen always felt this exhilarating wilderness behind his cramped in-teriors. In *A Doll's House* we glimpse it as winter weather and black water. In *The Lady from the Sea* it is the cold ocean, with its whales and its gulls. In *The Wild Duck* it is the northern marshes, with wildfowl but no people. In the last scene of *Ghosts* it is, of course, the bright snow-peaks, which may mean Mrs. Alving's quest in its most disembodied and am-bivalent form; very much the same sensuous moral void in which Wagner, having totally rejected the little human foreground where Ibsen fights his battles, unrolls the solitary action of passion. It is the "stage of Eu-rope" before human exploration, as it might have appeared to the first hunters.

There is a kinship between the fearless and demanding spirit of Kierkegaard, and the spirit which Ibsen tried to realize in Mrs. Alving. But Mrs. Alving, like her contemporaries whom Kierkegaard described, will not or cannot accept any interpretation of the spirit that drives her. It may look like the *Weltgeist* when she demands the joy of living, it may look like the Holy Ghost itself when one considers her appetite for truth. And it may look like the spirit of evil, a "goblin damned," when we see the desolation it produces. If one thinks of the symbols which Ibsen brings together in the last scene: the blank parlor, the wide unexplored world out-side, the flames that consumed the Alving heritage and the sunrise flaming on the peaks, one may be reminded of the condition of Dante's great rebel Ulysses. He too is wrapped in the flame of his own consciousness, yet still dwells in the pride of the mind and the exhilaration of the world free of people, *il mondo senza gente*. But this analogy also may not be pressed too far. Ulysses is in hell; and when we explore the Mountain on which he was wrecked, we can place his condition with finality, and in relation to many other human modes of action and awareness. But Mrs. Alving's mountains do not place her anywhere: the realism of modern realism ends with the literal. Beyond that is not the ordered world of the tradition, but *Unendlichkeit,*[1] and the anomalous "freedom" of undefined and unin-formed aspiration.

Perhaps Mrs. Alving and Ibsen himself are closer to the role of Dante than to the role of Ulysses, seeing a hellish mode of being, but free to move on. Certainly Ibsen's development continued beyond *Ghosts,* and toward the end of his career he came much closer to achieving a consistent

---

[1] [Endlessness.]

theatrical poetry within the confines of the theater of modern realism. He himself remarked that his poetry was to be found only in the series of his plays, no one of which was complete by itself.

BROADWAY—AND THE ALTERNATIVE

ERIC BENTLEY

Probably not many would join Mr. Bennett Cerf in denying that the situation of the theater is today very problematic. Most discussions of the problem, however, go wrong—not in denying its existence but in regarding it as new and peculiar to our generation, and thus in attributing it to some localized cause, such as the rise of movies or the high Manhattan rents. It should be recognized that the theater is almost always a problem. Over a century ago Carlyle wrote: "Nay, do not we English hear daily for the last twenty years, that the Drama is dead, or in a state of suspended animation: and are not medical men sitting on the case, and propounding their remedial appliances, weekly, monthly, quarterly, to no manner of purpose?" Such statements are to be found not only in times of dramatic drought but also in the harvest seasons. Looking back on the eighteen-nineties today, we regard them as years of considerable dramatic achievement; Bernard Shaw's *Dramatic Opinions,* written at the time, tell another story. We think of the Restoration as the age of Congreve, yet the great comedian was very inconspicuous in his own day, and his now acknowledged masterpiece was a total failure on the stage. Shakespeare, the most read and the most performed of all dramatists, was probably best known in his lifetime for his cheapest and rawest plays, and a contemporary editor boasts that one of his best plays was "never clapper-clawed by the hands of the vulgar."

The theater is always in trouble because its success depends upon too rare a set of coincidences. A poem needs only an author and a reader. A sonata needs a composer, a performer, and a listener. Closer to the drama is the symphony, which requires teamwork, co-ordination at the hands of a conductor, a large audience, and a heap of money. The drama, however, boasting of being a meeting place of all the arts, requires a too rare con-

junction of economic, social, and artistic elements. Especially in its synthetic manifestations, which include everything in musical-choreographic-
spectacular-mimetic-rhetorical theater from the Greeks to *Tannhäuser* and
beyond, drama is the most impossible of the arts.

Yet the very citation of titles reminds us of its possibility. The fact
is that, while high theater has a harder time than any other high art, the
popular theater, dedicated to entertainment, and today functioning chiefly
on the screen and over the air, is perpetually the most flourishing of the
arts. It is the art which most excites children, savages, and all who are
least conscious of artistic leanings. It seems to be an inextinguishable and
indispensable art, an addiction more universal than smoking. It followed
the doughboys to foxholes on tropical islands. It followed the dehumanized,
doubly "mechanized" divisions of the Third Reich. It lures the schoolboy
twice a week to the movies; it entices the student to turn on the radio while
supposedly studying.

Entertainment means the redemption of leisure time by a pleasing
titillation of the senses and of that small part of the brain which the
simplest jokes call into play. Entertainment is an infinitely complex industry devoted to the evocation of the crudest responses. In its modern
form it presupposes an audience that is already tired, inclined to be bored,
probably not educated and certainly not cultured, yet not totally illiterate,
but acquainted with that segment of knowledge and sensibility provided
by the radio and the press. The power of entertainment in modern life is
shown by the fact that even the knowledge presupposed in entertainment
is acquired through entertainment, for what is modern reporting and propaganda if not a cunning use of histrionic method in the commercial, political, and educational spheres? All information is nowadays supposed to
be "entertainingly" presented, and the results are evident in radio news
reports and radio advertising, in the screen popularization of musical and
literary classics, and in schools where the pupils expect to be entertained
by the teacher. The founders of democracy hoped and expected that universal suffrage would mean a sober presentation of issues to a people
which would soberly weigh them. A recent development, however, is the
setting of political slogans to hot jazz choral music and the staging of vast
political pageants that would be the envy of a Roman emperor. At the
center of these entertainments is the very symbol of entertainment itself,
the man-god, hero, and totem animal of modern civilization, the film
star.

The techniques of the theater, run wild, have taken over every other
branch of public communication, especially in countries where industrialism and mechanization have gone furthest. The Salvation Army began

the application of the methods of mass entertainment to religion, and visitors to Aimee Semple MacPherson's Los Angeles Temple know how far the idea has been carried since the days of General Booth. Northcliffe and Hearst pursued the same art in politics, and Goebbels turned their skill into an industry. A Nazi rally, where masses of soldiers saluted and applauded and sang at given signals, where music, spectacle, and oratory combined in a macabre *gesamtkunstwerk*,[1] and where the master tragi-comedian himself played systematically upon every group prejudice and stock response—this was at once the apotheosis and the nemesis of entertainment.

Entertainment has almost been the death of all the arts. How could music hope to survive the onslaughts of the popularizers? What room is there for Beethoven in a world where a hundred hacks make his music "more entertaining" by removing his individuality? How could literature survive the *Saturday Evening Post?* Recently a writer in that journal defended himself with the argument that Shakespeare also was a popular writer, not afraid to use as material the cliché absurdities of current convention. Great writers, he argued, come out of the hard school of commercial writing, not out of coteries. The hard-headedness of the remark and its one per cent of truth give it the color of plausibility, and while criticism remains unhistorical the argument is not easily disposed of. But history supplies the answers, and they are germane to our theme. To be popular in an aristocratic culture, like ancient Greece or Elizabethan England, is quite a different matter from being popular in a middle-class culture. Like Dr. Johnson, our critic is suspicious of those who do not write for money. And there is nothing wrong with money. It all depends on what is demanded of you in return. To earn his living Shakespeare had, for example, to acquire a highly complex literary language, far above the usage of his native Stratford; to earn his, the modern *Post* writer has to unlearn anything he might have learned from acknowledged classics, or from the depths of personal experience, and acquire the crude, vacuum-concealing lingo which titillates the miseducated sensibility.

That is only one factor among many, but it permits us to glimpse the difference between Elizabethan and modern culture. Industrialism, capitalism, and the democratic movement created an unprecedented cultural situation; its problems are the subject of all the anti-industrialist, anti-capitalist, and antidemocratic literature which lovers of the arts have written in the past hundred and fifty years. The essence of the matter is that the extension of literacy to the previously illiterate majority created, not a

---

[1] [Mass spectacle. Literally, "combined work of art."]

nation of philosophers, but a nation of newspaper readers. In this context popularity takes on a new meaning.

Popularity is a very flexible term and an impossible criterion. Medieval and Chinese drama are "popular" in that they appeal to a totally illiterate populace; the "popular" *Post* is read by many college graduates and, perhaps, hardly at all by the least educated classes for whom the funnies and the pulps suffice. The pulps are "popular"; so is Somerset Maugham. The difference can be appreciated only by those who recognize the cultural stratification which has taken place in recent generations. While changes in the mechanics of communication and the promotion of democratic and religious ideas have in modern times brought men closer together, other forces have wrenched them apart. One need hardly mention nationalist politics, imperialist economics, and racial ideology. The same technology which brought men closer through mechanized transport and telegraphy kept them apart by the mention of their manufacture, mass production. The kind of man they created was portrayed by Charlie Chaplin in *Modern Times.*

There is no need to linger over the general matter of middle-class culture. The point is that if the new conditions have significance for the culture as a whole, they have all the more significance for the drama, which has had the closest link with the people, possibly, of all the arts. In the days before general literacy, the drama was, with the sermon, the great bond between verbal culture and the people; in books on the drama one constantly reads that drama is the least esoteric, the most democratic of the arts. Drama critics are indeed never tired of asserting that great drama belongs to the people, and that obscurity and "rareness" are out of place on the stage; theorists of the drama insist on the communal character of theatrical experience and cite LeBon on the psychology of the crowd. Well and good. But what becomes of the drama in an age like ours when popular taste is debauched, when "entertainment" has a monopoly of public attention, when greedy capital controls production and consumption alike? Lowbrow writers will repeat their argument that art, particularly dramatic art, is always an adjustment of an artist's purpose to public demand. But, as I have said, it all depends on what is demanded: if the public's demands, or the plutocrat's demands, are degrading, we shall not have dramatic art at all; which is the situation on Broadway today. To be sure, drama depends on an audience, upon common human experience, upon crowd psychology; but there are crowds and crowds. There is a difference between an audience of Athenians at a time when the Athenian citizenry represented, so we are told, one of the peaks of human and social development, an audience for whom a play was also an important rite, and a crowd of oddly miseducated twentieth-century folk who for years have been subjected to half-baked ideas and cheap sensations.

At this point someone will say that, at times when drama flourished, audiences were not always Periclean. They were often illiterate or frivolous or both. When Stanislavsky's audiences changed from the sophisticated upper classes of Tsarism to the ignorant peasantry and proletariat of the early Soviet years, this very aristocratic director was, after initial apprehension, delighted by the spontaneity and keenness of the latter, even when the play performed was *The Cherry Orchard*. Such facts prove that an ignorant audience can enjoy a great play. They do not prove that all ignorant audiences would enjoy that play or that even the same ignorant audience would enjoy every great play. They do not reveal how far such an audience understands the play, nor do they help us to settle what for us is the great problem, the problem not of the ignorant and illiterate but that of the half-literate, the possessors of the little knowledge which is a dangerous thing, the readers of the pulps and the Hearst press, and even the comparative high-brows who read *Collier's* and the *Saturday Evening Post*. Today it is almost inconceivable that any drama would satisfy the canons of the most exacting criticism and also be popular. Already in the nineteenth century, Matthew Arnold wondered whether drama had become an impossibility. The vulgarization and consequent social stratification of culture had gone too far, he seems to have thought, and modern British society in particular lacked the homogeneity which drama requires. Some critics have met the situation by lowering their standards. They consider the exacting critics *too* exacting, and erupt occasionally in jibes against high-brows, aesthetes, sophisticates, and coteries. More disconcerting are the arguments of those who are distressed by mediocrity yet who are reluctant to draw revolutionary conclusions.

Theatre Arts, the only theatrical magazine of repute in the English-speaking world, frequently publishes such arguments. One of its most intelligent writers, Mr. George Beiswanger, has gone so far as to discourage us from even *trying* to make a home for drama in America. The drama, he observes, has little past and little present here, and there is no reason to suppose that it will have a future—"which may or may not be too bad," he adds; "after all, there is no moral compulsion, is there, for any one type or branch of art to continue in existence?" Mr. Beiswanger thinks that vaudeville will do instead of drama. "Such a masterpiece" as *Oklahoma!* possesses a "perfection" which has "deep subconscious roots." At last the Composite Art Work has triumphed:

There is one stage today on which all the theater arts unite in happy combination to produce theater that is sheer, ample, and without inner tension or quarrel. I refer again to the musical stage, to such natural triumphs of the American theater imagination as *Lady in the Dark* and *Oklahoma!* Grant that these are not Shakespeare nor Euripides nor Dante. But they come close to being Aristophanes or Mollière. Increasingly they approach opera. And they are our own, genuine outpourings of American temperament, honest mirrorings of what we are. An age cannot fight itself. It has to make what theater it can. . . .

Here is a revived and jazzified Wagnerism which does not omit Wagner's nationalism and praise of the soil nor his belief in the historical inevitability of his success. One is tempted to meet assertion with assertion by retorting bluntly: *Oklahoma!* is *not* in the same class as *Tartuffe,* commercial musical comedy does *not* approach great opera. . . . And what can an age do except fight itself? The great minds of the modern age are the great fighters against the modern age. An age can and must fight itself.

But the point in Mr. Beiswanger's argument which most concerns us here is less fundamental. Mr. Beiswanger rejoices in song and dance and *décor,* in the *élan* of stage performance which, though indescribable, may yet be stronger in one's experience than many a playwright's mere words. The playwright's work Mr. Beiswanger, following professional usage, calls a "script," and it is, he tells us, the mere shadow of the theatrical reality. Mr. Beiswanger's way of looking at things is symptomatic. His remarks remind us of the fact that popularized Wagnerism is probably the most widespread dramatic theory—or the most widely held preconception— of our day. The assumption is that theater is primarily a musico-visual art, an art of spectacle, movement, and melody. It is ballet, it is opera. But it is not drama. The actor is never at more than one remove from the dancer. Unity and character are imposed upon this composite art work by an artist-director.

Since the decline of Zolaist Naturalism some such theory has underlain much of the most adventurous theatrical endeavor. So as not to place all the responsibility of it on Mr. Beiswanger—who does not subscribe to every article of the doctrine—we can call the theory *theatricalism.* It goes back to Max Reinhardt, who made the theatrical director the artistic dictator in the world of drama (though like dictators in politics he was subject to approval by the men of money). Max Reinhardt began as an actor, and when he turned to dramatic dictatorship he at first produced those plays which his actor's good instinct led him to approve: he introduced Wilde, Maeterlinck, Wedekind, and Strindberg to a large public. Theatricalism, however, led him astray, and he introduced a yet wider public to *The Miracle* and a Shakespeare with elephantiasis. The name of Gordon Craig should also come in again here. Where Reinhardt elevated the director, Craig elevated the stage-designer above the dramatist, and in one of his most vigorous flights of theatricalism he succeeded in subordinating the twin genius of Ibsen and Duse to the megalomania of Craig. The final refutation of Craig was that so many of his designs could not be executed at all; they were pretentious fantasies. Reinhardt's theatricalism ended by his losing contact with the drama, Craig's by his losing contact with the theater itself. The wheel had come full circle.

The theatricalist view is even more suspect in its relation to the actor. It is of course refreshing to realize anew that the art of acting is akin to dancing, yet the devotion of actors to psychological analyses should not be interpreted as a passing fancy of nineteenth-century realism. From the Greeks to Ibsen the actor has represented, by elocution as well as by movement, human character and human destiny. There is no apparent reason why he should forfeit the riches of his heritage even for a dancer's birthright. When drama takes on the abstract character of pure music or pure dance it ceases to be drama; when, as a compromise, it tries to combine the abstract with the concrete it is invariably the drama, the words, that suffer. The words are the weakest element in *Oklahoma!* They are the weakest ingredient in the Wagnerian brew, though Wagner guarded against the weakening by projecting as much as possible of the drama into the music.

The theatricalists try to make drama without the help of a dramatist. Even where the high theater has had most scope—in Soviet Russia and Weimar Germany—there has been more theatrical and technical than dramatic and creative talent. Such dramatists as Georg Kaiser scarcely exist without the boon of a modernistic staging; it is the poverty of such an imagination that does indeed justify the critic in speaking of scripts and libretti. Twenty years ago dozens of books announced a theatrical renaissance which had either just begun in Russia or Germany or was about to flower in America or England. The evidence of the renaissance was chiefly drawn from stage-design and directing; ten years later it was found in the rightness (*i.e.* leftness) of the author's social philosophy. Now many productions in these decades equaled or surpassed *Oklahoma!* and retained also a certain seriousness—at least of intention. *Oklahoma!* insofar as it is unorthodox at all, represents the experimentalism of the earlier decades degraded, now that the faiths and affirmations of those years are out of favor, into "middle-brow" terms. Lacking the seriousness of purpose, the sternness of outlook, the originality of yesterday's experiments, *Oklahoma!* proclaims the bankruptcy of theatricalism.

I have already formulated the truth that few have cared to assert, as follows: *a drama not verbalized is a drama not dramatized.* The dramatist

not only charts out a plan of procedure, he conceives and realizes a work
of art which is already complete—except for technical reproduction—in
his head, and which expresses by verbal image and concept a certain
attitude to life. He is a writer, a poet, before he is a musician or a chore-
ographer. Wagner of course showed that many dramatic elements can be
embodied in orchestral music; silent movies showed how much can be done
with the visual element alone; but if you add Wagner to Eisenstein and
multiply by ten you still do not have a Shakespeare or an Ibsen. This is not
to say that drama is *better* than music, dancing, or the visual arts. It is
different.

The comparison of a script to a musical score is apt insofar as performance is the proper mode of presentation for both; and it is true that
the director's function is properly that of the conductor, namely, to be
utterly faithful and subordinate to the composer. Yet if the comparison be
submitted to the crude test of common experience it is manifestly inexact.
Even the professional musician does not read scores with ease or relish;
but from our childhood we have innocently cherished the "scripts," however shadowy, of Shakespeare. Are we to forfeit that pleasure at the bidding of even very unacademic theorists?

Here we abut upon the old and vexed theme of the reading of plays
as opposed to seeing them in the theater. The spokesmen of "theater
arts" have rendered good service in insisting that good drama is always
good theater and should therefore be performed; but Mr. Beiswanger gives
the show away (almost literally) when he argues that good theater is
always good drama or that, if it is not, drama does not matter anyway.
The defenders of the arts of the theater are infected by the commodities
of the theater once they forget that all of the arts of the theater are means
to one end: the correct presentation of a poem. It goes without saying that
a dramatic poem is a particular kind of poem; that the dramatic poet must
visualize stage action in all its intricacy; and that there is undramatic poetry
as the theatricalists always remind us; I am reminding them—since they
end by throwing out poetry altogether—that there is also *dramatic* poetry.
Now poetry which is dramatic, being shaped to the human throat, and directed at the human heart and head, cannot but be readable. What are
the great theatrical pieces which make boring reading? Is *Oklahoma!* an
instance? If so, it is comforting to know that the plays of Shakespeare,
Congreve, Molière, Ibsen, and Shaw are not. Even O'Neill, the prince of
melodramatists, is highly readable. It seems that the dichotomy of theatrical
and dramatic is questionable. Closet dramas, the dramas which supremely
are offered to us as dramatic reading matter, are seldom good poems of
any kind and therefore are seldom good reading; yet—to confuse us

further—one classic instance of this genre, Tennyson's *Becket,* was a stage favorite of that most theatrical and theatricalist genius, Henry Irving.

What is behind theatricalism? The dichotomy of theater and drama existed as early as the eighteenth century. As the public was stratified into what we now call high- and low-brows, the theater was similarly split. While Iffland and Kotzebue found it easy to amuse the public with their cheap wares Goethe learned to look upon the theater, well as he served it, with a certain disdain, and when the duke's mistress insisted on staging a play featuring a performing dog Goethe left the theater for good. The younger generation of German writers (and I pick out Germany because it was at that time theatrically the most flourishing country) made of literature an antithesis to drama. They followed Goethe in writing plays that were too cumbersome for production; but they did not inherit any of his genius, and the literary play earned at this early date a name for dullness and pedantry. In this situation, as in ours today, the one thing needful was a reaffirmation of dramatic essentials. Two more Germans, Otto Ludwig and Friedrich Hebbel, provided it in the forties and fifties. Though these two proficient playwrights and superb dramatic theorists were antagonists, they had a common goal; to appeal from the drama or artifice to an as yet unborn drama of substance. Since then every serious dramatist has had to run the gantlet between those who feared that he was too theatrical to be poetic and those who feared that he was too poetic to be theatrical. In our own time T. S. Eliot was provoked by the antipoetic William Archer into reaffirming that poetry is not necessarily undramatic. Bertolt Brecht goes yet further in denying that lyric and narrative verse are necessarily out of place on the stage.

In the arts, as in religion, no single, double, or triple reaffirmation is ever enough, and today we need reminding of the essentials as much as ever. I have been arguing that the part of the devil has in our time been played by theatricalism, which has now penetrated as far from Broadway as the literary quarterlies. Of course a play is a play, but this simple axiom —which is the only truth behind theatricalism—should not need so much promotion. Studies, such as Stark Young's, of the artistic values in the subsidiary arts of the theater are useful if you have also Mr. Young's literary sense. Today we see the results of placing the emphasis on the arts of the theater—on each separate instrument, or on the conductor, but not on the composition. After a moving performance of *Rosmersholm* at the Yale Drama School, I heard the drama students comment on everything except Ibsen's lines and Ibsen's meaning. The young men and women could lecture you on lighting, costumes, *décor,* acting, direction, but it seemed not to matter what was being lit, costumed, decorated, acted, and directed. Textbooks on drama remain bad. Such criticism as exists is impressionistic or inspirational, and one reads such evasive sentimentalities as: "The best criticism of a play is a production of it." Criticism is not a substitute for a production; it ought to be a prerequisite for all participants in a production. Drama is now relegated to the colleges, but our modern professors are often more antiacademic than Broadway itself. Campus producers, who have the opportunity of presenting any play irrespective of the box office, voluntarily produce pure box-office commodities, lukewarm from Broadway, in the pathetic belief that this is real theater and not mere literature.

What are the simple essentials to which we should return and what are the revolutionary conclusions to which we are impelled? I have said that drama is the most exacting of the arts, and if we think on the usual scale and on the usual lines this is undeniable. Yet there is point too in recalling Goethe's remark to the effect that the essentials of theater are two boards, four barrels, and a handful of actors. In some way the theater is incredibly complex and will remain so; in others it is simple to the point of crudity, and the theatricalists have dressed up a wide-eyed lass in the garb of a courtesan. Otto Ludwig put Goethe's thought slightly less simply when he said that the drama consists of uniting the two arts of poetry and acting. Two arts; and they do not include the arts of directing and stage-design. *The dramatist is a poet*—that is, an imaginative writer of verse or prose—*who transmits his work through gesturing elocutionists*. Keep close to these simple elements and you will be able to maintain an essential distinction between drama and the pure spectacle of silent movies. The sound movie is different. There might be drama on the talking screen, though the attempted elimination of acting in current movies is one of the nondramatic elements which distinguish them from drama proper. There is of course character acting in most movies, but the "normal" parts are just stars presenting themselves in different costumes. On the stage the "straight part" is also transmitted through the actor's own personality, but the interest of his performance consists in the compromise he makes between himself and his role (synthesis might be a better metaphor) in the practice of a craft which we are aware of as such. Eventually the screen may unlearn its illusionism, yet the stage will retain immense advantages in nonillusionistic performance, advantages arising from the "psychic" contact between the living actor and his audience.

Hollywood has been expert in many ways, but it has never attended to the two basic requirements of drama: it is against poetic imagination and it will not let actors act. (Such an achievement as Victor McLaglen's performance in *The Informer* is a rare event indeed.) But should the screen be dramatic? We all know the party line of the Higher Critics of the movie: plays should not be transferred to the screen, so runs the tale, for the screen will develop its own art forms according to its own potentialities. There can be no objection to this line of thought even though we suspect that the antiliterary prejudice—which is a prejudice against culture itself —is again at work. Only what *are* the potentialities of the talking screen? They differ from those of the silent screen in adding the dimension of dialogue—which, potentially, is poetry. Actually the screen has suffered not by being literary but by being theatricalist. Every MGM movie is a Reinhardt show.

To obtain the simple essentials—trained acting and a real dramatic "script"—one revolutionary conclusion is needed: the repudiation of the theater as it is now financed and organized, which means, positively stated, the acceptance of a special, limited audience. This is not a snobbish plan, for the special, limited audience may consist of trade-unionists or of college students or of unemployed. It may well be a more earthy audience than that of Broadway where the cheapest seat is usually $1.20. The audience at a "popular" Broadway play is not popular. It consists of a fairly well-to-do class of citizens who insist on their usual diet; if they enjoy an unusual dish (as I noticed at a performance of *The Skin of Our Teeth*) it is for the wrong reasons. Nor is the provincial audience much better. Many amateur groups that began with good intentions soon submitted to pressure and started giving Broadway plays. At this point theatricalism is seen in its true colors: it is a "high-brow" rationalization of "low-brow" taste in drama. Since the pundits are all theatricalists now, there is no one to give a lead. You may study drama for years in drama departments and still be unable to tell a good play from a bad. To prefer Wedekind to Maxwell Anderson would be thought outrageous snobbery by many professors (if they had heard of Wedekind at all). Of course the problems of a college drama department are peculiar. The kind of student who "takes" drama is seldom concerned with the imagination of a Shakespeare or a Sophocles. He is more often an exhibitionist and an aspiring movie star. Nevertheless I shall quite deliberately harp on the college in this discussion of the present plight of drama because I am convinced that the campus is one of the few places where something might be done about it. On some campuses much has been done already. Not on many. I spent some time at one of the most artistic and experimental colleges in the country, and saw for my pains Sutton Vane's *Outward Bound,* Barrie's *Twelve Pound Look,* and worse. Alas!

Elsewhere I have tried to show that Henrik Ibsen, the so-called father of modern drama, was never more a poet than in his last prose plays, which are highly subjective and obscure. If we follow the history of high drama since Ibsen we shall find that most of it is minority drama, written for small theaters, demanding from its audience considerable sophistication, knowledgeability, and refinement, if not also such a command of politics, economics, philosophy, or religion, as the readers of popular magazines would not care to be cumbered with. After Ibsen came Strindberg, who founded his Intimate Theater at Stockholm and, taking a tip from Reinhardt, invented the Chamber Play on the analogy of chamber music; his preface to *Miss Julia,* a document as rewarding to the student of modern theater as Aristotle's *Poetics,* and his *Dramaturgy* lay down the principles of the new art. The great organization through which we have a modern drama at all—the Théâtre Libre, Freie Bühne, Independent Theater, the Abbey Theater, the Moscow Art Theater, the Provincetown Players, were all minority organizations, and most of them not very "successful" at that. In performing the modern masterpieces in improvised conditions before a handful of enthusiasts in a Little Theater one is fully in the spirit of the modern dramatists. One is succeeding. It is those who go to the academy to study Broadway who fail.

IV

Biographies and Bibliographies

1. Short Biographies of Contributors

MATTHEW ARNOLD (1822–1888) Educated at Rugby, where his father was headmaster, and at Balliol College, Oxford, Arnold published his first volume of poems in 1849. The essay in this volume was published in 1865. His principal critical works are included in two volumes: *Essays in Criticism* (1865) and *Essays in Criticism, Second Series* (1888).

IRVING BABBITT (1865–1933) Professor of Comparative Literature at Harvard until his death, Irving Babbitt was the leader of a group known as Neo-Humanists, which flourished in the 1920's and early 1930's. His chief critical studies were *Masters of Modern French Criticism* (1912) and *Rousseau and Romanticism* (1919). The essay in this volume is from the former.

MONROE C. BEARDSLEY (1915–) Educated at Yale University, A.B. 1936, Ph.D. 1939, Beardsley now teaches at Swarthmore College.

R. P. BLACKMUR (1904–) The author of two collections of critical writings, *The Double Agent* (1935) and *The Expense of Greatness* (1940), Blackmur teaches at Princeton University. He was formerly an editor of *Hound & Horn*.

ERIC RUSSELL BENTLEY (1916–) Born in England, Bentley studied at Yale University and taught at the University of California at Los Angeles, Black Mountain College, and the University of Minnesota. His books include *Playwright as Thinker* (1946), where the essay in this volume appears, *Bernard Shaw* (1947), and *The Importance of Scrutiny* (1948), which he edited.

MAUD BODKIN An English scholar and critic, Miss Bodkin is author of *The Quest for Salvation in an Ancient and a Modern Play* (1941) and *Archetypal Patterns in Poetry* (1934). The essay in this volume is Chapter One of the latter book.

CLEANTH BROOKS (1906–) Formerly editor, with Robert Penn Warren, of *The Southern Review,* Brooks is author of *Modern Poetry and the Tradition* and *The Well-Wrought Urn;* co-editor with Warren of *Understanding Poetry* and *Understanding Fiction,* and with Robert B. Heilman of *Understanding Drama.* He taught at Louisiana State for many years, but now is at Yale.

KENNETH BURKE (1897–)   Educated at Ohio State University, Burke was music critic for *The Dial* (1927–1929) and for *The Nation* (1933–1935). His critical works include *Permanence and Change* (1935), *A Grammar of Motives* (1945), and *A Rhetoric of Motives* (1950). At present he teaches at Bennington College. He is represented in this volume with an article from *A Grammar of Motives*.

SAMUEL TAYLOR COLERIDGE (1772–1834)   Born in Devonshire and educated for the Church, Coleridge became a leading English poet and critic. His chief contributions to criticism were his lectures on Shakespeare and the *Biographia Literaria* (1817), of which the excerpt in this volume is Chapter XIV.

MALCOLM COWLEY (1898–)   Born in Pennsylvania and educated at Harvard and in France, Cowley was for many years literary editor of *The New Republic*. He is the author of *Exile's Return* (1934) and editor of *The Portable Faulkner* (1946) and *The Portable Hawthorne* (1948). The essay included in this volume appeared first in *Sewanee Review* (1945) and was reprinted in *A Southern Vanguard* (edited by Allen Tate, 1947).

BENEDETTO CROCE (1866–)   An Italian philosopher of international reputation, Croce's interest in problems of aesthetics has made his works of great interest to literary critics. Available in English are *Aesthetics* (1919) and *The Defense of Poetry* (1933). The latter, which was a lecture delivered at Oxford University, is reprinted in this volume. His "The Breviary of Aesthetic" (1915) was delivered as a lecture at Rice Institute and published as a Rice Institute Pamphlet (2).

T. S. ELIOT (1888–)   Born in St. Louis and educated at Harvard, the Sorbonne, and Oxford University, Eliot won the Nobel Prize for Literature in 1948. His published criticism includes *The Sacred Wood* (1920), *For Launcelot Andrewes* (1928), *Selected Essays* (1932; revised, 1950), *The Use of Poetry and the Use of Criticism* (1933), *After Strange Gods* (1934), *Elizabethan Essays* (1934), *Essays Ancient and Modern* (1936), *The Idea of a Christian Society* (1939), and *Notes toward a Definition of Culture* (1949).

WILLIAM EMPSON (1906–)   Graduated from Cambridge University where he studied with I. A. Richards, Empson is now lecturer in English literature at Peking National University. The author of *Seven Types of Ambiguity* (1930) and *Some Versions of Pastoral,* known in America as *English Pastoral Poetry* (1935), he is now engaged upon a work to be called *The Structure of Complex Words*.

FRANCIS FERGUSSON (1904–)   Educated at Harvard, Fergusson taught at Bennington College, and is now at Princeton University. He was dramatic critic for *The Bookman* (1930–1932). He has contributed to *Hound & Horn, The American Review, Kenyon Review,* and many others. He is the author of *The Idea of a Theater* (1950), from which the article included here is reprinted.

NORMAN FOERSTER (1887–) Graduated from Harvard in 1910, where he was a student of Irving Babbitt, Foerster has taught at the universities of Wisconsin, North Carolina, and Iowa. Among his critical works are *American Criticism* (1928) and *Towards Standards* (1930). The article in this volume was delivered as a lecture at Princeton University and published in *The Intent of the Critic* (1941).

E. M. FORSTER (1879–) Primarily a novelist, Forster is author of a significant book on fiction, *Aspects of the Novel,* which originated as a series of lectures delivered at Trinity College, Cambridge, in 1927.

WALLACE FOWLIE (1908–) After teaching at Harvard, Yale, and the University of Chicago, Fowlie is now at Bennington College. His books include *Clowns and Angels* (1943), *Rimbaud* (1946), and *Jacob's Night* (1947). He has appeared in *Kenyon Review, Partisan Review, Western Review, Accent,* and many foreign periodicals. The article in this volume appeared in *Focus,* an English publication edited by B. Rajan.

REMY DE GOURMONT (1858–1915) Although few of his works are available in translation, this French critic has been particularly influential upon critics in England and America. J. M. Murry's *The Problem of Style* (1922) is essentially a restatement of Gourmont's famous work of the same title. Two translations published in America are *Selections* (edited by Richard Aldington, 1928) and *Decadence* (1921). The selection in this book is from the latter volume.

THOMAS ERNEST HULME (1883–1917) Hulme's critical notebooks were edited posthumously as *Speculations* (1924) by Herbert Read. He was killed while serving with the British artillery in World War I.

HENRY JAMES (1843–1916) Born in New York, but spending much of his time abroad, James became a British subject in 1915, in protest against America's failure to enter the war as Britain's ally. His criticism is contained primarily in *Partial Portraits* (1888), which contained the essay included in this volume, and in his famous prefaces to the New York edition of his works. These prefaces have since been published separately as *The Art of the Novel* (edited by R. P. Blackmur, 1934).

L. C. KNIGHTS (1906–) Professor of English at the University of Sheffield and a member of the editorial board of *Scrutiny,* a leading British critical journal, Knights is the author of *Drama and Society in the Age of Johnson* (1937) and *Explorations* (1946).

F. R. LEAVIS (1895–) ·A fellow of Downing College, Cambridge, and Director of English Studies, Leavis has been an editor of *Scrutiny* since its beginning in 1932. He is the author of *New Bearings in English Poetry* (1932), *For Continuity* (1933), *Revaluations* (1936), *Education and the University* (1943), and *The Great Tradition* (1948). He has also edited two volumes of critical essays: *Towards Standards in Criticism* (1933) and *Determinations* (1934).

HARRY LEVIN (1912–) Professor of Comparative Literature at Harvard, Levin is the author of *James Joyce* (1941), from which the article in this volume is taken, *Toward Stendhal* (1945), *Toward Balzac* (1947), and edited *The Portable James Joyce* (1947).

PERCY LUBBOCK (1879–) Educated at Cambridge, Lubbock is best known for his *The Craft of Fiction* (1921), from which the article in this book is excerpted. He is also the author of *Roman Pictures* (1923), *The Region Cloud* (1925), and *Portrait of Edith Wharton* (1947).

F. O. MATTHIESSEN (1902–1950) A teacher at Harvard University until his death, Matthiessen was the author of *The Achievement of T. S. Eliot* (1935), *American Renaissance* (1941), and *Henry James: The Major Phase* (1944). He also contributed articles to many magazines and edited selected works of Melville and James. The article in this volume is from *Henry James: The Major Phase*.

EZRA POUND (1885–) Born in Idaho and educated at the University of Pennsylvania and Hamilton College, Pound has, since 1908, spent almost all of his time in England, France, and Italy. In 1924 he settled in Rapallo, where he remained until he returned to the United States as a prisoner of the U.S. Army following World War II. During his years abroad he exerted a powerful influence upon contemporary letters. He is at present a patient in St. Elizabeth's Hospital, Washington, D.C. The article in this volume is from *Polite Essays* (1937).

JOHN CROWE RANSOM (1888–) Editor of *The Fugitive* (Nashville, 1922–1925) and a member of the so-called Fugitive Group of southern poets and critics, Ransom has edited the *Kenyon Review* since 1939 and taught at Kenyon College. His principal criticism has appeared in two volumes: *The World's Body* (1938) and *The New Criticism* (1941). Uncollected articles have appeared in many magazines. The article in this volume was originally a lecture delivered at Princeton University and printed in the volume *The Intent of the Critic* (1941).

HERBERT READ (1893–) Educated at the University of Leeds, where he also received an honorary D. Litt., Read is the author of many books of poetry, literary and art criticism, and one novel. Best known of his literary criticism are *In Defense of Shelley* (1935), *Collected Essays* (1939), and *Phases of English Poetry* (1929, 1951).

I. A. RICHARDS (1893–)   Formerly of Cambridge, Richards now teaches in the College of Education at Harvard. His interest in literary criticism grew in part from his concern, as a psychologist, with the effects of language. His critical volumes include *Principles of Literary Criticism* (1924), *Science and Poetry* (1926), *Practical Criticism* (1929), and *Coleridge on Imagination* (1934). The article in this volume is from *Science and Poetry*.

GEORGE SANTAYANA (1863–)   Born in Spain and now living in retirement in Italy, Santayana for many years taught philosophy at Harvard. His principal works dealing with aesthetics are *The Sense of Beauty* (1896), *Interpretations of Poetry and Religion* (1905), and *Three Philosophical Poets* (1935).

MARK SCHORER (1908–)   Graduated from the University of Wisconsin and now teaching at the University of California, Schorer is an editor of *Criticism* (1948) and of *The Story* (1950). The first is an anthology of critical articles, and the second a critical anthology of short fiction. He is the author of *William Blake: The Politics of Vision* (1946). The article reprinted in this volume first appeared in *The Hudson Review*.

ALLEN TATE (1899–)   Originally associated with the Fugitive Group of Nashville, Tate has lectured at Princeton University and New York University. Equally respected as a poet and critic, he has also written a fine novel. His criticism has recently been collected into a single volume *On the Limits of Poetry* (1948). Included in it is work from three separate volumes: *Reactionary Essays* (1936), *Reason in Madness* (1941), and *The Hovering Fly* (1948). He was editor of *Sewanee Review* from 1944 to 1946.

E. M. W. TILLYARD (1889–)   Master of Jesus College, Cambridge, since 1945, and author of books on various writers, including Lamb, Wyatt, Milton, and Shakespeare, Tillyard is best known for *Poetry: Direct and Oblique* (1934, 1945), *The Personal Heresy* (with C. S. Lewis, 1939), and *Five Poems, 1470–1870* (1948), from which the article in this volume is taken.

LIONEL TRILLING (1905–)   A native of New York, Trilling teaches at Columbia University and has published a collection of critical articles under the title *The Liberal Imagination*, from which the article in this book is taken. He has also published studies of Matthew Arnold (1939) and E. M. Forster (1943).

AUSTIN WARREN (1899–)   After teaching at Boston University and The State University of Iowa, Warren is now at the University of Michigan. He is the author of *Pope as Critic and Humanist* (1929), *The Elder Henry James* (1934), *Crashaw* (1939), and *Rage for Order* (1948); he is co-author with René Wellek of *Theory of Literature* (1949). The article in this volume is from *Rage for Order*.

ROBERT PENN WARREN (1905–)   Co-editor with Cleanth Brooks of *The Southern Review* (1935–1942) and of *Understanding Poetry* (1938) and *Understanding Fiction* (1943), Warren is also a respected poet and novelist. He has taught at Vanderbilt, Louisiana State University, and the University of Minnesota. His critical articles have not been collected, but he published a long critical study, *The Rime of the Ancient Mariner* (1946). The article in this volume appeared originally in *Kenyon Review*.

EDMUND WILSON (1895–)   After education at Princeton, Wilson has served as an editor of *Vanity Fair, The New Republic,* and *The New Yorker* and has edited writings of T. K. Whipple, F. Scott Fitzgerald, and John Peale Bishop. His books of criticism include one anthology, *The Shock of Recognition* (1943), and four original works: *Axel's Castle* (1931), *The Triple Thinkers* (1938), *The Wound and the Bow* (1941), and *The Boys in the Back Room* (1941).

W. K. WIMSATT, JR. (1907–)   A teacher of English at Yale University, Wimsatt has published one book, *Prose Style of Samuel Johnson* (1941), and articles in various journals. "The Intentional Fallacy" (with M. C. Beardsley) appeared first in *Sewanee Review*.

YVOR WINTERS (1900–)   Educated at the University of Colorado and Stanford University, Winters now teaches at Stanford. He is the author of *Primitivism and Decadence* (1937), *Maule's Curse* (1938), and *The Anatomy of Nonsense* (1943). He has also published a critical study of Edwin Arlington Robinson (1947). The first three books have been collected in a single volume entitled *In Defense of Reason* (1947).

MORTON DAUWEN ZABEL (1901–)   A former editor of *Poetry* magazine and a teacher at the University of Chicago, Zabel is the editor of *Literary Opinion in America* (1937) and of *The Portable Conrad* (1947). The article in this volume appeared first in the Stevens number of the Harvard *Advocate*.

2. Books of Literary Criticism

AMES, VAN METER, *Aesthetics of the Novel.* University of California, 1928.
——, *Proust and Santayana.* Willett, Clark, 1937.
ARNHEIM, RUDOLF, *et al., Poets at Work.* Harcourt, Brace, 1948.
ARVIN, NEWTON, *Melville.* Sloane, 1950.

BABBITT, IRVING, *The New Laokoön.* Houghton Mifflin, 1910.
——, *Masters of Modern French Criticism.* Houghton Mifflin, 1912.
——, *Rousseau and Romanticism.* Houghton Mifflin, 1919.
BARZUN, JACQUES, *Romanticism and the Modern Ego.* Little, Brown, 1943.
BASLER, ROY P., *Sex, Symbolism and Psychology.* Rutgers University, 1948.
BATES, H. E., *The Modern Short Story.* Nelson, 1942.
BEACH, JOSEPH W., *The Twentieth Century Novel.* Appleton-Century-Crofts, 1932.
——, *American Fiction, 1920–1940.* Macmillan, 1941.
BEER, THOMAS, *Stephen Crane.* Knopf, 1923.
BENTLEY, ERIC R., *The Importance of Scrutiny.* George Stewart, 1948.
——, *The Play, a Critical Anthology.* Prentice-Hall, 1951.
——, *The Playwright as Thinker.* Reynal & Hitchcock, 1946.
——, *Bernard Shaw.* New Directions, 1947.
BERGSON, HENRI, *Time and Free Will.* Macmillan, 1910.
——, *Matter and Memory.* Macmillan, 1919.
BISHOP, J. PEALE, *Collected Essays.* Scribner, 1948.
BLACKMUR, R. P., *The Double Agent.* Arrow Editions, 1935.
——, *The Expense of Greatness.* Arrow Editions, 1940.
BOAS, GEORGE, *A Primer for Critics.* Johns Hopkins University, 1937.
BOGAN, LOUISE, *Achievement in American Poetry, 1900–1950.* Regnery, 1951.
BOUDOIN, CHARLES, *Psychoanalysis and Aesthetics.* Allen & Unwin, 1924.
BOURNE, RANDOLPH, *The History of a Literary Radical.* Viking, 1920.
BOYD, ERNEST, *Criticism in America.* Harcourt, Brace, 1924.
BOYNTON, PERCY, *Some Contemporary Americans.* University of Chicago, 1924.
——, *More Contemporary Americans.* University of Chicago, 1927.
——, *The Challenge of Modern Criticism.* Follett, 1931.
BOWRA, C. M., *The Heritage of Symbolism.* Macmillan, 1943.

BRENNAN, J. G., *Thomas Mann's World*. Columbia University, 1942.

BROD, MAX, *Franz Kafka*. Sohn, 1937.

BROOKS, CLEANTH, *Modern Poetry and the Tradition*. University of North Carolina, 1939.

———, *The Well-Wrought Urn*. Reynal & Hitchcock, 1947.
See also under Warren, R. P., and Heilman, R. B.

BROOKS, VAN WYCK, *The Ordeal of Mark Twain*. Dutton, 1920.

———, *The Opinions of Oliver Allston*. Dutton, 1941.

BROWNELL, W. C., *American Prose Masters*. Scribner, 1909.

———, *Criticism*. Scribner, 1914.

BURGUM, E. B., *The New Criticism*. Prentice-Hall, 1930.

BURKE, KENNETH, *Counterstatement*. Harcourt, Brace, 1931.

———, *Permanence and Change*. New Republic Books, 1935.

———, *The Philosophy of Literary Form*. Louisiana University, 1941.

———, *A Grammar of Motives*. Prentice-Hall, 1945.

———, *A Rhetoric of Motives*. Prentice-Hall, 1950.

BUTLER, E. M., *Rainer Maria Rilke*. Cambridge, 1941.

CALVERTON, V. F., *The New Grounds of Criticism*. University of Washington Bookstore, 1930.

CASSIRER, ERNST, *Philosophie der Symbolischen Formen*. Cassirer, 3 vols., 1923–1931.

CAUDWELL, C., *Illusion and Reality*. Macmillan, 1937.

CAZAMIAN, LOUIS, *Criticism in the Making*. Macmillan, 1929.

CENTANO, AUGUSTO, *The Intent of the Artist*. Princeton University

CHASE, RICHARD, *Herman Melville*. Macmillan, 1949.

CHENEY, SHELDON, *Expressionism in Art*. Liveright, 1934.

CLAUDEL, PAUL, *Ways and Crossways*. Sheed & Ward, 1933.

CONNELLY, CYRIL, *Enemies of Promise*. Macmillan, 1948.

COWLEY, MALCOLM, *Criticism in America*. Harcourt, Brace, 1924.

———, *Exile's Return*. Norton, 1934.

———, *After the Genteel Tradition*. Norton, 1937.

CROCE, BENEDETTO, *The Breviary of Aesthetic*. Rice Institute, 1915.

———, *Aesthetics*. Macmillan, 1919.

DAICHES, DAVID, *The Novel and the Modern World*. University of Chicago, 1939.

———, *Poetry and the Modern World*. University of Chicago, 1940.

DAMON, S. FOSTER, *William Blake*. Houghton Mifflin, 1924.

DAY-LEWIS, C., *A Hope for Poetry*. Oxford, 1936.

DEUTSCH, BABBETTE, *This Modern Poetry*. Norton, 1935.

DEVOTO, BERNARD, *Mark Twain's America*. Little, Brown, 1932.

———, *The Literary Fallacy*. Little, Brown, 1944.

DREW, ELIZABETH, *The Modern Novel*. Harcourt, Brace, 1926.

———, *Directions in Modern Poetry*. Norton, 1940. With J. L. Sweeney.

DUPEE, F. D.,   *The Question of Henry James*. Holt, 1945.
———,   *Henry James*. Sloane, 1951.

EASTMAN, MAX,   *The Literary Mind*. Scribner, 1931.
ELIOT, T. S.,   *The Sacred Wood*. Knopf, 1921.
———,   *For Launcelot Andrewes*. Doubleday, 1928.
———,   *Selected Essays: 1917–1932*. Harcourt, Brace, 1932.
———,   *The Use of Poetry and the Use of Criticism*. Harvard University,
      1933.
———,   *After Strange Gods*. Harcourt, Brace, 1934.
———,   *Poetry and Drama*. Harvard University, 1951.
ELTON, OLIVER,   *The Nature of Literary Criticism*. Manchester University,
      1935.
EMPSON, WILLIAM,   *Seven Types of Ambiguity*. New Directions, 1947.
———,   *English Pastoral Poetry*. Norton, 1938.
———,   *The Structure of Complex Words*. New Directions, 1951.

FARRELL, JAMES T.,   *A Note on Literary Criticism*. Vanguard, 1936.
FERGUSSON, FRANCIS,   *The Idea of a Theater*. Princeton University, 1949.
FERNANDEZ, RAMÓN,   *André Gide*. Corrêa, 1931.
FLORES, ANGEL,   *The Kafka Problem*. New Directions, 1946.
FOERSTER, NORMAN,   *American Criticism*. Houghton Mifflin, 1928.
———,   *Humanism and America*. Rinehart, 1930.
———,   *Reinterpretations of American Literature*. Harcourt, Brace, 1938.
FORD, FORD MADOX,   *The March of Literature*. Dial, 1938.
FORSTER, E. M.,   *Aspects of the Novel*. Harcourt, Brace, 1947.
FOWLIE, WALLACE,   *Rimbaud*. New Directions, 1946.
———,   *Age of Surrealism*. Swallow & Morrow, 1951.
FREEMAN, JOSEPH A.,   *American Testament*. Rinehart, 1936.
FRY, ROGER,   *The Artist and Psychoanalysis*. Hogarth, 1924.

GARROD, H. W.,   *Scholarship: Its Meaning and Value*. Cambridge University,
      1947.
GATES, LEWIS E.,   *Studies and Appreciations*. Macmillan, 1900.
GIDE, ANDRÉ,   *Imaginary Interviews*. Knopf, 1944.
GLASGOW, ELLEN,   *A Certain Measure*. Harcourt, Brace, 1943.
GOLD, MICHAEL,   *The Hollow Men*. International, 1941.
GORMAN, HERBERT S.,   *James Joyce*. Rinehart, 1948.
GOURMONT, REMY DE,   *Decadence*. Harcourt, Brace, 1921.
GRATTAN, C. H.   *The Critique of Humanism*. Brewer & Warren, 1930.
GREGORY, HORACE,   *Pilgrim of the Apocalypse: D. H. Lawrence*. Viking, 1933.
———,   *The Shield of Achilles*. Harcourt, Brace, 1944.
———,   *A History of American Poetry: 1900–1940*. Harcourt, Brace, 1946.
      With Marya Zaturenska.
GRIGSON, G.,   *Psychology and Art Today*. Bodley Head, 1935.

GUERARD, ALBERT, *Literature and Society*. Lothrop, Lee & Shepard, 1935.
———, *André Gide*. Harvard University, 1951.
GUERARD, ALBERT, JR., *Joseph Conrad*. New Directions, 1947.
———, *Thomas Hardy*. Harvard University, 1949.
GUGGENHEIMER, R., *Creative Vision in Artist and Audience*. Harper, 1950.
GUSTAFSON, ALRIK, *Six Scandinavian Novelists*. Princeton University, 1940.

HACKETT, FRANCIS, *Horizons: A Book of Criticism*. Viking, 1918.
HALL, JAMES, *The Permanence of Yeats*. Macmillan, 1950. With Martin Steinmann.
HAZLITT, HENRY, *The Anatomy of Criticism*. Simon & Schuster, 1933.
HEARN, LAFCADIO, *Appreciations of Poetry*. Dodd, Mead, 1916.
HEILMAN, ROBERT B., *This Great Stage*. Louisiana University, 1948.
———, *Understanding Drama*. Holt, 1948. With Cleanth Brooks.
HENDERSON, PHILIP. *The Novel Today*. Bodley Head, 1936.
———, *The Poet and Society*. Secker & Warburg, 1939.
HICKS, GRANVILLE, *The Great Tradition*. Macmillan, 1935.
HOFFMAN, FREDERICK J., *Freudianism and the Literary Mind*. Louisiana University, 1945.
———, *The Modern Novel in America, 1900–1950*. Regnery, 1951.
HORTON, PHILIP, *Hart Crane*. Norton, 1937.
HOSPER, JOHN, *Meaning and Truth in the Arts*. University of North Carolina, 1946.
HOWGATE, G. W., *George Santayana's Philosophy*. University of Pennsylvania, 1938.
HULME, T. E., *Speculations*. Harcourt, Brace, 1936.
HUNEKER, JAMES G., *Iconoclasts*. Scribner, 1905.
———, *Promenades of an Impressionist*. Scribner, 1910.
HYMAN, STANLEY E., *The Armed Vision*. Knopf, 1948.

JAMES, HENRY, *The Art of the Novel*. Scribner, 1934.
———, *Notebooks*. Oxford University, 1947.
JONES, HOWARD M., *The Theory of American Literature*. Cornell University, 1948.
JOSEPHSON, MATTHEW, *Portrait of the Artist as American*. Harcourt, Brace, 1930.

KAZIN, ALFRED, *On Native Grounds*. Reynal & Hitchcock, 1942.
KNIGHTS, L. C., *Explorations*. George Stewart, 1947
KRUTCH, J. W., *The Modern Temper*. Harcourt, Brace, 1929.
———, *Five Masters*. Cape & Smith, 1930.
KUNITZ, STANLEY, *Living Authors*. Wilson, 1931.
———, *Twentieth Century Authors*. Wilson, 1942. With H. Haycraft.

LAWRENCE, D. H., *Studies in Classic American Literature*. Boni, 1923.
LEAVIS, F. R., *Determinations*. Chatto & Windus, 1934.

————, *New Bearings in English Poetry*. Chatto & Windus, 1938.

————, *Revaluations*. George Stewart, 1947.

————, *The Great Tradition*. George Stewart, 1949.

LEAVIS, Q. D., *Fiction and the Reading Public*. Chatto & Windus, 1932.

LEMAÎTRE, G. E., *Four French Novelists*. Oxford University, 1938.

LEVIN, HARRY, *James Joyce*. New Directions, 1941.

————, *Toward Stendahl*. New Directions, 1945.

————, *Toward Balzac*. New Directions, 1947.

LÉVY, JULIAN, *Surrealism*. Black Sun, 1936.

LEWIS, C. S., *The Allegory of Love*. Clarendon, 1936.

LEWIS, WYNDHAM, *Time and Western Man*. Harcourt, Brace, 1928.

LEWISOHN, LUDWIG, *Expression in America*. Harper, 1932.

LIDDEL, ROBERT, *A Treatise on the Novel*. Cape, 1947.

LOWES, JOHN L., *Convention and Revolt in Poetry*. Houghton Mifflin, 1919.

————, *The Road to Xanadu*. Houghton Mifflin, 1927.

LUBBOCK, PERCY, *The Craft of Fiction*. Peter Smith, 1947.

————, *Portrait of Edith Wharton*. Appleton-Century-Crofts, 1947.

MACLEISH, ARCHIBALD, *The Irresponsibles*. Duell, Sloan, & Pearce, 1940.

McMAHON, PHILIP, *The Meaning of Art*. Norton, 1930.

MANN, KLAUS, *André Gide and the Crisis of Modern Thought*. Creative Age, 1943.

MANSFIELD, KATHERINE, *Novels and Novelists*. Knopf, 1930.

MARITAIN, JACQUES, *True Humanism*. Scribner, 1939.

————, *Art and Poetry*. Philosophical Library, 1943.

MATTHIESSEN, F. O., *The Achievement of T. S. Eliot*. Oxford University, 1935.

————, *American Renaissance*. Oxford University, 1941.

————, *Henry James: The Major Phase*. Oxford University, 1944.

————, *Theodore Dreiser*. Sloane, 1951.

MENCKEN, H. L., *A Book of Prefaces*. Knopf, 1917.

MERCIER, L. J. A., *The Challenge of Humanism*. Oxford University, 1933.

MILLE, GEORGE DE, *Literary Criticism in America*. Longmans, Green, 1931.

MILLETT, F. B., *Contemporary American Authors*. Harcourt, Brace, 1940.

MONROE, HARRIET, *Poets and Their Art*. Macmillan, 1926.

MONROE, N. E., *The Novel and Society*. University of North Carolina, 1941.

MORE, PAUL ELMER, *New Shelburne Essays*. Princeton University, 3 vols., 1928.

MUIR, EDWIN, *The Structure of the Novel*. Hogarth, 1947.

————, *Essays on Literature and Society*. Hogarth, 1948.

MULLER, HERBERT J., *Modern Fiction*. Funk & Wagnalls, 1937.

————, *Science and Criticism*. Yale University, 1943.

MUMFORD, LEWIS, *Herman Melville*. Harcourt, Brace, 1929.

MUNSON, GORHAM B., *Style and Form in American Prose*. Doubleday, 1929.

MURRY, JOHN MIDDLETON, *The Problem of Style*. Oxford University, 1922.
———, *Discoveries*. Collins, 1924.
———, *Son of Woman; The Story of D. H. Lawrence*. Cape, 1931.

NEIDER, CHARLES, *The Stature of Thomas Mann*. New Directions, 1947.
———, *The Frozen Sea* (on Kafka). New Directions, 1948.
NUHN, FERNER, *The Wind Blew from the East*. Harper, 1942.

O'CONNOR, W. V., *Forms of Modern Fiction*. University of Minnesota, 1948.
———, *Sense and Sensibility in Modern Poetry*. University of Chicago, 1948.
———, *Wallace Stevens*. Regnery, 1950.
OGDEN, C. K., *The Meaning of Meaning*. Harcourt, Brace, 1923. With I. A.
    Richards.
ORTEGA Y GASSET, JOSÉ, *La Déshumizacion del Arte*. Revista de Occidente,
    1925. English translated edition, Princeton University, 1948.

PARETO, VILFREDO, *The Mind and Society*. Harcourt, Brace, 4 vols., 1935.
PARKES, H. B., *The Pragmatic Test*. Colt, 1941.
PARRINGTON, V. L., *Main Currents in American Thought*. Harcourt, Brace,
    3 vols., 1930. One-volume edition, 1930.
PEACOCK, RONALD, *The Poet in the Theatre*. Harcourt, Brace, 1946.
PEPPER, S. C., *The Basis of Criticism in the Arts*. Harvard University, 1946.
PEYRE, HENRI, *Writers and Their Critics*. Cornell University, 1944.
POTTLE, FREDERICK, *The Idiom of Poetry*. Cornell University, 1946.
POUND, EZRA, *The Spirit of Romance*. Dutton, 1910.
———, *Instigations*. Boni, 1920.
———, *How to Read*. Harmsworth, 1931.
———, *Make It New*. Yale University, 1935.
———, *Polite Essays*. New Directions, 1937.
———, *The Letters of Ezra Pound*. Harcourt, Brace, 1950.
PRALL, D. W., *Aesthetic Analysis*. Crowell, 1936.
PRAZ, MARIO, *The Romantic Agony*. Oxford University, 1933.

RAHV, PHILIP, *Image and Idea*. New Directions, 1949.
RAJAN, B., *Focus* (Critical Annual). Dobson, 1945–1947.
RANK, OTTO, *Art and Artist*. Knopf, 1932.
RANSOM, JOHN CROWE, *God without Thunder*. Harcourt, Brace, 1930.
———, *The World's Body*. Scribner, 1938.
———, *The New Criticism*. New Directions, 1941.
READ, HERBERT, *Reason and Romanticism*. Faber & Gwyer, 1926.
———, *The Sense of Glory*. Harcourt, Brace, 1929.
———, *Form in Modern Poetry*. Sheed & Ward, 1932.
———, *Meaning of Art*. Faber & Faber, 1935.
———, *In Defense of Shelley*. Heinemann, 1936.
———, *Collected Essays*. Faber & Faber, 1938.
———, *Phases of English Poetry*. New Directions, 1950.
RICHARDS, I. A., *Science and Poetry*. Norton, 1926.

——, *Practical Criticism*. Harcourt, Brace, 1930.

——, *Coleridge on Imagination*. Harcourt, Brace, 1935.

——, *The Meaning of Meaning*. Harcourt, Brace, 1936. With C. K. Ogden.

——, *Principles of Literary Criticism*. Harcourt, Brace, 1948.

ROBERTS, MORRIS, *Henry James' Criticism*. Harvard University, 1929.

ROSENFELD, PAUL, *Men Seen*. Dial, 1925.

ROURKE, CONSTANCE, *American Humor*. Harcourt, Brace, 1931.

RUSSELL, PETER, *An Examination of Ezra Pound*. New Directions, 1950.

SAINTSBURY, GEORGE, *The Collected Essays: 1875–1920*. Dutton, 4 vols., 1923–1924.

SANTAYANA, GEORGE, *The Sense of Beauty*. Scribner, 1896.

——, *Three Philosophical Poets*. Harvard University, 1927.

——, *The Genteel Tradition at Bay*. Scribner, 1931.

SAVAGE, D. S., *The Personal Principle*. Routledge, 1944.

——, *The Withered Branch*. Eyre & Spottiswoode, 1950.

SCHORER, MARK, *Criticism: The Foundations of Modern Literary Judgment*. Harcourt, Brace, 1948. With McKenzie and Miles.

SEDGWICK, W. E., *Herman Melville: The Tragedy of Mind*. Harvard University, 1945.

SELINCOURT, E. DE, *Oxford Lectures in Poetry*. Clarendon, 1934.

SHERMAN, STUART P., *The Main Stream*. Scribner, 1927.

SHIPLEY, JOSEPH T., *The Quest for Literature: A Survey of Literary Criticism*. Richard R. Smith, 1931.

——, *A Dictionary of World Literature*. Philosophical Library, 1943.

SLOCHOWER, HARRY, *Three Ways of Modern Man*. International, 1937.

——, *No Voice Is Wholly Lost*. Creative Age, 1945.

SMITH, BERNARD, *Forces in American Criticism*. Harcourt, Brace, 1939.

SNELL, GEORGE, *Shapers of American Fiction*. Dutton, 1947.

SPARROW, JOHN, *Sense and Poetry*. Yale University, 1934.

SPENCER, THEODORE, *A Garland for John Donne*. Harvard University, 1931.

——, *Shakespeare and the Nature of Man*. Macmillan, 1942.

SPENDER, STEPHEN, *The Destructive Element*. Houghton Mifflin, 1936.

——, *Life and the Poet*. Secker & Warburg, 1942.

SPENGLER, OSWALD, *Decline of the West*. Knopf, 1932.

SPINGARN, J. E., *Criticism in America*. Harcourt, Brace, 1924.

SPITZER, LEO, *Linguistics and Literary History*. Princeton University, 1948.

SPURGEON, CAROLINE, *Shakespeare's Imagery and What It Tells Us*. Macmillan, 1935.

STALLMAN, R. W., *Critiques and Essays in Criticism*. Ronald, 1949.

——, *The Art of Modern Fiction*. Rinehart, 1949. With Ray B. West, Jr.

——, *The Critic's Notebook*. University of Minnesota, 1950.

STARKIE, ENID, *Arthur Rimbaud*. Norton, 1940.

STAUFFER, DONALD, *Intent of the Critic*. Princeton University, 1941.

——, *The Nature of Poetry*. Norton, 1946.

STEIN, LEO, *The A.B.C. of Aesthetics*. Liveright, 1927.

———, *Appreciation: Painting, Poetry and Prose*. Crown, 1947.

STOLL, E. E., *From Shakespeare to Joyce*. Doubleday, 1944.

SYMONS, ARTHUR, *The Symbolist Movement in Modern Literature*. Dutton, 1919.

TATE, ALLEN, *Reactionary Essays on Poetry and Ideas*. Scribner, 1936.

———, *Reason in Madness*. Putnam, 1941.

———, *On the Limits of Poetry*. Swallow & Morrow, 1948.

TILLOTSON, GEOFFREY, *Essays in Criticism and Research*. Macmillan, 1942.

TILLYARD, E. M. W., *Poetry Direct and Oblique*. Chatto & Windus, 1945.

TINDALL, W. Y., *Forces in Modern British Literature*. Knopf, 1947.

TRAVERSI, D. A., *Approach to Shakespeare*. Paladin, 1937.

TRILLING, LIONEL, *Matthew Arnold*. Norton, 1939.

———, *E. M. Forster*. New Directions, 1943.

———, *The Liberal Imagination*. Viking, 1950.

TURNELL, MARTIN, *The Poetry of Crisis*. Paladin, 1938.

———, *The Classical Moment*. New Directions, 1948.

———, *The Novel in France*. New Directions, 1951.

TUVE, ROSAMUND, *Elizabethan and Metaphysical Imagery*. University of Chicago, 1947.

UNAMUNO Y JUGO, MIGUEL DE, *The Tragic Sense of Life in Men and Peoples*. Macmillan, 1921.

VALÉRY, PAUL A., *Variety*. Harcourt, Brace, 1927. Second series, 1938.

VAN DOREN, CARL, *The American Novel*. Macmillan, 1921.

———, *Contemporary American Novelists*. Macmillan, 1922.

VAN DOREN, MARK, *The Poetry of John Dryden*. Harcourt, Brace, 1920. Reissue, Holt, 1946.

———, *Edwin Arlington Robinson*. Literary Guild, 1927.

———, *The Noble Voice*. Harcourt, Brace, 1946.

WAGGONER, HYATT H., *The Heel of Elohim*. University of Oklahoma, 1950.

WARREN, AUSTIN, *Richard Crashaw*. Louisiana University, 1939.

———, *Rage for Order*. University of Chicago, 1948.

———, *Theory of Literature*. Harcourt, Brace, 1949. With René Wellek.

WARREN, R. P., *Understanding Poetry*. Holt, 1940. With Cleanth Brooks.

———, *Understanding Fiction*. Appleton-Century-Crofts, 1943. With Cleanth Brooks.

———, *The Rime of the Ancient Mariner: An Essay*. Reynal & Hitchcock, 1946.

WEBER, BROM, *Hart Crane*. Bodley Head, 1948.

WELLEK, RENÉ, *The Rise of English Literary History*. University of North Carolina, 1941.

———, *Theory of Literature*. Harcourt, Brace, 1949. With Austin Warren.

WEST, R. B., JR., *Writing in the Rocky Mountains.* University of Nebraska, 1947.

————, *The Art of Modern Fiction.* Rinehart, 1949. With R. W. Stallman.

WESTON, JESSIE L., *From Ritual to Romance.* Cambridge University, 1920.

WHARTON, EDITH, *The Writing of Fiction.* Scribner, 1925.

WHIPPLE, T. K., *Study Out the Land.* University of California, 1943.

WHITEHEAD, ALFRED, *Science and the Modern World.* Macmillan, 1925.

————, *Symbolism: Its Meaning and Effect.* Macmillan, 1937.

WILSON, EDMUND, *Axel's Castle.* Scribner, 1931.

————, *The Triple Thinkers.* Oxford University, 1938.

————, *To the Finland Station.* Harcourt, Brace, 1940.

————, *The Boys in the Back Room.* Colt, 1941.

————, *The Wound and the Bow.* Oxford University, 1947.

WINTERS, YVOR, *Primitivism and Decadence.* Arrow Editions, 1937.

————, *Maule's Curse.* New Directions, 1938.

————, *The Anatomy of Nonsense.* New Directions, 1943.

————, *In Defense of Reason.* Swallow & Morrow, 1947.

————, *Edwin Arlington Robinson.* New Directions, 1946.

WOOLF, VIRGINIA, *The Common Reader.* Hogarth, 1929.

————, *The Death of the Moth.* Harcourt, Brace, 1942.

————, *The Second Common Reader.* Harcourt, Brace, 1947.

————, *The Moment.* Harcourt, Brace, 1948.

YEATS, W. B., *A Vision.* Macmillan, 1938.

————, *Dramatis Personae: 1896–1902.* Macmillan, 1936.

YOUNG, STARK, *The Flower in Drama.* Scribner, 1923.

————, *The Theatre.* Doran, 1927.

ZABEL, M. D., *Literary Opinion in America.* Harper, 1937.

3. Criticism in
Uncatalogued Periodicals

Periodicals included here are not elsewhere catalogued. For periodicals not included, see *A Reader's Guide to Periodical Literature* and *The International Index of Periodicals*. Since 1950, two of the periodicals included (*Partisan Review* and *Kenyon Review*) have been catalogued in *The International Index,* but not for the years preceding. Most of the periodicals below have been indexed for the years 1948 and 1949 in the *Index of Little Magazines* (Alan Swallow, Denver, 1949 and 1950). Symbols used to identify the periodicals included in this bibliography are listed below. Volume number and date of publication are listed in each case.

AB—*American Bookman* (New York, N.Y.), Accent—*Accent* (Urbana, Ill.), AP—*American Prefaces* (Iowa City, Iowa), BQ—*Briarcliff Quarterly* (Briarcliff Manor, N.Y.), Chimera—*Chimera* (New York, N.Y.), Critic— *The Critic* (London, England), Furioso—*Furioso* (Madison, Conn., and Northfield, Minn.), HR—*Hudson Review* (New York, N.Y.), Kenyon— *Kenyon Review* (Gambier, Ohio), MQ—*Maryland Quarterly* (College Park, Md.), NMQR—*New Mexico Quarterly Review* (Albuquerque, N.M.), Partisan—*Partisan Review* (New York, N.Y.), Pers.—*Perspective* (Louisville, Ky.), P&L—*Politics & Letters* (London, England), QRL—*Quarterly Review of Literature* (Chapel Hill, N.C., New Haven, Conn., Annandale-on-the-Hudson, N.Y.), RMR—*Rocky Mountain Review* (Salt Lake City, Utah), Scrutiny—*Scrutiny* (Cambridge, England), UKCR—*University of Kansas City Review* (Kansas City, Mo.), WR—*Western Review* (Lawrence, Kans., and Iowa City, Iowa).

ABEL, DARREL, Strangers in Nature: Arnold and Emerson. UKCR. 15. 1949.
ABELE, RUDOLPH VON, "The Scarlet Letter": A Reading. Accent. 11. 1951.
AIVAZ, DAVID, The Poetry of Dylan Thomas. HR. 3. 1950.
ALDRIDGE, JOHN W., The Metaphorical World of Truman Capote. WR. 15. 1951.
ALLEN, CHARLES, The Dial. UKCR. 10. 1943.
AMYX, CLIFFORD, The Aesthetics of Allen Tate. WR. 13. 1949.
ANDERSON, QUENTIN, Henry James and the New Jerusalem. Kenyon. 8. 1946.
———, Henry James, His Symbolism and His Critics. Scrutiny. 15. 1947.
ARENDT, HANNAH, Franz Kafka: A Revaluation. Partisan. 11. 1944.

———, What Is Existenz Philosophy? Partisan. 13. 1946.

ARMS, GEORGE, William Cullen Bryant. UKCR. 14. 1948.

———, A Note on Explication. WR. 15. 1950.

ARROWSMITH, WILLIAM, English Verse Drama. HR. 3. 1950.

ARTHOS, JOHN, Ritual and Humor in the Writing of William Faulkner. Accent. 9. 1948.

ARVIN, NEWTON, Melville's Shorter Poems. Partisan. 16. 1949.

AUDEN, W. H., Yeats as an Example. Kenyon. 10. 1948.

AUERBACH, ERICH, Stendhal, Balzac, Flaubert: In the Hôtel de la Mole. Partisan. 18. 1951.

BABEL, ISAAC, Guy de Maupassant. Partisan. 17. 1950.

BAKER, JOSEPH E., Using Our Regional Past. AP. 7. 1942.

———, The Ageless Region. AB. 1. 1944.

BALDENSPERGER, FERNAND, Complacency and Criticism. AB. 1. 1944.

BANTOCK, G. H., Arthur Koestler. P&L. 1. 1948.

BARRETT, WILLIAM, Writers and Madness. Partisan. 14. 1947.

———, A Present Tendency in American Criticism. Kenyon. 11. 1949.

———, American Fiction and American Values. Partisan. 18. 1951.

BAUDELAIRE, CHARLES, Madame Bovary. Partisan. 13. 1946.

BEACH, JOSEPH W., The Sacred and Solitary Refuge. Furioso. 3. 1947.

———, Sartre's Roads to Freedom. WR. 12. 1948.

BEACH, LEONARD, Washington Irving. UKCR. 14. 1948.

BECK, WARREN, William Faulkner's Style. AP. 6. 1941.

———, Virginia Woolf. AP. 7. 1942.

BELITT, BEN A., A Reading in Kirkegaard. QRL. 4. 1947.

BENTLEY, ERIC R., D. H. Lawrence, John Thomas, and Dionysos. NMQR. 12. 1942.

———, Wagner, Siegfried, and Hitler. NMQR. 13. 1943.

———, I. A. Richards: An Autopsy. RMR. 8. 1944.

———, The Theatres of Wagner and Ibsen. Kenyon. 6. 1944.

———, Pirandello and Modern Comedy. RMR. 10. 1945.

———, What Is Epic Theatre? Accent. 6. 1946.

———, The Meaning of Robert Penn Warren's Novels. Kenyon. 10. 1948.

———, Monsieur Verdoux as Theatre. Kenyon. 10. 1948.

———, Chekhov as Playwright. Kenyon. 11. 1949.

———, Eduardo de Filippo and the Neapolitan Theatre. Kenyon. 13. 1951.

BERLAND, ALWYN, Henry James. UKCR. 17. 1950.

———, Sherwood Anderson and the Pathetic Grotesque. WR. 15. 1951.

———, Violence in the Poetry of Allen Tate. Accent. 11. 1951.

BERRYMAN, JOHN, F. Scott Fitzgerald. Kenyon. 8. 1946.

BEWLEY, MARIUS, Kenneth Burke as Literary Critic. Scrutiny. 15. 1948.

———, The Poetry of Wallace Stevens. Partisan. 16. 1949.

———, James's Debt to Hawthorne. Scrutiny. 16. 1949.

BISHOP, JOHN PEALE,   Obscurities. WR. 12. 1948.
————, Reflections on Style. HR. 1. 1948.
BLACKMUR, R. P.,   The Idiot of Dostoievski. Accent. 3. 1942.
————, Crime and Punishment; A Study. Chimera. 1. 1943.
————, Language as Gesture. Accent. 3. 1943.
————, Four Categories in Criticism. Critic. 1. 1947.
————, Hans Castorp: Small Lord of Counterposition. HR. 1. 1948.
————, In the Birdcage: The Possessed. HR. 1. 1948.
————, For a Second Look. Kenyon. 11. 1949.
————, Anna Karenina. Kenyon. 12. 1950.
————, The Politics of Human Power. Kenyon. 12. 1950.
————, In the Hope of Straightening Things Out (Eliot). Kenyon. 13. 1951.
————, The Lion and The Honeycomb. HR. 3. 1951.
————, The Loose and Baggy Monsters of Henry James. Accent. 11. 1951.
————, Madame Bovary: Beauty out of Place. Kenyon. 13. 1951.
BLUM, MORGAN,   John Crowe Ransom, Critic. WR. 14. 1950.
BOGAN, LOUISE,   Popular and Unpopular Art. Partisan. 10. 1943.
BOWLING, L. E.,   Faulkner: Technique of the Sound and the Fury. Kenyon.
        10. 1948.
BRADBROOK, M. C.,   Notes on the Style of Mrs. Woolf. Scrutiny. 1. 1932.
BRADBURY, JOHN M.,   Auden and the Tradition. WR. 12. 1948.
————, Ransom as Poet. Accent. 11. 1951.
BRICKELL, H.   The Contemporary Short Story. UKCR. 15. 1949.
BROOKS, CLEANTH,   Empson's Criticism. Accent. 4. 1944.
————, Miss Marianne Moore's Zoo. QRL. 4. 1948.
————, My Credo: The Formalist Critic. Kenyon. 13. 1951.
BROWN, ROBERT,   The Poetry of William Carlos Williams. NMQR. 11. 1941.
BROWN, STUART G.,   Emerson. UKCR. 15. 1948.
BROWN, W. CABLE,   The Heresy of the Didactic. UKCR. 11. 1945.
————, Mr. Eliot without the Nightingales. UKCR. 14. 1947.
————, A Poem Should Not Mean but Be. UKCR. 15. 1948.
BURGUM, EDWIN B.,   John Crowe Ransom. RMR. 8. 1944.
BURKE, KENNETH,   Motives and Motifs in the Poetry of Marianne Moore.
        Accent. 2. 1942.
————, The Tactics of Motivation. Chimera. 1. 1943.
————, Ideology and Myth. Accent. 7. 1947.
————, The Imagery of Killing. HR. 1. 1948.
————, Othello: An Essay to Illustrate a Method. HR. 4. 1951.
————, Three Definitions. Kenyon. 13. 1951.
BURNHAM, JAMES,   Observations on Kafka. Partisan. 14. 1947.
BUSH, DOUGLAS,   My Credo: The Humanist Critic. Kenyon. 13. 1951.
BUTTERFIELD, H.,   History and the Marxian Method. Scrutiny. 1. 1932.

CADY, EDWIN H.,   Howells in 1948. UKCR. 15. 1948.
CAMPBELL, H. M.,   T. S. Eliot. RMR. 8. 1944.

————, Dostoievski and the Modern Temper. RMR. 10. 1945.

————, Merezhkovsky's Christ and Antichrist. WR. 13. 1948.

CARPENTER, F. I., Modern Philosophical Criticism. UKCR. 11. 1945.

————, Thomas Wolfe: The Autobiography of an Idea. UKCR. 12. 1946.

CARRIER, WARREN, Meaning in the Poetry of Lorca. Accent. 10. 1950.

Case of Ezra Pound. Partisan. 16. 1949.

CHASE, FREDERICK, The Vanishing Literary Story. UKCR. 11. 1944.

CHASE, RICHARD, History vs. The City of God. Partisan. 11. 1944.

————, The Sense of the Present. Kenyon. 7. 1945.

————, An Approach to Melville. Partisan. 14. 1947.

————, The Brontës. Kenyon. 9. 1947.

————, Dissent on Billy Budd. Partisan. 15. 1948.

————, Faulkner's Light in August. Kenyon. 10. 1948.

————, New vs. Ordealist. Kenyon. 11. 1949.

————, Melville's Confidence Man. Kenyon. 11. 1949.

————, Art, Nature, Politics. Kenyon. 12. 1950.

CHIARMONTE, NICOLA, Bernanos and Christian Liberty. Partisan. 11. 1944.

————, Malraux and the Demons of Action. Partisan. 15. 1948.

CHURCHILL, R. C., Dickens, Drama, and Tradition. Scrutiny. 10. 1941.

————, Arnold Today. P&L. 1. 1947.

CIARDI, JOHN, Peter Viereck: The Poet and the Form. UKCR. 15. 1949.

CLARK, ELEANOR, The World of Jean Genet. Partisan. 16. 1949.

COHEN, GUSTAVE, Le Cimetière Marin. QRL. 3. 1947.

COLEMAN, ELLIOTT, Proust as Moralist. WR. 15. 1951.

COLINS, ALICE, The Meaning of Poetry. QRL. 3. 1947.

COLLINS, CLIFFORD, Theme and Conceptions in Wuthering Heights. Critic.
1. 1947.

————, The Distinction of Riders to the Sea. UKCR. 13. 1947.

COOK, REGINALD, Robert Frost: Poet in the Mountains. WR. 11. 1947.

————, Thoreau in Retrospect. UKCR. 14. 1947.

CORMICAN, L. A., Medieval Idiom in Shakespeare. Scrutiny. 17. 1951.

CROCE, BENEDETTO, Criticism in Italy. Kenyon. 10. 1948.

DANIEL, ROBERT, Poe's Detective God. Furioso. 6. 1951.

DAVIS, ROBERT G., Art and Anxiety. Partisan. 12. 1945.

DOUGLAS, KENNETH, Paul Valéry, Mysticism. QRL. 3. 1947.

DOUGLAS, WALLACE W., The Professor and the Ode. WR. 13. 1948.

DOWNER, ALAN S., The Life of Our Design. HR. 2. 1949.

DUFFEY, BERNARD I., Kenneth Burke's Theory of Poetry. WR. 12. 1948.

EBERHART, RICHARD, Empson's Poetry. Accent. 4. 1944.

————, Pound's New Cantos. QRL. V. 1945.

EDWARDS, CALVIN, Hamlet and Ulysses. WR. 15. 1950.

ELIOT, ALEXANDER, Melville and Bartlesby. Furioso. 3. 1947.

ELIOT, T. S., The Music of Poetry. Partisan. 9. 1942.

————, Paul Valéry. QRL. 3. 1947.

————, From Poe to Valéry. HR. 2. 1949.

ELLMANN, RICHARD,   W. B. Yeats: The End of Youth. Furioso. 3. 1948.

————, W. B. Yeats, Magician. WR. 12. 1948.

————, Joyce and Yeats. Kenyon. 12. 1950.

EMPSON, WILLIAM,   Proletarian Literature. Scrutiny. 3. 1934.

————, Emotion in Words Again. Kenyon. 10. 1948.

————, A Doctrine of Aesthetics. HR. 2. 1949.

————, Wit in the Essay on Criticism. HR. 2. 1949.

————, The Verbal Analysis. Kenyon. 12. 1950.

————, Sense in the Prelude. Kenyon. 13. 1951.

ENRIGHT, D. J.,   The Case of Stefan George. Scrutiny. 15. 1948.

FAIRLEY, BARKER,   Goethe: The Man and the Myth. Partisan. 16. 1949.

FARRELL, JAMES T.,   Fiction and the Philistines. UKCR. 11. 1945.

————, History and War in Tolstoy's War and Peace. UKCR. 13. 1946.

FERGUSSON, FRANCIS,   Action as Passion. Kenyon. 9. 1947.

————, Oedipus Rex. Accent. 8. 1948.

————, Racine's Berenice. HR. 1. 1948.

————, The Theatricality of Shaw and Pirandello. Partisan. 16. 1949.

————, Hamlet. HR. 2. 1949.

FIEDLER, LESLIE,   Toward an Amateur Criticism. Kenyon. 12. 1950.

FJELDE, ROLF,   Time, Space, and Wyndham Lewis. WR. 15. 1951.

FLANAGAN, JOHN T.,   Eugene Field after Fifty Years. UKCR. 11. 1945.

FLEMING, RUDD,   Quidditas in the Tragi-Comedy of Joyce. UKCR. 11. 1945.

————, Cultural Anxiety and the Romantic Audience. Partisan. 17. 1950.

FLORES, KATE,   Franz Kafka and the Nameless Guilt. QRL. 3. 1947.

FLUCHÈRE, HENRI,   Surrealism. Scrutiny. 1. 1932.

————, The French Novel of Today. Scrutiny. 2. 1933.

FORD, BORIS,   A Case for Kipling. Scrutiny. 11. 1942.

FOSTER, RUEL E.,   Dream as Symbolic Act in Faulkner. Pers. 2. 1949.

FOWLIE, WALLACE,   Swann and Hamlet. Partisan. 9. 1942.

————, A Note on Crane and Rimbaud. Chimera. 2. 1943.

————, The Meaning of Manon Lescaut. WR. 11. 1946.

————, La Jeune Parque. QRL. 3. 1947.

————, The French Literary Mind. Accent. 8. 1948.

————, Under the Equanimity of Language. QRL. 4. 1948.

————, André Breton in the Age of Surrealism. WR. 14. 1949.

FRANK, JOSEPH,   Spacial Form in Modern Literature. Sewanee. 53. 1945.

————, Reaction as Progress. HR. 2. 1949.

————, Romanticism and Reality in Robert Penn Warren. HR. 4. 1951.

FREUD, SIGMUND,   Dostoievski and Parricide. Partisan. 12. 1945.

FREYER, GRATTAN,   The Little World of J. M. Synge. P&L. 1. 1947.

————, The Politics of W. B. Yeats, P&L. 1. 1947.

FROHOCK, W. M.,   The Prolapsed World of Jean-Paul Sartre. Accent. 7. 1946.

FROST, ROBERT,   Education by Poetry. AP. 6. 1940.

FRYE, NORTHROP, Levels of Meaning in Literature. Kenyon. 12. 1950.

————, A Conspectus of Dramatic Genres. Kenyon. 13. 1951.

————, My Credo: The Archetypes of Literature. Kenyon. 13. 1951.

GARDNER, W. H., The Religious Problem in Hopkins. Scrutiny. 6. 1937.

GHISELIN, BREWSTER, D. H. Lawrence. WR. 11. 1947.

————, Hart Crane. Partisan. 16. 1949.

GILLET, LOUISE, Joyce's Testament: Finnegans Wake. QRL. 1. 1943.

GIRAULT, NORTON R., An Analysis of All the King's Men. Accent. 7. 1947.

GLICKSBURG, C. I. The Furies in Negro Fiction. WR. 13. 1949.

GODWIN, MURRAY, Three Wrong Turns in Ulysses. WR. 15. 1951.

GOLDGAR, HARRY, A Note on Charles Dobzynski. WR. 15. 1951.

————, Yeats and the Black Centaur in France. WR. 15. 1951.

GOLFFING, F. C., Tristan Corbière. QRL. 2. 1945.

————, Jules Laforgue. QRL. 3. 1946.

GOODMAN, PAUL, Advance-Guard Writing, 1900–1950. Kenyon. 13. 1951.

GORDON, CAROLINE, Notes on Faulkner and Flaubert. HR. 1. 1948.

GRABO, CARL, An Experiment in Criticism. UKCR. 10. 1943.

GRAHAM, W. S., Notes on a Poetry of Release. QRL. 3. 1947.

GREGORY, HORACE, Edgar Allan Poe. Partisan. 10. 1943.

————, The Vein of Comedy in E. A. Robinson's Poetry. AB. 1. 1944. With M. Zaturenska.

————, On Paul Elmer More. Accent. 4. 1944.

GRENE, MARJORIE, Kierkegaard: The Philosophy. Kenyon. 9. 1947.

GROETHUYSEN, B., Apropos of Kafka. QRL. 2. 1945.

GUTERMAN, NORBERT, Kierkegaard and His Faith. Partisan. 10. 1943.

HALL, JAMES B., Moby Dick: Parable of a Dying System. WR. 14. 1950.

HAMOLIAN, LEO, Mr. Eliot's Saturday Evening Service. Accent. 10. 1950.

HARDING, D. W., Coherence of Theme in Donne's Poetry. Kenyon. 13. 1951.

HARDWICK, ELIZABETH, Faulkner and the South Today. Partisan. 15. 1948.

————, Elizabeth Bowen's Fiction. Partisan. 16. 1949.

HEILMAN, ROBERT B., Poor Naked Wretches in Proud Array. WR. 12. 1947.

————, The Sight Pattern in King Lear. QRL. 4. 1947.

————, The Two Natures in King Lear. Accent. 8. 1947.

————, The Turn of the Screw as Poem. UKCR. 14. 1948.

————, A Critical Method for Poetic Drama. Pers. 1. 1948.

HEMPHILL, GEORGE, Hemingway and James. Kenyon. 11. 1949.

HEPPENSTALL, R., Jean-Paul Sartre. QRL. 4. 1948.

HERBST, JOSEPHINE, Miss Porter and Miss Stein. Partisan. 15. 1948.

HERSHLEIFER, P., As Whirlwinds in the South: Light in August. Pers. 2. 1949.

HOFFMAN, F. J., Infroyce: Joyce and Psychoanalysis. UKCR. 11. 1944.

HOLMES, MARY, Metamorphosis and Myth in Modern Art. Pers. 1. 1948.

HONIG, EDWIN, The Poetry of Federigo García Lorca. NMQR. 11. 1941.

HOOK, SIDNEY, God, Geometry, and the Good Society. Partisan. 11. 1944.

HOWE, IRVING, James T. Farrell as Critic. Partisan. 14. 1947.

———, Sherwood Anderson and D. H. Lawrence. Furioso. 5. 1950.

———, The Book of the Grotesque. Partisan. 18. 1951.

———, Sherwood Anderson: An American as Artist. Kenyon. 13. 1951.

HYMAN, STANLEY E.,   Van Wyck Brooks and Biographical Criticism. Accent. 7. 1947.

———, Modern Literary Criticism. NMQR. 18. 1948.

———, The Psychoanalytic Criticism of Literature. WR. 12. 1948.

———, John Peale Bishop. Accent. 9. 1949.

HYNES, SAM,   Robert Penn Warren: The Symbolic Journey. UKCR. 17. 1951.

JACK, PETER M.,   A Review of Reviews of Eliot's Four Quartets. AB. 1. 1944.

JARRELL, RANDALL,   Stages of Auden's Ideology. Partisan. 12. 1945.

———, The Obscurity of the Poet. Partisan. 18. 1951.

———, Reflections on Wallace Stevens. Partisan. 18. 1951.

———, A View of Three Poets (Wilbur, Lowell, Williams). Partisan. 18. 1951.

KALLEN, H. M.,   Jefferson's Garden Wall. AB. 1. 1944.

KALLICH, MARTIN,   F. Scott Fitzgerald: Money or Morals. UKCR. 14. 1949.

KAZIN, ALFRED,   On Melville as Scripture. Partisan. 17. 1950.

KENNER, HUGH,   Baker Street to Eccles Street. HR. 1. 1949.

———, Eliot's Moral Dialectic. HR. 2. 1949.

———, The Rose in the Steel Dust. HR. 3. 1950.

KERMAN, JOSEPH,   Some Leitmotifs in Franz Kafka's Work Psychoanalytically Explored. UKCR. 13. 1946.

KERN, A. C.,   Dr. Oliver Wendell Holmes Today. UKCR. 14. 1948.

KLEIN, A. M.,   The Black Panther: A Study of Joyce. Accent. 10. 1950.

KLINGOPULOS, G. D.,   Arthur Koestler. Scrutiny. 16. 1949.

KNIGHTS, L. C.   The Ambiguity of Measure for Measure. Scrutiny. 10. 1942.

———, Notes on Comedy. Scrutiny. 1. 1933.

———, Scrutiny of Examinations. Scrutiny. 2. 1933.

———, Shakespeare's Sonnets. Scrutiny. 3. 1934.

———, Tradition and Ben Jonson. Scrutiny. 4. 1935.

———, Shakespeare and Profit Inflation. Scrutiny. 4. 1936.

———, Prince Hamlet. Scrutiny. 9. 1940.

———, The Politeness of Racine. Scrutiny. 9. 1941.

———, On the Social Background of Metaphysical Poetry. Scrutiny. 13. 1944.

———, On the Tragedy of Antony and Cleopatra. Scrutiny. 16. 1949.

KRIDL, MANFRED,   Russian Formalism. AB. 1. 1944.

KOESTLER, ARTHUR,   The Intelligentsia. Partisan. 11. 1944.

KOCH, VIVIENNE,   An Approach to the Homeric Content of Joyce's Ulysses. MQ. 1. 1944.

———, The Peaceable Kingdom of Miss Moore. QRL. 4. 1948.

———, The Poetry of Allen Tate. Kenyon. 11. 1949.

LaDriere, Craig,   Annotated Bibliography of Criticism. AB. 1. 1944.

Landsberg, Paul L.,   Kafka and the Metamorphosis. QRL. 2. 1945.

Langer, Susanne K.,   The Principles of Creation in Art. HR. 2. 1950.

Leavis, F. R.,   What's Wrong with Criticism. Scrutiny. 1. 1932.

————,   Milton's Verse. Scrutiny. 2. 1933.

————,   The Poetry of Pope. Scrutiny. 2. 1934.

————,   English Poetry in the Seventeenth Century. Scrutiny. 4. 1935.

————.   Shelley. Scrutiny. 4. 1935.

————,   Wordsworth. Scrutiny. 3. 1935.

————,   English Poetry in the Eighteenth Century. Scrutiny. 5. 1936.

————,   Antony and Cleopatra and All for Love. Scrutiny. 5. 1936.

————,   E. M. Forster. Scrutiny. 7. 1938.

————,   Arnold as Critic. Scrutiny. 7. 1939.

————,   Coleridge in Criticism. Scrutiny. 9. 1940.

————,   Joseph Conrad. Scrutiny. 10. 1941.

————,   Literature and Society. Scrutiny. 12. 1943.

————,   Johnson as Critic. Scrutiny. 12. 1944.

————,   Imagery and Movement. Scrutiny. 13. 1945.

————,   Doctor Johnson. Kenyon. 7. 1946.

————,   George Eliot. Scrutiny. 13 and 14. 1946 and 1947.

————,   Henry James and the Function of Criticism. Scrutiny. 15. 1947.

————,   The Novel as Dramatic Form. Scrutiny. 14. 1947.

————,   The Novel as Dramatic Poem. Scrutiny. 15. 1948.

————,   The Novel as Dramatic Poem. Scrutiny. 17–18. 1950–51.

Leavis, Q. D.,   The Critical Writings of George Santayana. Scrutiny. 4. 1935.

————,   Lady Novelists and the Lower Orders. Scrutiny. 4. 1935.

Levin, Harry,   Literature as an Institution. Accent. 6. 1946.

————,   Flaubert. Kenyon. 10. 1948.

————,   Observations on the Style of Ernest Hemingway. Kenyon. 13. 1951.

Lewis, R. W. B.,   Casella as Critic: A Note on R. P. Blackmur. Kenyon. 13. 1951.

————,   The Hero in the New World: William Faulkner's The Bear. Kenyon. 13. 1951.

Lewis, Wyndham,   Ezra: The Portrait of a Personality. QRL. 5. 1949.

Literature and the Professors. Kenyon. 2. 1940.

Loose, Gerhard,   On the Marble Cliffs. Furioso. 3. 1947.

Lorca, Federico García,   The Poetic Image in Don Luis de Gongora. QRL. 16. 1951.

Macauley, Robie,   The Good Ford. Kenyon. 11. 1949.

————,   Fiction of the Forties. WR. 16. 1951.

MacDonald, Dwight,   Kulturbolschewismus. Partisan. 8. 1941.

Magalaner, M.,   The Myth of Man: Joyce's Finnegans Wake. UKCR. 16. 1950.

Magny, Claude-Edmonde,   French Literature since 1940. Partisan. 13. 1946.

MALLAN, LLOYD, The Poet, the People, and the Hemisphere. NMQR. 11. 1941.

MALLARMÉ, STEPHANE, Art for All. AB. 1. 1944.

MARCH, RICHARD, Psychology and Criticism Scrutiny. 5. 1936.

MARITAIN, JACQUES, Poetry's Dark Night. Kenyon. 4. 1941.

MARTIN-CHAUFFIER, LOUIS, Proust and the Double "I." Partisan. 16. 1949.

MASON, H. A., Camus and the Tragic Hero. Scrutiny. 14. 1946.

———, F. R. Leavis and Scrutiny. Critic. 1. 1947.

MASTERS, CHARLIE, Some Observations on Burnt Norton. AP. 6. 1941.

MATTHIESSEN, F. O., Eliot's Quartets. Kenyon. 5. 1943.

———, Katherine Anne Porter. Accent. 5. 1945.

———, The Problem of the Private Poet. Kenyon. 7. 1945.

———, Phelps Putnam: 1894–1948. Kenyon. 11. 1949.

MAYHALL, JANE, The Modern Poet and the Devil's Circumstance. UKCR. 15. 1949.

MILES, JOSEPHINE, The Language of the Donne Tradition. Kenyon. 13. 1951.

MILLER, MILTON, Milton's Imagination and the Idyllic Solution. WR. 13. 1948.

MIZENER, ARTHUR, The Fathers and Realistic Fiction. Accent. 7. 1947.

———, Fitzgerald in the Twenties. Partisan. 17. 1950.

———, The Novel of Manners in America. Kenyon. 12. 1950.

———, How to Write for Practically Nothing a Year. WR. 16. 1951.

———, My Credo: Not in Cold Blood. Kenyon. 13. 1951.

MOORE, MARIANNE, Ezra Pound. QRL. 5. 1949.

MORGAN, FREDERICK, Symbolism in Dante and Shakespeare. Chimera. 1. 1943.

———, Notes on the Joseph Novels. HR. 1. 1949.

MORRIS, BERTRAM, Art and Society. NMQR. 13. 1943.

MUNSON, GORHAM, The Real Thing: A Parable for Fiction Writers. UKCR. 16. 1950.

NAGEL, ERNEST, The Historian as Moralist. Partisan. 9. 1942.

NEIDER, CHARLES, Kafka and the Cabalists. QRL. 2. 1945.

———, Thomas Mann. RMR. 9. 1945.

———, Two Notes on Franz Kafka. RMR. 10. 1945.

———, The Secret Meaning of Kafka's The Castle. WR. 11. 1947.

NEMEROV, H., A Note on the Terms of Kenneth Burke. Furioso. 2. 1947.

———, The Phoenix in the World: R. P. Warren. Furioso. 3. 1948.

———, On the Poetry of Allen Tate. Furioso. 3. 1948.

O'CONNOR, WILLIAM V., War Poetry: The Promised Idiom. UKCR. 10. 1944.

———, The Poet's Private Reality. QRL. 3. 1946.

———, The Poem as Vision. UKCR. 13. 1947.

———, The Poet as Aesthetician. QRL. 4. 1948.

———, The Politics of a Poet. Pers. 1. 1948.

———, Wallace Stevens and Imagined Reality. WR. 12. 1948.

——, Social and Activist Criticism: A Chapter in American Criticism. NMQR. 21. 1951.

O'Donnel, W. G., Kierkegaard: The Literary Manner. Kenyon. 9. 1947.

O'Donnell, D., Graham Greene. Chimera. 5. 1947.

——, The Pieties of Evelyn Waugh. Kenyon. 9. 1947.

——, The Temple of Memory: Péguy. HR. 3. 1951.

Olbrich, Marshall, Rilke and the World of Feeling. QRL. 2. 1945.

Olson, Charles, David Young, David Old. WR. 14. 1949.

Olson, Elder, Sailing to Byzantium: Prolegomena to a Poetics of the Lyric. UKCR. 8. 1942.

Ortega, Joaquin, A Colombian Poet in New Mexico. NMQR. 12. 1942.

Ortega y Gasset, José, In Search of Goethe from Within. Partisan. 16. 1949.

——, On Point of View in the Arts. Partisan. 16. 1949.

Orwell, George, Critic and Leviathan. P&L. 1. 1948.

Parkes, H. B., The Tendencies of Bergsonianism. Scrutiny. 4. 1935.

——, The Philosophy of Marxism. Scrutiny. 7. 1938.

——, The American Cultural Scene: Criticism. Scrutiny. 8. 1939.

Pearson, Norman H., Both Longfellows. UKCR. 16. 1950.

Peery, William, Does the Buskin Fit O'Neill? UKCR. 15. 1949.

Pepper, Stephen C., The Outlook for Aesthetics. Kenyon. 8. 1946.

Peter, John, The Family Reunion. Scrutiny. 16. 1949.

Phillips, William, Dostoievski's Underground Man. Partisan. 13. 1946.

Picon-Salas, Mariano, Literature and Life in Spanish America. AB. 1. 1944.

Pinto, V. de S., The Street Ballad and English Poetry. P&L. 1. 1947.

Pitcher, Seymour, Return to Nobility. AP. 7. 1942.

Poggioli, Renato, Italian Literature between Two Wars. BQ. 3. 1947.

Powell, Sumner C., William Faulkner Celebrates Easter, 1928. Pers. 2. 1949.

Praz, Mario, Hemingway in Italy. Partisan. 15. 1948.

Pritchett, V. S., The Future of English Fiction. Partisan. 15. 1948

Putnam, Samuel, The Making of an Expatriot. BQ. 3. 1946.

Quinn, Sister M. Bernetta, Ezra Pound and the Metaphysical Tradition. WR. 15. 1951.

——, The Poetics of Hart Crane. Pers. 4. 1951.

Rahv, Phillip, The Dark Lady of Salem. Partisan. 8. 1941.

——, On the Decline of Naturalism. Partisan. 9. 1942.

——, James and the American Fate. Partisan. 10. 1943.

——, Concerning Tolstoi. Partisan. 13. 1946.

Rajan, B., Georgian Poetry: A Retrospect. Critic. 1. 1947.

Ransom, John C., Yeats and His Symbols. Kenyon. 1. 1939.

——, The Pragmatics of Art. Kenyon. 2. 1940.

——, Art Worries the Naturalists. Kenyon. 7. 1945.

——, Poetry: The Final Cause. Kenyon. 9. 1947.

————, Poetry: The Formal Analysis. Kenyon. 9. 1947.

————, On Being Modern with Distinction. QRL. 4. 1948.

————, The Understanding of Fiction. Kenyon. 12. 1950.

————, William Wordsworth. Kenyon. 12. 1950.

————, The Poetry of 1900–1950. Kenyon. 13. 1951.

READ, HERBERT, The Present State of Poetry. Kenyon. 1. 1939.

————, The Present Situation of Art in Europe. HR. 1. 1948.

————, The Critic as Man of Feeling. Kenyon. 12. 1950.

————, Jung at Mid-Century. HR. 4. 1951.

Religion and the Intellectuals. Partisan. 17. 1950.

REMENYI, JOSEPH, Creative Uprootedness. UKCR. 10. 1944.

————, Lorinc Szabo, Hungarian Poet, WR. 14. 1950.

RICE, PHILIP B., George Santayana: The Philosopher as Poet. Kenyon. 2.
     1940.

————, Thomas Mann and the Religious Revival. Kenyon. 7. 1945.

RICHARDS, I. A., The Chinese Renaissance. Scrutiny. 1. 1932.

————, Troilus and Cressida and Plato. HR. 1. 1948.

————, The Places and the Figures. Kenyon. 11. 1949.

RIOSECO, A. T., On Contemporary Spanish American Poets. AP. 7. 1942

RODITI, EDOUARD, Critical Principles of the Troubadours. AB. 1. 1944.

————, Proust and Nerval. QRL. 1. 1944.

————, Paul Valéry: Poetics as an Exact Science. Kenyon. 7. 1945.

————, Oscar Wilde and Henry James. UKCR. 15. 1948.

ROSENTHAL, M. L., On the "Dissidents" of the Thirties. UKCR. 17. 1951.

ROTH, RUSSELL, The Brennan Papers: Faulkner in Manuscript. Pers. 2. 1949.

————, William Faulkner: The Pattern of Pilgrimage. Pers. 2. 1949.

SANDEEN, ERNEST, The Writer as American. AP. 7. 1942.

SARTRE, JEAN-PAUL, Writers and Responsibility. Partisan. 12. 1945.

————, Commitment in Literature. P&L. 1. 1947.

————, For Whom Does One Write? Partisan. 15. 1948.

————, Literature and Communism. Partisan. 15. 1948.

————, What Is Literature? Partisan. 15. 1948.

SAVAGE, D. S., The Aestheticism of W. B. Yeats. Kenyon. 7. 1945.

————, E. M. Forster. RMR. 10. 1945.

————, D. H. Lawrence as Poet. BQ. 2. 1945.

————, Ernest Hemingway. HR. 1. 1948.

————, Two Prophetic Poems. WR. 13. 1949.

————, The Innocence of Evelyn Waugh. WR. 14. 1950.

————, Swift. WR. 15. 1950.

SCHERER, OLGA, Illogical Moralist: Albert Camus. Pers. 2. 1948.

SCHILLER, ANDREW, Shakespeare's Amazing Words. Kenyon. 11. 1949.

SCHWARTZ, DELMORE, The Writing of Edmund Wilson. Accent. 2. 1942.

————, T. S. Eliot as the International Hero. Partisan. 12. 1945.

————, The Literary Dictatorship of T. S. Eliot. Partisan. 16. 1949.

————, Grapes of Crisis. Partisan. 18. 1951.

SEELEY, CAROL, Notes on the Poetry of Paul Eluard. WR. 14. 1949.

SHATTUCK, CHARLES, A New Reading of Joyce's Dubliners. Accent. 4. 1944. With Richard Levin.

SHELLEY, ROBERT, John Frederick Nims: A Palmtree of Steel. WR. 15. 1951.

SHORT, R. W., Melville as Symbolist. UKCR. 15. 1948.

SLOCHOWER, HARRY, Mann's Latest Novels. Accent. 3. 1943.

————, Eugene O'Neill's Lost Moderns. UKCR. 10. 1943.

————, André Malraux. QRL. 2. 1945.

————, Franz Werfel and Sholom Asch. Accent. 5. 1945.

SMITH, GROVER, Eliot's Death by Water. Accent. 6. 1946.

————, Yeats, Minnaloushe, and the Moon. WR. 11. 1947.

SMITH, WINNEFRED, The Worker as Hero. AB. 1. 1944.

SNELL, GEORGE, Edmund Wilson: The Historical Critic. RMR. 8. 1944.

————, William Faulkner. WR. 11. 1946.

SPENDER, STEPHEN, War and the Writer. Partisan. 9. 1942.

————, The Life of Literature. Partisan. 15. 1948.

————, My Credo: On the Function of Criticism. Kenyon. 13. 1951.

STAFFORD, JEAN, The Psychological Novel. Kenyon. 10. 1948.

STALLMAN, R. W., A Selective Bibliography on the Criticism of Poetry, 1920–1942. UKCR. 10. 1943.

————, John Peale Bishop. WR. 11. 1946.

————, Robert Penn Warren. A Checklist. UKCR. 14. 1947.

————, Cleanth Brooks. A Checklist. UKCR. 14. 1948.

————, Kafka's Cage. Accent. 8. 1948.

————, Conrad and the Secret Sharer. Accent. 9. 1949.

————, Structure and Symbolism in Conrad. WR. 13. 1949.

STANFORD, DEREK, Rilke and His Exclusive Myth. QRL. 4. 1948.

STAUFFER, DONALD, The Making of a Lyric Poem. Kenyon. 11. 1949.

STEIN, ARNOLD, Structures of Sound in Donne's Verse. Kenyon. 13. 1951.

STEWART, RANDALL, The Moral Aspect of Henry James's International Situation. UKCR. 10. 1943.

SWALLOW, ALAN, Induction as Poetic Method. NMQR. 11. 1941.

————, Subjectivism as Poetic Method. NMQR. 13. 1943.

————, Yvor Winters. RMR. 9. 1944.

SYPHER, WYLIE, The Metaphysicals and the Baroque. Partisan. 11. 1944.

————, Wallace Stevens. Partisan. 13. 1946.

TATE, ALLEN, The Post of Observation in Fiction. MQ. 1. 1944.

————, John Peale Bishop, A Personal Memoir. WR. 12. 1948.

————, Longinus. HR. 1. 1948.

————, A Note on Autotelism. Kenyon. 11. 1949.

————, Our Cousin, Mr. Poe. Partisan. 16. 1949.

————, To Whom Is the Poet Responsible? HR. 4. 1951.

————, Johnson on the Metaphysicals. Kenyon. 11. 1949.

———, *et al.,* Teaching and Study of Writing. WR. 14. 1950.

TAYLOR, FRAJAM, Keats and Crane. Accent. 7. 1947.

THEALL, D. F., Traditional Satire in Eliot's "Coriolan." Accent. 11. 1951.

THOMPSON, FRANCIS I., Finnegans Wake: A Portrait of the Artist Asleep. WR. 14. 1950.

TINDALL, W. Y., The Symbolism of W. B. Yeats. Accent. 5. 1945.

———, Dante and Mrs. Bloom. Accent. 11. 1951.

TOYNBEE, PHILIP, The Novels of Henry Green. Partisan. 16. 1949.

TRAVERSI, D. A., Coriolanus. Scrutiny. 6. 1937.

———, Piers Ploughman. Scrutiny. 5. 1937.

———, Giovanni Papini and Italian Literature. Scrutiny. 7. 1939.

———, Troilus and Cressida. Scrutiny. 7. 1939.

———, The Development of Modern Italian Poetry. Scrutiny. 10. 1941.

———, Henry the Fifth. Scrutiny. 9. 1941.

———, Henry IV, Part 1. Scrutiny. 15. 1947.

———, Henry IV, Part 2. Scrutiny. 15. 1947.

———, The Tempest. Scrutiny. 16. 1949.

TRILLING, LIONEL, Literary Aesthetic. Kenyon. 2. 1940.

———, A Note on Art and Neurosis. Partisan. 12. 1941.

———, The Sense of the Past. Partisan. 9. 1942.

———, The Life of the Novel. Kenyon. 8. 1946.

———, Art and Fortune. Partisan. 15. 1948.

———, Wordsworth and the Iron Time. Kenyon. 12. 1950.

TROY, WILLIAM, Stendhal: In Quest of Henri Beyle. Partisan. 9. 1942.

———, Scott Fitzgerald: The Authority of Failure. Accent. 5. 1945.

———. Limits of the Intrinsic. HR. 2. 1949.

———, Poet and Mystifier. Partisan. 16. 1949.

TURNELL, MARTIN, Literary Criticism in France. Scrutiny. 8. 1939.

———, Postscript on Verlaine. Scrutiny. 9. 1940.

———, Flaubert. Scrutiny. 13. 1945.

———, The Writer and Social Strategy. Partisan. 18. 1951.

TUVE, ROSAMOND, On Herbert's Sacrifice. Kenyon. 12. 1950.

TYLER, PARKER, Kafka and the Surrealists. Accent. 6. 1945.

———, Hamlet as the Murdered Poet. QRL. 3. 1946.

———, The Impressionism of Marcel Proust. Kenyon. 8. 1946.

———, The Poet of Paterson Book One. BQ. 3. 1946.

UNGER, LEONARD, T. S. Eliot's Critics. Pers. 1. 1948.

———, Keats and The Music of Autumn. WR. 14. 1950.

VALÉRY, PAUL, In Memory of Henri Bergson. Partisan. 11. 1944.

———, Literature. HR. 2. 1950.

VIERTEL, BERTHOLD, Bertolt Brecht, Dramatist. Kenyon. 7. 1947.

VIGNERON, ALFRED, Genesis of Swann. Partisan. 8. 1941.

VIVAS, ELISEO, The Objective Correlative of T. S. Eliot. AB. 1. 1944.

———, Don Alonzo to the Road Again. WR. 11. 1946.

————, The Objective Basis of Criticism. WR. 12. 1948.

————, Criticism and the Little Mags. WR. 16. 1951.

VORTREIDE, WERNER, Rabelais, Stendhal, and Gide. UKCR. 15. 1948.

VOSS, A. W. M., James Russell Lowell. UKCR. 14. 1948.

WAGGONER, H. H., The Legend of Ezra Pound. UKCR. 10. 1944.

————, Hart Crane and the Broken Parabola. UKCR. 11. 1945.

————, Poet and Scientist. UKCR. 13. 1946.

————, Poets, Test-Tubes, and the Heel of Elohim. UKCR. 12. 1946.

————, Nathaniel Hawthorne. UKCR. 14. 1948.

————, Hawthorne's Beginning. UKCR. 16. 1950.

————, Sermon for Critics. WR. 14. 1950.

WALCUTT, C. C., Critic's Taste or Artist's Intention. UKCR. 12. 1946.

————, The Naturalistic Novel. QRL. 3. 1946.

————, Frank Norris and the Search for Form. UKCR. 14. 1947.

WALLINGHAM, CALDER, A Note on James T. Farrell. QRL. 2. 1945.

WALTON, GEOFFREY, Andrew Marvell: A Summing Up. P&L. 1. 1948.

WARREN, AUSTIN, The Case of Vachel Lindsay. Accent. 6. 1946.

————, My Credo: The Teacher as a Critic. Kenyon. 13. 1951.

————, The Style of Sir Thomas Browne. Kenyon. 13. 1951.

WARREN, ROBERT PENN, The Snopes World. Kenyon. 3. 1941.

————, Katherine Anne Porter. Kenyon. 4. 1942.

————, Melville the Poet. Kenyon. 8. 1946.

————, Hemingway. Kenyon. 9. 1947.

WATKINS, W. B. C., The Kingdom of Our Language. HR. 2. 1949.

WATTS, HAROLD H., Jules Romains. RMR. 10. 1945.

————, The Sense of Regain: A Theory of Comedy. UKCR. 13. 1946.

————, The Poet's Place. QRL. 3. 1947.

————, Mann's Myth for His Times. QRL. 4. 1948.

————, The Devices of Pound's Cantos. QRL. 5. 1949.

WEISS, PAUL, Prophetic Blake. QRL. 3. 1947.

WEISS, T., The Nonsense of Winters' Anatomy. QRL. 1. 1944.

————, Gerard Manley Hopkins. Accent. 5. 1945.

————, Kenneth Patchen and Chaos as Vision. BQ. 3. 1946.

WELLEK, RENÉ, Literary Criticism and Philosophy. Scrutiny. 5. 1936.

————, Van Wyck Brooks and a National Literature. AP. 7. 1942.

WERFEL, FRANZ, Realism and Inwardness. AB. 1. 1944.

WEST, RAY B., JR., R. P. Blackmur. RMR. 8. 1944.

————, Four Rocky Mountain Novels. RMR. 10. 1945.

————, Three Rocky Mountain Poets. NMQR. 16. 1946.

————, Katherine Anne Porter. Accent. 7. 1947.

————, Truth, Beauty, and American Criticism. UKCR. 14. 1947.

————, The Boys in the Basement. WR. 13. 1948.

————, Mark Twain's Idyl of Frontier America. UKCR. 15. 1948.

————, Atmosphere and Theme in A Rose for Emily. Pers. 2. 1949.

————, Ezra Pound and Contemporary Criticism. QRL. 5. 1949.

————, Europe and the American Writer. WR. 15. 1950.

————, Literature and the American Writer. WR. 14. 1950.

————, The Craft of the Short Story: 1951. WR. 15. 1951.

————, The Tiger in the Woods: Five Contemporary Poets. WR. 15. 1951.

WHEELWRIGHT, PHILIP, Dogmatism—New Style. Chimera. 1. 1943.

WILLIAMS, MENTOR L., Whitman Today. UKCR. 14. 1948.

WILLIAMS, RAYMOND, The Soviet Literary Controversy. P&L. 1. 1947.

————, The Exiles of James Joyce. P&L. 1. 1948.

WILSON, EDMUND, Flaubert's Politics. Partisan. 4. 1937.

————, The Myth of the Marxist Dialectic. Partisan. 6. 1938.

WINTERS, YVOR, Gerard Manley Hopkins. HR. 1 and 2. 1949.

————, The Audible Reading of Poetry. HR. 4. 1951.

WORMHOUDT, ARTHUR, A Psychoanalytic Interpretation of The Love Song of J. Alfred Prufrock. Pers. 2. 1949.

YOUNG, VERNON, Joseph Conrad. HR. 2. 1949.

ZABEL, M. D., The Poet on Capitol Hill. Partisan. 8. 1941.

4. Recent Articles
by Contributors

BEARDSLEY, M. C.,   Phenomenalism and Determinism. Journal of Philosophy.
39. 1942.
———,   Rationality in Conduct: Wallas and Pareto. Ethics. 54. 1944.
See also Wimsatt, W. K., Jr.
BENTLEY, ERIC R.,   D. H. Lawrence, John Thomas, and Dionysos. New
Mexico Quarterly Review. 12. 1942.
———,   Literature in the Third Reich. Nation. 156. 1943.
———,   The Second Best Bed. RMR. 7. 1943.
———,   Wagner, Siegfried, and Hitler. NMQR. 13. 1943.
———,   Bernard Shaw's Fabian Platonism. Saturday Review of Literature.
27. 1944.
———,   Modern Hero-Worship. Sewanee Review. 52. 1944.
———,   I. A. Richards: An Autopsy. RMR. 8. 1944.
———,   Romanticism—A Re-evaluation. Antioch Review. 4. 1944.
———,   The Theatres of Wagner and Ibsen. Kenyon. 6. 1944.
———,   Pirandello and Modern Comedy. RMR. 10. 1945.
———,   Broadway Today. Sewanee Review. 54. 1946.
———,   What Is Epic Theatre? Accent. 6. 1946.
———,   Broadway and Its Intelligentsia. Harper's. 194. 1947.
———,   The Meaning of Robert Penn Warren's Novels. Kenyon. 10. 1948.
———,   Monsieur Verdoux as Theatre. Kenyon. 10. 1948.
———,   Chekhov as Playwright. Kenyon. 11. 1949.
———,   Eduardo de Filippo and the Neapolitan Theatre. Kenyon. 13. 1951.
———,   Pretensions of Pantomime. Theatre Arts. 35. 1951.
BLACKMUR, R. P.,   Conrad Aiken. New Republic. 61. 1930.
———,   Chaos Is Come Again. Southern Review. 6. 1941.
———,   Humanism and Symbolic Imagination. Southern Review. 7. 1941.
———,   Between Myth and Philosophy. Southern Review. 7. 1942.
———,   The Idiot of Dostoievski. Accent. 3. 1942.
———,   Crime and Punishment: A Study. Chimera. 1. 1943.
———,   Language as Gesture. Accent. 3. 1943.
———,   The Novels of Henry Adams. Sewanee Review. 51. 1943.
———,   The Economy of the American Writer. Sewanee Review. 53. 1945.

———, Notes on Four Categories of Criticism. Sewanee Review. 54. 1946. See also Critic. 1. 1947.

———, Hans Castorp: Small Lord of Counterposition. HR. 1. 1948.

———, In the Birdcage: The Possessed. HR. 1. 1948.

———, For a Second Look. Kenyon. 11. 1949.

———, Anna Karenina. Kenyon. 12. 1950.

———, The Politics of Human Power. Kenyon. 12. 1950.

———, In the Hope of Straightening Things Out (Eliot). Kenyon. 13. 1951.

———, The Lion and The Honeycomb. HR. 3. 1951.

———, The Loose and Baggy Monsters of Henry James. Accent. 11. 1951.

———, Madame Bovary: Beauty out of Place. Kenyon. 13. 1951.

BROOKS, CLEANTH, The Reading of Modern Poetry. American Review. 8. 1937.

———, The Poem as Organism. English Institute Annual: 1940. New York. 1941.

———, Empson's Criticism. Accent. 4. 1944.

———, New Criticism: A Brief for the Defense. American Scholar. 13. 1944.

———, History without Footnotes. Sewanee Review. 52. 1944.

———, Shakespeare as a Symbolist Poet. Yale Review. 34. 1945.

———, Criticism and Literary History. Sewanee Review. 55. 1947.

———, Miss Marianne Moore's Zoo. QRL. 4. 1948.

———, Homage to John Crowe Ransom. Sewanee Review. 56. 1948.

———, Milton and Critical Re-estimates. PMLA. 66. 1951.

———, Absalom, Absalom: The Definition of Innocence. Sewanee Review. 59. 1951.

———, Milton and the New Criticism. Sewanee Review. 59. 1951.

———, My Credo: The Formalist Critic. Kenyon. 13. 1951. See also Stallman, R. W., Cleanth Brooks: A Checklist. UKCR. 14. 1948.

BURKE, KENNETH, Freud and the Analysis of Poetry. American Journal of Sociology. 45. 1939.

———, On Musicality in Verse. Poetry. 57. 1940.

———, Character of Our Culture. Southern Review. 6. 1941.

———, On Motivation in Yeats. Southern Review. 6. 1941.

———, Motives and Motifs in the Poetry of Marianne Moore. Accent. 2. 1942.

———, Flowerishes. RMR. 7. 1943.

———, The Tactics of Motivation. Chimera. 1. 1943.

———, Container and Thing Contained. Sewanee Review. 53. 1945.

———, Kinds of Criticism. Poetry. 68. 1946. See also Golffing, F. C., Poetry. 67. 1946.

———, Ideology and Myth. Accent. 7. 1947.

———, The Imagery of Killing. HR. 1. 1948.

———, American Scholar Forum: New Criticism. American Scholar. 20. 1951.

————, Othello: An Essay to Illustrate a Method. HR. 4. 1951.
————, Three Definitions. Kenyon. 13. 1951.

COWLEY, MALCOLM,   Angry Professors. New Republic. 62. 1930.
————, The Poet and the World. New Republic. 70. 1932.
————, A Hope for Poetry. New Republic. 82. 1935.
————, Literature and Politics. New Republic. 81. 1935.
————, Thomas Wolfe's Legacy. New Republic. 99. 1939.
————, Writing in Wartime. New Republic. 105. 1941.
————, Spender, Auden and After. New Republic. 107. 1942.
————, William Faulkner's Human Comedy. New York Times Book Review. Oct. 29, 1944.
————, Return of Henry James. New Republic. 112. 1945.
————, William Faulkner Revisited. Saturday Review of Literature. 28. 1945.
————, Walt Whitman. New Republic. 114. 1946.
————, A Natural History of American Naturalism. Kenyon. 9. 1947.
————, Hawthorne in the Looking Glass. Sewanee Review. 56. 1948.
————, American Scholar Forum: New Criticism. American Scholar. 20. 1951.
————, Fitzgerald's Tender; the Story of a Novel. New Republic. 125. 1951.
CROCE, BENEDETTO,   Criticism in Italy. Kenyon. 10. 1948.

ELIOT, T. S.,   Ulysses, Order and Myth. Dial. 75. 1923.
————, Literature, Science, and Dogma. Dial. 82. 1927.
————, Isolated Superiority. Dial. 84. 1928.
————, The Poems of Richard Crashaw. Dial. 84. 1928.
————, Literature and the Modern World. AP. 1. 1935.
————, The Music of Poetry. Partisan Review. 9. 1942.
————, The Poetry of W. B. Yeats. Southern Review. 7. 1942.
————, In Praise of Kipling's Verse. Harper's. 185. 1942.
————, Notes toward a Definition of Culture. Partisan. 11. 1944.
————, The Man of Letters and the Future of Europe. Sewanee Review. 53. 1945.
————, Ezra Pound. Poetry. 68. 1946.
————, What Is Minor Poetry? Sewanee Review. 54. 1946.
————, Paul Valéry. QRL. 3. 1947.
————, Milton. Sewanee Review. 56. 1948.
————, From Poe to Valéry. HR. 2. 1949.
————, The Aims of Education. Measure. 2. 1951.
————, Poetry and Drama. Atlantic. 187. 1951.
————, The Three Provincialities with a Postscript. Essays in Criticism. 1. 1951.
See also Unger, Leonard, T. S. Eliot; Matthiessen, F. O., The Achievement of T. S. Eliot.

EMPSON, WILLIAM,   Proletarian Literature. Scrutiny. 3. 1934.
————,   Thy Darling in an Urn. Sewanee Review. 55. 1947.
————.   Emotion in Words Again. Kenyon. 10. 1948.
————,   Structure of Complex Words. Sewanee Review. 56. 1948.
————,   A Doctrine of Aesthetics. HR. 2. 1949.
————,   Donne and the Rhetorical Tradition. Kenyon. 11. 1949.
————,   Wit in the Essay on Criticism. HR. 2. 1949.
————,   The Verbal Analysis. Kenyon. 12. 1950.
————,   Sense in the Prelude. Kenyon. 13. 1951.
        See also Accent. 4. 1944.

FERGUSSON, FRANCIS,   D. H. Lawrence's Sensibility. Hound & Horn. 6. 1933.
————,   Action as Passion. Kenyon. 9. 1947.
————,   Oedipus Rex. Accent. 8. 1948.
————,   Racine's Berenice. HR. 1. 1948.
————,   The Theatricality of Shaw and Pirandello. Partisan. 16. 1949.
————,   Hamlet. HR. 2. 1949.
FORSTER, E. M.,   Does Culture Matter? Spectator. 165. 1940.
————,   Art of Virginia Woolf. Atlantic. 170. 1942.
————,   Books That Influenced Me. New Statesman and Nation. 28. 1944.
FOWLIE, WALLACE,   Novels of Jules Romains. Southern Review. 7. 1942.
————,   Swann and Hamlet. Partisan. 9. 1942.
————,   A Note on Crane and Rimbaud. Chimera. 2. 1943.
————,   The Meaning of Manon Lescaut. WR. 11. 1946.
————,   La Jeune Parque. QRL. 3. 1947.
————,   The French Literary Mind. Accent. 8. 1948.
————,   Under the Equanimity of Language. QRL. 4. 1948.
————,   Homage to Valéry. Sewanee Review. 56. 1948.
————,   Mauriac's Dark Hero. Sewanee Review. 56. 1948.
————,   Mallarmé's Afternoon of a Faun. Tiger's Eye. No. 7. 1949.
————,   André Breton in the Age of Surrealism. WR. 14. 1949.
————,   Three Masks of Mallarmé. Zero. 1. 1949.
————,   Art of Saint-John Perse. Poetry. 79. 1951.
————,   Jules Laforgue. Poetry. 78. 1951.
————,   Mallarmé as Ritualist. Sewanee Review. 59. 1951.

KNIGHTS, L. C.,   Notes on Comedy. Scrutiny. 1. 1933.
————,   Scrutiny of Examinations. Scrutiny. 2. 1933.
————,   Shakespeare's Sonnets. Scrutiny. 3. 1934.
————,   Tradition and Ben Jonson. Scrutiny. 4. 1935.
————,   Shakespeare and Profit Inflation. Scrutiny. 4. 1936.
————,   Prince Hamlet. Scrutiny. 9. 1940.
————,   The Politeness of Racine. Scrutiny. 9. 1941.
————,   The Ambiguity of Measure for Measure. Scrutiny. 10. 1942.
————,   W. B. Yeats: The Assertion of Values. Southern Review. 7. 1942.

————, On the Social Background of Metaphysical Poetry. Scrutiny. 13. 1944.

————, On the Tragedy of Antony and Cleopatra. Scrutiny. 16. 1949.

LEAVIS, F. R., What's Wrong with Criticism. Scrutiny. 1. 1932.

————, Milton's Verse. Scrutiny. 2. 1933.

————, The Poetry of Pope. Scrutiny. 2. 1934.

————, English Poetry in the Seventeenth Century. Scrutiny. 4. 1935.

————, Shelley. Scrutiny. 4. 1935.

————, Wordsworth. Scrutiny. 3. 1935.

————, Antony and Cleopatra and All for Love. Scrutiny. 5. 1936.

————, English Poetry in the Eighteenth Century. Scrutiny. 5. 1936.

————, E. M. Forster. Scrutiny. 7. 1938.

————, Arnold as Critic. Scrutiny. 7. 1939.

————, Coleridge in Criticism. Scrutiny. 9. 1940.

————, Hardy the Poet. Southern Review. 6. 1940.

————, Joseph Conrad. Scrutiny. 10. 1941.

————, Literature and Society. Scrutiny. 12. 1943.

————, Johnson as Critic. Scrutiny. 12. 1944.

————, Imagery and Movement. Scrutiny. 13. 1945.

————, Doctor Johnson. Kenyon. 7. 1946.

————, George Eliot. Scrutiny. 13 and 14. 1946 and 1947.

————, Henry James and the Function of Criticism. Scrutiny. 15. 1947.

————, The Novel as Dramatic Form. Scrutiny. 14. 1947.

————, Teaching of Literature. Sewanee Review. 55. 1947.

————, The Novel as Dramatic Poem. Scrutiny. 15. 1948.

————, The Novel as Dramatic Poem. Scrutiny. 17 and 18. 1950 and 1951.

LEVIN, HARRY, Pseudoxia Academica. Southern Review. 6. 1940.

————, Jonson's Metempsychoses. Philological Quarterly. 22. 1943.

————, Everybody's Earwicker. New Republic. 111. 1944.

————, Falstaff Uncolted. Modern Language Notes. 61. 1946.

————, James Joyce. Atlantic. 178. 1946.

————, Literature as an Institution. Accent. 6. 1946.

————, Flaubert. Kenyon. 10. 1948.

————, Some European Views of Contemporary American Literature. American Quarterly. 1. 1949.

————, Observations on the Style of Ernest Hemingway. Kenyon. 13. 1951.

————, What Is Realism? Comparative Literature. 3. 1951.

MATTHIESSEN, F. O., Eliot's Quartets. Kenyon. 5. 1943.

————, Katherine Anne Porter. Accent. 5. 1945.

————, The Problem of the Private Poet. Kenyon. 7. 1945.

————, Communication. Sewanee Review. 54. 1946.

————, Poe. Sewanee Review. 54. 1946.

————, American Poetry: 1920–1940. Sewanee Review. 55. 1947.

——, Homage to John Crowe Ransom. Sewanee Review. 56. 1948.
——, Phelps Putnam: 1894–1948. Kenyon. 11. 1949.

RANSOM, JOHN C., The Aesthetics of Regionalism. American Review. 2. 1934.
——, Characters and Character. American Review. 6. 1936.
——, Mr. Empson's Muddles. Southern Review. 4. 1938.
——, T. S. Eliot as Dramatist. Poetry. 54. 1939.
——, Yeats and His Symbols. Kenyon. 1. 1939.
——, Honey and Gall. Southern Review. 6. 1940.
——, The Pragmatics of Art. Kenyon. 2. 1940.
——, Yvor Winters: The Logical Critic. Southern Review. 6. 1941.
——, Irish, the Gaelic, the Byzantine. Southern Review. 7. 1942.
——, The Inorganic Muses. Kenyon. 5. 1943.
——, Bases of Criticism. Sewanee Review. 52. 1944.
——, Art Worries the Naturalist. Kenyon. 7. 1945.
——, On Shakespeare's Language. Sewanee Review. 55. 1947.
——, Poetry: The Final Cause. Kenyon. 9. 1947.
——, Poetry: The Formal Analysis. Kenyon. 9. 1947.
——, Literary Criticism of Aristotle. Kenyon. 10. 1948.
——, On Being Modern with Distinction. QRL. 4. 1948.
——, The Understanding of Fiction. Kenyon. 12. 1950.
——, William Wordsworth. Kenyon. 12. 1950.
——, The Poetry of 1900–1950. Kenyon. 13. 1951.
See also Matthiessen, F. O., Homage to John Crowe Ransom. Sewanee Review. 56. 1948.

READ, HERBERT, Psycho-Analysis and the Critic. Criterion. 3. 1925.
——, The Present State of Poetry. Kenyon. 1. 1939.
——, Culture and Liberty. Nation. 152. 1941.
——, The Present Situation of Art in Europe. HR. 1. 1948.
——, Coleridge as Critic. Sewanee Review. 56. 1948.
——, The Critic as Man of Feeling. Kenyon. 12. 1950.
——, Jung at Mid-Century. HR. 4. 1951.
——, York Mystery Plays. New Statesman and Nation. 41. 1951.

RICHARDS, I. A., Gerard Hopkins. Dial. 81. 1926.
——, Literature, Science, and Dogma. Dial. 82. 1927.
——, The Chinese Renaissance. Scrutiny. 1. 1932.
——, Emotive Meaning Again. Philosophical Review. 57. 1948.
——, Troilus and Cressida and Plato. HR. 1. 1948.
——, The Places and the Figures. Kenyon. 11. 1949.

SCHORER, MARK, Blake as a Religious Poet. Sewanee Review. 54. 1946.
——, Fiction and Matrix of Analogy. Kenyon. 11. 1949.

TATE, ALLEN, Poetry and the Absolute. Sewanee Review. 35. 1927.
——, Modern Poets and Convention. American Review. 8. 1937.
——, Hardy's Philosophic Metaphors. Southern Review. 6. 1940.

———, Miss Emily and the Bibliographer. American Scholar. 9. 1940.

———, Literature as Knowledge. Southern Review. 6. 1941.

———, Dostoievski's Hovering Fly. Sewanee Review. 51. 1943.

———, The Post of Observation in Fiction. Maryland Quarterly. 1. 1944.

———, Techniques of Fiction. Sewanee Review. 52. 1944.

———, The New Provincialism. Virginia Quarterly Review. 21. 1945.

———, Reading of Keats. American Scholar. 15. 1946.

———, John Peale Bishop: A Personal Memoir. WR. 12. 1948.

———, Longinus. HR. 1. 1948.

———, Johnson on the Metaphysicals. Kenyon. 11. 1949.

———, A Note on Autotelism. Kenyon. 11. 1949.

———, Our Cousin, Mr. Poe. Partisan. 16. 1949.

———, American Scholar Forum: New Criticism. American Scholar. 20. 1951.

———, To Whom Is the Poet Responsible? HR. 4. 1951.

TILLYARD, E. M. W., Note on Donne's Extasie. Review of English Studies. 19. 1943.

TRILLING, LIONEL, Mr. Faulkner's World. Nation. 133. 1931.

———, Literary and Aesthetic. Kenyon. 2. 1940.

———, The Victorians and Democracy. Southern Review. 5. 1940.

———, The Sense of the Past. Partisan. 9. 1942.

———, A Note on Art and Neurosis. Partisan. 12. 1945.

———, The Life of the Novel. Kenyon. 8. 1946.

———, Art and Fortune. Partisan. 15. 1948.

———, Contemporary American Literature in Its Relation to Ideas. American Quarterly. 1. 1949.

———, Wordsworth and the Iron Time. Kenyon. 12. 1950.

———, Virginia Woolf: The Novel of Sensibility. The Symposium. 3. 1952.

WARREN, AUSTIN, The Criticism of Meaning. Sewanee Review. 46. 1938.

———, Kosmos Kafka. Southern Review. 7. 1941.

———, Religio Poetae. Southern Review. 7. 1942.

———, The Case of Vachel Lindsay. Accent. 6. 1946.

———, Achievement of Some Recent Critics. Poetry. 77. 1951.

———, My Credo: The Teacher as a Critic. Kenyon. 13. 1951.

———, Religion as Self-Therapy: Emerson in Another Perspective. Measure. 2. 1951.

———, The Style of Sir Thomas Browne. Kenyon. 13. 1951.

WARREN, ROBERT P., T. S. Stribling: A Paragraph in the History of Critical Realism. American Review. 2. 1934.

———, The Hamlet of Thomas Wolfe. American Review. 5. 1935.

———, The Snopes World. Kenyon. 3. 1941.

———, Katherine Anne Porter. Kenyon. 4. 1942.

———, Cowley's Faulkner. New Republic. 115. 1946.

———, Melville the Poet. Kenyon. 8. 1946.

——, Hemingway. Kenyon. 9. 1947.

——, Nostromo. Sewanee Review. 59. 1951.

See also Stallman, R. W., Robert Penn Warren: A Check List. UKCR. 14. 1947.

WILSON, EDMUND, The Literary Class War. New Republic. 70. 1932.

——, The Ambiguity of Henry James. Hound & Horn. 7. 1934.

——, The Canons of Poetry. American Mercury. 153. 1934.

——, The Literary Left. New Republic. 89. 1937.

——, Flaubert's Politics. Partisan. 4. 1937.

——, The Myth of the Marxist Dialectic. Partisan. 6. 1938.

——, H. C. Earwicker and Family. New Republic. 99. 1939.

——, Dickens and the Marshalsea Prison. Atlantic. 165. 1940.

——, Literary Criticism and History. Atlantic. 168. 1941.

——, Poe as Literary Critic. Nation. 155. 1942.

——, Paul Rosenfeld: Three Phases. Commentary. 5. 1948.

WIMSATT, W. K., JR., Poe and the Mystery of Mary Rogers. PMLA. 56. 1941.

——, Johnsonian Generality and Philosophic Diction. Philological Quarterly. 22. 1943.

——, The Structure of the Concrete Universal. PMLA. 62. 1947.

——, Poetry and Morals. Thought. 23. 1948.

——, Rhetoric and Poems: The Example of Pope. English Institute Essays: 1948. New York. 1949.

——, The Affective Fallacy. Sewanee Review. 57. 1949. With Beardsley, M. C.

——, History and Criticism, a Problematic Relationship. PMLA. 66. 1951.

——, Samuel Johnson and Dryden's Du Fresnoy. Studies in Philology. 48. 1951.

——, The Substantive Level. Sewanee Review. 59. 1951.

WINTERS, YVOR, Holiday and Day of Wrath. Poetry. 26. 1925.

——, The Poetry of Louise Bogan. New Republic. 60. 1929.

——, Robinson Jeffers. Poetry. 36. 1930.

——, The Lyrics of Robert Bridges. Hound & Horn. 5. 1932.

——, Poets and Others. Hound & Horn. 5. 1932.

——, Robert Frost. Sewanee Review. 56. 1948.

——, The Poetry of Gerard Manley Hopkins. HR. 1 and 2. 1948 and 1949.

——, The Audible Reading of Poetry. HR. 4. 1951.

ZABEL, MORTON D., The Lyrics of James Joyce. Poetry. 36. 1930.

——, Towards Standards of Criticism. Poetry. 45. 1934.

——, Varieties of Poetic Experience. Southern Review. 3. 1938.

——, The Condition of American Criticism. English Journal. June, 1939.

——, Example for Critics. Nation. 151. 1940.

——, Hardy in Defense of His Art. Southern Review. 6. 1940.

——, The Whole of Housman. Nation. 150. 1940.

———, The Poet on Capitol Hill. Partisan. 8. 1941.

———, Conrad: The Secret Sharer. New Republic. 104. 1941.

———, Conrad in His Age. New Republic. 107. 1942.

———, Yeats in the Autobiographies. Southern Review. 7. 1942.

———, Graham Greene. Nation. 157. 1943.

———, Henry James's Place. Nation. 156. 1943.

———, Joseph Conrad: Chance and Recognition. Sewaneee Review. 53. 1945.